HOLLYWOOD AND WAR,
THE FILM READER

Hollywood and War, the Film Reader brings together key theoretical texts from multiple critical approaches to broaden the reader's understanding of the relationship between war and cinema.

Contributors examine how the images, narratives, and myths that war movies provide have been pivotal to America's social, political, and economic development since the late nineteenth century.

The reader is divided into five thematic sections, each with an introduction by the editor:

- **War as a way of seeing** examines the way we think about and process images, and how this may depend on representational media practices, and the depiction of war on screen, both politically, and morally
- **Early formations of war cinema in the United States** considers the history of war cinema, with special reference to World War I and the Spanish-American war.
- **The apotheosis of the Hollywood war film** discusses how movies have been used as propaganda, and looks closely at World War II cinema.
- **Shadows of ambivalence** analyses war in the modern period, in Vietnam and Korea, and looks closely at antiwar and brainwashing film.
- **Hollywood and war: contemporary formations** draws the collection to a close by bringing the reader to the present, and situating war cinema within the media arena where representation fights reality

These essays uncover the ongoing relationship between Hollywood and war, and are essential reading for any student investigating cinema, politics and history.

Contributors: Jeanine Basinger; Jean Baudrillard; Gregory D. Black; Lynda Boose; Robert Burgoyne; James Castonguay; John Whiteclay Chambers II; Leslie Midkiff DeBauche; Thomas Doherty; Bernd Hüppauf; Michael Isenberg; David E. James; Douglas Kellner; Geoff King; Geoffrey Klingsporn; Clayton R. Koppes; Lary May; Steve Neale; George H. Roeder, Jr.; Melani McAlister; Michael Rogin; Michael Ryan; Thomas Schatz; Pierre Sorlin; J. David Slocum; Paul Virilio; Charles Young; Marilyn Young; Slavoj Zizek

J. David Slocum is Associate Dean of the Graduate School of Arts and Science and Visiting Associate Professor of Cinema Studies in the Tisch School of Arts, both at New York University. His previous edited collections include *Terrorism, Media, Liberation* (2005), *Rebel Without a Cause* (2005) and *Violence and American Cinema* (2001).

IN FOCUS

In Focus: Routledge Film Readers
Series Editors: Steven Cohan (Syracuse University) and Ina Rae Hark (University of South Carolina)

The In Focus series of readers is a comprehensive resource for students on film and cinema studies courses. The series explores the innovations of film studies while highlighting the vital connection of debates to other academic fields and to studies of other media. The readers bring together key articles on a major topic in film studies, from marketing to Hollywood comedy, identifying the central issues, exploring how and why scholars have approached it in specific ways, and tracing continuities of thought among scholars. Each reader opens with an introductory essay setting the debates in their academic context, explaining the topic's historical and theoretical importance, and surveying and critiquing its development in film studies.

Exhibition, The Film Reader
Edited by Ina Rae Hark

Experimental Cinema, The Film Reader
Edited by Wheeler Winston Dixon and
Gwendolyn Audrey Foster

Hollywood Comedians, The Film Reader
Edited by Frank Krutnik

Hollywood Musicals, The Film Reader
Edited by Steven Cohan

Horror, The Film Reader
Edited by Mark Jancovich

Movie Acting, The Film Reader
Edited by Pamela Robertson Wojcik

Movie Music, The Film Reader
Edited by Kay Dickinson

Queer Cinema, The Film Reader
Edited by Harry Benshoff and Sean Griffin

Stars, The Film Reader
Edited by Marcia Landy and Lucy Fischer

Technology and Culture, The Film Reader
Edited by Andrew Utterson

Transnational Cinema, The Film Reader
Edited by Elizabeth Ezra and Terry Rowden

Color, The Film Reader
Edited by Angela Dalle Vacche and Brian
Price

Hollywood and War, The Film Reader
Edited by J. David Slocum

HOLLYWOOD AND WAR,
THE FILM READER

Edited by J. David Slocum

Routledge
Taylor & Francis Group

NEW YORK AND LONDON

First published in the USA and Canada 2006
by Routledge
711 Third Ave, New York, NY 10017

Simultaneously published in the UK
by Routledge
2 Park Square, Milton Park, Abingdon, Oxon OX14 4RN

Routledge is an imprint of the Taylor & Francis Group, an informa business

© 2006 J. David Slocum

Typeset in Novarese and Scala Sans by
Keystroke, 28 High Street, Tettenhall, Wolverhampton

Library of Congress Cataloging in Publication Data
A catalog record for this book has been requested

British Library Cataloguing in Publication Data
Hollywood and war : the film reader / edited by J. David Slocum.
    p. cm.
  Includes bibliographical references and index.
  ISBN 0–415–36779–4 (hardback : alk. paper) – ISBN 0–415–36780–8 (pbk. : alk. paper)
  1. War films–United States–History and criticism. I. Slocum, J. David (John David)
  PN1995.9.W3H65 2006
  791.43′658–dc22   2006017729

ISBN10: 0–415–36779–4 (hbk)
ISBN10: 0–415–36780–8 (pbk)

ISBN13: 978–0–415–36779–0 (hbk)
ISBN13: 978–0–415–36780–6 (pbk)

Contents

Acknowledgments

1. Steve Neale, *Hollywood and Genre* (New York: Routledge, 2000), pp. 125–33. Reproduced by permission of Taylor and Francis Books Ltd.

2. Geoffrey Klingsporn, "War, film, history: American Images of 'real war,' 1890–1925." © Geoffrey Klingsporn 2006. Used with permission of author.

3. Paul Virilio, *War and Cinema: The Logistics of Perception*, trans. Patrick Camiller (New York: Verso, 1989; 1984), pp. 68–89. Reprinted by permission of Verso Books. All rights reserved.

4. Bernd Hüppauf, "Experiences of Modern Warfare and the Crisis of Representation," *New German Critique* 59 (Spring/Summer 1993): 41–76. Reprinted by permission of Telos Press Ltd.

5. George H. Roeder, Jr., *The Censored War: American Visual Experience During World War Two* (New Haven: Yale University Press, 1993), pp. 81–104. Used by permission of Yale University Press.

6. Michael Rogin, "'Make My Day!': Spectacle as Amnesia in Imperial Politics." © 1990, by the Regents of the University of California. All rights reserved. Printed from *Representations*.

7. Slavoj Zizek, *Welcome to the Desert of the Real: Five Essays on September 11 and Related Dates* (New York: Verso, 2002), pp. 5–32. Reprinted by permission of Verso Books. All rights reserved.

8. James Castonguay, "The Spanish-American War in U.S. Media Culture." © James Castonguay 2006. Used with permission of author.

9. Leslie Midkiff DeBauche, "The United States' Film Industry and World War One." From Paris, Michael. *The First World War and Popular Cinema: 1914 to the Present.* Copyright © 2000 by Rutgers, the State University. Reprinted by permission of Rutgers University Press.

10. Michael Isenberg, *War on Film: The American Cinema and World War I, 1914–1941* (East Brunswick, NJ: Associated University Presses, 1981). Reprinted by permission of the publisher.

11. Pierre Sorlin, "War and Cinema: Interpreting the Relationship," *Historical Journal of Film, Radio, and Television* 14.4 (1994): 357–66. Reproduced by permission of Taylor and Francis Books, Ltd.

12. Thomas Schatz, "World War II and the Hollywood 'War Film,'" in Nick Browne, ed., *Refiguring Film Genres: Theory and History* (Berkeley: University of California Press, 1998), pp. 89–128. Reprinted by permission of the author.

13. From *Projections of War: Hollywood, American Culture, and World War II* by Thomas Doherty. Copyright © 1999 Columbia University Press. Reprinted with the permission of the publisher.

14. Reprinted with the permission of The Free Press, a Division of Simon and Schuster Adult Publishing Group, from *Hollywood Goes to War: How Politics, Profits & Propaganda Shaped World War II Movies* by Clayton R. Koppes and Gregory D. Black. Copyright © 1987 by The Free Press. All rights reserved.

15. From *The World War II Combat Film: Anatomy of a Genre* by Jeanine Basinger. Copyright © 1986 Columbia University Press. Reprinted with the permission of the publisher.

16. Lary May, *The Big Tomorrow: Hollywood and the Politics of the American Way* (Chicago: University of Chicago Press, 2000), pp. 141–57. Used by permission of the University of Chicago Press and the author.

17. John Whiteclay Chambers II, "All Quiet on the Western Front (U.S., 1930)," pp. 13–30, from *World War II: Film and History*, edited by John Whiteclay Chambers II et al., © 1996 by Oxford University Press, Inc. Used by permission of Oxford University Press, Inc.

18. Charles Young, "Missing Action: POW Films, Brainwashing and the Korean War, 1954–1968," *Historical Journal of Film, Radio, and Television* 18.1 (1998): 49–74. Reproduced by permission of Taylor and Francis Books, Ltd.

19. "Film and the War: Representing Vietnam." © 2006. David E. James. Reprinted with permission. All Rights Reserved.

20. Michael Ryan and Douglas Kellner, *Camera Politica: The Politics and Ideology of Contemporary Hollywood Film* (Bloomington and Indiana: Indiana University Press, 1988), pp. 194–216. Used by permission of Indiana University Press.

21. Robert Burgoyne, *Film Nation: Hollywood Looks at U.S. History*, pp. 16–37. Copyright © 1997 The University of Minnesota Press. Used with permission of the University of Minnesota Press. All Rights Reserved.

22. Lynda Boose, "Techno-Muscularity and the 'Boy Eternal': From the Quagmire to the Gulf," in Amy Kaplan and Donald Pease, eds., *Cultures of United States Imperialism* (Durham: Duke University Press, 1993), pp. 597–611. Copyright, 1993, Duke University Press. All rights reserved. Used by permission of the publisher.

23. Geoff King, *Spectacular Narratives: Hollywood in the Age of the Blockbuster* (New York: I.B. Tauris, 2000), pp. 117–41. Reproduced by permission of the publisher.

24. Jean Baudrillard, *The Gulf War Did Not Take Place* (Bloomington: Indiana University Press, 1993), pp. 61–87. Used by permission of Indiana University Press.

25. Marilyn Young, "In the Combat Zone," in *Radical History Review*, Volume No. 85, pp. 253–64. Copyright, 2003, MARHO: The Radical Historians Organization, Inc. All rights reserved. Used by permission of the publisher.

26. Melani McAlister, "A Cultural History of War Without End," *Journal of American History* 89.2 (2002). Copyright © Organization of American Historians. Reprinted with permission.

General Introduction: Seeing Through American War Cinema

J. DAVID SLOCUM

This volume explores America's "war cinema" as a discursive formation constituted and sustained through complex relationships among individual motion pictures, filmmaking as a major American industry and cultural institution, and militarization and national security as recurrent, if shifting, aspects of U.S. social life. Contributors here examine how mass cinema has reflected and shaped wide-ranging changes in American life wrought by militarization and a preoccupation with war in the twentieth century. Crucial to those processes of reflection and shaping is the very use of the word "war": especially in the era of continuing "small wars," insurgencies, and regional conflicts, it is necessary to recognize that "war" is a negotiated category, indeed a kind of social institution, that confers status to some organized behavior or collective conflict yet withholds it from other violent situations (Allen 1999). Such a basic problem of classification for political scientists or international relations scholars extends to film and media scholars whose analyses range from narrative forms and genres overtly involving military combat to the processes of psychological, informational, and technological mobilization and control that are arguably ongoing in a modern society defined by violent conflicts.

The claim here is neither that all attitudes, behaviors, and representations in modern life should be subsumed under the term "war," nor, conversely, that all films or film industry operations are intrinsically related to militarization and conflict. It is, however, to assert that important, guiding, and sometimes defining linkages have existed since the late nineteenth century between the development of military technologies and the repeated mobilization of U.S. society *and* the evolution of cinema as a representational technology, commercial enterprise, and cultural institution. Consequently, following historian Michael S. Sherry's use of the term militarization as "the process by which war and national security became consuming anxieties and provided the memories, models, and metaphors that shaped broad areas of national life," the suggestion is that American cinema has played an ongoing and privileged role in that process (Sherry 1995: xi). To shed light on that process entails, moreover, the scrutiny not only of visual symbols or storytelling patterns but a whole range of narrative and discursive practices that resonate with, and correspond to, the approaches adopted by individuals and society to engage the world of social and, especially, political relations and conflicts. Again, this is not meant to imply that a monolithic framework for understanding war has been imposed by and through Hollywood productions. Rather, the goal of this volume is to provide ready access to classic writings about U.S. war cinema and, through them, to submit that the images, narratives, and myths this cinema provides have been pivotal to the nation's film, social, political, and economic histories since the late nineteenth century.

Images and narratives of war have been consistent staples of U.S. film production since the emergence of motion pictures. As Robert Eberwein has recently written, from the earliest films of the Spanish-American War, productions documented events related to military conflicts and their effects on combatants and others, reenacted decisive or affecting events, created stories about what happens before, during, and after combat, and advanced political and ideological claims about military action (Eberwein 2004). These films also emerged from the complex institutional relations between Hollywood and the U.S. military, government, and American society that have been continually reproduced and recast from the Spanish-American War, World War I, and World War II, through the Korean War and Vietnam to conflicts in the Gulf and the current war against terrorism. By examining these cinematic, historical, and institutional relations, the contributions here illuminate how the tensions pervading more than a century of war cinema have consistently constructed and contested our predominant cultural "ways of seeing" war on screens and in the actual world. Put differently, the production of, and perceptual processes shaping, military images and narratives on screen are approached as being intrinsically related to U.S. political involvement in actual violent conflict. Since war is the most overt illustration of how violence is deployed by the modern nation-state in the name of order and civilization, the framing of such deployment in motion pictures has far-reaching implications for how we understand military events and the people, societies, and nations participating in them.

A necessary opening question in popular and critical responses has concerned the classification of productions and what constitutes a war film or war cinema, especially during wartime. Generic norms are crucial to the organization and experience of cinema. Film genres "represent an aesthetic and social contract between audiences and filmmakers," and provide, in Matthew Bernstein's pointed formulation, "the most revealing link between film and society" (Bernstein 1999: 3). Yet by nature, genres are subject to revision and subversion. They require ongoing revision to remain culturally relevant; and it is precisely the tension between normative structures and variations that enables genres to exist and evolve. The refiguration of genres, both aesthetically and socially, has been especially pronounced and active in times of national crisis and has consistently relied on dynamic on-screen representations. Genres thus evolve in ways identifiable from changes in the relationships between viewers, Hollywood, and the broader society. In fact, elements more typically associated with other genres, including epic, historical, Western, espionage, foreign correspondent, genocide, and even comedy films, are also often central to the analysis of war cinema and blur or complicate the process of classification. As critical viewers have sought greater clarity of understanding of individual films through comparative reference to generic groupings, such categorizing remains slippery and often politically determined by assumptions about what war is in the first place. Through these critical debates, however, it has been the combat experience of World War II—what Thomas Schatz called "Hollywood's military Ur-narrative"—that has remained at the heart of most models and historical understandings of the Hollywood war film as genre and war cinema as discourse (Schatz 2002: 75). The nature of the enemies of the United States and of battle in the late twentieth century and early twenty-first may have changed and prompted modifications in the cultural understanding of militarization and national security, in other words, but the experience of the Second World War, particularly as imagined in Hollywood cinema, has remained formative.

Steve Neale spells out the basic parameters of the war film genre in his contribution here: "war films are films about the waging of war in the twentieth century; scenes of combat are a requisite ingredient and these scenes are dramatically central" (Neale 2000: 125). Such focus on Hollywood war films typically involves only a narrow range of productions and historical and cultural concerns inordinately focused on the experiences of World War II and Vietnam. Often excluded from direct consideration as "war films" are productions about historical (i.e., pre-cinema-era) battles, including the Civil War, the wartime homefront, the Holocaust, and the Cold War. The contemporary war on terrorism, one without major, conventional battles or state antagonists, presents its own challenges for categorization, as Melani McAlister notes in her contribution here on the idea of "the war without end." One result of these difficulties is that the vision of war fostered by Hollywood dwells on actual combat even as the experience of wartime of most filmgoers in the U.S.—and beyond—during the twentieth-century has been much broader and embraces the homefront, varied industries and institutions, and, ultimately, attitudes and beliefs about war itself.

To proceed with an examination of how films about combat relate to the broader society and wider experiences of military conflict assumes that Hollywood produces more than entertainment for passing consumption. Indeed, the wider assumption here is that the cinema is a social institution that both reflects and shapes the ways we see and understand the world and our role and place within it. Hardly a straightforward process, the cinematic medium has obviously evolved over the last century, prompting enormous changes, for instance, in film industry relations with the government and military. In parallel there has been an extraordinary evolution in storytelling and viewing practices, special effects technologies, ideas about realism and aesthetics, and the politics and economics of production, distribution, and exhibition. While the following pages primarily focus on narrative productions in order to analyze the complex relationship between the U.S. film industry and military, political, and historical events, many of the issues raised are both relevant to and, in turn, illuminated by close attention to other film and media forms, including documentary, photography, and journalism. An aim of this volume is to demonstrate how narrative films made by the U.S. film industry for mass viewing capture and construct broadly relevant ways of seeing wars and shaping experiences of faraway events and military conflicts.

A brief history of U.S. War combat films

To explore cinematic and cultural understandings of war, the writings collected here focus on battlefield combat, the site of the predominant American visual experience of war, and the tensions and ambivalences around it. Photography was a major precursor to the visual experience afforded by cinema and the understandings of military conflict from the mid-nineteenth century of the Crimean War and the U.S. Civil War were formative for filmmakers and audiences alike. Also inherited from earlier representational forms like literature were longstanding myths and narratives of war like the camaraderie and male-bonding that emerge in battle, the expression of moral and political beliefs through actions on the battlefield, and the values associated with democracy, civilization, home, family, and femininity in whose name fighting is often undertaken.

The Civil War occupies an uneasy yet unavoidable place in the history of U.S. war cinema. Waged from 1861–1865, the conflict itself obviously predated the emergence of cinema. Yet the war was memorably documented in still photography that contributed technologically to the emergence of the new medium of motion pictures three decades later. As Geoff Klingsporn argues in his contribution here, the continuity between the two media appeared not only in visual iconography but complex social and economic changes related to the consumption of amusements. Compared with productions about other conflicts, relatively few films about Civil War battles have been made. In 1911, D.W. Griffith made *The Battle*, possibly the earliest motion picture featuring combat from the war between the states. His racist epic about the war and the era of Reconstruction, *The Birth of a Nation*, followed four years later and demonstrated the possibility of large-scale battle sequences and their box office potential as the U.S. film industry was consolidating narrative film production practices as well as distribution and exhibition arms (in the midst, recall, of World War I). Thematically, Griffith's film celebrated ideas of heroism, chivalry, and gallantry in combat and on the homefront that would become standard in later productions. Among later major films about the war are the 1939 epic *Gone With the Wind* (Victor Fleming), the 1951 anti-war picture (and box-office flop) made from the Stephen Crane novel, *The Red Badge of Courage* (John Huston), the critically well-received *Glory* (Edward Zwick 1989), *Gettysburg* (1993) and *Gods and Generals* (2003, both Ronald F. Maxwell), and *Cold Mountain* (Anthony Minghella 2003).[1]

Pivotal in the emergence of cinema in the United States, as Jim Castonguay's essay here details, was the Spanish-American War of 1898. Most of the motion pictures about the conflict were exceedingly brief and no films were made of actual combat in Cuba. Many of the images therefore were reenactments of known events like *Roosevelt's Rough Riders* (1898), portraying a charge by the famous horse soldiers (though actually shot by Biograph in Tampa). Other films, like the *Burial of the 'Maine' Victims* (1898), photographed by Edison in Havana harbor, showed the emotional aftermath of well-known events. Another grouping of films presented scenes of general military experience; the appearance of the three-minute *Love and War* (James H. White 1899), a tale of parents worrying about their son at war, his injury in battle, and eventual return home to a girlfriend has been called the "earliest surviving narrative film about the war" (Eberwein 2004: 3). Still other productions were patriotic entertainments, like *Raising Old Glory Over Moro Castle* (Edison 1899), that captured some of the developing power of cinema both as a "visual newspaper and as propaganda" (Musser 1990: 261).

Motion picture technologies and storytelling practices developed rapidly in the years leading up to World War I. U.S. audiences had seen newsreels of the Mexican Revolution and documentaries from the European war. During the war years (1914–1918), films reflected popular sentiments that ranged, early-on, from remaining isolated from the conflict "over there" (*On the Belgian Battlefield* [1914]) to being prepared for American entry (*The Battle Cry of Peace* [J. Stuart Blackton 1915]) to later demonizing German aggression (*The Kaiser, Beast of Berlin* (1918) and supporting American boys (*The Unbeliever* [Alan Crosland 1918]). Whatever their ostensible politics, the eventual features dealing with combat—be they pacifist epics (*Civilization* [Thomas Ince 1916]) or patriotic romances (*Hearts of the World* [D.W. Griffith 1918])—relied on increasingly standardized storytelling forms. In April 1917, President Woodrow Wilson created the Committee on Public Information (the "Creel Committee") to coordinate the presentation of information to the public and to shape its opinions and emotions. Such close relations with the government, as well as the lack of competition from European filmmakers during the war, helped U.S. cinema to consolidate industrially and expand its social place and global reach.

Immediately after the armistice, films about the war almost completely disappeared. By the mid-1920s, several major productions, including *The Big Parade* (King Vidor 1925), *What Price*

Glory? (Raoul Walsh 1926), and *Wings* (William A. Wellman 1927), revisited the war and, despite showing camaraderie and patriotism, conveyed disenchantment with war's horrors. In 1930, Lewis Milestone directed the antiwar masterwork, *All Quiet on the Western Front*, from Erich Maria Remarque's novel. Around the same time occurred one of the crucial transitions in the history of cinema, to sound movies, enabling filmmakers to enhance their portrayal of battle with the sounds of gunfire, explosions, and anguished voices. Sound amplified the experiences of the aerial dogfights in Howard Hughes' *Hell's Angels* (1930) and the futility of combat in Howard Hawks' drama of trench warfare, *The Road to Glory* (1936). Productions about the Great War continued to appear throughout the 1930s and were used, famously in *The Fighting 69th* (1940) and *Sergeant York* (Howard Hawks 1941), to comment on the U.S. political conversion from isolation from to intervention in World War II. Among the trickle of subsequent productions has been the profound indictment of military leadership in Stanley Kubrick's *Paths of Glory* (1957).

The December 1941 attack by the Japanese on Pearl Harbor prompted U.S. entry into the war and intensified engagement by Hollywood filmmakers and exhibitors in the new war effort. As Tom Schatz's contribution here makes plain, Hollywood was already consistently involved in making war-related productions before the formal declaration of war (and depiction of Americans fighting). While the emphasis in this volume is on the layered social and cultural meanings of films about combat, it is difficult not to consider almost any Hollywood production of the following four years, featuring combat or not, in terms of the nation's war effort. Contrary to the popular memory generated in succeeding decades by mostly postwar productions, only relatively few feature-length films made during the war itself directly portrayed the training of servicemen or military combat. Of more than 1,400 features released by major studios between 1941 and 1945, the number of productions dealing significantly with basic training is around 30 while those about armed forces in a "combat environment" released before war's end total between 25 and 30, and several films count in both categories.[2] Many other movies foregrounded conventional Hollywood fare—light romances, comedies, musicals—with war in the background (Schatz 1997). During the same years, other forms of motion pictures, including documentaries, newsreels, shorts, and animation, filled out theatrical programs and often dealt directly with the war effort at home and in combat areas (Doherty 1993).

The experience of battle on land, at or under the sea, or in the air was at the heart of war cinema. During actual hostilities, it was war in the Pacific—based partly on the racist demonization of the Japanese enemy—that was the subject of the majority of combat films. Most of this combat, furthermore, was set on land, featured the courageous efforts of GIs, and appeared in titles like *Wake Island* (John Farrow 1942), *Bataan* (Tay Garnett 1943), *Guadalcanal Diary* (Lewis Seiler 1943), *Cry Havoc* (Richard Thorpe 1943), *Gung Ho!* (Ray Enright 1943), and *Objective, Burma!* (Raoul Walsh 1945). Naval-related battles appeared in the submarine film, *Destination Tokyo* (Delmer Daves 1943), and the John Wayne PT-boat drama, *They Were Expendable* (John Ford 1945). *Thirty Seconds Over Tokyo* (Mervyn LeRoy 1944) was a quintessential picture about the war in the air. Films about the European theater, including the Atlantic and North Africa, included the Humphrey Bogart vehicle *Sahara* (Zoltan Korda 1943); the story of infantry soldiers as told by correspondent Ernie Pyle, *The Story of G.I. Joe* (William A. Wellman 1945); the submarine drama *Crash Dive* (Archie Mayo 1943); and Howard Hawks's tale of a B-17 Flying Fortress crew, *Air Force* (1943). As had happened in World War I, Hollywood worked closely with government agencies, this time notably the Bureau of Motion Pictures and the Office of War Information, to coordinate the political (and patriotic) messages communicated through its films.

After the end of the war, combat experience was briefly coupled with the return home of veterans, as in *The Pride of the Marines* (Delmer Daves 1945). 1949 marked the re-appearance of the combat film with *Battleground* (William A. Wellman), *The Sands of Iwo Jima* (Allan Dwan), and *Twelve O'Clock High* (Henry King). Among many productions of the 1950s were psychological dramas about the war like *Attack!* (Robert Aldrich 1956) and *The Enemy Below* (Dick Powell 1957), and, especially, command, in *Battle Cry* (Raoul Walsh 1955) and *Flying Leathernecks* (Nicholas Ray 1951). If films made during the war celebrated enlisted men, Peter Biskind has observed, "the heroes of fifties war films were officers" (Biskind 1983: 60; see also, Landon 1989). The following decade saw epics (*The Longest Day* [Darryl F. Zanuck 1962] and *The Battle of the Bulge* [Ken Annakin 1965]), antiwar dramas (*Beach Red* [Cornel Wilde 1967]), and offbeat action adventure films about the war (*The Dirty Dozen* [Robert Aldrich 1967]). Later treatments included Franklin J. Schaffner's ambivalent portrait of its eponymous warrior and war itself, *Patton* (1970), the U.S.-Japanese co-production *Tora! Tora! Tora!* (Richard Fleischer, Kinji Fukasaku, Toshio Masuda 1970), the all-star *Midway* (Jack Smight 1976), the epic *A Bridge Too Far* (Richard Attenborough 1977), and Samuel Fuller's cautionary tale about infantry, *The Big Red One* (1980). The 1990s saw renewed attention to World War II with the fiftieth anniversary of many of the war's key events. In 1998, the infantry dramas *The Thin Red Line* (Terrence Malick) and *Saving Private Ryan* (Steven Spielberg) appeared, along with the Academy Award-winning Holocaust film, *Life is Beautiful* (Roberto Benigni). More recent productions include the special effects-laden epic romance, *Pearl Harbor* (Michael Bay 2001), and the story of American Indian soldiers—and military multiculturalism—*Windtalkers* (John Woo 2002).

Called by some "the forgotten war," the conflict in Korea from 1950–1953 was the subject of only sporadic interest by Hollywood (Blair 1987). Of the ninety-one films identified by Robert Lentz in his filmography of the war, twenty were made during actual fighting and the majority of the rest produced in the remaining years of the decade (Lentz 2003). Some of these featured conventional narratives about squads on missions facing combat, from *The Steel Helmet* (Samuel Fuller 1951) and *Retreat, Hell* (Joseph H. Lewis 1952) to *Pork Chop Hill* (Lewis Milestone 1959). Besides films featuring small units in battle, at least three other types of Korean War film can be identified (Edwards 1997). The "psychological trauma film," like *Fixed Bayonets* (Samuel Fuller 1951) and *War Hunt* (Denis Sanders 1962), dwelled on the conflicted relationships between U.S. troops that symbolized wider American struggles over race, between liberals and conservatives, and between military "lifers" and those serving temporarily. "The POW/brainwashed film" is exemplified by *Prisoner of War* (Andrew Marton 1954), with Ronald Reagan as a soldier who allows himself to be captured to learn more about the communist menace in POW camps, and *The Manchurian Candidate* (John Frankenheimer 1962), about brainwashing by the Chinese with the ultimate aim of assassinating a U.S. Presidential candidate. A final grouping, films about the homefront and training, such as *Take the High Ground* (Richard Brooks 1953), spoke to domestic concerns more than combat. A notable later film about the Korean War was Robert Altman's black comic vision of war and military life, *M*A*S*H* (1970).

U.S. military involvement in Vietnam emerged from the Cold War policy of "containment" meant to prevent communist expansion. After sending advisors as early as 1954, the United States first deployed infantry units to South Vietnam in 1965 to counter insurgent activity and political instability. During the succeeding ten years, as military operations seemed marked by defeat and miscalculation and the domestic debate about the conflict increased, television became the principal conduit for providing the public with information about what was later called "the living-room war" (Arlen 1982). The U.S. government did not coordinate the production of war information with Hollywood as it had during previous wars, but enabled print and television journalists access in the field. Filmmakers did nevertheless add their own stories and images of battle, often using documentary forms, to a complicated range of contemporary war-related productions. Looking at the years 1967–1969, for instance, it is common to acknowledge that the depiction of combat was limited to the studio release in 1968 of only one film, John Wayne's *The Green Berets*. Yet dozens of productions that Jeremy Devine has categorized into "four fluidly defined subgenres" "helped reflect and create a consciousness concerning the war." They are "the traditional war story, the combat film"; "stories of returning veterans"; "the counterculture of the late 1960s and early 1970s"; and, films "set in different locales or time periods that are about or highly influenced by the Vietnam War" (Devine 1995). Like the estimation of "war-related" films made during the years of World War II, it is difficult to view many productions from these later years without acknowledging some influence of, or attention to, the Vietnam conflict.

Motion pictures featuring narratives explicitly about the war arrived in numbers only following the final withdrawal of the U.S. from Vietnam in the spring of 1975. At the end of that decade, *The Boys in Company C* (Sidney J. Furie 1978), *The Deer Hunter* (Michael Cimino 1978), and *Apocalypse Now* (Francis Ford Coppola 1979) imagined the horrors of war from the level of individual soldiers to that of the ideologies underlying U.S. involvement. But it was in the mid-1980s that Hollywood participated in a larger cultural re-evaluation of the American experience of war in Southeast Asia. Some of these stories, like *Rambo: First Blood Part II* (George P. Cosmatos 1985) and *Missing in Action* (Joseph Zito 1984), were fantasies about returning to Vietnam to fight again and rescue comrades left behind. Others sought to return to the war years themselves and, in the process, question both political and military decisions *and* previous cultural standards for heroism in and filmic storytelling about combat. These included dramas about the experience of training and battle: *Platoon* (Oliver Stone 1986), *Hamburger Hill* (Jon Irvin 1987), *Full Metal Jacket* (Stanley Kubrick 1987), *Born on the Fourth of July* (Oliver Stone 1989), and *Casualties of War* (Brian DePalma 1989). A more recent production about the early battle of Ia Drang, *We Were Soldiers* (Randall Wallace 2002), has been called the first "straightforwardly pro-Vietnam war film" since John Wayne's three and a half decades before (Carruthers 2003: 170).

Following the end of the Vietnam War in 1975, the United States military has engaged in various battles. Yet the political conflicts during these years, and especially in the post-Cold War era, have changed their scope and become more narrowly targeted. At the same time, the proliferation of twenty-four hour news services via cable and satellite television and the internet has exponentially increased the stories and images immediately available about them. For Hollywood, these conditions have presented new challenges for cinematic re-telling. A few films about the 1991 Gulf War that liberated Kuwait from Iraqi occupation have addressed the role of women in the military and combat (*Courage Under Fire* [Edward Zwick 1996]), the status of soldiers and civilians alike in contemporary war (*Three Kings* [David O. Russell 1999]), and the futility for individual soldiers of basic training and deployment (*Jarhead* [Sam Mendes 2005]). *Black Hawk Down* (Ridley Scott 2001) focused on battle rather than politics in its re-enactment of a single mission gone wrong during the 1993 U.S. intervention in Somalia. *Behind Enemy Lines* (John Moore 2001) followed a Navy flier downed in the Balkans and caught in the political contradictions of U.S. military involvement in that region. As of early 2006, the U.S. invasions of Afghanistan and Iraq had produced several documentaries but no Hollywood narrative films. The wider "war on terrorism" of which these operations were officially part—by definition, a wider campaign without a traditional military enemy or conventional battles—returns us squarely to the problem of classifying political conflicts and media productions about them.

Surveying analyses of War cinema (I): individuals and nations, morality and myth

There has been an immense body of writing, spanning journalistic reporting and reviews, academic studies, industry guidelines, government laws and policies, and public discourse, which address the vast number of film productions relating to war. This work has fed abiding anxieties about war and national security ever since filmmakers accompanied the "yellow press" to Cuba in 1898. Yet it was the public and journalistic debates about violence and reconsideration of the social role of Hollywood cinema during the Vietnam era that initiated more probing analyses of war in American history and culture. By the late 1970s and 1980s, four importantly related developments occurred. First, the institutionalization of film studies and the turn toward analysis of media in the academy opened critical spaces vital for the sustained and rigorous examination of cinema. Second, Hollywood's long-repressed direct engagement with the Vietnam War erupted on film screens in productions like *Platoon* and *Casualties of War* and compelled public discussion about the meaning of that conflict, and of war generally, in American history and experience. Film scholars responded by investigating the cultural myths and representational codes underlying the Vietnam conflict and cinematic efforts to capture it and to assess their historical significance (Ryan and Kellner 1988; Jeffords 1989; Wood 1986; Dittmar and Michaud 1990; and Anderegg 1991). Third, scholars also began to produce a new and more sophisticated body of work on World War II (Kane 1982; Dick 1985; Basinger 1986; Polan 1986; Koppes and Black 1987). Such critical attention often cast the cinematic and cultural experiences of World War II and Vietnam in a dialectical, or at least generational, opposition. This relationship was reinforced by, and indeed mapped onto, the entrenchment of contrasts between "old" or classical and "new" Hollywood that were affirmed by the publication in 1986 of *The Classical Hollywood Cinema: Film Style and Mode of Production to 1960* (Bordwell, Staiger, and Thompson 1986). Fourth, still another cultural turn sparked by the 1960s and 1970s and institutionalized in subsequent academic research was a cluster of related theoretical concerns—gender studies, political economy, trauma studies, and cultural imperialism—that were brought to bear on the historical and cultural specificities of U.S. war cinema.

A central concern about Hollywood war films is the motivations, attitudes, and behavior of individuals preparing for or immersed in combat. To an extent, this concern derives from Hollywood cinema's broader emphases on individual characters (and the stars often portraying them), and their decisions, relationships, behavior, and conflicts as the bases of dramatic action and narrative coherence. The motivations of protagonists and others range broadly from the personal to the social, from the pursuit of excitement or heroism, duty, faith, and revenge to love, friendship, camaraderie, and belonging. How individuals behave, how they interact in groups from the squad to the nation, and what values or beliefs they stand for in the midst of extreme situations, may shift over time in ways arguably reflecting the changing social relations and anxieties. Oftentimes, military experiences, particularly the liminal, transitional experiences of basic training and combat, serve as rites of passage for young soldiers into full manhood.

Whatever their diverse motivations, individuals in war cinema confront objectives greater than their own and either reject them or, more conventionally, adopt them and become part of a cohesive fighting group. The melting pot platoon has been a narrative device well-suited to the needs of moviemakers to strike a balance between the exigencies of storytelling focusing on individuals and the imperative to represent the values and stake of American society in films about the nation going to war. Writing of the cinematic reconciliation of individual and community interests in productions like *Thirty Seconds Over Tokyo*, *Guadalcanal Diary*, and *Wake Island*, Robert Ray consequently observes that "the wartime mood [of WWII] prompted the American cinema's normally camouflaged ideology to become more overt" and combat films to reaffirm "the myth that proposed the compatibility of individual and communal values" (Ray 1985: 89, 125). Whatever the surface image of selflessness or conspiracy, the insistent focus on the exceptional "great man" or, more often, the initially reluctant "everyman" emerges as individual conflicts are foregrounded while the wider political issues are simplified and relegated to the background. This tendency, too, derives from Hollywood norms for seeking emotional or psychological explanations for social and economic problems. Put differently, the individual soldier or commander might be presented as heroic and noble or flawed and ineffective, but the study in character itself, however seemingly representative of historical experience, often averts attention from the ideological or structural aspects of the war in which he is fighting.

If war films and cinema turn most significantly on narratives and representations of individuals, another crucial, defining element of these individuals' ineractions is romance. War cinema frequently amplifies the stylized American masculinity of its characters through romance and the life-and-death decisions and actions of its heroes. On one level, romance here means the heterosexual love interest of the soldiers that typically coincides with (and serves as the private analogue for) the interest in public order sought through military training and battle. The presence of women in films about war, like the girl back home who is the subject of friendly rivalry in *What Price Glory?*, symbolizes for some critics the feminine or domestic sphere for which battles among men are fought. Women can also be viewed as feminizing influences, figures of vulnerability, who soften the resolve of soldiers or, worse, emasculate them; this latter threat can occur during wartime, as in *Thirty Seconds Over Tokyo*, or returning to domestic life, as in *The Pride of the Marines* or *Coming Home*. Whatever their symbolic meaning, the presence of women in war cinema foregrounds both the masculine nature of the institution of war and the parallels, emotional and physical, between attempts at heterosexual conquest and military triumph (Renov 1988). On another level, as presented in the sexualized narrative of *Full Metal Jacket*, the romance of war refers to the bonding that occurs between male soldiers through their training and, especially, shared experience of combat. Sometimes the emphasis is the camaraderie among a "band of brothers" loyal to each other; in other cases, relationships are framed as rivalries ingrained in military customs, hierarchies, and generational relations. On still another level, these relationships are homo-erotic and feature intense and even intimate emotional exchanges and physical proximity between men otherwise prohibited in Hollywood cinema or other normative social spaces (Eberwein 2001; DeBona 2003; Donald 1992). A final level of romance and perhaps the most troubling that appears in war cinema (and the actual experience of war) is an irrational attachment to what has been called the "destructive sublime." While we will return to this later, it is worth noting here the intense and even perverse fascination with sensation and death that can mark viewers' relationships with war cinema that also appears in narratives as war lovers; early on, these were enemy characters like the evil Hun or diabolical Jap, but more recently, psychotic or bloodthirsty GIs, like Tom Berenger's Sergeant Barnes in *Platoon*, have also appeared. Fundamental to all of these relationships is their occurrence amid intense experiences transcending those of everyday life. War cinema arguably relies on a consistent linkage between these dual aspects of individual development in extraordinary conditions through which norms for social behavior, interaction, and belonging are clarified.

The relationship between the individual and the group showcases the actions of the former but inevitably casts light on the values and beliefs of the latter. In war cinema, the group on-screen may range from a squad or platoon to the combined military services, but it usually somehow stands in for the American nation. How the group is constituted and behaves can consequently be seen to express something of how society makes sense of its place in the world and in history. Myths can be understood as adaptable narratives that, over time, distill this process of cultural sense-making and symbolize collective values, beliefs, and moral principles; in the process, myths function as the basis for identity claims by individuals and communities. Essential to the myths and rhetoric of Hollywood war cinema is the assumption that the United States, as a free and democratic society, has a unique mission in the world and in history to advance human progress and the promise of spiritual salvation. "One of the most significant and obvious forms of national mythology [are] the war stories of the nation-state. In the twentieth-century United States, the narrative forms that have molded national identity most profoundly are arguably the western and the war film, genres that articulate an image of nation that, in the words of Anthony D. Smith, has been 'beaten into national shape by the hammer of incessant wars'" (Burgoyne 1997: 7–8; see also Anderson 1991; and Smith 1981). Various films based on "the lost patrol," from *The Lost Patrol* (John Ford 1934) to *Bataan* (1943) to *Steel Helmet* (1951), epitomize this American mythology of individuals converted into a cohesive unit who, by seeking to fight against unforgiving odds in a savage land, fulfill the nation's founding mission of bringing civilization to a wilderness.

Nation-based myths have long been contested, of course, in narratives and images critical of war or nationalism. More thoroughgoing are questions raised about how cinema has functioned to make and perpetuate myths. In a famous review, Renata Adler wrote, "*The Green Berets* is a film so unspeakable, so stupid, so rotten and false that it passes through being funny, through being camp, through everything and becomes an invitation to grieve not so much for our soldiers in Vietnam . . . but for what has happened to the fantasy-making apparatus of this country" (Adler 1969: 199–200). Later scholars have developed this concern more systematically, arguing that films have become largely self-referential commodities. In the process, national myths or cultural codes of representation are eroded and left as little more than surface markers to orient viewers in their consumption of a steady stream of otherwise largely undifferentiated images.

Especially in the post-Cold War era, related questions have been posed by scholars about the emergence (or re-emergence or re-figuration) of American empire inscribed in, and possibly extended by, war cinema. Some responses to war cinema have engaged both imperial issues abroad and social and cultural concerns at home. In his discussion of the Spanish-American War, Jim Castonguay thus attends to concerns ranging from the savage, racialized foreign enemy and typically white masculine American heroes on-screen to the complexity of media production about war and the variety of filmgoers responding to those media images and narratives. Such articulations of social difference substantiate and drive the "war stories of the nation-state" at the heart of American mythology. These articulations often proceed from the overt imaging of sameness and belonging or otherness and separation that mythologize antagonisms with distant enemies. Yet recent criticism has also sought to *de*-mythologize the wartime unity of American fighting forces and, more, the coherent national society they are presumably fighting for. The melting pot ideal that celebrates the nobility of individual heroes has therefore also revealed the inequity of the multiethnic and, later, multiracial group (and the multicultural nation for which it stands). Even more, the hypermasculinity of soldiers, illustrated in characters from John Wayne's Sergeant Stryker in *The Sands of Iwo Jima* (1949) to Sylvester Stallone's John Rambo in the trilogy of the 1980s, has been questioned. Women, too, have occasionally entered combat and the consideration of their gender has been the basis for similar critical treatment. Mary Pickford was an inadvertent heroine on the battlefields of France in *The Little American* (Cecil B. DeMille 1917), nurses like Margaret Sullavan and Claudette Colbert proved their mettle under fire on the Pacific front in *Cry Havoc* (Richard Thorpe 1943) and *So Proudly We Hail* (Mark Sandrich 1943), Margi Gerard's Marine doctor fought the VietCong in *The Siege of Firebase Gloria* (Brian Trenchard-Smith 1989), and Meg Ryan's helicopter commander in *Courage Under Fire* (1996) was ultimately shown to be heroic in the first Gulf War. Racial, gender, class and other forms of social difference may be foregrounded and even critiqued, in other words, but traditional assumptions about difference tend to remain powerful background standards for narrative filmmaking (Eberwein 2004). It is also necessary to recognize that these forms of difference are sometimes significant for their absence or invisibility. The race of African-Americans (and, ultimately, their status as slaves) has, for example, been called by Thomas Cripps the "absent presence" motivating the military conflict of Civil War movies but often excluded, as in *Gettysburg* and *Gods and Generals*, by filmmakers dwelling on individual gallantry or romance (Cripps 1994). Put briefly, while often grounded in forms of difference like race, gender, and class, the layered "politics of representation" in play in war cinema ultimately reveal the inequitable power relations and boundaries of difference that mark and maintain American narrative cinema and social institutions—including the military and Hollywood itself (Koppes 1995; see also, Bates 1996).

War cinema is not only produced through characterization, storytelling patterns, production values, special effects, or association with national, imperial, or mythical frameworks. The repetition of these elements breeds crucial familiarity with audiences and guides the marketing and exhibition campaigns of the film industry as a social, economic, and cultural institution. The analysis of the production of war movies has consequently included attention to individual filmmakers from Howard Hawks, Lewis Milestone, and John Ford to Stanley Kubrick and Oliver Stone, as well as actors like John Wayne or Robert Mitchum, who have shaped the generic representations with their individual styles and values. Generic repetition emerges from (and also evidences) industrial practices and institutional contexts that have led scholars to dwell on the operation of the film industry, its place in society, and its relations with the U.S. government and armed forces or through a given conflict. Relevant here is the evolution of censorship by both government and industry of war-related images and stories (see, for example, Koppes 1997; and Jeffords and Rabinowitz 1994). More generally, scholars have examined the linked questions of government participation in individual film productions and of the possible industry complicity in the growth of militarization and national security (Suid 2002; Shull and Wilt 1996). Perhaps most broadly, Hollywood's national and global ascendance has, from its beginnings, been linked by film historians to war, particularly the years of World War I in which the U.S. film industry, as David Bordwell has written, effectively "defined commercial filmmaking" (Bordwell and Thompson 1994: 76; see also, Kelly and Lawrenson 1998).

The social role of the film industry assumes special significance when the question is posed about how a motion picture positions itself vis-à-vis a specific conflict, the government or nation waging it, or the institution of war generally. Part of the difficulty stems from the ambiguity of being for or against war and from the fact that both tendencies can exist in the same film. As two critics wrote about Steven Spielberg's 1998 production, *Saving Private Ryan*, particularly its juxtaposition of the horrors of combat in its famous opening sequence of the D-Day invasion with the laudable story of personal commitment to duty, the film offers "the best of both worlds" by being "an antiwar film that celebrates those who fought the war" (Wetta and Novelli 2003: 875). Similarly problematic is the category of Hollywood itself: over time, the nature of the film industry has changed radically, such that feature films that at one time were developed and made in-house by a studio came later to be produced by multinational teams (*Tora! Tora! Tora!*) or financed independently (*The Boys in Company C* and *The Deer Hunter*). Related to the debates about how film functions for or against war and the nation is the educational function attributed to cinema. Particularly during the first half of the twentieth century, Hollywood positioned itself as a social institution with an important and patriotic dual role, both providing entertainment to distract civilians and soldiers from the grave realities of conflict *and* disseminating information about how and why the war was being fought. The narratives of *Gung Ho!* (Ray Enright 1943) and (anachronistically) *The Green Berets* (1968) illustrate this didacticism, showing and telling why U.S. involvement, and the fictional spectacles that the films feature, are justified.

Beginning with Harold Lasswell's groundbreaking study, *Propaganda Technique in the World War*, propaganda emerged as the subject of substantial critical attention related to war cinema (Lasswell 1927; see also, Culbert 1990; Winkler 1978; Fyne 1994; and Nornes and Yukio 1994). More frequently, the very norms of narrative storytelling extended the reach of Hollywood's messages and, in John Belton's words, "filtered its polemical arguments" about war "rather than presenting them directly" (Belton 2005: 213). Since the Vietnam era and the proliferation of television and later the internet as sources of news about distant wars, cinema has played a lesser role in supplying image-based accounts of war. Politically, too, the orientation of filmmakers has become more mixed, as the emergence of New Hollywood in the 1960s raised heretofore unprecedentedly critical visions of U.S. militarization and war-making.

While propaganda and the filtering or regulation of information about war poses questions about the ethics of filmmakers and governments, critics have used war cinema to raise more basic concerns about the morality of a given conflict or of combat itself. The battlefield thus becomes a setting in which morality is either absent or in abeyance (leaving combatants to behave according to primal motivations like self-preservation or the death drive) or crystallized into profound tests (unlike any available in the everyday world) (McMahon 1994). In films of World Wars I and II, the enemy, like Erich von Stroheim throwing a baby to its death in *The Heart of Humanity* (Allen Holubar 1918) or the Japanese raping of women in occupied China in *Behind the Rising Sun* (Edward Dmytryk 1943), perform the most heinous acts—and, in doing so, justify American retaliation. Later films feature a suspension of morality for Americans as well, as in the kidnap, rape, and killing of the Vietnamese girl in *Casualties of War*. Running through war cinema is a presumption that the extreme situations involving life and death, duty and responsibility, which are common to the pitched narrative conflicts of combat, often constitute morality tales. Yet the superficiality and contrivance of many of the moral frameworks in which these choices appear fail to correspond to the complexity of either the collective moral cases made by a nation for war or the individual decisions faced by actual combatants. The moral calculus of Hollywood's fighting man is, as with Gary Cooper's decision to set aside his religious scruples in the name of duty to country and fight the Germans in *Sergeant York*, often inseparable from an elaboration of the justness of the nation's military campaigns that rests on moral and political tenets. Beyond examining decisions made about specific wartime events, films often explore the legitimacy of combat and even war as a social institution (see, for example,

Wood 1986; Ryan and Kellner 1988; Dittmar and Michaud 1990; and Kelly 1997). In the wake of the Gulf War, and especially resonant for the discussion here, sociological and media analysts have approached more critically the longer history of popular cinema's legitimation—and occasional condemnation—of militarization and warfare (Combs 1993). Where films fit in the larger process of legitimating or de-legitimating prevailing ways of waging or experiencing war remains a pressing question.

Surveying analyses of War cinema (II): realism and repression, history and memory

Besides the standards of morality or justness of the individual or collective actions portrayed in film narratives (or the act of producing the films themselves), the most common basis of claims of the legitimacy of war cinema may be the standard of "realism" being employed. Putative authenticity of, and fidelity to, the lived experience of men in training or combat have long been standards employed in making and studying war films. A difficulty of these debates is the variety of levels of experience—physical, psychological, political, aesthetic—one can claim defines war authentically. The psychic and emotional violence of war, for example, marks representations of the battlefront and homefront alike as unstable, anxiety-fraught, and disruptive of ordered, often pre-war social relations. As Jeanine Basinger has written, "the complaint of 'unreality' in Hollywood war films can be connected best to its narrative content: the senti-mentalizing of relationships (both on the home front and in combat), the propagandizing of motives (which was part of the war on all fronts), and the presentation of battle violence that could not logically re-create the true battle experience" (Basinger 1998). Consider, too, the controversy that erupted over *The Deer Hunter* (Michael Cimino 1978). Critics of the film, including veterans, assailed the dramatically central use of Russian roulette as utterly fictional; no documentary evidence existed that the Vietcong played, and forced Americans to play, the deadly game. Yet others countered that Russian roulette was an accurate metaphor for U.S. involvement, especially that of many individual soldiers, in the long war; some claimed that the scenes of futile and self-destructive behavior enacted a "larger truth" about the U.S. experience of the war. Even if we allow both positions, the debate underscores the importance not only of the content or complexity of particular historical representations but of their *representativeness* and how, through them, cinema shapes viewers' understanding of war. At the same time, it is through the cinematic and critical privileging of specific standards of realism—that is, of image-based authenticity grounded, finally, in the visceral, personal experience of battle and not the overarching power relations organizing war and militarization—that war cinema also reinforces the representational practices aligned with the prevailing social order (Slotkin 1992; Shohat and Stam 1994).

Standards of realism or authenticity, that is, of the putative reality of different levels of experience of the same war, themselves change over time. Thus the important issue of the *simultaneity* in war cinema arises when considering how films made during times of actual conflict differ from those made afterward. Major productions about World War I such as *The Big Parade*, *The Crowd*, and *The Four Horseman of the Apocalypse* appeared years after the 1918 armistice—and the jingoistic productions of the war years—and were critical of the psychological and emotional tolls suffered by soldiers during the war and by society afterwards; likewise, the waves of pictures about the conflict in Vietnam that first appeared in the late 1970s, like *Apocalypse*

Now and *Go Tell the Spartans*, and then the mid-1980s, with *Platoon* and *Full Metal Jacket*, condemned the human costs, bureaucratic incompetence, and even absurdity of war that had surfaced in Southeast Asia. While common to observe that attitudes toward war often change and grow more sober after hostilities end, it is also necessary to add that both simultaneous and retrospective viewpoints have integrity. The authenticity of military activity, and of its representation, evolves even as the experiences of war—training and build-up, battle itself, coming home, looking back—do.[3]

A related concern that has grown especially prominent over recent decades is the role of cinema in the production of history and memory. Updating his standard cultural history of American movies in 1994, Robert Sklar wrote, "the question of historical memory has become the touchstone of movies' cultural power, as myths and dreams had been in the Great Depression and World War II" (Sklar 1994: 358). Sklar's observation came following a series of war films, including *Platoon*, *Born on the Fourth of July*, and *Schindler's List* (as well as other historical productions like *Salvador* [Oliver Stone 1986], *JFK* [Oliver Stone 1991], and *Malcolm X* [Spike Lee 1992]) that showcased the efforts of Hollywood and individual filmmakers to shape popular historical discourse. The greater role of movies in influencing understandings of historical events raises profound questions about the roles both of technological media and of more traditional, especially archive- and written text-based modes of approaching the past. Beyond recognizing the historical claims made by, and familiar representational forms used in, contemporary films in their depiction of certain events, the challenge is to explore how the representation of historical experience affects viewers' relationship to cinema and cinema's relationship to the society the history pertains to.

Positing the significance of mediated understandings of past wars to contemporary attitudes is hardly a new phenomenon. In fact, one can track a generational process of literary and cinematic influence across the major conflicts engaged in by the United States. Joanna Bourke has written about how the recounting of nineteenth century wars, especially on the Western frontier, fashioned soldiers' attitudes toward World War I; Paul Fussell has argued for Hollywood productions as a basis for understanding the behaviors of GIs in World War II; Tom Engelhardt and others have probed the dissolution of belief in so-called "victory culture" engendered in World War II films for Vietnam era soldiers; and, most recently, Anthony Swofford wrote about the significance of screen images of Vietnam and action heroes like Sylvester Stallone to the imaginings of combat of soldiers in the first Gulf War (Bourke 1999; Fussell 1989; Engelhardt 1998; Swofford 1993). Cinema has been pivotal to these processes both on and off-screen. In Alan Crosland's 1918 film about World War I, *The Unbeliever*, the father fondly recalls his own service in the Civil War as his son departs for Europe, for example, and a much-discussed scene early in Sam Mendes's *Jarhead* (2005) shows Marine recruits rallying for battle by watching Francis Coppola's *Apocalypse Now*.[4]

The cumulative impact of motion pictures appeared especially pronounced in the differing representations of World War II and Vietnam. As suggested earlier, the contrasting cinematic renderings of the two wars have come to constitute a dominant framework for cultural and narrative understanding of all war films and, in the process, reinforced their own priority while marginalizing other experiences. Lloyd Lewis quoted Vietnam soldiers as suffering from the "John Wayne Wet Dream Syndrome" in which their expectations of battle were found in Wayne's World War II films (Lewis 1985). Yet the cinematic linkages between the two wars are much more profound and far-reaching. World War II arguably occasioned the apotheosis of Hollywood as a cultural institution operating in tandem with the state, other social institutions, and the public realm. The complex industrial, stylistic, and ideological transition from classical, or old, to New Hollywood during the 1960s was defined, in part, precisely by a willingness to reflect upon and rework longstanding cinematic conventions.[5] Even more, the proliferation of television, and its expanded role in juxtaposing recycled images of previous wars while providing and framing images of contemporary conflict, altered the social role of cinema in shaping viewers' understandings of war.

Vietnam also coincided with the beginnings of a critical turn toward confronting the idea of history itself. For some, including film scholar Timothy Corrigan, film narratives from the late 1960s and 1970s came to betray a more thoroughgoing breakdown in the way a past, especially a coherent, mythic past, could be understood. Thus *The Deer Hunter* "accurately reflects the contemporary trouble with representing *any collective history* for an audience that, at least since Vietnam, has only the most temporary sense of itself as a singular historical image among an unprecedented plethora of cultural and historical images" (Corrigan 1991: 15). Approached from a different conceptual vantage, Linda Dittmar and Gene Michaud cast light on this narrative ambiguity by suggesting that "the Vietnam War is presented as something that happened, not as something that was done." Instead of narrative closure that enables "healing" to take place, "repression is often made to stand in for it" (Dittmar and Michaud 1990: 12; see also, Wood 1986). Whether by challenges to a coherent past or to a past actively determined by American policies and will, film scholars posited in their analyses of Vietnam-era cinema a heretofore unprecedented instability of historical discourse and traditional strategies for making meaning and generating understandings of the past (Ankersmit 1994).

By the late 1980s, historians were addressing the status of film history in the context of more far-reaching reassessments of how to understand the past. Robert Rosenstone argued that since pure historical truths, "History—with a capital H," could no longer be trusted, multiple approaches to past events and social changes, including Hollywood films, ought to be more fully considered (Rosenstone 2004: 202; see also, *American Historical Review* Roundtable 1988; Ferro 1988; Kaes 1989). Rosenstone and others claimed that historical discourse is larger than empirically-based norms of traditional historians' written scholarship; his call to expand the understanding of past experience accordingly embraces the condensations, symbolizations, invented characters and dialogue, and creation of dramatic situations and coherent narratives essential to filmmaking. Starting in 1989, a series of fiftieth anniversaries of many of the key events of World War II coincided with a reconsideration of the relations not only between the war film and society but between Hollywood cinema, traditional written history, and popular memory (Rosenstone 1995; Toplin 1996; Burgoyne 1997; Sobchack 1996). The box-office and critical success of Steven Spielberg's *Schindler's List* in 1993 galvanized public attention around the questions of memory of the Holocaust while raising more general questions about the role of cinema in shaping public understanding of the past (Loshitzky 1997). Many considerations of "film and history," needless to say, have turned on representations of war, political violence, and military conflict.

Mark Carnes spells out an exemplary contrast between actual experiences of past behavior and events and the "reel" history presented through cinema by emphasizing the inherent visuality of cinema so important to the cinematic depiction of war. He observes that, "filmmakers chiefly justify their assertions of truthfulness by claiming that their movies replicate the costumes and settings of the past. Directors think mostly in visual terms; hence a movie that *looks* like the past *is* like the past. . . . Hollywood films, consequently, offer remarkably accurate . . . evocations of how the past *looked*" (Carnes 2004: 47). To this, we might add the centrality of claims of emotional and linguistic and aural truth, which, as the stuff of dramatic conflict, also define filmic visions of the past. Finally, a focus on war cinema, which turns on depictions of the risk and often enactment of violent injury and death, underscores the significance of bodily behavior and practices of incorporation to social memory (Connerton 1989). Close attention to familiar dramatic conventions and the primacy of the visual raise questions about who has authority over history or memory and which standards we employ to engage and understand the past as individuals and societies.

Such far-reaching questions redound upon filmmakers and traditional historians alike and touch on matters like the selectivity of treatments of the past, mythmaking, and historical revisionism. Writing about the 1993 production, *Gettysburg*, Trevor McCrisken and Andrew Pepper conclude that the film's "desire to make every soldier on the battlefield sympathetic by emphasizing their manly courage and moral reserve ends up obscuring the complex reasons and motivations that underpin the conflict in the first place" (McCrisken and Pepper 2005: 65). Likewise, in later productions like *Black Hawk Down* and *We Were Soldiers*, more is at stake than recasting either the general memory of the wars or the history of specific battles. The implication is not only that these events "were actually victories, misconceived as defeats," but, as Susan Carruthers argues, that ultimately it is pointless to question military ventures: "All that matters is obeying orders; fighting courageously to save one's life and, more heroically, those of other men. War is reduced to a primal struggle to stay alive, to get back home, to 'leave no man behind.' And while specific wars may not amount to sacred duties, nevertheless, by definition doing one's duty is *good*" (Carruthers 2003: 182, emphasis in orig.). War, in these terms, transcends politics and military action is held outside ideological debates about policies in the present or the lessons of the past. The heroism of men, and the glory (or horror) of battle become timeless and apolitical. Rather than merely emphasizing individual action over political, economic, or structural context as earlier productions may have, these films evacuate meaningful attention to culturally or historically-specific causes or motivations for the conflicts being depicted; they participate, through their replication of spectacle, in what Michael Rogin describes here as a process resulting in "cultural amnesia." War cinema in these recent years emerges as self-referential, concerned not just with a nostalgia for, or appropriation of, previous combat films but a consistent set of values and behaviors transposable to any number of visually distinct but otherwise historically undifferentiated conflicts.

Mediating war

The importance of nostalgia and amnesia, like that of broader questions of film, history, and memory, is how they have shaped—and themselves been shaped by—the shifting viewing practices, cultural production, social relations, ideologies, and visual regimes constituting war cinema. To speak of visual regimes here points to more than the repetitive patterns of film narratives and images. The emergence of cinema in the late nineteenth and early twentieth centuries coincided with the cultural developments and historical transformations that constituted modern life. Ways of seeing and experiencing the world arguably shifted during this period of increasing mechanical reproduction, urban culture, and mass consumption. Commercial motion pictures can be seen to epitomize many of these far-reaching changes, not least in their use of machines to represent distant experience, their stimulation of visceral reactions among viewers, and their creation of publics from these viewers. One needs only return to the early films of air war, *Wings* or *Hell's Angels*, to witness the exuberance and energy of mechanical flight as well as the images that such flying made possible. Film historian Ben Singer's advocacy of a "neurological conception of modernity" in these terms implies "a fundamentally different register of subjective experience, characterized by the physical and perceptual shocks of the modern urban environment" (Singer 1995: 72).

Characterized by ceaseless mechanical shocks and sensation, the modern military environment was every bit as revealing of these different modes of perception and experience (Coker 1993; Joas 2002). Order, be it psychological, social, national, or global, accordingly arrives through the deployment of technology. That quest for order, moreover, has legitimized combat and rationalized the destructiveness of war. On a more individual level, the violence of war was seen as a singular experience in which one could feel most completely alive through the simultaneous empowerment and susceptibility wrought by modern military equipment (Huyssen 1993). This trope of transcendent experience was enhanced by individual action and recast by the sophistication and reach of military technology and weaponry. In fact, the suggestion of battle as an ineffable experience points to another basic concern of modernity that has special resonance in considerations of war cinema: namely, the claim that, increasingly, the "real" can be apprehended only through its representation even as representations rely on their semblance to reality (King 2005: 54). Especially since Vietnam, this dialectical relationship has highlighted the inscrutability of battle; as Michael Hammond has recognized, recent films such as *Rules of Engagement* (William Friedkin 1999) or *Courage under Fire* are investigations into the often traumatic, for some unrepresentable, experience of combat (Hammond 2002).

If questions of history and memory emphasize the meaning of war across and even beyond time, questions of mediation also foreground issues of space and the relation of viewers to distant conflict. Among those pressing issues are how films and related visual technologies re-cast the distant experience of war for viewers and how those viewers re-make themselves, their own subjectivities, and their societies in the process. As we have discussed, the cultural function of war cinema has involved, from its beginnings, "making sense of war and its organized, if often random violence" (Chambers and Culbert 1996: 148; see also, Winter 1989). At the same time, a less rational, more emotional and compelling aesthetic and political operation is underway: watching battle, its pain and carnage, from a distance sufficient to maintain one's own physical safety produces a "terrible beauty" and the basis of intense and seductively enjoyable sensations that have been called the "destructive sublime."[6] Yet both the sense-making and visual pleasures have always been complexly related to the ideological preoccupations imparted through specific representational, institutional, and commercial practices and strategies. Cinematic representation provides neither a neutral lens through which to observe war nor a straightforward reflection of the political or economic predispositions of the historical period of production.

Hollywood has long sought to make invisible its formal conventions and, especially, the political, cultural, and ideological preoccupations they reinforce. Through repetition, the presumption of viewers is that the visual representation of events on screen—whatever the superficial politics of narrative conflict being presented—is a transparent process. For war cinema, these tendencies toward invisibility strongly inscribe and code representations of violence as well as deeper political and moral rationales for military action. As a result, Hollywood filmmaking creates and sustains formal and ideological frameworks for cinematic spectacles of destruction and death that through repetition have become naturalized for viewers. Even as war cinema ostensibly depends on simplistic political and moral justifications to explain its narrative conflicts, character motivations, and spectacular violence, films employ consistent techniques to order images of destruction and map the world in terms of violence and civilization. Less conspicuously, but upon close analysis no less definitively, these techniques frame and orient perceptions of a world of socially, economically and morally unequal civilizations.

As suggested above, critics have devoted special attention to how technologies of war and representation conduced with other social and commercial changes in modern life during World War I and II to alter the nature of human perception and experience. Over the last three decades, scholars have asserted further shifts in prevailing modes of perception and experience linked to advances in military and media technologies. Bruce Franklin, writing after the first Gulf War, observed that the conflict had been projected "from the point of view of the weapons," building on Hollywood's tradition of "warplane romances," like *Strategic Air Command* (1955), starring Jimmy Stewart, and creating "the impression of a 'clean' techno-war, almost devoid of human suffering and death, conducted with surgical precision by wondrous mechanisms" (Franklin 1994: 25–43). Essential here for film and media analysts old and new is the idea that technological developments have not merely upgraded military and media hardware or even furthered the strategic purposes of diplomats and military planners but transformed how individuals and societies experience distant combat as an economic and perceptual event. Manuel De Landa thus talks about a "war-game mentality" that blurs differences between simulation or make-believe and reality, corrupts actual data to fit the games, and neglects such human-level concerns as soldiers' morale and motivation or the enemy's mindset (De Landa 1991: 100–01). Also addressing war games, James Der Derian contends that late twentieth- and early twentieth-first century "infowar" is "more a weapon of mass persuasion and distraction than destruction . . . [in that it] targets civilian as well as military populations and its exchange-value as a deterrent outweighs its use-value as an actual weapon" (Der Derian 2003: 47).

This line of thinking has to do with more than propaganda or media distraction from actual events. Pushing it to an extreme, Jean Baudrillard made his provocative claim that "the Gulf War Did Not Take Place." At issue in his piece with that title is not whether military attacks physically took place or material damage was done by the United States in the Gulf but what comprehension of these events can exist for the West outside of mediated experience of twenty-four hour news television news coverage. If, for soldiers and civilians alike, military operations are executed using media technologies that enhance vision and rely on simulations, what other approach to these events is possible? The measure of the authenticity of experience in these terms thus shifts, for some, fundamentally. For Jordan Crandall, "the reality of representation is substituted for the representation of reality. That is, authenticity arises less from the authenticity of reality, per se, than the authenticity of the means by which reality is portrayed" (Crandall 2003). Technologies of weaponry and media, and their attendant practices of visual repre-sentation, are complicit in this substitution and the re-making of viewers' experiences of war which they enable. Returning to the opening query of this Introduction, the very definition of war becomes destabilized as one's ability to recognize and apprehend violence and conflict is refigured by mediation.[7]

In closing, it might be useful to urge approaching war cinema's ongoing enterprise as one of wide-scale, semi-participatory, techno-perceptual socialization. To be sure, concerns persist about the repetitive and circumscribed meanings of Hollywood narratives of combat, the ideological preoccupations they perpetuate, and the commercial and perceptual practices they reinforce. While the understanding and even history or memory of experiences of battle are put in question by cinema, in other words, the very attitudes and behaviors animated by viewers are influenced by war cinema and contribute to the socializing or civilizing process that sociologists see molding and constraining attitudes and behaviors alike (Slocum 2005). Attitudes toward, and understandings of, social relations and violent interactions are the most obvious. The larger implication of a convergent military and media ordering of information and mobilizing of attention, though, is that the same drill and distraction characteristic of military regimentation works to re-shape and mobilize other social processes of mediation and viewing practices (Kittler 1999; 1986). At issue here is how practices of viewing, consumption, and subject-positioning are regulated and constrained by war cinema—and then the extent to which viewers are (or can be) active participants. Yet as Mark Lacy cautions, it is also a matter of understanding *on what terms* that activity might operate: "cinema has been concerned with normalizing the idea of war as the natural order of things," he has remarked, and, in the process, with developing "distancing techniques [that] are deployed to create moral indifference to suffering" (Lacy 2003). As the essays in this volume make clear, the engagement or detachment attendant to given instances of war cinema have varied over time and for individual viewers.

Invoking the moral underscores an urgency about comprehending the representational and viewing practices constituted through processes of mediation. In fact, for individual viewers especially, war cinema demands positioning oneself as morally engaged with, or morally indifferent to, distant political violence and spectacle-based media. Many of the analysts who see military and media technologies as pacifying viewers and normalizing the idea of war claim that corporate or institutional processes of production or consumption allow only for moral indifference to, or detachment from, combat and carnage. Like the process of dismantling meaningful history amidst the suggestion of timeless and apolitical military attitudes and behaviors of concern, the distancing and amoralizing processes of war cinema can potentially bracket meanings attributed to war by viewers. These processes can readily deflect any meaningful attention to the social and power relations at the root of political violence and the production, even definition, of war.

Threading through the essays here, whether they ostensibly address matters of narrative politics or industrial practices or visual form, are a fuller range of questions of how individual viewers can engage the frequently distant violence and suffering of war. What are the perceptual processes, representational patterns, and moral dimensions involved in war cinema? And how are they relevant to individual viewers, their acts of engagement, and the mediations of war in which they participate? The goal of this volume is to survey essential scholarly writings about Hollywood's war cinema and, in doing so, to suggest that cinema constructs war as a way of seeing the world built upon distance, the interaction of commercial media practices and militarization, and, finally, the circumscription of moral and political meanings of violence. The hope, in turn, is that through these readings viewers might reflect on their own positions and become more fully engaged with the power relations that have for more than a century shaped—and been shaped by—war and cinema alike.

Notes

1   See Cullen 1995, and Chadwick 2001. Probably the most important media production of the second half of the twentieth century about the war was Ken Burns' *The Civil War*,

an eleven-hour documentary shaped by still photographs, dramatic narration, and contemporary filming of historical sites, which first appeared on U.S. television in the fall of 1990.

2   This is the total offered by both Basinger 1986: 281–93; and Shull and Wilt 1996: 162. In another, more nearly contemporary estimate, Dorothy B. Jones claims that 374 films, or roughly 30 percent of the industry output, "were directly concerned with some aspect of the war"; her subsequent categorization of these productions does not include "combat films" but motion pictures about "why we fought," "the enemy," "our allies," "American production," "the home front," and "our fighting forces" (Jones 1945).

3   Technological advancements in television and internet presentation of distant conflict have fundamentally altered the question of simultaneity since the 1980s. Journalistic coverage has been most directly re-shaped, yet fictional treatments also been affected. *Over There*, a weekly television drama series debuting on the FX cable channel in August 2005, followed a fictional U.S. Army unit, and their friends and families at home, through their arrival in Iraq and subsequent operations in Iraq. Despite positive critical responses, the show was cancelled in November 2005 after its initial 13-episode run.

4   The complex interplay between the representation in 2005 (in the midst of the Iraq War) of Marines in training in 1990 (for the first Gulf War) watching the 1979 film (about the Vietnam War) merits thoughtful unpacking. While against or, at least, ambivalent about war, *Apocalypse Now* features several rousing battle sequences, most famously the attack of a Vietnamese village by the U.S. air cavalry, accompanied by the playing of Wagner's "Ride of the Valkyries." That the later generation of soldiers could appropriate such a sequence at cross purposes with the intention of their original maker raised for several critics the quandary of whether any cinematic depiction of combat, with its intense, stimulating, even eroticized images of death and destruction, could be viewed as anti-war. (See, especially, Weschler 2005).

5   For Gilles Deleuze, the key transition in film history is between the wartime cinema that culminated in the 1940s ("linked to the organization of war, state propaganda, ordinary fascism") and the postwar cinema that conspicuously reveals itself first in the Italian neo-realism of Rossellini, De Sica, and others that immediately followed hostilities. The "extremes" or "everyday banality" of this latter cinema called attention to "the unities of situation and action that [could] no longer be maintained in the disjointed post-war world." The resulting "pure optical and sound situations" were also evident to Deleuze in many productions of the 1960s, like Godard's *Les carabiniers* (1963), a film critical of war reportedly made in response to the Hollywood D-Day epic, *The Longest Day* (Ken Annakin, et al. 1963). (Deleuze 1989: 165; Tomlinson and Galeta 1989: xv).

6   "Terrible beauty" is William Butler Yeats' description from his poem, "Easter 1916" (Yeats 1997: 182). The notion of the "destructive sublime" goes back at least to Edmund Burke, who held pain to be a more severe and intense sensation than pleasure. Burke's conception of the sublime is linked to a source, often visual and realistic, able to produce feelings of pain, terror, or dread. Subsequent writings on politics of visual pleasure have subsumed what Burke distinguished as pain and pleasure (Burke [1757] 1968). In terms of war, specifically, the notion was cited more recently by Chris Hedges, who writes of carnage and destruction in the "rush of battle" as a seductive, "potent and lethal addiction" (Hedges 2002: 3). J. Glenn Gray goes further, connecting destruction with the visual as arguably two of the three "secret attractions" he cites compelling men to go to war: "the

delight in seeing, the delight in comradeship, and the delight in destruction" (Gray 1970: 28–29; see also, Turgovnick 2005: 30).

7   This refiguration is arguably an aspect of a larger re-structuring of advanced industrial society. Ulrich Beck, the German sociologist renowned for his formulations about the "risk society," thus writes how, in contemporary life, "relations of definition are to be conceived analogous to Marx's relations of production" (Beck 2000: 224).

War Films

STEVE NEALE

War films

For the most part, the category 'war film' is uncontentious: war films are films about the waging of war in the twentieth century; scenes of combat are a requisite ingredient and these scenes are dramatically central. The category thus includes films set in the First World War, the Second World War, Korea and Vietnam. And it excludes home front dramas and comedies and other films lacking scenes of military combat. However, as with most generic categories, there are a number of ambiguities, some stemming from the generically untidy nature of some of the films, others from changes in their dominant conventions, still others from changes in the way films have been labelled or defined.

For example, the term 'war film' was first used in the industry's relay to describe films set in the Civil War or in the Indian Wars of the nineteenth century. These films included *The Empty Sleeve* (1909), described as a 'war picture' by the *Moving Picture World* (5 June 1909: 754), and *Clarke's Capture of Kaskaskia* (1911), advertised in the *Moving Picture World* as 'A new kind of War picture, taking us back to the pioneer days on the Frontier' (29 April 1911: 9). Films about the Indian Wars soon came to be treated as westerns. Some Civil War films did too, though films with a Civil War setting tended to form distinct and different generic alliances, and later Civil War films like *The Red Badge of Courage* (1951) and *Advance to the Rear* (1964) are in fact closer in look, tone and structure to contemporary war films than they are to contemporary westerns. (On early Civil War films, see Bowser 1990: 177–9 and Koszarski 1990: 186. On Civil War films in general, see Kinnard 1998. The term 'alliances' derives from Leutrat 1985.)

The criterion of combat, meanwhile, has exercised a number of theorists, critics and historians. Taking his cue from the inclusive nature of the surveys of war-related films conducted on behalf of the Office of War Information (OWI) by Jones in the 1940s (1945), Shain has argued for a broad definition of the war film. 'A war film', he writes, deals 'with the roles of civilians, espionage agents, and soldiers in any of the aspects of war (i.e. preparation, cause, prevention, conduct, daily life, and consequences or aftermath).' War films therefore 'do not have to be situated in combat zones' (1976: 20). Service comedies can be included, but 'not all films with military characters are on the list' (ibid.). On the other hand, Basinger, like Kagan (1974) and Kane (1982, 1988), argues that broad definitions are too vague. Proposing that 'The war film does not exist in a coherent generic form' (1982: 10), she restricts herself to films with a Second World War setting and substitutes the term 'combat film' for war film in order to mark combat itself as a central defining criterion: '"War" is a setting, and it is also an issue. If you fight it, you have a combat film; if you sit home and worry about it, you have a family or domestic film; if you sit in board rooms and plan it, you have a historical biography or a political film of some sort' (ibid.).

Issues of terminology have also been raised by those wishing to distinguish between films in terms of their attitudes to war. Chambers (1994), for example, suggests that 'antiwar film' might be a more appropriate term than 'war film' for films like All Quiet on the Western Front (1930). Thus there seems to be an assumption in some of the writing on war films that generic terms and definitions should be governed by logic: that the category 'war film' should logically include all films with a wartime background, that 'combat film' is the logical term for war films which focus on combat, and that 'antiwar film' is the logical term for films with an antiwar attitude. However, as Basinger in particular is otherwise the first to acknowledge, Hollywood's genres and terms are governed by custom, convention and history rather than logic. And custom, convention and history dictate that 'war film' implies a degree of focus on combat whatever attitude to war is adopted (Belton 1994: 164; McArthur 1982: 881; Springer 1988a. Belton compares the role of combat scenes in war films with the role of musical numbers in musicals; Springer discusses them in terms of their formal characteristics and of the ideological ambivalence their 'excess' can often generate). They also dictate that service comedies, spy films and home front dramas possess their own separate conventions and terms.

Some of the confusion here may stem from an awareness of the extent to which generic overlap can occur, of the extent to which a service comedy like The Wackiest Ship in the Army (1960) can culminate in scenes of serious combat or to which a 'combat film' like Battle Cry (1955) can include scenes of personal drama. Some may stem from the fact that scenes of combat can occur in other genres and films, that their dramatic functions can therefore differ, and that war films themselves can vary the number of combat scenes they include, as well as their duration, location and scale. In war films, combat with the enemy, however infrequent, usually determines the fates of the principal characters. That is why films like Pride of the Marines (1945) and Coming Home (1978), in which combat determines the physical condition of the central male characters but not their ultimate fates, are not normally considered as war films. That is why combat scenes nearly always occur towards the end of war films, at the point of dramatic climax. (Films like All Quiet on the Western Front, Apocalypse Now and Paths of Glory (1957) vary convention by having the fates of major characters determined by the actions of a single sniper, by the actions of a covertly commissioned assassin, and by the actions of a military court respectively. However, the ironies involved are in each case dependent on an awareness of generic convention, and this awareness is cued by the presence of extensive scenes of combat earlier on.) And finally, given the life or death outcome of combat in particular and of wartime conditions in general, that is why writers like Kaminsky (1974: 229) and Belton (1994: 164–5) argue that war films are as much about the fragilities and conditions of physical survival as they are about war – or wars – as such.

Confusion may also stem from the tendency to focus on films with a Second World War setting. Basinger suggests that 'Different wars inspire different genres' (1986: 10). Like Kane (1976, 1988), she is concerned with the distinctive conventions of the 'World War II combat film'. Thus although she herself maintains that 'At bottom, both WWI and WWII films are about death' (1986: 87), she argues that their differences outweigh their similarities and that they should be treated as separate genres. However, aside from noting Koszarski's argument that *The Big Parade* (1925), a First World War film, helped establish the convention of 'the variegated platoon' (1990: 186), and aside from noting Isenberg's argument (1981: 89–90) that this particular convention, which Basinger and others associate specifically with Second World War films, was established even earlier, during the course of the First World War itself,[1] it is possible to mount an alternative argument. It is possible to maintain that the Second World War film, however specific its conventions, is and was a variant on the same basic genre, and that the foundations of this genre were laid during the course of the First World War, when the criterion of combat inherent in earlier uses of terms like 'war picture' first came to be focused on films about modern war.

Two books have been written on the First World War and Hollywood's films, by Isenberg (1981) and by DeBauche (1997). Neither is straightforwardly focused on fictional war films, and both have specific agendas. Isenberg is interested in the relationship between film and public opinion. He therefore spends some time detailing the history of government involvement in film production during the war itself, the activities of the Committee on Public Information (the CPI or 'Creel Committee') as the government's principal propaganda agency, collaboration with the military (especially in terms of the provision of advisers, extras and equipment, a key aspect since then of nearly all Hollywood's war films as Shain (1976), Suid (1978, 1979) and others have noted), and the nature and production of documentaries and training films as well as of fictional features. Like most commentators, he argues that there was a transition from pacifist antiwar films like *In the Name of the Prince of Peace* (1915) and *Civilization* (1916) to bellicose anti-German propaganda films like *Daughter of France* (1918) and *The Kaiser, The Beast of Berlin* (1918). He also notes, though, that the apparently straightforward nature of this transition was complicated by the early production of martial adventure and 'war preparedness' films like *The Battle Cry of Peace* (1915) and *The Hero of Submarine D-2* (1916). (A number of war-preparedness serials were made in 1916, most of them featuring action heroines and serial-queens. Examples include *The Secret of the Submarine* and *Pearl of the Army*. See Dall'Asta (1995). Isenberg (1981) suggests that all three of these strands were governed by Victorian codes of gentility, manifest in the general avoidance of bloodshed and carnage, in the emphasis on honour, duty and valour in the second and third of these strands, and in the influence of contemporary liberal values in the first. He also argues that democracy and democratization were common themes and points of reference in films made both during and after the war, at their strongest in films about the army and at their weakest in films about the air force.[2]

Isenberg goes on to discuss the influence of changing attitudes to the First World War in the 1920s and 1930s, the extent to which the revisionist accounts produced by novelists, poets and playwrights affected Hollywood's films, the extent to which Victorian codes were challenged or had broken down, and the extent to which the war itself featured as background in romances like *The Enchanted Cottage* (1924) as well as foreground in war films as such. He argues that Victorian codes were by no means totally rejected, its codes of valour, honour and duty often co-existing with a revisionist verisimilitude in the treatment of battle scenes and in the use of 'hardboiled' language, and that 'Not until 1930, and then in only a very few films, did moviemakers come to a realistic grip with modern war in a mood of disillusionment which approached that of literature' (1981: 114–15). Until then, routine 'war-inspired regeneration' films like Dangerous Business (1921) and Dugan of the Dugouts (1928) were produced in great numbers alongside road-shown specials like The Big Parade and Wings, films in which the contradictory effects of the interaction between Victorian codes and revisionist devices are, he argues, especially apparent.

Both here and elsewhere (1975), Isenberg suggests that revisionism remained only partly and intermittently visible in Hollywood's films. Even amidst the pacifism and isolationism of the 1930s, films like Journey's End (1930), The Road to Glory (1936) and both versions of The Dawn Patrol (1930 and 1938) continued to manifest contradictions like these, while a cycle of heroic aviation films that included Hell's Angels (1930) and Hell in the Heavens (1934) served to perpetuate the tradition of war as adventure. By the end of the decade, as the adventure tradition continued with films like Submarine Patrol (1938), a series of preparedness films for a new war began to appear (Basinger 1986: 110–13; Dick [1985] 1996: 65–100; Leab 1995).

DeBauche covers similar chronological ground, though she focuses in more detail on the 1910s. This is in keeping with her parallel aims: to deal not only with films with a First World War setting, but also with the impact of the war on the US film industry and with the history of the industry itself. As a result, she pays as much attention to the activities of the National Association of the Motion Picture Industry (NAMPI) as she does to those of the Creel Committee. She is keen to stress the commercial advantages of 'practical patriotism' (1997: 29). And she is much more precise than Isenberg about the nature of the industry's output and its relationship to the industry's practices. She notes that 'War-related feature films' did not become 'a significant factor in "List of Current Film Release Dates," until September 1918, two months before the signing of the Armistice' (ibid.: 38). (It was in March 1918 that Daughter of France and The Kaiser, The Beast of Berlin were released, to be followed in subsequent months by To Hell with the Kaiser and others. The most extreme anti-German propaganda films were therefore seen by the American public at, near or even after the end of the war.) However, while 'a minority of all films in distribution in 1917 and 1918 were war-related' (ibid.: 48), about half of these were specials and road shows and would thus in publicity and public-relations terms have been disproportionately visible.

The nature and duration of production schedules meant that over fifty war-related feature films were released in 1919. Numbers dropped severely in 1920 and 1921, increased slowly between 1922 and 1924, then increased rapidly in 1925 and 1926. For DeBauche, the war films of the 1920s 'displayed striking innovations. They were told from the soldier's point of view and foregrounded battle over any other wartime experience' (1997: 171). In addition, they 'eliminated or significantly reduced the role of women as causal agents in their narratives' as 'a clear divide was created between the "love story" and the war scenes' and as 'war was defined as combat' (ibid.: 172). Thus they came increasingly to resemble war films made later, in the 1930s and 1940s, though it should be noted that Isenberg argues that in films like The Mad Parade (1931) and She Goes to War (1929) 'women were almost indistinguishable from men as warriors' (1981: 198).

Basinger provides the most detailed account of the war film and its history from the 1940s through to the late 1970s. However, although she discusses films about the First World War, the Korean war and Vietnam, and although she also discusses musicals, dramas and comedies, her account is centred on the Second World War, not just as subject matter but also as the period during which the conventions she identifies as basic to her principal concern, the 'World War II combat film', were forged. Moreover, despite her willingness to discuss marginal examples, exceptions, and hybrids, to recognize variations, and to acknowledge the generic untidiness of Hollywood's output, she is wedded to a very particular notion of the combat film. 'I had a prior conception of what the genre would be', she writes,

> What I knew in advance was what presumably every member of our culture would know about World War II combat films – that they contained a hero, a group of mixed types, and a military objective of some sort. They take place in the actual combat zones of World War II, against the established enemies, on the ground, the sea, or in the air. They contain many repeated events, such as mail call, all presented visually with appropriate uniforms, equipment, and iconography of battle.

(Basinger 1986: 23)

As a result, she treats the combat film not as a particular generic paradigm but as the only true genre of war; hence, for all its apparent comprehensiveness, her account is very specific in its focus; and so the films she sees as central are often outweighed by those she sees as marginal, especially (and ironically) when she comes to consider those made during the Second World War itself.

Basinger begins here by noting 'how few actual combat films were released': 'From December 7, 1941 to January 1, 1944, the primary list of pure combat films . . . contains only five films, and none of these appears before 1943' (1986: 24). Because they lack an exclusive setting in combat zones, an appropriate iconography and/or a hero, group and military objective, films like *Wake Island* (1942) and *Desperate Journey* (1942) are not considered 'pure combat'. Pure combat only begins to emerge, and is in fact only truly represented prior to 1945, by just two films, *Air Force* (1943) and *Bataan* (1943), the former serving as the template for films marked by journeying, movement and victory, the latter for those marked by stasis, last stands and defeat. Thus *Action in the North Atlantic* (1943), *Destination Tokyo* (1944) and others serve principally as further examples of generic impurity until *Air Force* and *Bataan* are joined in 1945 by *Objective, Burma!*, *They Were Expendable* and *The Story of G.I. Joe* and in 1946 by *A Walk in the Sun*. These films are canonic. For Basinger they are important because they are the first to display and exploit generic awareness, an awareness 'that they are all one type' (ibid.: 123). They also provide the focus of Kane's book, which uses them along with *Guadalcanal Diary* (1943) and *Air Force* to construct a structural model of the combat film in which narratives can result in victory or defeat and in the integration or disintegration of the combat group, and in which dualities such as war and peace, savagery and civilization, democracy and totalitarianism, humanity and inhumanity and duty and self-interest are played out within and across a basic conflict between Americans and their allies and their enemies. (Usually Japan and Germany rather than Italy, as Fyne 1992: 311, among others, points out.)

With the coming of peace, the production of war films of all kinds promptly ceases until the appearance of *Fighter Squadron* in 1948 and of *Command Decision*, *Battleground* and others in 1949. These films inaugurate a 'third wave' of combat films which persists in large numbers until 1959. This third wave is marked by the purity of its conventions and by various forms of generic awareness. It is also complicated and augmented by the Korean War and the Cold War. In the Korean films, iconography is adjusted to accommodate Korean terrain and the use of new weapons like jet planes, the mixture of the group is adjusted to accommodate a wider variety of minorities, and narrative patterns are changed to focus for the most part on stalemate or retreat. Basinger argues that an uncertainty about war aims and the necessity of leaving recently established homes and families to fight overseas is accompanied by 'a new cynicism toward war and those who plan it and lead it' (1986: 188). However, this effect is felt as much on First World War films like *Paths of Glory* (1957) and on Second World War films like *Attack!* (1956) as it is on Korean films themselves, and it is preceded in the early years of the Cold War by films like *Twelve O'Clock High* (1949) and *The Caine Mutiny* (1954) which, like a number of contemporary novels and plays, focus sympathetically on the stresses, strains and values of command (Jones 1976: 67–86; Kane 1988: 95; Lundberg 1984: 386; Walsh 1982: 138–42). Shain argues that the realignment of allies and enemies brought about by the Cold War and the consequent realignment of Hollywood's overseas markets brought about changes in the depiction of the Japanese and the Germans and thus indirectly encouraged revisionist trends (1976: 92–128). He also argues that these trends were accompanied by changes in the image of hero, that the 'socially responsible citizen' of the 1940s and the 'professional warrior' of the 1950s increasingly gives way to depictions of a hero who rejects 'long range political, social, and military goals in favor of immediate personal considerations' (ibid.: 210).

Trends like these are especially marked in the fourth and fifth phases, which run overall from 1960 to 1975. Here an augmented cynicism, evident as satirical comedy and generic deconstruction in films like *What Did You Do in the War, Daddy?* (1966), in the stress on the waste and absurdity of war in films like *None But the Brave* (1965), and in the undermining of conventionally selfless motives in 'dirty group' films like *Kelly's Heroes* (1970), runs alongside 'epic reconstructions' like *The Longest Day* (see Ambrose 1994) and large-scale 'war-as-adventure' films like *The Guns of Navarone* (1961) and *Where Eagles Dare* (1968). Reactions to the war in Vietnam help further augment revisionist trends. However, depictions of armed combat in Vietnam itself are few and far between. Following *China Gate* (1957), *A Yank in Vietnam* (1964), *To the Shores of Hell* (1966), *Marine Battleground* (1966), *The Green Berets* (1968) and *The Losers* (1970), most of them both generically and industrially marginal, are the only films to represent combat in Vietnam in any form and to any great extent until the late 1970s.

Basinger discusses some of the films set in Vietnam towards the end of her book (1986: 212–13). Alongside the observations she herself makes there now exist numerous studies of Hollywood's films and the Vietnam war, and with them a set of standard explanations for the paucity of Vietnam war films prior to the late 1970s and a standard account of the evolution and characteristics both of films which refer to the war and of Vietnam war films as such. It is generally argued that Hollywood was reluctant to make war films with a Vietnam setting in the 1960s and early 1970s because the war was publicly divisive, because the industry was in crisis and seeking to appeal to younger sectors of the population who were largely hostile to the war and because the military were unwilling to provide facilities for films which criticized the war. Defeat and withdrawal from Vietnam in the early 1970s challenged the tenets of America's 'victory culture' (Engelhardt 1998), ensured that its participation in the war remained deeply controversial, posed questions as to how the war could or should be represented, and rendered the paradigms associated with the Second World War combat film at least temporarily inappropriate. For all these reasons, the war was alluded to in neighbouring genres like the western and in figures like the maladjusted veteran far more often than it was represented directly on screen (Adair 1989: 7–76; Auster and Quart 1988: 23–55; Berg 1990: 47–60; Klein 1990b: 19–22; Martin 1990b: 134–57; Richman 1991: 1–105; Scarrow 1991: 1–67; Suid 1991: 100–98; Walker 1991).

Along with *Apocalypse Now*, the appearance of *Go Tell the Spartans* (1978), *The Boys in Company C* (1978) and *The Deerhunter* (1978), all of them independently financed and produced, put Vietnam back on Hollywood's agenda. These particular films varied widely in form and convention and are often seen as experimenting with ways of representing the war in the light of America's defeat. Some were modelled on the more cynical combat films of the 1950s and 1960s. Others echoed much more distantly some of the films set in the First World War or attempted to find a format of their own. However, along with a further cycle of films about veterans, they all tended to stress loss and impairment – the loss or impairment of American moral, political and military superiority as well as of the lives, bodies, innocence or sanity of its troops – as fundamental hallmarks of the war and its aftermath (Adair 1999: 77–120; Auster and Quart 1988: 55–73; Berg 1990: 55–6; Klein 1990: 22–3; Martin 1990b: 148–68; Richman 1991: 106–202; Scarrow 1991: 68–73, 121–3; Suid 1991: 199–233).

Finally, in the context of a decisive political turn to the right in the 1980s, the American military, the Vietnam war, victory culture and the Vietnam veteran were rehabilitated in an array of cycles which included sci-fi action-adventure films like *The Empire Strikes Back* (1980), films about the training and ethos of military officers like *Taps* (1981) and *The Lords of Discipline* (1983), films about the rescue by Vietnam veterans of American prisoners-of-war in Southeast Asia like *Uncommon Valor* (1983) and *Rambo: First Blood Part II* (1985), and later in the decade, a short-lived though much-debated series of films which revived and modified the conventions of the combat film, and which included *Platoon* (1986), *Hamburger Hill* (1987) and *Full Metal Jacket* (1987).[3]

Rehabilitated too, some have argued, was a traditionally defined masculinity (Britton 1986: 24–7; Jeffords 1989, 1994; Ryan and Kellner 1988: 217–43; Wood 1986: 172–4). Coinciding with a renewed interest in the topic of masculinity in Film, Media and Cultural Studies, war films of all kinds have been studied since then, not only in terms of their Oedipal dynamics and their sado-masochistic scenarios, but also in light of the fact that the war film is one of the few genres in which, as *Saving Private Ryan* (1998) has recently confirmed, male characters are regularly permitted to weep as a means of expressing their physical and emotional stress and hence their physical and emotional vulnerability (Belton 1994: 167–9; Easthope 1986: 61–8; Fuchs 1990; Jeffords 1988; McMahon 1994; Modleski 1988; Neale 1991: 53–7; Newsinger 1993; Scarrow 1991: 161–78; Springer 1988b; White 1988). This is not the only conventional but otherwise unusual feature of the Hollywood war film. Its close relationship to US foreign policy, its regular stress on cooperative goals, its frequent critiques of extreme individualism and its routine emphasis on the extent to which its characters lack knowledge and control of their environment, their activities, their enemies and their fates all tend to make it the exception rather than the rule among Hollywood's genres.

Notes

1   Given the importance accorded the collective and variegated nature of the combat group in writing on war films, its history as a convention is clearly important. Most commentators see it as a Second World War invention, stressing the role of the OWI in its

promulgation. However, while it is clear that the OWI played a part in advocating cooperative devices and multi-ethnic variegation (Koppes and Black 1987), it is also clear that small-scale combat groups and variegation of one kind or another can be found in at least some films made before the Second World War. What seems to change is the nature and extent of the variegation involved and the role allotted to the individual within the group and its various activities.

2   This point dovetails with Basinger's acute observations about

> the various spaces assigned . . . to the three basic formats of combat: air, sea, and land. Those who fly can return to safe havens and the occasional foray into night-clubs or private homes . . . The spaces they occupy tend to be *professional*: offices, barracks, briefing rooms. On the ocean when not in combat, men occupy *domestic* spaces: their bunks, bedrooms, kitchens, galleys . . . On land, men occupy foxholes or tents, which are purely *combat* spaces. Consequently, the air force film is often about *professionalism*, the pressure of duty, the responsibilities of leadership. The navy film is often about *domestic strife*, not only the kind that grows up among men on board (as in family life), but also the kind they left behind with women who resent their long months at sea. The land/infantry film is about *combat*.
>
> (Basinger 1986: 21–2; emphases in original)

Basinger makes these points about Second World War combat films, but it applies (with one or two modifications) to films with a First World War setting as well.

3   The literature here is extensive. It includes Adair (1999: 121–86), Auster and Quart (1988: 92–147), Berg (1990: 61–3), Corrigan (1991: 39–47), Doherty (1988/9), Haines (1990), Klein (1990: 23–36), McMahon (1994), Martin (1990b: 168–93), Porteous (1989), Richman (1991: 203–48), Rist (1988), Ryan and Kellner (1988: 194–216), Scarrow (1991: 123–60), Studlar and Desser (1990), Traube (1992: 39–66), Waller (1990), Walsh (1988) and Whillock (1988: 249), who argues that because of the heterogeneity and paucity of the films, there is 'no Vietnam war genre' as such.

PART ONE

WAR AS A WAY OF SEEING

This section gathers essays that explicitly discuss how the relationship between Hollywood and war has oriented and framed understandings of military activity and more broadly American society and history. Narrative and storytelling practices and the nature of spectacle are analyzed here as bases for establishing conceptual linkages between cinema and politics. Likewise explored are the persistent notions of "propaganda," "realism," and "truth" as standards for adjudging war films and the role played by war films in the construction and evolution of history and memory.

The convergence of the military and entertainment media has an effect that reaches far beyond contributing to the soldier's basic training or even combat experiences to re-shaping the sensorium of nearly all media viewers. Though some of the writers in this volume argue over the degree of cultural or spectatorial negotiation possible amidst the onslaught of technological media, they tend to agree on the thoroughgoing re-orientations of perception, social relations, and subjectivities that have occurred with the century-long development of war cinema. To speak of war as a way of seeing, then, is to recognize the emergence of perceptual and discursive fields that has coincided with the increasing social priority of militarization. Particularly over the twentieth-century history of cinema, during which electronic media have proliferated and become the basis for communicating information about distant events and societies, seeing comes to be about participating in thoroughly mediated processes of framing and organizing experience. To propose war as a way of seeing is ultimately to posit a way of subject-making and being in a world that has arguably changed with the conjoined evolutions of weaponry and cinema.

Geoff Klingsporn opens the section by looking at the roots of visualizing the experience of battle and the "harvest of death" it produces for the camera; historically, he argues, the emergent cinematic medium appropriated, reworked, and institutionalized "ways of seeing" battle from still photography and made them consumable commodities. The second contribution is from Paul Virilio's seminal 1985 *War and Cinema*. In that work, he wrote, "the history of battle is primarily the history of radically changing fields of perception. In other words, war consists not so much in scoring territorial, economic or other material victories as in appropriating the 'immateriality' of perceptual fields" (Virilio 1989: 7). The next essay, by Bernd Hüppauf, considers the links between modern forms of visual representation, including the cinematic, and the "logistics of perception" required by technological warfare. Like Virilio, he begins early in the twentieth century and focuses on World War I but then posits the important priority of these ideas to subsequent war cinema and war making. A fourth piece, from which the section takes its title, provides George H. Roeder's reading of how Hollywood importantly framed popular understandings of the experience of battle in World War II. In the fifth piece, the late Michael Rogin elucidates the "imperial" politics of representing late twentieth-century wars as spectacles to be consumed and forgotten. The final selection, from Slavoj Zizek, asserts that the de-realization so shocking in World War I had become, by the early twenty-first century, a commonplace, indeed, the "reality" through and in which we lived. The tragedy of 9/11 reveals for him how complete has been the inversion of the de-realized and the real in the contemporary, thoroughly mediated and militarized world.

War, film, history: American images of "real war," 1890–1920

2

GEOFFREY KLINGSPORN

Twenty years ago, Paul Virilio's assertion that "there is no war . . . without representation" seemed like provocative French theory. More recently, the convergence of war and media has become a journalistic commonplace. The New York Times worries about "the temptation to fight the last war movie" in Kosovo, while internet pundits note that "successfully delivered Allied ordnance are simply media of communication. A missile is a missive." Even glossy technology lifestyle magazines trumpet a new form of military-industrial complex: "There's no longer much 'industrial' about it. Its name these days is the 'military entertainment complex' . . . Hollywood and the Pentagon—the logistics of images and the logistics of weapons—the two things postmodern America does best."

Proclaimed in tones ranging from fear to celebration, the message is clear and achingly self-conscious: war can no longer be distinguished from its mediation.[1] But this phenomenon is hardly new. While Virilio traced its origins as far back as World War I, in the United States the intertwined histories of commercial (particularly visual) media and modern (mechanized, total) war began much earlier, in the photographic legacy of the nation's Civil War.[2] But these Civil War photographs, so familiar to Americans now, were "lost" until the end of the nineteenth century. In fact, the decades around the turn of the twentieth century witnessed a remarkable coincidence: photographic images of war became widely available for the first time, at the same moment in which the medium of cinema and the profession of History were born. What are the shared origins of war, film, and History, and what does this tell us about our "weapons of perception?"

Consider the following example from 1919.[3] With two photographs—one labeled "A Civil War Photographer with Portable Darkroom and Equipment," the other a "Photograph of a Shell Explosion in No-Man's Land"—a national advertisement from the Eastman Kodak Company looked back to the Civil War to validate the Great War. The ad's copy invokes Mathew Brady, a figure it assumes is familiar to the reader: "[t]rundling his horse-drawn darkroom from battlefield to battlefield" to create "his great picture history of our Civil War." Emphasizing the limits of Brady's equipment, the ad goes on to praise the relative speed and precision of modern Kodak technology. Now, it claims, the photographic "truth" of war can be captured on film: "And so now are recorded, in both still and moving pictures, the rush of men, the sweep of airplanes, the sudden, tremendous upheaval of shell explosions, all with the detailed accuracy of truth itself."

Such superior images, the ad concludes, are in the service of not only truth but history: "current war pictures form a chapter of history as yet in the writing. Long after we have won the war, other generations may still see today's battles refought across the screen." Photographs and history alike (indeed, the line between the two terms is intentionally blurred) become a kind of vicarious, mediated experience of war.

Kodak's advertisement embodies paradoxes of war and filmic representation that still trouble us. New visual technologies continually promise access to the "truth of war" (or the "real war"), while in the form of weaponry they make that "reality" ever more abstract and in many ways invisible. Simultaneously, the commercial media most responsible for reproducing and distributing these images, and which make the most elaborate use of the new technologies, are faulted for relying on outdated, "romantic" conventions to depict war to their audiences. Kodak's use of the halftone process to reproduce photographic images of war, its employment of such images to sell goods, its location in a national magazine, its rhetoric of photographic realism and its choice of Mathew Brady as an icon of that realism are all keys to the history of war pictures in the United States. Located at the extreme limits of violence, nationalism, and representation, war challenged the ability of photographers, filmmakers, and historians to define and represent the "truth." Producers of war pictures found a solution that relied as much on personal authority as photographic objectivity—a successful response that offered both a challenge to and a model for the historical profession.

War in the age of mass illustration

The sheer number of surviving war photographs from the late nineteenth and early twentieth centuries testifies both to the capability of photographic producers to mobilize their resources to capture war, and to the range of outlets through which these images were made available to American consumers. War photography appeared in magazines and newspaper supplements, postcards, stereograph sets, shop window displays, magic lantern slides, and in popular history books—a quantity and variety of images so immense as to frustrate any attempt to define a representative sample, much less a complete survey. Yet the corpus of war photography was only one of many tributaries to the torrent of images at the turn of the century. The halftone and the cinema, along with other new methods of reproduction and distribution, filled the everyday lives of Americans with images of all kinds, colors, and subjects. War photographs in the late nineteenth and early twentieth century existed alongside illustrations, posters, advertisements, museums, panoramas, and the rest of the attractions and distractions of an increasingly visual age. Almost no photographs would have reached a wide American public audience, however, had it not been for the "magazine revolution" of the late nineteenth century.[4]

The magazine as we know it first appeared in the late nineteenth century. Until then, American magazines had for the most part been operated by and for a literary elite. As industrial growth, commercial pressures and technical advances drove down the cost of periodical publishing, however, "editors locked up their ivory towers and came down into the marketplace."[5] The new magazines, like the urban penny press, were heavily pictorial and largely subsidized by advertisers. Unlike the newspapers, however, magazines tried to avoid the appearance of yellow journalism and scandalous illustration. Furthermore, while newspapers remained necessarily local in scope, magazines depended on nationwide circulation to attract the brand-name advertising upon which they relied. With the help of these advertisers (and the advances in transportation and communication which made such markets possible), turn-of-the-century magazines became the first national mass medium— a position they held virtually unchallenged until after World War I.[6]

Photography and war were two of the most visible components of the new magazines. Together, photography and the halftone process were "a double revolution": they offered a new kind of visual content as well as an inexpensive technology for reproducing all kinds of illustration.[7] The low cost of the halftone (around one-fifth that of a woodcut) reduced production expenses and made the five- or ten-cent magazine a viable proposition.[8] At the same time, photographs were used editorially as a means to distinguish these journals from the penny press: given photography's reputation for truthfulness and objectivity, "the new halftone photographs assumed an important place in these magazines as a way of presenting to readers an image of timeliness and authenticity."[9] These years between the thirtieth and fiftieth anniversaries of the Civil War witnessed a "boom" in martial imagery, tied to the birth of a new and modern US nationalism.[10]

In the decades following Reconstruction, Alan Trachtenberg tells us, America was "a word whose meaning became the focus of controversy and struggle during an age in which the horrors of civil war remained vivid."[11] America's increasingly "incorporated" culture both created and supplied a huge market for soldiers' memoirs, novels, and histories of the Civil War. An entire "vernacular culture" developed around war nostalgia, including plays, novels, magazine stories and serials as well as public rituals surrounding Decoration Day, July 4th, soldiers' reunions, and battle anniversaries. This was a period of "the militarization of social thought and the purification of memory," in which the political origins of the conflict were subordinated to the public's fascination with war and its high esteem of veterans.[12] For the most part, these narratives of heroism and tragedy, broken families and girl spies followed the familiar conventions of romance. But consumers of Civil War nostalgia were also in search of the unfamiliar; they sought to vicariously experience the war, whether through first-hand documentary accounts or realistic fiction and illustration.

The popular audience for halftones of war developed along with the new national magazines, which became the most important means of distribution for these mass-reproduced images. The *Century*, the "leading magazine of the nineteenth century" and one of the few "quality magazines" to successfully navigate the journey from ivory tower to marketplace, was perhaps the best example. Although it later fell behind its rivals in graphic innovation, in 1884 the *Century* was among the first American serials to adopt the halftone for illustration. In the same year, the *Century* began its "risky and expensive" Civil War series, "Battles and Leaders of the Civil War," which ultimately continued for three years and doubled the magazine's circulation. *McClure's* and the *Review of Reviews*, both of which ran their own Civil War series in later years, imitated this successful mix of war, photography and history, and the war remained a favorite topic throughout the period.[13]

One result was the rediscovery of Mathew Brady (who died penniless and unknown, a few years too early) and the transformation of the war's photographic archive into a popular consumer product. In recent decades, Brady's authorship of most of the war photographs attributed to him has been widely and successfully challenged, and his manipulation of the subjects of some of his most famous images clearly established. But a century ago, his credibility was untouched; his reputation as *the* photographer of the Civil War—and the first "photographic historian" remains unshaken even today.

Harvests of Death[14]

Photographs of the dead have come to dominate the modern memory of the Civil War so thoroughly that "to think of the Civil War at all is for many Americans to recall A *Harvest of Death* . . . with its bloated corpses flung across a misty field."[15] But the history of this famous war photograph is almost entirely a post-war story. Unlike most of the photographs taken that day at Gettysburg, this one was never published as a stereograph or *carte-de-visite* during the war. It remained unpublished for three years until Gardner later included it in his *Sketch Book of the War* (1866), giving the image its famous title in a hortatory caption that read, in part:

> Slowly, over the misty fields of Gettysburg—as all reluctant to expose their ghastly horrors to the light—came the sunless morn, after the retreat by Lee's broken army. Through the shadowy vapors, it was, indeed, a "harvest of death" that was presented . . . Such a picture conveys a useful moral: It shows the blank horror and reality of war, in opposition to its pageantry. Here are the dreadful details! Let them aid in preventing such another calamity falling upon the nation.[16]

Even in this form, the image never reached a wide audience: due to its prohibitively expensive positive prints, Gardner's *Sketch Book* was limited to editions of only 100–150.[17]

The privileged, popular status of "A Harvest of Death" is an artifact not of the Civil War but of the late nineteenth and early twentieth centuries—the age of mass reproduction. Its place in modern memory is due not so much to its compelling vision but to its consistent visibility: that is, to the fact that this image is "perhaps the most frequently reprinted of all Civil War photographs."[18] The career of "A Harvest of Death" in reproduction reveals how the image lost its specificity of time, place, and even medium, becoming available for use in other wars and by other means of visual communication—ultimately, a crucial part of the visual grammar for representing modern war, an icon of "real war."

Dissociated from the original *Sketch Book* image, and popularized in mass-market photographic histories, Gardner's metaphor was applied to similar images from current conflicts. War photographs depicting dead soldiers published in the popular press from the early years of the First World War, and even as late as the Spanish Civil War, echoed "A Harvest of Death" in their titles and captions as well as composition. The survival of Gardner's agricultural metaphor in captions and titles is relatively easy to uncover; more elusive and significant is its long career as a visual convention for picturing the war dead without this explicit textual reference.

The influence of Civil War photographs upon American war photography at the beginning of this century is strikingly evident—no more so than when photographers attempted to picture the dead. Images of corpses always represented a distinct minority of war photographs, but those that exist tend to frame their subject in similar fashion: the dead are shown from ground level, viewed frontally from a "respectful" distance (like a nineteenth-century portrait), receding into the horizon where a level field meets the sky.[19] The nature of modern war, censorship, notions of propriety and technological limitations all affected the look of these photographs, but none explain the consistency of this visual trope of dead soldiers lying in a field. From 1898 to 1918, across two decades of technological changes and wars on three different continents, photographs of war that were presented to an American audience depicted the dead with this iconography developed in the 1860s.

A few examples must suffice to trace this iconography through the first decades of this century. When the famous war correspondent and photographer Jimmy Hare photographed the Russo-Japanese War, his pictures of the wounded tended to be taken from close range. But Hare's photograph of "Russian Dead Awaiting Burial in the Outskirts of Port Arthur" steps back into the longer perspective of Civil War photographs.[20] The horse-drawn cart in the middle distance even echoes the figures on horseback in Gardner's original image. Less than a decade later, when photographers went to Europe to cover the Great War, they returned to this distant image of dead men lying in a field. By this time, technologies and standards had changed sufficiently to allow much closer views of the victims of war (especially foreign or enemy casualties). Yet examples of gruesomely intimate views simply serve to underscore the continuing influence of Civil War iconography: even with the opportunity, the tools, and the license to take new kinds of photographs, photographers continued to frame their pictures of the dead in much the same way as their mid-nineteenth century counterparts. From newspaper correspondents, to photo services like Underwood & Underwood, to the official photographers of the Signal Corps, each planted their tripods and composed their views in ways to make their subjects look like the dead on the battle-fields of the Civil War.

Neither the harvest metaphor nor its iconography was confined to still photographs. The popularization of Civil War halftones also had an immediate impact on the cinema, quickly becoming an even more influential form of visual history. Publicity for one Civil War film of 1911, for example, openly capitalized on the appeal of the Brady archive and the best-selling *Photographic History of the Civil War*:

> . . . you'll think the great Brady took a moving picture camera South with him and we discovered his long-lost reel. Certainly, all the re-discovered Brady Collection of war photos will not surpass this motion film as an accurate picture of Rebellion time. Only the knowledge that moving pictures are a late invention will convince you that the reel wasn't done in the actual battle days of '61.[21]

Accordingly, early cinematic depictions of war carried Gardner's phrase into this new medium. A 1915 dramatization of *The Life of Abraham Lincoln* includes an intertitle that reads: "1862. Lincoln sees the harvest of death, and with a breaking heart, feels that he has failed in his effort to preserve the Union."[22] In a postwar twist that returned to Gardner's somber but triumphant use of the metaphor in the *Sketch Book*, the 1919 Committee on Public Information film *The Price of Peace* introduced a series of battlefield panoramas with the title: "The harvest of the guns—the price the enemy paid—and lost."[23] A split-screen image in 1918's *My Four Years in Germany* bore the legend "DOUBLE HARVEST," over a Bradyesque image of the Great War dead.

Cinema producers adapted familiar Civil War imagery as a means to add "realism" to their attempts to dramatize war, and the "harvest of death" became a common piece of cinematic synecdoche. The influence of Civil War photographs upon the films of D. W. Griffith is a well-known example, but this convention was limited neither to Griffith nor to films about the Civil War.[24] Thomas Ince's 1916 pacifist drama, *Civilization*, also features corpse-strewn fields in its vision of war, as do numerous other First World War-era films, both pro- and anti-war, fiction and documentary.[25] Ince's earlier feature-length version of *The Battle of Gettysburg* (now lost) relied heavily on the photographic archive for its reconstruction of battle scenes and their aftermath, provoking this telling response from one reviewer: "Enough of the memorable features of the sensational three day's engagements are introduced to give the play verisimilitude to the spectator." For the vast majority of those spectators (especially by 1913, a half-century after the battle), this visual memory was necessarily vicarious. The film's verisimilitude depended on its adherence not to the history of the battle, but to the experience of its images.[26]

In these films, the "harvest of death" icon is abstracted from both its original medium and its allegorical title, yet remains as a visual shorthand, a reference to a familiar and "authentic" body of evidence that has come to represent death in war, and "the reality of war." Even today, in newscasts and blockbuster war films alike, this effect can be seen whenever the action stops to allow the camera to pan across a field of motionless casualties, perhaps stopping altogether to focus on a single corpse, lying as it fell.

Brady's heirs

The "rediscovery" of the Civil War photographs also recast Brady and his fellow photographers as the fathers of photojournalism, and thus as models for future photographers of war. Edward Steichen, who would become the Great War's most famous photographer, recalled his enlistment in precisely these terms: "I wanted to be a photographic reporter, as Mathew Brady had been in the Civil War . . . When I found that the Signal Corps was charged with photography, I went to them and was accepted."[27] Like Steichen (and Kodak), the Signal Corps saw Brady as both a model to emulate and a standard to surpass: "The best pictorial records that have been handed down to us from the days of the Civil War are the still photographs taken in the Union Army by an operator named Brady."[28] The Signal Corps clearly expected to join Brady's example with fifty years of technical advances in photography and the invention of motion pictures: the author of the Photographic Division's "historical file" was also confident that: "future generations will prize these photographs and movies of the American Army's march from Hoboken to the Rhine with all the high esteem that the present-day historian has for the precious records that Brady collected in the Civil War."[29]

But as the photographers of World War I were to discover, authenticity and references to Brady were not sufficient to communicate the war to their audience. Wartime correspondence reveals constant dissatisfaction in Washington with the images sent back from France. During the nineteen months of war the Photographic Division was repeatedly restructured and threatened with the loss of its monopoly on battlefield photography. "Generally speaking," wrote the exasperated director of the War College Pictorial Section in June, 1918, "the official U.S. pictures which have been coming here are not as good as they ought to be. They appear scrappy and inconsequential."[30] The country's propaganda agency was equally displeased; the director of the pictorial division of the Committee on Public Information complained to the Signal Corps that: "we have been exceedingly embarrassed by lack of material with which to show, not only to America, but to the world, that America *is* in the war, that she *has* men in France, and that they *are actually* doing something."[31]

Production of images was not the problem. The Signal Corps faced many difficulties, among them a shortage of cameras and a lack of well-trained personnel. But even with these disadvantages, the Signal Corps produced tens of thousands of photographs and hundreds of thousands of feet of motion picture film.[32] Rather, the inability of anonymous government cameramen to meet their audience's photographic expectations of the real lay with the lack of "romantic," thrilling individuals and narratives to go with the pictures. Captain Edwin Cooper described his difficulties filming the war with a reference to the most famous motion picture director of the time: "Mr. Griffith with his wonderful war pictures, (as it is not fought), had educated the public to such a degree that we felt we might at this juncture satisfy them, and tried to get the spectacular, but the modern warfare makers did not take into consideration the photographer."[33]

Note, however, that the attempt was still made; the desire for thrilling or "spectacular" pictures was not reserved for bloodthirsty civilians or superiors in the rear. And the standard here remains the photographic history of the Civil War (the famous Birth of a Nation serving as a cinematic "harvest of death").

Grappling with absolute truth

Throughout the decades surrounding the turn of the twentieth century, Americans expressed, displayed, and sold their nationalism to themselves in media that were increasingly dominated by the visual. Not far into the new century, J.A. Hobson found it "obvious that the spectatorial lust of Jingoism is a most serious factor in Imperialism." If there existed a popular "militarist imagination" around the turn of the century, it was most assuredly visual. Such a situation was obviously open to manipulation, and the visual spectacle of war was easily blamed for duping the public. "The dramatic falsification both of war and of the whole policy of imperial expansion required to feed this popular passion," wrote Hobson, "forms no small portion of the art of the real organizers of imperialist exploits."[34] Subsequent scholarship on these imagined wars has followed much the same course, pointing out falsehoods and interpreting the ideological motives behind them.

War pictures challenge the historian's typical divisions between film and History, and the separation of each from the "real war" they attempt to represent. The simultaneous emergence of the halftone, the cinema, and the historical discipline in an era of militarized nationalism and consumer culture reveals, first, that the lines between war and film have been blurred since the beginning: picture not only Brady's doctored images later taken as "reality," but also Captain Cooper hurriedly trying to set up his camera and capture something that looked like a Griffith film. Secondly, the hybrid nature of war pictures—at once consumer goods, objective records, the products of dashing and adventurous young men —represents not only a challenge to traditional history but a suggestion that historians and cameramen share not only goals and materials but methods as well.[35] The publishers of The Photographic History of the Civil War advertised their collection of "real photographs" in these terms, presenting Brady and his colleagues as superior historians (if not better men): "Unafraid and determined the photographers went to the very front armed only with clumsy photographic outfits. . . . With cameras alone they did what no other historians have succeeded in doing—grappled with absolute truth, conquered it, and gave it as a heritage to the American people for all generations."[36]

A similar impulse is reflected in the continuing reluctance of scholars to approach photographs of war in the same way as other kinds of images. While the objective "realism" or indexicality of the photographic image may be a dead issue in most recent studies of visual culture, discussions of war persistently revolve around issues of realism and authenticity. Take for instance W. J. T. Mitchell's *Picture Theory*, a crucial influence on recent scholarship in visual culture. The final paragraphs of *Picture Theory* also exemplify the reluctance of many critics to extend such insights to images of war. When it comes to critical responsibility or "intervention," war pictures mark the end of playful theory or historical relativism: Mitchell concludes by warning that war pictures require particular attention from scholars of visual culture—not as critics but as guardians, "preservers of the historical record."[37] This impulse to privilege war photographs over other kinds of images—in a sense, to take them more seriously—derives from assumptions about war's enhanced "reality."

Scholars should beware such reductions in an age in which photographic technologies have become inextricable from the practice of history, as well as the waging of war. A large part of war's cultural power, its attraction and seeming inevitability, is rooted in the belief that war is a privileged path to reality.[38] In war photography, this fallacy is effectively doubled. The urge to exalt war as somehow more real than normal everyday existence combines with our tendency to see the photographic image as transparent. The result is a realism that appears self-evident—which seems to speak for itself (in a universal language) even though literally mute, with the silence of the photographic print and the silence of the dead. But the possibility must be considered that our respect for such images has contributed to the violence of this century: that by treating them as "undeniable truth" we have perpetuated the allure of combat; that by failing to analyze them as part of consumer culture, we have strengthened the myth of war as an antidote to the discontents of that culture.

Notes

1   Paul Virilio, *War and Cinema: The Logistics of Perception*, trans. Patrick Camiller, Originally published as *Guerre et Cinéma*, Paris: Cahiers du cinéma/Editions de l'Etoile, 1985 (London: Verso, 1989), 6; Jacob Weisberg, "Bombs and Blockbusters," *New York Times Magazine*, 11 April 1999, 17–18; "The Internick", "Nothing but Bombs," (1999); McKenzie Wark, "Pop Politics," 21•C 1997, 24–30, 28.

2   On issues of representation and violence during the Civil War, see Charles Royster, *The Destructive War: William Tecumseh Sherman, Stonewall Jackson, and the Americans* (New York: Random House, 1991), especially Chapter 6, "The Vicarious War," 232–95.

3   Eastman Kodak Co. advertisement, *American Magazine* (March 1919), 136. As the lead time for the magazine was at least three months, the ad must have been submitted in December, 1918, just weeks after the Armistice (or perhaps even earlier, given the indeterminate tense of the final paragraph). See David Reed, *The Popular Magazine in Britain and the United States, 1880–1960* (Toronto: University of Toronto Press, 1997), 115.

4   The scholarship on this mass culture is nearly as old as its subject, and the importance of visual images has long been acknowledged. For a pithy summary of mass culture criticism, see T. J. Jackson Lears, "Mass Culture and Its Critics," in Mary Kupiec Cayton, Elliott J. Gorn, and Peter W. Williams, ed., *Encyclopedia of American Social History* (New York and Toronto: Scribner, 1993), 1591–610; on contemporary objections to the "expanded pictorialism in mass culture," see Neil Harris, "Pictorial Perils: The Rise of American Illustration," in *Cultural Excursions: Marketing Appetites and Cultural Tastes in Modern America* (Chicago and London: University of Chicago Press, 1990), 337–48.

5 Frank Luther Mott, A History of American Magazines, Volume IV: 1885–1905 (Cambridge, Mass.: Belknap Press/Harvard University Press, 1957), 2. My discussion of the "magazine revolution" and the context of war photographs are indebted to a large secondary literature on the topic. Mott's multi-volume work is still the definitive study, but recent years have seen a new burst of interest in the turn-of-the-century popular magazine: Theodore P. Greene, America's heroes; the changing models of success in American magazines (New York: Oxford University Press, 1970); Richard Ohmann, "Where Did Mass Culture Come From? The Case of the Magazines," reprinted in The Politics of Letters (Middletown, Conn.: Wesleyan University Press, 1987), 135–51; Matthew Schneirov, The Dream of a New Social Order: Popular Magazines in America, 1893–1914 (New York: Columbia University Press, 1994); and David Reed, The Popular Magazine in Britain and the United States, 1880–1960 (Toronto: University of Toronto Press, 1997).

6 Ohmann, 139–45; Schneirov, 11–12.

7 Mott, 153.

8 Mott, 3–4; Reed, 36. The shift to halftones occurred years before the other major economic innovation of the magazine revolution—the reliance on advertising revenues rather than subscription rates.

9 Schneirov, 123. Jussim, Visual Communication, is the most complete discussion of this effect; see also Harris, "Iconography and Intellectual History," 305–06; Ohmann, 149–50.

10 John Pettegrew, " 'The Soldier's Faith': Turn-of-the-century Memory of the Civil War and the Emergence of Modern American Nationalism." Journal of Contemporary History 31 (1996): 49–73.: 55–56.
    Historians have often noted this trend in late nineteenth-century popular culture, but only recently analyzed it at length. The most complete accounts are Pettegrew's and Gerald F. Linderman, Embattled Courage: The Experience of Combat in the American Civil War. New York: Free Press, 1987: 275–97. Brief mention can also be found in Trachtenberg, 77; Lears, No Place of Grace, 98; G. Kurt Piehler, Remembering War the American Way. Washington, DC: Smithsonian Institution Press, 1995, 74–75; Cullen, Jim. The Civil War in Popular Culture: A Reusable Past. Washington and London: Smithsonian Institution Press, 1995: 18; Handlin, Oscar. "The Civil War as Symbol and as Actuality." Massachusetts Review 3 (1961): 133–43: 135; Thomas J. Pressly, Americans Interpret Their Civil War. New York: Free Press, 1965. 17. Directly relevant, though appearing after the writing of this article, is David W. Blight, Race and Reunion: The Civil War in American Memory (Belknap Press, 2002).

11 Alan Trachtenberg, The Incorporation of America: Culture and Society in the Gilded Age (New York: Hill and Wang, 1982), 7.

12 Linderman, 284.

13 Schneirov, 11, 76, 44–45; Reed, 36, 57–58. Schneirov's survey of magazine contents indicates that the Civil War was one of the two most popular topics from 1893 to 1903 (291 n. 38).

14 This section is adapted from my previously published article, "Icon of Real War: 'A Harvest of Death' and American War Photography," Velvet Light Trap 45 (Spring 2000), 4–19.

15 Jennifer Green-Lewis, Framing the Victorians: Photography and the Culture of Realism (Ithaca and London: Cornell University Press, 1996): 134.

16 Alexander Gardner, *Gardner's Photographic Sketch Book of the War*, reprint: New York, Dover Publications, 1959 (Washington, D.C.: 1866): Plate 36.

17 William A. Frassanito, *Gettysburg: A Journey in Time* (New York: Charles Scribner's Sons, 1975): 24–27; 198–228.

18 Alan Trachtenberg, *Reading American Photographs: Images as History, Mathew Brady to Walker Evans* (New York: Hill and Wang, 1989): 99.

19 See Joel Snyder, "Photographers and Photographs of the Civil War," in Joel Snyder and Doug Munson, ed., *The Documentary Photograph as a Work of Art: American Photographs, 1860–1876* (Chicago: David and Alfred Smart Gallery, 1976), 17–22: for a brief but suggestive description of the "formal attributes" of Civil War photographs.

20 James H. Hare, ed. *A Photographic Record of the Russo-Japanese War* (New York: P.F. Collier & Son, 1905); for examples of his treatment of the wounded, see 112–15.

21 Thanhouser Film Co. ad, *Moving Picture World* 8:12 (25 March 1911), 626.

22 *The Life of Abraham Lincoln* (Edison, 1915), Museum of Modern Art Film Library, New York; reel 2.

23 *The Price of Peace* |Part IV| (CPI, 1919), National Archives and Records Administration (200.70).

24 On Griffith and Brady, see Bill Brown, *The Material Unconscious: American Amusement, Stephen Crane, and the Economies of Play* (Cambridge, MA and London: Harvard University Press, 1996): 148; Evelyn Ehrlich, "The Civil War in Early Film: Origin and Development of a Genre," *Southern Quarterly* 19 (1981): 70–82: 178; and James Chandler, "The Historical Novel Goes to Hollywood: Scott, Griffith, and Film Epic Today," in Robert Lang, ed., *The Birth of a Nation: D.W. Griffith, director*. Rutgers Films in Print (New Brunswick: Rutgers University Press, 1994), 225–49: 236–37.

25 Examples include *My Four Years in Germany* (Warner Bros., 1918), *Joan the Woman* (Cecil B. DeMille, 1916); "Second Liberty Loan" short (Jesse L. Lasky, 1917); *The Unbeliever* (Edison, 1916), all at the Library of Congress; and *Official War Review #11* (CPI, 1918), NARA.

26 Review of *The Battle of Gettysburg* |Mutual, 1913|, *Variety* (27 June 1913); reprinted in *Variety Film Reviews* (New York: Garland, 1983). See also Frank Thompson, *Lost Films: Important Movies That Disappeared* (New York: Citadel Press, 1996), 19ff.

27 Edward Steichen, *A Life in Photography* (Garden City: Doubleday & Company, in collaboration with The Museum of Modern Art, 1963), |n.p.|.

28 |History of Signal Corps Technical and Administrative Services (Continued)|," 1919, Box 44, RG 120, NARA, 1.

29 History of Signal Corps Technical and Administrative Services (Continued), 4.

30 Major Kendall Banning to Captain William E. Moore, 20 August 1918, Folder "Photos—Correspondence War College," Box 6190, RG 120, NARA.

31 L.E. Rubel to Lieutenant Joe Marshall, 25 January 1918, Folder "Distribution—Com. on Pub. Inf.," Box 6189, RG 120, NARA.

32 |History of Signal Corps Technical and Administrative Services (Continued)|," 1919, Box 44, RG 120, NARA, 2.

33 "Extracts from Personal Narratives: Edwin H. Cooper, Captain," in "Miscellaneous 1919" folder, Box 44, RG 120, NARA, 156.

34 J. A. Hobson, *Imperialism: A Study*, originally published 1902 (Ann Arbor: University of Michigan Press, 1988), 215; quoted in Armand Mattelart, *Mapping World Communication: War, Progress, Culture*, trans. Susan Emanuel and James A. Cohen, Originally published as

La Communication-Monde. Histoire des idées et des strategies (Paris: Editions La Découverte, 1991) (Minneapolis: University of Minnesota Press, 1994), 29.

35 Robert Rosenstone, Visions of the Past: The Challenge of Film to Our Idea of History (Cambridge, MA: Harvard University Press, 1995).

36 Advertisement for The Photographic History of the Civil War, in American Magazine (January, 1913), 103.

37 W.J.T. Mitchell, Picture Theory: Essays on Verbal and Visual Presentation (Chicago: University of Chicago Press, 1994), 424–425. In the book's penultimate sentence, Mitchell warns his fellow image critics that: "the representations of war and mass destruction in narratives that simultaneously erase the memory of Vietnam and replace it with a fantasy replay of World War II should activate our responsibilities as preservers of the historical record and of cultural memory."

38 John Limon calls this "equation of combat and reality . . . the war synecdochic fallacy of war theory: . . . the assumption that . . . war is mute reality itself." Limon, 33.

3

A Traveling Shot over Eighty Years

PAUL VIRILIO

. . . If we remember that it was an optics professor, Henri Chrétien, whose work during the First World War perfecting naval artillery telemetry laid the foundations for what would become Cinemascope thirty-six years later, we can better grasp the deadly harmony that always establishes itself between the functions of eye and weapon. And, indeed, while the advance of panoramic telemetry resulted in wide-screen cinema, so the progress of radio-telemetry led to an improved picture: the *radar picture*, whose electronic image prefigured the electronic vision of video. From the commanding heights of the earliest natural fortifications, through the architectonic innovation of the watch-tower, and the development of anchored observation balloons, or the aerial reconnaissance of World War I and its 'photographic reconstruction' of the battlefield, right up to President Reagan's latest early warning satellites, there has been no end to the enlargement of the military field of perception. Eyesight and direct vision have gradually given way to optical or opto-electronic processes, to the most sophisticated forms of 'telescopic sight'. The strategic importance of optics was already clear in World War I, one indication being the dramatic rise during the war in French production of optical glass (for rangefinders, periscopes and camera lenses; for telemetry and goniometry) – from 40 tonnes to 140 tonnes a year, half the total Allied output.

The idea of war as fundamentally a game of hide-and-seek with the enemy was proved to the point of absurdity in those First World War earthworks where millions of men were entrenched and interred for four long years. With the appearance of what came to be called saturation weapons (repeating rifles, machine-guns, rapid-firing field guns) firepower alone determined who would be victorious – rather than the disposition of troops, the strict geometry of their movements. All efforts were made to conceal and disperse one's forces instead of deploying them in maximum concentrations. Hence those endless waves of sacrificial infantrymen who leapt over the parapets and crawled through the mud to their own burial – dead or alive, but anyway safe from enemy eyes and guns.

If the First World War can be seen as the first mediated conflict in history, it is because rapid-firing guns largely replaced the plethora of individual weapons.[1] Hand-to-hand fighting and physical confrontation were superseded by long-range butchery, in which the enemy was more or less invisible save for the flash and glow of his own guns. This explains the urgent need that developed for ever more accurate sighting, ever greater magnification, for *filming the war* and photographically reconstructing the battlefield; above all it explains the newly dominant role of aerial observation in operational planning.

In the wars of old, strategy mainly consisted in choosing and marking out a theatre of operations, a battlefield, with the best visual conditions and the greatest scope for movement. In the Great War, however, the main task was to grasp the opposite tendency: to narrow down targets and to create a picture of battle for troops blinded by the massive reach of artillery units, themselves firing blind, and by the ceaseless upheaval of their environment. Hence that multiplicity of trench periscopes, telescopic sights, sound detectors, and so on. The soldiers of the First World War may have been actors in a bloody conflict. But they were also the first spectators of a pyrotechnic fairy-play whose magical, spectacular nature some of them could already recognize (I am thinking especially of Ernst Jünger, Apollinaire and Marinetti). Ten years after the siege of Port Arthur, this was the inauguration of total war, a continuous performance, all day and all night.

Indeed, why should there have been any rest after dark? For the enemy's presence made itself known only through the flash of gunfire or the glow from the trenches, and daytime blindness was hardly any different from that which set in at nightfall. As a prelude to the lightning war of 1940, here was a *lighting war*, with the use of the first tracer bullets, flares that lit up no-man's-land for nocturnal targets, powerful searchlights with a range of nine kilometres, and early anti-aircraft defence systems. The old adage, 'The cavalry lights the way, the infantry wins the day', now well and truly belonged to the past. As the front settled into positional warfare, aviation took over the cavalry's functions and reconnaissance planes became the eyes of the high command, a vital prosthesis for the headquarters strategist, illuminating a terrain that was constantly being turned upside down by high explosives. Landmarks vanished: maps lost all accuracy, and as the landscape of war became cinematic, so the first on-board cameras came into their own. For only the lens-shutter could capture the film of events, the fleeting shape of the front line, the sequences of its gradual disintegration. Only serial photography was capable of registering changing troop positions or the impact of long-range artillery, and hence the capacity of new weapons for serial destruction.

Marey's interest in disclosing the successive phases of a body movement here becomes a concern to explain the sequence of a sudden disintegration of the landscape which is not fully visible to any one person. Aerial photography, cinematic photogrammetry – once again we find a conjunction between the power of the modern *war* machine, the aeroplane, and the new technical performance of the *observation* machine. Even though the military film is made to be projected on screen, thus obscuring the practical value of the successive negatives in analysing the phases of the movement in question, it is fundamentally a reversal of Marey's or Muybridge's work. For the point is no longer to study the deformations involved in the movement of a *whole body*, whether horse or man, but *to reconstitute the fracture lines of the trenches, to fix the infinite fragmentation of a mined landscape alive with endless potentialities*. Hence the crucial role of photographic reconstruction, and of those military films which were the first, little-known form of macro-cinematography, applied not (as with Painlevé after 1925) to the infinitely small but to the infinitely large. Thus, as the Hachette *Almanach* of 1916 put it, the techniques of representation proved their enormous importance during the war: 'Thanks to negatives and films, it was possible to retrace the whole front with the greatest clarity, from Belfort to the Yser.'

On the one hand, the secret of victory is written in the air by the ballistics of projectiles and the hyper-ballistics of aeronautics; on the other, it is negated by speed since only the speed of film exposure is capable of recording that military secret which each protagonist tries to keep by camouflaging ever larger objects (artillery batteries, railways, marshalling yards, and eventually whole towns as the black-out belatedly responded to the lighting war of 1940).

Just as weapons and armour developed in unison throughout history, so visibility and invisibility now began to evolve together, eventually producing *invisible weapons that make things visible* – radar, sonar, and the high-definition camera of spy satellites. The Duke of Wellington once said he had spent his life guessing what was on the other side of the hill. Today's military decision-makers don't have to guess: their task is to avoid confusing the forms of a representation which, while covering the broadest regions of the front, must take in the minute details always liable to influence the outcome of a conflict. The problem, then, is no longer so much one of masks and screens, of camouflage designed to hinder long-range targeting; rather, it is a problem of ubiquitousness, of handling simultaneous data in a global but unstable environment where the image (photographic or cinematic) is the most concentrated, but also the most stable, form of information.

The camera-recording of the First World War already prefigured the statistical memory of computers, both in the management of aerial observation data and in the ever more rigorous management of the simultaneity of action and reaction.

Was the Bofors predictor of the Second World War not the forerunner of the 'strategic calculator' of the immediate post-war period? In this anti-aircraft gun, which improved on telemetry by making the ballistic trajectory coincide with the target aircraft at a certain point in time and space, the deadly result was achieved by means of stereoscopic super-imposition, in real time, of the two flight images on a screen.

Thus, the theatre of operations of the Napoleonic Wars, where actors in the bloodbath moved in rhythm and hand-to-hand fighting was conducted by the naked eye and with bare weapons, gave way at the beginning of this century to a camera obscura in which face-to-face confrontation was supplanted by instant interface, and geographical distance by the notion of real time.

Military strategy had earlier involved the division of space, the building of permanent fortifications complete with ditches, ramparts and screens that added up to what one nineteenth-century general called 'a kind of box of surprises'. The twentieth century moved on to the division of time, where the surprise effect came from the sudden appearance of pictures and signs on a monitor, and where screens were designed to simulate, rather than dissimulate, a war that ever more closely resembled non-stop cinema or round-the-clock television. Only with the Second World War and the spread of radio-telephony, however, did the silent cinema of radiotelegraphy finally begin to talk. . . .

Although military force depends on its relationship to outward appearance, this power has over the years lost its verisimilitude in a profusion of camouflage, decoys, jamming, smoke-screens, electronic counter-measures, and so on. The offensive arsenal has equipped itself with new devices for a conflict in which optical and motor illusion have fused in the cinematic delirium of lightning-war. Here what counts is the speed at which objects, images and sounds travel through space, until the moment of the nuclear flash.

In the spring of 1940, unlike 1914–18, reconnaissance aircraft had a constant short-wave radio link with the ground, over a range that would increase from a few dozen kilometres to five hundred by the end of the war. In the autumn of the same year, RAF night-fighters became the first to have onboard radar which enabled pilots to see on cockpit screens a Dornier or Messerschmitt-110 flying through the dark over five kilometres away. The pilot's gift of double sight thus introduced a new doubling of the warrior's personality: with his head up, atmospheric transparency and ocular targeting; head down, the transparency of the ether, long-distance vision. Two military spaces, one close and one faraway, corresponded to a single battle, a single war. Later these technologies led to the development of over-the-horizon weapons systems.

As for the night-bombers, which had to face the blinding light of 200 million candlepower searchlights, they gradually acquired new resources and procedures to help them accomplish their mission. Whereas in 1940 the Luftwaffe dropped incendiaries to mark the bombing area in London and Coventry, in 1941 the Allies' 'Operation Millennium' used impact flare-bombs to sketch out in the darkness a rectangle of red lights for the Halifaxes and Lancasters to release their destructive load over Cologne.

Subsequently the Allies developed the magnesium flare and the electronic flash, which allowed USAF bombers not only to light up the ground but, more importantly, to dazzle enemy defences for a few moments. (Such innovations were taken further by Sam Cohen in the Vietnam War, when it became possible to blind the enemy for more than an hour: the latest development in this line is the stun grenade used against terrorists in Mogadishu and London.)

By 1942 ground-based electronic devices were able to direct Flying Fortress squadrons over a very long distance, helping them to drop their bomb-loads by day or night and under any weather conditions. The two ground stations involved were known as 'The Cat' and 'Mickey Mouse'. Aircraft fitted with a special receiver picked up the cat's beam and let themselves be passively guided to the vicinity of the target. The mouse, which had so far followed the operation in silence from a distance of some four hundred kilometres, then took over and, having calculated the moment when the bomber should release its load, transmitted the instruction by radar – all with a margin of error of a mere hundred metres.

This sophisticated electronic network covering Western Europe was first known as GEE. But as it continually improved, its name changed to the call-sign OBOE and finally, in 1943, to H2S, by which time it could give pilots not just a radar signal but a 'radar image', a luminous silhouette of the target over which they were flying. The bombing apparatus was equipped with a transmitter that beamed centimetric waves in a perpendicular line to ground level, the echoes then returning and forming on a cathode screen an electronic image of fifteen square kilometres. The system was used for the first time in Operation Gomorrah, which devastated Hamburg.

The visible weapons systems of artillery, machine-guns, and so forth thus became entangled with the invisible weapons systems of a continent-wide electronic war. No longer were objects on the ground invisible to pilots, who in the past had related to natural conditions both as a source of protective concealment from enemy fire and as a hindrance that masked their own target. Anti-aircraft defences benefited in turn from the ubiquitousness of war: the Kammhuber Line, for example, whose operational centre was at Arnhem in Holland, organized the German fighter response with an air-raid warning system that covered key areas from the North Sea to the Mediterranean. A network of 'panoramic radar' installations, each tracking a circle of three hundred kilometres, could cable an electronic image of the sky to the anti-aircraft batteries of *Festung Europa*. This total visibility, cutting through darkness, distance and natural obstacles, made the space of war translucent and its military commanders clairvoyant, since response time was continually being cut by the technological processes of foresight and anticipation.

The air-raid alert system also played a major psychological role on the Continent. Advance warning could be given to civilian populations as soon as enemy squadrons crossed the coast, and this was translated into a full-scale alert once they veered towards their target city. With the compression of space–time, danger was lived simultaneously by millions of attentive listeners. For want of space to move back into, their only protection was time given to them by the radio. . . .

In making attack unreal, industrial warfare ceased to be that huge funeral apparatus denounced by moralists and eventually became the greatest mystification of all: an apparatus of deception, the lure of deterrence strategy. Already in the Great War, as we have seen, the industrialization of the repeating image illustrated this cinematic dimension of regional-scale destruction, in which landscapes were continually upturned and had to be reconstituted with the help of successive frames and shots, in a cinematographic pursuit of reality, the decomposition and recomposition of an uncertain territory in which film replaced military maps.

Cinematic derealization now affected the very nature of power, which established itself in a technological Beyond with the space–time not of ordinary mortals but of a single war machine. In this realm sequential perception, like optical phenomena resulting from retinal persistence, is both origin and end of the apprehension of reality, since the seeing of movement is but a statistical process connected with the nature of the segmentation of images and the speed of observation characteristic of humans. The macro-cinematography of aerial reconnaissance, the cable television of panoramic radar, the use of slow or accelerated motion in analysing the phases of an operation – all this converts the commander's plan into an animated cartoon or flow-chart. In the Bayeux Tapestry, itself a model of a pre-cinematic march-past, the logistics of the Norman landing already prefigured The Longest Day of 6 June 1944.[2]

Now, it should not be forgotten that inductive statistics developed from the calculations that Marshal Vauban used to make during his long and repetitive journeys to the same place at different times. On each of these trips, Louis XIV's commissioner-general of fortifications became a kind of 'commissioner for displays'.[3] The kingdom paraded before his eyes, offering itself up for general inspection. This was not just a troop muster for the logistical benefit of the officer in charge of army comportment; it was a full-scale review of the country, a medical examination of its territorial corpus. Instead of the ordinary situation in which serried ranks used to pass back and forth before the watchful gaze of the king's administrator, it was the country's provinces, drawn up as on parade, which were passed in review by his inspector-general. However, these repeated trips, which caused the regional film to unwind, were no more than an artifice or cinematic trick for the sole benefit of the itinerant observer. Alone as he watched the situations and sequences dissolve, he gradually lost sight of local realities and ended up demanding a reform of fiscal law in favour of administrative norms.

Statistics brings us to the dawn of political economy, which rested on the persistence of the sign and of dominant trends, not on the merely chronological succession of facts. It is the same movement of ideas which led from the Enlightenment to photographic recording, Muybridge's multiple chambers, Marey's chronophotography and the Lumière brothers' film-camera, not forgetting Méliès, the inventor of the mystification of montage.

Winston Churchill, it is well known, believed that whereas episodic events used to have greater importance than tendencies, in modern wars the tendency had gained the upper hand over episodes. Mass phenomena do indeed elude immediate apprehension and can only be perceived by means of the computer and interception and recording equipment which did not exist in earlier times (hence the relative character of Churchill's judgement). We should therefore conclude that total war has made an essential contribution to the rise of projection equipment which can reveal and finally make possible the totalitarian tendencies of the moment.

The development of 'secret' weapons, such as the 'flying bomb' and stratospheric rockets, laid the basis for Cruise and intercontinental missiles, as well as for those invisible weapons which, by using various rays, made visible not only what lay over the horizon, or was hidden by night, but what did not or did not yet exist. Here we can see the strategic fiction of the need for armaments relying on atomic radiation – a fiction which, at the end of the war, led to the 'ultimate weapon'.

As we saw in the first chapter, many epilogues have been written about the nuclear explosions of 6 and 9 August 1945, but few have pointed out that the bombs dropped on Hiroshima and Nagasaki were *light-weapons* that prefigured the enhanced-radiation neutron bomb, the directed-beam laser weapons, and the charged-particle guns currently under development. Moreover, a number of Hiroshima survivors have reported that, shortly after it was detonated, they thought it was a *magnesium bomb* of unimagined power.

The first bomb, set to go off at a height of some five hundred metres, produced a nuclear flash which lasted one fifteen-millionth of a second, and whose brightness penetrated every building down to the cellars. It left its imprint on stone walls, changing their apparent colour through the fusion of certain minerals, although protected surfaces remained curiously unaltered. The same was the case with clothing and bodies, where kimono patters were tattooed on the victims' flesh. If photography, according to its inventor Nicéphore Niepce, was simply a method of engraving with light, where bodies inscribed their traces by virtue of their own luminosity, nuclear weapons inherited both the darkroom of Niepce and Daguerre and the military searchlight. What appears in the heart of darkrooms is no longer a luminous outline but a shadow, one which sometimes, as in Hiroshima, is carried to the depths of cellars and vaults. The Japanese shadows are inscribed not, as in former times, on the screens of a shadow puppet theatre but on a new screen, the walls of the city.

A-bomb, 1945; H-bomb, 1951. Korean War. . . . After the war everything speeded up: fire-power referred not just to firearms but to the jet-pipes of fighter aircraft. The sound barrier was crossed in 1952, the 'heat barrier' in 1956. As to the light barrier, that was for later. In the skies, Strategic Air Command bombers were in constant readiness, and Air Defense Command interceptors spread their protective umbrella for the eventuality of a Soviet long-range attack. The danger was all the greater in that the USSR exploded its first hydrogen bomb on 12 May 1953.

For the United States, it was becoming an urgent matter to have new information-gathering methods at its disposal. And so it was that Eastman Kodak came up with its Mylar-based film and Dr Edwin Land of Hycon Corporation with the high-resolution camera – both of which laid the basis for regular aerial reconnaissance over the Soviet Union. The sequel is well known. October 1961 saw the beginning of the Cuban crisis, with the threat of a third world war. On 29 August 1962, a U-2 aeroplane came back from a mission over Fidel

Castro's island with film evidence of Soviet missile installations. This sparked off the confrontation between Khrushchev and Kennedy which, after several months, led to a hot-line link-up between the two heads of state, an instant interface between their operations rooms.

We should remember that the U-2, still in service over Iran and the Persian Gulf, is fitted not only with photographic and electronic surveillance systems but also with a telescopic collimator or 'cine-drift indicator' which allows the spy pilot to follow ground contours at a height of more than twenty-five thousand metres.

Also in 1962, at a time when there were already ten thousand American advisers in Vietnam, the first electronic war in history was devised at Harvard and MIT. It began with the parachute-drops of sensors all along the Ho Chi-Minh Trail, and continued in 1966 with the development of the electronic 'MacNamara Line', consisting of fields of acoustic (Acouboy, Spikeboy) and seismic (Adsid, Acousid) detectors spread along the Laos access routes, around US army bases and especially the Khe Sanh stronghold.

At that time Harvard Professor Roger Fisher developed the strategic concept of a 'land-air dam', relying on up-to-the-minute technology to keep an effective watch on enemy movements. It would use infra-red devices and low-lighting television, combined with the most advanced means of aerial destruction such as the F-105 Thunderchief fighter, the Phantom jet, and the Huey-Cobra helicopter gunship. Transport aircraft (the Douglas AC-47 and, above all, the Hercules C-130) were converted into flying batteries with the latest electronic equipment: laser targeters capable of guiding bombs with absolute precision; a night-vision and image-enhancer system; and computer-controlled, multi-barrelled Minigums, descendants of the old Gatling gun which could fire six thousand rounds a minute.

With this sophisticated alert-system, made necessary by the fact that enemy movement usually took place by night, the black-out was a thing of the past, and darkness the fighter's best ally, while the daylight theatre also became a darkened cinema for the shadowy combatants. Hence the Americans' frenzied efforts to overcome this blindness by having recourse to pyrotechnic, electrical and electronic devices, most of which employed light intensification, photogrammetry, thermography, infra-red scanning, and even specially invented infra-red film. All these weapons systems resulted in a new staging of war, massive use of synthetic images, and automatic feed-back of data. They also gave rise to chemical defoliation, whereby it finally became possible to empty the screen of parasitic vegetation.

In October 1967, the Nakhon Phanom electronic surveillance centre in Thailand was picking up, interpreting and displaying on screen data sent from ground-interceptors and relayed by Lockheed Bat-Cat aeroplanes. In these offices, the new nodal point of the war, an IBM 360.35 computer automatically sorted the data, producing a 'snapshot' which showed the time and place when the interceptors had been activated. On the basis of this information, analysts drew up a schedule of enemy movement and passed on to fighter-bomber crews the 'Skyspot' combat data that enabled them to go into action with the greatest dispatch and precision. Most interesting from our point of view, however, was the pilotless Drone, an aircraft with a wing-span of approximately three metres whose camera could take two thousand pictures and whose onboard television could broadcast live to a receptor station 240 kilometres away.

'Il pleut mon âme, il pleut mais il pleut des yeux morts'[4] wrote Apollinaire in 1915, referring to enemy fire. With the advent of electronic warfare, this figure has become out of date.

Projectiles have awakened and opened their many eyes: heat-seeking missiles, infra-red or laser guidance systems, warheads fitted with video-cameras that can relay what they see to pilots and to ground-controllers sitting at their consoles. The fusion is complete, the confusion perfect: nothing now distinguishes the functions of the weapon and the eye; the projectile's image and the image's projectile form a single composite. In its tasks of detection and acquisition, pursuit and destruction, the projectile is an image or 'signature' on a screen, and the television picture is an ultrasonic projectile propagated at the speed of light. The old ballistic projection has been succeeded by the projection of light, of the electronic eye of the guided or 'video' missile. It is the life-size projection of a film which would have overjoyed Eugène Promio, the inventor of the travelling platform, and even more Abel Gance, who wanted to launch his cameras like snowballs into the Battle of Brienne.

Ever since sights were superimposed on gun-barrels, people have never stopped associating the uses of projectiles and light, that light which is the soul of gun-barrels. Recent inventions have included the photon accelerator and the light intensifier, and now there are the laser weapons, directed beams, charged-particle guns, and so on. Not content with barrel-mounting, the experts have inserted a sighting device into the inner tube of artillery in order to improve performance. At ballistic and aerodynamic research laboratories in both France and the United States, 'hyperballistic firing tunnels' nearly a hundred metres long can launch scale-models of 're-entry bodies' (the projectiles being tested) at a speed of 5,000 metres a second. 'Cineradiographic' flash equipment, with a capacity for 40 million images a second, is then used to visualize their path in the bore of the gun.[5] This takes us back to the origins of cinema, to Marey's first chronophotographic rifle which had a lens in the barrel and a cylinder for moving round the light-sensitive plate.

Since Vietnam and throughout the seventies, the mediation of battle has grown ever more pronounced. At the time of the Korean War a USAF Sabre already required more than forty kilometres to turn a Mig-15, but in Vietnam (as in the Six Days War) a Phantom needed an instrument-backed firing system if it was to have any hope of bringing down a Mig-21. The Phantom's targeting system subsequently led to the 'Fire and Forget' concept and to the Over-the-Horizon weapons systems which allow an attack to be conducted off the field. . . .

Today, techniques have improved still further and a 'dogfight simulator', consisting of two spherical cabins, can simulate an attack by two enemy aircraft. It should be noted at this point that simulation has long since spread to the other two branches of the military. The Sperry Corporation – one of the main manufacturers, together with Thomson, of this type of equipment – produces for armoured units as well as for the navy and the air force. Moreover, within the East–West framework of direct non-aggression that has resulted from the strategy of nuclear deterrence, military manoeuvres have also gradually taken on the aspect of large-scale electronic games, a Kriegspiel requiring whole territories over which the various procedures and materials of modern war are reconstituted.

In the Nevada Desert, a special practice range known as 'Red Flag' has been created to simulate exposure to a Soviet defence system. Authentic Soviet surface-to-air missiles and accompanying radar equipment – whether Israeli war booty or old supplies to Egypt – help to re-create a perfectly realistic electronic environment of radar beams, firing procedures, radio transmissions, and so forth, which the American crews are trained to recognize and then neutralize. The aerial force participating in such exercises includes an AWACS flying control-tower and an Aggressor Squadron made up of aircraft whose features are similar to those of the Mig-21 and Mig-23. Similarly, in the Mojave Desert in California, the Army's National Training Center simulates war in the most life-like way. Thanks to 'Miles' (the Multiple Integrated Laser Engagement System), the soldiers' weapons on both sides project laser or infra-red rays with a range and trajectory roughly comparable to those of real ammunition. The various targets, fitted with silicon plates, are linked up to 'black boxes'. Both the troops and their weaponry also carry sensitive plates on their most vulnerable surfaces, so that when one is hit by a laser beam, the micro-processor in the black box calculates the impact and communicates it to Headquarters, which then adds up the score. A host of other simulation devices and special film effects complete the picture.

In the same order of ideas we should mention the Tactical Mapping System, a video-disc produced by the Advanced Research Project Army. By speeding up or slowing down the procession of fifty-four thousand images, and changing the direction or season as one might switch television channels, the viewer is able to build up a continuous picture of the small Colorado town of Aspen. The town is thus transferred to a sort of ballistic tunnel for tank-pilots, who use this method to train in street combat. Let us not forget that the Dykstraflex camera made by John Dykstra for the film *Star Wars* – a camera in the service of a computer which records its own movements – was actually descended from a pilot training system.

The same kind of technological spin-off lies behind the SPAACE camera, an automatic tracking system that two Frenchmen developed for the cinema on the basis of an anti-aircraft radar platform. This new-style camera, with its powerful telephoto lens, can follow the actors' spontaneous movements without any difficulty, even locking on to the face of a jet pilot executing a low-altitude figure. The fact is that once the energy crisis had made the simulation industry profitable, the pace of technological innovation grew more frantic towards the end of the seventies and culminated in the automation of the war machine.

The complexity of manoeuvres, the ever greater air speeds, the assistance of satellites, and the necessity for ground-attack aircraft to fly supersonically at very low altitudes eventually led the engineers to automate piloting itself. On the F-16 'AFTI', for example, developed by Robert Swortzel, the pilot never touches the controls but navigates by voice. In return, an on-screen display keeps him informed of his flight plan and 'firing plan' and throws up on the windscreen the anticipated acceleration and countdown time, as well as the kind of manoeuvres that the pilot will have to execute. For the firing operation, the pilot has a special sighting-helmet linked to a laser and infra-red targeting system; all he has to do is fix the target and give a verbal instruction for the weapons to be released. This revolutionary apparatus, designed in 1982 for the United States Air Force, the Navy and NASA, combines a number of advanced technologies, particularly in the field of laser-targeting. The Eye-Tracked synchronization system fixes the pilot's gaze, however sudden the movement of his eyes, so that firing can proceed as soon as binocular accommodation is achieved.

Finally, there is the 'homing image', which joins together an infra-red ray and an explosive projectile fitted with a special device. This device acts in the manner of an eye, picking up the image of the infra-red-lit target. The projectile then makes its way towards the image – and thus towards the target for destruction – with all the ease of someone going home. This system, which is attached to the latest missiles, once again illustrates the fateful confusion of eye and weapon.

We can now understand better the concern on both sides to perfect weapons that are as undetectable as a submerged submarine – Stealth bombers, 'smart' missiles, invisible not just to the human eye but above all to the piercing, unerring gaze of technology. In the 1980s there was a significant shift or 'conversion' in global strategy, as East–West conflict passed into North–South confrontation. Notwithstanding the tensions in the Middle East and the Euromissiles controversy, military space is being shifted and organized around the oceans, in the Pacific, the Indian Ocean and the South Atlantic. Indeed, the Malvinas War can be seen as a rehearsal for a nuclear conflict, in the use of American and Soviet satellites, British nuclear submarines, and French missiles capable of destroying highly exposed surface-ships. But it was also a war of electronic countermeasures – naval decoys whose main feature was to superimpose upon the incoming missile's optical or infra-red radar image an entirely manufactured image that would appear both more important and more attractive than the real ship, as well as being equally credible to the enemy missile. Once this was achieved, the missile's automatic navigator locked on to the centre of gravity of the 'decoy-image-cum-ship-image', and all that remained was to exploit the spectre of the decoy to draw the missile far over the ship. The whole operation lasted barely a few seconds.

One could go on for ever listing the technological weapons, the panoply of light-war, the aesthetic of the electronic battlefield, the military use of space whose conquest was ultimately the conquest of the image – the electronic image of remote detection; the artificial image produced by satellites as they endlessly sweep over the surface of continents drawing automatic maps; life-size cinema in which the day and the light of film-speed succeed the day and the light of astronomical time. It is subliminal light of incomparable transparency, where technology finally exposes the whole world.

In the summer of 1982, the Israeli preventive war in Lebanon, baptized 'Peace in Galilee', drew on all the resources of the scientific arsenal: Grumman 'Hawkeye' aircraft-radar capable of simultaneously locating two hundred and fifty targets for F-15 and F-16 fighter-bombers; and, above all, the remote-piloted 'Scout' automata, with a wing-span of less than two metres, which were massively and systematically deployed for the first time in the history of battle. This toy craft, worthy of Ernst Jünger's *Glass Bees*, was a veritable Tsahal's eye fitted with TV cameras and thermal-image systems. As it skimmed the rooftops of the besieged city of Beirut, flying over the most exposed Palestinian districts, it provided images of population movement and thermal graphics of Palestinian vehicles for Israeli analysts sitting at their video consoles more than a hundred kilometres away.

In the autumn of 1982, the United States established a military high command for space and announced the impending launch of an early-warning satellite. In the spring of 1983, on 23 March to be precise, President Reagan painted a picture of an anti-ballistic-missile system employing nuclear energy, enhanced rays, directed beams and charged particles.

Last summer, on 5 July 1983, an American KC-135 aircraft fitted with a laser system shot down a Sidewinder missile travelling at 3,000 kilometres an hour.

Scan. Freeze frame.

Notes

1   To a large extent naval battles had long anticipated this type of practice.
2   For the Americans, the abstractness of their recapture of the Pacific islands made 'cinema direction' a necessity – hence the importance of the camera crews committed to the campaign.
3   The *commissaire aux montres* was the officer responsible for inspecting weapons and equipment under the Ancien Régime.
4   'It's raining my soul, it's raining, but it's raining dead eyes.' Guillaume Apollinaire, from 'La nuit d'avril 1915' in 'Case d'Armons', *Calligrammes*, Paris 1918.
5   See the report of the seminar '*Le cinéma grande vitesse* – instrumentations et applications', ANRT, Paris, December 1981.

Experiences of Modern Warfare and the Crisis of Representation

4

BERND HÜPPAUF

With the constant stream of films about the Vietnam War in the 1970s and 1980s, films which attracted millions of viewers the world over and seemed to give new significance to the cinema as a public space for collective memory, it soon became obvious that the war film genre had finally exhausted its critical potential. It has been argued in relation to films concerned with history that "the sheer mass of historical images transmitted by today's media weakens the link between public memory and personal experience. The past is in danger of becoming a rapidly expanding collection of images, easily retrievable but isolated from time and space. . . ."[1] This tendency of the photographic image to become isolated and – through reproduction, variation, and unlimited dissemination – ever more abstract, has been observed earlier (Bazin, Benjamin, Jünger), and is a precondition for the final disappearance of the binary division between war films and anti-war films. *The Deer Hunter*, *Apocalypse Now*, *Full Metal Jacket*, *Gallipoli*, and other films with an alleged anti-war commitment can be seen with equal justification as examples of a fascination with images of modern warriors, war technology, death, killing, and mass destruction. With the end of a clear moral divide in the war film genre, theses propounding a close structural relationship between war and film have became popular. Paul Virilio, for example, argues that war and cinema are linked by a structural homology which results in the "complete destruction of traditional fields of perception. . . . War is cinema and cinema is war."[2] Ignoring moral issues and focussing on aesthetic aspects, this extra-moral approach toward war and film has its precursor in theories about film and photography which emerged in the wake of World War I.

Ernst Jünger was involved in one of the numerous collections of photographs from World War I which appeared in Germany during the middle and late 1920s.[3] Jünger argued that the camera's cold and distanced view reflected the structure of the modern battlefield and that in turn human perception was changing and adapting to the view of the camera lens.[4] In the process of an unlimited unfolding of modern technology on the battlefield, the anthropological condition of human apperception was changing. The objective quality of photography could be seen, he argued, as the model of the new relationship between man's hardened senses and his world. The often denounced moral implications of this concept of perception, namely a glorification of war, were of little importance to Jünger. He refers instead to a simultaneous "process of decomposition" of bourgeois subjectivity and the emergence of a "cold and dispassionate view of the artificial eye" of the camera.[5]

Photography, he argues, presents to us radical images of the "decline of the individual and social physiognomy" significant of the emerging era of "the worker." This new era, he claims, is marked by a "deep connection between new machines and a new type of man."[6]

The degree to which Jünger distanced himself from emotions and kept the spheres of ethics and aesthetics apart is made evident by an entry in his diary in 1945. On January 11 he learned that his favorite son, Ernstel, aged 18, had been killed in action. Looking at photographs of his dead son, he developed "new ideas on photography," making the following comment:

> No photograph can compete with a good painting in the domain where art reigns and where ideas and consciousness are dominant. However, photographs have another, dark quality – the "sun-picture" is after all a shadow picture. It gives something of the substance of the human being, of his radiation, is an imprint of him. In this sense it is related to handwriting.[7]

While Jünger does not refer to the concept of a new man, hardened and emotionless, on the occasion of his son's death, he does confine himself to the sphere of reflection. In analogy to Ludwig Klages's concept of graphology, with which he was familiar, Jünger now emphasizes the active role of the object represented in photographs.[8] As in handwriting, the character of a person, his "substance," is present in his photograph as well, because it is mechanically produced by a camera and chemicals, similar to the way that quill and ink produce writing. His existence seems directly transferred onto the photographic image and then radiates from it without requiring his physical presence. Freed from limitations of time and space, photographic images create for Jünger a world which is at once the shadow of a reality lost forever and a construction following its own rules.

Jünger's brief comments point in a direction which theories of film and photography after World War II followed with considerable intensity. They can be read as both a radicalization of traditional positions and a turning point that leads away from them. Prior to the emergence of semiological approaches to film, André Bazin used the idea of "ontology" in his attempt to define the unique character of the photographic image:

> Originality in photography as distinct from originality in painting lies in the essentially objective character of photography. For the first time, between the originating object and its reproduction there intervenes only the instrumentality of a nonliving agent. . . . All the arts are based on the presence of man, only photography derives an advantage from his absence. . . . This production by automatic means has radically affected our psychology of the image. . . . In spite of any objections our critical spirit may offer, we are forced to accept as real the existence of the object reproduced, actually *re*-presented, set before us, that is to say, in time and space. Photography enjoys a certain advantage in virtue of this transference of reality from the thing to its reproduction. . . . The photographic image is the object itself, the object freed from the conditions of time and space that govern it.[9]

Bazin's position may be understood as an extension of the traditional belief in the objectivity of the photographic image. But what made it unique was its radical separation of this ontological position from all previous ideological contexts of realism, mimesis, truth claims, and their moral implications. In his view, it is not only the mechanical process itself, but also the viewers' knowledge of its nature that has changed the character of the image and its perception through a "transference of reality from the thing to its reproduction." Problems of representing modern warfare were instrumental in the development of radically new approaches to film and photography such as this one.

When Rudolf Arnheim claimed that pictorial representation should do more than mirror the represented object, he summarized an aesthetic position which gained considerable prominence with the unfolding of the "ontological" debate. In the age of film and photography, he argued, the onus was on the medium itself to show that representation is a product of the object itself, mechanically produced in the way objects of the physical world imprint their image onto the photographic plate.[10] From its early days on, photography had been commonly seen as a technique capable of duplicating visible reality. But with intensifying reflection on the specificity of the new medium, the focus moved away from the mere mechanical character of reproduction and toward the realization that photography created its own category of visual images. This unique category of images derived from the "independent" role played by the object in the process of reproducing and, more particularly, from the fact that the viewer was constantly aware of the "independence" of the object in its relation to both photographer and medium.

In a period increasingly dominated by the ideals of the "objective" sciences, photography was considered superior to all other forms of representation precisely because of the apparent absence of a consciousness mediating between the object and its representation. Photography therefore seemed to be the "medium of immediacy." The importance which this medium gained in everyday life, and in various scientific disciplines as forensic evidence, supported the common association of the photographic image with truth. Yet it is precisely its "documentary" character and the seeming absence of subjectivity which placed photography at the center of the crisis of representation. The specific object-medium relationship made photography particularly sensitive to changes in the object, that is, to changes in the physical or the imagined reality. It was soon observed that while they do not lie, photographs do not tell the truth either. Rather, they have to be seen as elements of a highly complex process in which both photographic techniques and the concept of reality have been dissolved. At one stage in this process of disillusionment, photography would be all but equated with falsification.[11] However, while falsification of photographs is an important issue, the close association of political and ideological doctrines with the distortion of reality in photographic representation tends to misconstrue the fundamental issue.

To the degree to which modern reality has succumbed to science and technology, and has become disjointed, opaque, and characterized by abstract mediation, the relationship between pictorial representation and linguistic accounts has become highly problematic. It is the abstract nature of modernity which seems to require conceptual modes of representation rather than a pictorial duplication of visible reality. Such a requirement does not correspond easily to the character and predominantly documentary image of photography, and more often than not has led to an uneasy relationship between the two. The representation of modern warfare in photography and film provides us with a disturbing example of the fading link between experience and knowledge, and manifests an asymmetrical relation between abstract and pictorial representation that is based upon an unresolved contradiction between images and structures.

This essay is based on the hypothesis that representations of modern warfare in film and photography are faced with a structural dilemma: their moral commitment is linked more often than not to a visual code which clashes with the requirements of visualizing a highly abstract modern reality. Juxtapositions of the human face and images of the destructive technological violence of modern warfare suffer in film and photography from an intrinsic contradiction: they aim to maintain a dichotomy between war and civilization. These attempts rely on a concept of humanity and nature which the very conditions of modern civilization – conditions only more exposed, accelerated, and condensed in warfare – are eroding. An iconography based on an opposition between the human face and inhuman technology oversimplifies complex structures. Films based upon such an iconography suffer from their attempt to ignore basic constitutive elements of modernity.[12]

The landscape of modern war is largely determined by communication technologies of the electronic age. At the same time, structures of modern warfare are constitutive elements in modern technology to such an extent that the aesthetic of a morally construed discourse (in contrast to an aesthetic of an extra-moral and technologically induced discourse) is in danger of rendering itself obsolete. This is a process in which photography, film, and the electronic media themselves have played a significant role.[13] War films with a moral commitment face the problem that the nature of their images and indeed their very structure of representation contradict the subject of representation: the destruction of humanity by modern technological-scientific means. The origin of this process of abstraction – which has finally led to the images of the Gulf War devoid of the space necessary for human experience, but highly fantastical and playful – can be traced back to the late 19th century. Its period of consolidation and first culmination was World War I and, in particular, aerial photography. . . .

When compared to traditional battle paintings or stylized images of battle formations, a fundamental difference in this new technique of representing the "reality" of war becomes obvious. Aerial shots do not represent sensuous or moral experiences of space, nor is the prescription for or analysis of military movements part of their iconic content. Without careful analysis they are silent, manifestations of a new mode of mediated perception and organization of battlefields, with huge concentrations of material and masses of soldiers in a vast space which no individual is capable of surveying. The war killed the natural landscape and replaced it with highly artificial and, within its own parameters, functional spatial arrangements. Aerial photography then, creating a metalevel of artificiality, further abstracted from the "reality" of this artificial landscape. It not only eliminated smells, noises, and all other stimuli directed at the senses, but also projected an order onto an amorphous space by reducing the abundance of detail to restricted patterns of a surface texture. In photographs taken from an certain altitude, only objects of a certain minimum size will be represented; smaller objects, in particular human bodies, will not be there, and cannot be made visible even with magnifying glasses or through extreme enlargements.[14] The morphology of the landscape of destruction, photographed from a plane, is the visual order of an abstract pattern.

Aerial photographs also developed an aesthetic of their own beyond their tactical and strategic functions. A cloud of mustard gas may produce an aesthetically attractive light, a grey shade on a darker grey background; and regular patterns of dark circles with sharp edges may result from the last long-range bombardment. But the sufferings inflicted on soldiers as a result of those gas attacks or bombardments are completely beyond the reach of the photograph. To a degree, the tradition of the picturesque retains its power to direct the eyes of the observer even in these abstract images. While their picturesque qualities contributed to the popularity of these photographs, their structure seems more like a modern version of abstract representations of warfare in primitive art. There, too, knowledge was required to decipher the shapes and colors associated with events, demons, totems, or tribes and their actions in tribal warfare. Visual representation of the modern battlefield in aerial photography is another example of the frequently observed return of archaic structures in the world of modern technology. Similar to the return of protective armor such as helmets and shields, and their association with magical protection, aerial photography led to a resurrection of primitive images disguised as high technology. Wilhelm Worringer based his reflections in *Abstraction and Empathy* on the opposition between an aesthetic that revolves around the psychological desire for empathy – part of the European classical and romantic traditions – and the tendency toward abstraction characterizing most works of art from both primitive civilizations and that of modernity.[15] He approaches the tendency toward abstraction in terms directly applicable to the aesthetic of aerial war photography:

> While the desire for empathy as the precondition for aesthetic experience finds its satisfaction in the beauty of the organic world, the desire for abstraction sees its beauty in the life-denying inorganic, crystalline world, generally spoken, in an abstract system of laws and needs.[16]

Combined with these "pure aesthetic" effects is a level of invisible "information" which can only be deduced from the represented topography and changes of its elements over time. On this level what is immediately visible is less important than the inferences which can be drawn from it. The code of the visible landscape of destruction has to be decodified and recodified in military terms. Only then will it be possible to decipher its geometrical symmetries and read pieces of information – logistics, ballistic paths, strategic plans behind changes of shapes – which lie hidden within the visible surface. This type of information is characterized by factors which contribute to the indirectness and abstractions of images. It involves, for example:

- long term developments which have to be monitored in order to become visible;
- indirect forces of change, such as strategic decisions taken at headquarters, the speed of transportation systems, etc.;
- wide spaces which transcend the perspective of an individual;
- the absence of an individual focus which is replaced by technical constructions.

Aerial photographs are symptoms of and at the same time forces in the process of changing the mode of perception by fusing pure aesthetic effects and highly functional military information. Their space is emptied of experience and moral content.

A reconstitution of the soldiers' identity went hand-in-hand with the destruction of experienced and morally charged space in war and its reconstitution in technical terms. The new landscape, a "dreamlike landscape like a furnace," as Ernst Jünger called it, provided no source for empathy. Identity, seen as a complex and continuous process of identifying with or rejecting other individuals, values, social and natural surroundings, was subjected to crisis very soon after soldiers experienced the conditions of the front. There was very little to identify with or to relate to. Soldiers felt cut off from real life.[17] Often no connection seemed possible between their lives in the trenches and the life they remembered back home. At first, looking at photographs of their families, wives, children, and girlfriends helped maintain connections and establish a sense of spatial and temporal orientation for their emotional landscape. After a while, they stared at these photos, and the photos remained silent. The soldiers' imagination was no longer able to create the context necessary for these photos to become suggestive parts in personal memories and stories. Often a few days' break in the environment of the base would enable them to regenerate these contexts of emotional orientation. But after a certain period of time spent in the landscape of destruction they tended to lose this ability.

There are numerous accounts of the disintegration of the culturally conditioned self in the wartime soldier, all produced years after the end of the war. These reports look back on a period in life when the awareness and self-reflection necessary to write about this process of disintegration had been lost. The decomposition of the soldiers' self was marked by the end of narratives. The silence which surrounded the images both photographic and immediate was often recalled many years after the end of the war, and caused the imagination of ex-soldiers to wander back to this disturbing experience. Shortly before his death, Edmund Blunden, commenting on his own experiences as a young man in World War I, could still claim: "My experiences in the First World War have haunted me all my life and for many days I have, it seemed, lived in that world rather than this."[18] The disintegration of subjectivity, a central theme in Nietzschean philosophical reflection on the modern condition, and in Freud's psychoanalysis, now left the confines of the upper middle class and the framework of philosophical reflection or psychoanalytic analysis and became a mass experience. Under the conditions of technological warfare, the destructive elements of modernity were condensed to the extreme and forcefully imprinted on the modern mind.

It is against this background that the heroic images of World War I reveal their ideological character as propaganda. It is not surprising that the most advanced technology of the war, the airplane, gave rise to the heroic imagery for the new times. Through mass distribution of photos, faces of young pilots came to be associated with the glory and splendor of warfare and gave visible expression to the desire to maintain an image of a kind of war that had ceased to exist with the advent of trench warfare. More than any other modern system of arms – including submarines and tanks (not to speak of gas-units) – planes and aerial combat were considered ideal for the creation of images of heroes. These heroes represented, in a war of mass armies and increasing abstraction, the ideal of the pure knight, the strong individual, and the master of both nature and the machine. A cult of young pilots emerged, based on portraits of the "aces" often photographed with symbols of their "nobility" (a leather cap, piece of equipment, or part of a plane), and made these lieutenants more prominent than generals, marshals, or chiefs of staff. On occasion this star cult would lead to public outbursts of emotion and identification. In 1916, German papers reported on their front pages the "triumphant burial" of one of these heroes, Max Immelmann, and printed photographs of the endless funeral procession curling through the streets of Dresden. The myth of the "red Baron" Manfred von Richthoven may have been even more powerful. In England and France enthusiasm for the heroes of the sky was equally strong and equally linked to reproduced images of the pure face of the modern hero. In public imagination the world of aerial combat comprised the idealized face of the young hero, the images of open duels with whole nations taking the place of the seconds, and a reinterpretation of the empty space of aerial photography in terms of individual experience and collective mythology. This anachronistic imagery, which used photography's power to create illusions that concealed the power of photography, played a significant role in the process of maintaining a moral framework for war propaganda. More than that, it was the mass reproduction of images of the pure human face which successfully contributed to the mystifications of modern warfare in the modern mind.

In contrast to this "humanist" vision of modern warfare, a vision of the faceless grey warrior emerged. Linked to the disintegration of the bourgeois ego and its meaningful psychological construction was the reconstitution of man as a fighting machine. The hardened man with his steel helmet, emotionless, experienced, with no morality apart from the value of comradeship and no obligation or attachment other than to his immediate group of warriors, fitted the imagery of futurism and soon degenerated into the fascist myth of a new man.[19] However, this ideological straitjacket, with its looming deformation into fascist attitudes and the Nazi killer mentality, was only the most openly menacing but short-lived political materialization of this experience. Jünger's idea of the *Arbeiter*, for all its now-dated characteristics, is a typified construction with considerable significance for western man in the second half of this century. Jünger's claim in 1963 that many of his observations are no longer surprising or provocative, but have become part of everyday experience, seems justified.[20]

The experience of the dissolution of subjectivity and its traditional patterns of orientation and values, the transformation of modes of perception, and the destruction of vast areas of landscape and experienced time and space have become constitutive elements of the modern consciousness. Although the destructiveness of modernity did not originate in World War I, this war was clearly experienced as a gigantic *rite de passage* into the modern condition. Once western civilization had undergone this experience, the binary oppositions between war and peace, production and destruction became obsolete and, as Blunden put it, modern memory has been *haunted* by this experience ever since. It seemed impossible to restore the human face after it had been mutilated beyond recognition in the outburst of destruction after 1914. Ernst Friedrich's collection of photographs, for all his humanist and socialist commitment, captured this inability to forget and restore the human face to its once God-like image, the inability to bridge time gap that separated a happier past from a disillusioned present. The photograph to which he gave the caption *The "Image of God" with a Gas Mask*[21] illustrates not only his satirical intentions but also his despair.

How could a civilization which was not only prepared to enter into such a carnage, but also determined to continue it for years, ever regain its human face? In the only conversation in Remarque's novel *All Quiet on the Western Front* (1929) that philosophically reflects upon the war, Paul Bäumer remarks that after having gone through two years of killing, devastation, and psychological regression, these young men will never again be the same as before. These sentences are repeated in Lewis Milestone's 1930 film based on Remarque's novel (also titled *All Quiet on the Western Front*). The anti-war message of this film is only too obvious, but its images fail to reflect Paul Bäumer's simple recognition of the irreversible changes brought about by the experience of this war.

It is this type of failure which underlies the structural contradiction in common anti-war discourse. Although they have become obsolete, traditional metaphors are revitalized and help maintain a language that is morally justified but largely incapable of reflecting the structural modernity of the war experience. Milestone's film, as well as *Westfront 1918* (1930) by G. W. Pabst, initiated a particular pictorial discourse on war by creating an imagery and language for the new medium of film which was designed to contribute to the international pacifist movement. By placing on the screen images of increasingly brutal war conditions and juxtaposing them with the human face, they established a visual code defined by political and humanist commitment. It seems beyond doubt that this emotionally powerful iconography differed from previous representations of wars in which violence and destruction were embedded in images of heroism and purpose. Yet the moral framework within which these images were created and are received largely excludes representation of the structurally inhuman battlefield of modern warfare. Moral imperatives continue to shape the majority of war films up to the present.

In anti-war iconography, the camera lens has adopted the position of the suffering soldier as a victim of war rather than exposing the structure of violence and presenting soldiers as elements of it. As a result, this iconography maintains a clear spatial and temporal distinction between home and front, peace and war, and the illusion that the destruction of the former by the latter can be reversed after the armistice. The complete restoration of a peaceful world is a matter of time and reason. The spatial or temporal distance between peace and war is marked by emotional images, such as photographs of a happy past, dreams, flowers, city streets (back at the base), or various images of mothers, sisters, girl-friends.[22] These images are associated with emotions and the longing to bridge the distance between present madness and senseless destruction, and past or future happiness, reason, and sanity. The resurrection of the peaceful world is a matter of traversing time and restoring reason. When in Milestone's film German soldiers spend a night with French girls, it is made obvious that their happiness is not to last. However, far from being presented as a mere illusion, the scene visually represents the continued presence of a world unaffected by the war despite the devastation of the surrounding tranquil countryside and the soldiers' experience of continuous destruction. . . .

. . . . The construction of war in analogy to aerial photographs would now have to be linked to the conception of non-emotional and basically empty space.[23] It is this geometrical and abstract space which makes possible the strategic mobility of mass armies amid related gigantic logistics. The effectiveness of the moral anti-war film, however, is based on the creation of a space of experience. In such a space, constituted through human action, emotion, and evaluation, no modern war could be conducted. While from the Trojan war to the wars of the late 19th century interaction with and attachment to structured space formed part of the warriors' identity, this is no longer required in modern warfare. As World War I after 1916 illustrated, modern warfare's complete devastation of an environment creates ideal conditions for the operation of modern armor, communication, and surveil-lance devices and is linked to a technologically induced desert of the mind. It was the anti-war film and photography which maintained an emotionally laden space and thus involuntarily contributed to the maintenance of obsolete images of war, because the space of suffering they represented is also the space in which outdated images of heroism have survived. They are separated by opposite political associations but they are also part of the dual structure of a moral space. Only mathematical space emptied of human experience but structured in abstract detail will provide the smooth sphere for the "pure" war of technology.

The moral code supporting attempts to develop an image of warfare that reflects the human ideal is linked to the need to create a space within which suffering and terror, caused by visible devices, can be both experienced by the victim and located and spatially assessed by the viewer. These images are based on the assumption that an anti-war mentality will never emerge without such an anachronistic framework. The modern technological definition of warfare, however, affords no room for experience and reduces time, space, and motion to abstract mathematical and physical quantities which enter into predictable, calculable operations. For missiles and their distant launchers, or for fighter pilots who have contact with their environment only through electronic screens, the space they need for movement is tendentially empty and completely void of objects fit for stimulating emotional reactions. Compared with this mathematic-strategic construction, the image which most anti-war films create of a space constituted by fighting, suffering, and dying soldiers, is an anachronistic image acting as a life support system for a threatened moral position. Laser beams, neutron bombs, and star wars games threaten to turn empty space into a space which, while structured, is completely devoid of life. There seems little room left for moral resistance apart from deliberately maintaining an anachronistic image of a space filled with the cries and groans and the flesh of the dying. But will a radical negativity in relation to advanced war technology achieve anything else but a simple repetition of the naiveté of 19th-century Luddites? It seems bound to remain equally inconclusive. Current abstract projections of a possible future war are ever more fantastical and playful: flight paths of beams and missiles, and electronic shields in space, without actors and victims. Displaced into empty interstellar space, SDI appears as the provisionally final version of abstraction in a life-denying crystalline world, to use Worringer's words. In World War I soldiers disappeared into their dugouts and an empty battlefield appeared on many aerial photographs. In the conception of warfare of the electronic age, human beings seem to have even less of a place, and a concept of experience seems to become ever more atavistic. It might therefore be tempting to charge film and the electronic media with the task of filling in the empty space and counterbalancing the technological vision of pure war. It seems unlikely, however, in the apparent absence of any justification other than than of an anachronistic morality, that the image of the human face will have an impact on the self-regulating system of technology. As early as 1927, Siegfried Kracauer argued that photography had become identical with a huge project aimed at replacing reality with images of reality.[24] Sixty years later, Baudrillard argues that contemporary reality *is* the interplay of signs and codes which follow their intrinsic semiotic rules with no external referent. Concepts such as "abstraction" and "simulation," he claims, are part of the past, as there is nothing *real* from which abstractions could be derived and no space in which simulation could refer to anything other than itself. "The real is produced from miniaturized units, from matrices, memory banks and command models – and with these it can be reproduced an indefinite number of times."[25] Photographic laboratories of World War I played a decisive role in the process of miniaturizing and producing reality from a matrix. This process has now entered into a new phase. Baudrillard argues: "Abstraction today is no longer that of the map. . . . Simulation is no longer that of a territory. . . ." Reality, he goes on, has become "the generation by models of a real without origin or reality: a hyperreal. . . . It is the real, and not the map, whose vestiges subsist here and there, in the desert. . . . The desert of the real itself."[26] Skepticism about the extravagant radicalism of such wordings seems appropriate. However, attempts aimed at educating or empowering the senses to resist absorption into the emptiness of a world made of "simulacra" have remained marginal, and the emergence of a more powerful project of a new aesthetic seems unlikely.

Notes

1   Anton Kaes, "History and Film: Public Memory in the Age of Electronic Dissemination," *History and Memory. Studies in the Representation of the Past* 2.1 (Fall/Winter 1990): 111–129; here 121.

2   Paul Virilio, *War and cinema*, trans. Patrick Camiller (London, New York: Verso, 1989) 26. Original version: *Guerre et cinéma, Logistique de la perception* (Paris: Editions de l'Etoile, 1984).

3   Ernst Jünger, "Krieg und Lichtbild," *Das Antlitz des Weltkrieges. Fronterlebnisse deutscher Soldaten* (Berlin: Neufeld & Henius, 1930) 9–11. See also: Ernst Jünger, "Das Lichtbild als Mittel im Kampf."

4   Ernst Jünger, "Über den Schmerz."

5   Ernst Jünger, *Der Arbeiter, Herrschaft und Gestalt* (Stuttgart: Cotta, 1982) 128. The first edition appeared in 1932, published by the Hanseatische Verlagsanstalt in Hamburg.

6   Jünger, *Der Arbeiter* 130.

7   Ernst Jünger, *Kirchhorster Blätter, Sämtliche Werke*, vol. 3 (Stuttgart: Klett-Cotta, 1979) 363. The German text reads: "Kein Lichtbild kann mit einem guten Gemälde wetteifern in der Domäne, in der die Kunst regiert und wo Ideen und Bewußtsein herrschend sind. Doch ist den Photographien eine andere, dunklere Qualität eigen – das Lichtbild ist ja im Grunde ein Schattenbild. Es gibt etwas von der Substanz des Menschen, von seiner Ausstrahlung, ist ein Abdruck von ihm. In diesem Sinn ist es der Schrift verwandt."

8   Ludwig Klages, *Ausdrucksbewegung und Gestaltungskraft* (Leipzig: Wilhelm Engelmann, 1921). The revised version appeared under the title *Grundlegung der Wissenschaft vom Ausdruck* (Leipzig: Barth, 1932).

9   André Bazin, "The Ontology of the Photographic Image," *What is Cinema?*, trans. and ed. Hugh Gray, vol. 1 (Berkeley: University of California Press: 1967) 9–16; here 13–14.

10 Rudolf Arnheim, "Systematik der frühen kinematographischen Erfindungen," *Kritiken und Aufsätze zum Film*, ed. Helmut Diederichs (Munich: Hanser, 1977).

11 Alain Jaubert, *Fotos, die lügen. Politik mit gefälschten Bildern* (Frankfurt/Main: Athenäum, 1989).

12 Sigmund Freud, in a letter to Albert Einstein in 1932, raises the radical question of whether war might not be an inevitable implication of the particular constitution of culture. See "Warum Krieg?" Studienausgabe, vol. 9 (Frankfurt/Main: Fischer, 1974) 272–286.

13 Based on the experience of World War II essays and films by Alexander Kluge have consistently emphasized the close links between perception and war: *Schlachtbeschreibung, Die Patriotin*. See also Oskar Negt and Alexander Kluge, *Geschichte und Eigensinn* (Frankfurt/Main: Zweitausendeins, 1981) 797–866. Cf. also Paul Virilio and Sylvère Lotringer *Pure War* (New York: Semiotext(e), 1983) and Paul Virilio, *La machine de vision* (Paris: Galilée, 1988).

14 Paul Virilio argues that aerial photography led to a new interplay of the human senses and their extensions: engine, eye, and armor are intricately linked to each other and form a collage of instruments vis-à-vis an equally functional and aestheticized reality. *Guerre et cinéma* 1: *Logistique de la perception* (Paris: Editions de l'Etoile, 1984).

15 Wilhelm Worringer, *Abstraktion und Einfühlung* (Munich: Piper, 1959). The first edition was published in 1908.

16 Worringer 36.

17 See Bernd Ulrich's recent observations in relation to the concept of "nerves" under the conditions of the front: Bernd Ulrich, 'Nerven und Krieg," Loewenstein 163–192.

18 Quoted in Paul Fussell, *The Great War and Modern Memory* (New York: Oxford UP, 1975) 256.

19 Cf. Bernd Hüppauf, "The Birth of Fascist Man from the Spirit of the Front," *The Attractions of Fascism*, ed. John Milfull (New York, Oxford, Munich: Berg, 1990) 45–76.

20 Ernst Jünger, "Vorwort," *Der Arbeiter* 8.

21 Ernst Friedrich, *Krieg dem Kriege!* – *War against War* (Frankfurt/Main: Zweitausendeins, 1981), 131.

22 In his reading of *Spanish Earth*, Thomas Waugh refers to an iconography of "water, blood and soil" and its opposition: "steel, planes, the sky." Thomas Waugh, "Water, Blood and War: Documentary Imagery of Spain from the North American Popular Front," *The Spanish Civil War and the Visual Arts*, ed. Kathleen Vernon (Cornell University: Western Societies Program, Occasional Papers No 24, 1990) 20.

23 For an original but highly uncoordinated discussion of advanced aspects of technology and modern ways of perception see Virilio, *La machine de vision*.

24 Siegfried Kracauer, "Die Fotografie," *Das Ornament der Masse* (Frankfurt/Main: Suhrkamp, 1963) 21–39.

25 Jean Baudrillard, *Selected Writings*, ed. Mark Poster (Stanford: Stanford UP, 1988) 166–184; here 166.

26 Baudrillard 166ff.

War as a Way of Seeing

5

GEORGE H. ROEDER, JR.

"The first casuality when war comes," said Senator Hiram Johnson in 1917, "is truth." Senator Johnson was only half right. Governments at war use the truth whenever it serves their purposes; it is ambiguity which they find intolerable. As Jean Bethke Elshtain concluded after studying war imagery from different places and times, to think in terms of this imagery "means seeing everything as existing in a state of extreme, Manichaean reduction, which erases all intermediate hues . . . and limits everything to . . . the primordial struggle of two forces—good and evil." The political scientist Harold Lasswell, along with other influential analysts of propaganda from the first world war, argued at the outset of the second that such reductionism was especially necessary in twentieth-century conflicts involving entire populations: "So great are the psychological resistances to war in modern nations that every war must appear to be a war of defense against a menacing, murderous aggressor. There must be no ambiguity about whom the public is to hate. . . . Guilt and guilelessness must be assessed geographically, and all the guilt must be on the other side of the frontier." Numerous individuals, institutions, and circumstances counterbalanced this tendency to oversimplification. But the most widely shared feature of the innumerable visual images created in the United States during the war years was their intention to present the conflict between the Allies and the Axis, and other war-related issues, in legible, unambiguous terms.[1]

To say that most of the images were intended to be unambiguous is not to say that they all communicated the same messages. They reflected the diverse viewpoints and interests of their many creators. In 1941 the government's "informational, promotional, and publicity activities" engaged the equivalent of 8,433 full-time workers, and their numbers swelled during the war, supplemented by many in the private sector engaged in similar efforts. The War Activities Committee of the motion picture industry encouraged production of visual material that publicized war needs and goals. The Graphic Arts Victory Committee, representing the manufacturers of printing materials, typographers, lithographers, and others involved in the graphic arts, insisted that their industry must "gear itself 100% to the war effort." The committee prepared a guide detailing why advertising and other printed material was "absolutely essential to the war effort" and explaining how companies could serve both their own and the country's needs through war-oriented promotional material.[2]

A glut of censors further complicated the task of coordination. In addition to the major responsibilities assumed by the Office of Censorship and the military public-relations branches, more than thirty other agencies were involved in censorship of one sort or another. Private organizations also had a say about which images reached the public. The Eastman Kodak Company continued its prewar practice of refusing to process films or photographs that the company deemed to be "criminal, obscene, and subversive matter." Thus diffused authority, conflicting interests, and the sheer volume of images doomed attempts to achieve coherence through centralized authority. An imperfect coherence was achieved, nonetheless, because these images presented the world as seen through the lens of war.³

Americans had much to see through this lens. World War II exposed them to more other peoples and cultures—domestic and foreign—than any previous event of such limited duration. Exposure came through direct experience and through the mediation of words and visual images. As James Covert, who grew up during the war years, observed, "To me World War II was like a gigantic stage production. It was as if I was a character actor on a global stage, watching this huge drama unfold around me." Several million Americans, many of whom had never before been out of the counties where they were born, journeyed across the Pacific or the Atlantic to play their part in the drama. Those at home were so avid to follow their travels that orders for National Geographic maps increased 600 percent. Before one of his first major addresses on the war, President Roosevelt suggested that his radio audience use a world map for reference as he spoke. Among the dozens of wartime films that oriented viewers with maps, usually presented in the opening sequences, were *Across the Pacific, Back to Bataan, Casablanca, The Immortal Sergeant,* and *Wake Island.* But the circumstances of wartime encounters with other cultures encouraged Americans at home and abroad to see these cultures through the narrowly focused lens of a bombsight, which reduced all things to one of two categories: that to be spared and that to be destroyed.⁴

In wartime imagery the United States destroyed only bad things. Accordingly, wartime films, photographs, posters, and comic strips celebrated the U.S. commitment to precision bombing. At the outset of *Bombardier,* a 1943 film made by RKO with assistance from the Army Air Forces, the proponent of a new bombsight amazed skeptical military officers and congressional leaders when he hit a small target from a plane flying so high that ground observers could not even see it. Viewers were assured that American technology allowed airmen to hit a barrel from an altitude of twenty-four thousand feet and dot an *i* from eighteen thousand feet. When a letter from his mother led one of the bombardier trainees to consider quitting because his activities would lead to the death of women and children, the unit leader assured him that the reverse would happen. By allowing Americans precisely to destroy enemy munitions factories, the new bombsight prevented production of truly murderous weapons.⁵

Initially American officials did strive for precision. From the outset of the war they knew they might need to form postwar alliances with some of the countries they were bombing. In a 1943 memo to "all air force commanders in combat zones" General H. H. "Hap" Arnold, head of the Army Air Forces, borrowing arguments used earlier by proponents of gas warfare, wrote that although war was always horrible, if used with precision the bomber "becomes, in effect, the most humane of all weapons." Whatever the merits of Arnold's reasoning, precision bombsights meant little when bombers were under enemy attack and smoke from earlier bombings obscured targets. Although in many cases American bombardiers hit specific targets, on the average American bombs dropped on visible targets hit only within a 1200-yard range (two-thirds of a mile), a large-enough variation to eliminate distinctions between schools and factories or between private houses and military barracks. When darkness or weather required use of radar for sighting, the range expanded to two miles. Given these limitations, and consistent with the practices of other major belligerents, American policymakers routinely designated large urban areas, rather than specific installations, as primary targets. By war's end the most common method was the use of incendiaries to ignite kindling created by dropping conventional bombs on densely built-up regions.[6]

Visual misrepresentation of the nature of Allied bombing led to misrepresentation of its consequences. American movies often showed the Axis powers using bombs against civilian populations. In *Thirty Seconds over Tokyo* Japanese pilots strafed a crowd of Chinese children, as they did in the 1945 film *God Is My Copilot*, where the children were accompanied by a priest. In another film from that year, RKO's *China Sky*, a hospital became one of the main recipients of Japanese bombs (American filmmakers granted the Japanese a high degree of precision in their bombing efforts when the targets were humanitarian institutions). In contrast were cartoons and animated features depicting American bombing, such as Walt Disney's 1943 *Victory through Air Power*. They gratified viewers with spectacular scenes of bombs destroying enemy munitions plants but excluded human bodies, or parts of bodies, from the debris that soared skyward after the invariable direct hit. The dialogue of some films acknowledged that American bombs killed many civilians. In *Thirty Seconds over Tokyo* bomber pilots expressed concern to one another that this was one of the grim, unavoidable consequences of the job they must do. The film did not show any of these casualties. When, as in *Bombardier*, wartime films did show the victims of American bombs, they always made it clear that they were enemy soldiers or male war workers. In reality the choice to focus the American bombing effort on German and Japanese population centers assured that a large majority of those killed would be women, children, and the elderly.

Many films and magazine features emphasized the care that went into the planning of American bombing missions in order to maximize military damage and minimize non-military casualties. None portrayed activities like those undertaken by the U.S. Army Chemical Warfare Service to develop incendiary bombs designed to cause unstoppable fires. Planning included testing the bombs against mockup German and Japanese towns and urban working-class districts built at proving grounds within the United States, complete with "curtains, children's toys, and clothing hanging in the closets." In some of the tests "teams of firefighters were brought in to quell the blaze with methods the Japanese would use." The tests indicated that when used against actual targets, the "'fires would sweep an entire community' and cause 'tremendous casualties,'" as indeed they did. Also completely invisible in wartime films were the actions of those crews which, failing to drop their bombs over a planned site and understandably not wishing to land with bombs on board, dropped them on whatever landscape they happened to pass over on the way back to base, even if it was the French countryside.[7]

Especially during the war's final months newspapers, newsreels, and magazines did show aerial views of entire cities that had been devastated by American bombs. Captions often gave them such designations as "urban industrial area." An editorial cartoon in the *Atlanta Constitution* that depicted bodies flying into the air after the bombing of Hiroshima carried the title "Land of the Rising Sons." Such captions helped distance viewers from the human meaning of the bombings, as did showing the cities as they appeared when viewed literally through a bombsight, a technique used in films made for war workers and war loan

organizers. Often films would further distance viewers from the violence of battle by depicting it through allegorical graphic animation. *Victory through Air Power* represented the war
in the Pacific by an American eagle attacking a malicious octopus that had stretched its
tentacles into areas where they did not belong. Such imagery seemed to have had an effect.
One American who was in college during the war years said that he "had never thought
of the people in bombed cities as individuals" until he read John Hersey's *Hiroshima*, a vivid
account, published a year after the event, of the experiences of a half-dozen people who were
in the Japanese city on August 6.[8]

Several filmmakers expended special effort to make the American planes that delivered
the bombs seem warm and friendly to movie audiences. In *Thirty Seconds over Tokyo*, when a
pilot learned while flying his B-25 that his wife was going to have a baby, the crew started
singing "rock-a-bye-baby" and the film cut to an external view that showed the plane gently
rocking from side to side as it flew. In *Sunday Dinner for a Soldier* (1944) a plane on the way
to a bombing mission made a marriage proposal, signified by the tipping of a wing as the
aircraft flew over the home of the aviator's beloved. This visual sanitation of American bombing had its verbal equivalent in President Harry S Truman's statement, as he announced
the use of the atomic bomb against the populous Japanese city of Hiroshima on August 6,
1945, that the target had been a "military base." And it was—as were Chicago, New York, and
London. Only a small fraction of the more than one hundred thousand people who died at
Hiroshima were in the Japanese military.[9]

It is hardly surprising that neither government officials nor private citizens who created
and selected images wished to call public attention to the indiscriminate destruction that
accompanied modern warfare. Those in similar positions made similar decisions during
World War I, and the governments of every other major participant in World War II controlled
the flow of visual images at least as tightly, although they often made different decisions as
to what to show. Early in the war, for purposes of intimidating the populations of other
countries, official German films showed some of the dreadful results of resistance to German
occupation. Soon after its involvement in the war began, the Soviet government released
pictures of some of that country's war dead, a decision reflecting different cultural traditions
concerning death and the need to rally a population under a direct German assault that
made keeping war death out of sight an impossibility in many parts of the country.

Nor is it surprising that propagandists consistently depicted the enemy as evil. Indeed,
polarization reached the extreme of suggestions that the enemy belonged to a separate
species. Americans almost always targeted such propaganda at the Japanese, whom movies
and other media usually had presented unfavorably in the prewar decades. Wartime imagery
compared them to rats, monkeys, snakes, and vermin. Among the thousands of such visual
comparisons were the covers of *Time* and *Collier's* depicting Japanese soldiers as apes, and
a float in a mammoth New York parade that included the American eagle "leading a flight of
bombers down on a herd of yellow rats which were trying to escape in all directions." Military
authorities censored photographs showing American soldiers treating wounded Japanese
soldiers, perhaps because these images of one human being helping another blurred the
visual distinctions considered necessary to a win-the-war attitude. John Dower noted in his
study of the imagery and reality of the American-Japanese conflict, *War without Mercy*, that "as
late as February 1945 the Pentagon was still blue-penciling scripts on the grounds that the
passages in question would evoke 'too much sympathy for the Jap people.'" Such policies,
as well as cultural prejudices and the desire to revenge Pearl Harbor, help explain why close

to half of all American soldiers agreed with the statement "I would really like to kill a Japanese soldier," but less than one in ten agreed when the soldier to be killed was German. . . .[10]

This dichotomized way of seeing linked images Americans devised of the enemy with those they devised of themselves. If the enemy was treacherous, cowardly, and heartless, Americans were fair, courageous, and caring. The enemy won only when they had great numerical superiority; when Americans won it was always by overcoming odds against them. The enemy was militaristic; Americans were reluctant to go to war but, like Sergeant York, invincible once aroused. Thus every war movie had at least one Pearl Harbor—type deceitful attack; the most heroic, effective, and unceasing American actions almost always came in response to some enemy outrage.

German Nazism, Italian fascism, and Japanese militarism supplied enough actual outrages to satisfy the needs of any propagandist. Repressive Axis policies invited emphasis on the contrasting diversity and openness of American life. Films in Frank Capra's *Why We Fight* series, for instance, showed authorities conditioning German children and Japanese soldiers to respond like automatons to their dictates, then showed Americans retaining their distinctive ethnic, religious, regional, political, and occupational identities even as they merged into an effective fighting force. A dominant theme of the images America presented to itself during the war years was that these individual differences led to stimulating variety but never to profound conflict. . . .

The persistence of the happy ending in some of the bleakest Hollywood war stories demonstrated the strength of forces bending wartime imagery into polarized patterns. The convention of a happy ending had reigned for decades before the war, but under different circumstances the war might have presented a severe challenge to it. The unconventional endings of some postwar *film noir* productions might be seen as a delayed response to just such wartime challenges, but more often ways of seeing encouraged by the war helped entrench the tradition of a happy ending, as in the contrived conclusions of *Happy Land* and *The Fighting Sullivans*. Sometimes the widely known facts of contemporary events required a deferred happy ending. In *Wake Island* and *Bataan*, although all American defenders were dead, captured, or about to be killed at the end, no viewer could doubt that their heroic resistance would contribute to the victorious outcome of the war. *Bataan* closed with a vision of the Americans captured there marching out of captivity with worn but determined and thankful looks on their faces. Consistent with the movement toward less evasive imagery as the war progressed, the number of films with somber endings increased, but all suggested that whatever the war's costs, all was for the best. At the end of the 1944 film *Tender Comrade* Ginger Rogers was in grief after having received word of the death of her husband in the war; but with their baby, Chris, as an uncomprehending audience, she explained that his sacrifice was worthwhile because it would make a better world for Chris. A tough film from the war's last year, *Pride of the Marines*, though it conveyed much of the terror, pain, and emotional agony suffered by blinded Marine hero Al Schmid, intimated at the end not only that his life was enriched by a perfect love, but that his sight might be returning. Hollywood did not make up this ending; the real Schmid returned to his prewar sweetheart and did recover some vision in one eye. But that was part of the reason Warner Bros. chose to film his story.[11]

In most cases the government neither encouraged Hollywood to concoct happy endings nor worked them into officially produced material. Indeed, OWI and other agencies guarded against creating within the public the expectation that each of their personal segments of the shared war story would have painless outcomes. Perhaps to avoid stirring false hopes among the hundreds of thousands of other American families who would not enjoy a miraculous reversal of the bad news they had received, BPR did not release a photograph showing the joyous reunion with his family of a coastguardsman erroneously reported killed. Nonetheless the government's wartime messages, like those of Hollywood, suggested that neither the war nor the conditions of American life presented citizens with situations for which the probable outcome was a tense, imperfect, temporary resolution, rather than a satisfying and definitive one.[12]

The sharpest challenge to maintenance of clear distinctions between allies and enemies required by polarized wartime ways of seeing came from the presence in the country of a few hundred thousand Asian-Americans. Henry R. Luce, born of missionary parents in China, was especially concerned lest Americans confuse residents of Japanese and Chinese ancestry. Shortly after Pearl Harbor the magazines he published, Time and Life, ran detailed, illustrated articles, based on highly dubious assumptions about connections between ethnicity and behavior as well as appearance, on "How to Tell Your Friends from the Japs." Filmmakers found easier ways of identifying the ethnic affiliations of characters so that the audience could sort out good and bad. Among the onlookers at a military parade depicted in Shores of Tripoli was a spectator who waved an American flag and wore a sign that said, "Me Chinese." Newsreels featured stories such as "Chinatown Hails Captured Jap Sub" to emphasize the difference.[13]

Not even the Constitution could restrain the imperative to maintain clear distinctions between enemy and ally. The government violated at least half of the ten amendments comprising the Bill of Rights with its decision to remove Americans of Japanese ancestry, the majority of them U.S. citizens, from the communities where they lived and worked, and to place them in guarded camps in sparsely inhabited areas of the West. This move was dictated primarily by political expediency (the action won widespread approval) and fears, later discredited, of espionage. Other reasons for this action included concern over violent attacks on Japanese-Americans by hostile neighbors, and the greed of some of these same neighbors, who because of the relocation were able to buy at greatly reduced prices much of the detainees' property. But a consequence of the relocation was removal of 110,000 living reminders that the bestial Japanese faces that glowered from wartime posters and cartoons did not tell the whole visual truth.[14]

The government acknowledged visual motivations for its actions. An OWI bulletin sent to the motion picture industry emphasized that Japanese-Americans were sent to relocation centers partly because they "look like our Japanese enemies." Relocation actually complicated the types of visual distinctions Luce had tried to maintain. Because it placed actors of Japanese ancestry behind barbed wire, it assured that the omnipresent Richard Loo and other Chinese-American actors would be cast in roles such as the interrogating Japanese general in Purple Heart. It also meant that when Twentieth-Century Fox filmed Little Tokyo, U.S.A., it used neon signs in Los Angeles's Chinatown as a substitute for those in that city's Japanese business and entertainment district, which had been darkened by the internment. But most moviegoers probably were unaware of these inconsistencies. Because relocation was more about perceived threats and differences than about substantive ones, it helped maintain the wartime illusion of clear distinctions.[15]

Many Americans resisted this compulsive wartime need to suppress ambiguity. If one purpose of the Allied effort was to allow people to make informed choices about their own destinies, then among the war's heroes were journalists, entertainers, artists, and public officials who used visual means to open up an honest dialogue on the war's nature and meaning. For those who sought to give firsthand reports on the conflict, the dangerous undertaking of getting in a position to be able to see and record the war was just the beginning of the process. . . .

One difficulty surpassed all these others: finding ways to communicate the enormity of the experience of war. Innumerable veterans insisted in memoirs and interviews that those who were not there could not really understand this experience. It encompassed more than the obvious horrors. It included aggressive impulses raised then given no outlet during long stretches of waiting with no clear-cut action. It involved encounters with a wide range of distinctive smells, sounds, and other sensations, some the result of living in inexpressible filth. Communicating truths about the pain and death of war presented Americans with a particularly difficult challenge. Their culture had no common language of visual communication for dealing with these phenomena, which seldom received frank discussion or straightforward portrayal in peacetime society.

For a century before War Department personnel established the Chamber of Horrors, death had been drifting toward the periphery of American visual experience. During the nation's early years almost all Americans died at home, where members of the family prepared them for burial. By 1941 increasing numbers of Americans died in hospitals. The practice of using professional "funeral directors" to prepare a corpse for viewing had spread from the upper middle-class enclaves in the Northeast, where it took root in the mid-nineteenth century, to become common practice in urban areas, where the majority of the population lived. Moreover, this farm-to-city population shift, along with the disappearance of the horse as an urban beast of burden, reduced visual encounters with the death of large animals. The spread of photography in the United States after 1839 at first led to the common practice of making photographic records of loved ones within hours of their demise. Soon, however, this new medium, through its offshoot of the 1890s which set images in motion, was employed more often to bring Americans images of strangers simulating death—albeit strangers whose visual presence became familiar as they attained the status of movie stars. These stylized images of death proved inadequate to convey the sights of modern war.[16]

The incomprehensible scale of the carnage compounded the problem. War linked the histories of mass production and mass destruction. During the American Civil War the concept of a "billion" first entered the language of production, when Secretary of War Edwin M. Stanton estimated Union needs at 1,022,176,474 short-arm cartridges. Even before the development of manufacturing techniques that made possible such ten-digit requisitions, humanity had shown a marked talent for destroying life and property, as in the Thirty Years War (1618–1648), which eliminated half of the population and most of the livestock, towns, and buildings of large regions in Central Europe. Not until World War I, however, did "tens of millions" become a useful unit for measuring obliteration of human lives during a short time period, with 20 million killed during its four years, when all participants applied their most advanced industrial and organizational techniques to the manufacture of one commodity, corpses. With the toll reaching 50 million during the six years of World War II, photographers and other visual artists and reporters had to deal with their version of a problem recognized earlier in the century by the French writer Philippe Berthelot: "When a man dies, I suffer; when a million and a half die, that's statistics."

The ability of combat to redefine the meaning of ordinary experiences created another barrier to communication. One soldier told the photographer Margaret Bourke-White that he had "come to hate moonlight . . . ever since my best friend was killed on a moonlight night." Many World War II combat veterans came to associate lush green fields of grass with maiming land mines. Thus "for years after the war, ex-soldiers seized up when confronted by patches of grass and felt safe only when walking on asphalt or concrete." World War I had elicited many similar responses. Before becoming one of the twenty thousand British soldiers killed on the first day of the 1916 battle of the Somme, Second Lieutenant William Ratcliffe had written to his parents, "Everywhere the work of God is spoiled by the hand of man. One looks at a sunset and for a moment thinks that that at least is unsophisticated, but an aeroplane flies across, and puff! puff! and the whole scene is spoilt by clouds of shrapnel smoke." World War I made such transformations a staple of contemporary literature, but visual records of that war seldom expressed such complexities. . . .[17]

Those who rejected polarized ways of seeing war could incorporate a revealing sense of irony into their visions. Totalitarian states and conventional American propagandists used irony as a weapon of war. An example of this commonplace use of irony came in the film *Bombardier* when Japanese soldiers used a stretcher whose markings indicated clearly that it had been donated by the United States when Japan needed medical assistance at the time of the 1923 Tokyo earthquake. This was not the irony of self-reflection, but merely added ingratitude to the list of the enemy's sins. When a Paramount newsreel told how thread spun by the black widow spider had proven to be the ideal material for making the crosspiece for American bombsights, the narrator told the story with the unqualified enthusiasm accorded all American technical advances during the war, again without any self-reflexive irony.[18]

John Huston's 1945 film *San Pietro* offered a contrast. Early in this U.S. Army documentary he recites from a prewar guidebook that called attention to San Pietro's beautiful old church. As Huston read, the camera showed the viewer that as a result of the German occupation and American assault on this seven-hundred-year-old Italian village, the church had been reduced to an empty, half-broken shell. The film, a powerful tribute to the American soldier, made clear that modern combat required destroying many things that the war was fought to preserve. *San Pietro* acknowledged cinematically the contradictions Huston later stated in discussing the film: "Nobody ever wanted to kill Germans more than I did. And I thought it was anti-war to do it, in order to stop Hitler."[19]

Irony reminded viewers how easily human actions could lead to unexpected outcomes. Images that documented limitations on the ability of humans to predict and control thereby acknowledged the limitations present in all human products, including the images themselves. Photographers and filmmakers who felt compelled to communicate such complexities could find allies in government. Elmer Davis thought that most of the public, like most soldiers, were moved not by "flag-waving" patriotism but by their recognition of the war as "something grim, unpleasant, but unavoidable" which they wanted to end as soon as possible. Davis's lack of government experience, influential allies, and clear-cut authority often hampered his efforts to translate his convictions into official policy. Davis took the job in partial awareness of these difficulties. Like a soldier going into battle, he could not fully appreciate the obstacles until he encountered them firsthand. . . .

The populace sometimes demanded conformity and sometimes challenged polarized ways of seeing. Wartime public pressures helped bring about both the abuse and protection of the constitutional rights of American citizens, as shown by the contrasting examples of incarceration of Japanese-Americans and maintenance of a relatively free press. Before the end of the first year of American involvement an OWI survey reported on an insistent public demand "that the Censor discard his rose-tinted glasses." According to the survey many Americans resented "being treated like babies" and expected the government to recognize that "they can take bad news and want to be treated like full partners." Another survey reported that "press and public are convinced that censorship is rigid beyond any requirements of security." Wartime polls showed slightly more people in support of than opposed to publication of grim photographs. The month after the first photographs of dead Americans were released an OWI survey asked people if they wanted more pictures with this type of "realism": 45 percent responded yes, 8 percent yes with some qualifications, 42 percent no, and 5 percent had no opinion. Later in the war larger majorities responded favorably.[20]

Staffers within OWI who pushed for more forthright portrayal of the realities of combat strengthened their position by citing this and other evidence that audiences favored candor and resisted blatant manipulation. When OWI previewed Darryl Zanuck's At the Front in Los Angeles, "at one showing before a kid audience cries of 'fake' were forthcoming in some scenes." As noted, Roosevelt had rejected a military proposal for "complete censorship of publications, radio, and motion pictures within the U.S.A." in part because he believed the American public would not accept it. During the war the military temporarily withdrew from circulation one film in the Why We Fight series, The Battle of China, because it went so far in its attempt to show China as united and strong that it completely ignored the intense internal conflict that consumed that ally's leaders, and therefore would have no credibility for viewers with any awareness of what was going on there. The experience of the American veteran and Holocaust witness Joseph Kushlis indicated that doubts about the reliability of government-produced imagery remained strong at the war's end. He noted that audiences took his reports more seriously when they learned that his photographs of the death camps had been "taken by a strict amateur photographer in which there could be no doctoring of scenes and no faking of film."[21]

Soldiers were the toughest audience. The Marine veteran William Manchester remembered "John Wayne being booed in a Hawaiian hospital by an audience of wounded Marines from Iwo Jima and Okinawa, men who had had macho acts, in a phrase of the day, up their asses to their armpits." Manchester also reported that after seeing an advertisement in an American magazine that jauntily declared "Who's afraid of the big Focke-Wulf" |a German fighter plane|, pilots at one base wrote "'We are" and "followed it with the signatures of every airman there, including the commanding officer, and mailed it to the sponsoring firm." Near the end of the war the most publicity-conscious of all American generals, Douglas MacArthur, refused to appear in a government-produced film explaining that American soldiers were fighting for "peace for ourselves, our children, and their children." MacArthur argued against making such films because "the reaction of the troops is cynical and resentful as they regard |them| as propaganda." A G.I. in Rome complained that "stuff like Humphrey Bogart whipping a whole German armored-car column singlehanded gives us pains in the pratt because that kind of crap gives the folks at home the wrong kind of idea about what we are up against." During the war few American soldiers made recorded comments concerning depiction of its horrors. Most who did agreed with the colonel who told George Biddle that he should draw a recently killed soldier because "the people at home ought to see things like that."[22]

At the same time, soldiers did not want to increase the anxieties of those waiting for them to return. Thus the novelist and veteran James Jones reported that almost every soldier was able "to perk up enough so that whenever he saw a reporter with a pencil or a photographer with a camera, he could be ready with the wisecrack and make the toothy smile for the folks back home." Meanwhile, back at home, soldiers' families were among those pushing hardest for full and honest disclosure of war news. In November 1942 about one hundred members of a midwestern Marine Fathers Group held a protest meeting in Chicago to call attention to excessive censorship of news from military areas. Such protest meetings were rare during the war, although numerous individuals and groups wrote to criticize various aspects of government information policy. The controversy caused by Patton's slapping a shell-shocked soldier brought forth perhaps the largest number of letters to the government and the press; a substantial majority condemned not only Patton's action but also early attempts to suppress information about it. More unusual were letters like the one sent by Edith Huntington Snow of New York to OWI objecting that newsreel pictures of battle were "softened and made unreal" by the upbeat music that accompanied the images. . . .[23]

Attitudes such as this, which contained both skepticism and willful indifference, could help or hinder those who sought to make visible revealing wartime images. The same was true of the public in general, which could react adversely both to those who tried to challenge conventional understandings or practices and to those perceived as withholding or distorting information. If the historian Lee Kennett is correct, limits in the public ability to understand war's painful necessities sometimes cost lives, as when the U.S. Army, knowing that one death during basic training outraged the public more than a dozen during battle, established training procedures that reduced fatalities in the short term but ultimately led to more deaths by leaving soldiers less adequately prepared for combat. Kennett's claim seems plausible, but so does the wartime belief of Elmer Davis that the public desire for truth was one of the most valuable resources he had to draw on in his battle against excessive restrictions on the flow of information.[24]

Whatever the wisdom of the competing policies of restriction and openness, the war as presented gave many Americans an enlivened sense of purpose. Despite significant contributions to dialogue made by individual effort, free speech traditions, and the diversity of the American population, wartime imagery reinforced those aspects of the culture that encouraged thinking of international relations in simple terms of right and wrong. Because of its consequences, this encouragement of polarized ways of seeing must be calculated as one of the costs of the war.

Notes

1   Jean Bethke Elshtain, *Women and War* (New York, 1987), 256; Lasswell, *Propaganda Techniques in the World War*, p. 47, quoted in Willard Waller, ed. *War in the Twentieth Century* (New York, 1940), 449.

2   Bound folder marked "Organization of Information Activities for Defense and War, 1940–42" by Harold F. Gosnell, in La Mar Seal Mackay Papers, box 1, Hoover; *Guide to Essential Wartime Printing and Lithography* (New York, n.d.).

3   La Mar Seal Mackay papers, box 1, Hoover; Byron Price papers, notebooks, p. 15, in box

3; SHSW; AG's office to Kodak, 2 September 1941, in file marked "AG 000.73–8–26–41," RG407, entry 360, box 4, NA.

4   Covert interview in Harris, Home Front, 72. Burns, Roosevelt: The Soldier of Freedom, 212. On overseas travel see Kennett, G.I., 111, and Spector, Eagle Against the Sun, 382.

5   For the fullest and best account of changing official and popular attitudes toward aerial bombardment, as well as of actual changes in the capabilities in American air power, see Michael Sherry, The Rise of American Air Power: The Creation of Armageddon (New Haven, 1987).

6   Arnold memo, 10 June 1943, from Arnold Papers, Official Files, Jacket 36, Bombing; my thanks to Michael S. Sherry for this document. On the accuracy of the Norden bomb-sight, which made the idea of precision bombing seem plausible, see Spector, Eagle Against the Sun, 15. For some spectacular and often deadly examples of wartime blunders see Fussell, Wartime, 19–35.

7   Sherry, Air Power, 226–27; the air veteran Gibson Byrd described the indiscriminate disposal of bombs in an interview with the author, May 1974.

8   New York Times, 11 March 1945, p. 1; on "rising sons" see Paul Boyer, By the Bomb's Early Light: American Thought and Culture at the Dawn of the Atomic Age (New York, 1985), 13; for an example of a bombed city shown from great height see "Victory Loan Trailer," in LC; student quoted in Hess, United States at War, 133.

9   The exact death toll at Hiroshima will never be known, but all of the most recent and thorough estimates put the number at well over one hundred thousand people.

10 John Dower, War Without Mercy: Race and Power in the Pacific War (New York, 1986), 19, 86–93; Hess, United States at War, 74. For an example of a censored photo showing American soldiers helping a wounded Japanese soldier see 16 October 1942 photograph #80-G-12463 in SPB, NA. See also memo, General Hdq, Southwest Pacific Area to WD, 3 March 1945, which requests a waiver of an earlier policy restricting release of photographs in which the features of individual "Japs" were identifiable (the request was granted), 062.1–66, Public Information Div, RG165, entry 499, box 67, NA. This policy was partly due to the army's concern that photos of recognizable Japanese soldiers might yield useful information to Japanese intelligence agencies; see Curtis Mitchell to Navy PR Office, 23 August 1943, 062.1–666, ibid., box 25.

11 On the real Al Schmid, see Life, 22 March 1943, p. 35.

12 Returning sailor photo #N31565 in RG208, SPB, NA.

13 Time, 22 December 1941, p. 3; newsreel from c. 8 November 1942 described in file "United News," RG208, entry 285, box 1520, NA.

14 On widespread public support for the relocation see Hadley Cantril, ed., Public Opinion, 1935–1946, prepared by Mildred Strunk (Princeton, 1951), 380.

15 Special Bulletin, 24 October 1942, OWI Bureau of Motion Pictures, in Film Study Center, Museum of Modern Art, New York (emphasis in original). The Office of Censorship reviewed in advance all stories and pictures of the camps where Japanese-Americans were confined. See letter from N. R. Howard Press Div, to Gen. A. D. Surles, Director, BPR, in PR Div, RG165, entry 499, box 10, NA. On Little Tokyo and other ironies of wartime film imagery of Chinese and Japanese see Koppes and Black, Hollywood Goes to War, 72–74, and Lingeman, Don't You Know, 180–81.

16 On changing attitudes toward death see Philippe Aries, Western Attitudes toward Death from the Middle Ages to the Present (Baltimore, 1974).

17 Bourke-White, *Purple Heart Valley*, 65; on fear of grass see Fussell, *Wartime*, 279; Ratcliffe quoted in Fussell, *Great War*, 55. Fussell notes that "dawn has never recovered from what the Great War did to it" (*Wartime*, 63).

18 Paramount newsreel for 5 January 1944, NA; on the heavy-handedness of German use of humor see, for example, Leila J. Rupp, *Mobilizing Women for War: German and American Propaganda, 1939–1945* (Princeton, N.J., 1978), 165.

19 Huston quoted in *Film: Book* 2, p. 29. For revealing documents related to the production of *San Pietro* see Culbert, *Film and Propaganda in America*, 3:227–319.

20 Lucien Warner to Alan Barth, 9 October 1942, in file marked "Correspondence Panels Miscellaneous," USIS, BSS, RG44, entry 149, box 1711, NA; 13 November 1942 memo, "Developing Situation—Governments Information Policy Antagonizes Public and Press," ibid., box 1710; poll figures from "OWI Current Surveys," issue 27 (27 October, 1943), ibid., box 1715. See later poll from Cantril and Strunk, *Public Opinion*, 487.

21 On Los Angeles audience see note from Howard Langley, April 1943, in RG208, item 215, box 1063, NA; Roosevelt memo, 20 February 1941, in file marked "AG 000.7–1/22/41," RG407, entry 360, box 3, NA; concerns over *Battle of China* in memo, Maj. Gen. F. H. Osborn, Information and Education Div, to Gen. George C. Marshall, 1 November 1944, 062.2 (case 36), Army Chief of Staff, RG165, entry 13, box 133, NA. Kushlis quoted in Robert H. Abzug, *Inside the Vicious Heart: Americans and the Liberation of Nazi Concentration Camps* (New York, 1985), 138.

22 Manchester, *Goodbye Darkness*, 12; Manchester, *Glory and the Dream*, 285; cable from MacArthur to WD, 15 April 1945, 062.2 (case 44), Army Chief of Staff, RG165, entry 13, box 133, NA; Morella, Epstein, and Griggs, *Films of World War II*, 61; George Biddle, *Artist at War* (New York, 1944), 207. In *Up Front*, 131–32, 169–70, Bill Mauldin described the resentment of soldiers at phony wartime advertisements. For one example of soldiers' criticism of a misleading photograph during World War I see Moeller, *Shooting War*, 149. Although most soldiers rejected glorified representations of combat, and only 13 percent could name as many as three of the "Four Freedoms" which Roosevelt identified as central to the war effort, they overwhelmingly supported that effort. In one large survey 65 percent expressed the belief that they were fighting to "guarantee democratic liberties to all peoples of the world." See Larrabee, *Commander-in-Chief*, 625–26.

23 Jones, *World War II*, 76; on Marine Fathers Group see Report from Director, Intelligence Div, Hdq Sixth Service Command, Chicago, 29 November 1942, 0000.73–43, Public Information Div, RG165, entry 499, box 6, NA; Snow to Lowell Mellett, 21 March 1942, in file marked "Newsreel Coverage," RG208, entry 285, box 1518, NA.

24 Lee Kennett, *G.I.: The American Soldier in World War II* (New York, 1987), 51–52.

"Make My Day!": Spectacle as Amnesia in Imperial Politics

6

MICHAEL ROGIN

. . . . World War II laid the structural foundations in politics for the modern American empire. First, the good war established the military industrial state as the basis for both domestic welfare and foreign policy. Second, it made surveillance and covert operations, at home and abroad, an integral part of the state. Third, it drew the political parties together behind an interventionist, bipartisan foreign policy directed by Democrats during the major wars (World War II, Korea, and Vietnam), and by the former Democrat, Ronald Reagan, in the 1980s. Fourth, the good war's popularity linked the mass public to the structures of power. Mass enthusiasm for the national security state could not be mobilized for subsequent hot wars and was actually threatened by them. Nevertheless, only for a few years during and after the American defeat in Vietnam were the fundamental assumptions about America's role in the world established during World War II ever challenged by significant sectors within American politics. Finally, World War II celebrated the undercover struggle of good against evil, and thereby prepared the way for the covert spectacle.

World War II slid easily into the Cold War, as Communism replaced Nazism and one Asian enemy, China, took the place of another, Japan (so that the Japanese demons of World War II movies could be recycled within the decade as Hollywood North Koreans and Chinese).[1] But the Cold War was fought mainly with symbols and surrogates. It organized politics around ideology and conspiracy (Communists in government at home, secret interventions abroad) just as ideology was supposed to be coming to an end. It may be, as Fred Block argues, that the state recognized its need to play a foreign, economic role as the alternative to domestic social reconstruction, and recast economic challenges as Cold War and military ones to mobilize popular support. In any case, Richard Barnet suggests, the permanent mobilization of the American population—to sustain high taxes, foreign aid, interventionist state policies, and ongoing international alliances—marks a fundamental break with the peacetime past. The worry in the now famous National Security Council memorandum no. 68 as the Cold War began—that America would be crippled by internal weakness at the moment of its greatest strength—reflected the state's new economic and security role and the fear that the population would not support it. Genuinely covert actions were one response to fears of popular flaccidity; the politics of spectacle as political mobilization was the other.[2]

The spread both of covert operations and of foreign policy as spectacle responded to the tensions among economy, state, organs of public opinion, and instruments of nuclear war that emerged in the shift from World War II to the Cold War and that were accentuated at the end of the first Cold War period with the American defeat in Vietnam. Postwar worries about the weakness of the American state nonetheless presumed an American hegemony that more recent economic and political developments have called into question. A multinational-dominated internationalized economy that resists state control sets the stage for defensive, American nationalism. The sources for that nationalism lie in state structures that lack the power either to control the economy or to mobilize the populace and so turn to covert action and the spectacle; in the political economy of the military-industrial complex; in a nuclear-dominated military strategy, where weapons function as symbols of intentions in war games rather than as evidence of war-fighting capabilities; and in the permeation of public and private space by the fiction-making visual media.[3]

Public anti-Communist mobilization operated alongside genuinely covert operations in the early Cold War years, the one to engage masses, the other to serve the interests of elites. That separation broke down with John Kennedy, however, for whom the theory and practice of foreign interventions served less to preserve imperial interests than to demonstrate the firmness of American will. Vietnam functioned as the most important theater of destruction, from Kennedy's Green Beret adventurism through Nixon's expansion of the war to test our resolve to meet a future "real crisis."[4] But Vietnam failed as symbolic foreign policy, not just because the United States lost the war but also because American suffering and turmoil could not immediately be dissolved into spectacle.

The full-fledged absorption of American foreign policy by symbolic gesture, therefore, awaited the Reagan presidency. The men whose consciousness was formed by World War II revived the American empire after Vietnam—Paul Nitze and the other members of the Committee on the Present Danger, who prepared the ideological ground for the Reagan administration; William Casey, who moved from the wartime OSS to direct first Reagan's presidential campaign and then the CIA (and, as he shifted from electoral spectacle to secrecy, to subordinate intelligence collection to covert activities); and Reagan himself, who made training and morale movies during the war and who met the crisis in his personal and professional life after it by leading the fight against Hollywood Communism.[5] The Reagan Doctrine—inspired by the ideological adventurer Jack Wheeler, known as the "Indiana Jones of the right"[6]—recuperated in political theater what had been lost in imperial substance. A foreign policy run from the expanded, hidden, militarized National Security Council aimed, by reversing Vietnam ("Do we get to win this time?" Rambo wants to know), to reenact the good war as a movie.

The covert spectacle thus reflects the persistence of dreams about American dominance in the face of the erosion of the material and ideological sources for American preeminence in the world. The budgetary and political demands that the American government inflicts on its people in the name of military and national security contribute, to be sure, to trade and budget deficits and economic decay. But at the same time the decline in a solidly based American preeminence has generated efforts at symbolic recovery that center around military and national security. This combat with the Soviet Union takes two forms: a visible military buildup in weapons that cannot be used, and low-intensity (as they are called) military interventions in the Third World. Together these demonstrate American resolution without substantial risks at home. Foreign policy is conducted by theatrical events—Grenada invasion, Libyan bombing, Persian Gulf flagging, Honduran "show of force"—staged for public consumption. These interventions may well succeed, but their significance lies less in stopping the local spread of "Communism" than in convincing elite and mass publics that America has the power to have its way. Substituting symbols for substance, these staged events constitute the politics of postmodernism, so long as one remembers that symbols produced for consumption at home and abroad have all too much substance for the victims of those symbols, the participant-observers on the ground in the Third World.[7]

Individual covert operations may serve specific corporate or national-security-clique interests, and the operations themselves are often (like Iran/Contra) hidden from domestic subjects who might hold them to political account. But even where the particular operation is supposed to remain secret, the government wants it known it has the power, secretly, to intervene. The payoff for many covert operations is their intended demonstration effect. The covert spectacle is a form of therapeutic politics. By focusing attention on itself, it aims to control not simply political power but knowledge.

Most obviously, the specular relation to political life has implications for democratic governance. Spectators gain vicarious participation in a narrative that, in the name of national security, justifies their exclusion from information and decision making. Covert operations as spectacle pacify domestic as well as foreign audiences, for they transform the political relation between rulers and citizens from accountability to entertainment. Vicarious participation, moreover, is also granted to the rulers themselves, for those who sponsor and promote covert action almost never place themselves at risk. Vicarious participation in the spectacle of the covert heals in fantasy and preserves in fact the separation of those who plan from those who kill and are killed, the separation that Richard Barnet has called bureaucratic homicide.[8]

Secrecy is a technique not just for vicarious inclusion and political exclusion, however, but also for defining the real. Covert actions, obscured by disinformation, require the state to lie. When John Poindexter denied that the Libyan bombing aimed to kill Qaddafi, and defended the spread of disinformation about alleged Libyan terrorism as a strategy to keep the Libyan leader off balance, he also had a domestic purpose. He was orchestrating an entertainment that, in winning popular applause, would underline for the mass audience the need for secret planning, accountable to no one and to no standard of truth outside itself. Poindexter wanted a mass public that stopped asking what was true and what false because it knew which side it was on. The term for the psychology at which Poindexter aimed is *identification with the aggressor*. Destabilizing orienting cues from any source, the state was to become the single anchor in the midst of the shifting realities it displayed. And that would increase trust in government, for the less one experiences alternatives to power, the more one needs to see it as benign.

Aggression is thus not opposed to intimacy but rather a technique for producing it —much as, conversely, intimacy in the American president normalizes the violence he authorizes. The benign version of spectacle plays on our ontological insecurity by offering trust in the sources of information. That answers the question James Lardner recently asked in his review of *Broadcast News*: "Why are the networks' anchormen so much more vivid to us than the stories they present?"[9] Presidential intimacy, as in the "giant womb" Garry Wills described at the 1984 Republican convention, or Bush's call for a "kinder, gentler nation" four years later, offers us the security of trusting the head of state as much as we trusted Walter Cronkite.

The form promoted by political infantilization is reliance on central power; its content is reassurance that we can continue to live in the (fantasized) past. Aspirations to appropriate basic trust may well fall short, into mass cynicism and withdrawal. But they do succeed in investing the imaginary with as much truth effect as the real—or rather, I have been arguing, the other way around. Where political spectacles compel attention and are not turned off, they acquire the power of fiction. For why should the mass audience be able to tell the difference between TV series and movies and the political spectacles that also appear on the screen, so long as the reality principle never reaches, directly and forcefully, into their lives (as it did, for example, in the 1930s depression or the 1960s draft)? The spectacle aims either to keep the reality principle entirely at bay (Star Wars as invisible shield) or to seize control of the interpretations placed on its intrusions (Star Wars shifts the terms of political debate from aggressive American preparations to win a nuclear war to the pros and cons of nuclear defense).

The covert spectacle thus breaks down the distinction between politics and theater (or rather, movies)—from the one side in police, spy, adventure, and science-fiction thrillers (including old movies starring Ronald Reagan) where the audience is privy to the hidden world of counterinsurgency warfare, and from the other side in Reagan's invocation of lines from such movies and reenactments of their plots—in his praise to Oliver North on the day he fired him that the events that had made North a "national hero" would "make a great movie."[10]

This movie reenactment of history, whether directed from Hollywood or from Washington, puts few Americans at risk. Instead of actually refighting the Second World War, it enlists Third World peoples as surrogates. The covert spectacle is thereby grounded in the history of American expansion, not eastward against established European powers but westward and southward against vulnerable racial others. But the 1960s, by recovering imperial history in the civil rights struggle and Vietnam, challenged the racial constitution of American national identity. The Reagan doctrine had to forget, therefore, the moment in which American history was remembered. . . .

"The crisis in ideological confidence of the 70s, visible on all levels of American culture and variously enacted in Hollywood's 'incoherent texts,' has not been resolved," writes Robin Wood in *Hollywood from Vietnam to Reagan*. "Instead it has been forgotten." Wood is referring to the shocks administered to the dominant (white male) politics and culture by black protest, Vietnam, and the emergence of a mass-based feminism. Two 1967 Sidney Poitier movies, as Ed Guerrero has argued, represented Hollywood's last effort to incorporate race into liberalism. These twin celebrations of the black, middle-class professional, *Guess Who's Coming to Dinner* and *In the Heat of the Night*, together won seven Academy Awards. But Hollywood containment exploded the next year—in the Tet offensive, on the streets of America's inner cities, at the Chicago Democratic National Convention, and with the assassinations of Robert Kennedy and Martin Luther King, Jr. Wood analyzed the Hollywood movies that registered cultural breakdown without being able to resolve it. Ella Taylor has offered a comparable interpretation of the (more domesticated) space opened up on 1970s television, undercutting the traditional family and finding refuge in imagined workplace communities. The Carter presidency would lend itself to similar treatment.[11]

The Reagan regime put America back together again by exploiting and disavowing the 1960s. On the one hand, Reagan capitalized on the sharpest electoral polarization in American history along race and gender lines. Beginning in 1968, a large majority of whites (overwhelming in every election but 1976) has opposed the presidential choice of a large majority of peoples of color. Beginning in 1980 men have voted more strongly Republican for president than have women. No president since James Monroe has received as enormous a share of the white male vote as Reagan received in 1984—75 percent by my rough calculation, if Jewish voters are excluded—and the gap between men and women was as large or larger in the presidential vote four years later. On the other hand, since the 1960s subversive, colored, and female voices have called into question the racial and political demonology that often silenced such voices in the past.

The response to this double pressure, which undercuts the Reagan regime's claims to universality as they are being made, is regression. 1980s Hollywood has been dominated, writes Wood, by "children's films conceived and marketed largely for adults," an analysis that applies to Washington as well. Even if not technically science fiction (like *Star Wars*, the movie, and *Star Wars*, the weapon), 1980s films restore traditional race and gender divisions by abandoning pretensions to verisimilitude. "The audiences who wish to be constructed as children also wish to regard themselves as extremely sophisticated and 'modern,'" Wood explains, and they do so by admiring the skills with which they have been infantilized. Production is not hidden as the real source of power; it rather appears on the surface as one more display. Taking pleasure from production numbers, in film terminology, from the special effects of spin doctors, in the language of political campaigns, audiences enjoy at once the effects produced on them and the way those effects are produced. "We both know and don't know that we are watching special effects, technological fakery," Wood writes, suggesting that being in on the infantilizing tricks allows one to regress and enjoy them.[12]

The self-aware quality of the mass spectacle, to which postmodernism points, should thus be read not as a sign of maturity but as an escape from troubling depths so that their residues can safely appear on the surface. As the mass public withdraws from political engagement to spectacles, lo and behold it watches self-ironizing—*Indiana Jones*—or self-pitying—*Rambo*—displays of racial demonology. Fredric Jameson once distinguished entrapping displays of nostalgia, which emphasize the beauty and accuracy of surface reproductions, from self-knowing forms of pastiche that create distance from the past.[13] He wrote before the politics and the movies of the Reagan years used self-knowingness to allow us to return to the past (or go *Back to the Future* in another movie invoked by the president) without having time travel remind us of what we now know we must not do. When an imperial white male wins a white woman in violent combat with evil, dark tribes, as in the Indiana Jones movies, everyone knows that these surface cartoons are not meant to be taken seriously. So we don't have to feel implicated in their displays, can think they are sendups of 1930s serials rather than precipitates of current covert operations, and forget what we have seen. "Go ahead. Make my day!"

George Bush might have borrowed his film criticism during the 1988 campaign from Robin Wood. "We have turned around the permissive philosophy of the 70s," Bush boasted, so that a society that once enjoyed movies like *Easy Rider* now prefers "Dirty Harry" films. "Clint Eastwood's answer to violent crime is 'Go ahead, make my day,'" Bush continued. "My opponent's answer is slightly different. His motto is, 'Go ahead, have a nice weekend.'" Bush was invoking, of course, the Massachusetts weekend furlough program under which Willie Horton, the black convicted murderer, had been allowed to leave prison. Horton, as the Bush campaign was making sure every American knew, had terrorized a white couple and raped the woman. The black criminal and white rapist whom Eastwood had dared to make his day had merged in the figure of Horton; Bush was casting Dukakis as the impotent liberal who could not protect his wife. The buddies who went seeking America, according to the advertising campaign for *Easy Rider*, and "couldn't find it anywhere" had in Bush's movie reviews turned into Dukakis and Horton.[14]

Bush's campaign was not the first attempt to organize American politics around the specter of interracial rape. Repeated ads showing a revolving prison door, combined with the Horton victim's well-advertised campaign tour for Bush, reproduced *The Birth of a Nation*.[15] Attacking Dukakis as weak on defense as well as on violent crime, moreover, the Bush campaign linked imperial to domestic racial politics, for the Dukakis of Bush's television ads would make Americans vulnerable to aliens abroad and at home. Open racist appeals were now forbidden, however, and Bush (and his supporters in my presidency class) denied that Bush's version of "Make my day!" had anything to do with race. But the Republican candidate had succeeded in replacing Jesse Jackson with Willie Horton as the dominant black face in the campaign. For the first time, several of my students then remembered the racial and sexual context for "Make my day!"

That memory of the racial antagonism he promoted posed a problem for Bush, however, to which he offered a solution after his victory. The solution was amnesia. Along with two other movie phrases popularized by President Reagan—"Win one for the Gipper," from *Knute Rockne, All American*, and "the Evil Empire," from *Star Wars*—"Make my day!" will be included in the new edition of *Bartlett's Book of Famous Quotations*. If Bush has his way, however, the words will be severed from their meaning. "The American people," the new president reassured us after his election, "are wonderful when it comes to understanding when a campaign ends and the work of business begins." Bush wanted Americans to believe that his campaign spectacle would have nothing to do with his conduct of government. He was making his business that "great act of American amnesia," as political scientist James Barber called it on election night, by which our politics forgets the forces that drive it. The new president brushed off Barbara Walters's questions about the campaign on the eve of his inauguration. "That's history," said George Bush. "That doesn't mean anything any more."[16]

Notes

An earlier version of this paper was presented in the series "The Peculiarities of the American Empire," sponsored by the History Department, Rutgers University, 29 April 1988. The title of the session for which this paper was written was "The Postmodern Empire." I am grateful for the responses of Richard Barnet, Fred Block, Victoria de Grazia, and Michael Schaffer, who share responsibility for the differences between the paper they heard and this one. I have also benefited from the comments of Ann Banfield, Kathleen Moran, H. Bradford Westerfield, and members of the *Representations* editorial board.

1 Tom Engelhardt, "Ambush at Kamikaze Pass," *Bulletin of Concerned Asian Scholars* 3 (Winter-Spring 1971): 64–84.
2 Fred Block, "Empire and Domestic Reform" (Paper delivered at the conference on "The Peculiarities of the American Empire," Rutgers University, 29 April 1988); Richard Barnet, comments at the same conference; James Fallows, *National Defense* (New York, 1981), 162–63.

3 Of the enormous literature on these subjects, I have found particularly helpful Jonathan Schell, *The Time of Illusion* (New York, 1975); and Fallows, *National Defense*.

4 Cf. Garry Wills, *The Kennedy Imprisonment* (Boston, 1982); Bruce Miroff, *Pragmatic Illusions: The Presidential Politics of John F. Kennedy* (New York, 1976), 35–166; Schell, *Time of Illusion*, 90–95.

5 See Robert Scheer, *With Enough Shovels: Reagan, Bush, and Nuclear War* (New York, 1982); and Michael Rogin, '*Ronald Reagan*', *the Movie, and other Episodes in Political Demonology* (Berkeley, 1987), 27–37.

6 Ben Bradlee, *Guts and Glory: The Rise and Fall of Oliver North* (New York, 1988), 153–55.

7 Richard J. Barnet, "Reflections (National Security)," *New Yorker*, 21 March 1988, 104–14; "Talk of the Town," *New Yorker*, 4 April 1988, 23.

8 Richard J. Barnet, *The Roots of War* (New York, 1972).

9 James Lardner, "Films," *Nation*, 28 January 1988, 94–98.

10 *New York Times*, 30 November 1986, 12-Y.

11 Robin Wood, *Hollywood from Vietnam to Reagan* (New York, 1986), 162; Edward Villaluz Guerrero, *The Ideology and Politics of Black Representation in U.S. Narrative Cinema* (Ph.D. diss., University of California, Berkeley, 1989), 68–79; Ella Taylor, *Prime-Time Families* (Berkeley, 1989).

12 Wood, *Hollywood*, 163–66.

13 Fredric Jameson, "The Shining," *Social Text* 4 (Fall 1981): 114.

14 Maureen Dowd, "Bush Boasts of Turnaround from 'Easy Rider' Society," *New York Times*, 7 October 1988, A-11; Elizabeth Drew, "Letter from Washington," *New Yorker*, 31 October 1988, 94; Wood, *Hollywood*, 228.

15 Cf. Michael Rogin, "'The Sword Became a Flashing Vision': D.W. Griffith's *Birth of a Nation*," in "*Reagan*," *the Movie*, 190–235. Having written on the political significance of *Birth*, I was suffering from amnesia, and the connection between *Birth* and Willie Horton was pointed out to me by Martin Sanchez-Jankowski.

16 *New York Times*, 28 November 1988, B-4; *New Yorker*, 21 November 1988, 41; *International Herald Tribune*, 21 January 1989, 4.

Passions of the Real, Passions of Semblance

SLAVOJ ZIZEK

When Brecht, on the way from his home to his theatre in July 1953, passed the column of Soviet tanks rolling towards the *Stalinallee* to crush the workers' rebellion, he waved at them and wrote in his diary later that day that, at that moment, he (never a party member) was tempted for the first time in his life to join the Communist Party. It was not that Brecht tolerated the cruelty of the struggle in the hope that it would bring a prosperous future: the harshness of the violence as such was perceived and endorsed as a sign of authenticity. . . . Is this not an exemplary case of what Alain Badiou has identified as the key feature of the twentieth century: the 'passion for the Real (*la passion du réel*)'?[1] In contrast to the nineteenth century of utopian or 'scientific' projects and ideals, plans for the future, the twentieth century aimed at delivering the thing itself – at directly realizing the longed-for New Order. The ultimate and defining moment of the twentieth century was the direct experience of the Real as opposed to everyday social reality – the Real in its extreme violence as the price to be paid for peeling off the deceptive layers of reality. . . .

And is not so-called fundamentalist terror also an expression of the passion for the Real? Back in the early 1970s, after the collapse of the New Left student protest movement in Germany, one of its outgrowths was the Red Army Faction terrorism (the Baader–Meinhof 'gang', and so on); its underlying premise was that the failure of the student movement had demonstrated that the masses were so deeply immersed in their apolitical consumerist stance that it was not possible to awaken them through standard political education and consciousness-raising – a more violent intervention was needed to shake them out of their ideological numbness, their hypnotic consumerist state, and only direct violent interventions like bombing supermarkets would do the job. And does the same not hold, on a different level, for today's fundamentalist terror? Is not its goal also to awaken us, Western citizens, from our numbness, from immersion in our everyday ideological universe?

These last two examples indicate the fundamental paradox of the 'passion for the Real': it culminates in its apparent opposite, in a *theatrical spectacle* – from the Stalinist show trials to spectacular terrorist acts.[2] If, then, the passion for the Real ends up in the pure semblance of the spectacular *effect of the Real*, then, in an exact inversion, the 'postmodern' passion for the semblance ends up in a violent return to the passion for the Real. Take the phenomenon of 'cutters' (people, mostly women, who experience an irresistible urge to cut themselves with razors or otherwise hurt themselves); this is strictly parallel to the virtualization of our environment: it represents a desperate strategy to return to the Real of the body. As such, cutting must be contrasted with normal tattooed inscriptions on the body, which guarantee the subject's inclusion in the (virtual) symbolic order – the problem with cutters, is the opposite one, namely, the assertion of reality itself. Far from being suicidal, far from indicating a desire for self-annihilation, cutting is a radical attempt to (re)gain a hold on reality, or (another aspect of the same phenomenon) to ground the ego firmly in bodily reality, against the unbearable anxiety of perceiving oneself as nonexistent. Cutters usually say that once they see the warm red blood flowing out of the self-inflicted wound, they feel alive again, firmly rooted in reality.[3] So although, of course, cutting is a pathological phenomenon, it is none the less a pathological attempt at regaining some kind of normality, at avoiding a total psychotic breakdown.

On today's market, we find a whole series of products deprived of their malignant properties: coffee without caffeine, cream without fat, beer without alcohol. . . . And the list goes on: what about virtual sex as sex without sex, the Colin Powell doctrine of warfare with no casualties (on our side, of course) as warfare without warfare, the contemporary re-definition of politics as the art of expert administration, that is, as politics without politics, up to today's tolerant liberal multiculturalism as an experience of the Other deprived of its Otherness (the idealized Other who dances fascinating dances and has an ecologically sound holistic approach to reality, while practices like wife beating remain out of sight . . .)? Virtual Reality simply generalizes this procedure of offering a product deprived of its substance: it provides reality itself deprived of its substance, of the hard resistant kernel of the Real – just as decaffeinated coffee smells and tastes like real coffee without being real coffee, Virtual Reality is experienced as reality without being so. What happens at the end of this process of virtualization, however, is that we begin to experience 'real reality' itself as a virtual entity. For the great majority of the public, the World Trade Center explosions were events on the TV screen, and when we watched the oft-repeated shot of frightened people running towards the camera ahead of the giant cloud of dust from the collapsing tower, was not the framing of the shot itself reminiscent of spectacular shots in catastrophic movies, a special effect which outdid all others, since – as Jeremy Bentham knew – reality is the best appearance of itself?

And was not the attack on the World Trade Center with regard to Hollywood catastrophe movies like snuff pornography versus ordinary sado-masochistic porno movies? This is the element of truth in Karl-Heinz Stockhausen's provocative statement that the planes hitting the WTC towers was the ultimate work of art: we can perceive the collapse of the WTC towers as the climactic conclusion of twentieth-century art's 'passion for the Real' – the 'terrorists' themselves did not do it primarily to provoke real material damage, but *for the spectacular effect of it*. When, days after September 11, 2001, our gaze was transfixed by the images of the plane hitting one of the WTC towers, we were all forced to experience what the 'compulsion to repeat' and *jouissance* beyond the pleasure principle are: we wanted to see it again and again; the same shots were repeated *ad nauseam*, and the uncanny satisfaction we got from it was *jouissance* at its purest. It was when we watched the two WTC towers collapsing on the TV screen, that it became possible to experience the falsity of 'reality TV shows': even if these shows are 'for real', people still act in them – they simply play themselves. The standard disclaimer in a novel ('Characters in this text are fictional, any resemblance to real-life characters is purely accidental') also holds for participants in reality soaps: what we see there are fictional characters, even if they play themselves for real.

The authentic twentieth-century passion for penetrating the Real Thing (ultimately, the destructive Void) through the cobweb of semblances which constitutes our reality thus culminates in the thrill of the Real as the ultimate 'effect', sought after from digitalized special effects, through reality TV and amateur pornography, up to snuff movies. Snuff movies which deliver the 'real thing' are perhaps the ultimate truth of Virtual Reality. There is an intimate connection between the virtualization of reality and the emergence of an infinite and infinitized bodily pain, much stronger than the usual one: do not biogenetics and Virtual Reality combined open up new 'enhanced' possibilities of *torture*, new and unheard-of horizons of extending our ability to endure pain (through widening our sensory capacity to sustain pain, through inventing new forms of inflicting it)? Perhaps the ultimate Sadeian image of an 'undead' victim of torture who can bear endless pain without having the escape into death at his or her disposal is also waiting to become reality.

The ultimate American paranoiac fantasy is that of an individual living in a small idyllic Californian city, a consumerist paradise, who suddenly starts to suspect that the world he is living in is a fake, a spectacle staged to convince him that he is living in a real world, while all the people around him are in fact actors and extras in a gigantic show. The most recent example of this is Peter Weir's *The Truman Show* (1998), with Jim Carrey playing the small-town clerk who gradually discovers the truth that he is the hero of a permanent twenty-four-hour TV show: his home town is in fact a gigantic studio set, with cameras following him everywhere. Among its predecessors, it is worth mentioning Phillip K. Dick's *Time out of Joint* (1959), in which the hero, living a modest daily life in a small idyllic Californian city in the late 1950s, gradually discovers that the whole town is a fake staged to keep him satisfied. . . . The underlying experience of *Time out of Joint* and of *The Truman Show* is that the late-capitalist consumerist Californian paradise is, in its very hyperreality, in a way *unreal*, substanceless, deprived of material inertia. And the same 'derealization' of the horror went on after the WTC collapse: while the number of victims – 3,000 – is repeated all the time, it is surprising how little of the actual carnage we see – no dismembered bodies, no blood, no desperate faces of dying people . . . in clear contrast to reporting on Third World catas-trophes, where the whole point is to produce a scoop of some gruesome detail: Somalis dying of hunger, raped Bosnian women, men with their throats cut. These shots are always accompanied by an advance warning that 'some of the images you will see are extremely graphic and may upset children' – a warning which we never heard in the reports on the WTC collapse. Is this not yet further proof of how, even in this tragic moment, the distance which separates Us from Them, from their reality, is maintained: the real horror happens *there*, not *here*?[4]

So it is not only that Hollywood stages a semblance of real life deprived of the weight and inertia of materiality – in late-capitalist consumerist society, 'real social life' itself some-how acquires the features of a staged fake, with our neighbours behaving in 'real' life like stage actors and extras. . . . Again, the ultimate truth of the capitalist utilitarian despiritual-ized universe is the dematerialization of 'real life' itself, its reversal into a spectral show. Among others, Christopher Isherwood gave expression to this unreality of American daily life, exemplified in the motel room: 'American motels are unreal! . . . They are deliberately designed to be unreal. . . . The Europeans hate us because we've retired to live inside our advertisements, like hermits going into caves to contemplate.' Peter Sloterdijk's notion of the 'sphere' is literally realized here, as the gigantic metal sphere that envelops and isolates the whole city. Years ago, a series of science-fiction films like *Zardoz* or *Logan's Run* forecast today's postmodern predicament by extending this fantasy to the community itself: the isolated group living an aseptic life in a secluded area longs for the experience of the real world of material decay. Is not the endlessly repeated shot of the plane approaching and hitting the second WTC tower the real-life version of the famous scene from Hitchcock's *Birds*, superbly analysed by Raymond Bellour, in which Melanie approaches the Bodega Bay pier after crossing the bay in a little boat? When, as she approaches the wharf, she waves to her (future) lover, a single bird (first perceived as an indistinguishable dark blot) unexpectedly enters the frame from above right, and hits her on the head.[5] Was not the plane which hit the WTC tower literally the ultimate Hitchcockian blot, the anamorphic stain which denaturalized the idyllic well-known New York landscape?

The Wachowski brothers' hit *Matrix* (1999) brought this logic to its climax: the material reality we all experience and see around us is a virtual one, generated and co-ordinated by a gigantic mega-computer to which we are all attached; when the hero (played by Keanu Reeves) awakens into 'real reality', he sees a desolate landscape littered with burnt-out ruins – what remains of Chicago after a global war. The resistance leader, Morpheus, utters the ironic greeting: 'Welcome to the desert of the real.' Was it not something of a similar order that took place in New York on September 11? Its citizens were introduced to the 'desert of the real' – for us, corrupted by Hollywood, the landscape and the shots of the collapsing towers could not but be reminiscent of the most breathtaking scenes in big catastrophe productions.

When we hear how the attacks were a totally unexpected shock, how the unimaginable Impossible happened, we should recall the other defining catastrophe from the beginning of the twentieth century, the sinking of the *Titanic*: this, also, was a shock, but the space for it had already been prepared in ideological fantasizing, since the *Titanic* was the symbol of the might of nineteenth-century industrial civilization. Does not the same hold also for these attacks? Not only were the media bombarding us all the time with talk about the terrorist threat; this threat was also obviously libidinally invested – just remember the series of movies from *Escape from New York* to *Independence Day*. That is the rationale of the often-mentioned association of the attacks with Hollywood disaster movies: the unthinkable which happened was the object of fantasy, so that, in a way, America got what it fantasized about, and that was the biggest surprise. The ultimate twist in this link between Hollywood and the 'war against terrorism' occurred when the Pentagon decided to solicit the help of Hollywood: at the beginning of October 2001, the press reported that a group of Hollywood scenarists and directors, specialists in catastrophe movies, had been established at the instigation of the Pentagon, with the aim of imagining possible scenarios for terrorist attacks and how to fight them. And this interaction seemed to be ongoing: at the beginning of November 2001, there was a series of meetings between White House advisers and senior Hollywood executives with the aim of co-ordinating the war effort and establishing how Hollywood could help in the 'war against terrorism' by getting the right ideological message across not only to Americans, but also to the Hollywood public around the globe – the ultimate empirical proof that Hollywood does in fact function as an 'ideological state apparatus'.

We should therefore invert the standard reading according to which the WTC explosions were the intrusion of the Real which shattered our illusory Sphere: quite the reverse – it was before the WTC collapse that we lived in our reality, perceiving Third World horrors as something which was not actually part of our social reality, as something which existed (for us) as a spectral apparition on the (TV) screen – and what happened on September 11 was that this fantasmatic screen apparition entered our reality. It is not that reality entered our image: the image entered and shattered our reality (i.e. the symbolic co-ordinates which determine what we experience as reality). The fact that, after September 11, the openings of many 'block-buster' movies with scenes which bear a resemblance to the WTC collapse (tall buildings on fire or under attack, terrorist acts . . .) were postponed (or the films were even shelved) should thus be read as the 'repression' of the fantasmatic background responsible for the impact of the WTC collapse. Of course, the point is not to play a pseudo-postmodern game of reducing the WTC collapse to just another media spectacle, reading it as a catastrophe version of the snuff porno movies; the question we should have asked ourselves as we stared at the TV screens on September 11 is simply: *Where have we already seen the same thing over and over again?*

The fact that the September 11 attacks were the stuff of popular fantasies long before they actually took place provides yet another case of the twisted logic of dreams: it is easy to account for the fact that poor people around the world dream about becoming Americans – so what do the well-to-do Americans, immobilized in their well-being, dream about? About a global catastrophe that would shatter their lives – why? This is what psychoanalysis is about: to explain why, in the midst of well-being, we are haunted by nightmarish visions of catastrophes. This paradox also indicates how we should grasp Lacan's notion of 'traversing the fantasy' as the concluding moment of the psychoanalytic treatment. This notion may seem to fit perfectly the common sense idea of what psychoanalysis should do: of course it should liberate us from the hold of idiosyncratic fantasies, and enable us to confront reality as it really is! However, this, precisely, is what Lacan does *not* have in mind – what he aims at is almost the exact opposite. In our daily existence, we are immersed in 'reality' (structured and supported by the fantasy), and this immersion is disturbed by symptoms which bear witness to the fact that another, repressed, level of our psyche resists this immersion. To 'traverse the fantasy' therefore, paradoxically, means *fully identifying oneself with the fantasy* – namely, with the fantasy which structures the excess that resists our immersion in daily reality. . . .

This means that the dialectic of semblance and Real cannot be reduced to the rather elementary fact that the virtualization of our daily lives, the experience that we are living more and more in an artificially constructed universe, gives rise to an irresistible urge to 'return to the Real', to regain firm ground in some 'real reality'. The Real which returns has the status of a(nother) semblance: *precisely because it is real, that is, on account of its traumatic/ excessive character, we are unable to integrate it into (what we experience as) our reality, and are therefore compelled to experience it as a nightmarish apparition.* This is what the compelling image of the collapse of the WTC was: an image, a semblance, an 'effect', which, at the same time, delivered 'the thing itself'. This 'effect of the Real' is not the same as what Roland Barthes, way back in the 1960s, called *l'effet du réel*: it is, rather, its exact opposite: *l'effet de l'irréel*. That is to say: in contrast to the Barthesian *effet du réel*, in which the text makes us accept its fictional product as 'real', here, the Real itself, in order to be sustained, has to be perceived as a nightmarish unreal spectre. Usually we say that we should not mistake fiction for reality – remember the postmodern doxa according to which 'reality' is a discursive product, a symbolic fiction which we misperceive as a substantial autonomous entity. The lesson of psychoanalysis here is the opposite one: *we should not mistake reality for fiction* – we should be able to discern, in what we experience as fiction, the hard kernel of the Real which we are able to sustain only if we fictionalize it. In short, we should discern which part of reality is 'transfunctionalized' through fantasy, so that, although it is part of reality, it is perceived in a fictional mode. Much more difficult than to denounce/unmask (what appears as) reality as fiction is to recognize the part of fiction in 'real' reality. (This, of course, brings us back to the old Lacanian notion that, while animals can deceive by presenting what is false as true, only humans (entities inhabiting the symbolic space) can deceive by presenting what is true as false.) And this insight also allows us to return to the example of cutters: if the true opposite of the Real is reality, what if, then, what they are actually escaping from when they cut themselves is not simply the feeling of unreality, of the artificial virtuality of our lifeworld, but the Real itself which explodes in the guise of uncontrolled hallucinations which start to haunt us once we lose our anchoring in reality?

Notes

1   See Alain Badiou, Le siècle, forthcoming from Éditions du Seuil, Paris.
2   On a more general level, we should note how Stalinism – with its brutal 'passion for the Real', its readiness to sacrifice millions of lives for its goal, to treat people as dispensable – was at the same time the regime most sensitive about *maintaining proper appearances*: it reacted with total panic whenever there was a threat that these appearances would be disturbed (say, that some accident which clearly revealed the failure of the regime would be reported in the media: in the Soviet media there were no black chronicles, no reports on crime and prostitution, let alone workers' or public protests).
3   See Marilee Strong, *The Bright Red Scream*, London: Virago 2000.
4   Another case of ideological censorship: when firefighters' widows were interviewed on CNN, most of them gave the expected performance: tears, prayers . . . all except one who, without a tear, said that she does not pray for her dead husband, because she knows that prayer will not bring him back. Asked if she dreams of revenge, she calmly said that that would be a true betrayal of her husband: had he survived, he would have insisted that the worst thing to do is to succumb to the urge to retaliate . . . there is no need to add that this clip was shown only once, then disappeared from the repetitions of the same interviews.
5   See Chapter 3 of Raymond Bellour, *The Analysis of Film*, Bloomington: Indiana University Press 2000.

PART TWO

EARLY FORMATIONS OF WAR CINEMA IN THE UNITED STATES

This section includes essays that aim to pinpoint the distinctive elements and characteristics of Hollywood war cinema—as film genre, industrial product, cultural commodity, register of politics, morality play, expression of national myth, and symbolic carrier of memory and history. The appearance of these elements occurred during the concurrently formative years of cinema and of modern warfare at the end of the nineteenth century and opening decades of the twentieth. Contributors here address the interrelations between textual and narrative patterns on-screen and the industrial and social contexts beyond that were contested and, in some cases, consolidated during these years. To do so, the pieces illustrate different approaches to the study of Hollywood and war, ranging from more traditional archival research to broadly-conceived cultural and media analysis. As a result, attention to the broader historical backdrop casts light on the contemporary formation of discourses of nation, civilization, and freedom that informed filmmaking and war-making alike.

Cinema emerged in a late nineteenth-century moment of growing U.S. military power, international ambition, and imperial politics. Early cinema, especially war cinema with its images and then narratives of battle and military activity, coincided with and contributed to a complex cultural negotiation over the meaning and extent of America's militarization and international politics. Such on-screen negotiation, of course, could not but effect the development of cinema itself as cultural production and social institution. Whatever the racial, gender, or imperial politics of the moment, it is necessary to note the concurrent ordering of American society and industry that had begun in the decades following the Civil War (Wiebe 1966; Trachtenberg 1982). Much of the early history of cinema turns on the evolution of corporate control over specific patents for filmmaking technologies, the merging and expansion of various production companies, and, finally, the integration of production, distribution, and exhibition by the end of World War I. These changes were emblematic for a nation with both growing global political and economic ambitions and an increasingly modern, urban, and consumer domestic society.

World War I was a turning point for U.S. cinema. The reduction (or cessation) of production by other national cinemas during the war enabled what became Hollywood to achieve a pre-eminent status in world markets. This was accompanied by the consolidation and predominance of a coherent set of narrative filmmaking practices. For our discussion, the films about World War I appear at the intersection of larger political, industrial, and formal or stylistic changes.

While hardly an exclusive type of production at the time, the resulting films about war can therefore be seen to epitomize the range of possibilities for then contemporary cinema. Despite reflecting disparate attitudes toward the war, these variations operated within what had quickly developed into a circumscribed range of political and narrative possibilities for the cinematic engagement of war.

A final concern in this section is the linkages formed between early filmmakers and the military services. Amidst the political, technological, and ideological overlaps that shaped early war cinema, World War I, especially, also witnessed the forging of an institutional partnership between Hollywood and the U.S. government that was seen by both as mutually valuable. This was the foundation of a much longer and more complicated relationship between filmmakers and the military that moved beyond the provision of men and materiel as the basis of images on screen. The relationship would grow to include the more overt development of technologies for ways of seeing and understanding actual and cinematic wars alike.

Pivotal in this relationship was the emergent citizen-spectator. Film studios and armed services could strike mutually advantageous agreements, in other words, but to be meaningful their interactions required the participation of individuals and groups whose political and viewing positions were being reoriented accordingly. While theorists have varied widely in their attribution of significance, activity (or passivity), and volition to individuals, the citizen-spectator as figure both marking and enabling the convergence of processes of militarization and mediatization appears even in the earliest formations of war cinema.

James Castonguay's first essay situates early films and related accounts of the Spanish-American War in the contemporary historical landscape of expanding media and consumer culture. Leslie DeBauche's contribution to this section discusses the complex relationship that developed between the U.S. government and the burgeoning film industry during World War I. She explains here how the "form" and "function" of movies about the war changed in the 1910s and 1920s, shifting from an emphasis on "preparedness" before U.S. entry into the conflict in April 1917 to patriotic narratives after that demonized the "bestial Hun," dramatized the threat to women and American soldiers and then, in the years after the 1918 Armistice, to depictions of the harsher realities of combat faced by soldiers and the conclusion that war itself was the enemy (DeBauche 1997: 196). In the third selection, historian Michael Isenberg offers a series of insightful summary observations about how filmmakers imagined the enemy, the homefront, and women and even used humor in order to represent the Great War. The fourth essay samples Pierre Sorlin's exploration of specific, enduring images of battle that cinema helped to establish.

The Spanish-American War in United States Media culture[1]

8

JAMES CASTONGUAY

The world is nearly all parceled out, and what there is left of it is being divided up, conquered, and colonized. To think of these stars that you see overhead at night, these vast worlds which we can never reach. I would annex the planets if I could.
— Cecil Rhodes, "Last Will and Testament"

It has been a splendid little war; begun with the highest motives, carried on with magnificent intelligence and spirit, favored by that fortune which loved the brave.
— John Hay, American ambassador to Great Britain, to Colonel Theodore Roosevelt in the wake of the Spanish-American War

What a marvel, indeed, would be a moving photograph of a duel between two warships, American and Spanish, terminating, of course, in the destruction of the enemy's vessel, exhibited on a stereopticon screen before wildly enthusiastic audiences from Boston to San Francisco.
— "Photos of the Conflict," June 6, 1898, *Indianapolis News*

Introduction

The commercial cinema was barely two years old when the United States declared war against Spain in April of 1898. Judging from the work of leading film historians, it would be difficult to overestimate the importance of the Spanish-American War to a fledgling U.S. film industry in the wake of cinema's putative novelty year. According to Charles Musser, "with the onset of the Spanish-American War the motion picture industry discovered a new role and exploited it, gaining in confidence as a result. . . . It was the ongoing production of a few firms [e.g., Biograph and Edison] that provided the commercial foundation for the American industry, and it was the war that gave this sector new life" (*Emergence of Cinema* 225). Robert C. Allen argues that film became the "star attraction in vaudeville [during the Spanish-American War] as the American motion picture took on a new role: that of visual newspaper" (*Vaudeville and Film* 139), and Douglas Gomery concludes that "no genre of pro-gramming could be developed to match the consistent drawing power of the images of the

Spanish-American War" (*Shared Pleasures* 16).[2] While this film scholarship is invaluable for increasing our understanding of the economic, technological, and aesthetic aspects of early American film production and exhibition, descriptions of Spanish-American War films—and their place in early cinema history—unwittingly present a nostalgic picture of a Spanish-American "|W|ar film craze" (Allen) that existed during cinema's early "heyday" (Gomery 1992) when exhibitors exploited a "patriotic wave that tossed Biograph to new heights" (Musser, *Emergence* 241), even transcending class conflict and ideological differences plaguing the industry and exhibitors (Musser and Nelson).

Given the central importance of the Spanish-American War to the early film industry, then, it is surprising that the field of early cinema studies has underemphasized the ideological implications of the cinema's role in the war's cultural production.[3] Indeed, as Ella Shohat and Robert Stam note, "Of all the celebrated 'coincidences'—of the twin beginnings of cinema and psychoanalysis, cinema and nationalism, cinema and consumerism—it is |cinema's| coincidence with the heights of imperialism that |remains| least explored . . ." (100).[4] Through an investigation of film's role in the larger mediation of the first U.S. war exhibited on film to the U.S. public, I begin to fill in this gap in film studies scholarship, while also increasing our understanding of pre-nickelodeon cinema and the emergence of *fin-de-siècle* mass culture in the United States.

Intermediality, early cinema, and the Spanish-American War

As Leo Charney and Vanessa Schwartz point out, during the pre-nickelodeon period, "cinema constituted only one element in an array of new modes of technology, representation, spectacle, distraction, consumerism, ephemerality, mobility, and entertainment—and at many points was neither the most compelling nor the most promising one" (1). In the late 1890s, vaudeville, newspapers, and film were inextricably bound together as vaudeville and the theatrical medium's method of variety programming provided early film producers with an existing format through which they could exhibit their films (Allen *Vaudeville and Film*), and newspapers provided a narrative context for the earliest films, which were often less than one minute in length.

In the case of the Spanish-American War, several communication technologies in addition to film were used by the military, the news media, the entertainment industry, and citizens to mediate the war with Spain, including newspapers, telephones, telegraphs, stereographs, magic lantern shows, and phonographic cylinder recordings.[5] For example, the *Milwaukee Journal* published an illustrated column about the use of battlefield telephones in Cuba, while an advertisement for a "commission stockbroker" in Worcester, Massachusetts sold "news and gossip on the situation" he received "over |his| private wires." The *Worcester Telegram* announced that "while . . . one story was being hustled into shipshape, a special diamond-tipped wire was clicking off the latest news from Havana and the editorial department was pressed into service taking |reports| from the telephone" (February 19, 1898). Indicative of many newspapers' self-fashioned participatory role during the war, the *Telegram* also boasted that its reporters were assisting divers in the battleship *Maine* investigation, which, in turn, made celebrities out of many Spanish-American War journalists covering the "correspondents war," such as Stephen Crane, Frances Scovel, Richard Harding Davis, Frederic Remington, and even a young Winston Churchill.[6]

By emphasizing its new role as a visual newspaper, the film industry became an active participant in the war effort through its complicity with leading American publishers, most notably through the partnership between leading film producer Thomas Edison and *New York Journal* publisher William Randolph Hearst. *The New York Clipper* included several advertisements touting the "unprecedented sensation of EDISON-JOURNAL CUBAN WAR FILMS" throughout the summer of 1898, and advertisements for Biograph in the *New York Clipper* also announced "authentic war views" from their "camera now following North Atlantic Squadron on the *New York Journal's* Anita." *War Correspondents*, a staged actuality showing several reporters dashing into the telegraph office to report war news, and *New York Journal Despatch Yacht "Buccaneer"* further demonstrate the synergy between a fledgling film business and the established newspaper industry.

To a large degree, Spanish-American War films can be located squarely within the dominant genres, style, and mode of reception of 1890s cinema. As Musser summarizes, "the film's subject or narrative was often already known by the spectators, . . . the spectator might rely on the exhibitor to clarify the film's narrative or meaning through a live narration and other sounds (music, effects, even dialogue added by actors from behind the screen), [and] spectators might easily find themselves in a position where they had to understand the film story without recourse to either special knowledge or the exhibitors' aid" (*Emergence of Cinema* 3). Although films comprised just one part of the intermediality of the 1890s, the Spanish-American War was inordinately well-suited to capitalize on early cinema's mode of reception given the ubiquitous presence of the images, stories, parades, speeches, songs, plays, and other intertextual raw materials concerned with the war circulating throughout U.S. popular culture.

At the same time, while Spanish-American War films fit nicely into our understanding of the existing modes of film production, exhibition, and reception at the turn-of-the century, I would like to emphasize the overall *militarization* of existing genres and conventions during the war. For example, the characteristic assault on the audience exemplified by trains rushing toward the camera is replaced with soldiers on horseback charging at the spectator (as in Biograph's *Roosevelt's Rough Riders*) or newspaper journalists running toward and past the camera in *War Correspondents*. Similarly, fiction or acted films like *A Romp in Camp*, in which a woman reveals her stockinged legs to soldiers, are also part of Spanish-American War imagery, representing a militarized example of early cinema's "scenario of exposure" exemplified by the staged actuality *What Happened on Twenty-third Street, New York City* (see Balides 1993). Like other scenes of everyday activities of military camp life, the actuality film *Soldiers at Play* (also staged for the camera) represents the further occupation of these genres by a masculinized and militarized mise-en-scène. Even George Méliès, the pioneer of the non-actuality genre of "trick films," produced at least one film inspired by the topicality of the Spanish-American War when he made an underwater reenactment of the Maine explosion shot with a model ship in an aquarium (see Gheorghuiu-Cernat 58).[7] Furthermore, during the Spanish-American War the various cinematic apparatuses battling for economic dominance in the 1890s were literally transformed into signifying war machines, standardized around the themes of imperialism and war. "The movies became so identified with war news," notes Allen, "that Edison renamed his Projecting Kinetoscope the 'Wargraph' for the duration of the hostilities" ("Movies in Vaudeville" 74). Other exhibitors provided similar, generic names for their projecting war machines (e.g., Warscope) through the turn of the century. The transformation of Howe's prewar Animotiscope and the ubiquitous image of a train in his promotional materials in 1897, to the War-graph and the new cinematic icon of the battleship a year later, also demonstrates the hypermilitarization of United States media culture during the Spanish-American War (see Musser and Nelson 84–91).

Receptions of war: the Spanish-American War film spectator

Charles Musser concludes his brilliant account of the production and exhibition of Spanish-American War films with the following provocative passage:

> [During the Spanish-American War] cinema had found a role beyond narrow amusement, and this sudden prominence coincided with a new era of overseas expansion and military intervention. Who can say what fantasies of power audiences experienced in those darkened halls, and how these emotions continued to resonate outside the theater?
>
> (*Emergence of Cinema* 261)

Spanish-American War films themselves can begin to answer Musser's vexing questions, since they reveal fantasies of power in relation to ideologies of race, gender, and empire. To offer just one example, the mise-en-scene of Edward Amet's 1898 allegorical tableau film *Freedom of Cuba* literally infantilizes Cuba and its people by showing a baby dropping a Cuban flag while reaching out to accept the hands of its beneficent protectors Uncle Sam (holding a rifle with bayonet) and Lady Liberty. The allegory thus presents the figure of the woman in a passive role as a surrogate supporter urging Uncle Sam to act or intervene on the "Cuban issue." The thematic of infantilization became a central trope in imperialist rhetoric during the war, reminiscent of Rudyard Kipling's "White man's burden" to protect and educate his "unciviliastic" little (brown) brothers.[8]

During the Spanish-American War, descriptions of war fever in many newspapers across the country reflected (and constructed) the ideologically charged *ethos* of wartime culture that in turn facilitated the "receptivity" of many early audiences. One could argue following Tom Gunning's description of an early "cinema of attractions" that Spanish-American War films became an especially powerful "attraction,"[9] intensified by the broader cultural narratives and the larger discursive continuum of the Spanish-American War. Illustrating this, one journalist speculated on audience reactions to hypothetical war films: "How the enthusiastic American audiences . . . would yell if they could see with their own eyes that monument to medievalism, Morro Castle, actually falling into a heap of its own debris before the fire-vomiting guns of Admiral Sampson's fleet. Then, like the Corbett-Fitzsimmons fight in its vitascope reproduction, they would behold the glorious performance again and again until satisfied that the Maine had been remembered sufficiently" (*Indianapolis News*, June 6, 1898).

This passage captures the anticipation of war and its images fanned by a belligerent yellow press in the wake of the explosion of the battleship *Maine* in Havana Harbor after years of sensationalist coverage of events in Cuba. More important for my purposes, this giddy anticipation of the new medium's novel ability to project motion pictures of real battles for the viewing pleasure of American consumers across the country also explicitly elides potential war actualities with sports contests and entertainment like *The Corbett-Fitzsimmons Fight*. This presentation of the impending war as potential entertainment and amusement reflects the overwhelming popularity of the war in many parts of the U.S., which was later fueled by Admiral Dewey's decisive naval victories and sensationalist media representations of events of the war.

Eagerly anticipated images of the realities of battle would never materialize during the Spanish-American War due to the technological and practical realities of 1890s warfare and conditions of film production. "Though one sees in the press of this period flamboyant notices for war films promising action galore," writes Stephen Bottomore, "in practice because of the new weaponry, most early cameramen couldn't get near enough to film any fighting, and so |were| satisfied with recording 'the human side of war,' showing troop movements, hospital scenes, and so on" (30). Film companies also compensated for the lack of "real" battle footage from Cuba by faking and staging war films using various methods. Edison immediately began filming actualities of Roosevelt's Rough Riders disembarking or charging on horseback toward the camera, and would later stage Rough Rider skirmishes and other battles in West Orange, New Jersey. J. Stuart Blackton made tabletop re-enactments with scale model ships in bathtubs (e.g. *The Battle of Manila Bay*), while other film companies and filmmakers (e.g., Lubin, Biograph, and Amet) staged their own battle scenes, re-enactments, and scenes of military life. Actualities of the U.S. battleship *Maine* and the Spanish ship *Vizcaya*—e.g., *Burial of the "Maine" Victims, Wreck of the Battleship "Maine," "Vizcaya" Under Full Headway, Wreck of the "Vizcaya"*—had especially strong consumer appeal and consequently the battle among film companies for exhibitors to purchase these films was keen. Film companies and exhibitors often promoted faked films as the real thing, and, not surprisingly, Edison's "War Extra Catalog" also tried to make even the most banal actualities of everyday camp life seem novel in order to sell its less exciting films to exhibitors.

While Stephen Bottomore contends that the lack of actual battle footage resulted in "some disappointment in the war films when they were screened back home" (30), he also insists that "whether they were the genuine article or fakes, war films drew huge audiences and were enormously emotive. The impact of such films was often increased by the use of music, patriotic commentary, sound effects of explosions and the like" (32). The power of Spanish-American War films could also have been increased by the exhibitor's arrangement of the films on the vaudeville bill, since a Spanish-American War film might be one act in a program that might include magic lantern slides of Cuba, a skit with a soldier going off to war, patriotic songs, and so forth. Finally, the arrangement of the films themselves also gave the exhibitor some control over the viewing experience or narrative trajectory of the film acts. For instance, an exhibitor might show "before and after" pictures of the *Maine* and *Vizcaya* or juxtapose films of the two ships against each other before concluding with *Raising Old Glory over Moro Castle* (see Musser and Nelson).

Despite the absence of films of actual battles, accounts of audience reactions to Spanish-American War films suggest that the *Indianapolis News* reporter's vision of ecstatic fans cheering on "our side" in the Spanish-American "War Show" (as Edward Amet would name his film exhibitions) and communally remembering the *Maine*, became a reality in many vaudeville theaters across the United States. In *The Emergence of Cinema*, Musser cites accounts of New York City spectators "shrieking their approval" at images of U.S. troops, the flag, and the battleship *Maine*, offering standing ovations when images of the Spanish warship *Vizcaya* were accompanied by a "huge illuminated sign . . . bearing the inscription: 'No hidden mines here.'" (244). Elsewhere Musser argues that "under such circumstances, the lecturer's spiel was unnecessary and would have been lost in the roar of the crowd" ("American Vitagraph" 43). As Musser has also pointed out, however, during the Spanish-American War, "the situation varied from city to city. In Rochester, where the biograph opened in late March, a film of the *Vizcaya* had to be eliminated from the program" because, according to the *Rochester Post Express*, "At first the audience hissed . . . with every performance . . . |but| |f|inally the gallery gods showed their disapproval with potatoes and other garden truck . . .". This response stands in marked in contrast to Boston, where "war fever |was| less pronounced" than many other places, and consequently "the biograph was given little prominence" (*Emergence* 244).[10]

In Indianapolis, the Grand Opera House advertised that its exhibition of the Corbett-Fitzsimmons fight film would be "especially attractive to the ladies" (*Indianapolis News*, March 19, 1898), while the competing Park Theater promoted "biograph pictures of the battleship Maine |and| . . . the Spanish Warship Vizcaya," both of which had been featured many times in war news in other sections of the paper. The Park advertisement also announced that "Large souvenir pictures of the Maine |will be| presented to all ladies on the lower floor during |the| engagement" (*Indianapolis News*, March 18, 1898),[11] thus echoing the explicit appeal to the female spectator and wartime woman consumer found in the advertisement for the *Corbett-Fitzsimmons Fight*.

A March 18, 1898, *Indianapolis News* article on "High Class Vaudeville at the Park" contains a description of audience's reaction to the Spanish-American War films, reporting that "the *Maine* was cheered lustily while the Spanish *Vizcaya* was as roundly hissed," and that "last night every seat was taken and there was a great house at the matinee." The April 2, 1898 edition of the entertainment trade journal *The New York Clipper* would later confirm "big business" for the Park Theater, while the "veriscope pictures of the Corbett Fitzsimmons contest |at the Grand Opera House| . . . had very light business," suggesting that war films were victorious in this battle for the historical female spectator and consumer.

Dan Streible has already shown that "the *Corbett-Fitzsimmons Fight* remains . . . an atypical example of early cinema, . . . |since its| format, fame, controversy, longevity, and profitability stood out from the increasing traffic of motion pictures. . . ." For Streible, "Even though the female clientele that may have taken an unintended pleasure in seeing the Veriscope pictures did so only during a brief moment in the early history of cinema, the fact remains that it was a significant rupture in the expected course of events." (47). In the case of Spanish-American War films, one could argue, perhaps, that the ability of women to view scenes of military life and combat, like their ability to see the *Corbett-Fitzsimmons Fight*, was politically progressive because in social reality women were excluded from military institutions. We might cast these women filmgoers as "G.I. Jane" spectators living out fantasies of military empowerment, or describe them as "Rosie the Riveter" consumers filling in the empty seats left by the male population at war seeking other attractions.

Regardless of specific historical and theoretical interpretations, I would argue that women's participation in the particular experience of viewing Spanish-American war films, and the entrance of women into the masculine sphere of militaristic imperialism—albeit "once removed" (to borrow Miriam Hansen's phrase)—has different ideological implications from the context of reception for The *Corbett-Fitzsimmons Fight*. Indeed, the female audience's cheers and jeers described in the *Indianapolis News* differ in important ways from the voyeuristic pleasures experienced by women at the *Corbett-Fitzsimmons Fight* (analyzed by

Miriam Hansen and Streible), while the example of the concurrent exhibition of the *Corbett-Fitzsimmons Fight* and Spanish-American War films in Indianapolis demonstrates that regional accounts of the exhibition and reception of early cinema can help us to modify existing theoretical models of historical spectatorship. I am not suggesting, of course, that the inclusion of women in cinema's public sphere is pejorative, but arguing instead that ideological opposition or resistance does not inhere in this new collective experience. It thus becomes necessary to examine what Hansen describes as specific "empirical constellations" ("Early Cinema" 228) of reception and representation in order to construct a fuller historical (and political) picture of the earliest cinema.

While the above example focuses on the female spectator in Indianapolis, other categories of cultural difference, including class, ethnicity, nationality, religion, race, region, and age (among others) affected the reception and meanings of Spanish-American War films. For instance, several states in the Deep South did not have widespread support for the Spanish-American War due in large part to their regional memories of the recent Civil War (see Silber). In addition, many mainstream Southern newspapers were more concerned about a possible "race war at home" and "colonization of [the South] by Negroes" than the Cuban situation (*Atlanta Constitution*, October 2, 1898).

Many African Americans, including Ida B. Wells-Barnett, saw the war and imperialism as a chance for African American men and women to prove their patriotism and as a window of opportunity for upward social mobility. At the same time, given the realities of increased lynching and "Jim Crow" in the South in the 1890s, many African Americans were ambivalent about, or militantly resistant to, joining the American cause (see Gatewood; Brundage).[12] Dissenting articles and editorials about the war in African American newspapers suggest a potentially resistant and active Spanish-American War spectator that is quite different from the war audience presented in film studies literature (see Castonguay). Consequently, if we accept the methodological premise that newspapers provided essential intertexts for constructing receptive Spanish-American War film spectators, then the alternative views expressed by the African American press suggest a potentially oppositional spectator.[13]

Conclusion: the politics of reception

According to Robert Sklar in *Movie-Made America*, "the War with Spain in 1898 gave regular film producers their first prime opportunity for spectacle. Patriotic fervor ran so high that it was easy to sense audience receptivity to films about the war, even if some were . . . obviously fabricated . . ." (22). I have suggested some of the ways that print media created and reflected both receptive and *non-receptive* film spectators—depending on the local contexts and "empirical constellation" (Hansen, "Early Cinema" 228) of reception. By doing so, I have tried to present a more complex picture of the cultural production and reception of the Spanish-American War and its films than is usually presented in the film studies literature on this period.

Inspired by the groundbreaking work of Roy Rosenzweig, Kathy Peiss, Elizabeth Ewen and others, social and feminist film historians have discussed cinema's public sphere as "alternative" and at times "oppositional," thus assigning a kind of alterity to early cinema (in opposition to later Hollywood narrative cinema) with varying concomitant degrees of political progressiveness. The reasons for the lack of sustained analysis of the political implications of Spanish-American War films are perhaps best understood in light of the question of whether or not early cinema "constituted an autonomous working-class public sphere or was the site for the absorption of hegemonic domination . . ." (Sklar, "Oh! Althusser!" 20).

Arguments for early cinema's radical alterity or "otherness"—often presented in opposition to the classical Hollywood spectator—tend to focus too narrowly on the films themselves and ground their concerns within the context of the dominant theoretical paradigms developed by film studies in the 1970s and 1980s. Consequently, the ideological, cultural, and historical functions of Spanish-American War films—especially in relation to audiences—have gone largely unexamined. At the very least, in the case of the Spanish-American War film spectator, one could argue that war films, while certainly encompassing the tropes, themes, and generic conventions of otherness discussed in early cinema studies scholarship, are also part of a much older history of military, screen, and social practices which, taken together, amount in large part to more of the representational and institutional same.

It may be that the Spanish-American War films and their reception do not lend themselves to radical historiography precisely because many accounts of wartime culture suggest "hegemonic domination" among many social groups and in many regions of the United States. Indeed, accounts in Euro-American newspapers demonstrate that the possibility of subversion was quite limited in some regions and for many readers and spectators in the months leading up to and during the Spanish-American War in 1898. Having said that, as I have argued, there were also important differences in experiences of, and attitudes toward, the war and its representations, and the cinema did not have a uniformly hegemonic role in the larger ideological process of recruiting support for imperialism and the war effort.

Notes

1   I am grateful to Philip Rosen, Patrice Petro, and Roy Rosenzweig for their helpful comments on earlier versions of this essay. Thanks also to David Slocum for his patience and helpful editorial suggestions. This research was supported by a University Film and Video Association Carole Fielding Research Grant and a Sacred Heart University Research and Creativity Grant.

2   Lauren Rabinovitz also argues that the "glut on the |motion picture| market might have led to movies' dismissal as only a passing fancy or fad had it not been for the outbreak of the Spanish-American War in 1898" (107). She acknowledges the ideological function of cinema during the war, claiming that through a "combination of journalism and patriotism, |Spanish-American War films| extended an ideological force . . . |that| spectacularized war and the concept of U.S. imperialism as had never before been accomplished" (108).

3   The important work of Tom Gunning, Miriam Hansen, and Lynne Kirby mentions the Spanish-American War only to support their more general arguments concerning the attraction, cultural appeal, and ontological power of early cinema. Although none of the contributors to The Birth of Whiteness: Race and the Emergence of U.S. Cinema discuss the prenickelodeon period, the editor does point out that "cinema's invention and early development coincided . . . with the United States' imperialist practices in the Caribbean and Asia" (Bernardi, "Introduction" 7).

4 This relative lack of focus on the historical relationship between cinema and imperialism (and Spanish-American War films) is symptomatic of the broader neglect discussed by Amy Kaplan in her introduction to *Cultures of United States Imperialism*. Kaplan's *The Anarchy of Empire in the Making of U.S. Culture* incorporates an insightful discussion of Spanish-American War films into her broader discussion of the "domestic" (in both senses of the term) effects of U.S. imperialism.

5 To offer just one example of this intermediality, Sigmund Lubin's 1898 projector combined a cineograph and stereopticon, thus embodying both the emerging tech-nology of the film projector while also retaining the residual technology from the established screen practice of the magic lantern slide show (see *The New York Clipper*, March 19, 1898).

6 As Richard Harding Davis would later write in *Harper's Weekly* about Stephan Crane, "[He was] quite as much of a soldier as [any] man," because under enemy fire he remained "as unconcerned as though he were gazing at a cinematograph" (160).

7 According to Musser and Nelson, the Méliès film *L'explosion du cuirassé "Maine" en rade de la Havane* served as "a highly emotional catalyst" in Lyman Howe's 1898 War-Graph exhibitions (88–89).

8 Political cartoons and newspaper articles celebrated the strengthening of Anglo-American relations during 1898, arguing that U.S. involvement in Cuba marked a return to the same ideological justification putatively assigned to the American Revolution (i.e., freedom from colonial oppression). According to these arguments, the Spanish-American War was fought not only to "turn the page" on the U.S. Civil War by reuniting the North and South, but also to reunite the U.S. and Great Britain through Anglo-Saxonism. In addition, the British government's support for the U.S. policy toward Cuba marked an important turning point in Anglo-American relations, which had grown increasingly strained since the Venezuelan border dispute in 1895. (I am grateful to Charles Musser for this last point.)

Symptomatic of the pervasive Anglo-Saxonism throughout the United States in the late nineteenth century, pseudo-Darwinian arguments were also harnessed to demonize the Spanish enemy. In May 1898, the *Milwaukee Journal* wrote of "The Degeneracy of the Spanish Race," claiming that the Inquisition "crushed intellect and blighted minds until a brutal and stupid race resulted," while a *Savannah Morning News* article on "The Spanish Temperament," stated that Spaniards "stab as readily as Italians [and] are about as brave as other Latin races." This ubiquitous nineteenth century discourse is present in the Edison's "war extra" catalog description of *Cuban Refugees Waiting for Rations*, which claims "the picture affords an exceedingly interesting racial character study" of the "listless and lifeless" reconcentrados (May 10, 1898, p. 4).

9 I am thus extending Constance Balides' claim that "the attraction of women within the cinema of attractions has political implications over and above those of a general—though certainly historical—conception of exhibitionism" (*Making Dust* 140), to include a consideration of Spanish-American War films and the female spectator.

10 In nearby Worcester, Massachusetts, which is less than forty miles from Boston, Spanish-American war fever ran rampant like in Rochester, and the biograph had been enjoying a long run in Worcester at the Bijou before the *Maine* explosion in January and into mid-February of 1898. The biograph was consistently presented in advertise-ments as the featured act on the bill until a fire destroyed the Bijou on on February 18,

1898—just three days after the U.S. battleship *Maine* exploded in Havana harbor. Headlines about the Bijou fire in the *Worcester Telegram* rivaled news of *Maine* disaster, as the biograph became the prime suspect of the arson investigation. This regional history in which the sole consistent site for the exhibition of movies in Worcester is destroyed the week of the *Maine* explosion is significant for the way it underscores the mode of exhibition and reception war films in the late nineteenth century. Even though the film apparatus remained intact after the fire, for Worcester residents there would be no exhibition of war films until September 1898, well after a U.S. victory was imminent and the preliminary peace agreement with Spain had been signed.

11 By mid-March the *Maine* had come to represent Spanish brutality, dead American soldiers, and the entire "Cuba libre" movement. The popularity and apparent success of the war facilitated the *Maine*'s commodification and the selling of war more generally— as advertisers modified popular war slogans (most famously "Remember the Maine! To Hell with Spain!") to capitalize on the war's popularity. Phrases like "War Declared on Prices" and "Remember the Main features of good laundry" appeared in newspapers across the country, thus conflating nationalist imperialism with late nineteenth century consumerism.

12 One of the more obvious resistant Spanish-American War spectators would be a member of the anti-imperialist movement. Although the mainstream anti-imperialist movement gained momentum during the Philippine-American War and even shortly after the events in Cuba in 1898, in the early months of 1898 the motivations and arguments for military intervention were perceived as morally just by many future prominent anti-imperialists who consequently saw the Spanish-American War as ethically justified. At the same time, many of the most vocal Euro-Americans against military involvement cast their anti-expansionist rhetoric in racist ideologies very different from the dissent expressed in African American papers. Alongside these essentialist discourses about the Spanish "race" were racist descriptions of their Cuban victims, exemplified by the following commencement speech to the class of 1898 by Stanford University President David Starr Jordan, who Richard Hofstadter argues is "probably the best known of all the peace advocates and anti-expansionists" (195):

> There are three things inseparable from the life of the Cuban people to-day, the cigarette, the lottery ticket, and the machete. These stand for vice, superstition, and revenge. . . . |T|hese people prefer the indolence of Spanish rule with all its brutalities to the bustling ways of the Anglo-Saxon. Many of them would take their chances of being starved or butchered rather than to build roads, wash faces, and clean up their towns. . . .

> ("Lest We Forget" 16–17)

13 Although African Americans were legally prohibited from viewing films in many theaters in the U.S. in 1898 and were not the primary audience for most exhibitors, it is certainly possible that many African Americans saw war films at legally and culturally segregated theaters and fairgrounds across the country (see Gomery; Waller). Given the ambivalence and anger many African Americans expressed about the war, one can speculate that images of America's imperial pursuits would have been received very differently among parts of the African American population. Spanish-American War films, including *Colored Troops Disembarking*, which features African American soldiers, would have different

meanings for African Americans than many other spectators in the North and the South, although certainly not uniformly, as the wide range of political positions expressed in African American newspapers suggests.

Matthew Frye Jacobson has also documented a wide range of political and emotional responses to the Spanish-American War by Irish, Polish, and Jewish immigrants in the Unites States. Although many immigrants were at times ambivalent about American imperialism during the 1898 war in Cuba, there was a large degree of support for the "Cuba libre" movement in the 1890s. It was mostly later as the war continued in the Philippines that immigrants' "denunciations of American expansionist policy became more . . . venomous" in response to the apparent hypocrisy of the U.S. presence in the Philippines (176).

Works cited

Allen, Robert C. (1977) "Vaudeville and Film 1895–1915: A Study in Media Interaction" Ph.D. Dissertation, The University of Iowa.
—— (1986) "The Movies in Vaudeville: Historical Context of the Movies as Popular Entertainment" in Tino Balio, ed., The American Film Industry, Madison: University of Wisconsin Press.
Balides, Constance (1993) "Making Dust in the Archives: Feminism, History, and Early American Cinema" Ph.D. Dissertation. University of Wisconsin, Milwaukee.
—— (1993) "Scenarios of Exposure in the Practice of Everyday Life: Women in the Cinema of Attractions" Screen 34.1.
Bernardi, Daniel (1996) "Introduction: Race and the Emergence of U.S. Cinema" in Daniel Bernardi, ed., The Birth of Whiteness: Race and the Emergence of U.S. Cinema, New Brunswick, NJ: Rutgers University Press.
Bottomore, Stephen (1995) "The Biograph in Battle" in Karel Dibbetts and Bert Hogenkamp, ed., Film and the First World War Amsterdam: Amsterdam University Press.
Brundage, W. Fitzhugh (1993) Lynching in the New South: Georgia and Virginia, 1880–1930 Urbana: University of Illinois Press.
Castonguay, James (1999) "The Spanish-American War in United States Media Culture" in American Quartely's Project for Hypertext Scholarship in American Studies, ed. Roy Rosenzweig. http://chnm.gmu.edu.aq.
Charney, Leo and Vanessa R. Schwartz, eds. (1995) "Introduction" in Cinema and the Invention of Modern Life. Berkeley: University of California Press.
Davis, Richard Harding (1995) "Our War Correspondents in Cuba and Puerto Rico" in Nathaniel Lande, ed., Dispatches From the Front: News Accounts of American Wars, 1776–1991 New York: Henry Holt and Company.
Gatewood, Jr. Willard B. (1975) Black Americans and the White Man's Burden, 1898–1903 Chicago: University of Illinois Press.
Gheorghiu-Cernat, Manuela (1983) Arms and the Film: War and Peace in European Films, trans. Florin Ionescu and Ecaterina Grundbock, Bucharest: Meridiane.
Gomery, Douglas (1992) Shared Pleasures: A History of Movie Presentation in the United States, Madison: University of Wisconsin Press.
Hansen, Miriam (1991) Babel and Babylon: Spectatorship in American Silent Film Cambridge, MA: Harvard University Press.

——— (1990) "Early Cinema—Whose Public Sphere?" in Thomas Elsaesser, ed., *Early Cinema: Space-Frame-Narrative* London: British Film Institute.

Hofstadter, Richard (1955) "Race and Imperialism" *Social Darwinism in American Thought*, rev edition, Boston: Beacon Press.

Jacobson, Matthew Frye (1995) *Special Sorrows: The Diasporic Imagination of Irish, Polish, and Jewish Immigrants in the Unites States* Cambridge: Harvard University Press.

Jordan, David Starr (1899) "Lest We Forget (An address to the Members of the Graduating Class of 1898, in Leland Stanford Junior University; delivered May 25, 1898)" in *Imperial Democracy* New York: D. Appleton and Co.

Musser, Charles (1983) "The American Vitagraph, 1897–1901: Survival and Success in a Competitive Industry" in John Fell, ed., *Film Before Griffith*. Berkeley: University of California Press.

——— (1990) *The Emergence of Cinema: The American Screen to 1907* New York: Charles Scribner's Sons.

Musser, Charles and Carol Nelson (1991) *High Class Moving Pictures: Lyman H. Howe and the Forgotten Era of Traveling Exhibition, 1880–1920* Princeton: Princeton University Press.

New York Clipper 1897–1899.

Rabinovitz, Lauren (1998) *For the Love of Pleasure: Women, Movies, and Culture in Turn-of-the-Century Chicago* New Brunswick: Rutgers University Press.

Shohat, Ella and Robert Stam (1994) *Unthinking Eurocentrism: Multiculturalism and the Media* London and New York: Routledge.

Silber, Nina (1997) *The Romance of Reunion: Northerners and the South, 1865–1900* University of North Carolina Press.

Sklar, Robert (1975) *Movie-Made America: A Cultural History of American Movies* New York: Random House.

——— (1990) "Oh! Althusser!: Historiography and the Rise of Cinema Studies" in Robert Sklar and Charles Musser, ed., *Resisting Images: Essays on Cinema and History* Philadelphia: Temple University Press.

Streible, Dan (1997) "Female Spectators and the Corbett-Fitzsimmons Fight Film" in Aaron Baker and Todd Boyd, ed., *Out of Bounds: Sports, Media, and the Politics of Identity* Bloomington: Indiana University Press.

Waller, Gregory A. (1995) *Main Street Amusements: Movies and Commercial Entertainment in A Southern City, 1896–1930* Washington, D.C.: Smithsonian Institution Press.

The United States' Film Industry and World War One

9

LESLIE MIDKIFF DEBAUCHE

When the United States entered World War One in April 1917, the film industry seized the opportunity to enlist in the government's efforts to rally the homefront.[1] A number of federal departments and agencies routed educational programmes and propaganda through the variety of channels the film industry made available. Throughout the nineteen months of American involvement in World War One, the government's needs to garner support for the war effort, to conserve food, to raise money and to recruit soldiers were met through the production of short instructional films, the public-speaking activities of movie stars, the civic forum provided by movie theaters and the administrative expertise offered by film industry personnel who had been assigned by their trade association, the National Association of the Motion Picture Industry (NAMPI), to work directly with governmental agencies.

The film industry also had much to gain from working closely with the United States government. In trade journals and in private correspondence, individuals representing all of its branches alluded to this belief. The War posed a direct challenge to the conduct of business as usual: the industry might have been deemed 'nonessential' and shut down for the course of the War, or it could have been subjected to government influence, which could easily have involved altering its product and disrupting distribution channels and timetables. The movies might have been decried as a frivolity not fitting to a nation at war. These threats were successfully countered in part through co-operative association with the government. Even more, the goodwill of both the movie-goer and the federal government which accrued to the American film industry on account of its war work served as a selling point in the 1920s when its major companies began to trade their stock on Wall Street, and it provided a buffer against national censorship when movie stars became embroiled in scandal. In addition, the War itself provided film producers with material for narrative films throughout the 1920s and 1930s.

The actions of the film industry, nearly from the moment war broke out in Europe, followed the precept of practical patriotism: it was appropriate and reasonable to combine allegiance to country and to business. In fact, it was understood that enlisting in the war effort on the homefront would likely benefit the film industry's long-range interests. It also reflected the attitude of many individuals working in the movies. I found the term 'practical patriotism' in a 1917 advertisement in the *New York Times* for a feature film called *The Bar Sinister*. As well as showing this movie, the manager of the Broadway Theater was also promoting a sweepstakes to give away a fifty dollar Liberty Bond. The ad ballyhooed this combination of entertainment and support for the country, and it urged theatre managers across the land to do likewise. 'One Bond given away daily in each of America's 16,000 picture theaters would place $5,000,000 a week in Uncle Sam's pocket and give strength to his mighty blows.'[2] Movie-goers were given a timely incentive to buy a ticket, the government gained fifty dollars to help support the war effort, and the theatre manager, who donated the Bond, likely made back his financial investment in addition to gaining useful public relations from his promotion. Cecil DeMille, director-general of the Famous Player Lasky Company, voiced the same sentiment later that summer. He wanted to go to Europe and entertain the troops by projecting movies. He had developed a portable generator for use at the front and only needed permission of his bosses, Jesse Lasky and Adolph Zukor, to embark. DeMille justified his plan by invoking practical patriotism. 'It would serve three great purposes: primarily the great good to the men: secondly, the great good to this firm; and thirdly, the great good to me.'[3] Lasky and Zukor denied DeMille's request. They felt the greatest good would be served if he remained in California directing films for the newly formed company.

The American film industry treated the exigencies of World War One as opportunities and raced to the aid of the federal government. Still, they helped without sidetracking regular production, distribution and exhibition of feature film programmes, and without converting the industry to the creation of only war-related product. In short, the film industry was able to fit its duties to the government within already existing categories of professional behaviour. In this chapter, I will survey the ways that film producers, distributors and exhibitors adapted standard business practices to meet the circumstances of wartime. The effects of the War on the film industry outlasted the nineteen months of US involvement in the conflict. American film assumed a position of pre-eminence in the world market and classical Hollywood cinema became a style other national cinemas emulated or reacted against for decades.

The War also survived as grist for film-makers. This chapter will conclude with a discussion of the way the war-film genre developed between the 1910s and World War Two. The changing narrative focus and thematic concerns of movies made about the Great war provide insight into the complex of influences on film production. D. W. Griffith's *Hearts of the World* (1918), advertised as the 'Sweetest Love Story Ever Told' was one of the most popular films of that year. The War was treated much differently by the mid-1920s when some film titles posed questions like *What Price Glory?*. The antiwar film, *All Quiet on the Western Front*, adapted from Erich Maria Remarque's international best-selling novel, won the third Academy Awards for production and direction in 1929/1930. Yet in 1941, *Sergeant York's* story of a young soldier's coming to terms with the job of war took the prizes for best actor and editing. Times had changed, the industry had changed, and the generic ways of telling war stories had also changed.

Film production, 1917–1918

American films of World War One were a mixed lot. Movies with war-related narratives included Hate-the-Hun propaganda exemplified by titles like *The Kaiser, the Beast of Berlin* and *The Prussian Cur*. In these films mustachioed German officers, already identified with

Erich von Stroheim, tossed babies out of windows, raped young women and murdered innocent civilians. Not all war stories were so virulent. In *The Little American* (1917) Mary Pickford plays Angela, an American born on the Fourth of July. She is in love with her German neighbour. After an ill-fated voyage to Belgium, and many plot twists, she liberates her love from a prisoner of war camp, brings him back to the United States, and presumably marries him.

While there were war films in release over the nineteen months during which the United States was engaged in World War One, the preponderance of movies playing in picture palaces and neighbourhood theatres across the land did not tell stories about the War. Comedy and drama, literary adaptation and original scenario, scripts with war-related narratives and, more frequent, scripts with no narrative relation to the War—all were offered by film producers to the exhibitor, and by the film exhibitors to their local clientele.

Film historian Benjamin Hampton described a three-to-six month production process as the norm for feature-length films. Studios could, if they chose, respond in timely fashion to the pressing issues of their day. Although they were produced and distributed in ever-increasing numbers over the months of US involvement in World War One, War-related narrative and documentary films never dominated other films. Instead, there was a slow yet steady increase in numbers of war-related feature films during 1917 and 1918. Working from the data base of films listed for distribution in the trade journal *Moving Picture World*, one finds eight dramatic features listed in May 1917, eighteen in October 1917, twenty-eight in March 1918, thirty-two in August 1918, and fifty-four in October 1918. This cautious consistency indicated that the production of war-related feature films was the result of decisions to respond tactically to the War through the timely adaptation of film narratives, and, further, that this decision was based at least in part on the testing of this type of film in the marketplace. There had been vociferous opposition to the US entry into the War, and it may have been the case that film producers were waiting to see what the popular consensus would be before committing themselves and their products to any single point of view. It is also the case that the most strident anti-German films appeared late in the War: *My Four Years in Germany* (March 1918), *To Hell with the Kaiser* (June 1918), and *The Prussian Cur* and *Kulture* (both in September 1918).

Still, numbers do not tell the whole story. All films in release were not equal: brighter stars, bigger promotional efforts and more elaborate exhibition differentiated film from film, creating a hierarchy ranging from (top to bottom) the special film to the programme picture. While films with war-related content were always the minority of all films in release, the conclusion does not follow that war-related films were insignificant. Certain of these film stood out. They received more press attention, and their audiences knew they were special. About half of the most prestigious and the most expensive movies released in 1917 and 1918 told war stories. In fact, one of the 'biggest' films of World War One was D. W. Griffith's *Hearts of the World* (1918).

Hearts of the World was the longest running and arguably the most prestigious film produced and released during the entire period of US participation in the War. This romance between the children of American neighbours living on the Rue de la paix in a French village was a good example of the way in which the War could be incorporated as a plot device in an otherwise conventional, melodramatic love story. An early inter-title introduced it as, 'an old fashioned play with a new fashioned theme'. Griffith also stated the theme in a later intertitle: 'God help the nation that begins another war of conquest or meddling! Brass bands and clanging sabres make very fine music, but let us remember there is another side of war.' *Hearts of the World* showed the other side of the Great War. The marriage plans of Lilian Gish and Robert Harron, the 'Girl' and the 'Boy', were interrupted by war. The Germans advanced on their village, the Boy's mother died, the Girl was mistreated at the hands of the enemy, and in a wonderfully eerie-made scene the Girl, clutching her wedding dress, roamed across a desolate battlefield searching for the Boy. The film's climax came as the Boy fought a German (playing by Erich von Stroheim), nearly lost, and was saved by the arrival of French and American troops. The film concluded in 'Happy Times'. 'America—returning home after freeing the world from Autocracy and the horrors of war forever and ever.' Viewers saw shots of American flags, followed by ships at sea, and a flag-draped portrait of President Wilson. *Hearts of the World* ended with a shot of the Boy and the Girl waving flags against a backdrop of bright light. Audiences loved it.

Programming the movie theatre, 1917–1918

World War One did have an impact on film production. Some of the most prestigious and some of the most memorable films made and released during 1917 and 1918 were feature-length films with war-related narratives. Still the impact of the War on the industry's production of its standard product was not pronounced, and genre is not the sole measure of how the American film industry incorporated the topicality of the War into its entertainment product. Film exhibitors also found ways to make their movie houses necessary to both their local patrons and the federal government. Like film producers, exhibitors accomplished this mission by adapting standard business practice: using their building, as well as the films and live acts on their bills, to woo customers and aid the war effort. As early as 1915, Epes Winthrop Sargent, author of *Picture Theater Advertising* (and a columnist for *Moving Picture World*), had urged managers to promote their theatre's as vigorously as they promoted their entertainment programs. 'Films are but a part of what you have to sell. Advertise all your features.'[4] In choosing films, both feature length and shorts, and in methods adopted to promote such film programmes, theatre managers reacted to the War, even while the strategies already in place for running their businesses remained constant. From Roxy Rothapfel, the trend-setting manager of the Rivoli Theater in New York City, to C. W. Martin at the Temple Theater in McCook, Nebraska, exhibitors' ultimate goal was to make their theatres an integral part of their communities. By participating in the War on the home front film exhibitors were simultaneously creating goodwill for their houses, and they knew it. Like film producers, they were operating well within the boundaries of practical patriotism. . . .

The following examples – which function as advertising designed to attract trade as well as propaganda for the government – show how exhibitors enlisted their theatres in the war effort. While war-related activities taking place in movie theatres informed citizens of governmental needs like food conservation and the purchase of Liberty Bonds, they simultaneously promoted the movie theatre sponsoring them. It is also important to note that home front programming was not necessarily part of a co-ordinated promotional campaign for a war film. Thus, the advertising value of allowing the Marines to set up an enlistment booth in the theatre lobby, and in permitting speakers to lecture about the causes of the War during a film's intermission, lay, first, in attracting customers to a specific theatre.

In programming and promoting their theatres during American involvement in World War One theatre managers had a great number of options. . . .

As the advertising value of donating money to civic projects was recognised and advocated as good theatre management, so the use of the lobby to attract trade had likewise been recognised. *Moving Picture World* published advertisements for such products as portraits of President Wilson: 'The President's face is done in water color and oils, and the American Flag is worked up beautifully in artistic reproduction of the proper shade of red and blue, giving in all a permanent display for the lobby.' The United States Food Administration also offered a six-color poster, suitable for framing and display in the theatres lobby. The Red Cross provided placards urging patrons to contribute, as well as coin boxes in which to place donations. Harold Edel wrote about how he had mounted a bronze plaque bearing the names of all Strand employees in the service in the lobby of his theatre.[5]

In addition to decoration, theatre managers could also add war-related presentations to their film programmes. Music roused patriotic feelings in yet another example of adapting existing exhibition practice to a timely situation. Sargent's *Picture Theater Advertising* had also noted that music could serve as an advertisement for the theatre. Some theatres reported playing the National Anthem at each screening, and the Alhambra in Milwaukee, Wisconsin, instituted the practice of 'Community Singing' of contemporary and topical songs at showings.[6] Prominent local folk, working under the auspices of the Committee for Public Information, made speeches at movie theatres during the War. Called Four Minute Men to invoke the American Revolution and to signal the time limit for their talks, these speakers used material generated in Washington to inform and persuade movie audiences during World War One. Topics included reasons to contribute to the first Liberty Loan, food conservation, ways of maintaining morale on the home front, and why Americans were fighting in the War.[7]

Once the houselights dimmed and the movie-goers' attention was directed to the screen, the theatre manager had a final opportunity to promote his theatre by striking a patriotic chord. An advertisement in *Motion Picture News* read: 'Attention Patriots Do Your Bit. Open or close every show with the Stars and Stripes. 60 feet or longer at only 10 cents a foot.' This patriotism by-the-foot was offered for sale by the American Bioscope Company. Slides were another option. The Excelsior Illustrating Company of New York sold 'a few of the other beautifully hand-colored patriotic slides, 25 cents'. Or exhibitors could make their own slides. Joseph Yeager, owner of a chain of theatres in Raton, New Mexico, showed slides of local men who had enlisted. Exhibitors also made use of newsreels showing hometown boys at boot camp. Later in the War 'smiles' films provided yet another way for exhibitors to connect their theatres to their community, their nation and the War in Europe. People were invited to stand on a particular street to be photographed by a cameraman, often employed by the local newspaper. The resulting film was to be sent to Europe and shown to the soldiers. These films were first screened in the local movie house, however, providing the exhibitor another time-honored way to attract trade.[8]

World War One presented film exhibitors with a set of challenges to their business, and they responded by attempting to turn those challenges into opportunities. Through advertising movie-goers were encouraged to see the theatre as a necessary, inexpensive and entertaining relief from the worries and inconveniences of the War, and, conversely, they were encouraged to consider attendance at the theatre as a way of participating in the war effort in that contributions to various war fund drives advanced the national cause.

The National Association of the Motion Picture Industry enlists

Clearly the film industry's desire to co-operate with the federal government was manifested in their product: films and theatrical entertainment. They also enlisted at the institutional level. Film producers, distributors and exhibitors, and such allied trades as suppliers of theatre fittings and publishers of theatre programmes joined in the US government's war effort on the home front. Combining the desire to help their country with the realisation that such help could further their own business goals, these various members of the film industry were willing to co-operate with government agencies. Only a structure was needed, and this was provided by the newly formed trade group the National Association of the Motion Picture Industry (NAMPI). NAMPI's co-operation with the government gave its members – the film companies, their leaders, their stars and theatre owners – the opportunity to integrate more fully with the many other industries mobilising the home front.

The National Association of the Motion Picture Industry was organised in July 1916 when the existing trade association for producers and distributors, the Motion Picture Board of Trade, proved unable to mediate a dispute between its members and the Motion Picture Exhibitor's League of America. NAMPI took as its mission to enrol representatives from all sectors of the motion picture industry. Its five classes of membership included producers, distributors, exhibitors, actors, insurance companies and advertising agents. Membership on the board of NAMPI ranged across the film industry, including such companies as Universal, Goldwyn, Bell and Howell, Pathé, Vitagraph and *Moving Picture World*, and such individuals as Adolph Zukor, Lee A. Ochs (president of the New York Motion Picture Exhibitors of America), N. C. Cotabish (National Carbon Company), William A. Johnson (editor, *Motion Picture News*), and D. W. Griffith. William Brady, of the production firm World Films, was elected president. It is significant that the board contained men who were gaining power and prestige within the film industry by conducting their business in a particular way: they were expanding, in part, through the acquisition of other companies. While NAMPI wanted a broad representation and a large membership, the make-up of its board of directors also reflected a desire to exercise control over that membership.

The stated goals of NAMPI represented the industry's main concerns: to facilitate discussion among all facets of the industry, to monitor government regulation of its business, to mediate disputes among members, and to serve a public relations function between the industry and the public. NAMPI's more specific goals and worries were manifested in its standing committees, which were focused on membership, finance, publicity, hostile legislation, censorship, taxation, fire-prevention regulations and insurance, foreign trade, copyrights and trademarks, standards and labour issues, among others. When the United States entered World War One, NAMPI added support for governmental initiatives to the list of its functions.[9]

Co-operation between the government and the film industry, represented by NAMPI, began as early as 23 May 1917, when its president, William Brady, acting in response to a request from Secretary of the Treasury McAdoo, called a meeting of representatives from the motion picture industry to discuss ways in which the film community could aid the First Liberty Loan Campaign. One month later *Exhibitor's Trade Review* reported that a War Cooperation Committee had been created 'to handle all matters in which the motion picture can be used to further the interests of the American Government in the world war'.[10] The government had contacted the industry through the one trade association comprising representatives from all its branches; NAMPI had responded to a specific request for help with the First Liberty Loan and had in the process willingly expanded its role.

Once appointed and introduced to Washington, the War Cooperation Committee went to work. Arthur Friend of Famous Players-Lasky was assigned to the Food Administration, where one of his first official acts was to send a memo 'To All Manufacturers and Distributors of Pictures' announcing that he was in Washington, and that he would be 'glad to consult and advise with anyone in the trade in regard to its |USFA's| future activities'. He also pledged to keep exhibitors and others in the industry informed of future plans by publicising the Food Administration's programmes in motion picture trade papers 'at the earliest possible moment'.[11] By 7 September 1917 the first Food Administration – film industry joint effort was underway.

A catalogue of the Food Administration's motion picture activities serves as a template for co-operation of the film industry with the federal government, and illustrates the active involvement of all sectors of the motion picture industry in the government's mission. The aid the film industry rendered took a variety of forms. Film producer Thomas Ince suggested that film and theatrical producers should refrain from using real food in their productions as a conservation measure. More important, the industry arranged for the distribution of Food Administration short-subject films through Universal, Pathé and Mutual newsreel distributors. Arthur Friend also enlisted film exhibitors to participate in the Food Administration's extensive Second Food Pledge Card Drive which took place from 21 to 28 October 1917. The Pledge Drive was a multi-media event. Exhibitors agreed to run a series of slides as part of their entertainment programme which would encourage audience members to conserve food by substituting fish for meat and corn for wheat, for example. In addition, the USFA sent out posters heralding 'Food Will Win the War'; exhibitors were encouraged to frame these and display them in the lobbies of their theatres. The Four Minute Men were scheduled to deliver talks on the need for a 'vast home army for conservation' the week of 21 October.[12]

By January 1918, the Film Division of the Food Administration added film advertisements called 'trailers' to its arsenal of advertising methods and in May short films called picturettes were also being distributed, with stars appearing in both. By this time the film exhibitor was the key purveyor of food conservation propaganda.

Co-operation between the film industry and the United States Treasury Department was also successfully manifested both in money and motion pictures. In June 1917, Lasky employees donated $75,000 to the First Liberty Loan, and in September the New York Times reported, 'A film production designed to help sell the next Liberty Loan was exhibited yesterday morning at the Strand Theater.'[13]

NAMPI named Adolph Zukor, of Famous Players-Lasky, Marcus Loew of Loew Enterprises, Jules E. Bruletour of Eastman Films, Walter Irwin of Vitagraph and George Spoor to its War Cooperation Committee which was assigned to the Treasury Department. While information regarding the activities of the Food Administration as it worked through the motion picture industry must be gleaned from archival documents, film industry co-operation with the Treasury Department can be found in the news, entertainment, rotogravure, and even the comics sections, of the nation's newspapers. The Treasury Department employed plenty of 'live interest' – movie stars – in its propaganda. The most popular actors and actresses in the business, including Mary Pickford, Douglas Fairbanks, Charlie Chaplin, Marguerite

Clark and Marie Dressler, travelled the country giving speeches urging their fellow-citizens to contribute to Liberty Loan drives. They made short films, like Chaplin's *The Bond* and Mary Pickford's *100% American*, designed to be shown in movie theatres to coincide with Bond campaigns. The Treasury Department also produced slides which were distributed to movie theatres in support of buying bonds. In October 1917, in fact, some 17,500 sets of slides, three slides to a set, were distributed to as many theatres. For the third Liberty Loan, NAMPI released 17,200 trailers, 17,200 sets of posters and a 'splendid patriotic film contributed by Douglas Fairbanks'.[14]

The film industry, co-ordinated by the War Cooperation Committee, went 'over the top' to promote the sale of Liberty Bonds. Many of the specific examples cited here were reported in the *New York Times*, the *Chicago Tribune*, the *Milwaukee Journal* and the *Minneapolis Tribune*, as well as other local newspapers. Movie stars, film companies and movie theatres all benefited from the image building that accompanied their war work. NAMPI also assigned film industry personnel to other departments in the federal government.

NAMPI assigned members of its War Cooperation Committee to the War Department, the Navy Department, the Department of Agriculture, the Department of the Interior and the Aircraft Division. Film industry personnel worked with the Committee on Training Camp Activities, the Shipping Board, the American Red Cross and the Commercial Economy Board. In August 1918, a committee of NAMPI was formed to aid Fuel Administrator Garfield find ways to help the film industry conserve fuel and to educate the public about ways to save fuel. On a less-grand scale, motion picture exhibitors aided the United States Army's 'pit and shell' drive. *Forward*, the paper of the Wisconsin Council of Defense, reported particularly good results among Midwestern theatre managers: 'One house in Indiana obtained four barrels of peach stones at one afternoon matinee.'[15]

The United States Army's pit and shell drive, the United States Food Administration, the Treasury Department and the Red Cross, among other agencies, benefited from the co-operation of the film industry during World War One. The film industry benefited too. The National Association of the Motion Picture Industry facilitated government–industry relations and increased its own membership during 1917 and 1918. Stars and other industry personnel, working through NAMPI, became identified by their war work as well as their movie making and achieved wider recognition and a brighter image.

Over the course of the War, NAMPI defeated most state and all federal attempts at censorship through its lobbying efforts and through a voluntary agreement allowing the National Board of Review to screen and approve all films for release. Stars, producing companies, NAMPI and local exhibitors, all received press coverage as they participated in the war effort. The film industry and the reformer were, for however brief a period of time, on the same side. As the image of the film industry improved, its potential for attracting a wider audience increased. World War One offered the film industry a greater number of selling points in advertising its product. Movie-going offered not only entertainment – important enough in this time of stress – but included in the price of admission a war tax that went directly to the government. The theatre functioned as a rallying point for the community. It was the place to be informed and inspired by the government's Four Minute Men, the place to be reminded about specific food conservation tactics, and the place to contribute to the Red Cross. In their advertising, exhibitors plugged these reasons for coming to the theatre as heartily as they promoted the feature film being shown. Film-producing companies also sent current movies overseas to be shown to soldiers.

Trade associations were primarily protective alliances which also helped to standardise business practices and foster good public relations with the consumer.[16] The National Association of the Motion Picture Industry followed these general guidelines and functioned with special effectiveness during the months from April 1917 until November 1918. As a result, both the government and the film industry benefited.

The American film industry at the end of the war

As film historian Janet Staiger points out, 'If there was a "golden age" of the studio, it was in full operation by 1917'.[17] It was not only the studio system's mode of production which had been established but also the foundations for the structure of the film industry, at least until 1948, were also set. Economic power was vested in the large integrated, or soon-to-be integrated, companies within all branches of the film industry. The traces of the future oligopoly were present. Pre-war trends, such as independent production, decreases in the number of small theatres and increases in the number of theatres in chains, continued and accelerated over the months of American involvement in World War One. The industry emerged from the War a big business, its stock bought and sold on Wall Street.

It had also become a reputable business. One of the abiding benefits for the film industry of its participation in the war effort on the home front was an enhanced public image, an effect that was felt in both tangible and intangible ways. The most prominent movie stars like Chaplin and Pickford, as well as lesser lights, had the opportunity for increased public exposure. They travelled the country speaking on behalf of Liberty Bonds: they appeared in picturettes for Herbert Hoover's United States Food Administration: they were regularly in the photogravure sections of newspapers working in their gardens, knitting for soldiers and donating ambulances to the Red Cross. These photo opportunities helped weave film personalities even more tightly into the fabric of popular culture. They became home-front heroes and heroines, and the goodwill they garnered almost certainly added to the audiences for their films. These activities also helped forestall potential criticism when their private lives got messy. When Pickford and Fairbanks divorced their mates to marry each other in March 1920, the public which had responded so generously to their Bond Drives revelled in their union.

William Gibbs McAdoo, Secretary of the Treasury, Director-General of the Railroad Administration and son-in-law of President Wilson, had met Pickford, Chaplin and Douglas Fairbanks during their work on the Third Liberty Loan. He would serve as counsel to United Artists, formed in 1919. The film industry also won the aid of Republicans. Will Hays, Republican Party chairman, and postmaster general in Warren Harding's administration, would join the film industry in 1922 as its point man – heading the Motion Picture Producer and Distributors Association. His task was to quell any federal censorship of the movies. Hays did his job well, with the industry instituting its own self-regulation.

Thus, World War One provided the film industry with the opportunity to enhance its goodwill with its market – the American public – and to win the goodwill of those in positions of power in the government. When Woodrow Wilson embarked for France to attend the Peace Conference, he carried fifteen movies with him for entertainment. 'The Famous Players-Lasky Corporation received a wire from Washington November 28 to supply the motion pictures . . .' The work of Douglas Fairbanks, Mary Pickford, D. W. Griffith and Dorothy Gish, among others, sailed with the American delegation on board the *George Washington*.[18]

War narratives: movies in the 1920s and 1930s

Throughout the 1920s, and up until World War Two, the Great War was used as narrative fodder in a variety of films. We can also see the foundations of the combat film genre established in a set of films about World War One made in the middle years of the decade. These films, including *The Big Parade* (1925), *What Price Glory?* (1926) and *Wings* (1927), told very different stories, featuring a new sort of hero than had been seen in the war films made in 1917 and 1918. When the War became the stuff of so pervasive and popular a medium as the Hollywood film, narrative conventions and industrial practice joined history and politics in shaping the image and meaning of World War One.

After the Armistice, the War found its way into a variety of genres whose films told contemporary stories. Threaded through the narratives and *mise-en-scènes* of two-reel comedies, westerns and big-budget dramas were reminders – as if the audience had ever really forgotten – that the Great War had been fought, and its effects were still felt. *Rolling Stone*, a Billy West comedy released in 1919, revolves around a jailbird who falls in love with the warden's daughter. Near the end we see Billy's two babies, in their cradle, dressed in military uniforms. Billy reads a newspaper, its headline – 'Wilson Sees End of War'. Another two-reel comedy, *The Detectress*, c. 1919 featured Gale Henry traversing 'Dirty Alley'. An inter-title explains, 'Dirty Alley was as peaceful as no mans land on a busy day.' Still another example is the 1928 short comedy *Vacation Waves*. In it, Edward Everett Horton, a train conductor who has just been shot in the backside, yells, 'War is over but if you shoot me again, I'll start another one.'

Comedy was not the only genre to incorporate references to the War into narratives and *mise-en-scène*. *The Stolen Ranch*, a 1926 western directed by William Wellman, shows two army buddies, Frank and Breezey, who survive the 'inferno' of the Western Front. The War cemented their friendship, and that relationship was the 'net profit taken from Flanders Fields'. Frank suffers from shell-shock, and Breezey must protect him from sudden loud noises which trigger flashbacks to battle. The two return home to find that Frank's ranch has been taken over by bad guys – presumably slackers who did not fight in the War. The *mise-en-scène includes flashbacks to battlefields where the two friends fought. Its iconography includes coils of barbed wire, airplanes flying overhead, bombs exploding, trenches and skeletal trees – a visual shorthand that had, by 1926, come to signify the Great War.*

Of the films touching in some way on the diverse experiences of World War One, those receiving the most critical attention in the 1920s, and those which served to influence the war-related films that would come in the 1930s and during World War Two, were movies that showed the experiences of the doughboy and the flyer in combat. Pictures like King Vidor's *The Big Parade* (Metro Goldwyn Mayer, 1925) and Raoul Walsh's *What Price Glory?* (Fox, 1926) replaced D. W. Griffith's *Hearts of the World* as the quintessential World War One war film in the 1920s. Building on foundations of narrative and *mise-en-scène* set in Charlie Chaplin's *Shoulder Arms* (First National, 1918), they focused on the ordinary soldier, his bleak and muddy life in the trenches (air combat movies like *Wings* [Paramount, 1927] would dominate the last years of the decade) and scenes showing basic training, mail call and soldiers going over the top or out on dawn patrol. While reiterating certain narrative characteristics – for example, sequences depicting life before and after the War – typical of the war-related pictures released during the War, the war films of the 1920s also displayed striking innovations. They were told from the soldier's point of view and foregrounded battle over any other wartime experience.

The function of women also changed dramatically. Combat films made in the 1920s eliminated or significantly reduced the role of women as causal agents in their narratives. In the war films of the 1910s the love story was central to the war story. Women were seen on the battlefield, and, more significantly, the War invaded their villages and homes. Both a domestic threat and a national threat were posed by the Great War. The worst thing Germans do, in the logic of these movies, is rape, or threaten to rape, the film's heroine, and, as in the propaganda posters of the era, soldiers enlist and fight to keep women safe. In the 1920s, however, characters like Melisande and Charmaine, or Mary, Clara Bow's character in Wings, still appeared in The Big Parade and What Price Glory?, but a clear divide was created between the 'love story' and the war scenes. Now, mothers and sweethearts lived on a distant home front where they wrote letters and were, most often, faithful; if overseas, they either drove ambulances or served as nurses. They might also be French villagers providing love and comfort behind the lines. Still, in most films made in the mid-1920s, war was defined as combat, and women were well out of the fray.

Realism was the main selling point in advertising these films, and it was a standard to which they were held by film reviewers. When The Big Parade opened in Boston the reviewer for the Boston Transcript praised the film and damned its cinematic predecessors. 'To watch it unroll is to realize anew all the shallow bombast, all the flatulency and all the saccharinity with which previous picture-makers have encumbered the trade of war.' Instead, he placed Vidor's film within the newer literary tradition of 'tough' stories about realistic dough-boys, 'soldiers nearer convention than Dos Passos's, less professional than Kipling's, and somewhat less pungent than Stallings's own marines in What Price Glory?'[19] New conventions for realism affecting story, intertitles, costume make up, setting and theme, among other aspects of film form, were being set and applied across theatre, literature and film. Women did not figure in this aesthetic of realism.

Thus, it is significant that the most influential war films of the 1920s and the novels and plays they resembled were written by a relatively small number of men who had served in the military during World War One. The review of the play What Price Glory? in the Women Citizen concluded by linking verisimilitude with authorial experience: 'Laurence Stallings, who, with Maxwell Anderson, wrote it, was a captain of marines, and lost a leg and won years of pain as a result of Belleau Wood. He ought to know.'[20] Stallings provided the story for The Big Parade – in which a young soldier loses a leg in a battle like Belleau Wood. John Monk Saunders, Second Lieutenant in the Signal Corps Aviation Section, contributed the story for Wings, The Legion of the Condemned (Paramount, 1928) and The Dawn Patrol (First National, 1930; 1938). Maxwell Anderson, co-author of What Price Glory? adapted Erich Maria Remarque's All Quiet on the Western Front for the screen. The stories these men told, based on their experiences in the War, were transformed into scenarios by other men and women, veterans not of combat but Hollywood. The result was a change in the conventions governing the way war stories were told – women and romance were removed to the subplot.

The combat films of the 1920s were also different in tone from 1917–1918 movies with war-related plots. The Big Parade, What Price Glory? and Wings were perceived, at least by movie critics, as being ambivalent in their attitude toward war. Even a perfunctory glance at titles like The Big Parade and What Price Glory? finds an irony absent from The Little American or Hearts of the World. Jim Apperson, the young rich man who enlists in 'the big parade' – the War – after being surcharged with enthusiasm by the rousing martial music he hears in a recruitment parade, comes limping home at war's end. He has lost a leg: his two buddies – a riveter and a bartender – are both dead. Jim's fiancée has taken up with his brother, who stayed home. The price paid by Apperson for a dubious glory is indeed high, and he knows it. An inter-title late in the film fairly shouts, 'What the hell do we get out of this war? Parades—who the hell cares?'

What Price Glory? was released as a roadshow in the year following The Big Parade. It tells of two career soldiers, Quirt and Flagg, who spend most of their time, and much of the movie, competing for the affections of women in China, the Philippines and, finally, in France. Although its ads promised that 'Women Love It's [sic] Daring—Its Romance and Its Uproarious Humor', the film also had, in addition to its quizzical title, a 'tragic note'.[21] This included what the reviewer for the New York Times called the 'Trench of Death' – a shell explodes in a trench and buries all the men positioned there. The scene closes on an image of bayonets spiking up through the rubble. The film's thematic terrain is equally bleak. After one of the young soldiers, an artist who spends much of his onscreen time writing home to his mother, dies in Flagg's arms, an inter-title describes a setting fraught with poignant irony: 'And all night long that wounded spiner in a tree screams for mercy. You talk about honor and courage and a man bleeds to death in a tree over your head.' Soon after, Quirt screams – in inter-title – 'What Price Glory Now?'

These influential films, plays and novels voiced a belief, broadly felt in American culture by the mid-1920s, that the government's wartime propaganda had been false. Stories of atrocities perpetrated in Belgium by bestial German combatants were unfounded, and the more high-toned metaphorical description of this War as the Great Crusade of Civilization against Autocracy was at odds with the soldiers' experience. Before the 1920s, war – at least at the movies – had been a necessary evil undergone in order to save the honour and chastity of women, to make the world safe for democracy, and to end all wars. In the 1920s, it was not so clear why men went 'over there'.

The war films of the 1930s and early 1940s, including All Quiet on the Western Front (Universal, 1930), Hells Angels (United Artists, 1930), The Down Patrol (1938), The Fighting 69th (Warner Bros., 1940) and Sergeant York (Warner Bros., 1941), show, at first a honing of the narrative conventions relating to the hero, the role of women and the themes set in the 1920s. Still, as the country moved closer to World War Two certain films began, as they had in the 1910s, to portray the redemptive possibilities of war.

The mode of production operating in the United States film industry in the 1930s is best described as producer unit. Within each studio, units comprising a producer, directors, technical staff, writers and actors, would work together on movies. Genre films were the norm in the studio system of the 1930s. Units worked together, over time, and honed both their visual style and generic conventions. Public disillusionment and the inclusion of war veterans in the production process help to explain the rather significant changes from the war film as historical spectacle made while the United States was at war to the war film as combat and coming-of-age tale in the 1920s. From the 1920s through the early 1940s I believe that genre was shaped more by the business of movie making than by ideology. As America verged on World War Two, the film industry again reframed its war stories to show what good could come out of war – even a war which had lost its lustre and whose aims had apparently failed. Young men could find God, could reaffirm democratic principles, and could experience a noble self-sacrificing love in the company of their comrades. Female characters did not fit in the trenches or in an airplane's cockpit: their romantic function only served to create division among friends and distractions from the soldier's job. Two men love the same woman in *Wings*, and a woman tries to come between brothers in *Hells Angels* – better to write them out of the story.

Conclusion: practical patriotism

Over the course of the Great War the film industry refined its product, and in the 1920s it set an international standard for film-making. It also continued along a path of corporate growth toward oligopoly which helped to ensure its profitability in the succeeding decade. There was no government-initiated censorship of the films, and, in fact, key figures in the government, like Will Hays, went to work for the film industry in the 1920s. The War did not divert the development of the craft or the business of film-making from its pre-war course.

While movies about the Great War never dominated the release schedules of film distributors, they did become a staple throughout the late 1910s, 1920s and 1930s, even though both their function and their form changed over time. Before the United States entered the conflict in April 1917, films told stories of the need for preparedness as well as the need to refrain from mixing in the problems of Europe. After American entry movies like *The Little American* and *Hearts of the World* showed movie-goers bestial Huns, endangered women, and brave, young, patriotic American men. Increasingly during the 1920s those films defined by the industry and the critical establishment as war films portrayed soldiers in combat – in the trenches and in the air. Here war was not depicted as a noble enterprise. In fact, in films like *The Big Parade*, *What Price Glory?* and *Wings*, it replaced the Hun as enemy. Still, the Great War on the screen did offer young men the opportunity to come of age and to act in noble ways. The films of the early 1930s, beginning with *All Quiet on the Western Front*, continue trends begun in the 1920s, especially the narrative focus on combat, and they deepen the cynicism about the War's aims and its results. Until, that is, World War Two looms large.

War films have been the most durable legacy of the participation of the United States' film industry in World War One. These movies were made by individuals working with and within the narrative conventions and modes of production sanctioned by that film industry. The films discussed here were neither idiosyncratic nor anomalous as they told war stories. Instead, the films of World War One made in the 1910s, 1920s and 1930s fit comfortably within the boundaries set by popular culture for depicting the War. The genre that developed always was, and remains, dynamic, responsive to creative film-makers, new technology, industrial practice and the influence of popular writers and historians.

Notes

1 Much of this chapter is taken from my book *Reel Patriotism: The Movies and World War One* (Madison: University of Wisconian Press, 1997). For more detailed analysis and explanatory case studies of selected films of World War One, please see this text.
2 Advertisement for *The Bar Sinister*, *New York Times*, 3 June 1917, sec. X.
3 Cecil DeMille to Jesse Lasky, 14 August 1917, box 240, folder 1, DeMille Collection, Brigham Young University Archives.
4 Epes Winthrop Sargent, *Picture Theater Advertising* (New York: Chalmers, 1915), p. 27.

5 Advertisement, *Moving Picture World*, 32.4, 28 April 1917, p. 630; United States Food Administration letter, 2 October 1917, National Archives, record group 4, 12 HC-A4, box 505; 'Fairbanks starts Red Cross fund', *Moving Picture World*, 33.1, 7 July 1917, p. 64; 'Strand places dedicatory tablet', *Moving Picture World*, 35.10, 9 March 1918, p. 272.

6 'Baltimore makes anthem obligatory', *Moving Picture World*, 35.2, 12 January 1918, p. 272; Advertisement, *Milwaukee Journal*, 14 July 1918, sec. 2.

7 For more information about the Four Minute Men see Bertram Nelson, 'The Four Minute Men', in Monteville Flowers (ed), *What Every American Should Know about the War*, (New York: Doran, 1918).

8 Advertisement, *Motion Picture News*, 28 April 1917, p. 2629; Advertisement, *Motion Picture News*, 5 May 1917, p. 2876 Epes Winthrop Sargent, 'Advertising for exhibitors', *Moving Picture World*, 35.9, 2 March 1918, p. 1235–6.

9 'Film men form temporary organization', *Moving Picture World*, 29.4, 22 July 1916, p. 612.

10 'Industry oversubscribes 2 1/2 million to Liberty Loan', *Exhibitor's Trade Review*, 23 June 1917, p. 173.

11 Arthur Friend, memo 8 August 1917, United States Food Administration Collection, record group 4, 12 HC-A4, box 504.

12 Maxcy Robson Dickson, *The Food Front in World War One* (Washington, DC: American Council on Public Affairs, 1944), p. 131; United States Food Administration letter to exhibitors, 2 October 1917, United States Food Administration Collection, record group 4, 12 HC-A4, box 504; William Clinton Mullendore, *History of the United States Food Administration*, 1917–1919 (Stanford: Stanford University Press, 1941), p. 87.

13 'Movies boom Liberty', *New York Times*, 19 September 1917.

14 'War achievements of the motion picture industry set forth in brief to federal officials by National Association', *Exhibitors Trade Review*, 20 July 1918, p. 552.

15 'Motion picture industry aids pit and shell drive', *Forward*, 2.9, 3 October 1918, p. 6.

16 Janet Staiger, 'Standardization and differentiation: The reinforcement and dispersion of Hollywood's practices', in David Bordwell, Janet Staiger and Kristin Thompson, *The Classical Hollywood Cinema: Film Style and Mode of Production to 1960* (New York: Columbia University Press, 1985), p. 104.

17 Staiger, 'Central producer system', in Bordwell, Staiger and Thompson, *Classical Hollywood Cinema*, p. 142.

18 'Paramounts and artcrafts to entertain peace party', *Moving Picture World*, 38.11, 14 December 1918, p. 1188.

19 'Watching the War from an orchestra chair', *Literary Digest*, 99.10, 6 March 1926, p. 38–42.

20 Review of *What Price Glory? The Woman Citizen*, 18 October 1924, p. 11.

21 Advertisements for *What Price Glory? Motion Picture News*, 28 October 1927, p. 1333.

War on Film: The American Cinema and World War I, 1914–1941

10

MICHAEL ISENBERG

The Threat: the Image of the Enemy

i

The images of the shadow-world of the screen are illusions which may or may not contain some basis in fact. What is important is that these images, repeated over and over with but little change in setting, eventually harden into stereotypes. Depictions of ethnic minorities, religions, national characteristics, and other easily stereotyped subject matter are expected by audiences to appear in a certain way. The image thus presented is both reassuring, since it reaffirms to the viewer what he knew before, and self-perpetuating, since it leads the viewer to expect more of the same. It took a filmmaker of rare initiative to depart from such a cycle in the days of the studio system. If he was successful, yet another cycle began.

Many stereotypes have been fostered by the motion picture. The visual immediacy of film has proved ideal for the simplistic depiction of national characteristics. The visual image of the German soldier, for example, is common coin today on movie screens and television sets, but it is often forgotten that Americans were first introduced to aspects of this image by the films of World War I. Films depicting an enemy nation, whether made during or after the war, tell us much about ourselves. This appears to be true both in a negative sense, i.e., enemy vices were the reverse image of our virtues, and in a positive sense, wherein the enemy was converted to American ideals. Both of these approaches were common.

Who was the enemy? Prior to 1917, this question never was answered clearly. Such producers as Blackton, the progenitor of *The Battle Cry of Peace*, and such authors as Dixon, who was responsible for *The Fall of a Nation*, certainly had no doubts. But their flirtation with the suggestion that a vague Teutonic monarchism was behind it all was never as explicit as they probably would have liked it to be. The American declaration of war released even moderate filmmakers from this false coyness. During the war years producers operating within the solid boundaries of national hatred chose to identify certain nationalities and individuals as the enemy. In the postwar period, the emphasis switched from the indictment of nationalities to the vilification of certain social classes.

The choice of enemy nationalities was narrowed down rapidly. Austrians were portrayed in only a handful of films. Pola Negri played a courageous Austrian woman in love with a

Hungarian officer in the first postwar production of *Hotel Imperial*. Lillian Gish was a more ethereal Austrian in *The Enemy*, having as her main task that of suffering nobly. *The Mysterious Lady* had an Austrian officer falling in love with a lady Russian spy. After much ado about little, the inevitable ending left viewers with the "final presumption . . . that the couple will be at home in Vienna."[1] An Austrian secret agent and yet another feminine member of the Russian spy corps fenced charmingly in *After Tonight*. And *A Woman of Experience* did little more than portray Vienna as a city of gaiety and light, the perfect background for star-crossed lovers. All this romantic folderol revealed that the use of Austrians as enemy material came after the war, and that even then Austrians never were opposed to American ideals. Plots using Austria as a war background settled there for exotic reasons, not because Austrians were in any way deemed culpable for the war in either cause or conduct. Only *The Enemy* hinted at this culpability, and it fell flat at the box office. Most other members of the Central Powers did not even fare so well. Bulgaria and Turkey were of little interest to Americans, and these nationalities were seldom if ever seen. Nationally speaking, only one enemy emerged—Germany.

There were several reasons for the selection of Germany as the enemy. By 1914 American attitudes toward Germany, which had been tolerably friendly since German unification in 1871, had shifted in a more hostile direction. The extensive publicity given German culture, German society, and the German cult of militarism tended to chill many Americans. A series of tensely polite international confrontations—in Samoa, China, the Philippines, and Latin America—seemed to illuminate the swaggering, imperialistic bellicosity of the Germans. Emperor Wilhelm II alienated many Americans by his truculent posturing on the international stage. In short, "at the beginning of the World's War the majority of the American sentiment was opposed to Germany."[2] Anti-German films, then, did not so much create this sentiment as they helped shape it into a more vicious and antagonistic emotion.

The country's considerable German-American population largely was ignored by the celluloid offensive. After 1917, virtually no films appeared that were sympathetic to the problems of this ethnic minority. When German-Americans were depicted, usually they were paragons of American virtue rather than schizoid national figures torn between two conflicting loyalties. The historian of this minority group has mentioned no films dealing with German-Americans.[3] They constitute the forgotten people in film's attack on the foe.

That they were not widely used as figures in film plots is due mostly to the fortuitous existence of evil incarnate in the shape of the fruits of the House of Hohenzollern. In spite of the outrageous attacks on the personal property and persons of many German-Americans by their fellow citizens, film did not advocate directly (with rare exceptions) this sort of thing. It did assist in creating a moral atmosphere in which such excesses were condoned for a period. But why use an ambiguous enemy at home when the perfect enemy existed abroad?

With the enemy thus specifically identified in national terms, moviemakers chose at first to present him individually. Here the choice could only light on one man. With his florid arrogant countenance, his bristling waxed mustachios, and his long record of international bluster and bombast, the Kaiser provided a ready target for celluloid bullets.

ii

Anti-monarchist pictures were nothing new to American audiences. But prior to the war, such films largely were given over to the gentle ridicule of royal and aristocratic ways. Now, with civilization seemingly hanging in the balance, the leader of the Germans appeared as the very incarnation of overweening imperial malevolence. The fact that crowned heads also existed in England and (for a brief period) in Russia was blandly ignored. The way had been prepared for the excoriation of the Kaiser by such films as *Civilization*, whose king wore a spiked helmet and rammed a declaration of war through his rubber-stamp parliament. The comparison of this mythical ruler with the Kaiser was made quite clear when the captain of one of the mythical king's submarines received a message to "Sink liner *Propatria* with full cargo of contraband of war. Passengers used as blind. Disregard sentiment."[4] *Civilization* obviously owed much to the *Lusitania* disaster, which had preceded its release only by a matter of months.

As America went to war, the gloves were taken off—rare was the war film that did not include at least an indirect and derogatory reference to the Kaiser, his family, monarchism, or aristocratic life. To begin with, in cinematic terms, the war was initiated at the instigation of the Kaiser. *Kultur* had Wilhelm decide "the time is ripe" for war. He then induced his "vassal monarch" of Austria to join him.[5] *To Hell with the Kaiser!*, released in 1918, claimed that the German emperor and his "war council" decided to violate Belgian neutrality as early as the spring of 1914. After the United States entered the war, this picture had the Kaiser partitioning the world, with America as the share of the Crown Prince. At the end, the Kaiser was ushered into a Napoleonic island exile, where he went mad and jumped into the sea. . . .[6]

Most of the films of the war period endorsed the axiom that the wearer of a German uniform was invariably a drunk, a looter, or a rapist, following the cue of his emperor. The American government encouraged this imagery in its Liberty Loan campaigns. Germans were caricatured in the grossest manner imaginable. They behaved like subhuman forms of animal life, with every appetite rapacious and compulsive. "In the Fall, a celebration in New York," read a caption in one Liberty Loan film, "and all American women will belong to German soldiers."[7]

There is considerable justification for the attitude that all this crudity was merely an irrational outpouring of vilification that contained little or no thought. On the other hand, the constant production of films that pilloried the Kaiser and his people was a suggestion that a good share of the American public acquiesced in a certain image of Germany. While the United States and Germany remained at war, this image was, ironically enough, closely linked with an image popular in Germany itself. But where many Germans saw in the prehistoric *Volk* only the simple goodness and purity of a hardy forest existence, Americans in their movie theaters received a vision of a primeval and destructive horde. German civilization, in this view, was only a thin veneer that vanished in the searing heat of war. Although many movie patrons did not know it, their Germany was that of Nietzsche, not of Goethe, and the German army they saw moved according to the principles of Attila rather than Von Moltke. At its extreme, the indictment of Germany extended from the Kaiser through the simplest uniformed peasant boy to the German civilian population. If this image was too irrational to enjoy favor for long, it was nevertheless a staple of the war era. . . .

As the twenties rolled on, the image of Germany in defeat came in part to supplant the familiar stereotypes of the war years. With the Kaiser and his military minions cast down from high places, a new sympathy arose, dictated by the struggles of the Weimar Republic. The martial image became softened and blurred. It remained to be seen if it could be erased. . . .

According to film, Germany was to all intents and purposes the only enemy America faced in World War I. As such, she was vilified from her Kaiser to her lowest peasant soldier during the war years. The German image of militarism, although it moved through various permutations with monarchism, aristocracy, and modern dictatorship, never softened on the American screen. It simply acquired the glossy sophistication of menacing decadence. For a period between the wars, the German people were viewed more as victims than as perpetrators of the war. But the coming of a new and greater conflict again erased any differences between rulers and ruled.

The comparison which comes most readily to mind is that with film's treatment of Russian communism in the decade following 1945. Communism was analyzed by many American films of the period as monolithic, power-hungry, and duplicitous to a fault. The sexual rapacity of the German menace, interestingly enough, tended to be transmuted into an intellectual seduction of idealistic young men (witness *Conspirator* and *My Son John*). At any rate, these later films are an indication that the strong stereotypes of the movie screen do not necessarily require the impetus of a shooting war.

These simple and often repeated images of Germany and of German life have left a residue of stereotypes which persist today in both motion pictures and television. It is difficult to estimate how much these films of World War I altered American views of Germany. It is sufficient to say that, taken as a whole, they did nothing to improve the image and a great deal to distort and defame it. As a vehicle for promoting international understanding, something fondly dreamed of by early supporters of the motion picture, the American film in this regard must be rated a conspicuous failure. . . .

We ourselves: the image of the home front

In its efforts to put the war on film, the American motion picture industry did not neglect the people at home. The perfection of the doughboy in performing his duty by defending his flag and capturing or killing Germans was duplicated by the folks he left behind. The call for patriotic sacrifice extended far beyond the Ardennes; it sounded in stateside training camps, public rallies, and in bond drives. The call crossed the doorstep of American homes and filtered into the commonalities of family life. The films that trumpeted forth the summons to participate reflected "reality" to the extent that they were both spurred on by the national war effort and sought to subsume the entire populace in that effort. They provided a firm index to the attitudes and ideals of a home front at war.

Many films issued during 1915–1917 had pressured American audiences to dedicate themselves to strengthening the country's defenses. One example from the many concerned the Triangle Film Corporation, which decreed that advertising for its production *The Flying Torpedo* be built around "preparedness" rather than "war features." The picture dealt with an invention which repelled an unnamed invader of the Pacific Coast in 1921. Triangle attacked the "peace-at-any-price man" and suggested that *The Flying Torpedo* could give exhibitors a chance to declare "Patriotism Week" at their theaters. According to the company, the government cooperated wholeheartedly in the promotion of the film by establishing recruiting stations in movie houses, lending actual torpedoes for exhibition, and arranging patriotic parades.[8] Here, as in so many other instances, films by offering their version of "reality" actually generated it.

By 1917, audiences were used to cinematic appeals to their loyalty, patriotism, and spirit of self-sacrifice. With the coming of the crisis, fully as much attention was paid to the home front as to the boys overseas. Not surprisingly, almost all of the films that created an image of the home front were produced in the years 1917–1919. As the external threat vanished, so too did the image invented to combat that threat. American attitudes turned inward upon the nation itself afford an opportunity to study through film the sacred ideals of a country at war. These ideals, while not necessarily accurate, were nonetheless so widespread on film as to indicate their popular acceptance.

Essential to the image was the notion of the value of hard work for the cause. No one was exempt from demands upon his devotion. The final title of *America's Answer* was addressed to home audiences and congratulated them on the fruits of their labor that they had just seen transmogrified on screen into mighty weapons of war. Both the government and private producers poured out miles of film destined for domestic consumption which showed the nation flexing its industrial muscles. . . .

Everyone was encouraged to "do his bit" by the film industry. From babes in arms to octogenarians, from fey dress designers to the most manly exemplars of democratic virtue, all were included in a vast consensus vis-à-vis the purpose of the war. Films of the home front tried to fasten a unity of purpose onto one of the most heterogenous of nations, and to a considerable extent they were successful. Their success, that is, their continuance as economic products, reflected an audience acquiescence in both wartime goals and patriotic ideals. The crisis of war seemed compelling enough for the cinema to insist that no one be allowed to shirk the cause of the moment. Devotion to the central aim of winning the war was rewarded; deviation from this goal was punished. The long months of preparedness advocation reached fruition in these pictures of domestic America at war. . . .

Certainly these pictures of the home front projected an image which was sharp and clear. Most importantly, everyone was expected to support the cause. For those who did not, there remained the choice of reform or of universal execration. The cardinal sin was the refusal to be involved—the reason for refusal was irrelevant. In the lexicon of the film world, pacifism was synonymous with cowardice. Any deviation from the norm was considered criminal in both a moral and legal sense. Any punishment suited such trespasses, the harsher the better. In this regard the motion picture industry proved itself to be perhaps the most intolerant of the mass media, none of which won medals for the dispassionate relaying of information or attitudes.

It was significant that the motion picture image of the home front was all-inclusive. Film synthesized the national will to fight in simple and well-defined terms. Continued audience toleration of such trite themes indicated a strong national consensus in favor of the cinema's version of "reality." Since the synthesis included both sexes, all ages, and virtually every important ethnic group (even, at times, the German-Americans), deviancy tended to stand out. The solidarity of the home front was composed of a wall of celluloid armor reinforced by the sense of external crisis. The crisis was permitted to become internal as well, both because dramatic convention demanded it and because of the notion that the depiction of skulduggery close to home would help to close the ranks even more. . . .

Through its movie cameras, the American public saw itself successfully resisting all onslaughts on its domestic riches. German agents, no matter how sly their plans or how nefarious their purposes, invariably came to grief when confronted by staunch heroes and heroines. The plots of films showing the dedicated defense of brilliant inventions, munitions plants, shipyards, naval bases, mines, and lumber camps were more than dramatic clichés. They showed those items Americans regarded as most necessary to the waging of the war. If people were expendable (unless they happened to be the leading man or leading lady), things were not.

This accent on materialism comes as no surprise. But the combinations of materialism and idealism displayed in these pictures of the home front illuminated two contrasting facets of the American character which seem to fuse successfully only in time of war. Ideals could be maintained at a fever pitch only by making the threat immediate, and this could be done only by placing the enemy in the very laps of the folks at home. For a time, it must have seemed that there were more Germans operating in the United States than in France. . . .

As the tides of crisis receded, the image of the home front dissolved. The crystal clear likeness of the screen version of wartime domestic life vanished overnight. It would not be seen again for two decades. Then, another international menace would give it new life within a different pattern.

At rare intervals in the interwar period pictures were released which included aspects of domestic America at war. But their plots were varied, their box-office success limited, and their concern for weathering a crisis already past was nil. A Belgian refugee unconvincingly prated about self-sacrifice to the home folks in *The Charmer*, shown in 1925. Three years later appeared *A Ship Comes In*, the sentimental story of an immigrant whose son lost his life in the war. Its tone was more that of its contemporary *Four Sons* than of any wartime film.

The following decade produced *Private Jones*, whose acerbic views of the domestic military establishment owed more to Depression bitterness than to a sense of historical actuality. An escape in another direction was provided by *Rendezvous*, a picture that gave the *coup de grâce* to the international menace. *Rendezvous* boasted deft and breezy performances by William Powell and Rosalind Russell, Powell as a newspaperman turned cryptographer-lieutenant and Miss Russell as a suffragist. Even the Germans almost faded from the picture; the "bad guys" out to break Washington's codes were scripted as "Marshovians."[9] There was no atmosphere of crisis as the stars went through their paces, only the witty nonchalance of a film which knew it could well afford an attitude of *savoir faire*.

The urgency underlying the image of the home front had vanished long before *Rendezvous* appeared. The pictures that made up the image suggested that a great majority of the American public were both rapid and efficient in closing ranks behind the war effort. Excluded from the domestic consensus were all enemy aliens, most German-Americans, and anyone who did not register wholehearted support for America's war aims. The only explicit exception to this attitude did not appear until 1933, when *Ever in My Heart* presented sympathetically the plight of a naturalized German professor and his American wife. This film weakened its argument, however, by having the professor become a German spy on the western front.

In addition these films, most of which have long since crumbled into celluloid rubble, provided America with a daguerrotype of an ethical system which rapidly was vanishing. The simplistic solutions to internal problems, the caricatures of the slacker, the coward, and the villainous knave, the rewards of political right-thinking and the punishments of ideological agnosticism—all these harked back to a calmer, more measured pace of life. Even as the nation careened into the problems and responsibilities of the twentieth century, its motion picture industry disseminated, for all its heroics and dramatics, wistful attempts to touch the past. It was a past freighted with materialism as well as idealism, but it was a useful past. It was a point of reference from which to repel the spies, saboteurs, and double-agents whom dramatic convention demanded must populate the country.

Civilian life remained the backbone of the democracy. Defense of country began at home, not in France. For the young gentlemen who fought valiantly on foreign fields, the motion picture had only praise and adulation. But the task was no less arduous or demanding for those who stayed at home. The film played its wartime part in internalizing the national will and purpose. It did its job in simple and universal terms and, since no opposition was allowed to appear, its efforts must be judged an unqualified success . . .

War and women

"War is a man's business," bitterly remarked the female principal of *The Story of Vernon and Irene Castle*. "Women only do what they're told."[10] Indeed, the common tendency of most cultures is to blot out female roles in time of crisis. Over and over again, cinematic war was presented as the aggregate of male experience. Women were present, of course, but they were there to be worshipped, fought over, defended, or violated. Women were excluded from the final camaraderie that made the threat of death the supreme male adventure. Thus the battling Quirt and Flagg, arms about each other, left their girl and struggled toward the front at the end of *What Price Glory*? The young protagonists of *Wings* were bound together by their common background and the romance of aerial war. And the two *Dawn Patrols*, with their depiction of lasting friendship in the face of almost certain death, remain the classic examples of the persistence of male bonding in crisis.

The friendship, loyalty, and devotion among men provided the staple for dozens of war plots. The test of manhood was not how one behaved toward the opposite sex, but toward one's brothers. The measure of maleness was taken from the relationship which helped to define the friend or the antagonist—not the mother, wife, or sweetheart. Only the rarest films, such as *All Quiet on the Western Front*, escaped this convention. As Karel Reisz perceptively has pointed out, the realistic depiction of death as a meaningless finality rather than a glorious finale tended to make men "break faith with (their) innate instinct of brotherhood."[11]

The traditional role of women in war was one which, for lack of a better term, may be defined as "inspirational passivity." Anthropologist Lionel Tiger has observed that under emotional stress, a community will allow its males to assume the most significant roles. "Adult males and females seeking defense from without or the maintenance of peace and order within respond positively to appropriate males and negatively to virtually all females."[12] Women might be exemplary, but they were seldom complete models for wartime heroism. Nevertheless, they provided males with reasons both for fighting and for fighting like gentlemen. This impossible ideal remained a rallying point from where the war could be viewed in the best possible terms until it was erased by the cynicism of the twenties. The country went to war with women in its hip pocket. . . .

Thus most women shared the male view of women as "natural pacifists," yet they also shared the militant sense of duty and the fervent idealism that animated their male counterparts. It is debatable whether the postwar world saw a reduction in their aroused militancy. With feminism at its "moral pinnacle" in 1920, all opposition seemed overcome. Yet women, once granted a place in public life, were not spectacularly different from men in their opinions on military issues. Jane Addams, for one, was to regret deeply the fact that many female members of Congress enthusiastically supported increased military appropriations.[13] The advances of women in the interwar period can be measured: as an increase in percentage of the labor force, as a small but growing increment in the professions, and in the increased divorce rate. But true feminine autonomy, as the sixties seem to have demonstrated, remained a will-o'-the-wisp.

The motion picture played an integral part in presenting women first in their traditional wartime role and then, as scenarists stretched for dramatic effect, as active participants in the conflict. It is to the movies, as much as to any other medium, that Americans owed the new vision of the partly emancipated woman. If she was not yet sexually free, she was divested of crinolines and scented handkerchiefs. While she was not yet "Rosie the Riveter" of World War II fame, she nevertheless could play a central role in the war effort. War on film was still a "man's business," but some women were losing their passivity and emerging as compatriots in the cause. The fact that women began to serve as adjuncts to a game formerly and exclusively male is one firm index of America's passage into the twentieth century. . . .

The most unwavering image of women in war films was that of the mother. If at times she grieved over her lost soldier boy, her role also was interlaced with the idealization of motherhood as a biological sanctification of the national spirit. Mothers, in fact, ran children a close second in the American lexicon of much-indulged ideal types. The country that could give the world Mother's Day (in 1907) was fully capable of stereotyping its movie Moms to the point of nausea.

Originally, mothers were linked with the fatherland-nation for which they bore sons to fight. Their fertility was sacred and their gentle saintliness revered. But this concept was more European than American. Feminist leaders in the United States tended to emotionalize the mother-child relationship instead of bowing proudly to Mars in the name of national service. Thus Alice Stone Blackwell reacted against the war in Europe by pleading for the "wishes of the mothers" to be heard.[14] In the scale of pacifism versus patriotism, the maternal instinct became doubly utilitarian.

It was as preachers of pacifism that women first reached America's wartime audiences. The culminating and the most sensational film of this kind was Lewis J. Selznick's War Brides, produced in 1916 and starring the famous tragedienne Alla Nazimova. Selznick paid his star $1,000 a day for thirty days and figured it was worth it; the picture grossed $300,000. Nazimova's hysterionics were perfectly suited to her role of a peasant wife rebelling against a mythical government's edict to marry and breed children for the army. She committed suicide upon hearing the King declare that war was perpetual. In retaliation, the nation's women took a page from Lysistrata and vowed to produce no more children until war was outlawed. War Brides was hysterically emotional and generated much debate, but it was rapidly withdrawn from circulation after America declared war.

War's aftermath tended to tone down the hysterical side of the maternal nature, leaving a residue of grief illumined by an honorable sense of duty. Never did the depiction of the mother, regardless of her nationality, slip from this mold. As the hero of The Big Parade went off to war, his mother cried; when he returned minus a leg, she was there to comfort him. The mother of the aviator in *Wings* who did not survive nobly chose to blame "war" rather than any individual for her son's death. And of course *Four Sons* pulled out all the stops, idealizing the mother's role in wartime to the absolute limit. Mother Bernle moved through John Ford's picture sustained by simple faith, able to endure the cruelest shocks for the sake of a happy ending. It was enough for most viewers that the film was a "simple story of mother love," with the aged heroine displaying the "fortitude of a true mother."[15]

With the thirties the portrayal of mothers was darkened by bitterness, but Mom remained a symbol of war's tragedy. Never did she put pacifism before patriotism to become an active opponent of military service. Thus young Paul's mother in *All Quiet on the Western Front* was oblivious to issues of state and concerned only with her son's safety and comfort. *Beyond Victory* showed the mother of a farm lad verbally resisting his enlistment, but doing nothing more. Sexual differentiation was displayed in *Broken Lullaby*, where German mothers softly mourned their sons while a German father was outraged by his boy's needless death. Some films made a maudlin spectacle of a mother's loss, as did *Pilgrimage*, which followed the journey of a Gold Star Mother to France to visit her son's grave. . . .

War clearly was the antithesis of motherhood. *Cavalcade* indicated that the use of the mother as a positive national symbol, never very strong in the United States, had vanished from the nation's screens. This may be seen as a mark of national maturity, the sign of a willingness to confront war through the spectacles of realism rather than idealism. "Has it ever occurred to you that there are women in the world who are going to become mothers?" queried the heroine of *The World Moves On*. "And you tell me the world is just getting ready to go to war again."[16] Although mothers continued to be shown as pacifists right up through *The Ramparts We Watch* and *Sergeant York*, they were more the emotional and sentimental counterweights to an unwelcome task that had to be done rather than vigorous proponents of peace at any price.

Having begun as the constant and patriotic companions-in-spirit of the male warrior, young American women moved rapidly into war-related occupations such as nursing and spying. The role of women in modern war was given a certain visual immediacy by these unrealistic films. In reality most American women did not capture spies, conduct bedroom acrobatics in the name of patriotism, or gun down Huns in the trenches. The dull routine of wartime factory work earned only a few documentary treatments during the war itself. Most of middle- and lower-class American womanhood remained immersed in home and family for the duration, an immersion that drowned the fires of wartime dramatics. Because of this, the screen's portrayal of women in war has an unreality perhaps greater than any other series of images discussed here. This unreality mirrors the national uncertainty over the increasing complexity of feminist issues in a society which was engaged in redefining a significant part of its moral code.

Hence the marked difference in the cinematic view of distinct feminine roles. It is important to note the sharp schism between the view of mothers in war and the view of younger (and thus romantically eligible) ladies. Where the mother worried, the girl encouraged; the loss belonged to the mother, the happy ending to the girl. While motherhood remained corseted in the bonds of Victorian conventionality, America's young women were striking out on new paths. . . .

If cinematic war was man's business, it was woman's opportunity. While her role as a mother bound her to home, family, and the genteel emotions associated with those relationships, she was able to find a more satisfactory ideal self as a wife and sweetheart. Movie portrayals of damsels battling German rapists dressing picturesquely modest war wounds, and trailing spies were a distinct departure from the vision of Grover Cleveland and his generation. The visual presentation of women in war spread the notion of increased feminine potential throughout the country.

Yet women never could shed the essence of their femininity. They might fire guns, wrestle saboteurs, and play with bombs, but they never achieved independence. As the turmoil of war subsided, receding first into revered memory and then into a dim past, females continued to move through the cinema conflict in dime-novel stories of tragedy. They were consistent symbols of the goodness that had vanished from a world at war. Not for them was the action-filled environment in which their elder sisters had reveled. They needed only a man to fulfill themselves. Even Lenin's girl secretary in British Agent finally avowed she was "too much of a woman" to be a Soviet patriot and an idealist. "You can't let political opinions come between us," pleaded her British lover[17]—and she didn't. Her story made a fitting epitaph. . . .

War and humor

Comedies using World War I as backdrop may seem at first glance to be misplaced in time and space. Yet their humor seldom was derived from the war itself. These films retained most of the comic mechanisms found in standard slapstick comedies or polite drawing room farces. Comic art is far more rewarding in terms of social analysis than is tragic art.[18] War comedies in fact contained social and intellectual themes that may be examined in the context of comic art. By asking the question "What was so funny about the war?" we may not arrive at answers to why the war was so funny, but we may achieve some idea of why Americans laughed.

In essence, the comedies of World War I used military "comic heroes" to explore questions of authority within the democratic system. In this guise, clowns in uniform commented endlessly on all of American society. That society, in spite of the boast and brag of its egalitarian tradition, has been like any other society a hierarchy of superiors, inferiors, and equals. Comedy has been called that "sanctioned doubt" which allows the claims of superiors to be deflated and the preposterous behavior of inferiors and equals to be reassuring.[19] In a sense, the society that denies itself comic art operates on artificial social planes. Comedy, while doubting, can close the gap between social theory and social practice by bestowing implicit approval on hierarchical social structures.

Most of the producers of these comedies probably never considered authority to be a central issue in the success of their films. Their comic heroes were clowns who specialized in exposing social vices to movie audiences who were both well aware that the vices existed and in agreement as to the need for exposure. Although they also were used to reject as well as support authority, the screen comedians who dueled against the authoritarianism of military life usually were harmless "safety valves" for moviegoers unable or unwilling to confront the growing bureaucratic impersonality of the twentieth century. In most of the war comedies authority received many blows to its pride and dignity, but it was never overturned. The comedies discussed in this chapter betrayed an uneasiness about military authority, a fear that the stern social gradations of uniformed life might be fastening themselves upon the rest of society. In upholding the shadow if not the substance of the egalitarian dream, these films were evidence that many Americans felt the dream threatened by forces over which they had no control.

In supporting authority, then, war comedies like other comedies made whatever threatened the social order appear ridiculous. In this way moviegoers could purge themselves of social tension while the actual hierarchy remained unscathed. Many of the pictures in this chapter thus may be described as "conservative," in the sense they advocated no social change. Institutions remained imperturbable under comic assault. If an individual soldier was a gross incompetent, the army remained the ideal of patriotic militancy.

All this seems quite removed from the war itself. In fact, producers never attempted what today would be called a "black comedy"—the examination of war's horror, futility, and absurdity through the devices of comic art. It would take a Hiroshima to produce a *Dr. Strangelove*. For this reason, comedies of World War I seldom ventured into the trenches, and if they got there the war was reshaped to fit comic routines, not vice versa. Instead, the comedies usually took place behind the lines or in training camps. This was an indication that the halo of serious purpose cast its aura around the battlefield itself, and that the fighting still was seen as part of a sacred cause well after the war had ended.

True to national ideals, the American comic hero was raffishly proletarian. Almost inevitably, in the military social structure, he was an enlisted man, one who blithely ignored the etiquette of military convention to comment endlessly on the foibles of his superiors, from corporals to generals. He at times was an example of the "comedy of reason," an ironic bird of discord piping notes that cast doubt on the social order. Thus a select few of the war comedies rose above their conservative function to offer the merest suggestion of the need for social change. The proletarian comic hero could more often play the fool, reassuring audiences by his blunders. Neither comic mode contained a hint of social revolution, which was the hallmark of a type of comic art not yet adapted to the screen.

Comedy plays an innately social function as a salve to soothe society's wounds. Democracies rightly value it among the most precious of their treasures, since it is so necessary to explain the incongruities which inevitably appear in professedly egalitarian social systems. Hugh Dalziel Duncan has explained it thus:

> We learn in comedy that the virtues of superiors are not so great after all, the humility and loyalty of inferiors are not without limits, and that friends and peers sometimes deceive us. But guilt lightens in laughter as I admit that if they are rascals, so too am I. We begin by laughing at others only to end by laughing at ourselves. The strain of rigid conventions, of majestic ideals, of deep loyalties, is lessened, for now they are open to examination. They can be questioned, their absurdities can be made plain. Now that we can openly express our vices, there is hope for correction. At least we now have company in misery; we are no longer alone and can take heart for another try. For when all is said and done, what do we have but each other? So long as we can act together we have all the good there is in life.[20]

There have been many attempts to explain film humor, but since nothing renders comedy less humorous than the explanation of it, this chapter does not attempt to analyze why some war comedies were funny and some were not. The central issue instead is the question of how authority is regarded by a democratic society. Even the crudest slapstick humor was not as far removed from this issue as one might think. When Mack Sennett exulted that "*Of course* comedy is a satire on the human race," he was talking about authority. "Our specialty was exasperated dignity and the discombombulation of authority," he remembered. "We whaled the daylights out of everything in sight with our bed slats, and we had fun doing it."[21]

Superficially, movie clowns provided an escape from everyday concerns. As early as 1914, a traveler in Europe reported a great demand for film comedies as an antedote to the horrors of war.[22] "Comedy is the thing," another observer noted two years later. "The soldier wants his thoughts to be taken away from the serious work ahead of him."[23] But the sloppy incompetence of most movie clowns went further than this, registering deeply with the American spirit. In their guise as pseudo-warriors, these funny-men took upon themselves the fear of not measuring up to the demands of a military organization caught up in a world war. They thus served as comic scapegoats for the society at large.

The comedies of World War I reflected a nervousness over the inadequacies of American social organization and the fear that these inadequacies were increasing rather than decreasing. The military was seen as a microcosm of society as a whole. Its well-ordered ranks, its unquestioning obedience to higher authority, and its meticulous attention to trivial details were aspects made for parody, just as they were uncomfortable reminders that the snake of social class continued to slither about in an egalitarian Eden. . . .

So the war survived attempts to make it funny. Even though the contrived screen humor presented to American audiences was comic distortion, the purpose of the nation's comic art went beyond a few moments of illusionary amusement. Democratic comedy, in fact, proved to be a bulwark of the egalitarian dream. Invariably, America's comic war heroes were "little men"—average guys with no distinguishing characteristics, save perhaps their ethnic personalities and their ability to become entangled in absurd situations. Keaton's aristocratic "Elmer Stuyvesant" in *Doughboys* was an exception which proved the rule. Although the nation's movie clowns were not proletarians in the sense political theorists might use the term, it is fair to describe them as such because of their role as mouth-pieces for depicting concern over and exasperation with authority and the claims of social class.

War comedies did not view the war as a laughing matter. The Great Crusade had not been conducted to be defamed by a few pies in the face or a well-placed kick in the rear. For this reason, no satires of the war itself—of its brutality, insanity, and meaninglessness—were forthcoming. *Shoulder Arms* was a noble attempt, made more so by the fact that it was issued while the war still raged, but it did not directly address itself to the aims and methods of the conflict. Either America's screen comic art was incapable of such a satire, or American audiences were not yet ready to see sacred ideals and institutions seriously challenged through the use of humor. The first possibility was unlikely, given men with the universal comic wisdom of Chaplin and Keaton. More probably, the nonexistence of true war comedies was absent proof of the nation's tendency to regard its conduct of the war as irreproachable.

What audiences preferred, then, were comedies with the ingredients of war in them. Uniforms, guns, drill sergeants, and now and then a little shellfire—these were sufficient to provide the illusion that somewhere, just off screen, a real war was taking place. In fact, what was taking place was the age-old ridicule of authority, placed in an ideal military setting. War humor attacked the pernicious arrogance of the authoritarian mind with every ego-deflating weapon at the hands of its proletarian clowns. In their average comic heroes, Americans found surrogates who satisfactorily pricked balloons of hot air which theoretically had no place among the cool breezes of a democracy.

But screen comedy held no final rebuttal for the inchoate forces which were slowly coalescing into The Lonely Crowd. Humor could irritate its main target; it might even delay the growth of institutionalized authoritarianism, but it could never completely quash it. Nor was this its primary purpose. Because the country's war comedies could never shake the sacred shackles of national institutions, they never seriously challenged authority. The recruits with two left feet, the white-toothed singing doughboys, and the stentorian topkicks were all permanent enlistees in a hopeless war, one that had little to do with World War I.

Notes

1   Unidentified clipping, folder, AMPAS.
2   These arguments are distilled from Clara Eva Schieber, "The Transformation of American Sentiment Towards Germany, 1870–1914," *Journal of International Relations* (July 1921): 50–74.
3   Carl Wittke, *German-Americans and the World War*, Ohio Historical Collections, vol. 5 (Columbus Ohio State Archeological and Historical Society, 1936).
4   *Civilization*, MOMA; quotation is from the film. The kingdom was identified, perhaps by a professional Welsh-baiter, as that of "Wredpryd."
5   *Moving Picture World*, September 28, 1918, p. 1922; see also *Motion Picture News*, August 17, 1918, p. 993.
6   *Moving Picture World*, June 22, 1918, p. 1762.
7   *Liberty Loan – National Association of the Motion Picture Industry*, LC; quotation is from the film.
8   *The Triangle*, March 4, 1916, pp. 1 ff.
9   Bella Spewack, Samuel Spewack, P.J. Wolfson, and George Oppenheimer, "Rendezvous," script ("Revised Dialog Cutting Continuity"), December 31, 1935, NYPL (LC).
10   Richard Sherman, Oscar Hammerstein II, and Dorothy Yost, "The Story of Vernon and Irene Castle," script ("Final"), December 16, 1938, with changes dated January 4, 10, 1939, p. 105 AMPAS.
11   Reisz, "Milestone and War," p. 13.
12   Lionel Tiger, *Men in Groups* (New York: Vintage Books, 1970), pp. 104–11.
13   A good statement of duty overriding pacifism is an unsigned editorial in *The General Federation of Women's Clubs Magazine*, June 1917, quoted in ibid., pp. 188–89. See also pp. 89, 92. Representative Jeannette Rankin of Montana, who voted against American involvement in both World Wars, was a much-publicized exception to the less well-known general voting pattern of women legislators.
14   Quoted in Kraditor, *Up from the Pedestal*, p. 287.
15   "*Four Sons* Wins Photoplay Medal For Last Year," *The Motion Picture*, December 1, 1929, p. 7; *National Board of Review Magazine*, March, 1928, p. 11.
16   Script, "The World Moves On," pp. 75–76.
17   *British Agent*, WCTR; quotations are from the film.
18   Duncan, *Communication and Social Order*, p. 438. The framework of this chapter is built around Duncan's insights into the nature of comic art.

19 Duncan, *Symbols in Society*, p. 60.

20 Duncan, *Communication and Social Order*, pp. 402–3.

21 Mack Sennett, *King of Comedy* (Garden City, N.Y.: Doubleday and Company, Inc., 1954), p. 90. Emphasis in original.

22 *The New York Times*, December 15, 1914, p. 13.

23 Dench, "Following the Movies to the Firing-Line and Back," 60.

War and Cinema: Interpreting the Relationship

11

PIERRE SORLIN

. . . . There are events that we experience immediately and events that we cannot apprehend but indirectly. When we deal with practical things, food or clothes, the words we use have a well-shaped significance but there is a fringe of meaning around other notions which is more akin to mental images or impressions than to defined concepts. Such is the case of "war". This is a highly imprecise term for which nobody has yet given a satisfactory definition. Let us begin by settling for what common sense tells: war is a conflict involving physical violence among nations, tribes or other large groups of people. Our awareness of what "war" is and of what any specific war was in the past century is closely linked to records which were made then. But, before photography, how was it possible to conceive of war in countries where most men and women had never witnessed an actual conflict? Some regions were regularly devastated but large portions of the world experienced no fighting for more than a century. Between the defeat of Bonnie Prince Charles (1745) and 1914, Britain waged dozens of battles but soldiers constituted less than 1% of the population and spent much more time in barracks than on battlefields. Information about fighting came from soldiers returning from the front, from books and magazines, from drawings and paintings. Hand-made illustrations can tell a lot but they are often short on facts. Goya's depiction of the Napoleonic war in Spain had a tremendous impact on imaginations all throughout Europe during the nineteenth century. Few people would dispute their ability to convey the atrocity of a merciless conflict but Goya tells us little about the actuality of war. Despite the invention of photography, the most popular kind of picture up to the end of the nineteenth century was still the cheap wood-engraving. Thousands of them, widely diffused in Europe, represented the wars fought during that period. Following very old patterns, these stereotyped fictions were more aligned to an earlier period than to their own. The dominant model was that of hand-to-hand fighting; gallant soldiers with bayonets confronted other soldiers: unreal, childish, terrifying and archaic.

I believe, where war is concerned, that something changed dramatically with the invention of the cinema. By 1914, city dwellers were used to attending regularly picture-houses all over the world; travelling shows went through most countries offering one-hour programmes consisting of news, documentaries and short stories. Films enabled spectators to see an imitation of life, to observe, for instance, an artillery fire or an infantry attack.

Cinema, as it appeared at the end of the nineteenth century, belongs to the past; it is already an historical subject as well as form of comprehending reality. Peter Rollins argues that the Gulf War was the first true television war since, for the first time, events were broadcast while they were occurring. In my view, the most important aspect of television is not its immediacy, but the fact that it reaches, simultaneously, millions of viewers. During the Vietnam War, there was a gap between the event and when it was seen, but Americans could still watch the same pictures at the same time. In this respect, cinema and television are two totally different media. When, at the end of the 1960s, movie producing companies stopped making newsreels, leaving visual information to television, the relationship between the spectator and the moving image was deeply transformed. When speaking of filmed information, we must remember that the newsreels presented in large cities at the beginning of a month reached the small towns only at the end of the month. Consequently, journalists were obliged to choose topics of general interest and omitted more current issues. Newsreels were a visual compliment to news already diffused by the press and radio which means that they were, in a certain sense, disassociated from the actuality of the situation. Newsreels cannot really be compared to television news.

A second point of considerable importance, at least for historians, is that, to a large extent, cinema was merely an extension of photography. There is no reason to marvel at the quick expansion of the new medium; it occurred because photographs encouraged people to become interested in analogous images. Photography had existed for a long time but expensive equipment restricted it to the well-to-do. Photographers were either rich or professionals most often asked to portray politicians and artists. The collotype process invented in 1890 made it possible to reproduce negatives in massive numbers. The press took advantage of this; the first decade of the twentieth century created a new journalistic category, illustrated reporting. There was also a profusion of postcards: on the eve of the First World War, some 600,000,000 illustrated cards were printed and sold every year in Britain. These types of pictures cannot be observed in isolation. Concentrating on films exclusively would be especially misleading for photography, painting and cinema overlapped each other. Since the beginning of the present century, life has been reflected in pictures and, however old we are, we were all born in societies where people's actions were recreated for them on the screen. Films are not only a mirror of what is permanently happening, they show us what we must know, they contribute in moulding our vision and telling us what our behaviour should be. Images tell us something about our surroundings and play a preeminent part in defining what we are.

Film was but one of the new images; right from the start, actuality filmmakers were hampered by the problems that photographers had previously faced. War correspondents [1] and photographers had been sent to various battlefields since 1856, but they had roughed it, they had seldom been allowed to visit the war zone and many of them had simply given up. Video equipment, as used today, is so light, and adapts so well to darkness, that it can operate virtually everywhere. Photographic or cinematographic equipment was heavy, cumbersome and costly; it was a burden for the cameraman, and later for the sound technician to bring equipment to where the action was. Good, efficient technicians were not easily replaced; furthermore, in the case of death, production studios might be liable for enormous damages. As a consequence, cameramen tended to film scenes which did not present particular difficulties. This resulted in the emergence of a few recurring patterns. There is no shortage of pictures about the conflicts of the second half of the nineteenth century, but we must look at them skeptically. Far from displacing the role of art and trying to catch "the real" directly, photography enhanced the appearance of people. Pictures of the time are thus primarily evidence not of how soldiers behaved but of what photographers were able to take.

The iconography of war, 1900

The iconography of war, *circa* 1900, can be divided into three main categories:

A. *Parades, gatherings, boardings and landings, military reviews, and farewells.* The classic picture is taken slightly from above, often from the roof of a warehouse. The troops are framed in the middle, with horse-soldiers or policemen delineating a square separating the civilians from the army. Such scenes look rather trivial; we need a caption to understand that the mounted rifles we see marching through the streets are about to leave for a far-away expedition.

B. *Fakes.* Take a photograph made in 1900, *Rescue of a Wounded Gunner*. It is so well framed, the horseman who assists his mate looks so quiet that it cannot be anything but a re-enactment. It is what Henry Luce later termed "fakery in allegiance to truth". But, while detecting what has been restaged, we must not be too critical. By 1900 most periodicals were still illustrated with drawings. A great many of the thousands of postcards inspired by contemporary wars were hand-made pictures which tried to look like snapshots and even, at times, imitated the fuzziness or the dots of a photograph. They showed scenes which could not be observed, *Routed: Boers retreating* or *The imperial Light Horse at Waggon Hill*, a dramatic picture of a small crew of exhausted privates, some of them badly wounded, resisting a final attack.

C. *"Authentic" documents*—with the caveat that it is hard to tell a forgery, arranged by the photographer with the help of the army, from a picture taken after an army spokesman has carefully chosen what could be photographed. All too often soldiers work, or look at the viewer so persuasively that it is tempting to think they have been chosen to make us believe that everything is under control.[2]

Cinema was a younger sibling of photography. However, while equally biased, at the beginning of the present century, it introduced viewers to a new conception of war. It is this paradox that must be emphasized. In 1900, postcards, drawings and photographs representing some aspect of military life made the company the key operational unit. Of course small groups are better adapted to the limited space of a postcard than regiments or divisions. But we must also take into account military theory which, during the last third of the nineteenth century, reshaped itself by reference to the pattern of colonial relief. Before the beginning of the Ethiopian expedition, an Italian tactician, Alberto Guglielmotti, defined a new style of war, "in which soldiers, harassing the foe from all sides, with careful firing, hold up its advance".[3] Cinema recreated this doctrine, showing again and again the self-contained, self-sufficient unit as appropriate to modern war. It celebrated small crews heroically defending a position or professionals leaping forward. War in the mind— imaginary war—was represented as the sum of heroic actions carried out by handfuls of individuals.

The early decades of the twentieth century, the years of the armaments race, brought complications which tacticians had to take account of. Films are significant inasmuch as they reflect part of these transformations while simultaneously concealing them. In all European countries, a new theme emerged with the presentation of Navy or army manoeuvres. Some were dramatised, such as *Invasion of England*, from March 1909, showing the quick advance by car from Hastings to London. This imaginary war was entirely concentrated on the front line, and especially on infantry or cavalry charges. Nothing was shown of the delivery of ammunition; soldiers seemed to carry with them all what was needed. The pictures themselves, even without commentary, indicated a short conflict won within a few days. There was nothing about firepower, nothing about the function of railroads in bringing up troops quickly, to stop attacks. Little footage from the Russo-Japanese war of 1904–05 was shot and no lesson learned, at least from cinema coverage. There was a congruence between the ideas of officers and the practice of filmmakers in accepting the cult of the offensive. In August 1914 all the armies launched massive offensives which resulted in terrible losses. A better strategy would have been to let men attack individually. But, as films show, such was not the conception of what an attack ought to be. In July 1914 nobody could foresee what was about to happen. Who could even have described it? Military representations showed regiments advancing with fixed bayonets. How is it that this misrepresentation surfaced so quickly after 1900? There is no one answer but certainly films helped spread the dominant image of massed battle.

1914 marked the opening of what has often been called the second Thirty Years War, 1914–1945. Cinema was mature enough to cover the event. Two days after the invasion of Belgium, Pathé announced it had filmed the exodus of civilians and was about to show it to cinema audiences. All countries, including the most backward, such as Austro-Hungary and Russia, set up military film crews. Quantitatively, the amount of visual evidence of the war is gigantic and, from a technical point of view, most footage is excellent. However, we are not surprised to see that this material is tediously repetitive, mostly parades, long lines of prisoners, or tracking-shots of the seemingly inexhaustible build-up of supplies accumulated before offensives. A few shots deal with military actions but, when scrutinizing them, we sense that they were taken during a period of training or reenacted.

Television has accustomed us to watching a series about the First World War. If we look at film catalogues, we are surprised to find few documentaries on the same period. Fictional films are more numerous, but not if compared with the number of films about World War II. Here is another paradox: the war was extensively filmed, seldom screened.

The paradox is even more puzzling than might at first be imagined. Jay Winter[4] and Samuel Hynes[5] note that most visual or literary accounts of the First World War were produced more than 10 years after the Armistice. There were of course exceptions: *Under Fire* published by Henri Barbusse in 1916 or King Vidor's *The Big Parade* released in 1925 but, until the end of the 1920s, knowledge of the horrors of the war was a grim secret whose communication was delayed. A fundamental difference between the two World Wars, at least in Europe is that, with the exception of Portugal, Sweden and Switzerland—Spain had had its own ordeal—nobody was spared while, in 1914–18, millions of men fought on a few limited sectors without affecting the majority of the population. As the war dragged on, soldiers at the front became increasingly bitter about those at home who did not seem to care about what they were suffering. Robert Graves confessed that while on leave he "found serious conversations with my parents all but impossible". *Under Fire* is filled with hostile references to the Rear. One of the characters complains: "We are divided into two foreign countries, the Front where there are too many unhappy and the Rear where there are too many happy".[6] After 1918, ex-servicemen were reluctant to speak because they did not believe they would be understood. It is something that we can easily conceive since it is still our problem: is there a way of speaking of the unspeakable, of the Holocaust for instance? Actual experience cannot be literally recreated, no matter hard we try. What form should it take? Veterans could not talk; Samuel Hynes stresses the similarity, afterwards, of soldiers who had been at the Front: "The accounts are composed mainly of things all rather small-scale, all randomly disposed and all rendered without judgment or expressed emotion".[7] Emotion could not be recreated, let alone shown on the screen. "Why didn't you tell them?" Leslie Smith asked Robert Graves, who answered: "You couldn't. You can't communicate noise. Noise never stopped for a moment".[8] "The roaring chaos of the barrage", Eric J. Leed comments, "affected a kind of hypnotic condition that shattered any rational pattern of cause and effect. This state was often described in terms of a loss of coherence".[9] There was also the stench of rotten flesh, urine, dead rats, sweat and verminous clothing which announced the Front a mile away; there was the mud, moisture and dirt. A few filmmakers attempted to fill the screen with filth and dampness but there remained an unbridgeable gap between film and reality. Most of the war was endured as endless waiting. There were attacks, at times, but there were many more empty days spent waiting for food to arrive, for shells to fall and kill, for the time on the front line to end. Cinema, until the 1960s, was a vehicle for narratives, a way of carrying fictitious characters from one place to another. The various "New Cinemas" have since introduced another conception of filmmaking more akin to the way we experiment the passing of life but that was not yet the case in the 1920s or 1930s. Every movie had, necessarily, its central character, from a group of comrades. Something had to happen—the spectator was taken toward an end which he expected whereas, on the Front, there was no predictable end except death.

There was, in short, no appropriate way of viewing a war which could not be represented. Yet paradoxically, an image of the war was created though it was felt by many people to be impossible. Some movies made the war a background for a plot set in a dugout (*Journey's End*) or in a prison camp (*Who Goes Next*, *Grand Illusion*). A handful of movies, *All Quiet on the Western Front* (USA, 1930), *Westfront 1918* (Germany, 1930), *The Wooden Crosses* (*Les Croix de Bois*, France, 1930), attempted to recreate the atmosphere of the Front. We have little evidence about the reactions of audiences but in the few cases where enquiries were made after the screenings we see that people attended in groups, veterans mixed with civilians, and that they came away deeply moved. This happened, I think, because those who had not been mobilized, but who had had one of their dearest killed, wounded or shocked wanted to "see" what had happened, to understand and at the same time to "participate". In his recent article on *The Battle of the Somme*, a documentary released in Britain after the failure of the long-awaited offensive which was meant to put an end to the war (July 1916), Roger Smither shows how anxious the British were to get "involved". After seeing *The Battle of the Somme*, Frances Stevenson, whose brother had been killed, wrote: "I am glad I went. I am glad I have seen the sort of thing our men have to go through". "It reminded me of what Paul's last hours were: I have often tried to imagine to myself what he went through, but now I know".[10] In many cases the screenings were ways of mourning collectively. The Front films were big hits and established a vision, a series of stereotypes endlessly reused to the present, to depict the First World War.

War photographs and the real world

What can we say about the relationship between photography and the actual world? A photograph is simultaneously reliable and deceiving. It is reliable because it is a reflection, a duplication of a fragment of our universe. It is deceiving because it isolates a portion of the continuous space we live in and freezes the flow of time. The images of war which emerged in the 1930s were neither true nor false; they were partial and limited. I call them "stereotypes" not because they lie but because they restrict the memory of war to a few recuring themes.

The first image is the trench. Of course trenches were a characteristic feature of the First World War, a defensive position which had seldom been used previously and was not systematically employed in subsequent conflicts. But, in many cases, the trench had an appearance of squalid improvisation, there was no parapet or sand bags or earth to protect the men from the enemy's fire and, sometimes, there was no trench at all. . . .

The repeated images of trenches are correct, but they are also incorrect. How can one film the men in their trenches without standing back from them? Characters must be clearly situated inside the framework of the picture so that spectators are led to believe that the trenches are quite wide and that soldiers could always hear each other. Trenches became symbols of another life, a hidden, subterranean life, opposed to the visible world of our homes, buildings, and monuments which stand above ground. Soldiers were underground beings.

The second image is a night patrol caught in barbed wire. Not an unlikely accident but one that men had learnt to avoid. Patrolling was a dangerous, organized operation but not necessarily fatal. Movies combine three cinematic devices: artificial lighting, close-ups of menacing barbed wire, plus the sound of human breath in an agonizing silence to create an impression of fear and despair. A good trick perhaps, but a trick nevertheless.

The third image is a denuded landscape with broken trunks, ruins, shell-holes and craters filled with water. This staggering view can be found in all photography archives but men could hardly see it because they had to lie down in holes or find shelter behind parapets. What soldiers could see was a restricted piece of ground shored up by branches and filled, in places, by dead rats, rations of food, discarded weapons and, sometimes, fragments of corpses. Above all there was the omnipresent mud that summer could not dry and which became a lake in September. It is possible to film the mud but one must, to make the take understandable, show a man walking knee-deep in slush or dirty water. In their trenches, soldiers could not move; they had to remain idle for hours, while dampness was seeping in from the ground.

A dominant pattern is also imaginary. It belongs more to the narrative. When the First World War films end, nobody has been spared. The characters introduced at the outset have been eliminated, one after the other; after the last has fallen the film continues on, showing upsetting images, taken at random by an anonymous camera. Compare the conclusion of First World War and Second World War movies. In the latter, someone, a friend, an officer, a comrade remembers: his companions, his men have been killed but that has not been in vain; their memory will survive. In First World War films nobody cares to tell what happened and there is no memory. The message is the more devastating for being delivered with no comment from the filmmakers. The emptiness of the shots give them an impact, an intensity that tends to overwhelm the spectator and to make us feel we have been caught up in some vast, impersonal, meaningless disaster.

Paul Fussell believes that the trauma of the Great War has moulded the self-consciousness of people belonging to belligerent countries.[11] War imagery supports and also qualifies his assumption. The stereotypes we have identified are forceful and weak, effective and fragile. Their strength can be seen in their periodic recurrence. Many decades after 1918 the same pictures, the same pattern, were reused by Kubrick (*Paths of Glory*, 1957), Monicelli (*La grande Guerra*, 1959), Losey (*King and Country*, 1964), Rosi (*Gli uomini contro*, 1970). However impressive they are, these pictures are unable to give us new understanding. Their verdicts are expressed in commonplaces as if the signs which allow us to identify the Great War had all been petrified. In pictures, the war has been turned to myth. It is like a Greek tragedy: we can describe the Great War again and again, we can create new characters and new circumstances but we can change neither the plot nor the signs which define the period. Complex films camouflage their background but, once one begins to look for it, simply repeat old images which cannot move us deeply since we have long been accustomed to them. Veterans' anguish is translated into a few visual formulas. . . .

The ambiguity of images

There is always an ambiguity in pictures which suggests a wide range of meanings. But, since ambiguity is also a part of our relationship to the social world, films may help us avoid clear-cut definitions and suggest more nuanced, less-definite interconnections among the data we try to observe. As historians, one of our tasks is to collect and interpret facts. Still none of us would reduce history to nothing but facts. Events cannot be understood unless they are returned to the context in which they happened. This context is partly factual (location, clothes, weapons) but it also includes elements which are not easily described in words. How is it possible to evoke the atmosphere in Europe at the time of the armaments race? It is necessary, if we want to understand the motivation of social action, to express pain, anguish or helplessness as well as hope or excitement. The Great War began in August 1914. The point is not only this fact, but the way people expected it, were told of it, understood it. Words such as "war", "fighting" "weapons" and "army" enable us to account for military situations. However, for contemporaries, for those who went through the Great War or the Korean War, these abstractions were related to clues that everybody, at the time, could identify. In dealing with a few cinematic representations of warfare I have tried to detect some of these images. In any society, besides written signs, we can identify a range of visual signs, of images, which document the hopes and fears of that group of people. Cinema is a language inasmuch as it enables us to communicate and send messages. What does humanity use language for? Simultaneously to make sense of the world which surrounds it and to conceal this world. Human beings cannot bear too much reality: hence the importance of euphemisms. We think we have gotten rid of them since we talk about sex overtly but reticence is obvious in other areas. Frankness and discretion are two systems of signs used to describe the same event. Films can reveal what is meant to be understood through euphemism, but only if we determine what is intended to be passed over in silence, that "real" war which is the quest of every historian and every cameraman.

Notes

1 The term "war correspondent" emerged during the American Civil War. "War film" appeared in 1897, less than two years after the first film was released, in the magazine *Animated Photography*. "War photography" came later, in 1907.

2 See the illustrations in THOMAS PAKENHAM (1979) *The Boer War* (London) where there is *no* picture of actual fighting.

3 *Vocabulario marino e militare* (1889).

4 *The Experience of World War I* (1989) (New York).

5 *A War Imagined: The First World War and English Culture* (1990) (London).

6 Many other references are to be found in PAUL FUSSELL (1991) *The Bloody Game. An Anthology of Modern War* (London). See also JOHN TERRAINE, *The Impact of War, 1914–1918* (1993 London) and JOHN GLOVER & JOHN SILKIN eds, (1991) *The Penguin Book of First World War Prose* (London).

7 Hynes A War Imagined, p. 423. This is confirmed by the testimonies collected by LYN MACDONALD (1983) in *Somme* (London).

8 Quoted in *The Listener*, 15 July 1971, p. 74.

9 *No Man's Land. Combat and Identity in World War One* (1979) (New York), p. 129.

10 "A Wonderful Idea of the Fighting": the question of fakes in "The Battle of the Somme" *Historical Journal of Film, Radio and Television*, (XIII, 2, 1993) p. 149.

11 *The Great War and Modern Memory* (1975) (New York).

PART THREE

THE APOTHEOSIS OF THE HOLLYWOOD WAR FILM

The essays in this section address how Hollywood war cinema became fully formed during and after World War II in movies about that conflict. Reworking institutional structures, viewing practices, and aesthetic and narrative strategies from the Great War as well as later modes of film production, war cinema grew more coherent in its on-screen articulations and more inclusive in its institutional reach. Motion pictures substantively shaped viewers' understanding of the morality and politics of this conflict and why it was being fought, but also influenced the meaning of war and its significance for Americans' self-understanding.

War cinema, as already indicated, involved much more than combat films. Productions with the war as theme or background but set on the homefront or elsewhere other than basic training or the battlefield proliferated before and especially after official U.S. entry into the conflict in 1941 (Schatz 1997; Doherty 1993). These included both narrative features and a wide range of other productions exhibited regularly as part of theatrical programs. Newsreels were thus a crucial source of information about faraway events; brief instructional films, so-called "Victory" shorts, explained issues of public concern from wartime conservation strategies to government taxation policy, and, most famously, the "Why We Fight" series offered justification for military action on various fronts. Even among features foregrounding conventional Hollywood fare —musicals, light romances, and comedies—that could otherwise be enjoyed as entertaining distractions from the life-and-death concerns of many filmgoers, the war often lingered unavoidably in the background.

Across these varied forms, Hollywood and its viewers together helped to shape what might be called the overall discursive experience of the war. The consolidation of existing storytelling practices and their deployment in characterizing contemporary events and political values relied on the sophistication of audiences familiar with these storytelling practices. Adapting existing narrative practices also suited the government's political aims of encouraging American unity and resolve while polarizing the conflict as between the Allies and the Axis powers. Through narratives about the battlefront and the homefront alike, cinema thus helped to position viewers not only relative to the current political environment but more broadly into a constructed realm of reassurance about timeless and empowering American values and, especially, the manifest destiny of the United States.

Proliferating linkages between government and media institutions coincided with the re-making of the citizen-spectator. Political and viewing positions both acceded to and pushed back against the patterned, often polarizing ways of seeing the rest of the world encouraged by many film productions. More practically, seeking to comprehend what was happening to loved ones in peril overseas and to reconcile the democratic values and mythologies of Hollywood and Washington with everyday realities, viewers played a crucial role in the contemporary consolidation of war cinema. Even as American society become more institutionalized, and institutions like the government and the film industry become more bureaucratic and intertwined, in other words, individuals remained more than passive viewers, consumers, or citizens. War cinema's ascendance during, and in the decade after, World War II is thus marked by the convergence of filmmaking practices, government and industry realignments, and active audiences.

The opening selection here, by Tom Schatz, describes the dual transition to wartime filmmaking from prewar conditions and from the widely-shared myths held over from World War I. In the second piece, Clayton R. Koppes and Gregory D. Black discuss the specific priorities employed by Hollywood and their newfound government collaborators (and regulators) for producing films to affirm and support the war effort. The third selection draws from Jeanine Basinger's influential book-length study by outlining the defining elements of the combat film genre and its "melting pot" platoon. The fourth piece, by Thomas Doherty, provides illustrative summaries of two historically important productions, *Sergeant York* and *Air Force*, that flesh out some of Basinger's general qualities but also link them directly to the historical entry of the United States, and Hollywood, into the war. Lary May's closing contribution discusses how narrative forms and priorities—namely of the conversion affirming American social values—can also be used to illuminate audience responses to the war effort more generally.

World War II and the Hollywood "War Film"

12

THOMAS SCHATZ

Prewar Hollywood and the changing movie marketplace

Though the Hollywood war film emerged virtually by government mandate after U.S. entry into the war, it's important to note that political and economic forces actually militated against war-film production in the late 1930s and early 1940s. As late as 1938–1939, with many overseas markets still open and isolationist sentiments at home still relatively strong, films criticizing fascism or advocating U.S. intervention in "foreign wars" were simply not good business. Hollywood did make occasional forays into war-related production in the late 1930s as conditions in Europe steadily worsened. The most notable of these, perhaps, was Warner Bros.' early-1939 release, *Confessions of a Nazi Spy*, a quasi-documentary thriller involving German espionage in the U.S. that well indicates the hazards of political film-making at the time. *Confessions of a Nazi Spy* won critical raves, with the National Board of Review naming it "the best film of the year from any country."[1] But the public was less enthusiastic, and the film did only moderate business in the U.S. Moreover, it was either banned or heavily censored in its overseas release, where it was a major commercial disappointment.[2]

This latter point was of considerable importance in the late 1930s, when the domestic market was still mired in a late-Depression recovery mode. At the time, foreign trade generally accounted for any net profits on major studio releases, and thus despite the myriad crises overseas, Hollywood relied much more heavily on foreign markets than did other major U.S. industries. As the *Wall Street Journal* noted, "The moving picture industry was one of the very few American businesses that had a vital stake in foreign trade when the war broke out [in September 1939]."[3] In fact, the Hollywood studio-distributors actually had benefited from the political and military crises in the late 1930s, which severely curtailed the production of feature films in England, France, Germany, and Italy, which were Hollywood's chief competitors overseas. These crises eventually undercut Hollywood's overseas trade, particularly in the Axis nations, which by 1937 were severely limiting both the number of U.S. film imports and the portion of box-office revenues "remitted" to the studios.[4]

By the time the war broke out in late 1939, Hollywood had all but lost the Axis markets on the Continent and in the Far East. But the studios still realized roughly one-third of their revenues from overseas, thanks largely to the United Kingdom. According to a *Variety* survey of the global marketplace in September 1939, Hollywood's chief overseas clients at the time were Britain (45 percent of foreign trade) and Australia (11 percent), with all of Continental Europe contributing roughly 20 percent.[5] With the escalation of the war and the fall of France in June 1940, Hollywood's European market would fall to virtually nil—leaving England standing alone by late 1940, not only in the face of Nazi aggression, but also as Hollywood's last significant foreign market.[6]

The studios had little trouble adjusting to these changing market conditions abroad, since Britain traditionally had been Hollywood's chief foreign client and generated the lion's share of Hollywood's overseas income.[7] Hollywood films historically had accounted for over 80 percent of the screen time in England, and by the late 1930s Britain was becoming something of a direct extension of the American market.[8] As the war intensified in 1940–1941, Hollywood was continually on the verge of writing off its British income. But once England survived the Battle of Britain and the German Luftwaffe's "London blitz" in 1940, it was clear that the nation was in for a long haul against the Nazis. It was clear, too, that England was undergoing a wartime boom in moviegoing, and that Hollywood would be the chief beneficiary of that boom.[9]

The steady increase of Hollywood's filmmaking and marketing focus on England in 1940–1941 coincided with Roosevelt's political and economic agenda. During this period, FDR developed his "lend lease" policy to support the British war effort against Nazi Germany (which gained congressional approval in March 1941), and the prospect of U.S. intervention on the side of Britain became increasingly likely—despite protests from isolationists and proneutrality advocates.

Roosevelt also initiated a massive defense buildup in the U.S. in 1940–1941, which revitalized the American economy and brought a definitive end to the Great Depression of the 1930s. The defense buildup marked the first stage of an extended war boom for the U.S. economy in general, with the motion picture industry among the prime beneficiaries. The boom was most acute in the urban-industrial centers where war-related production was gearing at a furious pace and where Hollywood did most of its business.[10] The full force of the defense buildup hit the movie industry in midsummer of 1941, and by the autumn the sustained box-office surge had become an accepted way of life for the studios and the nation's exhibitors.[11] Indeed, the prospects were virtually unlimited as new factories, urban labor migration, the draft, new army camps, and rearrangement of work schedules (night shifts, swing shifts, and the like) pushed movie attendance and ticket sales ever upward.[12]

This defense boom clearly indicated America's intensifying prewar mentality, which was further manifested by the public's growing appetite for news about the war overseas as well as U.S. "preparedness." By late 1940, Hollywood newsreels, documentary shorts, and features were increasingly devoted to war-related subjects. The public was buying, and in fact news-hungry audiences were changing the very nature of moviegoing. By spring 1941, theaters routinely interrupted their programs to provide news bulletins, and some houses began scheduling radio broadcasts of FDR's Tuesday evening "Fireside Chats," which were drawing total radio audiences of up to seventy million, fully one-half the U.S. population.[13] Another barometer of war-related public interest was the newsreel theater, which enjoyed its heyday before and during World War II. By late 1941, twenty-five of these theaters were in operation in the largest U.S. cities, with most of the news directly related to the war. . . .[14]

Hollywood's conversion to war production

In late December 1941, within days of the U.S. entry into World War II, Roosevelt appointed Lowell Mellett coordinator of government films. In that role, Mellett would act as liaison to the film industry and would advise the studios on war-film production. In the letter of appointment, FDR wrote: "The American motion picture is one of the most effective mediums in informing and entertaining our citizens. The motion picture must remain free in so far as national security will permit." This meant, in effect, that the industry could continue commercial operations without direct government control. But FDR clearly expected the industry's full support of the war effort, and he conveyed to Mellett six war-related subject areas that he wanted Hollywood to focus on in its films: the issues ("why we fight"), the enemy, the allies, the home front, the production front, and the U.S. armed forces.[15]

Washington eventually would formalize this "advisory" and monitoring process, creating the OWI in June 1942, with Mellett as head of the Bureau of Motion Pictures (BMP).[16] But by then the movie industry's voluntary support of the war effort was altogether evident. Indeed, it was nothing short of phenomenal, with every sector of the industry undergoing a rapid transformation. In the exhibition sector, movie theaters became wartime community centers, sponsoring events for the Red Cross, the March of Dimes, United Nations Relief, Army-Navy Emergency Relief, and many others.[17] Thousands of movie theaters became official bond "issuing agents" for the U.S. Treasury, and roughly one-fifth of the War Bonds sold during the war were purchased in theaters. Theaters also became collection centers for various "critical materials" such as blood plasma, rags and paper, copper, scrap metal, and rubber.[18]

In terms of distribution, the studios—mainly through the Hollywood-based War Activities Committee (WAC)—worked with the government to set up a worldwide distribution system, shipping 16 mm prints of nearly two thousand Hollywood features and another one thousand shorts in the course of the war to military bases, makeshift theaters, and "beachhead bijous" all over the globe.[19] By 1945, ten million military personnel per week saw Hollywood features under these conditions. WAC also helped secure distribution for government-produced documentaries and informational shorts—including, for example, Capra's "Why We Fight" films.[20]

Hollywood's conversion to war production in terms of actual filmmaking was equally impressive. Within weeks of Pearl Harbor, and with the Senate propaganda hearings only a few months past, Hollywood shifted from outspoken denial of any active promotion of U.S. involvement in the war to aggressive on-screen support of that effort. Within six months roughly one-third of the features in production dealt directly with the war, with a much higher proportion treating the war indirectly, as a given set of social, political, and economic conditions. In terms of the output of war-related films throughout the World War II era, consider these figures compiled by Russell Earl Shain.[21] Shain notes that during the sustained peak in Hollywood's war-related output from 1942 to 1944, one-fourth of all features (312 of 1,286 releases; 24 percent) dealt with the war. According to Shain, Hollywood released

Figure I. WWII-related Hollywood Features, 1940–1947

	Total War Films	Total Films	% War Films
1940	12	477	2.5
1941	32	492	6.5
1942	121	488	24.8
1943	115	397	29.0
1944	76	401	19.0
1945	28	350	8.0
1946	13	378	3.4
1947	2	369	0.5

340 war-related features during the four war years, or 20 percent of the industry total. Shain's figures relate only to films dealing directly with World War II and do not include films related to, say, World War I or the Spanish Civil War. Thus studies dealing with all war-related films indicate an even heavier overall output. Dorothy B. Jones of the OWI's Film Reviewing and Analysis Section found that over 28 percent of Hollywood's total output from 1942–1944 (376 of 1,313 releases in her sample) were war-related.[22]

Both Shain's and Jones's figures clearly indicate how rapid and aggressive Hollywood's conversion to war production after Pearl Harbor actually was. What they do not indicate, however, was the overall success of this effort in terms of both box-office revenues and popular response. In 1942, nineteen of the 101 films that returned at least one million dollars in rentals were war-related. The number and proportion of war-related hits more than doubled in 1943, when they comprised forty-one of the ninety-five releases returning one million dollars or more.[23] War-related films also included the top two hits in both 1942 and 1943: Mrs. Miniver and Yankee Doodle Dandy in 1942, and This Is the Army and For Whom the Bell Tolls in 1943. The war-related film's box-office currency peaked in 1944, when they comprised eleven of the nineteen releases returning three million dollars or more. For the entire wartime period, a remarkable thirty-two of the seventy-one three-million-dollar-returning releases were war-related—including ten musicals, nine combat films, and six home-front comedies or dramas.[24]

Considering the number of musicals and comedies in this total, it is clear that war-related films did not always depict combat or deal directly with war conditions. What Hollywood termed war themes were likely to show up in any number of genres, while the term war film took on steadily narrower connotations as Hollywood refined specific war-related formulas. The dominant formula was the combat film, although espionage films and home-front dramas involving military training or the day-to-day experiences of wartime Americans were significant cycles as well. Among the more interesting developments of Hollywood's war film production was the prominence of spy, espionage, and war-related crime thrillers in the early years of the war, especially 1942, and the subsequent surge in home-front dramas and combat films in the later war years. As the numbers from Shain's study clearly indicate, by 1944–1945 the combat film was by far the dominant war-related type (see figure 2).[25]

As we look at the reasons behind these figures, and especially the discrepancies between 1942 and the subsequent war years, it becomes evident that the first years of the war,

Figure 2. WWII-related film by type, 1942–1945

	1942	1943	1944	1945
espionage	59.5%	22.0%	15.6%	17.7%
combat	24.8	41.5	51.4	60.7
home front	16.0	36.7	32.7	18.0

and particularly the first six to eight months after Pearl Harbor, were a singularly odd, exceptional period in terms of Hollywood's war-film production. Predictably enough, perhaps, Hollywood's initial response to the war and to FDR's call to arms was to convert established stars and genres to war production. As noted earlier, Abbott and Costello stopped doing service comedies in late 1941 in deference to the war effort. That turned out to be a singular exception; the vast majority of stars and genres underwent just the opposite progression, converting to cinematic war production as soon as the U.S. entered the war. The result was a melange of genre hybrids and star-genre reformulations in 1942, with the term *war film* applying as little more than a useful generalization.

Significantly enough, most of the films directly related to the U.S. war effort were B pictures. Because Hollywood had been fairly tentative in its treatment of the war until Pearl Harbor, and because top features took nine to twelve months to produce and release, very few A-class pictures depicting U.S. involvement were released in 1942. *Casablanca*, for instance, was optioned within weeks of Pearl Harbor and went into immediate pre-production but did not go into general release until January 1943. Most of the war-related A-class films released in 1942 were initiated in 1941, and they tended to take one of three tacks: they focused on the British war effort (*Mrs. Miniver, This Above All*); they depicted Americans or "good" Europeans dealing with Nazis (*To Be or Not To Be, Desperate Journey*) or Japanese (*Somewhere I'll Find You, Across the Pacific*); or they featured American fliers fighting for other nations (England in *Eagle Squadron*; Canada in *Captains of the Clouds*).

There were B-grade versions of these trends in 1942 as well, such as MGM's *Journey for Margaret*, a low-cost knockoff of *Mrs. Miniver*, and Republic's *Flying Tigers*, with John Wayne leading a group of fighter pilots assisting the Chinese against Japan. The majority of B-grade war films in 1942, however, had little in common with Hollywood's A-class films, nor were they prone to historical accuracy or the depiction of actual combat. The B film's rapid production and penchant for exploitation enabled low-budget filmmakers to scoop their A-class counterparts in terms of war-related topicality; in fact, on-screen references to Pearl Harbor began turning up in B films within only weeks of Pearl Harbor.[26] But this invariably occurred in jingoistic celebrations of American heroism and superior know-how, depicted in terms of B-movie formula rather than the conditions at hand.

Hollywood's rapid conversion of various B-grade series to war production in 1942 was in its own way quite remarkable. Espionage and sabotage films dominated, as a result not only of genuine public concern but also of the easy reformulation of low-grade crime formulas. G-men and undercover cops simply turned their sights from gangsters to foreign agents, with the trappings of the story—from props, sets, and costumes to cast and plot structure—remaining much the same. A few A-class 1942 features dealing with spies and sabotage, notably Hitchcock's *Saboteur*, gave the formula a certain legitimacy. But shrill, jingoistic B-grade thrillers were far more prevalent. Gangster and spy formulas were refitted in pictures like *Sabotage Squad*, *Unseen Enemy*, and *Counter-Espionage*, while Sherlock Holmes and Dr. Watson were updated into wartime sleuths in *Sherlock Holmes and the Voice of Terror* and *Sherlock Holmes and the Secret Weapon*. B western series were recruited in films like *Valley of Hunted Men*, with Republic's Three Mesquiteers battling Nazi spies, and *Cowboy Commandos*, with Monogram's Range Busters pursuing Nazi saboteurs.[27] Even the Universal horror film was converted to war production in *Invisible Agent*, as Jon Hall's "invisible man" took on both Nazi and Japanese spies.

Many 1942 B-grade spy and crime thrillers exploited the American public's anger about Pearl Harbor and its anxieties about the Japanese threat—as evidenced by such titles as *A Prisoner of Japan*, *Menace of the Rising Sun*, *Danger in the Pacific*, and *Remember Pearl Harbor*. These and other 1942 Bs demonized the Japanese and embellished the "stab-in-the-back" thesis that was haphazardly applied to all Japanese—including Japanese-Americans.

The OWI was alarmed by these trends and issued a much-publicized report in September 1942 that openly criticized Hollywood's B-grade war films. "The emphasis of the entire industry is still too much on the exciting blood-and-thunder aspects of the war," asserted the OWI, and the report went on to note that thirty-one war-related espionage and sabotage pictures had been released in the previous six months, which "tended to give the public an exaggerated idea of the menace."[28] In October the OWI's BMP reported that seventy of 220 pictures in the past six months were war-related, but that few of these substantially advanced the war effort. A *Variety* headline in November blared, "OWI Frowns on 'B' Types," and the subhead noted the agency's "Drive to get the studios to lay off cops-and-robbers formula." That story noted that whereas six "saboteur-spy type" war films were released in October 1942, there were none in the OWI's "all-important 'The Issues—What Are We Fighting For' category."[29]

This latter refrain would persist throughout the war years, as Hollywood continually avoided dealing with the conflict in sophisticated social or political terms. As the OWI's Dorothy Jones pointed out in a 1945 assessment of Hollywood's war-related films, no more than fifty or so had "aided significantly, both at home and abroad, in increasing understanding of the conflict." Jones accused the Hollywood community of thinking only in terms of escapist entertainment, and that "when faced with the task of making films which would educate the public about the war, most Hollywood movie makers did not know where to begin."[30] The industry's defense, of course, was that the primary obligation of commercial filmmakers is to make pictures that sell. Walter Wanger, then the Academy president, outlined that rationale in the spring 1943 issue of *Public Opinion Quarterly*: "Film with a purpose must pass the same test that the escapist film more easily passes," said Wanger. "Theatergoers must want to see the picture." Convinced that the kind of pictures the OWI espoused "can effect no purpose except to empty theaters," Wanger argued that any "truths" about war-related issues "had better be skillfully integrated" into the drama.[31]

We should note here that Mellett and the OWI's BMP had become increasingly combative in their relations with the Hollywood studios and with the industry's self-censorship outfit, the PCA. Though Mellett generally abided by FDR's assurances that there would be no government censorship of movies, the BMP became actively involved in analyzing and evaluating movie projects, in actively promoting particular subjects and plot lines, and in applying various pressures on the studios to cooperate. By late 1942 the BMP had developed something of a "second production code" and a PCA-style review process in an effort to rectify the situation.[32]

The BMP and the PCA (and their respective codes) were politically and ideologically at odds, not only on the treatment of the war but on other issues as well, from their respective notions of a "good society" to their views of what constituted a "good movie." As Koppes and Black point out in *Hollywood Goes to War*, the PCA's extreme conservatism and obsessive concern over moral and sexual issues did not jibe with the OWI's ethos of "mild social democracy and liberal internationalist foreign policy."[33] "Moreover, the PCA had considerably more experience than the BMP in dealing with studio executives and filmmakers, and it also had a much clearer understanding of how to work social and political themes into films. Thus the OWI and the PCA often gave the studios conflicting and even contradictory input on the making of war-related films.

The OWI's ideological bent also conflicted with the views of Congress—particularly after the November 1942 election, which brought a more conservative-leaning group to Capitol Hill. The newly elected Congress viewed the OWI in general and the BMP in particular as blatantly pro-Roosevelt and dangerously liberal. And so in 1943 Congress cut off almost all funding for the OWI's domestic operations, which resulted in the resignation of Mellett and his key associates and left the BMP with little to do on the home front beyond the routine distribution of government shorts. But that did not mark the end of the BMP in Hollywood. On the contrary, the agency gained a stronger hand by shifting its liaison activities to its still-active overseas branch, which had developed a strong accord with the Office of Censorship. With its regulatory control over film exports, the Office of Censorship effectively put teeth in the BMP's advisory role, providing a post hoc threat to deny export to those films that blatantly disregarded the bureau's input on important political matters.[34]

Notes

This essay is excerpted and adapted from my book *History of the American Cinema*, Vol. 6: "Boom and Bust: The American Cinema in the 1940s," Charles Harpole, Series Editor. Copyright © 1997 by Thomas Schatz. Used with permission of Charles Scribner's Sons, an imprint of Simon & Schuster Macmillan.

1 *1940 Film Daily Year Book* (New York: The Film Daily, 1941), 81.
2 Clayton R. Koppes and Gregory C. Black, *Hollywood Goes to War* (Berkeley: University of California Press, 1987), 30. Warners released a similar film in September 1939, *Espionage Agent*, starring Joel McCrea; it too fared better critically than commercially, despite the outbreak of war in Europe that same month.
3 *Wall Street Journal*, 2 January 1941, p. 48.
4 *Motion Picture Herald*, 4 February 1939, p. 38; 11 March 1939, p. 6; 13 January 1940, p. 8; *Variety*, 19 July 1939, p. 11.
5 According to *Variety* (6 September 1939, p. 6), the market shares of Hollywood's overseas clients in September 1939 were:

    Great Britain—45 percent
    France and Belgium—13 percent
    Australia—11.2 percent
    Central and South America—9 percent
    Scandinavia—4.2 percent

Holland—1.5 percent

Bulgaria, Greece, and Turkey—1.2 percent

Neutral Central Europe—1 percent

Variety routinely reported that Hollywood realized up to half of its income from overseas. More conservative estimates placed the figure at about one third. The *Wall Street Journal* (3 October 1939, p. 1) reported: "The situation may be summed up as follows: American film producers obtain about 30 percent to 35 percent of their total film rentals from abroad. This varies somewhat from year to year. Around half of the foreign income . . . comes from Great Britain. South America supplies 10 percent to 15 percent and the rest is scattered. The Continent of Europe, due to government regulation and exchange difficulties, has provided little profit in recent years."

6 1941 *Film Daily Year Book*, 57. *Wall Street Journal*, 2 January 1941, p. 48.

7 *Wall Street Journal*, 2 January 1941, p. 48.

8 *Variety*, 4 January 1939, p. 5.

9 The major Hollywood studios took in nearly fifty million dollars in rentals in both 1940 and 1941—record figures that increased in the ensuing war years. *Motion Picture Herald*, 7 June 1941, p. 18; *Wall Street Journal*, 7 July 1941, p. 1.

10 On the impact of the defense buildup on the movie industry, see *Motion Picture Herald*, 22 June 1940, p. 8, and *Wall Street Journal*, 2 January 1941, p. 48.

11 See *Variety*, 9 July 41, p. 5; *Wall Street Journal*, 10 September 1941, p. 1.

12 *Motion Picture Herald*, 1 November 1941, p. 13; *Variety*, 26 November 1941, p. 7.

13 *Motion Picture Herald*, 3 May 1941, p. 9.

14 Douglas Gomery, *Shared Pleasures: A History of Movie Presentation in the United States* (Madison: University of Wisconsin Press, 1992), 152.

15 FDR's letter of appointment quoted in *Motion Picture Herald*, 27 December 1941, p. 17. See also Garth Jowett, *Film: The Democratic Art* (New York: Little, Brown, 1976), 311. According to several sources, Roosevelt himself specified the six subject areas.

16 Koppes and Black, *Hollywood Goes to War*, 58–60; *Motion Picture Herald*, 20 June 1942, p. 9.

17 *Look* magazine, *From Movie Lot to Beachhead* (Garden City: Doubleday, 1945), 204.

18 Ibid., 205; 1946 *Film Daily Year Book*, 145–46.

19 *Motion Picture Herald*, 29 July 1944, p. 9; *Motion Picture Herald*, 13 January 1945, p. 9; *Motion Picture Herald* 6, October 1945, p. 8; 1946 *Film Daily Year Book*, 147–48.

20 Garth Jowett, *Film*, 357; *Motion Picture Herald*, 3 January 1942, p. 16; 1946 *Film Daily Year Book*, 145.

21 Shain, *An Analysis*, 31.

22 Dorothy B. Jones, "The Hollywood War Film: 1942–1944," *Hollywood Quarterly* 1, no. 5 (October 1945): 2–3. Note that Shain's and Jones's total release figures for the period vary somewhat, which is not surprising given inconsistencies between the official and actual release dates.

23 *Variety*, 6 January 1943, p. 58; *Variety*, 4 January 1944, p. 54.

24 Figures are taken from an accounting of Hollywood's leading all-time box-office hits organized by decade in *Variety*, 24 February 1996, pp. 168–69.

25 Shain, *An Analysis*, 61. Note that the figures from 1945 do not total 100 percent; Shain does not explain this discrepancy.

26 The first reference, according to various sources, was in a Rapf-Schary B picture, A *Yank on the Burma Road*, which was reviewed in the *New York Times* on 29 January 1942. See Richard R. Lingeman, *Don't You Know There's a War On?* (New York: Putnam's, 1970), 176; and Jeanine Basinger, *The World War II Combat Film: Anatomy of a Genre* (New York: Columbia University Press, 1986), 26, 281.

27 Edward Buscombe, ed., *The BFI Companion to the Western* (London: BFI Publishing, 1988), 243–44; Koppes and Black, *Hollywood Goes to War*, 61.

28 *Motion Picture Herald*, 19 September 1942, p. 9.

29 *Variety*, 25 November 1942, p. 7.

30 Jones, "The Hollywood War Film," 12–13.

31 Walter Wanger, "The O.W.I. and Motion Pictures," *Public Opinion Quarterly* (spring 1943): 103–4.

32 *Motion Picture Herald*, 19 September 1942, p. 9.

33 Koppes and Black, *Hollywood Goes to War*, 69.

34 Ibid., 323.

Leni Riefenstahl's Contribution to the American War Effort

13

THOMAS DOHERTY

.... By 1945 any American who had been going to the movies for a long time knew the work of Leni Riefenstahl. Her two documentary masterpieces—*Triumph of the Will* (1935), the official record of the Nazi Party's Congress in Nuremberg in 1934, and *Olympia* (1938), a two-part chronicle of the 1936 Olympic Games in Berlin—had supplied the American screen with its most powerful and lasting images of the Nazis in full dudgeon. Spliced into newsreels, War Department orientation films, and Hollywood features, the awful beauty and repellent substance of Riefenstahl's footage gave an immortal motion picture life to the twelve-year Reich.

Like the Nuremberg rallies, filmmaking is a collaborative enterprise resisting the assignment of individual responsibility for the total production.[1] Without the architecture and lighting of Albert Speer, the geometric arrangement of troops drilled by Heinrich Himmler and Viktor Lutze, and the generative imagination of Hitler himself, no Nazi spectacle would be picture perfect. But Riefenstahl gave the iconography and rituals of Nazism a purely cinematic vitality. Her screen vision—the exultant compositions of brawny *Übermenschen* and budding *Hitlerjungen*, the night-for-night glow of Teutonic bonfires and torchlit parades, the worshipful low-angle shots and natural lighting silhouetting a deific Führer—imprinted the spectacular allure of the Nazi mythos in motion picture memory.

It also brought the director to the attention of an intrigued and appalled Hollywood. Attractive, talented, and female, Riefenstahl was a charismatic celebrity who under different patronage might have been feted and fawned over. She became instead a parable for the corruption of art by power. As an enemy propagandist, only (Paul) Joseph Goebbels surpassed her in infamy and insult. Around Hollywood, Riefenstahl may actually have edged him out. Reichsminister Goebbels presided over the complete range of mass media; Riefenstahl was of the movies alone and a genuine artist of the cinema at that. For the motion picture industry, the thought of a gifted and gorgeous filmmaker willfully in liege to Hitler inspired a Mephistophelian horror.

Riefenstahl was to become a representative figure, her work a dark mirror, because in motion picture (no less than in ideological or military) terms the war pitted stark alternatives against one another. "We have seen that the first act of tyranny anywhere is to make it impossible to see American films," proclaimed Charles Francis Coe, vice president and general counsel for the Motion Picture Producers and Distributors of America (MPPDA). "We know that no propaganda-laden picture can stand against American films. We know the first effect of vicious propaganda films is to empty theaters."[2] For the motion picture industry, the media-driven dimension of the Second World War structured the order of battle. Where the American military and GI everyman faced the challenge of the Wehrmacht and the Nazi superman, the studio system took on the Reichsfilmkammer and the popular artist fought the party hack. Matters of tactics and policy—democratic persuasion versus totalitarian manipulation, entertainment versus propaganda—were reflected in a contest of creative will and personal vision—Jack Warner versus Joseph Goebbels, Frank Capra versus Leni Riefenstahl.

The films that earned Riefenstahl ill-repute also made her reputation. Although never commercially released nor readily accessible in America during the 1930s, both Triumph of the Will and Olympia were well known around Hollywood—mostly by word of mouth, occasionally by sight.[3] Either overseas or at the Museum of Modern Art in New York, where film curator Iris Barry jealously guarded a 35mm print obtained from a German-American businessman, a select number of critics and directors had seen Triumph of the Will. Word of its dread impact circulated throughout the motion picture industry. Visiting Germany in 1938, director Josef von Sternberg told Riefenstahl he had caught a screening of Triumph of the Will at MOMA and praised it effusively.[4] "Mädchen," he rightly predicted, "this film will make film history—it is revolutionary." Siegfried Kracauer, working on his psychohistory From Caligari to Hitler, also studied the film at MOMA and wrote about it in a pamphlet, "Propaganda and the Nazi War Film," issued in 1942.[5] Like many viewers at the time and since, Kracauer's "deep feeling of uneasiness" at the "frightening spectacle" was the more acute for an aesthetic appreciation of its "sumptuous orchestration" of the elements of film grammar. . . .

Drawn on as "library footage" by the newsreels, incorporated and recast throughout Capra's Why We Fight (1942–1945) series, utilized as exposition and transition in Hitler's Children (1942) and Mission to Moscow (1943), Triumph of the Will was a consistent source of negative inspiration. It furnished the signature images of Nazism on the American screen even as it conferred a certain stylistic influence. Hitler's Children, a salaciously advertised and immensely popular proto-exploitation film, is downright fetishistic in its cultivation of swastika iconography and SS S&M. In low-angle two-shots of a uniformed Nazi in a loving clinch with his democratic girlfriend, the camera's awed gaze embraces some of the will to power the film's own dialogue condemns.

For Riefenstahl, meanwhile, the fortunes of war and antipathy from Reichsminister Goebbels thwarted further artistic development. At the very time Frank Capra's 834th Photo Signal Detachment and the Hollywood studios were making her work the American-approved, American-filtered version of the Nazis on screen, the director herself had fallen precipitously out of favor. Throughout the war, she stood on the propaganda sidelines, an absence that in Hollywood sparked the revealing rumor that she had been "liquidated."[6]

But though Riefenstahl was missing in action, Triumph of the Will commanded center stage for the duration. By war's end its images were likely better known in America than in Germany. The postwar denouement confirms the film's popularity and persistence. While public screenings of Triumph of the Will were banned for nearly fifty years throughout much of Europe (and can still spark a picket line in formerly occupied countries), its archival contribution to wartime America was taken up enthusiastically and extended throughout the 1950s and 1960s in feature films and television documentaries.[7] Standardized by recurrent usage, impossible to eradicate, Riefenstahl's images entered the select chambers of the American movie memory. In Stanley Kramer's *Judgment at Nuremberg* (1961), a crusty trial judge (played by Spencer Tracy) walks through the vacant Nuremberg Youth Stadium, now deserted but still haunted by the ghosts of rallies past. As Tracy gazes around the arena, up at the seats and across the field, the soundtrack mixes shouts of "Heil!" with the joyous call-and-response duet between *Volk* and *Führer*. Kramer did not need to screen a single frame of Riefenstahl's film for character and spectator alike to replay *Triumph of the Will* in the mind's eye.

Before the usurpation and containment, however, Riefenstahl's striking formal brilliance and Goebbels's sinister mass communications dexterity unnerved the motion picture industry at war. Just as the aura of battlefield invincibility surrounded the Wehrmacht, the cunning effectiveness of Nazi propaganda, particularly the exploitation of the art of cinema, suffused Goebbels's Reich Ministry for Popular Enlightenment and Propaganda. Understandably, Hollywood was at first uneasy about the matchup. On the propaganda canvas, after all, it was fighting out of its class. As unofficial and unselfconscious propagators of American culture, studio system filmmakers were the preeminent world champions; as official and conscious propagandists for the state, they were rank amateurs. When Army Chief of Staff George C. Marshall ordered Frank Capra to make what became the *Why We Fight* series, the ace director balked: "General Marshall, it's only fair to tell you that I have never before made a single documentary film. In fact, I've never even been near anybody that's made one."[8] By common agreement the Nazis enjoyed a competitive edge on their own field and possessed what an intimidated *Variety* reporter called "the slickest propaganda regimentation extant."[9]

Moreover, in a town where making documentaries was an esoteric practice, "propaganda" was a dirty word. Discredited in the American tradition by the hysterical Hun-baiting of the Creel Committee during World War I—a reputation now reinforced by the work of the Nazis—a designation once descriptive had become pejorative. In an address to the Chicago Rotary Club in 1943, War Activities Committee vice chairman Francis S. Harmon expressed the common sense: "I suppose the rank and file of people associate 'propaganda' either with outright falsehood or with something that is being put over by devious methods."[10] To one Hollywood artist, the already legendary director John Ford, the very word was anathema. Working in the Office of Strategic Services under Ford, lately put on active duty as a lieutenant commander in the Navy, film editor Robert Parrish was assigned to work on the combat report, *The Battle of Midway* (September 1942). Did Ford have in mind a propaganda picture, inquired Parrish? "Ford looked at me a long time, looked away and looked back at me," recalled Parrish, himself a petty officer second class. "Then he lit his pipe, which usually took about two minutes. This time it seemed more like two hours. Finally, he said, 'How do you spell that word?' I spelled it for him and he said, 'Don't you ever let me hear you use that word again in my presence as long as you're under my command.'"[11] Whatever the incidental ideological impact, American movies had been produced in service to a studio, not the state, and American moviemakers had mainly thought of themselves as doing a "job of work," not of political indoctrination.

In Hollywood's eyes, Riefenstahl's documentaries set the standard for a sustained celluloid assault directed by the Reichsfilmkammer, the coordinating board that in 1937 took full control of the German motion picture industry. In 1943 *American Cinematographer* conjured a frightening portrait of the machine works behind the cinematic blitzkrieg:

Dr Goebbels converted the Ufa Studio at Neubabelsberg—one of the largest and finest in the world—into an assembly plant for making propaganda for Nazism. Directors, technicians, and artists were put to work, three shifts a day, twenty four hours per day, grinding out films that glorified the Nazi ideals of the Super-race, of devotion to the State, and of hatred for the rest of the world. Shooting and production schedules were cut in half, sets were made to do double duty. Ufa's fourteen sound stages, twenty-one cutting rooms, and five private theaters hummed with day and night activity.[12]

Rolling off the production line were "topnotch battle films" showcasing the relentless Nazis in action-packed combat and glorious victory. In 1942 Variety shamefully acknowledged that American pictures of war production plants and troop training "look very pallid against shots of hard hitting Nazi tanks and Panzer divisions overcoming United Nations fighters on various fronts."[13]

Like a viral infection, Nazi films "softened up" and intimidated targets of opportunity, making democratic countries susceptible to Axis invasion by weakening the immune system of potential victims. Besides Triumph of the Will and special nation-specific segments of Olympia, Ufa newsreels and Reichsfilmkammer documentaries such as Der Feldzug in Polen (The Campaign in Poland) (1939) and Sieg im Westen (Victory in the West) (1940) presaged and assisted Nazi expansionism. "These films were shown to gatherings of foreign diplomats in practically every country in Europe, always prior to Nazi invasion," warned the Hollywood Reporter in 1942.[14] "Several weeks before the Nazi invasion of Yugoslavia and Greece these films were shown before high dignitaries of the two victims. Goering himself reportedly showed King Boris of Bulgaria many reels of Nazi conquests before that Balkan country signed on with the Axis." According to discomforting reports, the Nazis devoted no less than two full divisions of men "assigned strictly to obtaining a motion picture version of the war," which then got an expert "Nazified treatment" in postproduction.[15] In Divide and Conquer (August 1942), a Warner Bros. short utilizing captured enemy footage (not to be confused with Capra's Why We Fight entry of the same name), Nazi propaganda is accorded a plaguelike capacity to poison the polis with "mental confusion, indecisiveness, and panic."

Lacy W. Kastner of the overseas branch of the Office of War Information frankly acknowledged the propaganda gap. During extensive travels in prewar Europe, Kastner "saw and studied the screen technique of the Germans" and publicly, in 1942, praised it as superlative. "Sometimes after I came away from seeing one of those Nazi propaganda films, I was so impressed by the technical excellence of the picture that I had to remember it was Hitler we were fighting."[16] Ruefully observing how the Allied screen suffered by comparison, Siegfried Kracauer was also discouragingly blunt. "Owing to |the traditions of German cinema|, the Nazis knew how to use the three film media—commentary, visuals, and sound. With a pronounced feeling for editing, they exploited each medium to the full, so that the total effect frequently resulted from the blending of different meanings in different media. Such polyphonic handling is not often found in democratic war films."[17] When the Motion Picture Society for the Americas and the Office of Inter-American Affairs presented "Two Evenings of German Propaganda Films, 1934–1941" at Hollywood's Filmarte Theater in 1943, industry producers, directors, and writers packed the auditorium.[18] The propaganda neophytes came to learn from the master race.

Hollywood had nowhere else to turn for instruction. From Washington, studio professionals could expect little in the way of practical guidance. The state's entry into the motion picture business was as new as the industry's induction into the purposes of the state. In comparison to KINO and Ufa, the movie-making agencies under totalitarian regimes Leninist and Fascist, the American motion picture industry was conspicuously free of legal constraints and state-financed competition. As regulators and manipulators, the U.S. government had left cinema unfettered, untapped, and ill-considered. "Films are a field in which I am only dimly acquainted," Elmer Davis guilelessly confessed upon his appointment as director of the Office of War Information in June 1942. "I have no ideas at all as yet as to the part they should play in the war effort."[19] Lowell Mellett, head of the OWI's Bureau of Motion Pictures (BMP), was equally vague on specifics and even shorter on tact. During a tour of a studio sound-stage, he remarked to his executive guides that some of their movies had not been good for the war effort. Asked what titles he had in mind, the government official in charge of liaison with the motion picture industry replied, "I just can't mention the pictures, as I don't see many pictures. I'm too busy."[20] Col. Kirke B. Lawton, a former lawyer heading the Army Pictorial Service at least knew his limitations. "I can operate |my division| as an executive here in Washington, but as for making pictures, I know nothing about it," he admitted. "To take a man who knows nothing about the industry, who knows nothing about the research end, and send him out there |to Hollywood| would be like sending me out there."[21] Against the confirmed cineastes and frustrated auteurs of the Third Reich, the officials of the OWI and the War Department come off as visual illiterates.

During the course of the war, more in spite of government guidance than because of it, Hollywood filmmakers settled on an anti-Axis strategy suited to a mediawise and cinematically sophisticated culture. It was not a coordinated campaign or a rigorously enforced set of axioms; it was a commonsense recognition by popular artists of the background and values of an audience they had long been wedded to. By way of direct countermeasures, one line of attack confronted and rebutted Axis ideology. The other flank waged a subtler media-centered campaign that offered instruction in mass communications and propaganda techniques. Throughout both movements, Hollywood deployed the weapons it handled best, juxtaposing its own grammar and imagery with the enemy's cinematic vision of himself.

The first front explicitly responded to Axis provocations. The open avowal of American values and stacked-deck responses to Axis propaganda determine much of the structure of wartime orientation films, Victory shorts, and the more nakedly polemical of the Hollywood features. Commentators coo over breadbasket beneficence and crow about industrial might. Forward narrative action halts for magniloquent declarations of democratic verities and expressive montages of heartland tapestries. Hence too the compulsive inclusion of shots of captured German and Japanese troops in the newsreels and combat reports, defeated and deflated would-be conquerors who now, as RKO's narration to the Soviet documentary *Moscow Strikes Back* (1942) gloats, "seem less than supermen."

The second front was explicitly media-oriented. Audiences were educated to the ideological power of mass communications, flattered over their superior powers of apprehension, and assured of their democratic immunity to the falsehoods of Axis enticements. The appropriation and recasting of the Nazis' own widely disseminated images was the favorite guerrilla tactic. Redrawn to Allied specifications, hijacked enemy propaganda films supplied the raw material for the most clever and effective of American countermeasures. Announcing the screening of a reedited German film of the North African campaign, the London edition of the *Stars and Stripes* was airily nonchalant. "Sponsored by

Goebbels, the movie is entitled *Invincible*. Reservations may be obtained by telephone."[22] In the combat report *The Enemy Strikes* (March 1945), seized German footage of Field Marshal Gerd von Rundstedt's offensive during the Battle of the Bulge was recast for the domestic purpose of extinguishing homefront complacency. The Reichsfilmkammer film within the War Department film shows grimly determined Nazi soldiers smoking American cigarettes. The commentator expounds: "Germans smoked Camels and Chesterfields robbed from American dead and the Nazi cameraman filed it to amuse and reassure the moviegoers of Munich and Berlin."[23] Not all the hijacking was so somber. Circulated stateside by the newsreels beginning on January 15, 1942, the British import *Lambeth Walk* (1941), a two-minute travesty of *Triumph of the Will*, featured rewound and sped-up goosesteppers marching in time to a jaunty dancehall melody. . . .[24]

Fancying itself a more prestigious and technically complex medium, Hollywood cinema assumed a condescending and professorial tone when addressing its poor relations in mass communications. Look, the screen seemed to say, see how amateurish are the tricks, how easily exposed are the secrets, of these lesser media, so prone to manipulation and cheap effects: rely on the movies to open your eyes. By depicting the careful attention the Axis lavished on mass communications, laying bare the techniques and disrupting the presentation, wartime films illustrated how to see (and hear) through doctored photos, forged documents, and deceitful broadcasting.

Shockingly, the motion picture industry's chief media rival was especially inclined to treachery. Hissing in accented English, radio broadcasters from Tokyo to Berlin chortled over fictional battlefield victories and cast seeds of psychological discord over the air. Fortunately, radio transmissions were susceptible to celluloid exposure and democratic disruptions. Both *Once Upon a Honeymoon* (1942) and *Hitler's Children* include scenes in which live radio broadcasts are sabotaged to the consternation of Goebbels-like overseers. The fraudulence of Axis propaganda in print had only to be seen, not heard, to reveal its bold-faced prevarications. Flashbacking to the prewar innocence of undergraduate life at Texas A&M, Walter Wanger's *We've Never Been Licked* (1943) relies solely on twenty-twenty hindsight when a newspaper headline from late 1938 comes into focus: "'Germany Wants World Understanding and Peace'—Hitler." In *This Land Is Mine* (1943), directed by temporary exile Jean Renoir from a Dudley Nichols screenplay, the testimony is mute and the image speaks for itself. No shot is fired when the Nazis raise the swastika over an occupied French village, and no commentary is needed except the cold presentation of the Nazi truth: a propaganda poster ("Citizens! Trust the German Soldier") and a collaborationist newspaper with the headline "Hitler Speaks for United Europe."

Yet the danger of duplicity and misapprehension lurked also in the noblest of the media. In Axis hands the movies lied at twenty-four frames a second. During Darryl F. Zanuck's speculative courtroom drama *The Purple Heart* (1944), a Japanese prosecutor (Richard Loo) screens bogus motion picture evidence to a kangaroo court sitting in judgment of American POWs falsely accused of bombing civilian targets. In a darkened courtroom, he projects apparently authentic newsreel pictures of the bloody aftermath of the Doolittle Raid on Tokyo. As the prosecutor enunciates a deceptive voice-over ("The court will notice the wreckage of the Daijingu Shrine and the many civilian causalities"), forescreen, in the press gallery, a sympathetic newspaper correspondent objects. "That is not an actual air raid," he rasps sotto voce. "Those pictures were made during an air raid drill—before Japan was even at war. You know, we were all there!"

Perhaps the most polished inquiry into high-definition deception occurred in a lowbrow subgenre of wartime cinema. Released on the heels of *Hitler's Children* and exploited in like manner, RKO's anti-Japanese melodrama *Behind the Rising Sun* (1943) elaborately exposes the full scope of ideological awareness and mass communications smarts in Hollywood counter-measures. Its extended lesson in visual propaganda warrants a shot-by-shot breakdown; a plot summary may, or may not, provide necessary background orientation. In prewar Japan, Taro (Tom Neal), the handsome, Cornell-educated scion of Japan's sole surviving liberal patrician, returns to his militaristic homeland. He secures altruistic but self-fulfilling employment with the engineering firm of *gaijin* businessman O'Hara (Don Douglas) and embraces Western-style romantic love in the shape of the company's pretty Japanese secretary, Tama (Margo). But when Taro is drafted into the Imperial Army, he reverts to type as an occupying officer in ravaged China. One day he confronts an old acquaintance from his assimilationist time in Tokyo, a woman reporter who has been pushed, slapped, and insulted by guffawing soldiers under his command. She complains futilely to the now insensitive and fully Samurai-encoded Taro. At this point, the camera "matches" Taro's eyeline to initiate a deft cinematic exposure of Axis propaganda technique. As the sequence unwinds, the spectator receives a full education in the manipulation of the medium and the unreliability of the photographic image.

The exposé begins with what will be a repeated "core image," a medium shot of friendly Japanese troops handing out food packages to grateful Chinese civilians. In the course of the sequence, *Behind the Rising Sun* systematically reveals the reality behind a photographic image initially beheld and falsely perceived:

1. Taro (his eyeline gazing screen right)
2. From Taro's perspective, friendly Japanese soldiers hand out provisions to grateful Chinese women and children.
3. Taro (now holding a pocket camera). He sets up his photograph and takes a snapshot of the generous Japanese soldiers distributing food.
4. The core image—(2) above—constructed from Taro's perspective. The soundtrack mixes in the "click" of a snapshot being taken, and the screen freezes. The camera pulls back on the fixed, photographed image of Japanese soldiers giving out goods to reveal a hand holding what has now become a still photograph.
5. Back in Tokyo (in flash-forwarded, nonparallel action), Mr. O'Hara, the American businessman, and Tama, the girl back home, contemplate the snapshot:

   TAMA: "You see, Mr. O'Hara? They're really very nice to the Chinese children, aren't they?"
   O'HARA: (Scrutinizing the core image, skeptically):   ". . . Certainly seems so."

   After some talk about Taro and his family, Tama picks up the photograph again and gazes down at it.
6. The camera pulls in to a precise rendering of the core shot (shots 2 and 4 above) and "starts up" sound and action, flashbacking to the previous, China-set tableau. The reanimated Japanese troops continue to give out provisions to lines of smiling Chinese children. A girl grabs her package, pauses face-forward (before walking out of frame) and looks at what she has been given. Cut to:

7. Tight close-up of package label: "Imperial Japanese OPIUM monopoly."
8. Cut back to core set up. Frowning Chinese girl approaches Japanese troops.
9. Girl pushes package back into soldier's hands.

> JAPANESE SOLDIER: "What's this?"
> CHINESE GIRL: "We don't use opium here!"

10. Japanese Soldier: "You will eat what we give you—or you will not eat at all! Do you understand?" (Whereupon the Japanese soldier pushes the Chinese girl into oncoming traffic)

Eschewing verbal narration, with a slick cinematic dexterity suited to a fast lesson in photographic sleight of hand, *Behind the Rising Sun* delivers its media message in purely visual terms.

Clearly, the supreme magicians of screen propaganda no longer resided in the Ufa Studio at Neubabelsberg. Whatever anxieties the Reichsfilmkammer blitzkrieg and Riefenstahl triumphs had fostered in Hollywood at the onset of war had turned to serene confidence once the battle was truly joined. Capra's *Why We Fight* series alone had outmaneuvered and outstripped the once-feared "Nazified treatments" of the "slickest propaganda regimentation extant." By mid-war, evidence of the heightened mass communications smarts of American culture was daily visible on any motion picture screen— even in the unlikely precincts of *Behind the Rising Sun*.

The lately perfected dexterity on the American side had one unforeseen consequence. If the medium qua medium invited manipulation and deception, the potential for misapprehension could not be intrinsic to Axis cinema alone. Therefore, while the educational program in the treacherous techniques of enemy cinema proceeded apace, reassurances needed to be offered about the good intentions and fair dealing of Hollywood cinema. As an expression of trust and openness, the motion picture industry stopped safeguarding some its own secrets. Hollywood's trademark "invisible style," the studio system aesthetic that concealed the guiding hand of the filmmaker, was made visible for all to see. Increasingly after 1941, the newsreels, documentary shorts, and government information films spotlighted behind-the-scenes glimpses of Hollywood production and detailed reports on the techniques of motion picture photography, especially combat camerawork shot under fire. Feature films too began incorporating moments of instructive self-reflexivity. In *Pilot No. 5* (1943) a demagogic state governor rehearses a newsreel appearance with cameramen-cum-henchmen. Seated at his desk, oozing an affected homespun touch, he begins his on-camera presentation. The newsreel cameramen coach him to arise from his seat more slowly: "Remember, we have to pan up with you." During the subsequent take, the demagogue complies and a reverse shot reviews the lesson in film grammar by showing the newsreel cameras panning up. Contrasting the American with the Axis approach (and making generous use of the first-person plural), Lowell Mellett asserted the propaganda difference at the 1943 Academy Awards ceremony. "We have not sought to mesmerize the American people through the play of light and shadow upon their eyes and sound upon their ears," Mellett explained to the artists who devised the strategy. "We have not sought to goosestep the American soul."[25]

Far from having a mesmerized gaze or a goosestepped soul, the average American moviegoer circa 1945 had acquired a more alert, attuned, and skeptical eye than the circa

1941 model. Graduating from the four-year curriculum in motion picture technique and propagandistic persuasion was the first generation of moving-image spectators as accustomed to education as entertainment, as prepared for critical engagement as for cultural diversion. Axis cinema, endowed elsewhere with an almost hypnotic power of persuasion, could rightly be marked as crudely obvious and transparently deceptive to the discerning American whose Hollywood-trained vision was sharp enough to spot the con. "You are up to his tricks," Warner Bros.'s *Divide and Conquer* assures. "You can see through his technique." As for the deprived foreigners and occupied peoples who suffered prolonged exposure to the Reichsfilmkammer blight, the motion picture industry prescribed a predictable refresher course: its own features. As the *Hollywood Reporter* bragged: "Military authorities and OWI men are convinced that American films are the most important means of disintoxicating people in areas formerly occupied by the enemy from Axis propaganda and re-educating them to the knowledge of the free world and free people from which they have been cut off."[26] In selected cases the suspicion that should be accorded all images might be suspended.

Notes

1   Among the many studies of Nazi propaganda are Jay W. Baird, *The Mythical World of Nazi War Propaganda, 1939–1945* (Minneapolis: University of Minnesota Press, 1974) and David Welch, ed., *Nazi Propaganda: The Power and the Limitations* (London: Croom Helm, 1983). For a provocative analysis of the aesthetics of Nazism, see Peter Cohen's film *The Architecture of Doom* (1989).

2   "Coe Sees Films Helping to Win World Peace," *Motion Picture Herald*, August 7, 1943, p. 18.

3   On the international release and distribution of *Olympia* see Cooper C. Graham, *Leni Riefenstahl and Olympia* (Metuchen, N.J.: Scarecrow Press, 1986), pp. 154–249, esp. pp. 210–26 on the American market. Graham notes that *Triumph of the Will* was screened in German enclaves in the big cities and that *Olympia* was shown, probably in a pirated print, in New York in 1940.

4   The Josef von Sternberg quote is in Leni Riefenstahl, *Memoiren* (München: Albert Knaus, 1987), p. 300. Although von Sternberg's autobiography omits any plaudits for *Triumph of the Will*, he regally numbers Riefenstahl among "students of my work" and recalls that along with the rest of Weimar Germany, she hung around the set of *The Blue Angel*. Interestingly, he misremembers the film title as *The Will to Triumph*. Von Sternberg, *Fun in a Chinese Laundry* (New York: Macmillan, 1965), p. 144.

5   Siegfried Kracauer, "Propaganda and the Nazi War Film" (1942), reprinted in *From Caligari to Hitler: A Psychological Study of the German Film* (Princeton: Princeton University Press, 1947; London: Dennis Dobson, 1947), pp. 303, 278. Less cinematically minded observers were not as attentive to Riefenstahl's contribution. In a 1938 survey of the Nuremberg rallies for *Public Opinion Quarterly*, Thorton Sinclair makes no mention of either *Triumph of the Will* or Riefenstahl. Sinclair, "The Nazi Party Rally at Nuremberg," *Public Opinion Quarterly* (October 1938): 570–83.

6   Reports of Riefenstahl's "liquidation" are mentioned in Sgt. Alfred W. Rhodes, Jr.,

"German Propaganda Movies in Two Wars," *American Cinematographer* (January 1943), pp. 10–11, 28.

7 Richard Thompson, *Film Propaganda: Soviet Russia and Nazi Germany* (London: Croom Helm, 1979), p. 177.

8 Capra, *The Name Above the Title*, pp. 361–62.

9 "Film Biz Pressing Our Government for Better Coverage of the War," *Variety*, July 22, 1942, pp. 4, 18.

10 Francis S. Harmon, "Movies as Propaganda," in *The Command Is Forward: Selections from Addresses on the Motion Picture Industry in War and Peace* (New York: Richard R. Smith, 1944), pp. 8–9. In his 1945 account of the Hays Office, Raymond Moley offered a caveat that underlined the popular usage, "I have used the word 'propaganda' with no sinister implications." Moley, *The Hays Office* (Indianapolis and New York: Bobbs-Merrill, 1945), p. 112. A notable departure from Hollywood's traditional aversion to overt intrusion into politics occurred during Upton Sinclair's 1934 campaign for governor of California. With a sophistication and unscrupulousness worthy of the Reichsfilmkammer, MGM filmed bogus man-on-the-street interviews and presented the well-rehearsed anti-Sinclair smears as "newsreels" in theaters throughout the state. The spots were widely thought to have torpedoed Sinclair's chances. See Upton Sinclair, "The Movies as Political Propaganda," in William J. Perlman, ed., *The Movies on Trial* (New York: MacMillan, 1936), pp. 192–94.

11 Robert Parrish, "Fact Meets Fiction in a World War II Celluloid Face-off," *Smithsonian* (March 1986), p. 164. See also Parrish, "The Battle of Midway," in *Growing Up in Hollywood* (Boston: Little, Brown, 1976), pp. 144–51.

12 Rhodes, Jr., "German Propaganda Movies in Two Wars," p. 11.

13 "D.C. Brasshats' Short Sightedness on Propaganda Pix Nearing a Crisis," *Variety*, August 19, 1942, p. 47.

14 "Nazis Are Using Films for Conquest and Pacification," *Hollywood Reporter*, September 21, 1942, p. 7.

15 "Film Biz Pressing Our Government for Better Coverage of the War," *Variety*, July 22, 1942, pp. 4, 18.

16 "OWI Film Aim Is to Beat Nazis Among Neutrals," *Motion Picture Herald*, August 1, 1942, p. 16.

17 Kracauer, *From Caligari to Hitler*, p. 278.

18 "Propaganda Lesson," *Motion Picture Herald*, January 30, 1943, p. 9. During the segment from *Triumph of the Will*, the *Hollywood Reporter* heard chuckling from the crowd at "der Führer's strutting" and disapproved sternly of such "a prideful and frivolous reaction" to so "cunningly planned and darkly prophetic |an| example of threatening propaganda."

19 "Elmer Davis Says Mellett's Govt. Film Bureau Will Continue Its Function; Embarrassed by Praise," *Variety*, June 17, 1942, p. 4.

20 "Mellett's Trial Balloon Bursts; Prods. Stand Pat," *Hollywood Reporter*, December 21, 1942, p. 7.

21 Hearings Before the Special Senate Committee Investigating the National Defense Program, 78th Cong., 1st sess., February 16, 1943, p. 6903.

22 "American Soldiers See German Film of War," *Stars and Stripes*, January 29, 1943, p. 4.

23 "Propaganda in Reverse," *Motion Picture Herald*, March 3, 1945, p. 5.

24 "Hitler, Plus Lambeth Walk Equals a Panic," *Box Office*, January 17, 1942, p. 11.

25 "Academy Hears Mellett Make 'Faith' Award," *Motion Picture Herald*, March 6, 1943, p. 19.

26 "Axis Influence in No. Africa Being Overcome by U.S. Pix," *Hollywood Reporter*, January 18, 1943, p. 5.

Will this Picture Help to Win the War?

14

CLAYTON R. KOPPES and GREGORY D. BLACK

. . . . In the summer of 1942 the head of the Hollywood office of the Bureau of Motion Pictures, Nelson Poynter, and his staff assembled their suggestions in a "Government Information Manual for the Motion Picture Industry." The manual is a key document in understanding the relationship between film and propaganda during the war. More than a "how to" handbook, the manual was a comprehensive statement of OWI's vision of America, the war, and the world. That perspective derived from the liberal or left-liberal orientation of much of OWI's staff. Issued in loose leaf so that frequent up-dates could be incorporated, the manual affords an illuminating glimpse of how a key segment of American opinion understood the meaning of the war.

The only consensus about the war in America was that we had been attacked, that defeating the Axis was imperative, and that American might and right would triumph. That broad tent covered, however, sharp ideological cleavages about the nature of American right, and what American might should accomplish. Infinite shadings of opinion existed throughout the war, to be sure, but they tended to coalesce, like filings affected by magnetic forces, around two poles: Henry Luce's "American Century" editorial of 1941, and Henry A. Wallace's "Century of the Common Man" speech of early 1942. OWI marched under the banner of the common man. Wallace interpreted the war as a landmark in the revolutionary struggle for individual rights going back to Jesus Christ. The war was truly a struggle between light and darkness. America fought for the Four Freedoms worldwide. The vice president emphasized a decent standard of living for all, to be attained through government action in a mixed economy—in short, a world New Deal. Wallace wrote his speech as an answer to Luce. The publishing magnate wanted America to impose its power on the world for whatever purposes it saw fit; his blueprint was truly for a Pax Americana. He placed private enterprise ahead of social reform and evoked conservative constructs of stability, order, and economic freedom. In historian Norman Markowitz's phrase: "Luce had combined the Invisible Hand of Adam Smith with the benevolent imperialism of Rudyard Kipling to create the American Century."[1]

Believing every film was imbued with significance for the war effort, OWI asked film-makers to consider seven questions:

1. Will this picture help win the war?
2. What war information problem does it seek to clarify, dramatize or interpret?

3. If it is an "escape" picture, will it harm the war effort by creating a false picture of America, her allies, or the world we live in?
4. Does it merely use the war as the basis for a profitable picture, contributing nothing of real significance to the war effort and possibly lessening the effect of other pictures of more importance?
5. Does it contribute something new to our understanding of the world conflict and the various forces involved, or has the subject already been adequately covered?
6. When the picture reaches its maximum circulation on the screen, will it reflect conditions as they are and fill a need current at that time, or will it be out-dated?
7. Does the picture tell the truth or will the young people of today have reason to say they were misled by propaganda?

The manual was a virtual catechism of the world view articulated by Wallace in his "Century of the Common Man."[2]

1. *Why We Fight*. If one word summed up the struggle it was "democracy." That flexible term was used to provide a comprehensive explanation of why the Allies fought; it embraced both domestic politics and society and the international order. Democracy divided the world into two camps. The Allies were *ipso facto* democracies. This was a war for survival, since defeat meant slavery for all. The stakes of the war were so high that no compromise was possible. The manual quoted Wallace: "There can be no compromise with Satan." When Roosevelt announced the doctrine of unconditional surrender in 1943, OWI easily incorporated the idea. Ever mindful of the disillusionment that seared America after Versailles, the agency taught that we fought for a "worthwhile peace." Total victory would bring forth a "new world"—a world of the Four Freedoms to be shared by everyone, including the defeated Axis. The globe was, to use the term popularized by Wendell Willkie's bestseller of 1943, "one world." That world was indivisible; democracy must be universalized or these freedoms would "always be in jeopardy in America." The new world would be the community of the open door, "dedicated to the free flow of trade, ideas, and culture." The war was a continuation of revolutionary struggle; 1942 was an outgrowth of 1776.

This was, then, "a people's war," OWI proclaimed. Everyone had a stake in it, regardless of class, ethnic, or religious identification: everyone contributed according to his or her ability. "Show democracy at work," the manual said, "in the community, the factory, the army." Avoid stereotypes, such as blacks in menial or comic roles. Show loyal aliens, "glad of a chance to support and help the free land of their adoption." Few aliens were fifth columnists; they should be depicted as helping the war effort of "the free land of their adoption." Although this was a war for survival, "a worthwhile peace" would follow, based on the Four Freedoms—freedom of speech and religion, freedom from want and fear.

2. *The Enemy*. The enemy was not the entire German, Japanese, or Italian people, nor even the ruling elites. "The enemy is many people infected with a poisonous doctrine of hate, of might making right," said the propagandists. Enemies were ubiquitous. "This is total war," they wrote. "Everyone is either a friend or a foe." Abetting the fascists' spies and saboteurs, who could be readily unmasked, were the uncommitted, the pessimists, the buck-passers.

3. *The United Nations*. Thirty nations were allied against the Axis. The manual homogenized them into democratic societies which, whatever their peculiarities, shared a common anti-fascist goal. If an ally fell short of democracy, better to overlook that fact and concentrate on

its contribution to United Nations victory. British imperialism was glossed over with praise for the empire's "magnificent battle." More difficult was Stalin's Soviet Union. "Yes, we Americans reject communism," said the manual. "But we do not reject our Russian ally" and its heroic contribution to victory. Chiang Kai-shek's China, so badly misunderstood in the United States, was transformed into "a great nation, cultured and liberal." It had been "fighting our war since 1933" and we would be "closely bound" with her "in the world that is to come." Trujillo's Dominican Republic, Somoza's Nicaragua, and the Union of South Africa stuck out awkwardly, but as smaller nations they did not require specific whitewashes. The Allies should be given their due; the U.S. should not be shown winning the war single handedly. The people of the United Nations should be neither "peculiar creatures essentially unlike ourselves" nor "patently American types . . . in a foreign locale." Demeaning stereotypes were to be avoided at all costs.

4. *The Home Front*. American democracy was not perfect, OWI acknowledged. The country had its underprivileged, but they were becoming "less underprivileged" and hence had a stake in the war's outcome. Government programs—New Deal measures, though not so identified by the manual—brought slum clearance, curbs on "vicious tenant farming," rural electrification, and advances for blacks.

Unity became the byword of the civilian war effort. The movies should show everyone sacrificing cheerfully for the war. This might extend from uncomplaining payment of taxes and purchase of war bonds to such mundane practices as carrying one's own sugar when invited out to dinner or giving up seats on trains and buses to servicemen. Volunteer activities should be lauded, not belittled. Women should be shown in pictures as stepping forward, becoming war workers, donning armed forces uniforms, and assuming jobs formerly handled by men. They should also be depicted as coping without their husbands or sweethearts, even leaving their children at day-care centers. From production centers a stream of war goods flowed, implicitly promoting confidence in ultimate victory. The theme of all types of workers and management bosses contributing to victory—and achieving harmony through labor management committees—undergirded OWI's vision of a united home front.

5. *The Fighting Forces*. Although combat scenes naturally furnished an abundance of dramatic material, OWI urged the studios to use them for something more than melodrama. The agency hoped movies could stress all components of the armed forces, whether glamorous or not, show the careful training of G.I.'s, and prepare the public for casualties. The multi-ethnic platoon, "using names of foreign extraction" (what American names were not of foreign extraction?) and showing occasional black officers, would strengthen the impression of national unity. Finally, the public should be prepared for fatality lists by showing "why the sacrifice of their loved ones was worthwhile."

The OWI manual, augmented by revisions and "common law" decisions on particular films, constituted in effect a second code. Though not so rigorous or far-reaching as the Production Code Administration's canon, the OWI code served much the same function, instructing the moviemakers on the correct presentation of certain subject matter. The two codes coexisted uneasily, for they had different purposes. Both codes were designed to ensure that the movies reflected their sponsors' point of view, to be sure; but the challenge for the PCA code was more to remove material, that of the OWI to insert it. The two codes and the organizations interpreting them also differed in their political outlooks. They shared a certain conservatism in that they upheld the legitimacy and justice of American politics and society. OWI, however, demanded overt political positions while PCA tried to minimize them. And OWI through its embrace of the New Deal and the "Century of the Common Man" advocated a mild social democracy and liberal internationalist foreign policy that was anathema to the author of the PCA code and its chief interpreters. However, the PCA also recognized that the war created "extenuating circumstances" which would bring more violence and social and political subjects to the screen. Thus the explicitly political nature of the OWI code challenged an entrenched set of procedures, and thereby ensured controversy.[3]

Much of this potential for conflict was hidden in the summer of 1942. In a burst of patriotism the industry hailed the manual. Here was the recognition the movie colony had sought from the government. The manual was not filed and forgotten; the major studios duplicated copies or lengthy summaries of it for their staffs. The record of conferences between studio personnel and OWI indicates that many producers and writers gave it serious consideration as they planned productions. Not surprisingly, the manual, like OWI generally, found its friendliest response in liberal or leftist quarters. Warner Bros. was the most liberal studio and the most receptive. Nelson Poynter told the brothers Warner he was counting on them to blaze the trail in Hollywood. As a group writers were more left-leaning than the senior executives of the studios; some directors were also receptive.[4]

Even the writers and directors who were members of the Communist Party found the politics of the manual appealing. Some of them, such as Dalton Trumbo and John Howard Lawson, would become known during the Cold War as the "Hollywood Ten" when they ran afoul of the House Un-American Activities Committee. More politically conscious than many other writers, they were often chosen for war-related screenplays where they could put their expertise to work. This should not be misunderstood. There was little danger of "communist" ideas being slipped into wartime movies undetected. Whatever writers did, they were under the strict supervision of a top-heavy, usually conservative, studio hierarchy. Also, the Communist Party was in a phase in which its position was almost indistinguishable from that of European social democrats and advanced New Dealers. It was not that American liberals had moved left; it was more that, owing to the war, the Communist Party had temporarily moved right.[5]

What OWI was promoting in Hollywood, then, was an interpretation of American society and international politics that commanded assent from the center of the political spectrum to the left, but not necessarily from the right. That point of view, colored by wartime neces-sity and wishful thinking, raised as many questions as it answered. Consider the cornerstone of the edifice: "democracy." As a description of reality it fit only a few of the United Nations. As a measure of political aspiration, it was too specifically American to be extended to the myriad complexities of world politics. Faced with references to violence by the Spanish Loyalists in Paramount's *For Whom the Bell Tolls*, agency reviewers said: "Now it is necessary that we see the democratic-fascist battle as a whole and recognize that what the Loyalists were fighting for is essentially the same thing that we are. To focus too much attention on the chinks in our allies' armor is just what our enemies might wish. Perhaps it is realistic, but it is also going to be confusing to American audiences."[6]

OWI therefore retreated to a world of symbolism designed to evoke the desired responses. Concepts such as "democracy," "fascism," and "unity" conformed to what social theorist Robert Merton termed "sacred and sentimental" symbols—beliefs and opinions grounded in emotion, as is characteristic of patriotic and religious feelings. The use of such symbolism was all but irresistible because it seemed to evoke favorable results from large numbers of people. Therein lay the danger. Merton warned that so long as mass response was the goal, "the choice of techniques of persuasion will be governed by a narrowly technical and amoral criterion" This goal was dangerously manipulative because it encouraged "the use of whatsoever techniques work." Merton did not contend that all appeals to sentiment are manipulative. He offered, however, a distinction that is useful in interpreting OWI and Hollywood: "Appeals to sentiment within the context of relevant information and knowledge are basically different from appeals to sentiment which blur and obscure this knowledge. Mass persuasion is not manipulative when it provides access to the pertinent facts; it is manipulative when the appeal to sentiment is used to the exclusion of pertinent information."[7]

Through their use of sacred and sentimental symbols OWI and Hollywood tried to manipulate opinion by denying or clouding relevant information. The manual's seventh question correctly cited the heavy responsibility borne not only by Hollywood but also by OWI: "Does the picture tell the truth or will the young people of today have reason to say they were misled by propaganda?" The answer to that question, and its consequences, became clear as the sometimes competitive, but eventually collaborative, relationship between the propagandists and the commercial mythmakers unfolded. . . .

Notes

1   Henry A. Wallace, "The Price of Free World Victory: The Century of the Common Man," *Vital Speeches of the Day*, 7 (1942), 482–85; Henry Luce, "The American Century," *Life* (Feb. 17, 1941), 61–63; Norman Markowitz, *The Rise and Fall of the People's Century: Henry A. Wallace and American Liberalism* (New York, 1973), p. 50.
2   "Government Information Manual for the Motion Picture Industry," Summer 1942, box 15, OWI files. Revisions were made to keep the manual abreast of developments in the war, but this did not change the document's thrust. See the revisions dated April 29, 1943, and January 1944, box 15, OWI files.
3   Breen to Shurlock, Apr. 15, 1943, "Hitler's Madman," PCA Files, Academy Library.
4   Koppes interview with Poynter.
5   Ceplair and Englund, *The Inquisition in Hollywood*, pp. 177–83.
6   Script review, "For Whom the Bell Tolls," Oct. 14, 1942, OWI files.
7   Robert K. Merton with Marjorie Fiske and Alberta Curtis, *Mass Persuasion: The Social Psychology of a War Bond Drive* (New York, 1946), p. 186.

The World War II Combat Film: Definition

15

JEANINE BASINGER

Summary: elements of the genre

. . . From films of 1943 comes a list of elements to be found which repeat and recur in the combat genre. We know *Guadalcanal Diary* to be an on-the-spot-correspondent's account of an actual battle. And yet the story might as well have been thought up in Hollywood by someone who had never been there. Setting aside differences in military uniform and weapons, and thus the attendant differences in mission and type of combat, *Destination Tokyo*, *Bataan*, *Air Force*, *Sahara* and *Guadalcanal Diary* are the same movie. This "list" can be put into two forms:

A. As a "story" of a film—the "story" which becomes what everyone imagines the combat genre to be, but which, in fact, does not exist in a pure form in any single film. It is this "story" that the satirists use in TV skits, but it is also the thing that filmmakers would later use to create new genre films.
B. As an outline of elements and characteristics, to be used in analyzing films of the genre.

A. The "Story"

Here is the "story" of the universal World War II combat film, with its primary units in bold face and indications of how they can be varied without violating the basic definition in brackets.

The credits of the film unfold against a military reference. |A map, a flag, an insignia, a photo or painting of battle, a military song, for example.| **The credits include the name of a military advisor**.

Closely connected to the presentation of the credits is a statement that may be called the film's dedication. |It may be printed or narrated. It may be a reference to a military battle of the past or present. It may contain thanks to a military service which cooperated in the making of the film, or an emotional tribute to a gallant fighting force, our allies, or a quote from a famous World War II figure, with Churchill and Roosevelt being particular favorites.|

A group of men, led by a hero, undertake a mission which will accomplish an important military objective. [The group of men is a mixture of unrelated types, with varying ethnic and socioeconomic backgrounds. They may be men from different military forces, and/or different countries. They are of different ages. Some have never fought in combat before, and others are experienced. Some are intellectual and well-educated, others are not. They are both married and single, shy and bold, urban and rural, comic and tragic. They come from all areas of the United States geographically, especially the Middle West (stability), the South (naïveté but good shooting ability), New England (education), and New York City (sophistication). Favorite states are Iowa, the Dakotas, and Kansas for the Middle West; California and Texas for recognition; and Brooklyn. (In the war film, Brooklyn is a state unto itself, and is almost always present one way or another.) Their occupations vary: farmer, cab driver, teacher. Minority figures are always represented: black, Hispanic, Indian, and even Orientals.]

This group contains an observer or commentator. [A newspaperman, a man keeping a diary, or a man who thinks or talks out loud.]

The hero has had leadership forced upon him in dire circumstances. [The highest ranking officer may have been killed, placing him in command. He may have been forced into his role simply by having been drafted or having felt he had to volunteer for the role. He may have been a career military man who received an odious assignment. The assumption of enforced responsibility, however willingly or unwillingly accepted, is present.]

They undertake a military objective. [They may have to hold a fort and make a last stand. They may have to rove forward through jungle, desert, forest, the ocean, both on top and underwater, or in the air. But whether holding the fort or journeying to destroy the enemy's fort—or waiting for returning comrades or going out to rejoin comrades—the objective is present. The objective may have been a secret, or it may have been planned in advance, or it may have grown out of necessity.]

As they go forward, the action unfolds. A series of episodes occur which alternate in uneven patterns the contrasting forces of night and day, action and repose, safety and danger, combat and noncombat, comedy and tragedy, dialogue and action. [The variations are endless, as inventive as the writers can make them.]

The enemy's presence is indicated. [He may appear face-to-face, fly over in airplanes and bomb, sail by in other ships and shoot, crawl forward in endless numbers, assault from trees, broadcast on the radio, whatever. He is sometimes seen in closeup, and is sometimes faceless.]

Military inconography is seen, and its usage is demonstrated for and taught to civilians. [Uniforms, weapons, equipment, insignia, maps, salt tablets, K-rations, walkie-talkies, etc.]

Conflict breaks out within the group itself. It is resolved through the external conflict brought down upon them.

Rituals are enacted from the past. [If a holiday comes, such as Christmas, it is celebrated. If a death occurs, a burial takes place.]

Rituals are enacted from the present. [Mail is read, and weapons are cleaned. Philosophies of life and postwar plans are discussed.]

Members of the group die. [This has many variations, including the death of the entire group. The minorities almost always die, and die most horribly.]

A climactic battle takes place, and a learning or growth process occurs.

The tools of cinema are employed for tension (*cutting*), release (*camera movement*), intimacy and alienation (*composition*), and the look of combat (*lighting*) and authenticity (*documentary footage*).

The situation is resolved. |It will be so only after sacrifice and loss, hardship and discouragement, and it can be resolved either through victory or defeat, death or survival.|

THE END appears on the screen. |A "rollcall" of the combatants appears, either as cast names or pictures of the actors with their cast names or as a scene in which they march by or fly by or pass by us in some way, living and/or dead.|

The audience is ennobled for having shared their combat experience, as they are ennobled for having undergone it. We are all comrades in arms.

Anyone wishing to write a combat film can follow this story and make an appropriate script. Just to show how it can work, here is the first one-third of an imaginary combat film, entitled *War Cry!*

The insignia of the Marine Corps is seen, and "From the halls of Montezuma" is being sung by a male chorus. *War Cry!* jumps out from the screen. The credits appear, including the name of Col. Marcus B. Everson, Technical Advisor. As the credits finish, a map of the Solomon Islands is seen, and these words are on the screen:

"This film is dedicated to the ferocious fighting men of the American Marine Corps. From the halls of Montezuma to the shores of Tripoli . . . and now to the heat and humidity and horror of the Pacific . . . these men, ordinary people with extraordinary ability to fight . . . guard our American way of life. We owe them our deepest gratitude and greatest respect, because, no matter what, they always do the job with the rallying cry, " 'Marines Let's Go!!' "

Semper Fidelis . . .

On a troop ship heading into battle on the Pacific is a combat platoon consisting of Feinstein, O'Hara, Thomas Jefferson Brown, Kowalski, Rinaldi, Andy Hawkins, Bruce Martinson, Pop Jorgenson. They are under the command of Captain Charles P. Jenkins, and their tough professional soldier top sergeant is Kip McCormick. With them is war correspondent David C. Davis.

On board ship as they await battle, they talk of their lives and homes. Pop's feet hurt. He tells about the night before his first battle in World War I. Martinson, a Harvard graduate who had planned to go to medical school, is reading A *Farewell to Arms*. Feinstein talks about wishing he was back home going to Ebbetts Field to see the Dodgers, driving there in his cab. Hawkins, a young and unsophisticated boy, has never been away from home before, his home being his father's farm in the mountains of Tennessee. Kowalski and O'Hara hate one another, and are arguing about how to make a good stew. Kowalski says no potatoes, use cabbage. O'Hara says no cabbage, use potatoes. Thomas Jefferson Brown sings "Swing Low, Sweet Chariot," and Jenkins tells him how they always sang "Rock of Ages" at their little church in New England, but he guesses it's all just the same song. Jenkins notices the little dog Hawkins has hidden beside him, but decides to ignore it. Jenkins talks about his wife, a Sunday school teacher, and his two kids. Davis is keeping a diary. His voiceover talks about his fears of combat, and about how brave the other men seem. McCormick says nothing. He keeps his own counsel. Rinaldi is sleeping.

Going ashore, Jenkins is killed, and after their small band is isolated from the main group, McCormick assumes command. To survive, they must rejoin their main forces while avoiding the Japanese patrols. They have only enough salt tablets for half the group. Their maps were lost in the landing. Feinstein has been wounded and cannot walk. Kowalski and O'Hara prepare to carry him. Davis's voice is heard saying, "If we ever get out of this alive."

Here you have the first one third of a perfect combat movie, based on what you already know.

B. The Outline

Because so many variations of the basic definition can be created, and because of the process of evolution the genre will undergo, the story may be transferred into an outline form with which to compare films easily. Since characteristics can be the same, only different (group of mixed military forces, group of ethnic mixes, group of mixed international forces), and since what they represent will shift in the evolutionary process (how tragic to lose the good father leader, how good to get rid of the evil father who forced us to fight), we need an objective format with which to identify the basic definition:

The Outline
A. CHARACTERS
    1. The Hero
    2. The Group
    3. The Enemy
    4. The Women (if any)
B. SETTING
    1. The Theater of War (Date and Place)
    2. The Military Force Involved (Air, Sea, Ground)
    3. Relationship to History (True event or not)
    4. The Objective
C. NARRATIVE STRUCTURE
    1. Episodes
        a. Credits, Dedication, and Opening Sequence.
        b. Combat/Non-combat (Action and Repose)
        c. Familiar Events (This refers to events, such as mail call or Christmas celebration that occur from film to film.)
        d. Night/Day
        e. Comedy/Tragedy
    2. Organization of story pattern
        a. Time sequence (Present, past, use of flashback, etc.)
        b. Place sequence (Change of geographical location, etc.)
        c. Plot Sequence (Order of events)
        d. Narrative viewpoint (Objective/Subjective)
D. CULTURAL ATTITUDES
    1. Death/Sacrifice/Loss
    2. Propaganda
    3. Humor

4. Home/Family/Country
5. The Situation At Hand

E. LANGUAGE
   1. Film and visual language
      a. Technique (Cutting, camera movement, etc.)
      b. Image (Includes what is seen as event, gesture, action)
      c. Iconography (Includes all possible coded information)
   2. Dialogue

By using this outline and applying it to a particular film, the relationship of that film to the rest of the genre (its inconsistency or matching qualities) can be determined. Also, its position in the evolutionary process is established, as well as its overall relationship to history and reality. It demonstrates how a primary set of concepts solidifies into a story— and how they can be interpreted for a changing ideology. From the films came the list. From the list comes the story. Out of the story you can make a screenplay. Out of the total accumulated screenplays (films) can be made an outline. Out of the outline one can study the films to see where they differ and vary the basic pattern of the genre.

To simplify and condense, *Bataan* has been used here as the sample film from which to generate the list. In actual research, all the combat films screened were used for the basic definition. The important aspect of these characteristics is obviously not just the list itself. For a genre to live, it must in some way tell a story the audience needs to hear told after the war is over. This means its characteristics must contain meanings that an audience needs further information or involvement with in the postwar era.

Can the characteristics be made to represent the concerns of another era? We can see from the basic definition that the concepts may be varied, but that their function remains the same. Can they be varied and also have their functions inverted or adjusted ideologically, and still remain the genre? We know that genres have eras of particular popularity, and that some seem to disappear. Currently, we talk of the disappearance of the Western, and the suggestion is raised that, since the geographical frontier is no longer an important concept for filmgoers, we see no more Westerns but instead turn our attention to the science fiction movie and the new frontier of space. Of course we quickly see that the science fiction movie tends to give us the Western format in space clothes, but a discussion of that will come later.

Now we are concerned with basic definition. If the primary characteristics can be used to answer questions that are concerned only with the war, presumably the genre will have no use, no appeal, for viewers when the issue of the war is settled by its successful completion. When we look at the list of questions the war combat genre generates, it is obvious that some of them are settled once the war is over, but that most of them are basic to our understanding of ourselves and our history. They are eternal questions, and this makes the genre one that can (and, in fact, will) live on.

The primary questions which inspired the basic characteristics of the combat genre—the storytelling process of hero, group, objective—were straightforward concerns of a nation at war. Could we win it? What would we have to do to win? What was each individual's responsibility in the fight? We all would have to do our part—whether in combat or on the home front—but how? What things would we have to know in order not to become separated eternally from one another if some went to fight and others stayed behind? Who were these strange enemies, and what attitudes should we take toward them now? Since America was a nation of people from many countries, what would we do when some of us were suddenly designated as enemies? We had to be taught what to think, and what aspects of the enemy we should fear. In order to do this, we had to reconsider the concept of Americanism. What did it mean to be American? What was America's history, and who were her heroes? We had to think about what nice guys we were, and about how we always played fair and about how much we liked our moms and apple pie. If we were reluctant to fight, we had to be taught why we must. We were preserving our democratic system and our cultural attitudes. We were defending a precious and unique heritage. To do this, we were going to have to work together as a real group of equals, or we weren't going to make it. Oh, we needed the individual's bravery and guts, but only if it could be sacrificed to the good of the group. And if our families were separated and torn apart by war, this group could become our substitute family—a kind of big, national family of other Americans. More than anything else, we needed that group.

All these questions and lessons were basic to the war combat genre of World War II. When the war was over, however, these issues were resolved, and we had no further need for the information. If these had been the only questions ever asked by the World War II film, perhaps it would have died. But there were other issues involved in these stories, issues that made them of continued importance, because they were issues we would always need to think about. World War II films were all about living and dying. What makes a good life and what makes a good person? What should we be willing to die for—and how do you die right? If you had to die young, what would make you a noble sacrifice and what would make it all a waste? What about killing? If you had to do it, did that make you a killer? What about when the war was over, and you returned home, having killed? Would it change you forever? It was one thing to agree cheerfully to work in a group, and to accept the group over the individual for the war effort, but how did you do this? How did you resolve group conflicts and differences of opinion, background, and attitude? Could you really make family relationships and thus preserve a form of civilization in the midst of combat? How could you be a good American, and furthermore, was that really a good thing to be? Could you suffer loss and defeat and still survive? Could defeat really be victory in disguise? Was it wrong to be selfish, and not want to make sacrifices, or was it exhibiting sanity to reject wartime attitudes?

There are doubtless more questions, enough to fill a volume themselves. But in these one can see why the genre survived and was repeated. Long after the primary issues were resolved (we did win the war; we did learn to play our roles well; we taught the enemy they were wrong about it, etc.), the other issues have remained. The evolutionary process the genre has undergone happened because some of these issues are still relevant. We continue to need to learn what it means to be Americans, and if that is a good or bad thing. We continue to need to learn about living and dying, and about loss and defeat, and about what our way of life really means. Furthermore, these issues are flexible, and can be used to demonstrate differing ideology and political attitudes in the years to come. It can be bad or good to be American, right or wrong to kill. All this allows for the evolutionary process. And all this is typical of all genres, not just the combat film. It can be observed operating in the gangster films and Westerns over the years as they reflect a celebration of American violence or shame about it, as they repress women or liberate them, and as new wars come along to be understood and evaluated.

Since World War II is one of the biggest events of American history, it is natural that films about it would continue to be of interest. However, the same might be said about the Civil War, World War I, and even the Spanish American War.

Consider the films about other great wars of American history. We have almost no films about the Spanish American War although sometimes in Westerns or musicals the hero has to leave town to go fight it for a time, as in *Pursued* or *Stars and Stripes Forever*. The Civil War, too, has fewer actual combat films than one might suppose. It was *very* popular in silent films, but the two World Wars tend to crowd it off the screen. Although many Civil War films are set in the South, these are films about a way of life, and about issues such as slavery and sex more than they are about combat. The combat of the Civil War is actually seldom depicted on the sound screen. Perhaps the greatness of *The Birth of a Nation* took care of the presentation once and for all. *Gone with the Wind* has no actual combat, just its aftermath and the effect of renegade soldiers in the lives of women. *Horse Soldiers* (1959) is one of the few combat films of the Civil War, and the combat occupies perhaps half of its running time. It has a Westernized format, and is directed by a man closely associated with World War II films and Westerns, John Ford. *The Red Badge of Courage* (1951), that notorious flop, is a miniature patrol film, and its influence, both as a novel and as a film, might be felt, but the film was not released until *after* World War II. John Huston, its director, had already made documentary combat films, as he participated in the battle of San Pietro and went forward, camera in hand, to record the events. Here is a case of reality and fiction blurring indeed. Perhaps we do not care to see our Civil War depicted in any way but as what it is: a quarrel in the family over material matters. *Tap Roots* (1948) effectively carries this idea out by telling the true story of a Mississippi county that seceded from the secession. Thus, the combat is seen more as them-against-them than as us-against-us—a larger type of family quarrel. The World War I film, discussed in the next chapter, also seems relatively limited in appeal.

World War II seems to be the combat that speaks to the American soul. Perhaps it is our total victory, or the sense of our righteousness, or the conviction that it wasn't our fault, or the influence of technology on art—in which the ability to take cameras into the field created images of power that would and could not be forgotten—or the simple thing that a great many cracking good stories came out of WWII, or that the studio system was alive and well and could turn out many films. There are many possibilities and no doubt they all apply.

But all or nothing at all, as the World War II-era song says. Whatever the reason, the combat film was born in World War II, and it grew, lived, and evolved during the conflict.

Hollywood and the World War II Conversion Narrative

LARY MAY

Monopolizing the public sphere

To understand the transformation in American culture unfolding during World War II, it is important to realize that the call for unity generated a battle against the radical republican tradition that had pervaded national life ever since the early nineteenth century. After a decade of grassroots radicalism, ranging from unions to populist movements in the Midwest, South, and West, President Roosevelt announced that Dr. New Deal was being replaced by "Dr. Win the War." On the home front the major parties, including the Communists, agreed to postpone labor-capital conflict.[1] To back a popular war, labor leaders and big business agreed with government to arbitrate strikes, create price controls, and legitimize the spread of patriotic unions.

The film industry not only conformed to these strictures, but promoted films that gave meaning and purpose to the war. The unique status of the United States among all the allies heightened Hollywood's significance. Unlike the other nations, the United States remained isolated from the fighting and bombing. In these circumstances, leaders called on the Hollywood film industry to bring home the images of war to inspire the populace to support total mobilization. The central agency for coordinating this effort was the Office of War Information (OWI), which was guided by liberal, interventionist New Dealers who understood that the movies provided a mechanism to spur home-front morale. As the head of the OWI observed after Pearl Harbor, the "easiest way to inject propaganda ideas into most people's minds, is to let it go in through the medium of an entertainment picture when they do not realize they are being propagandized."[2]

Under the shadow of war, Hollywood recast national goals and purpose to satisfy the hopes that had emerged in the popular arts and politics of the New Deal years. The outlines of that shift emerged in the Manual for the Motion Picture Industry produced by the OWI. Written for all moviemakers creating films to promote the war, the manual noted that this conflict had to be portrayed as different from World War I. Where the battle against the Kaiser generated an Americanism rooted in Anglo-Saxon superiority, World War II was a crusade to defeat the "brutality, cruelty, treachery and cynicism" of the enemy.[3] Hitler and Mussolini thus embodied the tyranny of "Caesar and Pharaoh" that immigrants had left the Old World to escape. Victory would eliminate all "forms of racial discrimination or religious intolerance, for special privileges for any of our citizens are manifestations of fascism and should be exposed as such." The nation embodied a new "melting pot" of "many races and creeds that showed that people can live together in freedom and progress." To attain victory, the people must put aside "national, class or race war," opening the way for the country's fighting men to create a "new world free of fear and want" for the "common man."[4]

Disagreements would surface between the OWI and producers concerning how best to dramatize a society free of "want" and "race war," but it was clear that moviemakers proved willing allies. To begin with, the Depression was now a thing of the past: Hollywood profits had risen by a third and the audience had expanded by 20 percent. Since most studio heads descended from Jewish immigrants, the war against Nazi racism gained their support. Well before the attack on Pearl Harbor, Warner Bros. made *Confessions of a Nazi Spy* (1939) as a response to the murder of Joe Kauffmann, the studio's emissary in Berlin, because he was a Jew.[5] Similarly, film stars who had supported New Deal causes—James Cagney, Pat O'Brien, Edward G. Robinson, Myrna Loy, Carole Lombard, Bette Davis, Paul Robeson, Rex Ingram, Lena Horne, and John Garfield—participated in government-sponsored "Victory Parades," and screenwriters moved to Washington, D.C., to produce films that fused "characterization and the world struggle against fascism."[6] At the grassroots theater owners sold war bonds, generating over 20 percent of all bond sales. Linking the war to the people's heroes and heroines, the Department of Defense built ships named after the Cherokee Indian Will Rogers and Carole Lombard, while Lena Horne christened a Navy destroyer named for the black scientist, George Washington Carver.[7]

Many left-wing artists also envisaged the war as a chance to fulfill their reformist visions on a global scale. John Garfield, Lena Horne, Duke Ellington, and the black heavyweight boxing champion Joe Louis entertained the troops training to defeat the fascists. Bette Davis, known for her portrayals of rebellious women, challenged Army segregation and told news reporters that such stereotypes as Aunt Jemima and the comic butler Rochester had to give way to more dignified portrayals of blacks.[8] Similarly, the Jewish-American scenarist John Bright, author of *Public Enemy*, and the director Orson Welles, maker of *Citizen Kane*, joined forces to protect Mexican-American youths who were falsely accused by Los Angeles police in the Sleepy Lagoon murder. To justify the larger implications of these efforts, Welles became during the war a columnist for *Free World Magazine* where he wrote:

> Our Republican splendor in this new age will shine by its own virtues, not by contrasting it with tyranny abroad. . . . Much is against us on the records: we oppressed the Indian, we stole the Black Man from his home and held him in bondage. And the fragrance of American freedom rose over the stench of butchery. If the conquerors and the slavers left us a mad strain of hate . . . we've told our children this was hate from the old world, that in our climate this finally must perish.[9]

Writers on the left also saw the war as generating a restoration of faith and "manhood" against the defeats and humiliations of the Depression. According to Robert Rossen, the new chairman of a Hollywood writers' mobilization association, film narratives now expressed a "New Day." Those like himself who descended from immigrants and workers saw that after World War I and the corrupt twenties, "All our heroes had feet of clay and if they did not they weren't worth writing about." The Depression films had showed "corrupt, evil forces . . . crushing men and women." But the war turned all that around, revealing that the "people would win despite any conditions." In contrast to the dismal past, today the "average man sees and feels the difference between this and the last war." The "dark days are over," giving rise to a new character "who no longer despairs but has found dignity and a 'cause' worth dying for."[10]

The dream of renewed manhood paradoxically sanctioned the pluralistic inheritance of the thirties and identified the class conflict associated with that ethos as subversive and "un-American." Wartime show-within-a-show musicals like *This Is the Army* (1943), *Star Spangled Rhythm* (1942), and *Yankee Doodle Dandy* (1942) linked popular music to voluntary enthusiasm for the war. *This Is the Army* featured the black hero Joe Louis, while *Stormy Weather* (1943) featured Bill Robinson, Louis Armstrong, and Lena Horne. A *Walk in the Sun* (1945), written by Robert Rossen, depicted southerners and the children of the new immigrants defeating the Nazis, while *The Fighting Sullivans* (1944) dramatized the fate of an Irish Catholic family whose five sons die in battle against the Japanese. Similarly, eastern European laborers and factory owners voluntarily put aside class conflict in *Pittsburgh* (1942) and *An American Romance* (1944). Above all, American heroes in *Air Force* (1943), *Back to Bataan* (1945), *The Fighting 69th* (1940), and *Sahara* (1943) dramatized the formula of the "ethnic platoon" where blacks, Texans, Jews, and Italians cooperate to defeat the enemy. Similarly, *Lifeboat* (1944) spurred the black press to note that the black actor Canada Lee's disarming of a Nazi "did wonders for the morale of the Negro GIs who talked about it for days. To them it was the symbol of changing times, of acceptance, of full integration into the pattern of American life."[11]

Despite these gains, this pluralism bore a striking resemblance to the older ethos of assimilation defined by Anglo-Saxon opinion makers. True, members of formerly ostracized racial and ethnic groups gained acceptance, but historical memories and identities that collided with wartime nationalism had to be shed. Instead of finding their roots in the local community or an autonomous civic sphere, wartime heroes gave their loyalty to large "savior institutions" linked to the state or defense industries. To ensure unity, the OWI told moviemakers that those who "believe in the rightness of our cause" could no longer focus "attention on the chinks in our allies' armor." This type of criticism must be forbidden because that is precisely "what our enemies might wish. Perhaps it is unrealistic but it is going to be confusing to audiences."[12] Producers similarly labeled Lew Ayres, the actor who converted to pacifism after starring in *All Quiet on the Western Front*, a "disgrace to the industry" when he enlisted as a medic rather than a combat soldier. The president of MGM said, "As far as I am concerned . . . Lew Ayres is washed up with us since he washed himself up with the public." The FBI found it necessary to launch an investigation of Orson Welles since he engaged in radical causes and made *Citizen Kane*, a production critical of the newspaper magnate William Randolph Hearst. The FBI likewise labeled Philip Dunne a "communist" because he wrote the pro-union film *How Green Was My Valley* and supported progressive causes. Since he could not receive a security clearance to work with the director John Ford, now an admiral in the Navy, Dunne wrote:

> The hurt and the humiliation were not so easily exorcised. Apparently the only way citizens can be sure of remaining "clean" in the eyes of their own government is to abstain entirely from any political activity . . . abdicate their responsibilities as citizens in a democracy, and that is one of the worst crimes committed in the name of "security."[13]

Such crimes did not stop with the pre-production process. Frank Capra sought to re-release the 1937 film *Lost Horizon* during the war. In the thirties Capra had used the film in part to criticize imperialism in the Far East, but now the OWI cut a speech where the hero asks a British leader, "Did you say we saved ninety white people? Good. Hooray for us. Did you say we left ten thousand natives down there to be annihilated? No. No, you wouldn't say that. They don't count." Yet in the war years Capra dismissed writers from his own government-sponsored *Why We Fight* series (1942–1945) when the House Un-American Activities Committee (HUAC) investigated them for writing scripts that depicted the Japanese not as racial villains but as people who became imperialistic due to their unresolved class conflicts.[14]

Capra was not alone in encountering government censorship and subversion of wartime productions. The director John Huston found that his documentaries, *The Battle of San Pietro* (1945) and *Let There Be Light* (1946), were unacceptable to the Army because one portrayed men slaughtered by inept officers and the other showed that shell-shocked veterans were driven insane by combat. Yet not only government-sponsored documentaries drew the censors' attention. OWI officials considered *Mr. Skeffington* (1944), a film that dealt with anti-Semitism, "gravely detrimental . . . the Jewish question is presented in such a way to give credence to the Nazi contention that discrimination for which Americans condemn the fascists, is an integral part of American democracy."[15]

If censors believed that films critical of domestic life had to be eliminated, the war also created the conditions in which the large studios found it opportune to pay attention to their demands. Formerly moviemakers operated in a highly competitive public sphere open to the views and interests of marginal groups. A wide variety of independent films, some using foreign languages and experimental forms, appealed to diverse audiences. It was these independents who often pioneered gangster, fallen woman, social problem, and horror genres. So profitable were these productions that between one-third and one-half of all films made in the thirties came from independents. Yet during the war years the large studios gained the status of an "essential war industry," which allowed them access to raw film stock. When the smaller firms failed to attain that access, the number of independents declined from ninety-two in 1939 to fifteen in 1944. The result was that the large firms gained a monopoly, and foreign and independent films declined from half of all film production in 1939 to less than a fourth in 1944. Or to put it another way, independent productions decreased from 379 to 172 films, a decrease of more than 50 percent over five years.[16]

The decline of the independent film companies coincided with a closure of the public space between government censorship and the studios. No doubt censorship existed during the thirties, but the industry operated in a relatively autonomous manner and policed its own product through the Hays Commission.[17] When the OWI entered the equation, and the ranks of independents that skirted even industry censorship guidelines declined, the space between the state and the film industry collapsed. It was not just a matter of OWI influence. Rather, voluntary wartime cooperation by moviemakers with the OWI short-circuited the possibilities for dissenting views to gain visibility. As one director noted, "our primary responsibility was not to the box office, nor to our paychecks. It was a special responsibility . . . to the men who wore the uniform."[18] John Huston saw the film industry functioning in the war as the "conscience of our people," showing with a "blinding flash of truth" that we could overcome "race prejudice." Robert Andrews, the writer of *Bataan* (1943), saw the war as an extension of his career as a journalist who covered Chicago gang killings.

The purpose at that time was to "wake the good citizens to what they were up against. That's all I'm trying to do today. . . . And I am determined to write a picture so shocking that people would say to themselves, if this is what our men have to stand up to, we've got a job to do." Though the effect made audiences "depressed," they "find |themselves| getting angry— angry that such things are being done to us."[19]

Transferred to the screen, the revolt against things "done to us" yielded a shift in the nature of cinematic visual style. In the thirties, such directors as Michael Curtiz, Lewis Milestone, John Ford, Frank Capra, and William Wyler popularized a dialogic cinema where the moving camera described a world where different viewpoints appeared as within a cubist painting. To convey this multiplicity, directors often ensured that the foreground, background, and middle ground were lit equally, while the horizontal rather than vertical planes predominated to place characters in spatial relations of equality. These multiple spaces shown in simultaneous and receding forms allowed different views and voices to appear, enlisting viewers to choose between them.[20] In addition, a camera that moved inside the frame and compositions photographed at a diagonal angle often emphasized a world where movement rather than stasis predominated and things appeared to be interconnected.

But the war gave rise to dramas that pitted unquestioned good against evil, ensuring that a dialogical perception gave way to a fixed and monolithic mode of perceiving the world. Indicative of this sharply divided worldview, one writer noted "No longer is it necessary |to| cloak the more serious thoughts and aspects behind a melodramatic yarn or sugar coat the message. . . . Terms such as 'fascists' and 'appeasers' can be used without offense."[21] To convey that worldview, multiple viewpoints that asked the viewers to choose between different voices and views necessarily receded. In their place balanced com- positions came to the foreground, and the camera focused on one point. Directors ensured that viewers understood who was to be admired and who disdained through the utilization of sacred and fixed symbols of authority. The action might focus on preachers evoking the cause of the allies, while patriotic music, religious symbols, voice-over narrators, and maps told viewers exactly how to think about the action, giving a monolithic direction to their thoughts.[22]

Deradicalizing American myths and symbols

While wartime movies emphasized monolithic visual perceptions, and censors eliminated images that subverted state and business leaders, a central plot device—the conversion narrative—reversed the basis of cultural authority from the bottom to the top of society. In the thirties, the conversion narrative portrayed characters shedding dependency on the values promoted by the rich in favor of those of the "people" or the lower class. That transformation served to align the middle class with the lower class and revitalize America's traditional identity as a republic. But now films like *Casablanca*, the Academy-Award-winning film for best picture of 1943, portrayed the tragic consequences that flowed from having to convert to war: It meant the end of the republican dream where citizens controlled work and enjoyed a more inclusive and experimental culture and family life.[23]

Scripted by writers committed to New Deal reform, the movie opens with a montage of voices and maps that evoke images of a republic besieged. Refugees from Nazism seek to escape through Casablanca in North Africa. The moving camera stops on the frieze of a courthouse where the democratic ideals of the French republic, "liberté, egalité et fraternité," grace the exterior.[24] The camera then comes to focus on a hero who embodies the American side of that republican code. Operating in an autonomous civic sphere, Rick Blaine, played by Humphrey Bogart, is the ideal of the hero who came of age in the New Deal era. Merging cultural and social reform, he controls his property, "Rick's Café Americain," a nightclub where diverse peoples mingle in a pluralistic community and jazz music permeates the atmosphere, enacting dreams of a vernacular art and a more vital life. Rick also facilitates the escape of Jews from the Nazis, pays his employees high wages, and evokes the ideal of reciprocity across classes and isolation from Europe's quarrels that threaten to entrap the New World citizen.

In a scene that demonstrates Rick's merging of the modernized republican ideal of racial pluralism and resistance to the domestic oppressors of the New Deal era, he responds to a fellow nightclub owner's offer to "buy Sam," Rick's African-American piano player. Harking back to the producers' democracy of the abolitionist crusade, Rick says, "I don't buy or sell human beings." The audience also learns that Sam and Rick are friends who have forged ties across the races. Not only do they confide in each other, but Sam owns 25 percent of the Café Americain and has helped Rick escape from Nazis who "blacklisted" him and then put a "price on his head" since he ran guns to Ethiopia and Spain in support of African and Spanish citizens' battles to defeat fascist imperialism.

Above all, Rick couples the ideals of the producers' democracy with dreams of a more vital life, symbolized by his love affair with Ilsa, played by Ingrid Bergman.[25] When she appears on the scene and asks Sam to play "As Time Goes By," we learn that Ilsa and Rick were lovers in Paris, symbol of modern culture for a generation of Americans. Their love affair combined visions of a more passionate life with a commitment to social and cultural reform. Yet Rick believes that his lover deserted him, for when the Nazis invaded Paris, Ilsa disappeared. Amid his despair, Ilsa explains that their love had unfolded only when she believed her resistance-fighter husband, Victor Laszlo, had died in a Nazi concentration camp. When she discovered that he was still alive, she had to desert Rick to help Laszlo fight the Nazis.[26]

With Rick's faith restored that their love and mutual ideals had not been betrayed, he now acts again to fight tyranny and end his and, by extension, the nation's isolation from the fight. Yet that choice is seen as a tragic one, evoking a sense of the blues, which is associated more with black than white Americans, and is signaled by the haunting theme song "As Time Goes By," played at the piano by Sam. With blues music filling key scenes, Rick prepares for war by selling the Café Americain, symbolic of mass amusements rooted in the lower-class vernacular sensibility and of his autonomy. Knowing the full cost of his conversion narrative, Rick tells Ilsa they must shed their dreams of merging politics with a new culture and integrated selves.

Explaining why the new woman must return in wartime to the traditional family, Rick explains that "inside of us we both know you belong to Victor, you're part of his work, the thing that keeps him going. . . . I have a job to do, too. Where I'm going you can't follow. . . . I'm no good at being noble, but it doesn't take much to see that the problems of three little people don't amount to a hill of beans in this crazy world. Someday you'll understand that." When Ilsa asks what about "us," Rick explains that she must help her husband and restore traditional sexual roles. That is, to create the cohesion necessary for war, Ilsa has to channel her allure into the home. Laszlo reinforces their choice by saying to Rick, "Welcome back to the fight. This time I know our side will win."

The lovers acknowledge their commitments to the war, and musical motifs fill the sound-track with triumphant music of the French anthem the "Marseillaise," but the optimism is undercut by dark visuals, for Rick has to give up his dream of independence and a more vital life. As the camera penetrates through the night fog to show a sad Ilsa and Rick saying goodbye, Rick joins what he has disdained: a military organization grounded in hierarchy that has undercut his autonomy and personal freedom. To convey the ambiguity of that choice, Rick and the Vichy police chief (played by Claude Rains) move to the beat of the "Marseillaise." The dark scene, however, undercuts the music by evoking a deep undertone of loss beneath their commitment to the "good war."[27]

Within *Casablanca* are a series of narrative patterns that would recur in one form or another in the major films of the war: the need to shed oppositional values in favor of com-mitment to hierarchical institutions dedicated to saving the world. In film after film this choice converges with a deep undertone of rupture that the directors and writers try to overcome with a patriotic and optimistic commitment to defeating the enemy. On the home front American myths and symbols are deradicalized. Within the mainstream conversion narrative, subversive values belong to characters' earlier rejected selves. To shed guilt and prove one's patriotism, close friends and compatriots—whose beliefs mirror the protagonist's earlier loyalties—have to be destroyed.

Precisely because the need to convert the home front was so critical, the war in Hollywood films often takes place stateside as part of the quest to destroy "subversives." Take the case of *The Fighting 69th* (1940). Significantly, it featured the Irish Catholic actor, James Cagney, playing a role that evoked memories of his famous gangster rebel in *Public Enemy*. Drafted into the Army in World War I, the protagonist hates officers and subverts their power. Yet when his class and ethnic antagonism leads to the death of fellow soldiers, the antihero becomes a patriot by killing the Germans who attack the army he once disdained. Along similar lines, *Air Force* (1943) features a bomber crew flying to the Hawaiian Islands. On board are an Anglo-Saxon officer, a Jewish sergeant, and a Polish-American working-class tail gunner, Winocki, played by one of the classic "city boys," John Garfield. Like many an ethnic working-class man in the thirties, Winocki hates the Yankee com-mander, who he believes discriminated against him and denied him access to pilot training. Yet when the Japanese attack Pearl Harbor, this class antagonism dissipates in response to the need for unity. When Winocki turns his energies to killing "Japs," the screenwriter noted that he "has found something real to direct his embittered feeling against and his eyes grow hard." Similarly, in *Lucky Jordan* (1942) a gangster works to avoid the draft and makes money by stealing military secrets that he sells to criminals and German spies. Yet he ultimately shifts loyalties and violently destroys his former criminal friends, seeing them as tools of the enemy.[28]

Along with shedding class and ethnic identities, any earlier admiration for left-wing causes and the autonomy of minorities was seen as a tool of the enemy. *Americans All* (1941), a documentary made with the assistance of Louis Adamic, a promoter of minorities' inclusion in national life, opens with a narrator explaining that the country is proud of its racial and ethnic groups. The narrator warns, however, that Americans of Japanese, Italian, and German descent use the foreign language press and radio stations to support the goals of the enemy. The subversive threat most applies to black workers who participate in communist-led parades. Only when minorities turn over their former friends as subversives do unity and true Americanism predominate.[29] *Across the Pacific* (1942) advances a similar point. At the end Japanese plantation laborers revolt against white owners. Yet instead of portraying the laborers in valiant rebellion against oppressive plantation owners, the strikers' class antagonism aligns them to the Japanese army, which wants to build airfields to attack the American Canal Zone.

Besides condemning class conflict, moviemakers portrayed those who continued to advance left-wing populist causes as deadly traitors. In this vein, *Keeper of the Flame* (1942) tells the story of a reporter, played by Spencer Tracy, who deeply admires a public figure modeled on Huey Long and Charles Lindbergh. The reporter undergoes a conversion experience when he discovers that his populist hero, now dead, was really a Nazi agent. To dupe the people and aid the enemy, he had preached isolationism and attacked corporations. In *Mission to Moscow* (1943) isolationist traditions again aid the cause of Hitler. At the end an isolationist midwestern senator tells Congress, "And I say, gentlemen, not only can we do business with Hitler but we can make a nice profit doing so. . . . It's going to be Hitler's Europe and I say, what of it?" To top it off, any alternative sexuality was also seen as aiding the enemy. *The House on 92nd Street* (1945) depicts Nazi spies who steal secrets for a superweapon—one that resembles the atomic bomb. At the end they are revealed not only as traitors but as transvestites whose deviancy aids the enemy.[30]

All of these films depend upon linking subversive tendencies to protagonists' earlier beliefs and loyalties. But once they discover the folly of their pasts, the protagonists prove their patriotism by destroying those who represent parts of their early selves. Take the case of anti-imperialist values. In the thirties, Will Rogers criticized the colonization of nonwhite peoples as a product of American capitalist expansion. Similarly, films such as *All Quiet on the Western Front, Juarez, Ambassador Bill*, and *Mutiny on the Bounty* yoked European and American expansion to the exploitation of nonwhite people. Along the same lines Progressive historians like Charles and Mary Beard promoted isolationism as the means to prevent big business from advancing its class interests and power around the globe.

Now moviemakers equated the war with the liberation of colonial peoples and a holy cause to free the world. Yet if this were the case, how would one convert pacifists and anti-imperialists? One answer to the problem can be found in *Sergeant York* (1941). Using World War I as a metaphor for current events, the story charts the story of Alvin C. York, a Tennessee farmer. In the first part of the film York opposes large farmers who have monopolized land and converts to pacifism. But when the war comes, York goes to a mountain where he converts to a new patriotic cause. Seeing in the war a means to advance the cause of liberty, he, in one critic's words, "sets aside his religious scruples against killing for what he felt was the better good of his country and the lasting benefit of mankind." At the end York emerges as the most decorated soldier in the war, and the government supplies him with farmland. After the film's release, veterans groups feted its star, Gary Cooper, who won the best actor Oscar for the role, while President Roosevelt invited the real Sergeant York to the White House. The War Department noted that during the next few weeks it experienced a boom in enlistments.[31]

In other films the war promises to free people from colonial oppression around the globe. *Back to Bataan*, for example, takes place in the Philippines prior to the Japanese invasion. The enemy radio informs the natives that the Japanese have come to liberate them from the imperial United States. A U.S. officer, played by John Wayne, mobilizes the natives' resistance. The Japanese radio station asks the Filipinos why they are not joining with Asians to expel white imperialists. That question haunts the mind of the grandson of a Philippine patriot who had fought against American invaders in the 1890s. The grandson has resisted colonial power; moreover, his lover joins with the Japanese, serving as the radio announcer who calls on the Filipinos to side against John Wayne's troops. Once the Filipino patriots witness Japanese atrocities, however, they convert and join the American military to expel tyrants.[32]

By the third year of the United States' involvement in the war, Hollywood films equated the war effort with a transformation in national identity itself. Take the case of *The White Cliffs of Dover* (1944). It portrays a young American woman and her father who, while traveling by ship to England in 1914, express their disdain for the Old World where the people are not truly citizens but subjects of the upper classes.

When England goes to war, however, they realize that they must alter their views and join ranks with England to save Anglo-Saxon "civilization." In a similar vein, *Mrs. Miniver* (1942) focuses on a man who despises English aristocrats as decadent and lazy nonproducers. Yet when the war arrives, he marries an upper-class woman, and the final scene shows him, his wife, and his mother-in-law listening to a sermon that equates the war with a Holy Crusade to save Christianity from barbarians.[33]

More important, the conversion of American identity meant that the protagonists' attitudes toward race and the lures of mass culture had to undergo a dramatic alteration. Nowhere was that more evident than in the documentary *December 7th* (1943). Made in co-operation with the Navy by director John Ford and cameraman Gregg Toland, the story focuses on none other than "Uncle Sam" himself. Played by Walter Huston, known for his performance as Abraham Lincoln, Uncle Sam arrives in the Hawaiian Islands for vacation in December 1941.[34] At first Sam tolerates labor strikes and the Japanese Americans. Yet his conscience troubles him, for he knows that the hyphenated Japanese and their unregulated amusements breed subversion.

Why? Slowly the audience is shown that the Japanese Americans have bilingual schools and a Shinto religion, loyalties that attach them to the foreign emperor. Next viewers see that the Japanese spy on American ships, and Asian women use their sexual allure in nightclubs and bars to gain secrets from American sailors. These activities make it possible for the Japanese to attack the Pearl Harbor naval base, leading to disaster and defeat.

Drawing on the themes of fall and rebirth familiar in Depression-era filmmaking, the film shows men dying and battleships sinking. Uncle Sam undergoes massive guilt, leading to a conversion experience that yields a new America capable of defeating enemies within and without. Never recognizing that the United States' own involvement in imperialist com-petition with the Japanese and its colonial exploitation of Hawaii may have led to the war, Sam decrees that citizens can still be Asian racially, but must now become "One Hundred Percent American" culturally. The Japanese Americans shed their bilingualism and their Shinto faith, and bring unregulated amusements under patriotic guidelines. Now a unified nation emerges where immigrants look to white culture for a model of civilization. At the end they—"Americans all"—build the ships that will avenge Pearl Harbor and create on the home front a society devoid of racial and class difference.

The conversion narrative that dramatized such a dramatic rupture from older beliefs and values was not simply confined to the most prominent war films. On the contrary, a major alteration in popular values also took place. Calculations derived from our plot samples show that American myths were systematically reconfigured in World War II. With the enemy seen as outside rather than inside, the conversion narrative gave rise to a new vision of a classless society. In the thirties, stories wherein characters shed loyalty to the rich in favor of alliances with the lower class or oppositional identities informed more than 20 percent of all films in our samples. During the war this trend receded to zero, while over 30 percent of the plots dramatized characters shedding their earlier oppositional class identity in favor of loyalty to official institutions. Protagonists left behind participation in an autonomous civic sphere in favor of wartime identities as "patriotic heroes" who served in "savior institutions" such as the Federal Bureau of Investigation, the military, and defense industries. At the same time, the portrayal of subversives on the home front increased from less than 3 percent in 1940 to 20 percent by 1945. All in all, the conversion and subversion narratives acted as two sides of the same coin, informing over 50 percent of all films made in World War II.

The wartime conversion narrative ran parallel with the rise of a new cultural and class consensus. Portrayals of the rich as morally dangerous, for example, had informed over 50 percent of all films in the thirties; during wartime, however, such portrayals declined to 20 percent. Similarly, plots featuring big businessmen as villains had occurred in 20 percent of all Depression-era films, but declined to zero in the war. Fears of capitalism still remained; as noted, over 20 percent of films portrayed the wealthy as dangerous, and the spies in films such as *Keeper of the Flame* were aligned with corrupt businessmen. Still a pervasive trend was for patriotic businessmen and reformers to gain prominence in institutions that promised to save the nation; similarly, portrayals of minorities who helped to advance the cause also increased during the war era. All in all, these trends reinforced the view that formerly alienated groups had united behind the patriotic cause. . . .

Notes

1 See John Morton Blum, V *Was for Victory*. On labor's cooperation with management and the state and the pledge of the communists to avoid strikes, see Nelson Lichtenstein, *Labor's War at Home: The C.I.O. in World War II* (New York: Cambridge University Press, 1983) and George Lipsitz, *Rainbow at Midnight: Labor and Culture in the 1940s* (Urbana: University of Illinois Press, 1994).

2 See Dorothy Jones, "The Hollywood War Film: 1942–1944," *Hollywood Quarterly* 6 (1945–1946): 1–19; Clayton R. Koppes and Gregory Black, "What to Show the World: The Office of War Information and Hollywood, 1942–1945," *Journal of American History* 64 (1977): 88, and *Hollywood Goes to War: How Politics, Profits and Propaganda Shaped World War II Movies* (Berkeley: University of California Press, 1990).

3 On the shifting face of national identity, see Philip Gleason, "American Identity and Americanization," in *The Harvard Encyclopedia of American Ethnic Groups* (Cambridge: Harvard University Press, 1980), pp. 38–57. See also John Higham, *Strangers in the Land: Patterns of American Nativism* (New Brunswick, N.J.: Rutgers University Press, 1955) and *Send These to Me* (Baltimore: Johns Hopkins University Press, 1984). Chapters 8, 9, and 10 of the latter are critical for cultural pluralism. The fact that the war was fought in the name of realizing the dream of general abundance is the central theme of Blum, V *Was for Victory*.

4 K. R. M. Short, "Washington's Information Manual for Hollywood, 1942," *Historical Journal of Film, Radio and Television* 3 (1983): 171–180.

5 See editors of *Look* magazine, *Movie Lot to Beachhead: The Motion Picture Goes to War and Prepares for the Future* (Garden City, New York: Doubleday, Doran and Co., 1945), pp. 58–69, 82–96, 148–158, 204–215; Colin Shindler, *Hollywood Goes to War: Films and American Society 1939–1952* (London: Routledge & Kegan Paul, 1979). On the film industry and Jews, see Lary May, *Screening Out the Past: The Birth of Mass Culture and the Motion Picture Industry* (Chicago: University of Chicago Press, 1983), ch. 6. The death of Kauffmann is recounted in Otto Friedrich, *City of Nets: A Portrait of Hollywood in the 1940s* (New York: Harper and Row, 1976), p. 49.

6 Howard Koch, "The Making of Casablanca," in Howard Koch, *Casablanca: Script and Legend* (New York: Overlook Press, 1992), p. 19. See also *Movie Lot to Beachhead*. "Hollywood Victory Caravan" file, in AMPAS, has newspaper articles from around the country reporting the stars' victory parades.

7 Photographs of battleships named in honor of Will Rogers are on display in the Will Rogers Memorial, Claremore, Okla. For the amount of war bonds sold in movie houses, see *Movie Lot to Beachhead*, pp. 58–69. On Lena Horne, see Horne file, AMPAS.

8 On Davis, see *Los Angeles Daily News*, November 11, 1941, and *Hollywood Citizen News*, July 27, 1942, unpaginated clippings in the Bette Davis file, AMPAS.

9 See Sleepy Lagoon file, University of California at Los Angeles Special Collections Library (hereafter UCLASC); Orson Welles, "Race Hate Must Be Outlawed," *Free World Magazine* (July 1944), pp. 9–11.

10 Robert Rossen, "New Characters for the Screen," *New Masses*, January 18, 1944, in *Hollywood Directors*, ed. Richard Koszarski (New York: Oxford University Press, 1976), pp. 190–194.

11 All the cited films are on video. See Leonard Maltin, *TV Movies and Video Guide* (New York: Signet Books, 1999). The quotation can be found in Thomas Cripps, *Making Movies Black: The Hollywood Message Movie from World War II to the Civil Rights Era* (New York: Oxford University Press, 1993), p. 207.

12 This quotation derives from an OWI script review of *For Whom the Bell Tolls*, as cited in Koppes and Black, "What to Show the World," p. 92.

13 See Lew Bergen, "Lew Ayres Obituary," *The Manchester Guardian*, January 1, 1997, p. 12; James Naremore, "The Trial: The FBI versus Orson Welles," *Film Comment* (January–February 1991), pp. 22–27; Dunne, *Take Two*, p. 160.

14 Joseph McBride, *Frank Capra: The Catastrophe of Success* (New York: Simon and Schuster, 1992), pp. 356,451–501. For the revisions of *Why We Fight*, especially the Japanese sections, see John Dower, *War Without Mercy: Race and Power in the Pacific War* (New York: Pantheon Books, 1986), ch. 1.

15 John Huston, "The Courage of the Men: An Interview with John Huston," in *Film: Book 2*, ed. Robert Hughes (New York: Grove Press, 1962), pp. 22–35; K. R. M. Short, "Hollywood Fights Anti-Semitism," in Short, ed., *Film and Radio Propaganda in World War II* (London: Croom Helm, 1983), pp. 147–151. The *Mr. Skeffington* censorship story is recounted in ibid., pp. 160–162.

16 These collations and data derive from *Film Daily Yearbook* for 1916, 1918–1919, 1924, 1934, 1939, 1944, and 1954. I wish to thank my research assistant Michael Willard for tabulating and collating this complicated data. For a fine examination of the independents in the thirties, see Brian Taves, "The B Film: Hollywood's Other Half," in Tino Balio, ed., *Grand Design: Hollywood as a Modern Business Enterprise, 1930–1939* (New

York: Charles Scribner and Sons, 1993). There is some irony in having Taves's article in a book that basically argues that there was a monopolistic, closed Hollywood system in the Depression, since the independents often successfully challenged and competed with all the majors.

17 See May, *Screening Out the Past*, chs. 2 and 5, for censorship and the movies. See also Richard Maltby, *Reforming the Movies: Hollywood, the Hays Office and the Campaign for Film Censorship, 1908–1938* (New York: Oxford University Press, forthcoming).

18 Lester Koenig, "Back from the Wars," *The Screenwriter* 1 (1945): 23–25. On a larger scale this is also one of the central themes of Thomas P. Doherty, *Projections of War: Hollywood, American Culture and World War II* (New York: Columbia University Press, 1993).

19 John Huston, World Brotherhood Speech, in Huston Collections, AMPAS; Robert Andrews interview by Philip Scheur, *Los Angeles Times*, December 5, 1943.

20 See Irving Pichel, "Seeing with the Camera," *Hollywood Quarterly* 1 (1945–1946): 138–145; Irving Pichel, "Areas of Silence," *Film Quarterly* 3 (1947): 51–55.

21 *New York Times*, January 13, 1944, in Shindler, *Hollywood Goes to War*, p. 76.

22 Examples of this tendency can be found in *Back to Bataan, Bataan, Casablanca, The House on 92nd Street, Americans All, December 7th*, and almost all the war films cited in the chapter.

23 The original screenplay can be found in Howard Koch, *Casablanca, Script and Legend* (Woodstock, New York: The Overlook Press, 1992). It is also on video. See Maltin, *Video Guide*.

24 Howard Koch, *Casablanca*, p. 29.

25 Ibid., pp. 51, 65, 76, 108, 163–170, 185, 204–205.

26 Ibid., pp. 100–127.

27 Ibid., pp. 218–228.

28 Richard Slotkin, *Gunfighter Nation: The Myth of the Frontier in Twentieth Century America* (New York: Harper Perennial, 1992), pp. 318–326. All the films cited are on video. See Maltin, *Video Guide*. The quotation comes from Dudley Nichols, *Air Force*, ed. Lawrence Suid (Madison: University of Wisconsin Press, 1983), p. 73.

29 *Americans All* can be viewed at the Immigration History Research Archive, University of Minnesota.

30 See Maltin, *Video Guide*. All the cited films are on video and listed in this guide.

31 The film is on video. See Maltin, *Video Guide*; "World War Hero Makes Its Appearance at the Astor," *New York Times*, July 3, 1941. The account of York's visit to the White House is from "President Praises 'Sergeant York' to the Living Hero of the Picture," *News and Feature Service of Warner Brothers Studio*, in Sergeant York file, AMPAS.

32 See Maltin, *Video Guide*. This film and interpretation first came to my attention in the work of Jennifer Delton, "Sundered by Memory: Cold War Internationalism and the Problem of American Identity," senior thesis in the program in American Studies, University of Minnesota, Spring 1989.

33 Ibid.

34 A print of this film is in the United States National Archives, and the library of the American Studies program, University of Minnesota, has a copy. Jones, "Hollywood War Film," shows that the overwhelming majority of films focusing on the foreign enemy took place on the home front rather than in combat.

PART FOUR

SHADOWS OF AMBIVALENCE

This section deals with the longstanding ambivalence about war expressed in Hollywood films. Cinematic visions have expressed uncertainty about American involvement in every major military campaign waged by the United States since the late nineteenth century. Films have variously questioned the justness, necessity, humanity, and affirmative meanings of battle. Even more fundamentally, while war cinema may be seen to have defining links to the militarization of national life, institutions, and media, it can also be seen to betray a persistent uneasiness about warfare and its representation.

Expressions of ambivalence, especially in avowedly anti-war films, can also be tracked as cyclical and reflecting the cumulative history of war cinema. Several periods stand out in this history. The initial one followed World War I, when a spate of anti-war narratives reconsidered U.S. involvement in the seemingly senseless modern destruction of that conflict. Another appeared amidst the post-World War II glut of combat films that began in 1949 and ran through the 1950s. Here, ambivalence and complexity are often more accurate descriptors than "anti-war" for narratives.

Arguably the most sustained and far-reaching attempts to grapple with the meaning and legacy of individual and national participation in war were the motion pictures that erupted on screen in the late 1970s and 1980s to consider the American experience in Vietnam. Sharp-eyed and thoughtful critics contributed to an assessment of the war that illuminated the discourses of manhood, race, empire—and movies themselves—impelling the country's fateful involvement. In fact, the ambivalence that historians would express through their explication of films about war of the 1960s and 1970s such as *Patton* and *Apocalypse Now* reflected much deeper and more widespread uncertainties about cinema, its social role, and the cultural myths and narrative strategies constituting it (Tomasulo 1990; Toplin 1996). These "New Hollywood" decades were marked, in other words, by broader struggles to reconcile changes in social, industrial, and cultural conditions of classical, studio-era production that both subsumed and were crucially shaped by the visual and cinematic experience of Vietnam.

If war is a crucible for assessing the moral standing of individuals and society, the priority of deploying organized violence as political means, and the legitimacy of the state and existing power relations, war cinema takes on these issues and add concerns about how and to what end these elements should be reproduced and how viewers can or should participate. Films thus foreground overarching processes of militarization and mediation and the status of citizen-spectators in them. In doing so, films also call into question the standing, relevance, and even complicity of Hollywood as a social and cultural institution for negotiating myth-ologies of individual, media, military, and nation. What ultimately is suggested here is a thoroughgoing, intrinsic ambivalence pervading war cinema. Just as all jingoistic productions can be read against their grain to emphasize the horror, pretense, and arbitrariness of war, so putatively anti-war films, reliant as they often are on spectacles of carnage and destruction, can be approached as fantasies of militarization.

The first selection, by John Whiteclay Chambers, uses *All Quiet on the Western Front* to focus on the anti-war film as itself central to broader cinematic and cultural understanding of modern war. Charles Young, in the second piece, discusses brainwashing common to Korean War films and, by extension, a more general psychological threat or resistance in wartime. Tracking the widespread social resistance to Vietnam, David James, in the third essay, integrates the shifting relationship between film industry and society during the 1960s. The fourth piece revisits the late 1970s and 1980s, when, for Michael Ryan and Douglas Kellner, a renewed con-solidation of militarization and state power emerged that turned on discourses of gender, race, and colonialism. Robert Burgoyne, in the fifth selection, offers an incisive reading of the racial issues in play in representing the Civil War on screen in the early 1990s.

17

All Quiet on the Western Front (U.S., 1930): The Antiwar Film and the Modern Image of War

JOHN WHITECLAY CHAMBERS II

More than any other American feature film in the interwar years, All Quiet on the Western Front (U.S., 1930) came to represent the image of World War I. In a poignant saga of the life and death of a sensitive young German recruit, the film vividly portrays the senseless horror of trench warfare on the western front. Explosive sound effects accompany powerful visual images—it was one of the first "talking" pictures—to produce an emotionally wrenching viewing experience. It directly contributed to the widespread revulsion against such slaughter and against industrialized mass warfare in general.

All Quiet on the Western Front became the classic antiwar movie hailed as a brilliant and powerful work of film art and widely imitated.[1] It achieved that classic status for historical and political reasons as much as for the cinematographic excellence with which it brought to the screen the war novel of embittered young German veteran and writer, Erich Maria Remarque.[2] For the film speaks to ideology and history as well as to art.

Half a century later, the very title remains highly evocative. It has emotional significance even for those whose understanding of World War I comes primarily from sepia pictures in history books. Now blended in public memory, the novel and film have come, like the young protagonist, the schoolboy-soldier Paul Bäumer, to symbolize the transformative horror of the western front. It is a horror that remains embedded in Western consciousness as a consequence of World War I.

The film was based on the tremendously popular novel All Quiet on the Western Front (in the original German, Im Westen nichts Neues [literally, Nothing New on the Western Front]). The book was a semiautobiographical work, based on Remarque's brief experience in the German army in the last years of the war. It was also clearly a product of the disillusionment that he and many other veterans felt about the war and about the dislocations of the postwar era. . . .

The 1930 Hollywood version of Remarque's book was the result of the successful judgment of Carl Laemmle, an independent entrepreneur who had entered the industry by purchasing theaters and then expanding into distribution and finally into production, heading the Universal Pictures Corporation. All Quiet on the Western Front, directed by Lewis Milestone, starred both a young, relatively unknown actor, Lew Ayres, and a seasoned veteran, Louis Wolheim.[3] Ayres became personally identified with the film, for he perfectly captured the role of the protagonist, the sensitive, educated, young man, Paul Bäumer— the everyman trapped, corrupted, and destroyed by the horror of trench warfare. Like the book, the 1930 film continues to be available, now on videocassette. In 1979, an entirely new version, in color, was produced for television, starring Richard Thomas and Ernest Borgnine.

In August 1929, Laemmle rushed from Hollywood to his native Germany and acquired the film rights from the author.[4] He put his twenty-one-year-old son, Carl Laemmle, Jr., the studio's new general manager, in charge of production of *All Quiet on the Western Front*.[5] The younger Laemmle ("Junior," as he was called) hired Lewis Milestone as the director.

Born in Russia, Milestone had abandoned an education in mechanical engineering in Germany in 1913 at the age of eighteen and gone to New York City to pursue a career in the theater. He soon became an assistant to a theatrical photographer. When the United States entered World War I in 1917, Milestone enlisted as a private in the photography section of the U.S. Army Signal Corps. In the army, he first worked on training films in New York, then learned about editing at the film laboratory of the War College in Washington, D.C., where he worked with Victor Fleming, Josef von Sternberg, and a number of future luminaries in the motion-picture industry. Discharged from the army in 1919, Milestone became a U.S. citizen and soon moved to Hollywood. He worked as an assistant film cutter, a screenwriter, and, beginning in 1925, a director.[6] In 1927, *Two Arabian Knights*, a tale of two fun-loving American doughboys, earned Milestone the Motion Picture Academy Award for Best Comedy Direction.

Despite the objections of the younger Laemmle, Milestone hired Ayres, who was only twenty years old and largely unknown, for the starring role of Paul Bäumer.[7] Although inexperienced, Ayres had many of the qualities Milestone sought: he was handsome, earnest, intelligent, and somewhat broodingly introspective. Without a well-known actor in this leading role, the audience effectively saw the young soldier protagonist as a kind of everyman. Ayres's relative lack of experience was balanced by the veteran actor Wolheim, who personified Katczinsky (Kat), the knowledgeable, cynical, but compassionate oldtimer. It is Katczinsky who instructs the young recruits about how to try to survive in the deadly chaos of the front.

For the task of converting Remarque's novel into a screenplay for what the industry then referred to as a "talker," Milestone drew on a group of capable writers. Contrary to many accounts, playwright Maxwell Anderson was not responsible for the dramatic treatment; he simply wrote the first version of the dialogue.[8] Creating a chronological screenplay to replace the episodic form of the novel, Milestone and his associates helped give structure to a war-film genre: one that follows a group of young recruits from their entry into the military, through basic training, to the battlefront. In this case, the film begins with the young men together in the schoolroom just before they rush off to enlist, encouraged by their chauvinistic teacher, Kantorek, who shames them into enlisting and calls on them to become "Iron Men" of Germany.

The film, like the novel, emphasizes the war's senseless human waste, especially the waste of youth. The camera graphically illustrates the breakdown of romantic ideas of war, heroism, and defense of the nation in the squalor of the trenches and the brutality of combat. One by one, the young men are lost; finally death takes the veteran Katczinsky and shortly thereafter Paul himself. (Remarque ends his novel by stating that when Paul's body is turned over, "his face had an expression of calm, as though almost glad the end had come.")[9]

Milestone and his crew paid particular attention to the brutality and senselessness of war on the western front and to the sharp divergence between civilian and military society, between home front and battlefront. Civilian society is characterized by the strident chauvinism of influential males such as Paul's father and schoolteacher, or by the intense anguish of helpless women such as his mother and sister. In the training camp and at the front, civilian youths are transformed into soldiers. They form cohesive male fighting groups, bands of brothers. But the male bonding is not simply as a band of warriors but also, under the shock and pain of the war, as a family—caring, nurturing, even doing domestic chores—but a family without women.

The few women in this film have smaller roles. They, too, are victims. On home leave, Paul finds food in short supply, his mother ailing and out of touch with reality. At the military hospital, nurses and other medical personnel are overworked and unsympathetic. The book has little romantic interest, but Hollywood felt the need for some women and sex in the film. Indeed, one of the promotional posters used in the United States featured a pretty young French woman clearly alluring to the German schoolboy-soldiers as well as to potential ticket buyers. In a French village behind the German lines, three young women are so famished that they are willing to exchange sex for the soldiers' food rations. Although the book mentions this episode only briefly, Milestone expanded it into an important and moving sequence.

New motion-picture technology—sound equipment and more mobile cameras—gave "talkers" a distinct new feeling. Like many of the posters, paintings, and other art of the postwar period, film took on a new harder, sharper, more brutal aura. Milestone brought the brutal reality of the war to this picture. Together with his cinematographer, Arthur Edeson, the director used a combination of fast-moving sight and sound to heighten the impact of the violence of industrialized warfare. The two men built a number of powerful images: the pock-marked landscape of no man's land; flashes of artillery fire on the horizon; wisps of smoke and gas; soldiers climbing out of trenches and rushing into machine-gun fire and exploding artillery shells; bodies lying crumpled on the ground, hanging on barbed wire, or being hurled into the air by artillery blasts.

One of Milestone's most acclaimed—and imitated—photographic devices was a long, fast, parallel-tracking shot (moving sideways like a crab) along a German trench while maintaining its focus on the attacking French infantrymen. The shot was possible because Milestone mounted Edeson's camera on a giant wheeled crane so it could be rolled along behind the trench. In the film, for nearly a minute of uninterrupted camera movement, the picture travels rapidly along at eye level as machine-gun bullets mow down charging French *poilus*. When sound was added, the metallic staccato of the machine guns helped audiences believe they were *hearing* the authentic sounds of battle.

Milestone and Edeson drew on their experience in silent films to create appropriate visual imagery and movement. They shot the battle scenes with more maneuverable silent cameras, adding sound effects later. Outdoor dialogue scenes, however, were made with cameras and microphones. Edeson had been hired partly because he had developed a quieter camera whose whir would not be picked up by the microphone.

As cinematographer-historian George Mitchell has observed, Edeson used lighting and camera angles to particular effect.[10] He employed a low-key light level to emphasize the drama of the recruits' first nighttime barbed-wire duty and later to provide a claustrophobic effect of sustained artillery bombardment on the shell-shocked boys in their dugout. In one of the most important scenes—the shell-crater sequence—Edeson used a subtle but realistic lighting style to mark the passage from day to night to day again. At night, flashes of artillery fire light up the shell hole and its two occupants. With the morning light, a close-up reveals the dead French soldier's face, his eyes open and staring, as a wisp of smoke, a remnant from the battle, drifts into the frame. The camera cuts to Paul's anguished, pleading face. Thus the horror and remorse of individual killing is brought directly to the audience.

Universal worked to give an authentic World War I appearance to this historical drama, particularly since it was filmed in southern California, not northern France. Studio purchasing agents obtained actual French and German army uniforms as well as scores of tools, packs, helmets, rifles, machine guns, and even six complete artillery pieces. The focus on authenticity was in the visual details. As such, for example, the film illustrates the change in German army equipment during the war, from the initial spiked leather headgear (Pickelhaube) to the more practical steel helmets (Stahlhelm).

In the battle scenes, Milestone and Edeson produced some of the most effective pictures in the film. During the major attack sequence following the artillery bombardment, Edeson's main camera, mounted on a large crane, travels over the trenches as the German troops pour out of their dugouts and into position. It is joined by five other cameras shooting from different angles as French infantrymen charge toward the trenches and the mobile camera. Stern-faced German machine gunners open fire. The French are mowed down. Later in the editing room, Milestone repeatedly cut these shots with increasing brevity and speed. A hand grenade explodes in front of a charging poilu. When the smoke clears, all that remains is a pair of hands clutching the barbed wire. In the trench, Paul turns his face away in sickened revulsion. As the remaining French soldiers reach the trench, they lunge at the Germans with bayonets in hand-to-hand fighting. The Germans counterattack, but are temporarily halted by French machine guns. After taking the first line of French trenches, the German soldiers are ordered back to their own lines before the French can counterattack. The battle ends in a stalemate, each side exhausted and back in its original position.

Sound made action films such as All Quiet on the Western Front so powerful—the impact of music, the realism produced by the sound of rifle fire, the staccato rhythm of machine guns, and the deafening roar of exploding artillery shells. Milestone jolted his audience right onto the battlefield by simultaneously bombarding their senses and their emotions.

Milestone created powerful images of war for the public, but how did he, after having spent the war years in the United States, know the reality of combat? Milestone believed it had come from the year he spent in Washington, D.C., in the U.S. Army Signal Corps during World War I. There he had become quite familiar with photographic images of the war. As Milestone recalled in an interview published in 1969, "having examined thousands of feet of actual war footage while stationed at the Washington, D.C., War College during the war, I knew precisely what it was supposed to look like."[11] A decade later, he drew on that background in re-creating the battle scenes near Los Angeles. This is wonderfully suggestive phrasing by Milestone: what war was supposed to look like. He had never personally seen a battle or a battlefield. What he did was to draw on his experience with documentary photographic representation of the battlefront to create the "reality" for his dramatic representation of battle and the battlefront. He seems not to have questioned whether he was drawing on the illusions created by Signal Corps photographers, who were able to photograph battlefields only *after* the actual fighting.

The theme of disillusionment is heightened in *All Quiet on the Western Front*. The meaninglessness of the war is accentuated by having the front-line German soldiers discuss the fatuous nature of the official justifications from Berlin. However, it is most dramatically personalized in one of the key scenes of the film, the shell-crater scene. In the midst of battle, Paul, panic-stricken and hiding in a shell crater in the middle of no man's land, mortally stabs a French soldier who had leaped into the crater. While the Frenchman slowly dies, Paul begs his forgiveness, concluding that they are after all comrades forced to kill each other by the brutal mechanics of war. This certainly represents another powerful theme: all men are brothers.

The most unforgettable scene is the final one. On a quiet day shortly before the Armistice, Paul is killed by a French sniper's bullet as he reaches out to touch a butterfly just beyond the trench. Milestone juxtaposes the fragility and beauty of life against imminent death by means of ironic sound effects (a soldier's harmonica plays softly in the background) and by visual cross-cutting among shots of the French rifleman, Paul, and the butterfly. The camera focuses on a close-up of Paul's hand reaching out across the parched, lifeless earth to embrace life—the butterfly, which is also a symbol of Paul's lost innocence and youth, a reminder of his adolescent, butterfly-collecting days. But instead of life— death: the sharp crack of a rifle, the spasmodic jerk of Paul's hand, which slowly relaxes in death. The harmonica suddenly stops. The sensitive, young, schoolboy-soldier has become just another corpse in the trenches. It is, according to one observer, "one of the screen's most powerful, well-remembered moments."[12]

All Quiet on the Western Front was immediately hailed for its aesthetic excellence and trenchant realism. It officially premiered at New York City's Central Theater on April 29, 1930, a few days after opening at the Carthay Circle Theater in Los Angeles. Hearst's New York *American* reported that the film had played "before an audience stunned with the terrific power of stark, awful drama." The *New York Times* agreed that the spectators had been "silenced by its realistic scenes." "It is far and away the best motion picture that has been made . . . talking or silent," asserted the New York *Telegraph*.[13]

The film was a phenomenal financial success. "A money picture," reported *Variety*, the entertainment industry's weekly newspaper.[14] It actually cost $1.5 million to produce, a major sum for a motion picture at that time, and nearly double the $900,000 projected cost estimates. Universal was so embarrassed by the overrun that it publicized only $1.2 million.[15] Within two weeks after the premiere, however, it was evident that the studio would more than recoup its investment, even in the worst economic slump of the Great Depression. *All Quiet on the Western Front* broke box-office records and showed to sell-out crowds in city after city throughout the spring of 1930. . . .[16]

The success of *All Quiet on the Western Front*, the book and the film, convinced other studios to produce antiwar motion pictures. Two made in 1930 were particularly noteworthy both for their intrinsic merit and for their demonstration of the international nature of the phenomenon: *Journey's End* (Britain, 1930) and G. W Pabst's *Westfront 1918* (Germany, 1930). Although James Whale's sound-film rendition of English veteran Robert C. Sherriff's play proved highly popular with British audiences and American critics, its lack of battle scenes limited its mass appeal in America. More comparable to Milestone was Pabst, whose artistry and "near documentary realism" were widely recognized and whose antiwar film based on the novel *Vier von der Infanterie* (Four Infantrymen) drew large audiences on the European Continent.[17]

From its first showing, *All Quiet on the Western Front* was recognized as a powerful emotional force for opposition to war, particularly modern industrialized mass warfare. Its message received support from many pacifists, liberals, and moderate socialists throughout Europe and, to some extent, in the United States as well.[18] But there was also considerable hostility to the film in many countries. Some cultural critics decried its horrifying images and its "vulgarities." Military and political opponents argued that it distorted and demeaned the patriotism and heroism of soldiers of all nations and that it undermined nationalism, military defense, and the ability to wage war. They considered it subversive pacifist propaganda.

German sensibilities had been evident in reactions to Remarque's book, which had been vehemently denounced by conservative nationalist opponents of the fledgling Weimar Republic. Consequently, the initial German-dubbed version prepared by Universal, finally released in December 1930, had included, with Remarque's consent, a number of cuts to obtain the approval of the Berlin Censorship Board. These cuts were not concerned with aspects controversial in other countries—others had objected to the use of earthy language and latrine scenes, the oblique bedroom scene of Paul and a young French woman, or the scene of Paul stabbing a French *poilu* to death—but with the image of Germany and the German army. Thus Universal, in the initial German version, deleted scenes showing the recruits beating up their tyrannical corporal, Himmelstoss, a symbol of Prussian militarism; soldiers starving for food and eating ravenously; soldiers blaming the Kaiser and the generals for the war; the grim use of the boots of a dead comrade to show the loss of one soldier after another; and Paul's return to his former school and his antiwar remarks there.

Although *All Quiet on the Western Front* played to packed theaters in the United States, Britain, and a number of other countries, it was banned in Germany, first, for a time, by the Weimar Republic and then permanently in 1933 by the Nazi regime.[19] The German-dubbed film, which had opened to the general public in Berlin on December 5, 1930, almost immediately led to Nazi street demonstrations and theater disruptions.

Representatives of the German military and the War Ministry had already issued protests against the film for portraying German soldiers as ridiculous, brutal, and cowardly.[20] Now Nazi propaganda leader Joseph Goebbels took his brown-shirted toughs to the streets, directing a number of violent protests and demonstrations against what he characterized as "a Jewish film" filled with anti-German propaganda.[21] Inside the theaters, Nazis released snakes and mice and set off stink bombs.[22] Although both the Board of Censors and the government of Chancellor Heinrich Bruening denied that they were influenced by the Nazi demonstrations, the decision to ban the film was correctly seen as a capitulation to the right, including the Nazis. Pabst's antiwar film, *Westfront 1918*, produced in Germany, was being shown in many theaters without any disturbances or demonstrations, The Nazis had used the American film to force the issue, and they had won. Hailed in Germany by the nationalist press—Goebbels's newspaper called it "Our Victory"—the censorship decision was, nevertheless, denounced by most liberals and socialists there and throughout the West.[23]

The Bruening government's decision was vigorously attacked by the left-wing Social Democrats in Germany, but they were unable to lift the ban until late the following year. By

June 1931, Universal Pictures was willing to make concessions to gain access to Germany, with 5,000 theaters the second-largest market in Europe. The Board of Censors lifted the general ban in September 1931 after Universal had agreed to eliminate the scene of Corporal Himmelstoss's cowardice at the front as well as Paul's panic in the graveyard attack, and Paul's contrition for having stabbed the French soldier to death. The shortened film (cut by nearly 900 meters, or approximately 33 minutes) played with great success in Germany through early 1932. Indeed, in 1931 and 1932, All Quiet on the Western Front was the sixth most popular film in Germany.[24]

Nazi-inspired censorship of the film had a lasting impact long after the debate in Germany in the 1930s. Indeed, it apparently had a long-term effect on the film and its showings in many countries. In its eagerness to enter the German market, Universal Pictures had agreed to delete offensive scenes not only from the film shown in Germany but from all versions released throughout the world.[25] Thus the versions of Milestone's All Quiet on the Western Front seen by millions of viewers in many countries for years thereafter were versions "sanitized" to please the German censors in 1931.

The history of the various versions and releases of All Quiet on the Western Front from 1930 to the present, as reconstructed in part by film scholar Andrew Kelly, demonstrates that Universal Pictures was as responsive to national sensibilities and political constraints as it was to economic opportunities in the international marketplace.[26] The film was banned entirely in Italy, Hungary, Bulgaria, and Yugoslavia. Austria, also under pressure from the Nazis, followed Germany's lead. The version shown in France (beginning in October 1930) did not contain the scenes of French women entertaining German soldiers and had a drastically cut shell-crater scene in which Paul kills the French soldier. Paris banned this and other antiwar films in 1938—the eve of World War II. . . .[27]

Milestone's version of All Quiet on the Western Front had enormous impact. Its ideological message contributed to political debate about war and isolationism in the 1930s and later. And in its most lasting impact, it helped to shape public images and attitudes about trench warfare, about World War I, and, to some extent, about modern war in general. It also had an undeniable impact on the motion-picture industry. It encouraged directors to shift away from static, stage-like "talking pictures" and instead to combine sound with open, fluid, visual movement. Milestone's long tracking shots were widely and specifically imitated. Of broader and deeper influence was his effective combination of sight and sound to produce a new realism that became one of the most influential concepts of Hollywood in the 1930s.[28]

No wonder, then, that pacifists, antiwar activists, and isolationists—in the 1930s and in subsequent decades—have regarded the film as a powerful antiwar and antimilitary device. Its many subsequent rereleases (in 1934, 1939, and 1950)[29] and the creation of an entirely new version in 1979 both reflected and contributed to such tides of sentiment in the United States and perhaps elsewhere. Indeed, Lew Ayres was so affected by his role and by the antiwar sentiment of the 1930s that he became a conscientious objector in World War II, at first refusing to be a soldier, and only after much public censure, agreeing to serve as an unarmed medic in the Army Medical Corps.

Most important, All Quiet on the Western Front helped shape subsequent public perceptions of the nature of trench warfare and of World War I. In part, this was because the book and the film, the latter with its visual images matching—even exceeding—the inner power of Remarque's writing, were part of the outpouring of antiwar memoirs and novels of the period that recast and bitterly articulated the failure of the Great War in the story not of battles won but of individual lives lost—and lost for naught.

The popularity of *All Quiet on the Western Front* and some other antiwar films may also be due in part to more oblique reasons. Despite their so-called realism and their brutal images, the antiwar films of the 1930s about World War I may, as historian Jay M. Winter has suggested, actually have helped masses of people take the chaos and horror of the war and mentally organize them in a more understandable and manageable way. Most of these motion pictures, after all, focus on the surface of events, on action, on melodrama, usually even including some romance, or at least on a bit of comedy. In mythologizing the war (re-creating the conflict in a form more understandable and acceptable than the complex and chaotic event itself), such films offer a way to organize and contextualize events that are themselves fragmented and traumatic. They serve to "help people to bury the past and help people recreate it in a form they can accept," according to Winter.[30] In more generic terms and in a longer time frame, antiwar action pictures, from *All Quiet on the Western Front* to the anti-Vietnam War film *Apocalypse Now*, offer many viewers both the moral solace of a strong, antiwar message and the emotional appeal of an exciting, action-filled adventure.[31]

Regardless of how World War I is understood, it is clear that in cinematographic terms, the enduring public perceptions of the image of trench warfare were established in the 1930s. No single motion picture was more influential in fixing that visual representation than this one. After *All Quiet on the Western Front*, the "reality" of trench warfare in the public mind was a "reality" constructed in Hollywood.

Notes

1 See, for example, Martin Gilbert, *The First World War: A Complete History* (New York: Holt, 1994), p. 535; and Michael T. Isenberg, *War on Film: The American Cinema and World War I, 1914–1941* (London: Associated University Presses, 1981), pp. 30, 132, 138. Historical studies of the film's place in the larger political and cultural history of the period have been few and largely fragmentary—for example, Andrew Kelly, "All Quiet on the Western Front: Brutal Cutting, Stupid Censors and Bigoted Politicos, 1930–1984," *Historical Journal of Film, Radio and Television* 9, no. 2 (1989): 135–50; Jerold Simmons, "Film and International Politics: The Banning of *All Quiet on the Western Front* in Germany and Austria, 1930–1931," *Historian* 52, no. 1 (November 1989): 40–60; and Richard A. Firda, *"All Quiet on the Western Front": Literary Analysis and Cultural Context* (New York: Twayne, 1993), pp. 92–106. In a class by itself is Modris Eksteins, *Rites of Spring: The Great War and the Birth of the Modern Age* (London: Black Swan, 1990), pp. 368–97. A useful anthology is Bärbel Schrader, ed., *Der Fall Remarque: Im Westen nichts Neues: Eine Dokumentation* (Leipzig: Reclam-Verlag, 1992). An earlier, if longer, version of this chapter appeared as John Whiteclay Chambers II, "'All Quiet on the Western Front' (1930): The Antiwar Film and the Image of the First World War," *Historical Journal of Film, Radio and Television* 14, no. 4 (October 1994): 377–411.

2 On his early life, see Christine R. Baker and R. W. Last, *Erich Maria Remarque* (London: Oswald Wolff, 1979), pp. 5–17.

3 *All Quiet on the Western Front* (Universal Pictures, 1930). Original sound version is 138 or 140 minutes, black-and-white (a silent version with synchronized music and sound

effects ran longer). Carl Laemmle, Jr., producer; Lewis Milestone, director; George Abbott, Maxwell Anderson, and Del Andrews, screenplay; C. Gardner Sullivan, story editor; Arthur Edeson, director of photography; George Cukor, dialogue director; and David Broekman, music. The cast included Lewis Ayres (Paul Bäumer), Louis Wolheim (Katczinsky), George "Slim" Summerville (Tjaden), John Wray (Himmelstoss), Raymond Griffith (Gerard Duval), Russell Gleason (Müller), Ben Alexander (Kemmerick), Arnold Lacy (Kantorek), and Beryl Mercer (Mrs. Bäumer); in the silent version, Zasu Pitts (Mrs. Bäumer); Marion Clayton (Miss Bäumer); and Yola D'Avril (Suzanne).

4 "Confers on New War Film," New York Times, August 11, 1929, p. A8.

5 "Mr. Laemmle Returns [from Germany]. Universal's President Discusses Film All Quiet on the Western Front," New York Times, October 6, 1929, sec. 9, p. 8.

6 Lewis Milestone and Donald Chase, "Milestones" (typescript of unfinished autobiography in the Lewis Milestone Collection, Margaret Herrick Library, Academy of Motion Picture Arts and Sciences, Los Angeles [cited hereafter as Milestone Papers]); Joseph R. Millichap, Lewis Milestone (Boston: Twayne, 1981).

7 See the somewhat differing accounts of Ayres's selection in the interview with Lewis Milestone, in Charles Higham and Joel Greenberg, The Celluloid Muse: Hollywood Directors Speak (Chicago: Regnery, 1969), pp. 152–54; and William Bakewell, Hollywood Be Thy Name (Metuchen, N.J.: Scarecrow Press, 1991), pp. 71–72.

8 See, for example, Millichap, Milestone, p. 39. Maxwell Anderson acknowledged a less important role (Anderson, interview, May 10, 1956, Columbia University Oral History Collection, New York).

9 Remarque, All Quiet on the Western Front, p. 291.

10 George J. Mitchell, "Making All Quiet on the Western Front," American Cinematographer 66 (September 1985): 34–43.

11 Milestone, interview in Higham and Greenberg, Celluloid Muse, p. 151. He told this story many times.

12 Mitchell, "Making All Quiet on the Western Front," p. 42. Milestone tried several different endings during production. See mimeographed copies of the shooting script, November 20, 1929, Remarque Papers, Series 1, Folder 4; and the continuity script, undated, Film Studies Center, Museum of Modern Art, New York City.

13 Excerpts in an advertisement by Universal Pictures, Variety May 7, 1930, pp. 36–37.

14 [No first name given] Sime, Review of All Quiet on the Western Front, Variety, May 7, 1930, p. 21.

15 For the $1.2 million publicized figure, see ibid. The projected estimate was $891,000, according to "Estimated Cost Sheets," December 9, 12, 1929; the actual cost was $1,448,863.44, "Final Cost Sheet," May 7, 1930 (All Quiet on the Western Front file, Universal Pictures Collection, Doheny Library, University of Southern California, Los Angeles).

16 "Disappointments on [West] Coast Last Wk [sic]—'Western Front' Made Big Showing, $22,000 at $1.50 Top," Variety April 30, 1930, p. 9; "Only 'Western Front' at Over Capacity $21,957, in $2 Central," Variety, May 14, 1930, p. 8.

17 On Whale's film based on the R. C. Sherriff play, see D. J. Wenden, "Images of War 1930 and 1988 All Quiet on the Western Front and Journey's End: Preliminary Notes for a Comparative Study," Film Historia 3, nos. 1–2 (1993): 33–37. On Pabst's film, see Michael Geisler, "The Battleground for Modernity: Westfront 1918 (1930)," in The Films of G. W. Pabst, ed. Erich Rentschler (New Brunswick, N.J.: Rutgers University Press, 1990), pp. 91–102.

18 Modris Eksteins, "All Quiet on the Western Front and the Fate of a War," Journal of Contemporary History 15, no. 2 (April 1980): 355.

19 Simmons, "Film and International Politics"; Heiko Hartlief, "Filmzensur in der Weimarer Republik. Zum Verbot des Remarque-Films Im Westen nichts Neues: Eine Fallstudie im Geschichtsunterricht der gymnasialen Oberstrufe," Erich Maria Remarque Jahrbuch 3 (1993): 73–82.

20 U.S. Ambassador, Germany to Secretary of State, December 17, 1930, received January 3, 1931, in Foreign Relations of the United States, 1931 (Washington, D.C.: Department of State, 1931) vol. 2, pp. 309–10. (Hereafter cited as FRUS)

21 Diary entries, December 5–12, 1930, Joseph Goebbels, Die Tagebücher von Joseph Goebbels: Samtliche Fragemente, ed. Elke Fröhlich (Munich: Saur, 1987), vol. 1, pp. 641–45.

22 "Fascist Youth Riot as All Quiet Runs," New York Times, December 9, 1930, p. 17.

23 "Unser der Sieg! |Our Victory!|," Der Angriff December 15, 1930, p. 1; Guido Enderis, "'All Quiet' Banned by Reich Censors," New York Times, December 12, 1930, p. 12; New York Times, |editorial|, "Commercialism and Censorship," December 13, 1930, p. 20.

24 Simmons, "Film and International Politics," pp. 58–59; U.S. Ambassador, Germany, to Secretary of State, September 12, 1931, in FRUS, pp. 316–17; see also "Top 10 Films in Germany, 1925–1932" |table|, in Joseph Garncarz, "Hollywood in Germany: The Role of American Films in Germany," in Hollywood in Europe: Experiences of a Cultural Hegemony, ed. David W. Ellwood and Rob Kroes (Amsterdam: VU University Press, 1994), pp. 123–24.

25 U.S. Ambassador, Germany, to Secretary of State, September 12, 1931, FRUS, p. 316.

26 Andrew Kelly, "All Quiet on the Western Front: 'Brutal Cutting, Stupid Censors, and Bigoted Politicos, 1930–1984," Historical Journal of Film, Radio and Television 9, no. 2 (1989): 135–50.

27 Although some studies claim that the film was not shown in France until 1963, a silent version with French intertitles (and perhaps some simulated sound effects) opened there in October 1930. In December 1930, the German-dubbed sound version with French sub-titles brought the full impact of the battle scenes as well as the dialogue to enthusiastic French audiences. Apparently it was not until 1950 that a French-dubbed dialogue sound version was released. See "A l'Ouest, rien de nouveau vient d'être présenté à Marseille," La Cinématographie française, no. 624, October 17, 1930, p. 197; Fernard Morel, "Le Cinéma doit préparer la paix; on doit détaxer les films de ce genre," La Cinématographie française, no. 625, October 25, 1930, p. 49; "La Foire aux films," L'Humanité, November 23, 1930, p. 4; Emile Vuillermoz, "Le Cinéma: 'A l'Ouest, rien de nouveau,'" Le Temps, December 27, 1930, p. 5; and, for the rerelease, Henry Magnan, "Le Cinéma: 'A L'Ouest rien de nouveau' Durable chief-d'oeuvre," Le Monde, December 30, 1950, p. 8.

28 Millichap, Milestone, pp. 24–25; see also Michael I. Isenberg, "An Ambiguous Pacifism: A Retrospective on World War I Films, 1930–1938," Journal of Popular Film and Television 4, no. 2 (1975): 98–115.

29 Copies of the scripts for the 1930, 1934, and 1939 releases are in the New York Film Censor Records, New York State Archives, Albany New York. I am indebted to Richard Andress, archivist, for providing these.

30 Jay M. Winter, The Experience of World War I (New York: Oxford University Press, 1989), p. 328.

31 Milestone himself went on to direct a number of war and antiwar films, among them The General Died at Dawn (1936), The Purple Heart (1944), A Walk in the Sun (1946), Halls of Montezuma (1951), and Pork Chop Hill (1959).

Missing Action: POW Films, Brainwashing and the Korean War, 1954–1968

18

CHARLES YOUNG

The 1963 film *The Great Escape* (John Sturges, United Artists, US) is arguably the most exciting prisoner of war (POW) film ever made. Even if you have not seen the film, you have probably seen clips of Steve McQueen's motorcycle jump. McQueen is fleeing on a motorcycle from a World War II German prison camp. Soldiers close in from all sides, but McQueen uses an earthen embankment as a jump and just barely clears a 10 foot barbed wire fence. He is eventually recaptured, but repeated escape attempts fortify his spirit and inspire others who do get away.

The Great Escape is an archetype of the POW genre. POW camps are built in a heroic region of the cultural landscape, a place where natural motorcycle ramps abut barbed wire fences and where no-one gets dysentery. This adventure formula dominates every group of POW films except one: those set in the Korean War. The daring breakout is a defining element in *Stalag 17* (Billy Wilder, Paramount, US, 1953), *Von Ryan's Express* (Mark Robson, Twentieth Century Fox, US, 1965) and *The McKenzie Break* (Lamont Johnson, United Artists, US, 1970). The genre took on a new life in Vietnam POW/missing in action (MIA) films such as *Missing in Action* (Joseph Zito, Cannon, US, 1984), where commandos go back to free cinematic prisoners left behind at the end of the war. Valor comes so easily to the American POW that he can pause for jokes, such as in the long-running television series *Hogan's Heroes*. If it is a film set, the purpose of bars and wire is not to confine, but to provide something to escape through.

Almost invisible in prison camp adventures is the subject of collaboration. Informing and betrayal are fixtures of real incarceration; cooperation varies, but no-one gives just name, rank and serial number. The Hollywood image of captivity has such a hold on the imagination that it is difficult to counter, but in internal military documents, name, rank and serial number is known to be a myth. After Korea, the Army could not find 'any' former POW who gave only name, rank and serial number.[1] Because humans are mortal, they try to satisfy their captors. Resistance is common, even valorous, but rarely obstreperous. Most prisoners choose life and quietly cooperate as little as they think they can get away with.

Collaboration is ignored in POW films set in World War II and Vietnam; they feature the brave but rare event of escape and skip the compromises of everyday survival. *Stalag 17* came close, but its informer turned out to be a German spy educated in America, not a real turncoat. The adversary remained simple—the enemy without, not weakness within. The

Vietnam films often addressed betrayal—on the home front. Vietnam POWs are double-crossed by the CIA, politicians, the media and peaceniks, but do not themselves give in. Although the Vietnam films add the 'establishment' to the POW's list of opponents, he still battles external enemies, not his own character. With few exceptions, Hollywood concentration camps are places to celebrate masculinity, not question it.[2]

Sandwiched between the heroic films of World War II and Vietnam are a group of prison camp films that depart from convention in every case. This mostly grim subgenre depicted the American experience of captivity during the Korean War. Some form of collaboration with the enemy is a central issue in all six feature films about American soldiers imprisoned in Korea. These mostly forgotten films are, in chronological order, *Prisoner of War* (1954), *The Bamboo Prison* (1954), *The Rack* (1956), *Time Limit* (1957), *The Manchurian Candidate* (1962) and *Sergeant Ryker* (1968). The *Outer Limits* television episode 'Nightmare' (1963) also fits the pattern. Prompted by a misperception of whole-scale collaboration in Korean prison camps, these dramas were forced to flip convention on its head and acknowledge frailty, weakness and unfaithfulness. . . .

The glaring difference between Korean POW films and others is attributable to the prisoner image being melded to different aspects of the particular conflict. The attention put on POWs was due in part to the wider Korean stalemate which threw into question the resolve of the entire nation. America's inability to prevail was transferred to the prisoners' failure to do the same. We may have betrayed the POWs in Vietnam, but, in Korea, they betrayed us. The hypersensitivity over prisoner performance contrasts with World War II, where victory made introspection unnecessary. Prisoners are important in Vietnam lore, but to different ends. H. Bruce Franklin and Elliott Gruner explored the representation of the Vietnam POW/MIA.[3] The alleged abandonment of live POWs symbolized the government using men, then throwing them away when the effort became too costly. The Vietnam action film also emphasized the cruelty of captors, showing Americans to have been victims rather than perpetrators.

A different problem was raised by the Korean War, when the virtue of fighting communism in the less-developed world was barely questioned. American purpose was not impugned, only its strength and will. Korean War POW films reflected a crisis of national confidence during the early Cold War. Globalism brought new burdens, which seemed to have been fumbled during Korea. Although the Cold War consensus was broad, the POW films of the period reveal that domestic morale for the global crusade was problematic. Maintaining ardor for globalism was a complex affair, of which the Korean POW episode was no small part.

The prominence that prisoners and hostages have held since mid-century is an artifact of limited war. The modern prisoner became conspicuous only after America's rise to globalism brought friction in myriad regions of finite importance. In Korea, the American, Chinese and Soviet sponsors of the war did not want to risk a wider conflict; for this reason a negotiated settlement was reached. POWs are a footnote to conclusive conflicts because the winner dictates repatriation, but when decisive victory is too risky, as in Korea, the process of negotiation and compromise allows captives to become a source of contention. Limited war allowed a secondary issue like POWs to become the main sticking point during interminable negotiations and a major propaganda theme of both sides.

Fights that could not be finished introduced new difficulties in maintaining national morale during the Cold War. Americans traditionally go to war for high ideals in a Manichean universe. World War II was understood as a fight against the absolute evil of fascism and in the Cold War the concept of Red Totalitarianism was elaborated even further. Because Americans fought for survival and virtue, not *Realpolitik*, there was little room in the imagination for negotiation. If war is a contest between good and evil, then a negotiated settlement compromises virtue. Although the public had a simple understanding of the Korean conflict, government planners tempered their own impressions with a strategic conception of thrust and parry. Unlike World War II, there would be no goal of unconditional surrender. American interests in the Korean peninsula were limited; planners would cut their losses if the conflict undermined a global preponderance of power[4]. . . .

The decision not to widen the war suggested to many a failure of national nerve, in particular as the stalemate dragged on through endless peace talks. President Truman's failure to find a satisfying end to the war destroyed his hopes for re-election and gave birth to the myth of a lost victory. General Douglas MacArthur did much to advance the thesis that there was 'no substitute for victory'. A proponent of nuclear attack on China, his eventual dismissal resulted in hundreds of thousands of angry telegrams.[5] Although the myth of a lost victory began as an attack on the Democrats, it endured as Dwight Eisenhower also sought a negotiated end. 'We Can Win in Korea if We Want to', wrote General James A. Van Vleet in spring 1953, shortly after retiring as head of the Eighth Army in Korea. His article, printed in *Life* and *Reader's Digest*, denounced negotiations and called for military victory.[6] The position did not prevail, but it reflected and reinforced doubts about American will.

For Washington, the failure to succeed militarily was followed by the search for a 'substitute for victory', in the words of Rosemary Foot.[7] If large numbers of enemy POWs refused to return to communism, then the superiority of the West would be demonstrated even without military victory. As a condition of peace, Washington introduced 'voluntary repatriation', a novel interpretation of the Geneva Convention on the return of POWs which argued that individuals who chose to go elsewhere did not have to be repatriated.[8] The plan had great potential: many of the prisoners were re-educated nationalist soldiers of Chiang Kai-shek or Koreans with family ties to the south. Plenty of soldiers needed little persuading not to return home and Washington made a huge effort to convince the rest[9]. . . . Facing a public relations disaster, China was loath to accept voluntary repatriation and held out against the armistice for many months. Whether voluntary repatriation is considered humanitarian or opportunistic, it still prolonged the war; POWs remained at the center of events. . . .

By the end of the armistice talks, the war was about prisoners as much as anything else. Talks lasted more than half the war and with POWs the main sticking point, all eyes were on them. Prisoners of Korea returned to a country that had been unable to prevail against seemingly unworthy opponents, worried it might not have the fortitude to bear another international crisis. McCarthyism, spy hunts and the 'loss' of China were distressing even without Korea. It was commonly believed that American-born spies allowed the Soviets to catch up in the nuclear race and the development of the Russian hydrogen bomb was confirmed right in the middle of POW repatriation.[10] During the war, the germ warfare confessions suggested something odd was going on, but during the homecoming, these reports became dominant.

Unlike previous wars, Korea ended not with an atomic bang or conquest of a foreign capital, but when the last prisoner stepped off the boat. Under this kind of scrutiny and with no victory celebration for distraction, collaboration in prison camps could not remain the great unmentionable. Hints during the war of widespread collaboration became a flood as the POWs docked. It took a month to repatriate all the Americans, providing daily anecdotal evidence of treason. Each boat-load of returnees provided reporters with headlines like 'P.W.s Say Some G.I.s "Swallowed" Red Line, Bitter G.I.s Out to "Get" Informers Among P.W.s', or, simply, 'The Rats'.[11] By the most agitated estimate, one-third of all POWs were guilty of some sort of collaboration with the enemy. By another account it was one in seven.[12] Most disturbing were the defectors. Initially, 23 American prisoners chose communism over returning home[13]. . . . Collaboration was understood as a defect primarily in the individual, secondarily in the environment, but rarely as a predictable occurrence in wartime incarceration.

The thesis that Korean War POWs were particularly prone to collaborate has proven tenacious, despite being meticulously debunked as early as 1963 by Pentagon consultant Albert Biderman.[14] It was the captivity that was different, not the captives. In most conflicts, the frequency of collusion goes unspoken, but the Cold War put a premium on world opinion, a contest in which all Korea POWs starred. American prisoners were forced to broadcast confessions in Marxist jargon, rather than just quietly inform on fellows as in previous conflicts. The Korean War also included periods of incarceration as harsh as any in American experience—one-third perished—producing a highly coercive atmosphere. If there was more collaboration in Korea, it is best explained by the demands of the captors and the conditions of captivity, rather than a decline in the character of youth in the years since 1945.

Public innocence as to the reality of captivity was an important factor in the harsh judgment of the POWs. During World War II, it was axiomatic that prisoners were to give only their name, rank and serial number.[15] Every soldier, family and reader of comics knew that this was the measure of honor. Military planners, however, recognized this as a fiction, more for *élan* before capture than a commandment for after. Even without physical torture, the compulsion to say something, even a subterfuge, is great. . . . When prisoners returned from Korea, their country still expected them to have stuck to name, rank and serial number. When events conspired to expose the failure of this in every newspaper, the dismay was inevitable.

The high visibility and seeming pusillanimity of returned prisoners made them a target of frustration over America's lost victory. The perceived weakness of American youth in captivity became a staple of civic events and the chicken dinner circuit, where patriotic speakers lamented the deterioration of morals. Particularly active was Charles Mayer, a military psychiatrist by day, who gave talks and interviews into the 1960s. In a U.S. *News and World Report* interview entitled 'Why Did Many GI Captives Cave In?', Mayer used Korea for sweeping indictments of society: 'one third of prisoners lacked faith in America'; 'the American educational system is failing miserably'; 'we should develop more toughness'; and responsibility lies with 'people who raise and teach children'[16]. . . .

Lack of masculinity and national spiritual decline were the more reputable explanations for their susceptibility, while another was 'brainwashing', a term made common by the Korean War. The belief that the Reds had 'gotten' to many prisoners was particularly disturbing. Brainwashing explained the inexplicable. It was colloquially understood as preternatural control of thought; it spread as urban myth as much as in news reports. Brainwashing is generally understood to mean the forced removal of old ways of thinking and their replacement by new ideas. The victims of brainwashing are not simply obedient;

they become true believers. Its most extreme visualization was in the film thriller *Manchurian Candidate*, where a POW automaton kills on cue and remembers nothing. Tʰ breadth of belief in brainwashing was due in part to the anxiety of the times, but the termˊ. flexibility made it resistant to debunking. The *New York Times*, for example, used brainwashing as a synonym for the unusually systematic use of traditional methods of coercion: torture, starvation, filth and isolation.[17] An internal Army report used an even narrower definition based on the elaborate pressure put on a handful of prominent East European political prisoners. Too extravagant a process for mass use, the Army concluded there was not 'any' such brainwashing in Korea.[18] In public discourse, however, the term was commonly used with little qualification. Readers were free to understand it as new and diabolical or as old as bondage. Brainwashing by any definition was considered irresistible, which eventually complicated the jeremiad against alleged prisoner cowardice.

The idea of brainwashing was more significant in forming public attitudes than in permanently transforming souls. If the experience in Korea is taken as the working definition of brainwashing, the effect was transitory. Psychiatrist Robert J. Lifton made careful studies of repatriates and concluded that 'virtually all prisoners' gravitated back towards their old belief systems after returning home.[19] Even the defectors, who remained in the 'brainwashed' environment, became disillusioned. The 23 defectors almost immediately became 21 and over the years the rest trickled back home as well.[20]

While a permanent and profound revolution in thought patterns may not have occurred, POWs were still subjected to intensive indoctrination. These techniques accounted for much of the collaborative behavior that on the surface seemed like a transformation of personality and world-view. In the camps, officers were separated from the enlisted and 'natural' leaders were quickly transferred. Race, class and political differences were encouraged in order to abrade personal ties and group identity. Although the Chinese proclaimed a 'lenient policy' of persuasion, not force, the camps were inherently coercive places. Upon their return, freed prisoners displayed an almost casual familiarity with death. When debriefed, they rattled off the causes of fatalities with numbing repetition: dysentery, pneumonia, tuberculosis, malnutrition, and untreated wounds. 'No medical treatment' was a catch-all cause of death.[21] That simple answer was given to debriefers so many times that POWs seemed to categorize lack of treatment as a cause of morbidity, rather than the underlying malady. Disease made life precarious even for guards and collaborators; holdouts were last to receive scarce treatment. A decision not to sign a propaganda tract could easily kill a prisoner months hence. The need for medical care, food and patrons were daily inducements to cultivate the guards and compete with other prisoners.

In this fatal environment, the Chinese added a forum in which POWs could be minutely scrutinized for compliance: political education classes. These intensely monotonous sessions occupied a significant part of an average POW's day; prisoners hated them, but they left a mark. The sessions were notable for the extent that they used public scrutiny to challenge individual beliefs. Students were required to recite lessons and have them checked for soundness by the group. Chinese political trainers also used personal autobiographies and extensive public confessions to draw people out. These endless rounds of self-criticism exposed the building blocks of inner thought, allowing ideological correctives to be applied to each and every deviation. Prisoners became hyperalert to what views were expected of them and could give the appearance of a thorough conversion, right down to the class-struggle terminology in 'brainwashed' radio transmissions. 'Repetition, harassment,

humiliation were the principal coercive techniques the Communist enemy employed to
support indoctrination', concluded a US Army survey.[22] Once removed from the camps,
however, the prisoners no longer had cause to recite the dogma.

The Korean brainwashing episode was significant in elaborating the Cold War conception
of totalitarianism. As Abbott Gleason noted, it tangibly illustrated the state's 'holistic
reshaping of the individual' to conform to a new order. Gleason suggested brainwashing tales resonated particularly because of fears at home of the individual spirit being
overwhelmed by bureaucracy and institutions of modernity. The brainwashing issue helped
shift the concept of totalitarianism from the simple coercion of the police state to
'the enslavement of the helpless individual psyche'.[23] With Korea, the encounter with communism became an unusually personal and intimate battle with demons of thought.
Nationally, this encouraged the scrutinizing of the character of repatriates and, in Hollywood,
it helped transform the central themes of POW films. Captivity became an inner trial, not an
escape fable.

Returning prisoners of war became victims of American's crisis of confidence. Their
performance was exhibit A that the individual citizen was becoming weak and vulnerable.
Hollywood was quick to address the crisis of confidence after Korea. There was a clear
progression in film formulas as Hollywood searched for the best treatment for the subject.
Traditional heroic plots proved to lack verisimilitude to an audience aware of the record of
collaboration. Judgmental stories that blamed POWs for capitulating would be callous and
unentertaining. Scenes that focused on the torture and tribulations of incarceration were
too depressing and implicitly questioned whether war was worth it. The subgenre finally
settled on the courtroom drama as the best way to present the complexities of the Korean
POW experience.

The first POW films attempted to fit Korea into conventional adventure scenarios. The
1954 films *Prisoner of War* and *The Bamboo Prison* both featured stock heros who sneaked into
prison camps and only pretended to be collaborators so they could spy. The better-known
film is *Prisoner of War*, starring Ronald Reagan and directed by Andrew Marton. Released just
a few months after the real prisoners, the film was reportedly MGM's quickest production to
date. The military initially assisted production by providing former prisoners for interviews
and a repatriated officer as on-scene consultant. The Army also requested and obtained four
pages of script revisions.[24]

In the film, Ronald Reagan plays the fearless Web Sloane, who sneaks into a prison camp
to collect proof of violations of the Geneva Convention. He pretends to be a 'progressive',
the period term for collaborators, but the secret agent angle is drowned out by the film's
main theme, Communist torture, disturbing even by today's standards. In one scene, a
prisoner refuses to confess to germ warfare. Guards put his pet puppy in a burlap bag and
smash it with rifle butts. He still does not talk, but other prisoners are shown breaking under
horrible torture. In one frigid scene, guards dump buckets of water on a man and a grotesque
layer of ice forms around his head. In another, a haggard face is repeating name, rank and
serial number, the classic representation of resistance. The camera pulls back to reveal his
twisted arms weighted down with boulders. Prisoners are also shown boiling in the sun,
hanging from trees or capitulating before mock firing squads.

Prisoner of War flopped. The industry press, an authoritative judge of public tastes,
pronounced War Atrocities Pic Limited in Appeal.[25] The producers had tried for realism
by depicting documented incidents of torture, only to have it called 'a brutal, sadistic, and

thoroughly cheap attempt to exploit public interest'.[26] Although the film was almost universally hated by critics, the portrayals of torture were accepted as accurate. The reviewer for the Parent–Teachers Association (PTA) warned parents it should have been 'presented in documentary form to a prepared audience' rather than as entertainment. At least four persons used the word 'documentary' or a form of it in their reviews.[27] A telling explanation for why a seemingly realistic movie was a 'botch' came from Moira Walsh in *America* magazine, who called it an 'endless succession of physical brutalities' without balance from a 'counteracting moral and spiritual force'.[28] Portraying men breaking under torture was too pessimistic, it was necessary to believe that faith and masculinity provided honorable ways out of all situations. If captivity was examined too closely, a film undermined the morale it was supposed to improve.

Critics did not like the hopeless brutality, and also faulted the secret agent subplot, because the real record was considered shameful. The film 'shockingly suggests', wrote *Saturday Review*, 'that all the Americans who played along with the Communists . . . were really secret agents'.[29] The film claimed collaboration was a ruse or the result of extreme torture, not personal inadequacy. Treason, at the time the foremost association with captivity in the public mind, had been dealt with by denying it. . . .

The turncoats-as-agents plot was repeated later in 1954, but with an entirely different tone. *The Bamboo Prison* was a lighthearted B-movie. Unlike the Reagan film, this one was denied assistance by the Army from the beginning.[30] In *The Bamboo Prison*, a Sergeant Rand infiltrates a prison compound to gather proof of unreported prisoners so that negotiators at Panmunjom, Korea can demand them back. As in the earlier film, he pretends to be a progressive. Sergeant Rand spends most of the film in heat. His strategy is to seduce Tanya, the Russian-ballerina wife of a top Communist (an effete American from *The Daily Worker*) whose office might contain appropriate documents. When queried by a confederate as to how he will obtain the files, Rand explains 'I'm in the process, let's say, of climbing under the covers with the proletariat'. Tanya is responsive to American manhood and joins the scheme, believing that the Communists 'have ceased to be men'. The film ends with Tanya escaping to the West while Rand stays behind as an ersatz defector.

The Bamboo Prison did not follow the sober approach of similar films, but it was still very much a response to Korea's POW trauma. It was not just that in those unsure times American males would be pleased to be found more sexually desirable than Communist intellectuals. The real-life defections of soldiers to China added to the concern that Marxist ideology might have genuine appeal to the downtrodden, to which the film replied with cutting ridicule. In one scene, America's superior income is celebrated by a POW who rushes about the camp making car sounds like an 8 year old (he sells cars in civilian life). He manages to enrapture the camp commander with a vision of cruising in his very own American convertible, radio blasting. Unfortunately, his salary is only 100,000 Chinese yen. 'What's that in American money?' 'Four dolla twelve cents'. The car seller makes a face. During an interminable political education class for POWs, the camera pauses on a student's eyes. He blinks and the audience realizes he has been asleep—with eyeballs painted on the eyelids. During a recitation exercise on Marxism, the Chinese instructor calls on Arkansas, a gangly, endearingly mischievous youth. Arkansas recites class-struggle dogma in a mocking manner, which the pupils understand but the Chinese do not. The instructor is tipped off by a collaborator and he begins shouting wooden rhetoric at Arkansas: 'You have insulted the politburo. You have answered proletarian hospitality with bourgeois ingratitude'.

Arkansas feigns stupidity with his hillbilly accent, 'did Ah do ahll thaat?'. The film portrayed the sly earthiness of street wise proles, who despite coarse manners and little education, see right through Asiatic communism.

Although *The Bamboo Prison* is infectious as a period piece, it got very little notice at the time. One of the few reviews complained that its tone was 'incompatible' with the reality of the prison camps. Another critic, a Mrs Louis Bucklin of the PTA, was particularly disturbed that the film's most devious collaborator posed as a Catholic priest.[31] The Memphis Board of Censors sought to ban the film, citing the treasonous priest as an affront to the memory of Father Emil Joseph Kapaun, a heroic Army chaplain who died in captivity.[32] The script did not tap into the seriousness of concern in 1954. Bob Hope scratched plans for a farce after the Army refused to assist it.[33]

Neither realism, satire, nor heroic adventure were sufficient to address the POW crisis, so the Korean War POW subgenre adopted a new device: the courtroom drama. Three out of the next four POW films were court martial films. This paralleled real life, where the court martial became strongly associated with POWs. Although more sophisticated than adventure films, courtroom films brought new complications to using entertainment to address the POW issue.

Actual trials were few, but well publicized. Out of 4428 POWs returned, the conduct of 565 was seriously questioned. Most cases were dropped; others were sanctioned non-judicially with discharges, loss of rank or reprimands.[34] Only 14 ever went to trial,[35] though they were so publicized that they strengthened the perception of completely shattered discipline. The most chilling court martial served as an all-purpose example of POWs' failure of duty. Sergeant James C. Gallagher was convicted of murdering a dysentery victim by throwing him outside to freeze, reportedly because the man was too sick to clean him-self.[36] The men prosecuted were a staple of newspaper reports and editorials for several years. Their faces and stories made more impression than the scores of anonymous men allowed to go their way.

Interestingly, as media coverage of military prosecutions continued, a sympathetic backlash developed among a segment of the public who considered it unjust to punish victims of torture and brainwashing. The more the character of prisoners was challenged, the more their defenders pointed to the conditions of captivity. . . .

The emotional defense of repatriates presented a new challenge to Pentagon opinion managers and the film producers who chose to work with them. The unprecedented atten-tion on POWs, even if negative, gave greater currency to the agonies of captivity. Sympathy for the prisoners' dilemma was at odds with exhibiting them as proof of America going soft. The significance of the sympathetic backlash is underscored by the pains to which patriotic filmmakers and the Army's Motion Picture Branch took to address it. Realist torture was out, adventure yarns were out and now it seemed they could not even blame the prisoners who broke because it evoked empathy.

Hollywood responded by seizing this sympathy and turning it into support for patriotic renewal. The first Korean POW feature film that satisfied the Defense Department enough to give full assistance was released in 1956.[37] MGM, the studio responsible for *Prisoner of War* got it right with *The Rack*, starring Paul Newman as an Army officer returning from captivity. A moving, brooding, talky film, it was the most thoughtful of the bunch and favored by critics, but it offered nothing to the action market. *The Rack* explores treason, but with surprising empathy for the anti-hero. It suggests that honest men might collaborate and considers what should be done about it. Captain Hall (Newman) returns from prison camp as a psychiatric casualty. Although decorated for bravery before being captured, he is now about to be tried for collaboration. He is greeted by his father, who is a tough officer of the old school. And if that were not enough, Captain Hall's brother was heroically killed in battle. 'Why didn't you die like your brother did?', the father asks at one point.

Captain Hall wants only to plead guilty and get it over with. However, his kind attorney, puzzled by the early record of bravery, insists on a defense. During cross-examination the script reveals Hall's background and circumstances of aiding the enemy. He grew up lonely in a family bereft of warmth. His mother died when he was 10 years old and the father was cold and distant, not even kissing or touching his sons. The Chinese jailers exploited his emotional vulnerability by putting him in solitary confinement. Hall's anguish is wrenchingly communicated with in Newman's courtroom dialog; there are no prison flashbacks. Solitary confinement crushed Hall with hunger, cold and, worst of all, loneliness. After months of pressure, Captain Hall's jailers sensed a vulnerable moment and revealed the death of his brother in combat. They threaten to leave him alone forever; Captain Hall finally begins signing propaganda statements.

After setting up an empathetic premise, the Rod Serling script changes course and begins undermining Captain Hall's account. In a key sequence on the stand, Hall reveals the lone- liest day of his life, not in prison camp, but the day his mother died. The prosecutor points out that even after this, the worst day of his life, he still bounced back and became an officer, but in what was only the second worst experience, prison camp, he cracked. The prosecutor argues persuasively that the defendant was not at the limit of his endurance, it was his character that failed, rendering him culpable. In a nod to a debate of the day, the prosecutor adds in his peroration that even if society were remiss in preparing youths for the rigor of duty, it must not compound its error by failing to punish the guilty. 'If you find Captain Hall innocent of collaboration, you find all those other Americans who refused to collaborate guilty of stupidity.'

The Rack did not simply defend sympathy for collaborators, it sought to redirect it. In a scene near the end of the film, the father breaks down and acknowledges his emotional neglect of the family. The son forgives him in an embrace and the film seems to suggest that if only they had achieved such closeness earlier, Captain Hall, who was never physically tortured, would have had the spiritual strength to resist. By admitting that even well- meaning men can falter, The Rack added sophistication to the call for an unyielding Spartan code. The film's understanding tone showed respect for the backlash of sympathy for supposed collaborators, but civic mindedly tried to correct it. The Rack made compassion part of the rationale for unyielding discipline in captivity. Newman's spiritual pain did not come from the discomfort of a cell, but from his own failure to act heroically. The film called on society to steel its young soldiers for anything or face the shattered spirits who come home. The Rack optimistically concludes that valor is possible even during extreme isolation and deprivation. Surrender is still portrayed as a choice, character is the key variable, not the conditions of confinement. Captain Hall belatedly recognizes this and uses the court martial for atonement and a lesson to others. In a clear, strong, voice just before sentencing he says, 'I wish that everybody could feel the way that I feel now. Because if they did, they'd know what it's like to be a man who sold himself short'. He accepted the prosecutor's argument that he had given up faith in himself right when he needed it most.

The Rack informed a humiliated nation that a solution to the POW disgrace was already at hand: rededication to traditional values, as belatedly done by the Hall family. The message was well taken by critics. *Saturday Review* said *The Rack* showed 'the emotional and ideological unpreparedness of our own armed forces'. *Catholic World* called for 'better psychological background' for soldiers and approvingly noted the film's contrast between Newman and fellow-POW Lee Marvin, who did possess 'the inner resources' to maintain honor. *The New Yorker* added that the problem was society's inadequate nurture of children.[38] The only caveats came from reviewers who seemed to feel that empathy for alleged cowards strayed from a manly ideal. Collaborators were certainly 'more to be pitied than scorned', according to a *Nation* reviewer, but scriptwriter Rod Serling committed 'ethical mugwumpery' by not condemning them unambiguously. *Newsweek* made a similar point and compared it to a Broadway play called *Time Limit*.[39] The response to the prisoners of limited war remained divided between a sympathy that seemed to excuse weakness and a Spartan code that was unrealistic and heartless.

One year after *The Rack*, the play *Time Limit* (Karl Malden, United Artists, US, 1957) was remade into a film. In this variation of the court martial plot, a brave, selfless officer had collaborated with the enemy in order to save his men from mass execution. The film is a meditation on whether the officer (Richard Basehart) should be prosecuted for violating the military code to protect others. In weighing common decency against the exigencies of war, *Time Limit* was specifically addressing the lively public debate over the military's new Code of Conduct. In response to public anxiety, a Pentagon blue ribbon committee was appointed in 1955 to investigate the alleged collapse of discipline behind barbed wire. After lengthy and public deliberation, the Advisory Committee on Prisoners of War (also known as the Burgess Committee) produced a policy formalizing the traditional doctrine of name, rank and serial number. This time, the doctrine was made official in all military branches by an Executive Order and reinforced with more training. The public message of the committees's public report was one of firmness; the final sentence read 'The Korean story must never be permitted to happen again'.[40]

Although intransigence in captivity was emphasized, the drafters of the code appreciated the difficulty of actually following this. Name, rank and serial number would be the official slogan of martial *élan*, but in disciplinary proceedings there would be understanding. 'In the code there is no room for turncoats', President Eisenhower assured the country, 'but there is assurance of compassion and justice for those who yield only under torture'.[41] Although traditional policy was reaffirmed in 1955, it was not completely inflexible, contrary to common belief. It is not necessarily unforgivable to go beyond personal identification. When the code is read carefully, name, rank and serial number are mentioned as a minimum, not a limit. The key phrase accommodates a provision of the Geneva Convention which directs prisoners to identify themselves: 'Should I become a prisoner of war, I am *bound to give* only name, rank, service number, and date of birth'.[42] The code requires a POW to resist further interrogation 'to the utmost of my ability', a less-noticed phrase recognizing a finite nervous system.[43] Although the wording of the code had a dose of realism, the public presentation had little. During discussion in 1955, an Army general expressed the common, unforgiving understanding of the code this way: 'The tree of liberty thrives only when it is watered by the blood of patriots'.[44] The code attempted to accommodate two contradictory needs: getting the most resistance possible from captured troops, yet showing mercy for repatriates and respecting public sympathy for them.

Like *The Rack*, *Time Limit* built sympathy for a man accused of violating the code, yet still received an imprimatur from the Army's Motion Picture Branch. The accused officer had high motives: he made enemy propaganda to save the 16 men in his command. He felt that the lives of his subordinates should not be sacrificed for his own honor and reputation. The climatic clash between duty and sentiment is played out by a gruff general and the Richard Basehart character. In a somewhat involved element of the plot, it is revealed that the general's son had been murdered by other POWs for collaborating (despite enduring protracted torture). The general is appalled to learn his son died ignominiously: 'He was raised to know better'. Basehart pleads for understanding of prisoners situation. 'Your son was a hero for hundreds of days . . . And on only one day did he break. In the name of God, aren't all those other days worth something?' Basehart suggests there should be a 'time limit' on heroism.

Just when the script seems to favor the explanations of collaborators, the general is allowed his soliloquy. 'You talked to me of sixteen men. Multiply that by thousands. Try carrying that weight on your shoulders. Try sleeping with the cries of those wives and children in your ears. I've done that, Major, every war commander has, because until a better world is built, it's got to be done. That is why we have the Code, Major. The Code is our Bible and thank God for it.' On that note, it is decided not to drop charges against Basehart and the court martial proceeds. Like in *The Rack*, a nod was given to the defenders of the POWs. The film then explained that because the enemy would use our basic decency against us, harsh decisions were unavoidable. In order to minimize suffering in war, heroism had no upper limit.

It appears that some critics did not comprehend the military's rationale for assist-ing a production like *Time Limit*. Reviews reveal a debate locked into a simple-mindedly heroic conception of captivity. *Films in Review* called the story 'tendentious' for even considering a threshold for resistance. 'A time limit on heroism? . . . What an insidious implication!'[45]. *Newsweek* was just as unforgiving of the Basehart character: 'the Code of Conduct condones no collaboration of any sort under any circumstances. It is always the sad duty of an officer to sacrifice the lives of a few rather than risk the loss of many—in this particular case, the minds of many through false propaganda'.[46] Some had such a shallow appreciation of the realities of captivity that they denied that there was even a dilemma to consider. Robert Hatch wrote in *The Nation* that *Time Limit* conjured 'brain-teasing' choices just for enter-tainment, even though disloyalty in Korea resulted not from 'honorable dilemmas' but from 'confusion, ignorance and bad conscience'.[47] By looking seriously at the intensity of coercion, the film contradicted the view that collaboration was caused by gutlessness.

The negative reaction to a film approved by the military illustrates the trickiness of using POWs to stimulate patriotic verve. Respecting popular sympathy for the POWs seemed to violate the propaganda imperatives of the hard-liners. In order to be effective, a film had to address the public horror at enemy treatment of prisoners, the source of what the Advisory Committee on Prisoners of War referred to as 'misguided public sympathy'.[48] However, the revelation that strong, honest people can collapse, even without physical torture, threatened the heroic narrative which morale seemed to rest on.

An odd thing about both *The Rack* and *Time Limit* is that in real life, neither main character would have been court martialed. In actual disciplinary policy, collaboration in Korea was mitigated by duress. Internal Pentagon documents were explicit in saying that '*no disciplinary action*' was taken if POWs colluded under duress.[49] Strong penalties were carefully reserved for the most opportunistic.[50] However, common currency gave a dogged impression that name, rank and serial number was the test used for legal action. The very films favored by the Pentagon reinforced the perception that shattered young men were being tormented a second time.

The next feature, John Frankenheimer's *The Manchurian Candidate* (United Artists, US, 1962), does not fit easily with the other films, but it does support the belief that POWs were blameless because free will had been washed from their brains.[51] In this inventive fantasy, a young POW is brainwashed to the point that he can enter a memoryless state of suggestion and commit murder on cue. He is programed to murder a presidential candidate as part of an elaborate Communist plot. The completeness of brainwashing is displayed in a surreal scene early in the film. A group of young men, American POWs, are sitting in a hotel meeting room. A lecturer, a middle-aged woman in a colorful hat, drones on about hydrangeas to a ladies' flower club. The camera does a slow, 360° pan, showing the POWs sitting listlessly while the flower club members fan themselves. However, when the camera rotates back to the lecturer, she is no longer the flower lady, but a sinister-looking Chinese Communist named Yen Lo (actor Khigh Dhiegh, an all-purpose Asiatic villain who was also the camp commandant in *Time Limit*). Yen Lo explains to his real audience of malevolent, Communist officials that he has brainwashed the men (in 3 days!) to think they are at a hydrangea talk. The subjective camera view keeps cutting between middle-aged women with large hats and menacing men with scars, wearing jackboots. While the prisoners listen to flowers in the mind, Yen Lo reveals to his official audience the plan for the repatriated POW to assassinate an American leader. The effectiveness of brainwashing is proven by having a prisoner strangle a friend on stage.

The Manchurian Candidate is the only one of the films to do well then or since. Female lead Angela Lansbury got an Academy Award nomination for it. The success of the film demonstrates how deeply the fear of capture and absorption by an enemy organism resonated with the audience and how far the imagination might go to explain collaboration. One critic, Bosley Crowther, worried that although 'as wild a piece of fiction as any', the film might agitate the more 'anxious minds' of the day.[52] Another reviewer considered the film's robot assassin plot plausible enough to need a corrective: 'I do not believe', wrote Moira Walsh, 'that brainwashing . . . is as precise or efficient a process as the film makes it out to be'.[53] Like Jonathan Swift's A *Modest Proposal*, the premise was taken seriously enough to disagree with. Brainwashing was such a vital concern that even a paranoid extreme was compelling. Brainwashed prisoners could hardly be held responsible for their actions, bringing into relief the callousness of POW critics. . . .

The theme of Cold War America out of control is more explicit in the 1968 feature *Sergeant Ryker*. Lee Marvin is Sergeant Ryker, sentenced to death in the midst of the Korean War. (The name 'Ryker' is ironically similar to John Wayne's Sergeant Stryker in *Sands of Iwo Jima*.) Technically not a POW film (he is in prison here, not there), it still makes collaboration the central theme. The drama takes place concurrent with the second evacuation of Seoul, lending an air of hysteria and suggesting a rush to justice. The case against Ryker seems open and shut: Sergeant Ryker never denies joining the Red Army. However, as another compassionate defense attorney investigates, doubts and sympathy rise. A general warns the lawyer not to risk his career defending a man like Ryker, particularly while thousands of non-traitors are fleeing the capital. The establishment general is putting the system ahead of justice and it becomes clear Ryker is being railroaded. The betrayal theme is carried further by Ryker's wife, who would really rather be with the lawyer.

Eventually, cross-examination reveals that Ryker was a hero, not a turncoat. He had been on a secret mission when he crossed over, the truth known only by his superior officer, who was unfortunately killed in action. The real security breach turns out to be, significantly enough, an officer, whose Korean mistress is exposed in court as a spy. Ryker was not only falsely charged in court, he had been serving his accusing compatriots in a mission of extraordinary danger. The Chinese had believed his defection, it was his own people who did not. A moment of justice comes on the witness stand when Lee Marvin erupts in a marvelous hissing, spitting, tantrum. 'Go ahead and hang me, I risked my life for you brass types.' 'I only made one mistake, boys, I came back.'

Sergeant Ryker was originally a 1963 television film. A film distributor added outdoor shots to the courtroom dramatics and rereleased it to theaters in early 1968. The rerelease took advantage of the developing Vietnam anti-war audience by resurrecting an earlier episode of disillusionment.[54]

It was in the crisis of confidence of the Korean War that the POW first took a central place in modern military dramas. The danger of global engagement was highlighted by the high-profile prisoner of limited war. This representation of vulnerability has been reinforced by repeated captivity dramas, including Vietnam, the seizure of the Pueblo warship, the embassy takeover in Iran, kidnaps in Lebanon, Gulf War pilots and, not least, in popular fiction. The prisoner joined Pearl Harbor and the atom bomb as symbols of the nation's vulnerability to foreign evil. One of the most evocative representations of overseas involvement is one of victimization.

As the first limited war of its kind between East and West, Korea put unusual pressure on prisoners to cooperate publicly. A perception of whole-scale collaboration emerged that was too traumatic to be ignored, even in film entertainment. Loyalty, patriotism and commercial savvy encouraged producers to make films that would guide and reassure the audience. However, bringing a seemingly shameful episode to the screen was a delicate process, in particular since public attitudes were still evolving. Film makers tried different formulas and routinely turned to the Army's Motion Picture Branch for consultation and assistance with set materials. The series of Korean War POW films steered between the imperatives of propaganda and audience acceptance. Eventually, the subgenre arrived at a formula that acknowledged the pressure soldiers were subjected to, but still found a respectful way of demanding unending resistance. The films paralleled the development of public sentiment, where the initial shock at collaboration prompted an examination of captivity, followed by greater sensitivity, then disillusionment.

Korean War POW films were a significant departure from the adventure tales before and after. Escape, the principle theme of heroic captivity, was mentioned in few scripts and central to none. The preoccupation with collaboration reflected American insecurity about standing up to communism. However, feature films reveal more than just the self-doubt of the early Cold War. Hollywood producers and Pentagon film consultants joined other commentators in citing the supposed failure of the POW in a call for national renewal. However, as a symbol in service to Cold War morale, the POW proved difficult to manage. Extended attention on the obligations of captives, in film and elsewhere, gave a high profile to a less-recognized agony of war. A prisoner is a victim. Surrender is followed by dependence on the captor and often onerous conditions. This violated a maxim of public opinion management: war must never seem so horrible that it is not worth it.[55] Serious treatments unavoidably recalled the human cost of war, but the helplessness of the bound contradicted their use in a nationalist jeremiad. Chastising repatriates produced a backlash of sympathy and made official doctrine seem callous. The POW saga gave a dark hue to the Cold War mentality. This culminated in *The Outer Limits* and *Sergeant Ryker*'s sentiment that the POWs got a raw deal at home too.

The Korean War provided an early example of the difficulty of managing the image of the modern POW. As a symbol that must contain an implication of vulnerability, the POW can sow disillusionment as well as patriotic verve. Demanding more discipline and sacrifice by citing the demands of war accented the reality of sacrifice, moving some to question state sanctions rather than the repatriates. The disturbing course of the story revealed an inchoate fear of the Cold War's effect on human qualities at home. Prisoners are a reminder of the human price of conflict and indignation can switch from the jailers to the authorities that put them in harm's way. The dilemma of the prisoner of limited war rests ultimately on the disparity between the official and unofficial reasons for going to war. American mobilizations are justified as wars of survival against pure evil, but they are run according to the limited objectives of *Realpolitik*. Only wars of uncomplicated virtue justify the trial of captivity, so when a negotiated peace reveals a conflict to be of limited interest, the sparkling, martial adornment that distracts from the human cost is stripped away. Because the subject matter was so intractable, none of the films but one was ever very successful. Heroic films could not work and sensitive films hurt morale. The subgenre moved towards dissent, but, unlike the Vietnam war, there was never enough public protest over Korea to found a strong tradition of critical films. These POW films of Korea are more forgotten than the Forgotten War itself, but for much the same reason.

Acknowledgements

Thanks are due to John Chambers, Lloyd Gardner, Elliott Gruner, Bruce Franklin, David Oshinsky and Marilyn Young for comments about earlier versions of this article.

Notes

1 *Committee Documentation of the Secretary of Defense's Advisory Committee on Prisoners of War* (July 1955), Table 15a, Study Group I Problem D, Review of the Ives Committee Report, Air Force Plans Decimal File 1942–1954: 383.6; Entry 336 Box 441, Record Group 341, National Archives (hereafter RG 341).
2 *King Rat* (Bryan Forbes, US, Columbia, 1965) is a splendid exception. Set in the Pacific war, it does not address collaboration with the enemy, but it is about masculine vulnerability.
3 Elliott Gruner, *Prisoners of Culture: representing the Vietnam POW* (New Brunswick, NJ, 1993) and H. Bruce Franklin, *M.I.A. or Mythmaking in America* (New Brunswick, NJ, 1993).
4 On conceptualization of the Cold War, see Melvyn Leffler, *A Preponderance of Power: national security, the Truman administration, and the Cold War* (Stanford, CA, 1992).
5 Richard Barnet, *The Rockets' Red Glare: when America goes to war, the presidents and the people* (New York, 1990), p. 314.
6 James A. Van Vleet, 'We can win in Korea if we want to', *Reader's Digest* (July 1953), p. 1.

7   Rosemary Foot, A Substitute for Victory: the politics of peacemaking at the Korean armistice talks (Ithaca, NY, 1990).

8   A 'convincing' case can be made that voluntary repatriation violated articles 7 and 118 of the Geneva Convention, which required repatriation without delay and made no provision for release to third parties. Col. Walton K. Richardson, 'Prisoners of War as instruments of foreign policy', Naval War College Review, 23 (September 1970), p. 55.

9   Many officials were fiercely opposed to voluntary repatriation. C. Turner Joy complained that it cost another year of captivity for POWs and 50,000 American casualties in the field. In Joy's view, the policy put the welfare of former enemy soldiers above that of Americans languishing in prison camps or still fighting on the line. C. Turner Joy, How Communists Negotiate (New York, 1955), p. 152. Cited in Col. Walton K. Richardson, 'Prisoners of war as instruments of foreign policy', Naval War College Review, 23 (September 1970), p. 56.

10 Russian hydrogen bomb blast Aug. 12 confirmed by A.E.C., New York Herald Tribune (20 August 1953), p. 1.

11 New York Herald Tribune (14 August 1953), p. 3 and Newsweek (24 August 1953), p. 30.

12 One-in-three: Eugene Kinkead, In Every War But One (New York, 1959), p. 16. One-in-seven: preliminary findings on Army prisoners by the Human Resources Research Office, Committee Documentation of the Secretary of Defense's Advisory Committee on Prisoners of War (July 1955), Tab 12; Air Force Plans Decimal File 1942–1954, 383.6; Entry 336 Box 441, RG 341.

13 Twenty-three Americans, Time (5 October 1953), p. 33.

14 Albert Biderman, March to Calumny: the story of American POWs in the Korean War (New York, 1963). See also H.H. Wubben, 'American prisoners of war in Korea: a second look at the "Something New in History" Theme', American Quarterly, 22 (Spring 1970), p. 3. For the most developed example of the 'prisoners-were-traitors' theme see Eugene Kinkead, In Every War But One (New York, 1959). March to Calumny was a reply to Kinkead.

15 This is the common wording of the phrase, which I use for brevity and tradition. Formally, it is name, rank, service number and date of birth.

16 William E. Mayer, 'Why did many GI captives cave in?' U.S. News and World Report (24 February 1956), pp. 57–72.

17 For an example of this usage see Anthony Leviero, New York Times (14 August 1955), section VI, p. 12.

18 Facts page, Committee Documentation of the Secretary of Defense's Advisory Committee on Prisoners of War (July 1955), Table 12; Air Force Plans Decimal File 1942–1954, 383.6, Entry 336 Box 441, RG 341.

19 Robert J. Lifton, Thought Reform and the Psychology of Totalism,: a study of brainwashing in China (London, 1961), p. 150. Quoted in Abbott Gleason, Totalitarianism: the inner history of the Cold War (New York, 1995), p. 247. Gleason has an excellent chapter and bibliography on brainwashing.

20 When he returned decades later, the final defector stayed briefly in the home of David Buck, former editor of The Journal of Asian Studies. Conversations with author.

21 For accounts of the disease environment, see Interrogation reports of personnel returned to military control in Operation Little Switch, 1953. Box 1, Records of International and US Military Commands in the Pacific, 1947–headquarters, US Army Forces, Far East Office of the Assistant Chief of Staff, G-1, Office of the Adjutant General RG 497.

22 Communist Interrogation Indoctrination, and Exploitation of Prisoners of War, Department of the Army Pamphlet 30–101 (May 1956), p. 52. Box 19, RG 338.

23 Gleason, *Totalitarianism*, pp. 93 and 103.

24 'Defense Dept. won't back film on germ war issue', *New York Herald Tribune* (20 March 1954), p. 8.

25 *Hollywood Reporter* (24 March 1954), p. 3.

26 Arthur Knight, *Saturday Review* (17 April 1954), p. 24.

27 Mrs Louis L. Bucklin, *National Parent–Teacher*, 48 (May 1954), p. 40. Other 'documentary' references: Philip T. Hartung, *Commonweal*, 61 (9 April 1954), p. 15; *Harrison*, Library of Congress Motion Picture Clip File (undated, early 1954) and *Estimates*, Library of Congress Motion Picture Clip File (undated, Spring 1954).

28 Moira Walsh, *America*, 91 (22 May 1954), p. 229.

29 Arthur Knight, *Saturday Review* (17 April 1954), p. 24.

30 The Defense Department firmly prohibited any association with the film, specifying 'max dissemination' of the directive to 'ins|ure| compliance'. 15 December 1954 directive from CINFO; Adjutant General, Entry 363, Decimal File 062.2, Box 14, RG 407.

31 *Estimates*, Library of Congress Motion Picture Clip-File (18 November 1954). Mrs Louis L. Bucklin, *National Parent–Teacher*, 48 (December 1954), p. 39.

32 Box 1, Accession Number 59-A949, OASD(PA), WNRC-S. Included in Lawrence H. Suid, ed., *1945 and After*, Vol. 4 of *Film and Propaganda in America: a documentary history*, David Culbert, ed. (New York, 1991), pp. 274–275.

33 A letter to Hope's agent explained that the Army valued its previous collaborations with Hope, however, 'The subject is considered of too great importance and seriousness especially at this time to be treated in the farcical manner indicated by the outline'. Letter from Donald E. Baruch, Chief of Army Motion Pictures Section, to Louis Shurr Agency, 18 March 1954; Assistant Secretary of Defense, Office of Public Information, Motion Picture Section, Box 135, 1954, Entry 133, Decimal File 062.2, RG 330.

34 Service actions on repatriated Korean prisoners of war as of 30 June 1955, *Committee Documentation of the Secretary of Defense's Advisory Committee on Prisoners of War* (July 1955), Table 12; Air Force Plans Decimal File 1942–1954, 383.6, Entry 336 Box 441, RG 341.

35 Kinkead, *In Every War But One*, p. 65.

36 Kinkead, *In Every War But One*, p. 70.

37 Julian Smith, *Looking Away: Hollywood and Vietnam* (New York, 1975), p. 215.

38 Arthur Knight, *Saturday Review* (19 May 1956), p. 47; Robert Kass, *Catholic World* (May 1956), p. 145 and John McCarten, *The New Yorker* (17 November 1956), p. 102.

39 Robert Hatch, *Nation* (24 November 1956), p. 467 and *Newsweek* (4 June 1956), p. 99.

40 POW: *the fight continues after the battle*, Report by the Secretary of Defense's Advisory Committee on Prisoners of War (August 1955), pp. 18 and 32; G-3, Army General Staff, Assistant Chief of Staff for Operations, Box 270, Decimal 383.6 (POWs) 1955, RG 319.

41 Captive to give name, rank, number, age—mercy for tortured, *New York Times* (18 August 1955), p. 1.

42 Emphasis added. 'When questioned, should I become a prisoner of war, I am bound to give only name, rank, service number, and date of birth. I will evade answering further questions to the utmost of my ability. I will make no oral or written statements disloyal to my country and its allies or harmful to their cause.' From Biderman, *March to Calumny*, p. 279.

43 On tendentious interpretations of the Code, see S.L.A. Marshall, 'The code and the *Pueblo*—some questions and answers', *Air Force and Space Digest* (July 1969), p. 74.

44 *New York Times* (8 March 1955), p. 12.

45 John M. Bassett, *Films in Review* (November 1957), p. 463.

46 *Newsweek* (28 October 1957), p. 104.

47 Robert Hatch, *Nation* (9 November 1957), p. 332.

48 Statement of objectives, presentation to the Secretary of Defense part II, p. 7, *Committee Documentation of the Secretary of Defense's Advisory Committee on Prisoners of War* (July 1955), Table 13; Air Force Plans Decimal File 1942–1954, 383.6, Entry 336 Box 441, RG 341.

49 Original emphasis. Service actions on repatriated Korean prisoners of war as of 30 June 1955, Part II, p. 5, *Committee Documentation of the Secretary of Defense's Advisory Committee on Prisoners of War* (July 1955), Table 13; Air Force Plans Decimal File 1942–1954, 383.6, Entry 336 Box 441, RG 341.

50 Service actions on repatriated Korean prisoners of war as of 30 June 1955, *Committee Documentation of the Secretary of Defense's Advisory Committee on Prisoners of War* (July 1955), Table 12; Air Force 12 Plans Decimal File 1942–1954, 383.6, Entry 336 Box 441, RG 341.

51 *The Manchurian Candidate* was the only one of the six films in question to be nominated for Academy Awards, losing for best supporting actress and editing.

52 Bosley Crowther, *New York Times* (25 October 1962), p. 48:3.

53 Moira Walsh, *America*, 107 (24 November 1962), p. 1158.

54 *New York Times* (21 March 1968), p. 56:2.

55 Sanitizing of combat is ubiquitous, one example being the censoring of photographs of American casualties during World War II.

Film and the War: Representing Vietnam

19

DAVID E. JAMES

[handwritten annotation: film responses to viet? What impact does Vietnam have on film makers relationship to media/film]

> The document, then, is no longer for history an inert material through which it tries to reconstitute what men have done or said, the events of which only the trace remains; history is now trying to define within the documentary material itself unities, totalities, series, relations.
>
> Michel Foucault

> One day at the battalion aid station in Hue a Marine with minor shrapnel wounds in his legs was waiting to get on a helicopter. . . . "I *hate* this movie," he said, and I thought, "Why not?"
>
> Michael Herr

For the last half of the decade the war in Vietnam was the largest single determinant of other economic, social, and cultural developments in the United States, eventually becoming the master metaphor by which they were understood. As the imperial state declared itself in the ghettos, in the streets of Chicago, and on the campuses of the rest of the country, albeit with less ferocity than in the villages of Vietnam, Blacks and war protesters came to feel themselves to be fighting alongside the Vietnamese people in the same war of liberation. When Black Power's equation of the struggles of domestic minorities with that of the Vietnamese expanded to include other marginalized groups, then the notion of a unified Third World could stand in place of the largely absent class analysis, and acts of resistance against the state, especially as they became more violent in the Weatherman period, could be thought of as parallel to the Vietnamese resistance rather than simply ancillary or subordinate to it. The Progressive Labor Party's attack on North Vietnam's participation in the Paris peace talks as a betrayal of world revolution marks the extent to which the initially hegemonic confrontation in Asia could be re-contained in the political developments it engendered. Until this point, however, the operations in the Asian theater were the parent actions from which the "two, three, many Vietnams" of Che Guevara's injunction were spawned. Each of the special interest groups—students, GIs, the Vietnamese themselves, and indeed everyone conscious of the way his or her experience of capitalism, even at the psychic level of alienation from oneself, recapitulated the situation of Third World people—had thus a "Vietnam" of his or her own, a lived experience of imperialism.

This pandemic dispersal of the Vietnam War is the context for the specific issues faced by filmmaking that sought to intervene in it, either directly, by attempting to propagandize against it, or indirectly, but no less importantly, by confronting the establishment media's complicity in the social consensus that allowed the administration to fight the war on its own terms. Consideration of the way in which even the most dissident filmmaking was incriminated, on some level or other, in the international political system of which the Vietnamese decolonization struggle was the rupture eventually produced meta-cinematic reflections that argued themselves as the only politically valid filmmaking. As their only means of negating mass media representations which, however situated ideologically, only profited from the war, they refused to allow any unmediated image of Vietnam or any film practice engaged in its purview to pass without saturating it with the evidence of its own contradictions. Carried to their logical conclusions, such meditations would call into question the possibility of even making film, and so would open the road to a refusal that could authenticate itself only by espousing silence or self-destruction, or by totally recasting the practices under which cinema could be pursued. The filmic form of appearance of these cinematic issues is the tension between image and discourse in the documentation of the war. The inflection of general problems of representation by the specific question of representing the war imposed semiological crises upon the political crises involved in the dissemination of images and in the relation between such images and the institutions producing them. Contestation of the establishment definition of the war, of what constituted "Vietnam," thus inevitably involved contestation of the methods of representing it, of the agencies of representation, and hence of the relationship between media institutions and the other institutions of state power.

That the photograph manifests a stronger existential bond with reality than do most other forms of representation is accepted even by those semiologists who are most careful to insist that ostensibly transparent referentiality is in fact produced by means of the codes of visual language.[1] And so while Brecht's remark that by itself a photograph of the Krupp ironworks does not say very much may be true, one thing it does say is that the photographer has been there. In the case of motion pictures, this *"having-been-there"* of the still photograph "gives way before a *being-there* of the thing" (Barthes 1977: 45), but in both instances the assertion of one or another kind of presence is fundamental both to the rhetorical power of the higher levels of signification articulated by the image itself through the codes of its own legibility and to the other languages with which it is contiguous. In most sixties documentary war films, the resonances of the cinematic codes of World War II feature films that depend on this illusion of presence are amplified and directed by accompanying verbal languages—indirect speech, titles, direct speech, voice-of-God narration[2] —in which the image is encased. But even when such discursivity is not explicit, in genres like cinéma vérité that claim the aural and visual reproduction of nature as it is, the apparent iconicity only frames an intrinsic exposition. Thus presence and meaning—object and interpretation, denotation and connotation, representation and discourse—are the terms between which sequences of images argue a point of view while maintaining the semblance that their mediation is neutral, merely the articulation of what is implicit in the evidence they make present.

Bridging the pacific distance that kept the war in Asia from its production in the United States, the Vietnam War documentary exploits and compounds at two points especially the polemical assumptions of the documentary model in general: at the point where, to use

Bazin's inaugurating image, a photographic "impression" (Bazin, 1967: 12) is taken from the war by light and at the point where it is delivered to the public. The transactions involved at both points were scrutinized in the period in reflexive assaults on the theory of representational documentary, but in most Vietnam War documentaries, the precariousness of these moments when reality was transformed into film and when reality was recovered from it was typically supplied by a compensating excess of affirmation, so that the vehemence with which such and such film was offered as proof or disproof of the war's justification depended upon corresponding assumptions that the derivation of its images from situations of danger and horror empowered them with a more than ordinary authority. To invoke a metaphor used in one of the most rank exploitations of the war, those images secured from the heart of darkness were held to be simultaneously beyond language and the most eloquent. It is entirely appropriate that, as if in recognition of the centrality of this model of authority in the discourse of the Vietnam War as a whole, even Hollywood, in its only contemporary attempt to deal directly with the war rather than allegorizing it or displacing it into one of its adjacent issues, recognized that the politics of the Vietnam War were inseparable from the politics of its representation.[3]

Though a fictional feature, John Wayne's *The Green Berets* (1968), made when public opinion was already swinging against American presence in Vietnam, directly addressed the obligation of the press to produce domestic consensus. It dramatized the education of a skeptical journalist who is invited by a marine captain played by Wayne himself to go to Vietnam and share the day-to-day life of the Green Berets. The journalist becomes convinced of the necessity and indeed virtue of the U.S. defense of the south from communist aggression, not through argument of the historical process or explanation of the sequence of colonial penetrations that have produced the war, but by being brought face to face with National Liberation Front (NLF) atrocities. The wrenching visceral encounters he experiences—the sight of a murdered Montagnard chief, a GI horribly killed by a bamboo skewer booby trap, and finally the NLF attack on Fort Dodge—bring the war into focus for him as an altruistic response to a worldwide communist threat that only has been obfuscated by the cant of a liberal press. Though Wayne continuously interprets this evidence to ensure that the correct implications are construed, the journalist is essentially convinced by the nature of the atrocities themselves; they are, as it were, self-explanatory, conjuring a history and an ethics out of their own material presence. Like Eric Sevareid in 1966, like Morely Safer in 1967, he goes to Vietnam *to see for himself*, and he returns to the United States determined to report the truths that firsthand observation has made plain to him. He thus enacts the model role of the documentary filmmaker, even as intradiegetically he has enacted the role of the ideal audience for such a documentary.

Like *The Green Berets*, the typical Vietnam War documentary recreates a trip to the front; its transformation of the movie theater into the theater of war depends on the effectiveness with which the audience can be made to experience phenomenally the textures and terrors of battle. The crucial nexus is the GI, and, just as in the war itself he is our surrogate, so in the film he is intermediary between us and Vietnam.[4] His experience of the war, always weightier and more authoritative than ours and circumscribing any experience we can have, is proposed as the moment of authenticity and knowledge—of authenticity as knowledge—upon which the war can be evaluated and validated, just as his sacrifice is the war's justification, the proof of its virtue. Television specials like CBS's *Christmas in Vietnam* (1965) and films like Pierre Schoendorffer's *The Anderson Platoon* (1966–1967) and Eugene Jones's

A *Face of War* (shot in 1966 but not released until 1968) are representatives of such documentaries that propose the GI as the site of exemplary understanding.

For three months in 1966, Jones and his crew lived with a company of the Marine Corps that was unsuccessfully resisting the NLF's liberation of a small village. With as many as three cameras simultaneously, all equipped with radio microphones, the filmmakers followed the soldiers through all their activities. By virtue of the closeness of this surveillance and the crew's readiness to follow the soldiers into action, A *Face of War* does succeed in making available what is probably the most densely textured version of the GI's experience of the Vietnam War and of the day-to-day conditions under which it was fought Jones does not fall into the obvious formal and ideological trap of structuring his presentation dramatically upon the experience of a single hero and subordinating the remainder of the company in a hierarchy around him (and to this extent the concern of the film remains the generalized experience of the GIs almost as a historically representative class); still, some of them become sufficiently familiar that the remoteness of their civilian lives from the Asian front emphasizes both the poignancy of their attempts to make sense of Vietnam and the political mediation that lies between the GIs as individuals and the GIs as agents of an imperialism of which they have no understanding or real knowledge.

Inevitably the film's highlights are the points when these contradictions are greatest; in the combat scenes the cameramen's defensive reaction to enemy attack causes the coherence of the visual and aural fields to fall apart into the energized cacophony of the recording apparatus's own contact with violence, reproducing in the enunciation the chaotic violence of the exchange of fire and the cries of pain of the wounded. The film's overall structure exploits the tension between torturous and fearful silence and these sudden eruptions of filmic and profilmic violence, with collision montage used to juxtapose the terror and destruction of battle with the soldiers' attempts to befriend the peasants. The most powerful of these rapid shifts comes in a sequence showing the GIs providing medical care to the villagers when a truck is suddenly blown up by a land mine and a number of young soldiers are killed. In the jarring unpredictability of these alternations—the suddenness with which a silent march through empty paddies can be transformed into a miasma of destruction —Jones locates the essence of the GI's experience. And by following the soldiers into the heart of battle and by so fully subjecting himself to their risks that he was twice wounded —shooting so assiduously that he himself was shot—he appropriates for his film the authenticity of their extreme jeopardy.

While this most crucial assertion of Barthes's *"having-been-there"* does have its value, not the least of which is its unspoken but unmistakable conclusion that the GIs are as much victims as heroes, still the fallacies of the cinéma vérité model expose its naiveté. Its suppositious faith in the capacity of reality to reveal itself, the basis of its humanist pathos, is discredited by the clearly staged nature of many sequences, and especially by the self-consciously plangent, high-art photography of scenes such as that of soldiers on watch at dusk silhouetted by flares against coils of barbed wire, or of old women weeping as these same soldiers burn their homes. This implicit pleading on behalf of the military that finally only recapitulates the most egregious of the war's justifications comes to a head in the covert appropriation of World War II as a master metaphor. Most of the motifs A *Face of War* employs—the man on point listening to the jungle and waving his troop on, the chaplain's pre-battle address giving the imminent self-sacrifice a divine sanction, the football game in the mud, the communal bath in a natural pool, the smiles and gratitude of the natives, and even the birth of a baby—are recruited from Hollywood features; their silent intent is to rewrite imperialist invasion as the anti-fascist liberation of Asia from the Japanese, or of Europe from the Nazis.

As World War II supplied the model for understanding the Vietnam War, so Hollywood war movies provided the vocabulary for conducting it. Michael Herr's *Dispatches*, an attempt to write the soldiers' stories that was preempted by an artificiality that made the war for them already a movie (Herr, 1978: 188, 206), is only the most perceptive account of the war as a totally media-ted event, itself made over into the conventions of art. Such a Wildean mimetic inversion presents a particular problem for a would-be objective documentarist, for further transformations into language of an already aestheticized reality merely multiply the layers of reflexivity. What saves Herr himself from capitulation to total subjectivity and gives substance to his torrent of psychedelic flotsam is not appeal to the adequacy of any one story or to the actuality of events, for these are more bizarre than any trip; rather, it is the establishment of self-consciousness of the medium between events and any representation of them—the attention to language itself in the face of its attrition—that makes a place for understanding.[5]

Elsewhere that attrition, the dissolution of meaning into labyrinthine ironic jargon, facilitated the army's and the administration's use of the public media to present the war as non-ideological, as an apolitical, humane response to ideologically motivated aggression. Thus Jones, and in fact the establishment media at large, would have it that the intensity of the Vietnam experience was not only its own justification, it was also its own explanation. The affirmation of presence in the film image supposes a parallel aesthetic of empiricism, a repression of knowledge that can be countered only by an engagement with what it must suppress: history. As the war grew, the need for explanations of it was in no way lessened by the currency that television gave to hard-core imagery of its atrocities. Whatever value same-day footage of the bombardment of Khe Sanh or the fighting in Hue had in legitimizing the war or in authorizing an account of it became eroded by familiarity, but also by the disparity between the visceral overload and its lack of meaning. Films like A *Face of War*, which privilege the GI's trauma as the explanation of the war, were collusive with the tragedy they lamented. Suspended across the absent explanations of the historical events which produced the war, and by virtue of those absences contributing to public mendacity; they were collusive with the White House, which was able to prosecute the war for so long precisely by misrepresenting its causes.

The most important of the official apologies for the war was *Why Vietnam?* (1965), an extension of the Pentagon's World War II *Why We Fight* series. Scripted by the State Department to garner support for President Johnson's bombing of the north, its point of departure was a speech made by the president in July 1965 in which he cited a letter from "a woman in the midwest" who wanted to know why her son was in Vietnam. The answer, articulated both in Johnson's own words and in the extrapolation and commentary of a narrator, described a drama of aggression and appeasement: in the tradition of Hitler and Mussolini, Ho Chi Minh had invaded South Vietnam in a communist offensive aimed initially at the rice and the mineral industry, but with long-term ambitions stretching as far as East Pakistan. Blatantly misrepresenting history, Johnson argued in the film that Vietnam was a defensive war; the United States was simply "helping a free people to defend their sovereignty" against Ho and his plans for "a reign of terror." But his claims—Dien Ben Phieu had been a battle between communist and non-communist Vietnamese; at Geneva, Vietnam was divided into two in the pattern of Korea; there had been free elections in the south; the United States destroyers in the Gulf of Tonkin had been fired upon without provocation —are all apparently supported by documentary evidence. There is enough footage of fleeing peasants to prove the repressiveness of Ho's regime; shells with Chinese markings justify the assertion that the invasion is part of a global communist offensive; and though the enemy is as invisible in this film as he was reputed to be in the jungles of Vietnam, still the evidence of his presence is borne upon the bodies of the wounded American soldiers. Substituting for the indirect address of cinéma vérité the direct address of the narrator, and incorporating Johnson's discourse into its own even as it appropriates presidential authority, the mendacious history on the sound track closes the visual text and encloses the plenitude of meaning it is supposed to contain. In the 10,000 prints circulated through-out the country and shown to all GIs before departure to Vietnam, *Why Vietnam?* epitomizes the conjunction of a system of representation and a system of distribution—a film and a cinema—that together form the object radical film would have to contest. In that contestation, the representations of the Vietnamese and their methods of representation had a privileged role, one which may best be approached *via* their ideological and material absence from most Vietnam films.[6]

In *Fire in the Lake*, Frances Fitzgerald's perception that the war was a Vietnamese rather than simply an American event enabled her to collate the strategic crisis with the crisis in American misconception of the Third World in general. She suggested that the American command's absolute failure to understand the Vietnamese was matched by the soldiers' inability even to perceive their adversaries. Ignorant of the role of the village as the pivot of Vietnamese social life, the GI was incapable of knowing how the NLF had used that role to confound the distinction between combatant and noncombatant, drawing entire sectors of South Vietnam into its ranks and redefining the conditions under which the war could be fought. "In raiding the NLF villages, the American soldiers had actually walked over the political and economic design of the Vietnamese revolution. They had looked at it, but they could not see it, for it was doubly invisible: invisible within the ground and then again invisible within their own perspective as Americans" (Fitzgerald, 1972: 192). Running like a leitmotif through both the films and the other accounts of the war, the invisibility of the Vietnamese allowed them to be everywhere but also to be everywhere absent. It was a fact not only of the military experience but also of the media activity that reenacted it; and ironically so, since the privileged role of the Vietnamese as the verminous enemy or as the vanguard of the revolutionary resistance to imperialism endowed their images—representations of them and their representations of the war—with a peculiar authority.

Such images did have several kinds of use for the administration and the army, and in fact one of the most interesting of all the films produced by the war is *Know Your Enemy —The Viet Cong* (Armed Forces International Film 172), the U.S. Army's re-presentation of captured NLF footage of its own combat operations and non-military and propaganda work. In this film the army narrator, who is shown reviewing the footage, continually attempts to discredit scenes of NLF activity, for example, women and children transporting weapons on modified bicycles, casualties being met by doctors and nurses and assigned to underground hospitals, and the production of liberation newspapers—all scenes in which they appear to be proficient soldiers and fully human people—by warning the audience to remember that what they are seeing is "the Viet Cong as the Viet Cong would like to see themselves."

By and large, however, the White House and the corporate interests behind the war preferred to repress the Vietnamese peoples's view of themselves and of the war and so reproduce in the domestic theaters that invisibility which was so devastating in Asia. Whose interests were finally served by the media's decision to follow the military in conceptualizing the Vietnamese people only as body counts is difficult to tell. The dinner-time saturation of the American psyche with what became known as "'bang bang' coverage" (Arlen, 1969: 112) was by definition and structure piecemeal, and unable to deal in anything that could not be reduced to visual sensationalism; it probably did the administration as much harm as good, but certainly the media attempted to follow the official line. The networks regularly aired documentaries that parroted the government rationales, often under immediate direct pressure from sponsors and the White House (Barnouw, 1974: 273),[7] and they refused to show the many available documentaries that presented an opposite point of view.[8] Felix Greene's *Inside North Vietnam* is a case in point; although CBS sponsored it and supplied Greene with stock and laboratory services in return for an option, it deemed the film unshowable (ibid.: 281). Even Walter Cronkite's celebrated expression of reservations about the war on his visit to Vietnam in February 1968 merely reflected the shift in majority opinion that had happened eight months before.

With American and world support necessary for the continuation of the war, the media became as much the site of the war as the place where it was depicted, forcing the anti-war movement to adopt tactics whose decentralization, infiltration, and other strategies had a good deal in common with the NLF. Since access to images of the NLF was always a function of social power, a mark of a position in respect to the war mediated through specific relations with the army, with the State Department, and with the media institutions, and since wherever the Vietnamese people's struggle was supported or reenacted such images were most highly prized, the way they were handled was intrinsically so important that the contest of representation was inseparable from the contestation not only of the agencies of representation, but also of the modes of representation.

In this guerrilla media war these multiple interdeterminations demanded a new relation between image and exposition, between sight and sense, such as had, in fact, been developed by the NLF.

> The Viet Cong do use films, but not widely. However, they use filmstrips quite widely. All the Viet Cong films I've seen—captured propaganda films used in South Vietnam by the Viet Cong—are *silent*. These films are *accompanied by a narration delivered by a man during the projection*. It's as if this was an illustrated lecture. In that way he can *suit his content to the current local situation*.[9]

This extreme revision of cinema must have been substantially determined by material conditions, by the logistics of jungle warfare, by technological exigency, and by a limited cine-literacy on the part of the audience (and in any case it is not generalizable to all NLF films, some of which were extremely sophisticated). Still, it must be understood as a decisive and programmatic reorientation of the use of the apparatus. Indeed, it is in precisely such terms—and almost certainly drawing on the Vietnamese as a model—that the concept of a "Third Cinema" was formulated. In domestic attempts to reproduce this guerrilla cinema, supplantation of spectacle and consumption by the "film act," "A MEETING—an act of anti-imperialist unity . . . |in which the| film is the pretext for dialogue, for the seeking and finding of wills" (Solanas and Gettino, 1976: 62), together with other revisions of the social relations of film, is crucial. In their integration of cinema into the liberation struggle, the Vietnamese made concomitant modifications in the filmic.

The discovery that films "offer an effective pretext for gathering an audience, in addition to the ideological message they contain," and that "the capacity for synthesis and penetration of the film image . . . makes the film far more effective than any other tool of communication" (ibid.: 53) meant that formal codes had to be reconstructed accordingly. Interposing himself like the *benshi* between the film and its audience, the NLF spokesperson inserted his discourse between the image and its self-articulation. In doing so he contained its presence inside his presentation of it, inaugurating the possibility of a reading of the film and dispelling the unity of the diegesis into "a field of signs"[10] capable of further amplification and specification. Supplanting mimesis by the more fully articulate and situationally flexible verbal discourse, and retaining images only as subordinated illustration within that discourse, the NLF's rejection of theatricality in the reconstruction of cinema as an interactive educational and suasive process within a larger struggle against capitalism necessitated the destruction of the signifying procedures developed by capitalist cinema. The analogous American domestic guerrilla cinema developed by the Newsreels may be introduced by reference to the two most interesting attempts to engage the conditions of the discourse of liberation inside the largely unified hegemonic film text of Vietnam: Émile de Antonio's *In the Year of the Pig* (1969) and Nick Macdonald's *The Liberal War* (1972).

An intervention against the media's collusion in the administration's misrepresentation of the war, *In the Year of the Pig* differs from even establishment recognitions (like *Why Vietnam?*) that Vietnam had a history by emphasizing that history as the site of competing discourses rather than as a single unified text, a fact. The film is an assemblage of archival footage culled from East Germany, Hanoi, and the NLF offices in Prague, as well as from American companies such as ABC, UPI, and Paramount news, together with interviews with and speeches by over eighty politicians, and soldiers including Ho Chi Minh, Nguyen Huu Tho, Daniel Berrigan, Senators Wayne Morse and Everett Dirksen, Lyndon Johnson, Robert McNamara, and Generals LeMay and Westmoreland, as well as interviews with scholars like Paul Mus, David Halberstam, and Jean Lacouture. In its presentation of a history of the texts of Vietnam, the film contains scenes of colonial days followed by information on the life of Ho, on the Japanese occupation, on the expulsion of the French, and finally on the stages of American involvement.

Throughout, filmic documentation is not an authoritative showing forth of the truth so much as the occasion for interpretation. Eschewing the continuity of a single narrative voice, it replaces both the self-articulation of reality and the unified text of history with a collage in which visual information destabilizes and contradicts the verbal interpretations. For example, while Hubert Humphrey claims that prisoners are not being ill-treated, we see a Vietnamese beaten and kicked, and scenes of the self-immolation of Buddhist monks are juxtaposed with Madam Nu suggesting that it is a media event, not to be taken too seriously. The apologists for the war are betrayed by their own excess—General Patton's glee that his men are a "damn good bunch of killers," for example, or Curtis LeMay and General Mark Clark talking about the soldiers as "precious commodities." Other accounts are discredited by contradictory juxtapositions. *Why Vietnam?* presented the Gulf of Tonkin incident by means of a unified narrative consisting of footage of Johnson's speech, footage of American planes strafing and bombing, and a press conference in which, according to the omniscient voice-over that synthesized all these, "Secretary McNamara sets the record straight" by reiterating North Vietnamese provocation. In In the Year of the Pig, however, McNamara's flat assertion that the U.S. ships were reacting defensively to attacks on them is ruptured by testimony from a sailor from the Maddox who denies that these attacks ever took place. Setting one discourse against another, de Antonio calls into question all institutional versions of the war, especially discrediting the naive use of putative attacks on American soldiers to justify the administration's offensive. Consequently, the television network battle footage he eventually incorporates as his account moves into the present can no longer unequivocally manifest the war's propriety. His reconstruction of the history of Vietnamese liberation struggles and the competing ideological interests within them reveals the sacrifice of the GIs as a consequence of political maneuvering rather than of the innate perfidy of the NLF.

Nick Macdonald's homemade film The Liberal War (1972) abandons all pretense at realism and objectivity and, supplanting iconicity with symbolism, shifts presence away from the image to the voice of a narrator, who claims only that his account of the invasion of Vietnam and the genocide committed upon its peoples is "my own view, the way I see it." That narrational exposition is an account of the origin of the war during the Kennedy administration, in which it appears not as a mistake blundered into, but as the direct result and indeed logical implication of liberal policies. In illustration of the successive stages of the U.S. invasion, Macdonald supplies not scenes of soldiers or refugees, but models made out of toy soldiers and weapons, newspapers, and household bric-a-brac. Events and conditions are illustrated diagrammatically, often by literalizing the para-metaphoric language of the war's discourses: Diem's puppet regime is represented by a hand puppet with his face stuck on it; the difficulty of extricating American troops, by toy soldiers trapped in a narrow-necked bottle; the imprisonment of peasants in the concentration camp-like strategic hamlets, by plastic figures entombed in bricks; Kennedy's repression of the press, by cutting up the New York Times; the domino theory, by actual dominoes; and American financial interests, by coins on the map of Vietnam. When photographic images of the war do occur, it is their material nature as cultural signifiers that is stressed rather than the plangency of the represented scene; in illustration of napalm, it is a photograph rather than actual peasants that we see burning.

In its use of footage commonly available, The Liberal War exposes the social implications of de Antonio's archival footage and interviews almost as much as it does those of the "bang bang" aesthetic of the networks. It thus makes possible a critique of almost all use of front-line imagery as the trace of collusion with the institutional powers that control access to Vietnam. This is not pursued or made explicit by the film, but the domestic political implications of its own artisanal minimization of the cinematic apparatus are suggested by the film's fictional setting. While clues suggest that the narrative voice is Macdonald's own, his account is displaced hundreds of years into the future, so that it appears as a historical reconstruction made in an anarchist community that has transcended Kennedy's liberalism and authoritarian centralism in general. Imaged, in shots that open and close the film, as a natural paradise cleansed of technology, this utopian future is clearly a projection of sixties ruralism and carries with it all the contradictions of such idealisms. But although the intense rationality and social systematization of the Confucian bases of rural Vietnamese society would have no place in this Walden of the future, it is also in some sense Vietnam; the hostility to the city and to the instrumentalizing of social relations, the emphasis on self-discipline and decentralization, with a bricoleur's resourcefulness that can fabricate the model of the massive financial and technical complexity of the war from the odds and ends lying around the house, recapitulate the resourcefulness of the Vietnamese themselves—their ability to take apart American bombs and tanks and make such technological spillage over for their own purposes.

In Macdonald's refusal to represent the war iconically and his abstinence from imagery drenched in the presence of the military experience, a critique of the war becomes a critique of the media's use of it. The technical simplicity of his film, its articulation of its partisanship and subjectivity, its insistence on the discursiveness of historical interpretation, and its inevitable foregrounding of its own enunciation all reject the liberal languages of the war, as well as the liberal war itself. Though *The Liberal War* is not as explicit about the war's utility for the media as is *In the Year of the Pig*, in which, for example, the clear visibility of ABC microphones in interviews with soldiers lays bare the superimposition of station advertising upon ostensibly objective documentation, Macdonald's rejection of the technological resources and the language of the media industry allows him to project a *cinematic* alternative, displaced equally from hegemonic processes of cultural signification and from hegemonic cultural production.

Though implicit in both films' difference from the media practices that surround them, attention to their own mode of production or social location is not overt in either's critique of the communications industries. Confident and unselfconscious in their own formal mode, neither questions or even alludes to its own cinematic situation, though both were components in an alternative cinema and were used against the war. *In the Year of the Pig*, for instance, was "used as a tool by the Moratorium; it was a benefit for the Chicago Seven at the opening of their trial; the Australian anti-war movement used it as its primary film weapon" (de Antonio, n.d.: 37). Nevertheless, the films do not themselves articulate the issues of the alternative cinema. The remainder of this chapter is concerned with production that does manifest consciousness of itself as cinema and that confronts either intradiegetically or as practices of cinema not only institutional filmic codes, but also the hegemonic modes of cinematic production, consumption, and distribution. A summary of the issues of radical documentary film and a definition of the conditions under which a radical cinema could be established may be found in one of the most precise statements of the limits of the modern cinema, Jean-Luc Godard's section in Chris Marker's compilation film, *Far From Vietnam* (1967).

Far From Vietnam is compiled from several different kinds of representation of the war: Joris Ivens's footage of North Vietnam, a history of the war from the resistance to the French through the U.S. subversion of the Geneva agreements; a modified television address by General Westmoreland; interviews with the family of Norman Morrison, a Quaker who immolated himself on the steps of the Capitol; collages of television and magazine journalism; and documentation of protest activities in both Europe and the United States. This displacement of the war into its repercussions throughout the world is reciprocated in the displacement of the illusionist documentary mode into varying degrees of abstraction, discursivity, and reflexiveness. The questions of where the war is and of what an appropriate cinematic response to it is do come together, however, in Godard's section, which is a pivotal and seminal moment in modern film because it articulates a termination for modern cinema.

Introduced as "Camera Eye," the segment details a situation that is, in fact, exactly antithetical to Vertov's, for where Vertov's reflexivity flowers from his confidence in the role of the filmmaker in socialist society, Godard is paralyzed by the realization that in his society the impossibility of making a film about the Vietnam War means that film in general may be no longer possible. The newsreel footage, which Godard reproduces even as he admits that it is all he would have come up with had he been a cameraman for ABC in New York or for Soviet television, is only indirectly available to him, since the North Vietnamese correctly recognized that his ideology was "a bit vague" and refused him an entry visa. Obliged to remain in Paris, he realizes that the best thing we can do for Vietnam is to let Vietnam invade us and find out what part it plays in our everyday lives. The practical implementation of such a scrutiny would be for Godard to make films for and about the French working class —from whom he is as estranged as he is from the Vietnamese. The only film he can make— this one—comprises shots of the Mitchell studio camera, interspersed with fragments of newsreel footage and of his previous attempts to deal with Vietnam (the scenes from La Chinoise in which Juliet Berto as a Vietnamese peasant is attacked by U.S. planes). But the industrial camera is itself the site of contradictions, and scrutiny of it summarizes the contradictions faced by the film as a whole. A beautiful object, almost erotic in its responsiveness to his manipulations, the Mitchell is typical of the American technology with which the war is fought. But its instrumentality in the war goes beyond the analogy between the precision of its gears, the accuracy of its movements, and those of the war machine; as the means of production of American and French commercial film, it is the means by which U.S. cultural imperialism has stifled Third World cinema.

A function of his previous career in the industry and of his inability at that time to imagine a feasible alternative to it, Godard's impasse did make clear the need for an alternative cinema by which mass media collusion in imperialism could be contested, even though Godard was not himself capable of inaugurating it. The same imperatives define radical American film, which in its best instances produced a revolutionary, anti-industrial cinema that decolonized production and distribution, both participating in and enacting collective political action.

Notes

1 On this debate, see especially Eco's demonstrations of the limitations in the Peirceian concept of iconicity to refute Metz's assertion that, in its "perceptual literalness," the film image "reproduces the signified spectacle; and thus it becomes what it shows to the extent that it does not have to *signify* it" (Metz, 1974b: 75–76; Eco, 1976: 593–96).

2 The term was coined by Paul Rotha, but I take it from Nichols's taxonomy of documentary forms (Nichols, 1981: 170–208).

3 Although Hollywood's avoidance of the Vietnam War—by 1975 only four combat films had been set there (Smith, 1975: 3)—was indeed a function of the political complexities, the failure to represent accurately the Vietnamese and their position was a cinematic as well as an ideological problem that arose from the inapplicability of the anti-imperialist model of World War II and hence the inappropriateness of the codes of World War II movies. Thus, while it is an oversimplification, Julian Smith's witty summary, "Vietnam did not generate a great many films but it may have been America's first film-generated war, the first . . . war to grow out of attitudes supported, perhaps even created, by a generation of movies depicting America's military omnipotence" (ibid.: 4), correctly

points to the fact that representation was only half of Hollywood's role in the war. Writing after the rush of big budget Vietnam War films of the late seventies, Gilbert Adair is able to address some of the conditions which made them so amenable to revisionist histories of the war, refurbishing for the cold-war revival the imperialist rhetoric of the sixties (Adair, 1989).

4 Like representations of the GI in general, films about the GI's experience of the war reproduce his military instrumentality in his instrumentality in the political functions of the cinemas in which he is contained; hence his own extreme disenfranchisment, his exclusion from production. On the one hand, the films made by the army for Vietnam soldiers, the Armed Forces Information Films series, and The Big Picture series (many of which are still available) and, on the other, the various films made about or on behalf of veterans opposed to the war, such as Joseph Strick's *Interviews with My Lai Veterans* or the various documentations of the Wintersoldier hearings, and films made to counter the Army's own recruiting publicity, such as Newsreel's *Army*, are necessary adjuncts to the present discussion, especially in the way they fail to deal with the ambivalent location of the GI as simultaneously the agent and the victim of imperialism. The army indoctrination/training films are an especially interesting case of the politics of representation, in which the categorical servitude of the common soldier is reproduced in his absolute cinematic disenfranchisement.

5 Since by and large only those filmmakers who were favorably disposed to the administration's idea of the war either chose or were allowed to go to South Vietnam, there is no equivalent in film of Herr's awareness of the effect of the penetration and presence of the recording apparatus. Instead, as is argued below, the reflexive moment did not occur in American film until the object of documentation became the war at home.

6 Cf. "From *Saigon* to *The Green Berets*, American films set in Vietnam always emphasized American characters and did not create a single important Vietnamese who is not defined through his or her relationship to Americans" (Smith, 1975: 111).

7 For the Nixon White House's attempt to determine media coverage of the war, see also Gitlin (1980: 277–79).

8 Films from the NLF and North Vietnam that were available in the United States were listed in "Films in Vietnam" in 1969, and also in the various Newsreel catalogues. Four had been described by Peter Gessner in *The Nation* three years earlier (Gessner, 1966). Documentation of the North had been begun in 1954 with the Soviet Union's Roman Karmen's *Vietnam* (1955). After, escalation documentaries were available from both the NLF and North Vietnam, from Cuba (Santiago Alvarez's *Hanoi, Martes Trece* and *79 Primaveras* (79 *Springtimes*)), from East Germany, and from Japan. Most were suppressed in the United States. For Vietnam documentaries, see especially Barnouw (1974: 262–87). Television coverage of the war is summarized by C. Hammond (1981: 194–221). Because many of the films shot in North Vietnam, such as Newsreel's *People's War* (1969), Felix Greene's *Inside North Vietnam* (1968), and Santiago Alvarez's *Hanoi, Martes Trece* (1967), tended to recapitulate the aesthetics of presence, substituting the effects of U.S. bombing—the devastation of hospitals, the rebuilding of roads and bridges by peasants, individual bomb shelters, and burying the dead—for the village patrols, the booby traps, and the NLF dead shown in the establishment documentaries, they remain empirical and subjective; Greene's, for instance, subtitled "A Personal Report," is emphatically his presentation of the North's position.

9 The informant here was a United States Information Service (USIS) filmmaker who worked for two years in South Vietnam. He also noted that the improvisational quality of NLF films, their inevitable crudeness, gave the "impression of being the films of a revolutionary force" ("Films in Vietnam," 1969: 58). Consciously imitated for the same reason by radical filmmakers in the United States, such crudeness was ideologically loaded when assimilated with a war that culminated in a great victory over capitalist technology per se. In this respect the NLF's film *Young Puppeteers of Vietnam* is especially interesting. Showing how teenagers in liberated areas of Vietnam make puppets from bits of a downed U.S. plane and travel through the country putting on puppet shows that illustrate their resistance to the United States, the film is important in documenting the reconversion of the enemy's technology to instruments of liberation and also in documenting an art form largely supplanted by film in "advanced" societies.

10 Cf. "We may, in fact, consider the *benshi*'s entire discourse as a *reading* of the diegesis which was thereby designated as such and which thereby ceased to function as diegesis and became what it had in fact never ceased to be, *a field of signs*" (Burch, 1979: 79).

Vietnam and the New Militarism

20

MICHAEL RYAN and DOUGLAS KELLNER

Halloween and *Dressed to Kill* appear around 1978–1980, at the same time as *The Deer Hunter* and *Apocalypse Now*, two major conservative Vietnam films. All four are distinguished by regressive portrayals of women combined with assertions of male power and right-wing violence. That ideological conjunction, we suggest, is not accidental. It is symptomatic of a turn occurring in American culture at that time, a turn whose trajectory intersects eventually with the rise of the New Right as a force in American politics and with the renewal of militarism during the Reagan eighties. It is also symptomatic of the necessary connection between representations of paranoid projection in the horror genre as a reaction to feminism and representations of revived military might as a result of threats to national self-esteem. The psychological source was similar in each case as was the representational violence that emerged as its solution.

In American culture, film representations of military prowess seem inseparable from national self-esteem. For conservatives especially, greatness as a nation means the ability to exercise military power. In war, the strength and courage of the soldiers who represent male national prestige are tested and proven. In post-World War II cinematic representations of this ritual, proof of manhood was accompanied by a nationalistic idealism that pictured the American fighting man as a heroic liberator of oppressed people and as a defender of freedom. This ideal legend was justified by World War II, when American forces did indeed help defeat right-wing fascist regimes. After the war, however, the defense of political free-dom against the right-wing corporatism of the fascist movement was replaced by a defense of free enterprise capitalism against both Soviet communism and national liberation movements throughout the world, from Latin America to Southeast Asia. The legend of the freedom-defending U.S. fighting man soon began to be tarnished by the frequent sacrifice of political freedom and democratic rights that the defense of capitalism entailed. While the overthrow of democratic leftist governments in places like Guatemala and Iran could be tolerated in the Cold War climate of the fifties, in the sixties a new generation, nurtured in a more liberal cultural atmosphere and faced with having to risk their lives in the defense of capitalism overseas, began to question the right of a corporate controlled U.S. govern-ment to suppress democracy and socialism throughout the world in the name of "freedom." The equation of "freedom" and "democracy" with capitalism became increasingly strained because antidemocratic military dictatorships were more often than not U.S. allies in policing Third World liberation movements. During the 1960s, the Vietnam War became a focus of popular contestation. American youth refused to fight an unjust war, and by the early seventies, a majority of the people came to oppose the war. In addition, the army began to look increasingly incapable, undisciplined, and demoralized. In 1975, the United States suffered its first military defeat in its history with the liberation of Saigon. The loss created a lesion in the sense of national prestige, and it provoked a heated debate over American foreign policy.

We shall argue that Hollywood military movies of the seventies and eighties need to be read, first, in the context of the national debate over Vietnam, and, secondly, in the context of the "post-Vietnam syndrome," which was characterized by the desire for withdrawal from "foreign involvements" after the debacle in Vietnam and epitomized by the Clark Amendment forbidding intervention in Angola.

In the decade following the end of the war, America's military posture shifted from doubt to assertiveness, as the liberal tide of the mid-seventies receded and a rightist current came to dominate American political life. Films during the period articulate the arguments that led to this change and point the direction American culture was taking regarding the war long before actual political events confirmed the shift. Around the issues of Vietnam and war in general, the failure of liberalism took the form of an inability to transform the widespread antiwar feelings of the time into a permanent institutional change in foreign policy. Once again, in this regard as in economic policy, the liberals were victims of historical circumstances. As Carter and the Democrats staved off new military programs like the B-1 bomber, the Soviets invaded Afghanistan, the Sandinistas overthrew a U.S.-supported dictator in Nicaragua, and Iran's revolution led to the taking of American hostages all in 1979 and 1980. The American empire, which had lasted from 1945 to 1970, was crumbling, and the triumph of conservatism around military policy resulted from the ability of conservatives to take advantage of these circumstances to promote the sort of military buildup they favored. Many films of the period argue the conservative position.

One major factor in the conservative triumph was the social psychology of shame that was a significant motif of American culture after the military defeat in Vietnam. It is for this reason that the returned vet motif is so important in contemporary Hollywood film. Those whose self-identity is in part constructed through the internalization of representations of the nation as a military power no doubt felt a loss of self-esteem as a result of the nation's failure. That sense of loss generated resentment as well as a yearning for compensation. One aspect of the failure of liberalism is the inability of liberals to provide a redemptive and compensatory vision that would replace military representations as a source of self-esteem. Conservatives, on the other hand, managed successfully to equate self-restoration with military renewal.

1. Debating Vietnam

The posture Hollywood initially adopted toward Vietnam is best summed up in the title of Julian Smith's book—*Looking Away*.[1] With the exception of *The Green Berets* (1968), a jingoist war story, no major films dealt directly with the war until the late seventies. Nevertheless, war itself was a topic of great debate in films of the late sixties and early seventies, and many of these touch covertly on the issue of Vietnam. Blacklisted screenwriter Dalton Trumbo's thirties antiwar novel *Johnny Got His Gun* was made into a film in 1971, a time when opposition to the war was peaking, and films like M*A*S*H and *Soldier Blue* of the same period indirectly criticized Vietnam era militarism. A similar sort of indirect message from the conservative side was delivered in *Patton* (1970), a promilitarist film scripted by Coppola that supposedly helped inspire Nixon to bomb Cambodia. Indeed, Patton's opening speech, shot against an immense American flag, which exhorted Americans never to give up the fight, probably had a subliminal topical resonance for many prowar hawks.

The first major 1970s Hollywood film to deal directly with the issue of the war was the independently made feature documentary *Hearts and Minds* (1975), directed by Peter Davis. If *Patton* demonstrated that the conservative militarist pathology is inseparable from male self-aggrandizement, an authoritarian model of social discipline, and the skewing of the personality away from a composite of affectionate and aggressive traits and toward a hypertropism of violence, *Hearts and Minds* by combining clips from war films with scenes of football games, shows how militarism emerges from a culture that promotes aggressivity in young men and furthers a racist attitude toward the world. The film juxtaposes defenders and critics of U.S. policy, and the accompanying documentary footage of the ravages of war positions the prowar speakers as being arrogant and cruel. For example, General Westmoreland's remark that Asians do not value human life is juxtaposed to long and painful scenes of the Vietnamese mourning their dead.

The film is also significant for attempting to establish the historical context and social system out of which the war emerged. Unlike later fictional narrative war films, *Hearts and Minds* adopts a multiple perspective that undermines the power and the blindness of a monocular subjective position. What other films pose as an object (the Vietnamese), this film grants some subjectivity, as when the Vietnamese themselves express their anger and suffering. And it situates the war in a historical context that displaces the conservative concern for violent redemption or the liberal focus on the fate of individual (usually white, male) characters.

It was not until the war was over that fictional films began to appear that dealt directly with or were explicitly critical of the war. The first films to appear concerned returned veterans, frequently portrayed as dangerously alienated or violent (*Black Sunday*, *Stone Killer*). Later films take a more sympathetic point of view; films like *Cutter's Way*, *Who'll Stop the Rain?*, and *Some Kind of Hero* portray the vets as confused and wounded victims. Another strain of returned vet films use the motif as a springboard for justifying the kind of violent and racist disposition that initiated the war in the first place (*Rolling Thunder*, *First Blood*, *Firefox*). And finally, the vet motif in the eighties (*Uncommon Valor*, *Missing in Action*, *Rambo*) becomes a means of affirming the militarism of the new era.[2]

Liberal vet films focused on personal issues at the expense of the historical and global systemic concerns of *Hearts and Minds*. They criticized the war for what it did to good, white American boys, not for what ruin it brought to innocent Vietnamese. The first major liberal vet film—*Coming Home* (1978)—was also the first major Hollywood feature film to deal seriously with the issue of the war from a critical perspective. It skillfully manipulates the personalist and emotive codes of Hollywood to elicit sympathy for a wounded antiwar vet and to generate an empathetic yet critical stance toward a gungho soldier who is driven suicidal by the war experience. The scenes of the military hospital filled with the victims of war lifted a veil of silence, yet at the same time the film reproduces the traditional, Hollywood, sentimentalist vision of postwar experiences (as in, say, *The Best Years of Our Lives*).

Both *Who'll Stop the Rain?* (1978) and *Cutter's Way* (1981) use the figure of the returning vet to engage in social critique. In *Rain* a vet tries to help a buddy's wife who is victimized by drug dealers with whom her husband was involved. He is killed, and his death is cast in such a way as to evoke a sense of victimage. In addition, the fact that the final fight takes place in a carnival atmosphere suggests a critical parallel with the fruitless struggle in Vietnam. Passer's *Cutter's Way* is even bleaker. A bitter disabled vet becomes obsessed with revealing that a wealthy capitalist has murdered a young girl. He associates the man with the class he feels sent him to Vietnam to do its dirty work. Again, the vet dies, while riding a white horse through a lawn party on his way to have justice done. Such liberal vet films are distinguished by the hopeless vision they project, a vision reinforced in *Cutter's Way* by the use of somber color tones and confined spaces that suggest desolation and despair. Yet both direct the violence of the vet against groups or elites who clearly profited from the war at the expense of ordinary working-class soldiers. Conservative vet films turn shame into violent affirmation, but to do so they direct violence against the Vietnamese, in an attempt to win the lost war.

Rolling Thunder (1977) is an example of an extremely reactionary representation of the veteran issue. A veteran returns home to find his wife having an affair (a familiar cultural motif at the time expressed in the popular song "Ruby," concerning a woman who betrays a wounded vet). In this reprise of the post-World War II classic *The Blue Dahlia*, the wife and children are brutally murdered, and the veteran seeks out and kills the perpetrators with the aid of another veteran. Male bonding heals female betrayal, and violence, as usual, cures all ills. The wife's murder could be seen as a symbolic projection of the husband's revenge (his hand is mangled by the attackers, and the two events seem interrelated). And the rest of the violence is directed against non-whites. In this vision, the Vietnam War is not left behind; it is brought home to roost.

The film depicts the psychological basis upon which post-Vietnam Americans are enlisted into the new militarism. The hero is depicted as being shamed ("castrated"), and his reaction is to become violent against non-Americans. The shame associated with sexuality in the film is linked both to military defeat and to being deprived of money (the attack on his family is a burglary attempt). Thus, the denial of self-esteem around economic matters is also in part signaled as a source of resentment.

Returning veteran films range from the critical vision of films like *Coming Home* and *Cutter's Way* to the military revivalist vision of *First Blood*, *Firefox*, and *Rambo*. Films directly about the war experience itself are equally mixed, although, as in the returning vet subgenre, none adopts an explicitly oppositional posture toward the war.

Go Tell the Spartans (1978) and *The Boys in Company C* (1978) both criticize the U.S. involvement in Vietnam while forgoing more radical critiques of the military, U.S. foreign policy, or the values that support militarism. *Spartans* shows the army blundering deeper into the war during its early stages, and it stands as an allegory of the futility of the war effort as a whole. A small group of U.S. soldiers in a provincial outpost are ordered to occupy another, even more obscure position. They are overrun, and many are killed in the senseless action. Nevertheless, the critique of the war is executed against the standard of the "good war," which reproduces a traditional trope of critical Hollywood war films in that it criticizes a specific war while celebrating military values in general. *The Boys in Company C* suffers from a similar drawback. The story follows a platoon of young marines from boot camp through combat in Vietnam. Along the way, they discover that their officers are corrupt and only interested in high body counts. The film points to the futility and misguidedness of the American war effort. It criticizes both the U.S.-supported Vietnamese bourgeoisie and the Army high command that treated genocide against Vietnamese as a numbers game and as an excuse for using fancy high-tech weaponry. The common soldiers, in alliance with the Vietnamese people, symbolized by the children, are pitted against these two groups. They and the children are slaughtered in the end. The Boys in Company C constitutes one of the few overt statements against the war to come out of Hollywood, yet it resorts to the traditional Hollywood convention of valorizing "good grunt soldiers" over officers, and avoids criticizing the military as such.

Vietnam combat films like Spartans and Boys share the same limits as the liberal vet films. Liberals usually avoided the broader implications of the war, its origin in a desire to maintain access to Third World labor, markets, raw materials, etc., and to forestall the rise of noncapitalist sociopolitical systems. The traditional liberal focus on individuals implies a personalistic account that easily permits larger geopolitical issues to be displaced. And the sorts of self-replicating identifications that such an account invites usually evoke sentimentalist reactions to individual suffering rather than outrage at national policies of genocide. What needs to be determined is whether or not such personal evocations can translate into broader systemic lessons.

The rhetoric of liberal films nevertheless marks an advance on that used in conservative films. In simple thematic terms, the liberal films are critical of figures of authority, while conservative films like Patton metaphorically elevate such figures to an ideal position. There is a singularity of focus in conservative war films that is lacking in liberal rhetoric. Boys concerns a multiplicity of characters, and no one point of view is privileged. The "other" in Patton, a German officer assigned to study the general, is there simply to instantiate the implicit narcissistic male (self-)gaze, which takes the empirical form of the German's adulation for the great American hero. Boys draws Vietnamese into the narrative and grants them empathy not as admirers of the Americans but as their victims. Finally, Patton resorts to overwhelmingly metaphoric rhetorical strategies, while Boys is more metonymic in its approach. Patton assumes an ideal purity of character, and it even intimates a rather silly sort of universalism in the male militarist spirit. The trope of elevation and subordination fits easily with an authoritarian ideology in this film. In Boys, on the other hand, a representational strategy which emphasizes the equality of terms and their material, contiguous interconnections prevails. One soldier reprimands another for endangering all their lives; on the material level at which the soldiers are obliged to operate, metonymic connections are very real.

By the late seventies Vietnam was no longer an explosive issue. Conservatives decried the slow erosion of American international power in the face of Third World liberation movements, and in response to what they perceived as an expansionist USSR, they called for an end to the "post-Vietnam War syndrome." What began was a period of resurgent militarism, and Vietnam films of the time take part in the conservative backlash. They do so in part by rewriting history.

If, from a conservative political point of view, the period of the "post-Vietnam War syndrome" was characterized by national self-doubt, military vacillation, and a failure of will to intervene overseas, then the appropriate counter in the "post-syndrome" period of national revival was a triumph of the will, a purgation of doubt through action, and an interventionist military stance that brooked no restraint of the sort that led to the United

States' first military defeat, tarnished national prestige, and shamed American military manhood. Both *The Deer Hunter* and *Apocalypse Now* contribute to that revival by incorporating Vietnam not as a defeat from which lessons can be learned, but as a springboard for male military heroism.

The Deer Hunter, directed by Michael Cimino, won the Oscar in 1978. The film is more about the accession to leadership of the seer-warrior-individualist hero, Michael Vronsky (Robert DeNiro), than about the war. But this turning away from defeat, loss, and responsibility to an emblem of male strength might itself be symptomatic of a denial of loss through a compensatory self-inflation of the very sort that helped initiate and prolong the war.[3] Nevertheless, the film is multivalent politically. It appealed to working-class viewers who saw in it an accurate representation of the dilemmas of their lives. Radicals praised its implicit critique of certain male myths. And its bleak, ambiguous ending inspired many to read it as an anti-Vietnam-War statement. We respect all of these positions, but we read the film from the perspective of the critique of ideology, and in that light, it seems less progressive.[4]

The story concerns three steeltown buddies—Michael, Steve, and Nick—who are shown united in the first part in a highly ritualized wedding scene that conveys a sense of strong community. The church steeple, a symbol of unreflective faith, spontaneous adherence to hierarchy, and paternalistic authority, rises above the community as its guiding axis. It is returned to repeatedly by the camera, and the gesture underscores the church's centrality as a locus of social authority and an anchor securing community cohesion. All three men go to Vietnam, where they are reunited as prisoners of the Vietcong, who force them to play Russian roulette. Michael outsmarts the VC and saves his buddies. But Nick, apparently unhinged by his experience, remains in Vietnam playing roulette for money. Steve, now confined to a wheelchair in a stateside hospital, refuses to leave and return home. Michael returns to establish a relationship with Linda, Nick's old girlfriend. He forces Steve to overcome his shame, to be a "man" and leave the hospital. Then, Michael returns to Vietnam at the time of the fall of Saigon to witness Nick kill himself in his last roulette game. The film closes with Nick's funeral and the group of surviving friends singing "God Bless America."

Like so many films of the seventies, *The Deer Hunter* offers as a solution to complex political and social problems the exercise of power by a male individualist who is charged with saving a community through strong leadership. The community is patriarchal; women are present to be fought over, as bossy mothers, and in the role of not altogether faithful, weak, yet at the right moment supportive partners. War breaks the community, and its worst effect is the transformation of men into will-less weaklings (Steve) or addicted obsessives (Nick). It falls to Michael to exercise his natural power of leadership to restore the communal cohesion and order at the end of the film. That restoration requires the sacrifice of Michael's weaker counterpart, Nick, with whose funeral the film ends. The reaffirmation of male military power in the character of Michael is predicated upon the purgation of weakness, vacillation, and the obsessively suicidal behavior in which the country was engaged in Vietnam, all of which seem embodied in Nick. It is important that in the scene immediately following Nick's suicide, the audience sees documentary footage of the U.S. Army's "disgraceful" flight from Saigon. The juxtaposition associates Nick's weakness and self-destructiveness with the military defeat of 1975. The film, then, can be said to work in two dimensions. It concerns the restoration of community through strong patriarchal leadership.

And it offers an allegorical solution to the problem Vietnam poses by symbolically purging the source of defeat and proposing a way to renewed national strength and patriotic cohesion.

The call for strong leadership as a solution to historical crises is a political version of the aesthetic transformation in the film of actual history into a moral allegory. Just as the warrior-leader-savior resolves vacillation into a triumph of heroic will, so also the romantic, allegorical form of the film attempts to resolve the contradictions, meaninglessness, and ambiguity of the actual historical war into a meaningful and apparently noncontradictory quest narrative executed in a synthetic style that balances the unity of the individual leader with a formal or aesthetic unity. It is not surprising that a political ideology of the superior individual subject should seem inseparable from an aesthetic of romantic, quasi-mystical exaltation, since both are forms of empowerment. The romantic aesthetic overpowers history and incorporates it into highly subjective fantasy representations. The problem of realistically depicting history, which is linked to the political problem of acknowledging responsibility and loss as a nation, is solved by sublimating history into a stylized, ceremonial fusion of color, sound, and theme that elevates contingent events to a moral allegory of redemption and an ordinary human to secular divinity. It is important that the most stylized and allegorical representations appear while Michael is hunting. The aesthetic transformation of the mountains into a mystical temple (replete with choir) parallels the political and ideological elevation of the member of the gang into the strong, mystical leader, naturally destined to lead the lesser mortals around him. It is also, of course, a means of attaining the sorts of separation we have described as necessary to the more pathological forms of male sexual identity. Heightened mental representations of the sort evident in the mountain scenes are themselves ways of denying connection to the world and to others who might transgress the boundary between self and world which a reactive male sexual identity must establish. It is significant, then, that Michael is most alone in the mountain scenes, most separated from others, and most protected from them by a representational boundary that makes him seem transcendent, unique. Those scenes are also, of course, the most metaphoric.

Yet affirmations of transcendence are necessary only when the actual world is fallen (meaningless, hopeless, unhappy). "My country right or wrong" makes sense or is necessary only if the country can be or is frequently wrong. The quest for transcendence, for turning the everyday into the grandiose, the monumental, and the meaningful, presupposes the absence of the empirical equivalents of these spiritual ideals in the actual world. Indeed, the actual world has to be a positive negation of such things as fulfillment, self-worth, and significance for the quest for other-worldly, transcendent meanings to be activated. The metaphor exists in necessary tension with a more metonymic or worldly and material set of constraints which bring the metaphor into being as a reaction against them.

The transcendent moments of the film can thus be read either as successful enactments of the attainment of a spiritual ideal just short of the clouds that are the floor of heaven, or as the neurotic symptoms of this-worldly victimization, attempts to secure a sense of self-worth against a world that denies it nine to five and only allows a few leisure-time pursuits, like the male rituals of drinking and hunting, as metaphoric alternatives. The film depicts both, and our point is that its progressive potential resides in the fact that it cannot avoid this undecidability. The transcendental moments can only appear as such in contrast to a detailed description of a fallen everyday reality. This is why the film is so incredibly dense with ethnographic detail from everyday life, from the long marriage celebration to the scenes inside the industrial workplace. It is important, therefore, that the film opens in the factory, with an establishing shot from under a viaduct at night that makes the factory world seem enclosed and oppressive. The colorful mountain scenes of transcendence gain their meaning from their difference from the darkness of the workplace and the squalor of ethnic neighborhood life. And Michael's individuation is defined as a separating out, a denial of "weakening" social links of the sort that characterize his less strong male cronies.

Thus, the film permits a deconstruction of the premises of its idealization of Michael as the seer-leader. His elevation occurs through the metaphor of the deer hunt, which transforms a literal leisure-time activity into a higher ideal meaning that transcends literality, just as Michael comes to transcend the literal and material social texture, to rise above it. He must do so if he is to give it order, but the metaphor cannot fully rise above the literality that is its vehicle. Part of its literality is that it exists in metonymic or contiguous relation to the opening factory scene of fallen fire, confinement, and darkness where the men seem all alike. Michael's distinction as the superior individual who can read sunspots, like a shaman, or who knows the mystical meaning of a bullet ("This is this"), or who takes down deer with one shot like a true hunter has meaning only in differentiation from the other men, from their sameness in the factory. And the metaphor of transcendental leadership takes on meaning only in distinction from the workaday world; without that contrast, that determining difference, it makes no sense. Yet the film's ideology depends on the assumption that the metaphor subsumes the literal event into an ideal meaning which transcends worldly materiality and meaninglessness (nondistinction) entirely.

The film thus puts on display the interconnections between wage labor oppression and white male working class compensations for that oppression. In this film, a mythic idealization of the individual counters the reduction of all the men to faceless and impersonal functions in the industrial machine at the beginning of the film. An idealized meaning substitutes for the fallen reality of everyday life. The powerful emblem of the church, the extremely ritualized wedding, the mythologized hunt, and the strong bonding between the men should thus be seen as ways of counteracting the banality of life on the bottom of capitalism.

Like many populist films, this one therefore has a double valence. Its depiction of the accreditation of right-wing political leadership points to the way pre-class-conscious working class men can have their resentment against oppression channeled into conservative, even fascist forms in a highly individualistic and patriarchal cultural context that limits the means of attaining communal cohesion to strong male individual leadership. Yet it also points to potentially radical desires to transcend the cruel material conditions to which working class people are reduced (or were being reduced, in the late seventies particularly), conditions that deny a sense of worldly meaning or worth to people, who, as a result, overcompensate for those lacks by turning to either religious or political idealizations.

If both *The Deer Hunter* and *Apocalypse Now* indicate the reactionary way of dealing with the Vietnam War, they also testify to something amiss in the country's prevailing conception of itself. The need, demonstrated in these films, to repudiate the war as history and to transfer it into an allegory of militarist manhood is itself symptomatic of a wound, a sense of shame, that seems resistant to the sort of healing these films attempt. And the films merely reproduce the desire to realize a totality of American will in the world that reveals its own problematic anchoring in a web of serial, contiguous non-totalizable relations with other people the more it asserts itself so hyperbolically and hysterically.

By the mid-eighties, the Vietnam syndrome had been at least partially overcome, and conservatives once again felt a pre-Vietnam license to exercise U.S. military power overseas. Yet the country remained convinced by the experience of Vietnam, and it refused to back full-scale interventions that might lead to wars in places like Central America. Our poll suggests that American viewers tended to turn even conservative war films like *The Deer Hunter* into antiwar statements: 69% felt that it portrayed the war as a mistake, and 93% said that it confirmed their opposition to the war. The ending made 27% feel patriotic, while it made 51% feel disheartened. Perhaps the most disturbing result we found was that 74% felt that the representation of the Vietcong in the film was accurate. Even if Americans had learned some lessons regarding foreign wars, they still seemed to need to learn lessons regarding foreigners. And this perhaps accounts for the fact that, although they continued to oppose interventionism on a large scale, they overwhelmingly approved Ronald Reagan's strikes against Grenada and Libya during this period.

2. The military rehabilitated

One consequence of the Vietnam War and the draft that supplied it with men was an undermining of the U.S. Army. By the end of the war, soldiers were "fragging" (deliberately killing) their officers, rather than obeying orders to fight. As a result of this, as well as of the widespread opposition to war that the draft helped inspire, the draft was eliminated, and the army was transformed into an all-volunteer force. That new force was heavily minority, since nonwhite minorities in a retrenching capitalist society dominated by whites had few other career opportunities. Advertisements for the army began to appear on diversionary television shows (sports and MTV especially) that might attract working-class, unemployed, and minority viewers. The restoration of the army became a more pressing concern in the late seventies, when events such as the Soviet invasion of Afghanistan and the taking of U.S. hostages in Iran made it clear that American imperial interests were no longer going to be taken for granted or allowed to go uncontested in the world. Hollywood joined in the effort, and a number of early eighties films "humanize" the army by turning it into a scene for family melodrama, liberal ideals, and humor. The link seemed so overt that one suspected that some Hollywood filmmakers had not heard that culture is supposed to be at least relatively autonomous in relation to political power and the state.[5]

These films are generally liberal in tone; their humanization of the military is laudable in contrast to the more conservative exaggeration of the worst traits of the military—violence, discipline, intolerance, masculinism, etc—in such films as *Rambo*. Yet these films appear at a time when the country, in the hands of conservatives, was adopting increasingly militarist poses in the world theater and when a "culture of militarism" was developing (in the form of toys, magazines, TV shows, and films). Whatever the intention of these films, their political valence was reinflected in a conservative direction by their historical moment and their social context. Moreover, the liberal vision takes for granted the necessity of an institution like the military. Liberals fail to see the deep structural roots and systemic relations that link the military per se as an institution to the patriarchal socialization patterns that are partly responsible (as we have argued) for war. It is in light of a broader radical critique of the military itself that the liberal position must be judged. Such a critique would see the military as an instrument of class defense, as well as a machine for producing a model of a general social discipline of the sort capitalism (or any work-oriented, inegalitarian society) requires. In addition, the military from this perspective is less a protection than a threat. In the modern world especially, the very existence of the military poses a danger, and it is no longer possible, because of modern weapons, to justify the military as a defense against aggression. Defense and a war of total annihilation are no longer separable concepts.

The format of humanized military films like *Stripes*, *Private Benjamin*, and *An Officer and a Gentleman* consists of the transformation of an unsuccessful person into a very successful one. Thus, an affirmative personal narrative is laid over an attempt at institutional reconstruction, and, like the ads for the army on television ("Be all that you can be"), the films identify personal achievement with military life. In this way, the films seem to participate in an attempt in the culture to restore the army to its pre-Vietnam credit and, in certain instances, to reintegrate it with a lost patriotic vision of the United States.

Private Benjamin (1980) incorporates feminism into this process. It recounts the transformation of a dependent and ineffectual woman who is at a loss when her husband dies on the night of their wedding into a strong, independent figure. The change is marked by the difference between the first wedding scene, in which she is little more than a sexual servant of her husband, and the last, when she socks her husband-to-be on the jaw because he is a philanderer and stalks off alone. The ideological dimension of the film consists in intimating that the army is what has made her strong. Thus, a very antifeminist institution is made to appear an ally of feminism.

Stripes (1981) and *An Officer and a Gentleman* (1982) both concern the transformation of ne'er-do-wells into successful soldiers. But more important, both are allegories of the metamorphosis of the Vietnam generation, with its anti-bourgeois and anti-authoritarian dropout values, into the fighting machines of the eighties, who believe in patriotism, nationalism, and militarism. In *Stripes* an underemployed goof-off whose girlfriend has left him is transformed by the army into a good soldier who becomes a leader of his squad as well as a sexual success.

The most popular humanized military film, *An Officer and a Gentleman*, is neo-forties in outlook and tone; advertisements made it seem like a story out of the past, but that attempt to step back into the generic form and style of an older, more innocent male military ethos was very much a statement about the present. The film recounts the transformation of Zack (Richard Gere) from an undisciplined, motorcycle-riding, down-and-out tough guy into "An officer and a gentleman." Brutality saves, the film says, as the hammer shapes steel. Foley, Zack's black drill instructor (Lou Gossett), brutalizes him until he renounces his selfishness and becomes a team player. Zack stops treating women badly and does the honorable thing by carrying off his working-class girlfriend (Debra Winger) at the end. And he sacrifices his chance to set a new obstacle course record by returning to help a female classmate. The film elicits audience sympathy (even applause) at points like this. It plays on human, even liberal sentiments (integrationist and token feminist), but it does so in order to reinforce the military institution. Zack's military training seems to make him a better man, a "gentleman." We would argue that the film should be understood, then, as an allegory of a transformation being promoted by the Right in contemporary U.S. society. Zack represents a generation of youth who grew up disaffected with traditional institutions like the military. Through Zack, we see that generation overcome its alienation and accept such values as military honor and team play. The price is submission to discipline, authority, and brutality, but the prize is self-respect and love.

The love story is sweet and reassuring; its retreat from modernity to the sort of "torrid romance" of early Hollywood films invests libidinal energies into militarism—soldiers get the "girls," the film suggests. In a film where men must learn to be "men," it is fitting that the women's goal should be portrayed as "getting a man." The love story, in fact, depicts the real state of affairs of many working class women in a society that fails to satisfy real human needs and that makes women's survival often depend on men. Such romance has a double edge. It permits a hothouse closure to be established which reinforces the film's masculinist-militarist ideology. But romance also testifies to structural differences between male power and female dependency that could never be fully sublated to an ideological closure and are underscored, even as their reality is denied in a film like this. They remain outside such closure always, for they are the very things that make ideology necessary in the first place.

Films like *Officer* were some of the most successful ideological narratives of the era. Yet for that very reason, they are some of the most interesting for understanding the rhetorical procedures of ideology as well as the social system of militarism. They are open to deconstruction precisely because they seem such perfect exercises in ideology. Strong personal needs for romance or family are transferred metaphorically or by analogy onto the military. And by virtue of metaphoric substitution, the military stands in as the answer for the personal desires. Yet this exercise in metaphoric closure also signals literal connections between the realms which are joined metaphorically. The films do not merely compare male-dominated romance or the patriarchal family to the military; they inadvertently dramatize the real material or metonymic relations between these realms of socialization.

For example, in *The Great Santini* (1982), a narrative of intergenerational strife between a gung-ho old-style military man and his son is mapped over a justification of the military. The narrative proceeds as a movement toward a moment of recognition when the children finally see that the father was a good man despite his excesses. He becomes a locus of sympathy when he dies sacrificing himself so that a town will not be destroyed by his crashing jet. The son, who seemed to reject his father's values, dons his flight jacket, assumes his father's position at the driver's wheel of the family car, and begins to act like him. The gesture is indicative of the patriarchal character of the military. It is passed from fathers to sons, bypassing women, who serve in this film as breeders. If the family is not just a legitimating model by metaphoric analogy for the military, but also a literal seed-bed of militarist values, then this division of labor is not accidental. The socialization patterns of the two seemingly separate domains form a continuum.

Liberal films like *Taps* (1981) and *The Lords of Discipline* (1983) criticize military excess in the name of a humanized military, one in which militarism must be tempered by restraint and respect for life. Indeed, *Taps* thematizes this very position. Cadets at a military academy, in order to defend the existence of the academy, engage in an armed revolt, which results in the deaths of several of them. The most fervent apostle of military honor, an aging general, also dies, and his disciple, the young cadet who leads the revolt, learns that militarism must give way to good judgment. Yet the military itself is affirmed.

Films like this display the crucial ingredients of the failure of liberalism to develop a program for significantly transforming American society. Liberalism operates from within patriarchal presuppositions, which, like the similar procapitalist presuppositions liberals hold, limit the ability of liberals to see beyond the walls of the ideological prison in which they operate. Militarist patriarchs are okay, these films seem to say, though we'd be better off with nicer ones. But in a world in which one trigger-happy fool can send everyone to happy vaporland, even nice militarist patriarchs must be seen as pathological. It is such a shift of vision, whereby the most everyday assumptions of patriarchy and capitalism, especially the assumption that strong, rambunctious men are needed to lead and defend us, are relinquished forever, that lies beyond the capacity of liberals. Indeed, liberals should probably be defined as people incapable of such structural conceptualizations.

Liberals do not see the military as a social problem that must be eliminated, in part because they accept the patriarchal logic of the Cold War—that the only way to keep peace with an antagonist is through the threat of aggression or annihilation. Yet this position is itself a product of a patriarchal socialization to competition and power. In other words, if you only look at the world with sunglasses, you'll never see anything but a dark world. In order to perceive the military itself as an unnecessary and potentially dangerous institution, liberals would have to step outside their own socialization, exit from the structure they inhabit, question the very words that come automatically to their lips.

A more radical position would argue that the outlawing of armies and weapons is not a utopian dream; it is a precondition of the modern world's survival. Beyond patriarchal and capitalist socialization to competition, aggression, and domination reside alternative socialization possibilities, and alternate ideals of cooperation, demilitarization, and peaceful communal existence. But that would require a different set of structuring assumptions, as well as a different set of social institutions. If the problem of the military is wedded to the social institutions that justify it metaphorically, then it is not likely to change until they are changed. Indeed, one could say that something of that potentially emergent reality is signaled by even the ideology of some of the humanized military films. For by comparing the military with the family, they indicate the possibility of a breakdown of the boundaries that separate the two realms. The family is a patriarchal form, and for this reason, it can successfully legitimate the military. But it is also a communal form. The very "humanity" that it lends the military also threatens the military. The price of analogy is comparison. And in comparison to the family, the military can only ultimately appear as being inhumane. For if the family breeds children, the military murders them. *Taps* and *Lords* at least point this out. They just don't follow the point to its logical conclusion. And they couldn't, because of the very patriarchal assumptions which underwrite the military, assumptions which also limit any critique of the military by immediately branding accurate critiques as unreal, utopian, or, worse, not manly enough.

3. The new militarism

Liberals succeeded in stemming the growth of the military in the mid to late seventies, but they were incapable of turning the loss in Vietnam into a permanent structural reform of U.S. militarism. This was so in part because of historical events that made a renewed defense of the American empire necessary. That empire consisted of a network of client states overseas, in places like the Philippines and Iran, that were tied into the imperial economic and military system by treaty and corporate investment. These states helped assure that leftist or anticapitalist governments would not come to power in areas American corporations deemed necessary to their interests. Usually they brutally repressed liberation movements, in places like Indonesia and Chile, for example, and they protected the flow of raw materials and the supply of cheap labor for American firms. Military buildups within the United States were thus closely related to the status of the imperial client states, and they both have an economic dimension. In the late seventies and early eighties several client states fell to liberation movements (Nicaragua, Iran, the Philippines), others (South Korea, South Africa, El Salvador) were troubled by incipient liberation movements or unrest, and other U.S.-supported military regimes (Argentina, Brazil, Peru, Chile) were subject either to internal disturbances or to overthrow by democratic forces repulsed by the exercise of state terror in the name of defending capitalism. At the same time, several previously "secure" colonial nations became socialist—Angola, Ethiopia, Mozambique—as a result of revolutions. The empire was trembling, and the Iran hostage crisis of 1979–1980 heated up jingoist sentiment enough in the nation to give the new conservative power bloc the support it required to begin carrying out a momentous military buildup decked out in militarist and anticommunist rhetoric.

Yet public sentiment was not entirely homogeneous on the subject of militarism. Polls indicated that in general people opposed foreign interventionism. For this reason, perhaps, there was a cultural offensive to enlist support for the conservative ideals of an aggressive, combative defense of imperial interests. If the public didn't need to be whipped up, there would not have been so much whipping going on in the early to mid-eighties, especially in films.

The revival of militarism was not spontaneous, however. Conservative groups like the Committee on the Present Danger campaigned throughout the seventies for greater "defense" spending and for a firmer foreign policy. The new militarism is not an effect of the Reagan era; rather, Reagan himself is in part an effect of the culture of militarism born in the late seventies, with some help from Democrats like Jimmy Carter. *The Final Countdown* (1979) is an example of a film that prefigures the conservative military buildup of the early eighties. It concerns an aircraft carrier that travels through a time warp to emerge on the day before Pearl Harbor. The captain has to decide whether to intervene and change the course of history. The purpose of this historical displacement is to suggest that the United States needs a powerful military in order to prevent another Pearl Harbor. Indeed, in a number of new militarist films, the Vietnamese, the Russians, or the "enemy" are decked out in uniforms that markedly resemble Japanese and German World War II battle gear. This evocation of the notion of the past "just war" in the contemporary context recalls the American Right's persistent equating of communism with German Nazism, a movement which was in fact conservative and rightist in character as well as being devoted to the eradication of communism.

Militarism in the United States is inseparable from anticommunism. Although anticommunism has been a staple of post-World War II culture, after the late sixties, during the period of détente, it faded somewhat from American consciousness and from Hollywood film. But in the late seventies and early eighties it was revived and promoted in conjunction with the new militarism. It ranged from military revival allegories like *Firefox* to dance musicals like *White Night*. The new anticommunism worked either by projecting its own aggressive animus onto the "enemy," thus justifying itself as a "defense" against a hypothetically offensive Red Terror, or by dehumanizing the ideological adversaries of the United States through the use of racial and social stereotypes in such a way as to excuse the use of

violence against them. For example, *Megaforce* (1982) was a Pentagon-supported advertisement both for military hardware and for elite military manpower. It concerns an elite group
of fighters known as "Megaforce" (who look and taste like the Pentagon's Rapid Deployment
Force). They use some of the most sophisticated military technology available to fight
Castro-like, south-of-the-border bandits and their communist allies, who overthrow governments like dominoes, not for social ideals, but out of greed for money. The film presents
social revolutionaries as venal criminals. And this criminalization and dehumanization of
foreign people struggling for liberation from capitalism and feudalism seems to be essential
to the promotion of weapons designed for their liquidation.

Perhaps the most audacious anticommunist film of the era was John Milius's *Red Dawn*
(1984), about a hypothetical Soviet invasion of the United States. A group of youngsters hide
out in the mountains and become a successful guerrilla unit. In the end, they are all killed.
Along with the usual right-wing themes (the Soviets are subhuman concentration camp
guards, Latin American revolutionaries are merely their agents, the United States is the
last bastion of justice and freedom), the film is distinguished by certain ideological motifs
that hark back to fascist and national socialist ideologies of the twenties and thirties. At
one point, an intellectual liberal and a jock conservative fight over how to proceed in the
group. The liberal's call for democracy loses out to the conservative's assertion of his right
to command the others. The authoritarian leadership principle is linked to the assumption
that those with greater force or power should prevail—not those with the best principles
or rational arguments. Such force derives its authority from nature, from what the Nazis
called "blood and soil." The blood motif in the film appears as the ritual drinking of a deer's
blood as proof of one's warrior manhood; it refers to the Nazi fetishizing of powerful animals,
and it elaborates the conservative idea that human life is primitivist, a struggle for survival
in a civil society that is no different from nature. The soil motif appears at those moments
when Milius's camera meditates on nature, positioning it as a still, immense, unmoving
presence. The existential loneliness of the individualist warrior leader is associated with
expansive fields and high mountains, fetishes of power and strength.[6]

Thus, the film displays the close relationship between contemporary American right-wing
ideology and Nazism. Indeed, one curious dimension of the film's argument is that what
it poses against communism, depicted as totalitarian domination, is a social model of
authoritarian leadership. The authoritarian camp in the mountains is not much different
from the totalitarian "camp" in the town. At this point in history, conservatives like Jeane
Kirkpatrick argued for a distinction between totalitarianism (authoritarianism for the
sake of communism) and authoritarianism (totalitarianism for the sake of capitalism). The
film shows why such a distinction might have been necessary to avoid confusion.

While films like *Red Dawn* were not particularly successful at the box office, they are shown
repeatedly, for months on end, on cable television. In fact, this phenomenon points to the
breakdown of the distinction between film and television as well as to the eventual erosion
of the importance of box-office figures in the determination of the potential effects of films.
Since blockbusters must be kept off the market in order to maintain their scarcity and value,
lesser films arguably acquire a greater ability to influence audiences by virtue of saturation
showing on TV.

In the late seventies and early eighties, the "world communist conspiracy" becomes
associated with "terrorism," the use of non-state-sanctioned violence to gain political ends.
Conservative fantasists like Claire Sterling made careers out of tracing all violent opposition

to U.S. interests back to an "international terrorist network" emanating from Moscow. Numerous Hollywood films transcode this discourse, from Stallone's *Nighthawks* (1981) to *The Final Option* (1983), which suggests the peace movement is communist-inspired, and Chuck Norris's *Invasion U.S.A.* (1985), in which terrorists invade the United States. Norris and Stallone were also involved in promoting fantasies of veterans who return to Vietnam to free American POWs—*Missing in Action* (I and II) and *Rambo*.

In *Rambo* (1985), a veteran, who is depicted mythically as a super-killer, is enlisted to rescue missing POWs in Vietnam. He succeeds through heroic effort and a display of primitive violence that kills off numerous Russians and Vietnamese. The film satisfies several contemporary conservative prejudices. Asian communists are portrayed as subhuman. The film rewrites history in a way that excuses American atrocities against the Vietnamese. And it portrays Americans, not the Vietnamese, as the ones fighting for liberation. The overall significance of the film seems to be to try to make certain that the Vietnam War would be won in Nicaragua. It is less about an event than an attitude. The theme of betrayal that characterized the conservative attitude toward the liberal critics of the war (Reagan's remark that the army did not lose the war but was prevented from winning it)—and that is also reminiscent of post-World War I German attitudes that aided the rise of Nazism—appears in the way Rambo is misled by a Washington bureaucrat who wants him to fail in his mission so that the book can be closed on Vietnam. Yet we suggest that a film of this sort needs to be read as a symptom of victimization. A paragon of inarticulate meatheadedness, the figure of Rambo is also indicative of the way many American working-class youths are undereducated and offered the military as the only way of affirming themselves. Denied self-esteem through creative work for their own self-enhancement, they seek surrogate worth in metaphoric substitutes like militarism and nationalism. Rambo's neurotic resentment is less his own fault than that of those who run the social system, assuring an unequal distribution of cultural and intellectual capital.

We read the new militarist phenomenon as being both a psychological problem of patriarchal society and a problem of a threatened and defensive capitalism. Reagan's "hard line on defense," his stubborn hewing to a stern, punitive, and intolerant attitude toward the world, is symptomatic of patriarchal pathology, as much a matter of socialization as of social organization. *Rambo* is important because it displays the roots of that pathology. The male need to feel singular, to separate out from dependence on initial caretakers, is metaphorized in Rambo's mythic isolation. Because the social world is necessarily interdependent, such isolation is necessarily aggressive. Aggression separates, whereas affection binds and makes one dependent. The isolated male is therefore without affectionate ties. Freedom of action is his norm; it requires the repudiation of anyone who threatens his space or his sense of singular importance, from the communists to the federal bureaucrats—both enemies in the film. War is, as we have argued, in part a matter of representation, images that people identify with and internalize which mobilize action. Loss in war can in consequence be experienced as self-diminution, damage done to internal representations that have become inseparable from the self. Given the prevailing socialization patterns, such loss draws out male dependence and vulnerability, male "femininization." It is the rejection of this possibility, of its intolerable shame, that results in the sorts of hypertropic representations of violence in *Rambo*.

Yet within this problem lurk the rudiments of a solution. For the need for a confirmation of manhood signals a broader need for a feeling of self-worth of a sort that can only be provided by others. It depends on others' affection, just as all singularizing metaphors depend on contextualizing metonyms. To a certain extent, Rambo's violence is simply an expression of such a need. Such a radical compensation for lost self-esteem is in some respects a demand for a return of the other's recognition. If we call such needs "socialist" it is because the ideals of socialism are communal support, mutual help, and shared dependence. Even the male militarist's pathos articulates needs for such social structures. Even as he rejects dependence as shame, he affirms its necessity as the need for self-worth. And such unrecognized dependencies and unrealized desires cannot be recognized or realized in a patriarchal and capitalist social context. Indeed, this film is a testament to that reality.

One major consequence of this argument is that it is not only male sexualization that is at stake in militarism. Women, as they are socialized to be passive, to need strong men in order to survive, are complicit in the socialization process of men for war. This was made particularly clear to us at a viewing of Rambo. Women in the theater were especially loud in their demands for blood and vengeance. We were reminded of the housewives of Santiago de Chile who beat their pots at night to help bring down the leftist government. The sort of male self-display evident in Rambo requires an adulatory other in conservative women whose applause validates male violence. Thus, a reconstruction of male psychology is inseparable from a broader reconstruction of the patriarchal socialization system that produces both sexes.

The new militarism did not go uncontested. Films like War Games, Wrong Is Right, The Dogs of War, Blue Thunder, Full Metal Jacket, and Platoon opposed certain forms of militarism in the eighties. And several films like Testament and Countdown to Looking Glass during the same period criticized nuclear war policy. This cultural mobilization, in conjunction with public protests, had an effect. Reagan moved from statements regarding the feasibility of limited nuclear wars in the early years of his tenure to a defensive and somewhat disingenuous call for the avoidance of all nuclear war in his later years. Comedies also contributed to the continuing liberal critique, especially such Chevy Chase vehicles as Deal of the Century, a satire of the arms industry, and Spies Like Us, a satire of Reagan's "Star Wars" program (the "Strategic Defense Initiative") and of the militarist-Americanist mentality in general. In Spies, two trickster figures (played by Chase and Dan Ackroyd) overturn the military's plan to initiate a nuclear attack by the Soviet Union in order to use a new space defense system. The system fails, and one character remarks: "Such a short time to destroy a world." In the film's carnivalesque vision, military authority figures are little worthy of respect, and the irrationality of conservative nostrums ("To guarantee the American way of life, I'm willing to take that risk" |of nuclear destruction|) is underscored. What is noteworthy in this and other antimilitarist films is the attempt to depict alternative social attitudes (toward gays or sexuality, for example) that are necessary correlates of a post-repressive, post-militarist social construction. What the comedies underscore is the importance of irony and humor to such a process, since so many of the militarist films are distinguished by high levels of self-seriousness and an inability to engage in the plunge into indeterminacy that the carnivalesque inversion of hierarchy entails.

What all of this points to is that if militarism is a public projection of private or personal human relations and attitudes, then its reconstruction is something more than a matter of foreign policy. Liberal antimilitarist films like War Games, 2010, Testament, or Platoon frequently contain images of nonauthoritarian, nonexploitative, equal relations between people. Many conservative films offer just the opposite sorts of relations, and the positive relations are frequently oiled with sentimentalism, a form of alienated positive affect that often accompanies an equally alienated aggressivity that takes authoritarian and militarist forms. What this suggests is that one necessary route to a world free from militarism is a reconstruction of the alienated and skewed affective structures feeding the distrust and enmity that operate behind militarism. Militarism is a collective neurosis, not just a foreign policy alternative. The micrological or interpersonal dimension of human existence, therefore, is not apolitical, nor is it entirely distinct from the macrological dimension of political interaction. A different nonantagonistic structure of international relations, one purged of genocidal impulses, would be predicated in part on a different psychology and a different social construction of interpersonal affection and aggression.

Notes

1   See G. Adair, Hollywood and Vietnam: From The Green Berets to Apocalypse Now (New York: Proteus, 1981); L. Suid, Guts Glory: Great American War Movies (Reading: Addison-Wesley, 1978); J. Smith, Looking Away: Hollywood and Vietnam (New York: Scribners, 1975); A. Britton, "Sideshows: Hollywood in Vietnam," Movies 27–28 (1980–1981), pp. 2–23; and "Préparer à une troisième guerre mondiale: les films americains mènent campagne (1970–1980)," Cinethique (1981), pp. 1–36.

2   On returning vet films, see Adair, Hollywood and Vietnam; Smith, Looking Away; and A. Auster and L. Quart, "Man and Superman: Vietnam and the New American Hero," Social Policy (Jan.–Feb. 1981), pp. 61–64, and "The Wounded Vet in Political Film," Social Policy (Fall 1982), pp. 25–31.

3   F. Liebowitz, "Recycling American Ideology: The Second Coming of Michael Vronsky," Telos, no. 47 (Spring 1981), pp. 204–208.

4   See the provocative reading of The Deer Hunter as nihilistic tragic epic in F. Burke, "The Deer Hunter and Jaundiced Angel," Canadian Journal of Political and Social Theory (Winter 1980), pp. 123–31. Also, see R. Wood, Hollywood from Vietnam to Reagan (New York: Columbia University Press, 1986), pp. 270ff.

5   For a discussion of the relation between films about military life and the new militarism, see Tabloid, no. 4 (1981), pp. 3–17.

6   See G. Mosse, The Crisis of German Ideology: The Intellectual Origins of the Third Reich (New York: Grosset & Dunlap, 1964), pp. 55, 60, 62, 94, 281.

Race and Nation in *Glory*

21

ROBERT BURGOYNE

In resurrecting the forgotten story of a black Union Army regiment and its white leader, Colonel Robert Gould Shaw, *Glory* conveys a particularly complex understanding of the way racial and cultural identity is both bound up with and competes with the forces of national construction. Examining the historical construction of racial and national identity in the United States at a moment when concepts of nation were being fundamentally redefined, *Glory* emphasizes the tension between a civic ideal of nation conceived as a community of equals and the powerful appeal of ethnic and racial identities based on what Michael Ignatieff calls "blood and belonging."[1] Far from mediating or subduing ethnic concepts of nation, the Civil War, the film suggests, pulled potent structures of racial identification into visibility, promoting a sense of racial mobilization in white as well as in black America. *Glory* thus departs from the traditional themes of Civil War narratives, which typically focus on the emancipation of the slaves and the rebirth of national ideals of community and equality, to explore a subject that D. W. Griffith first considered from a rather different perspective: the struggle between competing ideals of nation, ethnic and civic, and their equally potent claims to recognition and belonging.

At first glance, *Glory* appears to be primarily concerned with the relation between what Cornel West has described as identity from above—identification with the nation-state—and identity from below—racial and ethnic identity. These two forms of identity, as West points out, are both defined by the most elemental concerns; they are fundamentally about desire and death. The desire for affiliation, for recognition, for visibility, is one of the most significant and visceral forces shaping both national and racial identity. But the construction of identity also involves the recognition of death, being willing to die for that identity, or being willing to kill others for it.[2] In *Glory*, this concept is dramatized in a strikingly literal way, as the struggle for racial visibility and recognition culminates in the spectacular assault and massacre of the film's final sequence, foregrounding the almost suicidal costs of aligning identity from below and identity from above. Underlining the theme of collective martyrdom with the sounds of choral music, the film idealizes the sacrifice of the black soldiers as the price of national affiliation, as if identity from above were in some way a mystical compact, authorized and conferred only in death. By invoking what Paul Gilroy calls "a mystic nationhood that [is] only revealed on the battlefield," the film further suggests that racial difference is dissolved in warfare, valorizing war as the defining moment when racial and national self-realization coalesce.[3]

But this thesis, in which national identity is presumed to dominate and displace the lived identity of race, is complicated by another, competing message in *Glory*. In counterpoint to the ostensible subject matter and theme of the film, which might be summarized in humanistic terms as the mutual reshaping and redefinition of identity from below and identity from above, the film also explores the more fractious subject of the failure of social movements to cut across racial identities, emphasizing the fear and hatred of the other as the constant feature of national experience. Although the central importance of national identity is asserted strenuously in the closing moments of the film, the body of the text seems to be concerned mainly with what I am calling identity from across: the non-symmetrical relationship between white identity and black identity that defines points of tension in *Glory* that have little to do with the unifying rhetoric of nation or the traditional Civil War topics of liberty, equality, and self-determination. And it is here that the film illuminates the hard kernel of historical truth that is slowly working its way through the various revisions of the dominant fiction that are currently being offered: the recognition that the achievement of new forms of collective coherence will require something other than an updated narrative of nation, and that only a historical narrative that, as the historian Peter Dimock writes, "is explicitly a collective narrative of social loss" will be able to address the present crisis of social belief.[4]

This secondary theme is articulated chiefly through the story of the white commanding officer, Colonel Robert Shaw, which serves in large part as a means of registering the dissonance between white racial identity and the imagined community implied by emancipation. Rather than merging whiteness and nation into a single myth, the film suggests that the historical coalescence of black identity during the Civil War forced apart the formerly seamless narrative of white identity, separating it from its traditional one-to-one correspondence with the concept of nation. With emancipation redefining the meaning of national community, the voice of white racial privilege could no longer be heard as the exclusive voice of national ideals. By inverted yet strangely similar paths, *Glory* comes to the same conclusion as D. W. Griffith's *Birth of a Nation*: white identity is defined and clarified by black identity, which forces "whiteness" into the open and compels it to speak in a language of its own.

As Richard Dyer has explained, white identity is an exceptionally elusive and difficult subject to analyze, for it represents itself not in terms of particular characteristics and practices, but rather as a synthesis of all the attributes of humanity. "The strength of white representation . . . [is] the sense that being white is coterminous with the endless plenitude of human diversity."[5] Just as the color itself is defined as a combination of all the other colors, white racial identity seems to have no substance of its own: "White power secures its dominance by seeming not to be anything in particular . . . as if it is the natural, inevitable, ordinary way of being human."[6] The invisibility of whiteness, its lack of specificity, masks it as a category; so thoroughly identified with the norm, white racial identity becomes difficult, especially for white people, to see and to represent.

One of the ways white identity does become visible, Dyer suggests, is in the contrast between white and nonwhite in narratives marked by ethnic or racial difference, narratives in which nonwhite characters play significant roles. In order to represent white identity, a "comparative element" seems to be required, for "only non-whiteness can give whiteness any substance." In such texts, the characteristics of whiteness can be inferred if not defined, understood by way of contrast with the stereotypes associated with nonwhite modes of behavior. In the films Dyer analyzes, the "presence of black people . . . allows one to see whiteness as whiteness." And the sense of whiteness is accentuated, Dyer notes, in films centering on situations where white domination is contested.[7]

These ideas offer an instructive approach to the representation of racial identity in *Glory*. The film uses the drama of the 54th Massachusetts Infantry, the first black regiment to be raised in the North, partly to pull white identity into visibility, detailing the practices and characteristics of the white Union military, emphasizing the "psychology" of whiteness, as seen through Shaw, and placing in relief the internal complacency and self-interest of the white establishment. The effective display of white identity, however, depends on a relation of rigid contrast with black identity, a contrast that recalls the absolute binarisms of racist thought. Stiff formality, an emphasis on individual agency and responsibility, and links to historical tradition are set out as clear markers of whiteness and explicitly set against the exuberance, collectivity, and sense of historical emergence that characterize the black soldiers. In keeping with the film's liberal themes and contemporary perspective, however, many of the features associated with whiteness are held up to scrutiny and subjected to criticism, partly through the voice-overs of Shaw himself. Ultimately, however, the traits identified as white are restored to dominance as Shaw overcomes self-doubt and gains the approbation and respect of the black troops.

As Dyer observes, the ability to resolve this kind of crisis of identity can also be seen as one of the attributes of whiteness; here, the hero restores his own fading sense of authority by appropriating the emotional intensity associated with the black soldiers, displaying an uncharacteristic passion in a series of scenes in which Shaw ferociously confronts the military establishment, dresses down his own officers, and, in an expression of solidarity with his troops, rips up his pay voucher to protest the unequal pay the soldiers have received, taking his cue directly from the black soldier Trip. In a subtle way, however, the emotional intensity common to the black soldiers is recoded in these scenes as part of human nature, latent but still accessible to the white Colonel Shaw. In contrast, when the black soldiers take on the rigor and discipline associated with the whites, it is a cultural attitude, not nature, that is absorbed. Where Shaw seems to require an infusion of natural passion to complete his character, the black soldiers require, in the logic of the film, the armature of certain cultural values associated with whites. Here, the film appears to reiterate conventional notions of blacks possessing more "nature" than whites, whereas whites command the sphere of culture. Thus, despite the superficial impression the film gives of a fluid crossing over of characteristics, the overall marking of racial differences is such that the boundary between black and white appears to be more fixed than permeable, and where mutual reshaping of identities does occur, the traits that are exchanged often play into well-worn stereotypes of racial difference.

Glory provides an especially good map of contemporary liberal thinking about race. In stressing the ways that white identity has been historically conferred, the film displays with exceptional precision the traditions, psychology, and behavior and practices of the white establishment during the Civil War period, underscoring the different ways whiteness, in both its progressive and reactionary aspects, has been shaped by the reality of an emergent black racial identity. In contrast, however, the film offers a portrait of black identity that is affirmative, but resolutely ahistorical, as if black history had to be remade by white hands and according to white ideas in order to release its most powerful messages.[8] Despite the positive accent the story of the black troops receives, the film's erasure of its actual historical figures, compared with its detailed reconstruction of the milieu of Colonel Shaw, ensures that the relations of racial identity here remain nonsymmetrical.

In general, the film uses two different paradigms to define racial identity, one of which is historical, the other folkloric and stereotypical, which are folded together or superimposed upon one another throughout the film. At several points in the narrative, the particularities of historical experience assert themselves in a powerful fashion, conveying a clear message that history has shaped racial identity in incommensurably different ways. For example, the film foregrounds the different meanings that blacks and whites assign to features of military life and specifically to the war against the Confederacy: military training and discipline, marching, and the climactic battle itself are viewed from a bifocal perspective that makes explicit the distinct optics that racial difference confers. At other points, however, this self-aware and careful dialogical principle gives way to a simple binarism in which racial difference is defined not in terms of historical experience but in terms of intrinsic differences, a tendency that rehearses essentialist patterns of racial representation. Seen in the most positive light, the film makes visible the way identity is constructed transitively, from across, using the binarisms of racial representation in a critical fashion and drawing from the dialogic encounter of black and white a reconsideration of the issues and traditions of national identity. But from another angle, the film hews uncomfortably close to old stereotypes, especially in its folkloric approach to black identity, which diminishes the actual historicity of black experience and identity.

In the pages that follow, I analyze the representation of racial identity in Glory from three different perspectives. First, I notice the contrast in the way the participants in the drama are defined and authenticated, a contrast that can be broadly described as historical versus folkloric. Second, I show how the film, despite its occasional lapses into stereotype, extends the dialogic principle discussed above—the foregrounding of the distinct viewpoints that racial difference entails—to encompass the historical process itself, represented in terms of two distinct historical trajectories, two competing narratives of history that are brought into conjunction in the imagery of the road and the march into the South. Third, I consider the messages the film conveys about racial identity and the national narrative from the perspective of the present, arguing that its seemingly traditional message of military valor and sacrifice opening up the "iron gate" to equality is counteracted by another message, signified by the closing shot of bootless corpses, which projects, like a kind of afterimage, a narrative of a nation imprisoned by its past as much as empowered by it.[9]

History versus folklore

By placing difference and conflict at the center of the national narrative, the film's approach to racial and national identity substantially changes the meaning of the story as it was known in the nineteenth century. Celebrated as one of the most renowned figures of the Civil War, Shaw, along with the 54th Infantry, had captured the imagination of the general public as well as the interest of the literary and political leaders of the period. Shaw's posthumous stature was such that Ralph Waldo Emerson and William James, among others, commemorated his "martyrdom" in verse and prose.[10] The recent treatment of the story, however, highlights Shaw in a different way, using him as a medium for registering the pointed racial animus of the Union military, as his idealism seems to bring into the open the underside of white racial identity, its basis in racial exclusion and fear. In large part, the text divides its affirmative and critical messages regarding racial identity in such a way that the Shaw narrative becomes the locus of a critical interrogation of white identity, now disjoined from its usual central position. The story of the black troops, on the other hand, who had been marginalized to such a degree that the "Shaw Memorial" in Boston had originally been designed with no black soldiers represented, is made the positive focus of the narrative, which treats the sacrifices of the 54th as the genesis of a black narrative of American history.[11]

In many respects, *Glory* reverses the usual codes of racial representation, portraying white identity for much of the narrative in an expressly critical way, while representing the narrative of the black soldiers as a drama of origins, the tracing of a heroic lineage. But in other ways, the film recapitulates many of the traditional stereotypes of race. Whereas the character of Shaw is heavily psychologized in a manner that emphasizes his self-consciousness and awareness, the black soldiers are portrayed in a resolutely nonpsychological fashion, and are associated instead, as if by way of compensation, with a kind of spirituality and resilience. Additionally, the historical dimensions and traditions of white identity are stressed: Shaw's actual historical existence is underlined by specific references to his abolitionist family and to the political and military leaders of the day and through the use of his correspondence, rendered in the form of several first-person voice-overs scattered throughout the film. The black soldiers, on the other hand, are represented as bereft of historical tradition: the actual historical figures who served in the 54th, which included Frederick Douglass's two sons, are replaced by entirely fictional figures. Whereas the historical individuality of Shaw is underlined, the black soldiers are represented in the form of an ensemble of stereotypes in which the "Wild Tom," the "Uncle Tom," the "Buppie," and the rural hick are plainly represented.

Another striking difference in the way white identity and black identity are portrayed is in the dissimilar styles of language that characterize the two groups. In the voice-over that opens the text, for example, Shaw draws direct links among language, history, and national identity. Comparing the Civil War to the War of Independence, he says: "How grand it is to fight for the country, like the old fellows did in the Revolution. Only this time we must make it a whole country so that all can speak." The voice-over continues over images of life in the military camp and scenes of dispossessed blacks on the road, at which point we hear that the war is being fought "for a people whose poetry has not yet been written, but which will presently be as renowned and enviable as any." The character finishes the monologue with a quote from Emerson, whose words, he says, provide him with strength and comfort. These lines are typical of the discourse of the white officers. The refined speech of Shaw and his colleagues connotes class privilege, a sense of social obligation, and a long, stable, and unified tradition, one that assumes a perfect congruence of white racial identity and national identity.

In contrast to the unified tradition of Shaw, the black soldiers exhibit a range of dialects, verbal patterns, and rhetorical styles; the "poetry" to which Shaw alludes conveys a diverse sense of origins and a loose, patchwork form of connection. Thomas, for example, the eastern-educated black volunteer, must have the patois of a Sea Island black translated for him by another black soldier. Similarly, the exaggeration and deadpan humor of Trip proves incomprehensible to Jupiter, a rural black. Moreover, the motley regiment comes equipped with a mute drummer boy, whose practice and mastery of his instrument serves as a kind of synecdoche for the unit's growing sense of cohesion. Whereas Shaw's voice-overs, together with the speech patterns of the white officers in general, are clearly marked as "historical," the black soldiers' speech patterns are marked as geographically diffuse, underlining the film's strategy of treating the story of the 54th as a narrative of emergence.

One of the consequences of this strategy, however, is the elimination of all but the most glancing references to black participation in the established political and social traditions of the period. A case in point is the portrayal of Frederick Douglass, who is depicted at the beginning of the film in a way that promises to counterbalance the traditional emphasis accorded Lincoln in stories of the Civil War. Contrary to expectation, however, Douglass appears only in the company of the white establishment, and is never mentioned by the black soldiers, who appear to be wholly unfamiliar with him. This aspect of the film contradicts the view of historians who aver that Douglass was widely known and revered among the black population of the Civil War period. The bracketing of Douglass from the portrait the film offers is compounded by its overlooking the fact that Douglass's two sons, Lewis and Charles, served in the 54th, with Lewis becoming sergeant major. Moreover, the film fails to indicate that the first black Medal of Honor winner was a member of the 54th.[12] Although it tries to make racial struggle a "formative and necessary part of the story" of American history, to use the words of Nathan Huggins, the film provides only fictional "types" among the black soldiers, rather than the actual historical figures, whose presence would certainly lend its historical portrait a heightened degree of authority.[13] Another omission is the role played by the black intellectual Charlotte Forten, who worked as a teacher and nurse in the area where the 54th was encamped in South Carolina, and who had gained the admiration of Shaw. To some degree, the film treats the black soldiers and citizens of the period as bereft of historical tradition, understood in the conventional sense. The story of the 54th is instead constructed as the genesis, the mythic origin, of black historical consciousness.

But the history of black identity during the Civil War period that *Glory* suppresses with one hand it restores with the other; what Frederick Douglass called the "fleshly diploma" of slavery—the whip marks and other signs of physical abuse inflicted on the slave's or the exslave's body—comes to express another kind of tradition, another kind of history, one that functions in counterpoint to the dominant tradition.[14] Although the film erases much of the actual history of the 54th, it succeeds in creating a picture of a historical world that is shaped by radically different historical experiences, implying that there are potentially many histories embedded in a given historical moment. Moreover, the film suggests that black history and white history in the United States determine and shape one another. At certain points, it illuminates with surprising subtlety the deep, structural connections between the dominant tradition and the suppressed and marginalized history of racial domination, a theme that allows us to glimpse the outline of a more fundamental rewriting of the narrative of American history than we might have expected from this film, a rewriting that works against the convenient myth that, as Nathan Huggins puts it, "American history—its institutions, its values, its people—was one thing and that racial slavery and oppression were a different story."[15] By articulating these stories together, the film echoes the approach of historians such as Huggins, whose words could almost serve as an epigram to certain sequences: "Whereas the master narrative detached . . . slavery and the slave experience from the central story . . . there can be no white history or black history, nor can there be an integrated history which does not begin to comprehend that slavery and freedom, white and black, are joined at the hip."[16]

These ideas are powerfully expressed in the flogging scene in *Glory*, as Trip and Shaw reenact a historical pas de deux that suggests that the stories of white and black in America are inseparable and mutually defining. Trip, the black soldier whose defiant character has already called forth particularly intensive disciplinary procedures, has slipped out of camp to acquire some decent leather boots. Caught and assumed to be a deserter, Trip is brought before Shaw and the assembled company to be flogged. Shaw insists on this punishment, over the protests of his second in command, determined to show his control over the men as well as his control over his own emotions. As Trip is readied for the punishment, the drill sergeant pulls the shirt off of Trip's back to reveal a torso covered with scars from previous whippings. Despite his evident shock and dismay, Shaw sticks to the order he has given. As the whipping commences, however, a certain reversal takes place. In a series of close-up reverse shots, Trip's self-discipline and control over his body are underlined, as he receives the flogging without "breaking down." Shaw, on the other hand, appears to lose authority with each stroke of the whip, as his rigidity is coded not as a form of strength but as inflexible adherence to a code that has suddenly been revealed to have two different meanings, one having to do with military discipline, the other with racial domination.

The flogging scene in *Glory* departs from actual history—flogging was banned in the Union military—to make a larger point about the way the historical past marks black and white differently, but with the same pen. The whip marks on Trip's body are the signifiers of the other national narrative, a history that, although suppressed and marginalized, challenges the master narrative itself. Here, the film uses the imagery of scarred and lacerated flesh as a historical text to be read in counterpoint or, better, to be read interlinearly with the dominant narrative, like a coded message in which every other line carries the principal meaning, a meaning that often explicitly contradicts the text taken as a whole.

The commonality of these two histories is underlined by the physical mirroring of Trip and Shaw. Consider the following passage from Frantz Fanon on the way master and slave, colonizer and colonized, act out a kind of mirrored identification:

> A world divided into compartments, a motionless, Manichean world, a world of statues. . . . The first thing the native learns is to stay in his place and not go beyond certain limits. . . .
>
> . . . he finds he is in a state of permanent tension. . . . The symbols of social order—the police, the bugle calls in the barracks, military parades and waving flags—are at one and the same time inhibitory and stimulating: for they do not simply convey the message "Don't dare to budge"; rather they cry out "Get ready to attack." The impulse . . . implies the tonicity of the muscles. . . . The settler . . . keeps alive in the native an anger which he deprives of an outlet; the native |is| inwardly in a state of pseudo-petrification.[17]

The flogging scene in *Glory* corresponds in an almost uncanny way to this description: the overall quality of motionlessness in its mise-en-scène, emblematized in the statuelike posture of Shaw versus the tensed, tight, muscular tonicity of Trip; the stiff formation of the soldiers; the trappings of military authority, the bugle call and the drum roll, which evoke here the contradictory emotions that Fanon describes—"Don't dare to budge," as well as "Get ready to attack"—producing an adrenalized stasis that is plainly represented in the body postures of Trip, the soldiers, and Shaw himself. Although the "symbols of social order" clearly mean different things for blacks and whites, the effects of power position Trip and Shaw in similarly fixed and inflexible roles. In an instructive analysis of Fanon's imagery, Homi Bhabha points out that the play of polarities in his description of colonial relations— Subject/Object, Self/Other, Oppressor/Victim, Power/Powerlessness—places both oppressor and victim in exceptionally similar predicaments: both are "pseudopetrified" in their antagonism.[18] In a similar fashion, Trip and Shaw become, in a sense, mirror images; in Trip, a continuous physical tension marks the conflict between the proscriptions of social reality ("Don't dare to budge") and the impulses of psychic reality ("Get ready to attack"), whereas in Shaw, the immobilizing effects of authority seem to mummify the character, marking his features and his body posture with a kind of rictus as he resolves to exercise the power of his office.[19]

Flogging scenes are a familiar staple of narratives set in the Civil War period; what sets this sequence apart is its dialogic quality. Rather than simply appealing to the masochistic or moral propensities of the viewer, the sequence is explicitly staged as a challenge to the dominant historical order and its way of perceiving race. Trip, a "graduate of the peculiar institution with |his| diploma written on |his| back," to apply the words of Frederick Douglass, has in effect "educated" Shaw about a history he had been insulated from, a history that transforms the punishment of Trip from the singular event that Shaw perceives it to be to the replaying of a historical pattern.[20] In a striking and pointed reversal, the scene suggests that it is Shaw's understanding of the historical past—and, by extension, white America's—that is mythological and folkloric. The dominant tradition, with its idealized conception of the American past, is itself a form of mythology insofar as it represses the history of race. As Huggins writes:

> The story of the United States is of the development of the North (read Puritan New England) rather than the South. It is of whites unrelated or unengaged with blacks. It is of freedom and free institutions rather than of slavery. It is as if one were to write a history of Russia without serious consideration of serfdom: a history of India ignoring caste. The distortion would be jarring did it not serve so well the national mythology and an idealized national character.[21]

Although the film appears at first to draw the most extreme contrast between the historicity of the white tradition and the folkloric nature of its version of black history, these terms end up being reversed, as one kind of historical knowledge confronts another.

Two historical trajectories

With the flogging scene, Glory produces a striking impression of "turning the tables" on the dominant tradition. But the overall thrust of the film—which is, I think, focused even more closely on white identity than on black—also channels the message of the sequence in another direction, bringing it back to the question of whiteness, to how the white hero will respond. The film uses this scene to instill in Shaw a layer of guilt that will be played on throughout the film. The linked themes of guilt, reparation, and reconciliation are from this point forward used to define the narrative of whiteness in a way that is distinct from the story of the black troops. Partly, this is a consequence of the psychologizing of Shaw, the focus on his emotions and sense of self-doubt. But it is also an aspect of the deeper fault line in the film, which configures the black narrative and white narrative along two different historical plotlines.

Like a painting with conflicting vanishing points, the film sets out different historical teleologies for blacks and whites. The narrative of collective emergence that characterizes the story of the African Americans is explicitly inverted in the story of Shaw, who we see discovering for the first time the hypocrisy of the white establishment. Continually confronted with venality, corruption, and lack of commitment in the military establishment, Shaw as a character becomes a way for the filmmaker to foreground the attenuation of the enlightenment narrative of history, of history unfolding in the service of liberty. With his continual wrestling with ethical dilemmas, and with the explicit message communicated through Shaw that the battle to be fought is not against an external enemy but rather against the internal complacency and self-interest of the whites, the Shaw narrative takes on the moral chiaroscuro more typical of the Vietnam film than the Civil War genre.

Nonetheless, Shaw is constructed as the hero of the narrative. Usually shown on horseback, often pictured in solitary contemplation of some distant horizon, Shaw is vested with the unmistakable iconography of the heroic. However, the film changes the meaning of his heroism from what it meant in the nineteenth century, for in *Glory* Shaw is constructed principally as a redemptive image of whiteness, a sacrificial figure who counteracts or "cleanses" the racial bias among the whites detailed throughout the film. Through Shaw, the narrative of whiteness becomes associated with social guilt and with the repayment of a historical debt. The theme of martyrdom, which dominated the Shaw legend in the nineteenth century, is here recoded to express a very different message of guilt and expiation.

In the scenes set on the road, the sense of a nation moving in two different historical directions is brought into relief. For example, one of the first shots in the film shows a mass of black families walking on the road near Antietam. As the film progresses, and as the soldiers of the 54th become increasingly disciplined and united in their resolve, the road is converted from an image of displaced drifting to a symbol of racial striving, with synchronized marching replacing images of wandering and admiring comments from bystanders supporting a sense of growing racial identity. One of the ways the film underlines the importance of the road motif is through its repeated use of close-up shots of running, marching, and bloodied feet. In a famous line, Frederick Douglass wrote, "My feet have been so cracked with the frost that the pen with which I am writing might be laid in the gashes."[22] The film reworks this image of wounded flesh, with its links to memory, into its own representational logic to signify the coalescence of a historical force and the beginnings of a new historical epoch, as the march of the black troops through the South clearly evokes the civil rights marches of the 1960s. From this perspective, the film corresponds closely to Mikhail Bakhtin's description of the "novel of historical emergence," in which the hero "emerges along with the world and . . . reflects the historical emergence of the world itself." The soldiers of the 54th Infantry of *Glory* are represented "at the transition point between two historical epochs," a transition that is accomplished, to paraphrase Bakhtin, in them and through them.[23]

The motif of the road conveys a very different sense of historical meaning, however, when viewed in terms of the character of Colonel Shaw. Rather than an image of collective emergence, the road represents something like a religious *via crucis* for Shaw, one that stretches from his near brush with death at Antietam to his actual death at Fort Wagner. The construction of Shaw as a purificatory figure culminates in the scene on the beach immediately prior to the assault on Fort Wagner. Here, in a solemn moment of poetic introspection, Shaw is shown gazing out to sea, in the company of his horse. In this scene, marked by solitude, interiority, and a sense of an approaching "end," there is little suggestion of an impending social transformation on the horizon. Instead, Shaw becomes the locus of a critical, post-Vietnam-style interrogation of individual and collective morality, especially the morality of white America. The message of historical emergence associated with the black troops thus meets a sense of historical closure in the character of Shaw, as the film projects a dualistic image of nation, one in which scenarios of continuity or dissolution seem equally available as possible futures that might be generated from the events of the past.

Racial identity into national identity

In what is clearly the summit of the film's aspirations concerning the recovery of African American history, Glory provides a long, detailed treatment of the collective religious ceremony called the shout, in which the black soldiers of the 54th define their own sense of collective identity. The filmmaker, Edward Zwick, has said that discovering the "voice" for this sequence was particularly difficult, and that he relied on the black actors and their experience of contemporary churches to fashion it.[24] Here, the film shifts to a different rhetorical style and mode of address—Zwick claims that it was done in an almost improvisational way—to underline the black "authorship" of the scene. And despite Zwick's seeming disclaimer as to its historical authenticity, both the imagery and the call-and-response pattern of the shout accurately render the communal practices of black people during the Civil War years, including black Union soldiers preparing for battle.[25] Music and religion, as Paul Gilroy notes, were the two resources of communication and struggle available to slave cultures: "The struggle to overcome slavery, wherever it developed, involved adaptations of Christianity and politically infused music and dance, which, in Du Bois's phrase, comprised 'the articulate message of the slave to the world.'"[26]

But the significance of this scene lies less in its historical authenticity than in the way it opens to larger themes of racial and national identity, especially the translation of racial identity into national identity. The shout in many ways functions as a kind of nerve center of the text, bringing the issues of race and nation, of identity from below and identity from above, into vivid conjunction. As the camera focuses on the troops assembled around a campfire, a lead vocalist is seen singing lyrics that communicate a double message: the story of Noah's Ark as an allegory of the slave ship. Certain lines of the song make this relation explicit: "He packed in the animals two by two; / ox and camel and kangaroo; / He packed them in that Ark so tight / I couldn't get no sleep that night." The song underlines the themes of diaspora and wandering that will be played up throughout the sequence, and poetically converts the experience of slavery and displacement to a message of survival and providential guidance.

As the scene continues, the historical analogies encoded in song and testimony also continue, with each character's testimony accenting the themes of history and identity in a different way. Jupiter, for example, an illiterate field hand at the beginning of the film whose tutoring by the well-educated Thomas has been subtly insinuated into several scenes, speaks of going into battle with "the Good Book in one hand and the rifle in the other." The link between the Bible and the rifle calls to mind the particular accent black people of the period gave to the image of Jesus. As Lawrence Levine notes, Jesus was ubiquitous in the spirituals, but it was not the Prince of Peace of the New Testament that was celebrated but rather a Jesus transformed into an Old Testament warrior: "The God I serve is a man of war."[27] Jupiter's words also imply an image of a future that will be made with both the rifle and the book; the book, the film suggests here, is a weapon as powerful as the rifle and can serve as an agent of community, in this case bringing the rural field hand and the educated easterner together.

Another character, Rawlins, also makes a comparison to the Bible when he says that he has left his young ones and his kinfolk "in bondage." The phrase calls up images of the Israelites and the historical affinity of the black slave narrative with the story of Exodus. Finally, Trip gives a statement about the value of collective endeavor, couched in terms of family. Bereft of kin, continually on the run, Trip here redefines his tragic past through his identification with a larger collective endeavor. At the end of the sequence, Thomas, the cultured friend of Shaw, becomes the focus of the camera's attention. Although Thomas doesn't speak in this scene, he begins singing the chorus of the spiritual, clearly marking his identification with his fellow volunteers. As the film has progressed, Thomas has taken on an increasing understanding of a specifically black consciousness. When he is wounded in battle, for example, he vehemently insists that he "is not going back." The phrase conveys a double meaning. Not only does he refuse to be sent back to Boston and a life of comfort, "a cup of decent coffee, sitting by a warm fire, reading Hawthorne," as Shaw reminds him, but he refuses to go back to being a favored black man in an all-white culture. Thomas here seems to have fully embraced a black identity.

Stuart Hall has written of black identity as something that must be constructed: "The fact is 'black' . . . has always been an unstable identity, psychically, culturally, and politically. It, too, is a narrative, a story, a history. Something constructed, told, spoken, not simply found. . . . Black is an identity that had to be learned and could only be learned in a certain moment."[28] The sequence of the shout strongly conveys this sense of identity being learned "in a certain moment"; black identity is "told" and narrated in such a way that a form of community emerges out of polyphony: a collective identity is here constructed from diverse voices and distinct trajectories. With Shaw manifestly excluded from the scene, the shout becomes a way for the potency and value of black collective life to pass directly to the spectator, as if the spectator were being invited to join in a dialogic ritual that, as Gilroy says, breaks down the division between spectator and performer. The signifiers of decline, isolation, and melancholy affixed to Shaw are directly countered by the vitality and exuberance of the black soldiers.

But as the film moves to its final, climatic scenes of battlefield carnage, this initial message of black identity as a dialectic of displacement and belonging is overlaid by the unifying paradigm of nationhood, in which the suicidal attack on Fort Wagner is configured as a necessary moment in the progressive unfolding of a plenary narrative characterized by racial and social advancement. In the ensuing scenes, the expressive form and language of the shout, which explicitly articulates a narrative of black diaspora, a narrative of dispersal, is placed in the service of a restored narrative of nation. Imagery that was used to express a fragmented, diaspora history is converted here to the expression of a coalescing nationalist sensibility. The variety of linguistic practices and the sense of geographic diffusion that have been associated with the black troops throughout the film are, in its closing scenes, renarrativized in terms of an exodus whose point of resolution is the nation-state. Although strong traces of African tradition can be found in the imagery and structure of the shout, the overall message that emerges is of a translation: vernacular black culture writing itself into, or being written into, the discourse of American nationalism.

The convergence of the theme of African American emergence with the theme of national identity is staged in a remarkably direct way. In the sequence that immediately follows the shout, the soldiers are depicted in tight, parallel formation, forming a corridor through which Shaw walks as he inspects the troops. After Shaw pauses to receive a Roman-style rifle salute from Jupiter, the film cuts to a high-angle close-up of the Stars and Stripes that literally fills the screen. Earlier, the symbolic meaning of "carrying the colors" had dominated a conversation between Trip and Shaw; Trip's refusal of this "honor" placed him on the far end of a continuum of identification and resistance that included Jupiter's eagerness to "wear the blue suits" and Rawlins's ambivalence about accepting the rank of sergeant major. But in the climactic attack on Fort Wagner, Trip has something like a battlefield conversion, seizing the colors and leading the charge, and immediately paying the price.

The "symbolic repertoire" of the community formed by the black soldiers has been portrayed in the film as relatively unfixed and still evolving, combining elements of Christianity, African tradition, local culture, and the codes of military life. But in the translation of this discontinuous history into a nationalist narrative, the film attempts to fix these symbols into universal meanings, capable of binding the whole "national community" together.[29] It attempts to assert, under the banner of the national, a sense of black and white "having a common story and necessarily sharing the same fate," an awareness of commonality that for Huggins, the author of this phrase, entails nothing less than a wholesale challenge and overturning of the master narrative of American history.[30] Glory takes this ideal as its goal, but stops far short of Huggins's conclusions, tying identity, instead, all the more securely to identification with the nation-state.

In the final scene, in which Trip and Shaw are buried together in a mass grave along with the other dead troops, the film refers to Griffith's Birth of a Nation and its very different tableau of racial brotherhood—the dying embrace of two white soldiers fighting for opposing sides. Seen as a dialogic response to Griffith, Glory can be said to push the question of race back into history; rather than seeing the persistence of racism and the legacy of slavery as forces that complicate or diminish the central American story, Glory treats them instead as necessary parts of the story, a point that is underlined by the ominous ending of the film, in which the Confederate flag is shown being raised over the bodies of the defeated troops. The overall political and historical context of emancipation is dramatized, then, not from the perspective we might expect, not as a privileged moment of decisive social change in which black and white came together, but rather from the viewpoint of the present, with its awareness of the relapses, resistance, and reactions that continue to plague the course of the struggle for racial equality in this country.

For all of the ways that Glory could be said to challenge racist ideology, however, its most resonant appeal is to forms of nationalism that are themselves "colored with racial connotations," reinforcing some of the ideologies the film seeks to challenge.[31] Although it restores, to some degree, the historical dimensions of black life in the United States, it also refurbishes national symbols of authority that require the renunciation of cultural particularity. And the links the film establishes among patriotism, militarism, and nationalism, its endorsement of a "mystic nationhood" revealed only on the battlefield, reinforce the dominant fiction at the site of its greatest potential harm, where it can have the most lethal consequences. Nevertheless, in its interstices, the film retains a quality of skepticism about the power of what Raymond Williams calls the "artificial order" of the nation-state in comparison to the more complete order of "full social identities in their real diversity."[32] In its unusually direct examination of identity from across—the particularities of white and black identity defined in relation to one another—the film makes evident the limits of its own nationalist solution to racial difference and antagonism, projecting in its closing images a message not about the end of slavery, but about the end of the nation as we know it. In the shots of the mass burial of the soldiers of the 54th that end the film, the national narrative is hauntingly evoked not as a triumphal story of social progress, but as a collective narrative of social loss.[33]

Notes

1 Michael Ignatieff, *Blood and Belonging: Journeys into the New Nationalism* (New York: Farrar, Straus & Giroux, 1993).

2 Cornel West, "A Matter of Life and Death," *October* 61 (Summer 1992): 20–23.

3 Paul Gilroy, *There Ain't No Black in the Union Jack* (London: Hutchinson, 1987): 52.

4 Peter Dimock, "Towards a Social Narrative of Loss," *Radical History Review* (Winter 1991): 54–56.

5 Richard Dyer, "White," in *The Matter of Images: Essays on Representations* (London: Routledge, 1993): 145.

6 Ibid., 141.

7 Ibid., 144.

8 Edward Zwick, the director of *Glory*, is probably best known as the cocreator of the TV series *thirtysomething*. In an interview in *Film Comment*, he describes the "anachronistic" scene in which Trip and Shaw converse about their parallel purposes as containing "a certain degree of liberal fantasy." See Armond White, "Fighting Black," *Film Comment* (January–February 1990): 26.

9 Frederick Douglass, *The Life and Writing of Frederick Douglass*, vol. 3 (New York: International, 1953): "The iron gate of our prison stands half open . . . one gallant rush . . . will fling it wide" (123).

10 Gary Scharnhorst, "From Soldier to Saint: Robert Gould Shaw and the Rhetoric of Racial Justice," *Civil War History* 34, no. 4 (1988): 308–22.

11 Ibid., 317–18.

12 See Peter Burchard, *One Gallant Rush* (New York: St. Martin's, 1965): on Douglass's sons, see 84, 139; on Charlotte Forten, see 116–17, 145–46. In the film, the black woman standing near Shaw in the Port Royal scene is, according to the screenwriter, Kevin Jarre, meant to represent Charlotte Forten.

13 Nathan Huggins, "The Deforming Mirror of Truth: Slavery and the Master Narrative of American History," *Radical History Review* (Winter 1991): 37.

14 Frederick Douglass, *My Bondage and My Freedom*, ed. William L. Andrews (Urbana: University of Illinois Press, 1987): 218–19.

15 Huggins, "The Deforming Mirror," 25.

16 Ibid., 38.

17 Frantz Fanon, *The Wretched of the Earth* (New York: Grove Weidenfeld, 1968): 51–53.

18 Homi K. Bhabha, "A Question of Survival: Nations and Psychic States," in *Psychoanalysis and Cultural Theory: Thresholds*, ed. James Donald (London: Macmillan, 1991): 98–99.

19 Ibid., 99.

20 Douglass, *My Bondage*, 218–19.

21 Huggins, "The Deforming Mirror," 31.

22 Frederick Douglass, *Narrative of the Life of Frederick Douglass, American Slave, as Written by Himself*, ed. Houston A. Baker Jr. (New York: Penguin American Library, 1982): 72; quoted in Stephanie A. Smith, "Heart Attacks: Frederick Douglass's Strategic Sentimentality," *Criticism* 34, no. 2 (1992): 197.

23 Mikhail Bakhtin, quoted in Gary Saul Morson and Caryl Emerson, *Mikhail Bakhtin: Creation of a Prosaics* (Stanford, Calif.: Stanford University Press, 1990): 411.

24 See White, "Fighting Black."

25 See Lawrence W. Levine, "Slave Songs and Slave Consciousness: An Exploration of Forgotten Sources," in *Anonymous Americans: Explorations in Nineteenth-Century Social History*, ed. Tamara K. Hareven (Englewood Cliffs, N.J.: Prentice Hall, 1971): 99–130.

26 Gilroy, *There Ain't No Black*, 159.

27 Levine, "Slave Songs," 120.

28 Stuart Hall, "Minimal Selves," in *Identity: The Real Me* (London: ICA, 1987): 45.

29 Gilroy, *There Ain't No Black*, 236.

30 Huggins, "The Deforming Mirror," 38.

31 Gilroy, *There Ain't No Black*, 26.

32 Raymond Williams, *Towards 2000* (Harmondsworth: Penguin, 1983); quoted in ibid., 50.

33 Variations of this phrase appear in Huggins, "The Deforming Mirror," and the separate "Responses" of Peter H. Wood, Peter Dimock, and Barbara Clark Smith, *Radical History Review* (Winter 1991): 25–59.

PART FIVE

HOLLYWOOD AND WAR: CONTEMPORARY FORMATIONS

The closing section features essays that address war cinema of the post-Vietnam era. The end of the Cold War, political and media institutional changes associated with so-called Reaganite entertainment of the 1980s, and the proliferation of new media and weapons technologies prepared the way for and constituted this change. The Gulf War of 1991, an event made more comprehensible to many through media contexts than political ones, evidenced the profound shifts in war cinema that had occurred—even as connections remained to histories of mili- tarization and mediatization extending back a century. Ongoing U.S. military actions in Afghanistan and Iraq following the attacks on the United States of September 11, 2001, have only confirmed how war and national security continue, through ever-evolving technological forms of mediation, to shape broad understandings of both past and current national life.

Upon its release in 2002, Tom Doherty wrote that *We Were Soldiers* was "Hollywood's first major Vietnam War film to portray American soldiers more concerned with killing the enemy than killing each other." "Unlike *The Green Berets* (1968)," he wryly observed, the film "makes Vietnam safe for the WWII combat film" (Doherty 2002: 6). That filmmakers would continue to revise the narratives of past wars by reworking the vast array of overlapping perspectives of cinematic and military histories should not surprise. Besides underscoring the familiar contrast between home and combat fronts, Randall Wallace's film deploys images of American domesticity to trump what are otherwise unusually far-reaching demonstrations of respect for the Vietnamese. While the film portrays America's foe as "highly motivated, professionally commanded, and strategically sophisticated," in other words, no images of Vietnamese domestic life or of the families of those soldiers are presented in juxtaposition with the portrayals of U.S. military families (Carruthers 2003: 174). The portrayals of camaraderie among fighting men in training and battle as well as of family lives at home worth fighting for unmistakably recall guiding tropes from the history of war cinema. Such nostalgia both urges reflection about why these specific values are being privileged now and reiterates the centrality of Hollywood to the construction of memories about war and wartime.

The thoroughly mediated geopolitics of the post-Cold War and, especially, post-9/11 world serve as an echo chamber for the evolution of processes of militarization and mediatization. *Black Hawk Down*, Ridley Scott's 2001 "extraction film" about an American military operation in Somalia that ended in the deaths of eighteen soldiers, was alternately viewed as an intense depiction of combat, a revealing document of post-Cold War racism and neocolonialism, and a well-intentioned humanitarian mission to the Third World turned tragic. This complexity follows from the layered representations of past wars. As Michael Ignatieff once remarked about television, the relations of Hollywood to peoples outside the U.S. and Europe "is a deeply complex mixture of willed amnesia, guilty conscience, moralizing self-regard, and real understanding." Notwithstanding what often appear condescending, xenophobic, or racist narratives, we might likewise say that cinema "does not suppress this ambivalence; it faithfully reproduces it in all its confusion" (Ignatieff 1997: 17). The strands of that political and discursive ambivalence or, better, polyvalence persist in inscribing narrative cinema. Many critics have responded by claiming, through analyses of empire, state and sovereignty, that the institution of the modern state may well be inseparable from war and that that condition is manifested, even upheld, by specific cultural forms (Agamben 1998; Hardt and Negri 2000; Kapferer 2004).

While such sweeping conceptual concerns exercise theorists, critics, and mediamakers, the pleasures offered viewers by cultural productions including cinema deserve special attention. One explanation offered by Mark Lacy is that dramatic films "provide moral security—the security that liberal democracies can bring justice and order to the world, affirming the sentiment that we are noble, responsible and good. These films work to construct the West not only as the main player in global politics, but as the legitimate and just source of authority in the global society." Put perhaps more directly, he goes on, "cinema provides the West with moral comfort food, the geopolitical feel-good factor" (Lacy 2003). Importantly, this comfort allays anxieties and fears that emerge both inwardly and outwardly. For a Hollywood cinema operating in the era of homeland security and less certain boundaries between the domestic and the global—in fact, a domestic realm arguably constituted by anxieties over technological, visual, and other commodity regimes of globalization—narratives can be culturally restorative and psychologically re-centering.

Such affirmation through media productions is, for some, illusory and even duplicitous. When Jean Baudrillard launched his polemic, excerpted here, that the "Gulf War Did Not Take Place," in 1991, a specific disagreement over the convergence of militarization and mediatization reached a pitch. Christopher Norris wrote a book-length response describing the "complicity that exists between such forms of extreme anti-realist or irrationalist doctrine and the crisis of moral and political nerve" prevailing among Western intellectuals (Norris 1992: 27). The nub of their disagreement, which addressed the Gulf War but occurred amidst the uncertain geopolitics of the early 1990s, was whether traditional moral positions and political values would continue to hold sway following the "end of history" pronounced by Francis Fukuyama after the United States' victory in the Cold War (Fukuyama 1992: 3). Indeed, Baudrillard's suspicion about political violence gathering meaning only from representation is ultimately an expression of concern about the evolution of social and media technologies and the shape and dynamics of the New World Order. His overarching claims are for social relations in which power derives less from the production of meaning by actual events or relations visible or invisible through media than from a locus of meaning shifted entirely to the ubiquitous visibility of media forms and representations themselves.

For many, Baudrillard's assertions, extended after 9/11 to address more explicitly the enlistment of media by terrorists whose acts are defined in resistance to globalization, are extreme and leave little if any space for active individual agency (Baudrillard 2003). Yet they can also be helpful in sketching out a contemporary trajectory of media analysis that emphasizes debates over the technological re-making or corrosion of social formations like civil society, the restoration or destabilization of national narratives and mythologies, the media-driven creation of memories or amnesia, the privileging of representation (or simulation) and, finally, the ennobling or interpellation of individual subjectivities. For the purposes of this volume, the claims about fundamental changes in media, social, and technological landscapes prompt, as well, questions about the future of Hollywood war cinema. James Der Derian has described the institutional consolidation of military and entertainment technologies in what he calls, "MIME-NET," the "military-industrial-media-entertainment network." Still a further set of questions engages the nature of military conflict itself. As Dean Lockwood argues, "Conflict in the twenty-first century is probably not going to be about blockbuster-style infernos." He goes on to conclude that, "the new terrorism will be waged invisibly, or, rather, it will frustrate the fantasy of total visuality" (Lockwood 2005: 77). Part of the aim of this volume is to suggest that linkages between changes in cinema and changes in war have evolved since the end of the nineteenth century. Amidst these many questions, the ultimate concern remains how we, as consumers, viewers, citizens, and moral beings, will respond.

In the opening selection here, Lynda Boose extends readings of the gender and cultural politics that she and others (notably Susan Jeffords) developed in light of Vietnam to the Gulf War. Geoff King looks in the second piece to the ambivalence of *Apocalypse Now* in order to understand *Saving Private Ryan*. In the process, he perceptively acknowledges the increasing relevance of action films to any elucidation of post-Vietnam war cinema. The third piece is from Jean Baudrillard's "The Gulf War Did Not Take Place." Next, historian Marilyn Young examines four recent productions as potentially engendering the beginnings of a new cycle that has Hollywood presenting war and U.S. military activity—in the past and present—as more politically and morally justifiable. The fifth piece, by Melani McAlister, extends these concerns with media and the dissolution of traditional politics (and wartime constructions) to the war against terrorism that we still wage. Her history of "the war without end" traces the political and filmic origins of a discourse of war against a non-nation-based, terrorist enemy.

Techno-Muscularity and the "Boy Eternal": From the Quagmire to the Gulf

22

LYNDA BOOSE

. . . . The Gulf War marks a particularly disturbing conjunction of interests. It marks the moment when the media, having suddenly recognized the boundless commercial potential of war, began, in columnist Sydney Schanberg's words, to look "more and more like an arm of the government's executive branch."[1] Thus it would be easy enough to locate the source of America's militant new "pride in itself" strictly in the government and the media. But consumers as well as producers participate in national mythmaking. As Richard Slotkin points out, the consumers of an ideology are "respondents capable of either dismissing a given mythic formulation, or affiliating with it."[2] Popular desires were complicit with governmental policies, each one acting to reproduce the other, in what Claude Lévi-Strauss calls the "will to myth."

The narrative of the unsung Norman Schwarzkopf, victimized by the ingratitude of the American public that did not give him a parade, is merely one of many more like it. However, Schwarzkopf's Vietnam story—much publicized during the Gulf War—contained just the patriarchal resolution to appeal to the anxieties of 1991 America: faced with a sister expressing reservations about the war in Vietnam, Schwarzkopf threw her out of the house. Yet when this story was first told me, the figures were reversed and it became Schwarzkopf who, upon return from the war, was thrown out of the house by his hippie, war protester sister. So familiar with the female-assigned rejection of Vietnam veterans had the public become that the story had been unconsciously rearranged into the pattern that told it "right."

In such revisionary narratives as this the most remarkable transposition lies in the way that the American soldier who fought in Vietnam—not the hapless two million Vietnamese who by choice or accident got in his way—has become the victim. The physically real violence routinely directed against war protesters—evidence of which the nation had been forced to witness via televised broadcasts of the 1968 Chicago Democratic Convention—had been displaced by stories of veterans victimized by words and gestures. And photographic images as vividly definitive of the Vietnam era as the killings at Kent State, the Vietnam Veterans Against the War hurling down their medals on the steps of the capitol, the napalmed Vietnamese girl running screaming toward the viewer, or the young Viet Cong soldier being shot in the head by the Saigon police chief—images that had once visually formed a seemingly indelible counternarrative to the thoroughly discredited official one—had been all but evacuated from the remembered story. Perhaps they faded because they were not finally "about" nor did they enhance the all-important national story of American male heroism that unconsciously conditions how Americans rank the importance of data they take in. The only "event" in the revised narration that the nation seemed to remember in 1991 was a narrative of American male subjectivity constructed by an act of collaborative imagination: as the nation reacted against a national guilt that it had tentatively begun to confront in the 1970s, the only image that America "saw" by the late 1980s was the convincing picture of itself as the proverbially innocent American soldier, returning from the war and being victimized by the insults of "spitting and jeering throngs."[3]

A *Los Angeles Times* editorial entitled "Vietnam Vets Weren't Feted by Parades" by Robert McKelvey is in many ways a paradigmatic 1991 account. In its opening comparison, former Marine Captain McKelvey bitterly measures the Marine Corps Commandant's idealized tribute to "our wives and loved ones supporting us at home" against the irony of his own wife's having "joined tens of thousands of others marching on the nation's capital to protest U.S. involvement in Vietnam." Two distinct narratives are at work here. In one, the veteran registers an uneasy awareness of the moral issues that prompted opposition to the war: "It was a divisive, unhappy time. Few people believed the war could be won or that we had any right to interfere in Vietnam's internal affairs." Nor does McKelvey himself ever argue that the war was morally—or even strategically—valid. We learn, in fact, that after returning and living with the Quakers, he "felt almost ashamed of the uniform I was still wearing. . . . |and| began to feel as if I had done something terribly wrong in serving my country in Vietnam." But that narrative is continually at odds with another, decidedly more pugnacious, eventually determining story. In this other narrative, his wife's failure to play out Penelope in a prescripted story that was always about not her but her husband comes to stand for everyone who was not "supporting us at home." Eventually, this becomes the site where all of the latent, internalized blame in his first narrative gets displaced.

> Even though our family and friends meant us no harm by protesting our efforts, and probably believed they were speeding our return, their actions had a very demoralizing effect. Couldn't they at least wait until we were safely home before expressing their distaste for what we were doing? But by then, the military had become scapegoats for the nation's loathing of its war, a war in which draft dodgers were cast as heroes and soldiers as villains. . . . I recalled stories of comrades who had been spat upon in airports and called "baby killers." . . . Watching the Desert Storm victory parades on television, I was struck by the contrast between this grand and glorious homecoming and the sad, silent and shameful return of so many of us 20-odd years ago. . . . |For us| there were no family, friends, well-wishers, representatives of the Veterans of Foreign Wars or children waving American flags. . . . The feelings aroused in me by the sight of our victorious troops marching across the television screen are mixed and unsettling. Certainly they deserve their victory parade. But there is also envy. Were we so much different from them? . . . Seeing my fellow Vietnam veterans marching with the Desert Storm troops, watching them try, at last, to be recognized and applauded for their now-distant sacrifices, is poignant and sad; . . . a sense of hurt still lingers on and, with it, a touch of anger. Anger that the country we loved, and continue to love, could use us, abuse us, discard and then try to forget us. . . . It was our curious, sad fate to be blamed for the war we had not chosen to fight when in reality we were among its victims.[4]

The issues that defined the first narrative—whether "we had any right to interfere in Vietnam's internal affairs" (or, for that matter, in the Middle East)—pale to inconsequentiality beside the all-consuming desire that not only motivates this memoir and determines the writer's affirmation of U.S. militarism in the Gulf but ultimately convinces him that he and his brother veterans were really the war's "used, abused, and discarded victims." To McKelvey, he and his brothers are victims because they did not get the applause that he imagines as every soldier's basic entitlement, irrespective of the morality of the war in which he served.

Ex-Captain McKelvey's letter is written from the world of boyhood—the boyhood of a white American male growing up in the glorious aftermath of World War II, imbued with the unconditional promises life seems to have made to all such little boys. Gone from adult consciousness is any historical recall of just how grotesquely inappropriate it really would have been to applaud a show of U.S. military strength in 1973 or in any way assist the Nixon government's attempt to displace the sober national mood with symbolic practices affirming U.S. actions in Vietnam. In McKelvey's reconstruction, the political is overwhelmed by the personal and adulthood by regressive desire: all that matters is that he and his comrades went to war and came back—for which they are entitled to be heroes who get a parade. Even his insistence that he/they should not be "blamed for the war we had not chosen to fight" seems especially telling, for as an officer in the U.S. Marine Corps, McKelvey cannot wholly be exculpated from "choosing to fight." What he did not choose— and what seems grossly unfair to him—was to be born to a generation that didn't get offered any good wars, but that got instead the war that may have bequeathed American males the opportunity for agonized moral wisdom but refused them the hero's glory they had grown up to expect.

Because heroism must be conferred by a woman—without whose cheers it cannot be constituted—this perceived injustice ends up being peculiarly the fault of his wife/women. Angrily, McKelvey envisions the war as a rewards system "in which draft dodgers were cast as heroes and soldiers as villains." To situate the draft dodgers as "heroes" loses sight of the father's approval essential to the cultural definition of "hero" and suppresses the price paid by those who left the country or went to prison. Nonetheless, the affiliation between draft resistance and the feminine—in this case, his wife's literal alignment with war protest— compels the victimized veteran script into such a polarity. The draft dodgers, like the unworthy suitors Penelope denied as she dutifully awaited the return of Ulysses, are traditional figures in this myth. They appear in the U.S. Army marching song "Sound Off" condensed into the figure of "Jodie," the imagined feminized male who stayed behind and has now "got" the soldier's wife, his sister, and his Cadillac,[5] all of which are signifiers of the real object of social desire, which is male heroism.

This male-constructed myth of heroic destiny—along with several other cherished American self-conceptions—failed catastrophically in Vietnam. But McKelvey's story unwittingly demonstrates how such unconsciously held mythic models, reinvoked for the Gulf War, served to polarize the Vietnam veteran against the anti-war movement with which he actually shared a crucial history.[6] By degrading the deeds of the collective and hence the individual soldier, the antiwar position that refused to praise the slaughter in Vietnam and defined it instead as a large-scale atrocity became the agent that deprived the Vietnam soldier of what, within the myth, is construed as his entitlement. And that negative position, imagined back to the scene of its origin, is the space of the withholding mommy.

In the new narration that has been under labored construction for the past decade, the patriarchal military state has been returned to its pre-Vietnam status of wise father. Its executive branch and military brotherhood have disappeared from the list of the culpable, and blame for Vietnam is associated almost exclusively with everything outside of those two masculine locations: the unsupportive home front, the Congressional curtailment of U.S. military potency, the peacenik press, and an effeminate Pentagon leadership that General Norman Schwarzkopf describes as "a cottage industry |that| developed in Washington, D.C., consisting of a bunch of military fairies that had never been shot at in anger."[7] The general's uninhibited invocation of the homophobic lexicon in itself says a great deal about how, in the wake of the Gulf War and its affirmation of masculine ideology, the categories of gender and sexuality had, in effect, been retooled into social bludgeons.

By all outward appearances, the American public in 1991 had come full circle back to a militarism built upon the reinvestment of a national/personal selfhood in the image of the American soldier. But playing out the prodigal son's return to the fold has proved complex for the generation of American sons caught up in that compulsion. For what the Vietnam War set in motion was the radical truncation of the oedipal journey: a narrative, ultimately, of hollowed-out paternity and perpetuated sonship. Besides meaning a war that was lost and an era of committed and bitter political division in the country, what "Vietnam" signifies is the site of a traumatic break between the men of one generation and those of another —between the fathers and the sons. Something dimly understood to be occurring even at the time and termed "the generation gap" proved to be a systemic rupture on the scale of mass culture. America emerged from the Vietnam War still a patriarchal system—but a patriarchy with an unoccupied and no longer occupiable center. Chronologically bracketed by the assassination of the national father at one end, marked in the middle by his successor's forced retirement and culminating in the disgraced resignation, a few steps ahead of impeachment, of the final father figure of the era, the battles that America's sons waged in and over the Vietnam War were played out against a history repeatedly defined by a both literal and symbolic evacuation of authority.

The expulsion of the father has not, however, served to liberate the sons. For America's post-Vietnam narrative is stamped with the intensity of a generation stuck in its own boyhood and now playing out, with increasing violence, an unconscious cultural myth that attempts to recover the father. Within the drama of manhood being staged across the psyche of American popular culture, the Vietnam veteran functions as proleptic historical signifier of the moment when the father was lost, the moment of refusing the father's dictates, and the moment of failing them. And the veteran's story of striving and rejection has come to be weighted with such significance not because it reflects the actual experience of most veterans, but because it captures the shared, symbolic truth of what happened to American males of the whole Vietnam generation, veteran and nonveteran. Inside the oedipal framework of the only narrative through which the culture has been able to imagine itself, this whole generation of men shared the same fate, regardless of which side of the war they were on: none of them got a parade, none got heroized, none earned the father's approval, and all were stranded in a never-completed transition to manhood, left poised in one gap en route to inheritance of the gap now signified by the father's vacated space.

The Vietnam War brought into being an historical collision of values that collectively compelled the nation's young men into severance from the fathers. Many severed themselves by rejecting their fathers' World War II reading of the Vietnam conflict, and many such sons were quite literally banished from their paternal houses. For defying the draft, some were forced into exile and others into federal prisons. But while back then the culture imagined the war protester versus the Vietnam soldier in terms of the classic Huck Finn/Tom Sawyer bad son/good son binary, the conditions of the Vietnam War made even the space of good son impossible. The young men of the Vietnam draft were forced by the dictates of the father-text to have to "choose," as a condition of masculinity among a sadistically constructed series of virtually self-annihilating options: to fight a war for which no plausible ethical justification existed; to refuse induction and, as criminals, serve hard time in prison; or to banish themselves from the father's house and flee hunted in exile from their country. And if the second and third choices more obviously signify the father-son rupture, the choice to fight in Vietnam proved incapable of preventing it. Ultimately, not even those men who sequestered themselves in draft exemptions could escape the culture-wide severance from paternal authority.

The father is synonymous with the law that dictates patriarchal society and sets out its inflexible requirements for masculinity. He is unforgiving. Thus despite even the readiness of the dutiful sons to prove themselves heirs to the patrilineal "line unbroken," even the sons who went to Vietnam failed. They did not return winners, as had their fathers from World War II, but left an unforgivable blot on the unblemished war record they inherited. And the fact that some 120,000 of those who returned have by now committed suicide—twice over the number that even the war managed to kill[8]—strongly suggests that some far more powerful source of rejection was at work in American society than any bra-less hippie shouting "baby killers" could account for. It suggests that the sons of patriarchy unconsciously hear and obey a silent but omnipresent commandment written out in ancient Sparta as the edict to return from a war with one's shield or on it.

The Vietnam generation was, furthermore, compelled into the revelation that patriarchy disallows: that they had been lied to and used by the fathers. They, the youth, had been used by the old men who either did not go to Vietnam or who, if they went, betrayed their task of leadership;[9] the young men had been asked in the name of a tradition that bound them to personal, national, and historical fathers to kill, to die, and to taint their souls for mystified ideals they later discovered were shrouded in political lies. Some, while yet in Vietnam, took aim with grenades or rifles and tried killing the father. But even those who tried not to see the lies returned to America to stony rejection for failing to keep the fathers' myths intact. The popular, politically useful story would have it that it was the antipatriot who met and reviled the returning soldiers, but the unspeakable truth is that returning veterans were treated as pariahs by the Veterans Administration and were probably more scorned by groups like the American Legion and the Veterans of Foreign Wars than they were by war protesters.[10] Moreover, the whole generation of men was scarred by the war, including even those lucky enough to be outside the reach of the draft. Having been given the opportunity to undergo patriarchy's "test by fire," they had failed, for Vietnam was the war of their generation, the heroic moment they had grown up to anticipate, and the only war they had. And it is not in the least uncommon today for men who happily avoided the war to look back on Vietnam and find themselves with "the distinct feeling that they had missed a critical 'rite of passage' in coming to terms with their manhood."[11]

As the example of Richard Rusk's fruitless reunion with his father should suggest, it is not just the men who fought in Vietnam who find themselves inexplicably caught up twenty years later in the rhythms of repetition and return that mark out the psychic landscape of the son's always impossible quest for the father. It is all the men caught in the ten-year-long war—the generation that has now moved into power in this country and the one whose psychic needs are now dictating everywhere the shape of a deeply regressive national master plot. The quest for the father—which might seem to be a reparative ideal—is dangerously regressive and invariably futile because what was required at the time of transition to adulthood cannot, by very definition, be incorporated twenty years later. For a short space in the 1960s and 70s, American culture set out on the difficult and uncharted quest for new masculine narratives that might move beyond the father and the patriarchal world he defines, but such a progression was always in contention with the seductive impulse toward repetition and return. The Gulf War gave the clearest possible evidence that America had turned back, with compulsive desperation, regressing into boyhood deeds that demonstrate masculine loyalties and contempt for the feminine—the conditions for earning the oedipal validation that time has already rendered moot. In the four "tests by fire" that the United States has staged since its defeat in Vietnam, the pattern has been one of a progressively escalating use of force and an increasing reliance on weapons of mass destruction demonstrably disproportionate to any imputed threat. For the rest of the world, America's *Bildungsroman* is dangerous, for the pattern strongly suggests a psychic quest that becomes compulsively more urgent with each successive proof of its impossibility.

Judging from such signs as America's heroized mythology of baby-faced gunfighters like Billy the Kid or from its traditional representation of its national historical self as the "young," "new," and "innocent" nation, one could say that this country has always valorized male adolescence. The choice of Audie Murphy as the national embodiment of the World War II American soldier reflects the attraction; and certainly for Henry James, adolescent selfhood was a definitively American trait, producing a brashly honest, stubbornly innocent American character that James finally found culpable for his refusal to grow up. But the positioning of the father strongly differentiates the film models of American boyishness clustered around World War II from those made in the post-Vietnam era.

In the fictions of the filmmakers of the Vietnam generation the father-son rupture gets repeatedly narrated, always from the consciousness of the son. Figures of authoritative, compassionate leadership like John Wayne's Sergeant Stryker of *The Sands of Iwo Jima* are simply gone, their absence narrated into post-Vietnam movies as either the father's betrayal of the son or the son's quest to revalidate the father or both. Films about World War II were generally organized as love stories and included girls/wives back home, but films about the Vietnam War—caught up in the regressions of the oedipal compulsion—are never love stories and their narratives are often violently inhospitable even to the presence of women. In these films the unresolvability of the father is frequently represented through an implicit accusation of him that is simultaneous with attempted exoneration, sometimes further complicated—as in *Apocalypse Now* and *Platoon*—by competition between several sites of vacated paternal authority within a narrative that impels the son to kill the father. In both these films the immediate position of the father is malevolently occupied and the good father displaced. But even when a benevolent father is put into the fantasy, as is the hero's mentor figure in the two Rambo films and Ron Kovic's father in *Born on the Fourth of July*, domestication has feminized him and his weakness and ineffectuality lead to a direct betrayal of the son anyway, leaving the father's position once again vacant. In the second Rambo film, blame is deflected away from the father by locating it with the pudgy, effeminate

Pentagon civilian; in Stone's film, it is shunted onto the castrating mother, who is blamed both for sending her son off to war and rejecting him when he returns.

Most of the footage of combat units in Vietnam films suggests a total vacuum of authority. In a film like *Casualties of War* or *Apocalypse Now* or *Full Metal Jacket*, the war is a chaotic moral landscape with no fathers on hand, a war fought by boys led by boys, a space abandoned to the rule of frightened and lethally armed adolescents. *The Deer Hunter*—one of the few to include a focus on the hometown—lacks fathers in even that space. There are only brothers. But while the law of the (absent) father—represented by the "one shot" model of male ethics—is offered on the one hand as the highest ethical code available and that which saves the oldest/strongest son (Robert de Niro), it proves lethal to the sensitive son (Christopher Walken). Furthermore, the older son's attempt to move into and redeem the space of the father by going back to rescue the other sons proves bitterly insufficient to save or return them whole. The film's one literal father/son pair offers a bleak comment on the transition of the Vietnam sons into any paternity of their own: in this pair, the paraplegic veteran cut off at his manhood and returned from the war to a state of near infantile dependency is symbolically situated as the putative father of a son who is not his. And though much in this film seeks resolution in regression back to the myths of frontier individualism in which American imperialism was born, the film is nonetheless radical in its understanding of "Vietnam" as signifying the end of the idealized nuclear family. *The Deer Hunter* and *Apocalypse Now* were among the first Vietnam war films that emerged belatedly at the end of the 1970s; and the bleak integrity of their father-son representations reflects something of the attempt to confront and get beyond the father—the response that could still be imagined in that first decade. By the time of *Uncommon Valor* (1983), the need to recuperate the father and resecure patriarchal authority had become so pressing that this film, which features a military father (Gene Hackman) going back to Vietnam to rescue the son, even tries to situate the Vietnam War and the sense of abandonment and exile it bequeathed to American sons inside of a good father narrative. But even this fantasy of paternal affirmation stops short of staging the father and child reunion, tacitly conceding its impossibility through a narration in which the son dies in captivity before the father arrives.

The film that carried the most overt fusion of father and military state was *Top Gun* (1989), which locates its narrative impetus squarely in the losses of the Vietnam War. This film proved literally the best recruitment device the U.S. Navy has ever helped to produce. In it the Vietnam War exists as a memory through which to enact, both on and off screen, the seduction of sons necessary for any militarist state. On screen, in shots of high-tech military aircraft and jet pilot maneuvers that packed in young males across the country, the son (Tom Cruise) becomes a warrior in order to recuperate the honor of a father whose death in Vietnam was enmeshed in obscure charges that have left his name (and thus, his son's) falsely dishonored. What was simultaneously under recuperation was the reputation of the U.S. military, likewise sullied in Vietnam. Through the logic that only by going to war and redeeming their fathers can the sons of the Vietnam generation lay claim to their own honor among men, an unconscious script was being valorized for a nation to do likewise.

Neither *Top Gun* nor *The Great Santini* (1979) is usually categorized as a "Vietnam War film," but both should be. In their representation of the peacetime military playing out a model of war as game and flight squadron as fraternity, these two offer especially acute visions of the ethos that traveled from the high-tech warrior cadres of Vietnam to define the wholly technologized U.S. military operation in the Gulf. In Vietnam as well as World War II films, the paradigmatic soldier is characteristically remembered as an enlisted army or marine corps grunt embodying a certain moral seriousness associated with his proximity to killing and dying. *Top Gun* and *The Great Santini* explore a radically different ethos, that of the elite technicians of war, the studied *sprezzatura* and gamesmanship of the high-flying macho men of the air who are almost always officers and who experience war from the detachment of button-pushing technology. It is the ethos behind the sports-heavy metaphors through which interviewed American pilots reexperienced their aerial devastation of Iraqi ground troops as the scoring of points in some competitive contest; ultimately, it became the moral and linguistic visor through which the American public—who experienced the war as a military talk show—likewise conceptualized it.

Robert Duvall's "Lt. Colonel Bull Mechum," alias the Great Santini, is a type of the well-loved hero particularly valued within the conformity of the military—a hero whose leadership fuses with the kind of little boy risk-taking, nonconformist contempt for the rules that made legends out of Patton and MacArthur. For air groups, the code also involves a Rabelaisian mockery of moral seriousness and a studied disregard for regulations and bureaucracies. A rigid family disciplinarian who reveres the marine corps, Bull Mechum is also a forty-plus-year-old adolescent whose boyish pranks perform the highly important American fiction of nonconformist individualism through rebellions that never seriously question or attempt to overthrow the status quo. No one belongs more completely to the established national norms than does Bull Mechum, whose pranks and rebellions merely play out the time-honored drama of son against father/authority; and Mechum is himself driven by obsessions about masculinity that not only compel his son to play sports and be a winner but also dictate the father's compulsive need to compete against and defeat his own son in order to hold on to the position of boy eternal.

Masculine game mentality is hardly unique to this country, but the manic level of it that Bull Mechum represents may be. No matter how old the male nor how inappropriate it may be for him to constellate his sense of selfhood around athletic prowess being able to defeat other males in various sports contests has become so overly invested a national feat that it quite openly affects even international interactions on the presidential level. Not only did George Bush thrive on setting up sports competitions as tests with which to challenge visiting foreign leaders but the mentality extended to even the parlance his administration coined for the device that launches nuclear war—a device inside of a black box that, with eloquent simplicity, became known as just "the football." For the president whose public fidgeting at world news conferences has been compared to that of an "elementary school student when [he gets] bored . . . a child inhabiting the body of an adult,"[12] the term presumably creates a nuclear sports joke about the nation's "quarterback" deciding to "throw the bomb."

It was through such a sports/game discourse with its underlying dictum of "win" that the American public was connected to the Gulf War. While the rest of the world may have been puzzled or even offended at hearing American pilots on C N N return from bombing runs and jubilantly relate the slaughter of Iraqi soldiers in terms of football and baseball metaphors, Americans understood the connections because they, too, had grown up in the uniquely American school system where sports take priority over academics, high schools produce sports heroes and colleges professional athletes, and the *real* curriculum that the system is tacitly organized to teach and test is one that could be called "Comparative (Competitive)

Masculinity." No one but Americans probably recognized the dedication of Superbowl 1991 to America's boys in the Gulf as a genuine tribute of high seriousness in the culture. Quite obviously, the Italian player on Seton Hall College's basketball squad who returned to Italy under physical threat from the fans did not understand what sacred premise he had violated in declining to participate in the team gesture of sewing an American flag on his uniform to signify support for America's Gulf troops. But Americans understood: the drive to make sports a part of the public educational curriculum had even originated in America at the end of the Civil War as a substitute to provide "the moral equivalent of war."[13] And if Americans who did not grow up male did not wholly grasp the sacred connections that link a team of players and their playing field to the nation's warriors out on a battlefield, they had the opportunity to learn a critical lesson from the public outrage and presidential denunciation that Roseanne Barr provoked after a San Diego Padres baseball game where her rendition of the National Anthem seemed, wittingly or not, to mock the nation's sacred masculine investments in baseball. At least in President Bush's eyes, her gesture had mocked all of America.[14]

In films like Big, Back to the Future, The Sure Thing, Dead Poets Society, Bull Durham, Field of Dreams, Home Alone, and myriad others, filmmakers of the 1980s and 1990s have been writing out a culture's regressive desires into big screen fictions of the boy eternal. The opening programs of the 1990 fall television season were so marked by a childish "elevation of behavior that can only be described as irresponsible" that the Baltimore Evening Sun's television critic insightfully assessed the season as "a clumsy attempt by baby-boomer-aged producers to translate the generation gap that formed one of the main conflicts in their lives into a contemporary setting."[15] The world imagined by this TV sitcom fare is one in which male adolescents, evermore in subject position, move through misogynist narratives marked by domineering mommies and either ineffectual or absent fathers: Get a Life, where a thirty-year-old paper boy who still lives with his parents persuades his best friend to play hooky from work and spend the day in the park eluding the friend's killjoy wife—illustrates a representative plot. Nor did the victory in the Gulf allay the need for such regressive fictions. Post-Gulf male fantasies could still be read through their projection onto big screen narratives of men's boyhood heroes, a repertoire that included 1991's Dick Tracy and Batman and in 1992 expanded to produce Captain Hook, the ultimate fantasy of suspended boyhood, produced for a target audience of middle-aged Peter Pans. Writing in The Washington Post, Andrew Ward recognizes the film's mirroring of cultural production seeing it as "of a piece with what my entire generation has done to childhood itself. We have ruined it by refusing to let it go."[16]

For the past decade, Americans have been devouring movie after movie about reclaimed sonships and perpetuated boys' rites of passage. But however enamored of the adolescent his own countrymen may be, all this boyishness in American behavior has costly consequences for the rest of the world. In Graham Greene's Vietnam novel, The Quiet American, the culpability of the boy-man version of American diplomacy is depicted through the fifty-five-year-old title American who is out planting bombs on bicycles in order to save the Vietnamese from communism, yet whose "young and unused face . . . gangly legs and his crew-cut and his wide campus gaze . . . seemed incapable of harm, . . . impregnably armoured by his good intentions and his ignorance. . . . as incapable of imagining pain or danger to himself as he was incapable of conceiving the pain he might cause others."[17] As Greene's novel about Vietnam of the 1950s prophetically recognized, America's "crew-cut" version of itself as the righteously innocent adolescent is a mythic self-image that allows the nation to behave in just such massively irresponsible ways as its foreign policies reflect. To the American boys on the sports field/battlefield and to Boy George, the overaged preppie in the White House whose film tastes run to the cartoon heroics of Stallone, Schwarzenegger, and Norris,[18] being a bully is apparently fun—as much fun, for instance, as the international American prank that was staged in Panama under direction from Washington with American soldiers bombarding the Papal Nuncio and his staff inside the Vatican Consulate with ear-splitting, round-the-clock rock music until Manuel Noriega was handed over from sanctuary. As for the some 1,000+ civilians who got in the way of America's little 1989 military Christmas show in Panama and were apparently then dumped in unmarked mass graves, the U.S. Army clearly felt annoyed by any imputation of moral responsibility. Leaving it up to the Panamanians to sort out the aftermath, America picked up its planes and trucks and went home to have a parade.

Yet even though such 1980s American "victories" were transparently the ego-driven posturings of an overgrown bully beating up the smaller kids, Americans in the late 1980s seemed incapable of registering anything but glee over actions that, in the mid-1970s, would more likely have provoked a challenge to the government that ordered them. Outside of remnant peace organizations that the press came increasingly to ignore, by 1990 the American public registered neither a sense of moral responsibility nor even curiosity about the price that civilian populations routinely pay for America's enjoyment of watching its own deadly technology go bang in the night. To be concerned for the plight of the many hundred civilians killed by a laser-guided hit on an Iraqi bomb shelter or to question the orders that selected that target would introduce exactly the kind of potentially emasculating ambiguity that war films educate their male viewers to discard. Ambiguities and doubts belong to the feminine; and American heroes from the western movie onward have always been heroes precisely because their masculinity depends on having the fortitude to stand firm against all such compromising complexities as those with which the "Vietnam syndrome" had threatened permanently to mar America's discourse of war.

The annihilation of the Iraqi army and the "Willie Horton" tactics of the 1988 U.S. presidential election together attested that winning—whenever and by whatever means possible—had clearly replaced all other possible ethics in America's reassertion of man-hood. But the compulsions that drove the "win" mentality signified anything but adulthood. The short-lived adulthood that had once visited the Vietnam generation, and through their experience had offered the nation a chance to grow up, had come in the form of sobering loss and painful self-knowledge, not as the movie ending of a cheering parade. The Gulf War provided the counteroffer of the parade. But in turning back to that option and enacting its regressive desires into full-scale war, what America produced and televised for the world to admire was, ironically, an all too appropriate depiction of the culture of American masculinity that the latter half of the twentieth century had shaped: an image of wanton boys, killing for their sport.

Notes

1   Sydney H. Schanberg's editorial for *Newsday*, "Another View of the Gulf War 'Victory,'" rpt., *Valley News* (Lebanon, N.H.) July 10, 1991, p. 16. The documentaries that Bill Moyers has

produced since the mid-80s—including "After the War," his June 1991 report on Gulf War television coverage and the film footage that none of the major channels would air— likewise indicate Moyers's growing concern over the increasing chumminess between the White House and the media.

2 Richard Slotkin, "Gunfighters and Green Berets: The Magnificent Seven and the Myth of Counter-Insurgency," Radical History Review 44 (1989): 65–90, 65. Of the various cultural assessments of Vietnam and its aftermath, The Vietnam War and American Culture, ed. John Carlos Rowe and Richard Berg (New York: Columbia University Press, 1991), offers a particularly rich collection.

3 The phrase comes from an otherwise unquoted letter to a local newspaper.

4 Robert McKelvey, editorial for the Los Angeles Times, "Vietnam Vets Weren't Feted by Parades," rpt. Valley News (Lebanon, N.H.), June 20, 1991, p. 22.

5 David Rabe invokes these lyrics in the first play of his Vietnam War trilogy, The Education of Pavlo Hummel. "Jodie" is likewise the name given to the Jon Voight figure—the war protester who, in the 1978 Vietnam film, Coming Home, does in fact "get" the wife of the soldier (Bruce Dern).

6 Here and elsewhere, my use of the term "the Vietnam veteran" refers to the public perception of such a figure that has emerged from dominant representation and whose image works to subsume the multiplicity of political perspectives that are, of course, actually held by the many different men and the women (never included in the public image of the veteran) who served at different times, places, and in widely different circumstances in Vietnam. As Cynthia Enloe points out, the model of "the Vietnam vet" has taken "15 years and a lot of celluloid and paper to create, but today he is a potent figure inspiring complex emotions, . . . |and| it is the unappreciated, alienated male Vietnam vet whose image looms over the present war" (as cited in note 19).

7 Quoted from Newsweek, May 27, 1991, p. 17.

8 Barry Romo, National Coordinator of Vietnam Veterans Against the War lecture, Drake University, Des Moines, Iowa, October 24, 1990.

9 The failure of any military leadership in Vietnam and the widespread careerism amongst senior officers is well documented. See esp. Loren Baritz's description in Backfire: A History of How American Culture Led Us into Vietnam and Made Us Fight the Way We Did (New York: Ballantine, 1985), pp. 276–318.

10 See esp. D. Michael Shafer, "The Vietnam Combat Experience: The Human Legacy," in The Legacy: The Vietnam War in the American Imagination, ed. D. Michael Shafer (Boston: Beacon Press, 1990), pp. 80–103. In discussing Vietnam veterans' "cruel . . . often callous treatment by the V A hospital system" Shafer points out how the acute care needs of the several hundred thousand young, seriously wounded Vietnam combatants were essentially ignored in favor of the chronic care needs of aging World War II veterans, the constituency that had numerical and political clout (96). The Legion and the V F W— veterans in the father position to the Vietnam returnees and also men who "strongly supported the American cause in Vietnam and often blame Vietnam veterans for defeat"—further protected such interests by aggressively lobbying to block funding of outreach, drug rehabilitation, and psychological counseling programs for Vietnam veterans (97).

11 Sam Brown, "The Legacy of Choices," in The Wounded Generation, ed. A. D. Horne (Englewood Cliffs, N.J.: Prentice-Hall, 1981); rpt. in The American Experience in Vietnam: A

Reader, ed. Grace Sevy (Norman, Okla.: University of Oklahoma Press, 1989), pp. 195–203, esp. p. 201.

12 Maureen Dowd, "Tame Latins and No Eggs Greeted Bush," *New York Times*, December 9, 1990, international ed., p. A3.

13 *Newsweek*, October 8, 1990, p. 64. Much has been written on the Gulf War and its sports metaphors. See, for instance, Molly Ivins, "Super Bowl in the Sand," *The Progressive*, March 1991, p. 46.

14 See "Chronicle," *New York Times*, July 27, 1990, p. B4; "Roseanne Strikes Out! The Whole Crazy Story of How She Turned into a National Disgrace," *National Enquirer*, August 14, 1990, pp. 28–29, 36; and Carolyn Marvin, "Theorizing the Flagbody: Symbolic Dimensions of the Flag Desecration Debate, or, Why the Bill of Rights Does Not Fly in the Ballpark," *Critical Studies in Mass Communication* 8 (1991): 119–38.

15 Michael Hill, "New Fall Season Glamorizing a Lot of Irresponsibility," for *The Baltimore Evening Sun*, rpt. *Valley News* (Lebanon. N.H.), September 11, 1990.

16 Andrew Ward, "Paunchy Peter Pans," editorial for *Washington Post*; rpt. *Valley News* (Lebanon, N.H.) December 31, 1991, p. 16.

17 Graham Greene, *The Quiet American* (London: Penguin Books, 1973), pp. 17, 179, 62.

18 *Newsweek*, April 16, 1990, p. 25.

Seriously Spectacular: "Authenticity" and "Art" in the War Epic

23

GEOFF KING

The practical effects gave us all – the crew, the actors, and myself – a feeling of actually being under combat conditions, and the actors couldn't help but react to it. Often we would walk away from a setup with our hands shaking, and it informed everyone's performance. It certainly reinformed me, from shot to shot, how I needed to tell the story.

Steven Spielberg[1]

I am violently, viscerally affected by *this* image and *this* sound, without being able to have recourse to any frame of reference, any form of transcendental reflection, or any Symbolic order. No longer does a signifying structure anticipate every possible perception; instead, the continual metamorphoses of sensation preempt, slip and slide beneath, and threaten to dislodge all the comforts and stabilities of meaning.

Steven Shaviro[2]

The door of a landing craft opens, exposing the troops inside to a hail of machine-gun bullets. An extremely unsteady hand-held camera puts us in the thick of the mayhem on board, blood spots flecking the lens. Soldiers eventually scramble ashore under unremitting gunfire, cowering behind anti-tank obstacles in a surf that soon runs red with blood. The camera stays close and highly mobile, to dizzying effect, following the troops up the beach, most of them falling on the way. A cacophony of bullet impacts and explosions pounds oppressively in the ears. Gore and agonized suffering fills the screen on all sides. We are made to endure this painful spectacle, shot tightly in close and mid shots, for a solid 20 minutes, with only the briefest moments of respite, before moving into a quieter interlude in which one infantryman sobs. The opening D-Day landing sequence of Saving Private Ryan (1998) is an assault on the viewer almost as much as on the beaches of Normandy.

Another war epic, Apocalypse Now (1979), starts with a rather different kind of spectacle. A long shot of a line of jungle trees is held for a full minute. Helicopters drift lazily past the camera in the foreground, the beat of their rotors slowed to create a dream-like mood. Wisps of smoke start to rise from the foreground. Music builds slowly, The Doors reaching a climactic 'This is the end' as the tree-line erupts into giant plumes of flame. The camera pans to the right to reveal more burning jungle before the image dissolves into the face of Captain Willard (Martin Sheen) lying in a sweaty hotel bed. A series of double-exposures place the image of Willard over a background of flaming jungle as we are only gradually relocated from the world of Vietnam combat to that of his tortured consciousness.

What do these sequences have in common, as Hollywood spectacles, and what distinguishes them within that category? War, like space or 'action' defined more generally, is an arena that lends itself to the spectacular impact sought by many contemporary Hollywood films. But the spectacle of war can be presented in a variety of ways. *Saving Private Ryan* and *Apocalypse Now* might be defined as, respectively, spectacles of 'authenticity' and of the 'artistic imagination'. Warfare also offers another opportunity for a return to versions of the American 'frontier' experience. Such an observation is hardly unique in relation to films of the Vietnam war, almost all of which have been injected with heavy doses of frontier mythology. This is worth another look if only because of the force with which the mythic/ideological recuperation has been asserted in this instance. It might also be related more directly to the transformation of the 'reality' of the Vietnam war, and others, into cinematic spectacle. The imposition of so familiar a framework might leave the viewer free to enjoy the sensual pleasures of the spectacle without being greatly challenged by less comfortable implications.

Hollywood action movies are relatively free to indulge in all sorts of death and destruction, often amounting to miniature wars of their own, without any great concern about issues of historical veracity or responsibility. Spectacular films based on real conflicts face a rather different, critical, and often self-imposed, agenda. Particular demands have to be met if Hollywood products are to be treated as 'respectable' representations of war rather than more 'lowly' works of action-exploitation. Films such as *Rambo* (1985) and the *Missing in Action* series (from 1984) are placed on one side of this divide. *Saving Private Ryan* and *Apocalypse Now* are among war films that locate themselves on the 'higher' ground opposite, in keeping with an epic tradition including works such as *The Bridge on the River Kwai* (1957) and *The Longest Day* (1962). One way they do this is through the brand of spectacle offered. Another involves the structure and underlying patterns of narrative.

There are obvious differences between the action cinema examined in the previous chapter and more 'serious' or 'respectable' war films, but they have some things in common. *Saving Private Ryan* and *Apocalypse Now* offer similar pleasures in important respects, but packaged to appeal to viewers who might shun the allegedly more 'gratuitous' impact of the action cinema. 'Serious' war films offer spectacular impact that satisfies the more general requirements of contemporary Hollywood production while allowing both audiences and filmmakers to distinguish themselves from more 'disreputable' aspects of popular culture. A similar effort was made by James Cameron to associate *Titanic* with the romantic epic tradition of *Doctor Zhivago* (1965) rather than less prestigious displays of special effects or melodrama.

Saving Private Ryan: the spectacle of 'authenticity' vs. Hollywood's 'same old story'

The Normandy landing sequence from *Saving Private Ryan* makes its bid for respectability in the name, above all, of 'authenticity'. We are not meant to wallow in the glorious sensual experience of Hollywood-created warfare but to be stunned by a sense of what the 'real event' must have been like. A decision was taken to 'risk not entertaining anyone or not having anyone attend any of the performances',[3] proclaimed the director Steven Spielberg. Such is the carnage that the film allegedly ran the additional risk of earning an NC-17 rating in the United States, a category usually viewed as commercial suicide. Spielberg has the industrial power to take such 'risks', given his general clout and the fact that the film was made jointly by his own company DreamWorks and Paramount. The same is true to a lesser extent of Francis Ford Coppola's position as architect of *Apocalypse Now*, a production for which he retained financial responsibility. The industrial dimension is a key determinant of the availability of one aesthetic strategy or another, in this case the ability of the film-maker to depart from some of the most immediate concerns about the potential response of a large audience.

The impression of authenticity constructed by *Saving Private Ryan* is offered on at least two levels. Spielberg's comments suggest an attempt to create a degree of authenticity in the pro-filmic event, the action staged in front of the camera. The sequence includes digitally-composed special effects added in post-production, but many of the effects are 'physical', created in the staging, and having an impact on performers and crew. Working in the midst of thousands of physical special-effects explosions and 'bullet impacts' provides, according to this account, an experience something like that of the original combat situation. Unusually, for Spielberg, he did not draw up storyboards in advance and shot the Omaha Beach sequence 'in religious continuity'[4] to maintain the illusion of a series of events unfolding according to their own logic rather than choreographed in advance.

If *Saving Private Ryan* seeks to create an impression of reality for those involved in the production, the aim, of course, is to increase the 'authenticity' of their performances and of the overall experience for the viewer. The formal devices used by Spielberg are designed to force us to share certain aspects of the experience of going into combat. Some of these devices are similar to those used in the cinema of action spectacle. Rapid and unsteady camerawork serve much the same purpose in both cases. The main difference in the landing sequence from *Saving Private Ryan* is that such techniques are used in a deliberate effort to make the viewer uncomfortable. The experience is claustrophobic, with few long or establishing shots. The viewer has to wait some 15 minutes before being given a relatively long shot in which the action on the beach can be seen in the context of the sea and a few ships framed behind. it is not until 36 minutes into the film – by which time the beach landing sequence has given way to the development of the 'saving Private Ryan' plot back in the United States – that we are given a grand vista of the entire beach, the sea, barrage balloons overhead and dozens of ships. This contrasts with the usual regime of the action movie, in which assaults on the viewer by aggressive bursts of 'in your face' spectacle are tempered by regular cuts to more 'objective' seeming perspectives and often undercut by comic quips. During the landing the viewer's perspective is tightly integrated with that of the troops. One of the first images is what appears to be a point-of-view shot, looking unsteadily from one landing craft to another alongside. The hand-held camera creates the same effect throughout the sequence. It bobs up and down, above and below the surface of the water, along with disembarking troops dragged under by the weight of their equipment. It maintains a very low angle and jerky motion throughout most of the movement up the beach. Blood again spatters the lens as medics attempt to stanch the flow.

With the exception of a couple of shots from the position of German machine guns, our perspective remains that of the troops on the ground. When the troops are pinned down behind a low ridge of sand near the top of the beach, so is the camera, its viewpoint not privileged above that of the protagonists. A 'documentary' type of effect is created, in other words, as if the camera were carried by one of the troops engaged in the assault.

One of the sharpest contrasts between the Normandy landing in *Saving Private Ryan* and the action-movie sequences examined in the previous chapter is the relative absence of editing. Impact effects based on cutting are generally eschewed in favour of camera movement, thus maintaining a greater sense of the substance of the pro-filmic event. Rapidity of movement combines with other photographic techniques to create a kinetic impact and disorientation effect as powerful as action-montage. Increased shutter speeds remove the element of blurring inherent in conventional camerawork, creating a strobing effect, noticeable especially in some of the rapid camera movements (an effect directly opposite to that achieved in Spielberg's *Jurassic Park*, in which an illusion of authenticity is created by the deliberate addition of motion-blur).[5] The impression given is that the cinematic technology is unable to keep up with the pace and violence of the events.

Some of the techniques employed involve a deliberate 'handicapping' of the means of representation, a denial of the full scope of the cinematic apparatus. A technology such as the Steadicam, which permits highly fluid mobile camera movements, is replaced here by a reversion to the precise opposite: a patenting, almost, of the radically 'unsteadicam.'[6] The 'documentary' effect is heightened by processing techniques used to desaturate colour from the images, which have a brownish tone vaguely reminiscent of historical footage. Such techniques are carefully contrived, of course, and the overall effect depends on digital augmentation of both image and sound, the latter playing an important part in the impact the sequence has on the viewer. 'Authenticity' remains itself a special effect and, like all special effects, can be viewed both as an absorbing recreation of reality and as impressive special effect in its own right. The strategic intention in *Saving Private Ryan* appears to be to emphasize the former and downplay the latter, again in the name of cultural respectability. Too much enjoyment of the spectacle might damage the film's claim to be something more than 'gratuitous' entertainment. How this really plays is open to question. Should Spielberg's comments about being willing to lose viewers be taken at face value or be seen as part of a strategic effort to position the film in the marketplace, to claim attention and distinguish it from the more 'disreputable' style of action-adventure? Does the unrelenting nature of the spectacle make it genuinely uncomfortable, or just allow the viewer to enjoy the dizzying hyperreal spectacle freed from any feelings of guilt? It is not easy to answer such questions with any certainty, although the issues might be clarified by examining the location of the beach landing spectacle within the broader narrative structure of the film.

The beach landing is presented as something like a solid 'slab' of recreated reality, seeking to immerse the viewer in the appalling chaos of the events. But this is still a Hollywood production, so there is a limit to how far this can be taken. The beach landing is the experience of a mass of men. The film respects this up to a point, highlighting moments of the nightmare endured by a fairly large number of soldiers. The principal mediation remains that provided by the star system, however, and the convention of focusing on a small group of individuals.

From landing craft to secured beachhead, the sequence is organized centrally around the perspective of Captain John Miller (Tom Hanks) and a few immediate colleagues. Miller is the first figure to be picked out as an important individual, in an early shot of the trembling hand that will become a signifier of human fragility. His perspective is especially privileged in two early slow-motion sequences in which the oppressive noise of battle is drowned out by the distant roar of his interior consciousness. The emphasis on what might be taken to be a representative sample is institutionalized by the narrative frame when we are introduced to the particular (fictional) story isolated from the broader scale of (historical) events. Miller and a small team are to locate Private James Ryan (Matt Damon), one individual paratrooper among hundreds mistakenly scattered around the French countryside. His three brothers have been killed in action, earning him a ticket home in the interests of family and compassion. The bruising spectacle of the beach landing is followed by the establishment of the 'Ryan' narrative. An overhead pan across the dozens of bodies comes to rest on the bag carried on one soldier's back and imprinted with the name of one of the dead Ryan brothers. Harsh realistic spectacle is replaced by more familiar Hollywood fare as gently melodramatic music plays over the sequence in which the coincidence of the three Ryan deaths comes to light, the mother is informed and the Chief of Staff General Marshall quotes from Abraham Lincoln to justify his order for the mission to 'save' the surviving brother.

The move from general scenes of warfare to a story based on a few particular individuals is the stuff of familiar Hollywood narrative. *Saving Private Ryan* ends up playing very much by the book. The way it does this, however, is worth closer examination. The issue of the relationship between the bigger picture and that on which the film focuses is explicitly taken up within the narrative. The initial and sustained reaction of Miller and his crew is that the mission to 'save' Private Ryan is an absurdity, a sentimental gesture made by the brass that risks the lives of eight men in the hope of saving one. Two of them die before Ryan is located. Their criticisms of the mission could apply equally to the narrative focus selected by the film: the business of winning the war is more or less ignored in favour of a small detail of no direct relevance to the bigger picture. The painful impact of the beach landing sequence is replaced by the working through of more familiar combat movie conventions focusing on the relationships between a small group of men. A questioning of the sentimentality of heartstring-tugging devices focused on individuals seems also to be implied in the scene where one member of the patrol dies after ignoring Miller's order not to take a child handed down by anxious parents from the ruins of one of the towns through which they pass. The soldier takes a risk in order to do what he defines as 'the decent thing', to help get a child to safety for the sake of its parents: in some respects an echo of the plot of *Saving Private Ryan*.

There is a contradiction, then, within the film that can be read to some extent as questioning its own narrative structure, its own complicity in a deeply sentimental project. Sentimental concerns, based on an excessive focus on a few individuals, are opposed to the business of larger life-and-death statistics not so easily grasped at a personal-emotional level, and thus less easily accommodated by the usual Hollywood frame. This is an issue central to the positioning not just of this film but of Spielberg himself, a populist filmmaker who has sought greater 'respectability' and gravitas in the pursuit of avowedly 'serious' projects such as *Ryan*, *Schindler's List* (1993) and *Amistad* (1997).

Miller describes how he has to 'rationalize' the death of men under his command: 94 deaths mean saving the lives of 10 or 20 times as many. That is how he weighs up the balance between the mission and the men. In this case, he is reminded – as the tagline for the film has already informed us – the mission *is* a man, a glib phrase that seems to sidestep the issue. The film contrives a way to reconcile the opposition. The unease expressed about the narrative from within seems to be in the name of remaining loyal to the aesthetic of authenticity so prominently displayed in the recreation of the beach landing. Maybe this is what Spielberg means when he talks about the impact of the filming having 'reinformed' him in how he needed to tell the story. The movement of both narrative and spectacular dimensions of *Saving Private Ryan* is towards a reconciliation of the two. The film ends with an even longer sequence of spectacular warfare, a climactic battle that lasts a good 30 minutes. Rather than standing opposed to the conventions of Hollywood melodrama, however, this sequence manages to combine elements of conventional narrative and the spectacular-authentic.

Private Ryan is eventually found among a band of troops protecting a bridge that has become a key strategic point in the Allied campaign. He declines to leave his post, declaring that his comrades there are the only brothers he has left. Miller declares that they have crossed a strange boundary: 'The world has taken a turn for the surreal.' If anything, the opposite is the case: the world of the film takes a turn for the conventional. Miller is left with little choice but to add his men to the complement defending the bridge, turning the remainder of the narrative into a familiar 'last stand' affair in which the outnumbered rag-tag band holds out against an assault by a much larger enemy equipped with tanks. Improvised 'sticky bombs' are used to disable one of the German tanks blocking the main street and delaying the advance sufficiently to enable the 'cavalry' of US aircraft and troop reinforcements to save the day, although not before Miller is killed.

The battle is shot in much the same style as the earlier beach landing sequence. It is a bruising encounter, again, for both fictional characters and filmgoers, but the aesthetic of 'authenticity' plays rather differently when the event has been framed in terms so conventional that the last holdout is labelled 'the Alamo'. It does not seem to be a question of the formal devices simply validating the more familiarly conventional action, or the cliché detracting from the power of the spectacle. Instead, the two seem to coexist, sitting together rather awkwardly or offering some measure of reconciliation of two dynamics that appear to be in competition during much of the film. It would be wrong to suggest that the more disturbing and visceral aspects of the film, especially on the beach, are entirely or simply 'contained' by the narrative frame. The experience of film viewing does not lend itself to such neat formulations. Audio-visual spectacle can have resonances not so easily pinned down or balanced by other dimensions of the text. It is not a question of mathematical calculations or equations, but of certain tendencies towards a reconciliatory dynamic that combines the aesthetic of authenticity with a more familiar narrative context.

If reconciliation is offered in *Saving Private Ryan*, its tenor is influenced by a prologue/epilogue framework constructed around the principal action. The film opens with the present-day Ryan visiting the war graves with his family. It concludes with a return to the family group and Ryan's expression of emotion at the cross marking Miller's grave. Miller's dying words to Ryan are 'earn this', to make the sacrifice on his behalf worth while. That Ryan has succeeded in doing so is implied in the epilogue by the presence of the family group in the background. Ryan is anxious for reassurance that he has led 'a good life' and is 'a good man'. His wife replies: 'You are', and the framing of Ryan with what appears to be an ideal family group, together with his humility, encourages us to believe her. The values of 'family life', the enshrining of which underpinned the 'illogical' mission to save Private Ryan, return, in other words, to validate the entire project. That this should be seen as a move to recuperate any doubts established earlier in the film is supported by the extent to which the effort to 'make sense' of the mission is overdetermined. One justification is the future trajectory of Ryan's life, and it seems significant that this includes bringing into the world descendants who are part of the generation of moviegoers today.

This way of structuring into the text an appeal to target audiences is an important aspect of Hollywood production. *Saving Private Ryan* has an inbuilt appeal to an older audience, despite the criticism it received from some of those involved in the historical events, but it is also structured to appeal to younger viewers.

The way these appeals are negotiated is rather similar in *Saving Private Ryan* and *Armageddon*, a film more clearly targeted at a primarily youthful audience. In *Armageddon* the characters of AJ and Grace are probably closest in age and attitude to the primary target audience. A tension results from the way they are initially set up in opposition to the older figure played by Bruce Willis, who is clearly the star and an important element of the film's box-office appeal; a tension that the film is careful to work out and resolve. *Armageddon* ends with the death of the father figure – but one still young, vigorous and sexy enough to appeal to a youth audience – and the delirious union of the young couple.

Saving Private Ryan also ends with the sacrificial death of a star who stands in the text as a father figure – a schoolteacher and mentor to the younger of his charges – but also retains an appeal for the younger viewer. Figures like Willis and Hanks are 'mature' enough to play paternalistic roles while maintaining a sufficiently glamorous movie-star aura to appeal to younger generations to whose more immediate representatives in the films they might seem opposed.

Stars, as Richard Dyer suggests, can themselves effect the kind of 'magical' reconciliation of apparently irreconcilable terms that appears to be offered so often in the narrative dimension of Hollywood films.[7] This is important in industrial terms, especially to the efforts of Hollywood to keep up with changing audience demographics.[8] Centre stage in the epilogue to *Saving Private Ryan* is given to the elderly Ryan and his wife, but it is the younger generations of Ryans in the background – and, by implication, some of their contemporaries in the audience – who are offered implicitly as what made the mission of saving Ryan himself worthwhile. As we have seen, however, the film has already given the mission more than adequate justification. If Miller and his crew had not gone in search of Ryan, the bridge might not have been saved from German control. It is Miller who designs the strategy used to hold out against the overwhelming odds, to make their limited resource count. However inadvertently, the Ryan mission ends up playing an important part in securing a key military objective, precisely the kind of factor in the 'bigger picture' from which it seemed a distraction. The narrative of *Saving Private Ryan* ends up conforming to a familiar Hollywood D-Day invasion movie device: a focus on the 'vital bridge' that serves as a microcosm of the broader conflict.

Apocalypse Now: hallucinatory spectacle and the 'art' of darkness

If *Saving Private Ryan* makes its claim to 'serious' respectability through an appeal to the authenticity of its spectacle, however much qualified by the demands of Hollywood-style narrative, *Apocalypse Now* might be viewed in terms of 'art', a creative interpretation of reality brought about by an act of visionary 'genius'. The quotation marks put around terms like 'art' and 'genius' will suffice for the moment to indicate their problematic nature. The issue is less a matter of whether such labels are justified or appropriate than how these films appear to have tried to position themselves.

Apocalypse Now has been criticized for failing to provide anything like an 'authentic' portrayal of aspects of the Vietnam war, a dimension in which most representations of the conflict have been found wanting. Unlike Saving Private Ryan, Apocalypse Now gives little indication of ever having been intended to do such a thing. Vietnam appears to be little more than a backcloth for an exploration of supposedly more 'universal' questions about 'good' and 'evil', the problem of distinguishing between the two, and the 'nature' of 'man'. The film is based partly on Joseph Conrad's novel Heart of Darkness (1902), from which it gains the resonances of a literary-artistic work.

The spectacular dimension of Apocalypse Now also appears to be structured to establish associations with the world of visionary 'art' rather than a texture of 'surface' authenticity. The opening sequence makes use of the startling imagery of fireballs so important to the genre of action-spectacular, but uses it rather differently. For one thing, the location of these images is far from certain, especially on first viewing. In retrospect, they appear to be a flash-forward to the air-strikes that will be called down on the Cambodian village ruled by the renegade Colonel Kurtz (Marlon Brando) after his assassination by Captain Willard. The song line 'This is the end' might help to confirm such a reading, but none of this is very clear at the time of watching. Steven Shaviro's characterization of the cinematic experience as one in which perceptions can shift and slip beneath stabilities of meaning seems to have some purchase here, although the case can be overstated. It is by playing up such protean qualities that a work distinguishes itself from the commercial mainstream, a lesson learned by filmmakers such as Coppola from post-war European 'art' cinema.

Rather than as a clearly locatable example of action-destruction, or part of more concrete representation of the horrors of war, the opening of Apocalypse Now is presented in terms of Willard's uncertain subjective state: very much the stuff of the cinema of 'art' rather than that of popular escapism. The film itself can be located as a product of the 'Hollywood Renaissance' period, from the late 1960s until the mid-to-late 1970s, in which a combination of particular social and industrial factors created a measure of space for the deployment of such strategies by a group of 'auteur' filmmakers of which Coppola was a leading member.[9] The overlapping images and the increasingly strange, disorienting noises on the soundtrack designed by Walter Murch create a nightmarish impression sustained throughout much of the film. In one of the most celebrated sequences – or one of the most notorious, depending on the viewer's perspective – Willard hitches a ride with an 'Air Cavalry' helicopter-based unit that attacks an enemy village to the accompaniment of Wagner's 'Ride of the Valkyries'. This is grand big-screen spectacle, a spine-tingling sequence that uses its 'high art' point of reference to create in the viewer something like the thrill the attack offers to some of the American participants.

The spectacle offered by Apocalypse Now is often one of incongruity: Wagner and aerial attack; a Colonel Kilgore (Robert Duvall) who insists on a demonstration of the attractions of a good surfing beach while still under fire; a religious service conducted in the foreground while a mobile flamethrower spews out flames and the conflict continues behind; the spectacle of a USO performance by Playboy centrefolds on a stage erected in the middle of nowhere; the weird sounds and images of the Do Long bridge, a chaotic realm and apparently the farthest American outpost, beyond which Willard must continue his odyssey.

With the exception of a couple of sequences rendered into a nightmarish slow motion, the viewer of *Saving Private Ryan* is battered over the head during the spectacular battle sequences, sometimes barely able to keep up with the disorienting motion of the image. *Apocalypse Now* offers a more contemplative and allusively textured spectacle. The pace and rhythm is at times closer to the pole represented by *2001: A Space Odyssey* than any of the other examples considered so far. In both cases the viewer is invited to enjoy the sensuous pleasures of unhurried spectacle. In *Apocalypse Now* this often takes the form of elaborate tracking or crane shots in which the nightmarish panorama unfolds before our eyes. Both films also draw the viewer into what are styled as 'profound' disquisitions on the nature of humanity.

This is also a feature of *The Thin Red Line* (1998), a close contemporary of *Saving Private Ryan* and another striking example of the 'artistic' war epic. *The Thin Red Line* offers a bruising spectacle of warfare, sold partly in terms of the 'realism' of its battle sequences. Warfare is rendered harsh and brutal, but the movement of troops up a deadly hillside under the eyes of machine guns is also given seductive qualities in sweeping passes of the crane-mounted camera through long, wind-blown grass. Above all, the film sets out to establish 'artistic' credentials, through a complex, multi-character structure of focus and a series of allusive voice-overs and flashbacks giving access to interior states manifested often in highly 'literary' form. The specific events of the Guadalcanal campaign of 1942 are largely subordinated to the supposedly 'universal' question of the origin of evil, signified by the intrusion of war into a seemingly timeless Pacific island paradise.

If *Apocalypse Now* shares some characteristics with *2001: A Space Odyssey*, its narrative structure remains a good deal more explicit. Much of the narration is done overtly. An early briefing scene sets out Willard's mission to 'terminate' the irregular operations of Colonel Kurtz. Throughout the film we are given Willard's voice-over commentary, both his own observations of events and the contents of briefing materials on Kurtz. The movement of the film could be seen as an alternation between moments of narration, in this form, and moments of lavish spectacle. The forward-moving narrative dynamic of the mission is interrupted by a series of elaborate set-pieces. The two dimensions are rather more integrated than that might suggest, however. Willard's narration continues through some of the more spectacular set-pieces, and its tone often seems to contribute to the atmosphere of hallucinatory spectacle, especially in the later stages of the journey up-river. Narrative and spectacle seem to interpenetrate to a considerable extent, as befits one of the major themes of the film: the merging of exterior and interior journeys, Willard s mission into the jungle and the exploration of his own self on the way.

Apocalypse Now is without doubt a powerful example of cinematic spectacle, and as such very much a product of the Hollywood landscape of the late 1970s. The release included a 70 mm version and was among the first generation to take full advantage of the extra dimension offered by the latest advances in stereo sound. But the film is also heavily overdetermined by a range of narrative frames. It has the structure of a quest, a narrative form with a long tradition. The same is true to a lesser extent of *Saving Private Ryan*. Both films take the viewer on a journey across a wartime landscape of suffering and chaos in search of an object of uncertain value. In each case we are introduced along the way to examples of absurdity: the surfing incident in *Apocalypse Now*, for example, and in *Saving Private Ryan* a troop-carrying glider that crashed because it had been weighted down with steel plates bolted to the underside to protect the seat of a general.

The exploration of such diversions gives the narrative something of a picaresque quality, a format well suited to the inclusion of spectacular set-pieces. In *Apocalypse Now*, the quest is pursued towards darker extremes, while *Saving Private Ryan* finds a more recuperative escape. The familiar trope of the 'bridge mission' central to the more conventional dynamic of *Saving Private Ryan* is undercut in *Apocalypse Now*. The Do Long bridge is a signifier not of an important strategic objective, but of the absurdities of which the American effort in Vietnam was often accused: destroyed every night by the enemy and rebuilt each day just to enable the brass to say the road is open. Blowing up a bridge is the kind of 'heroic' behind-the-lines mission on which Willard is assumed to be engaged by a member of the boat crew assigned to take him up river, not the morally ambiguous task of assassinating an American officer.

Apocalypse Now has been widely criticized for an apparent narrative 'weakness' in its later stages at the jungle temple compound where Kurtz mutters darkly and quotes from Eliot's *The Hollow Men*. The film's literary-artistic aspirations are rather openly on display here, including what Gilbert Adair describes as the 'rather too artfully composed still-life shot' in which Kurtz's bedside reading is exhibited: Jessie Weston's *From Ritual to Romance*, an influence on the work of Eliot, and James Frazer's early anthropological classic, *The Golden Bough*.[10] What some take for a 'failure' of narrative might further strengthen the modernist or 'artistic' credentials of the film as a complex text that refuses to deliver the satisfaction of an immediate climactic pay-off. The narrative is crowded with mythical and literary illusion, including references to the Bible and to Dante's *Inferno*. The co-writer John Milius cites a list in which Willard is cast variously as Adam, Faust, Dante, Aeneas, Huckleberry Finn, Jesus Christ, the Ancient Mariner, Captain Ahab, Odysseus and Oedipus.[11] Willard's laconic voice-over adds to the mix the 'lower' cultural narrative forms of detective fiction and *film noir*.

The existence within *Apocalypse Now* of such a diversity of narrative frameworks and potential allusions has left the film open to a variety of readings. Michael Ryan and Douglas Kellner convict the film of expressing a 'quasi-fascist' version of conservative ideology.[12] The narrative focus, they suggest,

> is on Willard's progressive identification with Kurtz's power and ruthlessness and on his concomitant transformation into an effective warrior. The point is made, through Willard's increasing disgust with the ineptitude of the leaderless army and his admiration for Kurtz, that the latter's brand of authoritarian warrior leader is needed as a solution to the disarray of the war.[13]

Ryan and Kellner conclude that the confusion and doubt that characterize much of the film are eventually resolved into certainty and authority, through Willard's identification with Kurtz and his eventual acquisition of Kurtz's power. The 'meaning' of the film seems rather less stable than this suggests, however. Willard does grow increasingly to respect and to be intrigued by Kurtz. He finds it hard to see any clear distinction between warfare as practiced by 'madmen' such as Kurtz or the officially sanctioned Colonel Kilgore. A recognition of the moral ambiguity of all such judgements seems to characterize Willard's response more than any clear-cut process of identification with Kurtz. The landscape through which he travels offers images of chaos and of authoritarian leadership, neither of which appear to be endorsed unambiguously.

Apocalypse Now has it both ways, as Frank Tomasulo suggests, especially in terms of its political resonances. Ambiguity may be a quality often associated with complex works of art, but it can also be a feature of more popular cultural products that seek to appeal to large audiences by leaving themselves open to more than one reading. Such a requirement may have been particularly acute for a project such as *Apocalypse Now*, one of the first in a wave of films to deal directly with the contentious subject of the Vietnam war. Thus, for Tomasulo, the film 'is filled with double binds and mixed messages in its attempt to have it both ways'.[14] Many scenes 'depict the absurdity and outright lunacy of America's Vietnam policies, as well as the machinations of high-level military commanders'.[15] Other aspects of the content and style have the opposite effect. Tomasulo is not the only critic to have questioned the film on the grounds of the 'aestheticization of violence' in spectacular sequences such as Kilgore's helicopter attack, the structure of which he describes as implicating the audience cinematically 'in the exhilarating superiority of the American attack'.[16]

The sequence remains more ambiguous in some details, as both Tomasulo and Adair suggest. The village attacked is declared to 'belong' to the Viet Cong, yet it is shown immediately before the raid to be a peaceful place filled with schoolchildren. Kilgore's principal motivation for the assault is to put on a display of surfing, yet the village is shown after all to be armed and its population includes a woman who hides a grenade in her hat to destroy a helicopter picking up the American wounded. The sequence does indeed 'have it both ways', a pattern repeated through much of *Apocalypse Now*.

If the film is to be enjoyed primarily on the level of its spectacular attractions, it may be that one side of this equation will be favoured over the other. The thrill of the spectacle seems to override the impact of passing details such as the procession of schoolchildren glimpsed in the village square. This appears to be a more grand and upmarket version of the action spectacle, the 'higher' cultural tone of which – together with its location in a more 'serious' narrative framework – might make its enjoyment more acceptable to some audiences. The spectacle of combat might be inherently ambiguous. Combat sequences offer an exhilarating adrenalin rush, the implications of which cannot be determined by the nature of the spectacle alone, Claudia Springer suggests:

> they elicit both intellectual and heightened emotional responses, and spectators have to sort out their own responses based on their predispositions to the events represented. This would explain why it is possible for an antiwar viewer to praise a combat sequence for powerfully depicting the horrors of war, while another viewer might respond to the same film as if it were a wartime adventure filled with exciting action.[17]

The filmmaker who wants to present an antiwar statement has to do so clearly in the narrative dimension, 'for it has to compensate for the more ambiguous signifying system of spectacle'. The provision of large-scale spectacle is one way Hollywood films can avoid nailing their colours too clearly to any particular mast, since the visceral thrills offered can be open to multiple readings. The destruction of landmarks such as the White House or a famous Manhattan skyscraper might be a source of horror or of undisguised glee. Either response is available. If this ambiguity is a more general characteristic of cinematic spectacle, it is of particular relevance in such potentially controversial territory as representations of the war in Vietnam.

Overall, Tomasulo's conclusion on *Apocalypse Now* seems convincing: 'By subordinating content to style and foregrounding aesthetic ambiguity and richness, the director secondarized the ideological implications of a deeply political question – the Vietnam War.'[18]

Tomasulo criticizes Coppola on this ground, calling for a more 'forceful' and politically unambiguous statement about the war. This is all very well from a political point of view. *Apocalypse Now* is 'guilty' of substituting dehistoricized mythical resonances for any analysis of the more concrete realities of the Vietnam war. The reasons for this need to be understood, however. A rather muddy and ambiguous blend of narrative components and hallucinatory spectacle served two purposes rather well. It gave the film the aura of serious 'artistic' respectability while courting audiences by avoiding a commitment to any one political perspective on the war. Another source of this ambiguity may have been Coppola's own reported confusion during the production about where the film was headed, although the terms in which this has been expressed tend to underline the status of the film as the work of a tortured and visionary artist. . . . [19]

'The last stand'

Saving Private Ryan ends with a 'last stand', in which the heroes are heavily outnumbered by the enemy. This guarantees a spectacular set-piece battle, a climactic pay-off that is found in most examples of contemporary Hollywood spectacle, although denied to many viewers of *Apocalypse Now* as part of its more 'artistic' credentials (the film has been seen in versions with several different endings, only one of which ends explicitly with the fiery destruction of Kurtz's compound). Whatever narrative themes these films pursue they are more or less obliged to provide this kind of pay-off if they are to seek a position in the commercial mainstream. The importance of such imperatives in shaping this kind of cultural product should not be underestimated. In *Saving Private Ryan* the final battle is even more protracted than the earlier landing sequence. . . .

The 'last stand' supplies the necessary spectacular climax but is also a narrative device rich in associations with the American frontier experience. In its original shape, taken from the events at the Alamo in Texas in 1836 and Custer's fall at the Battle of Little Big Horn in 1876, the 'last stand' was a signifier of 'heroic failure'. As such it seems readily transferable to the mythic recuperation of American involvement in the Vietnam war. 'Heroic failure' is certainly a flattening way of conceptualizing American defeat in Vietnam. . . .

This lapse into solipsism is rather typical of the myopic perspective that appeared to play a part in the American defeat in Vietnam. The myth of the 'last stand' might be able to contribute towards the film's assertion that internal divisions can to some extent be overcome. That, in Richard Slotkin's reading, was one reason why Custer's 'Last Stand' gained such metaphorical power, becoming one of the most frequently depicted moments in American history. The 'Last Stand', Slotkin suggests, was open to different interpretations: 'The Conservative/Democratic tendency saw Custer as a martyr to Indian savagery empowered by soft-headed philanthropic liberalism; the radical/Republican tendency saw Custer as the "real savage" in his representation of the values of racial bigots and aficionados of violence.'[20] The 'last stand' provided a narrative framework within which different readings of the frontier experience could be unified. It is also important to note that the defeats at both the Alamo and Little Big Horn proved to be only temporary reverses against enemies that were soon defeated.

Metaphorical reworkings of the 'last stand' or the 'Alamo' complex are not new to Hollywood films set during the Second World War, but more usually associated with the early stages of war in the Pacific theatre, where American troops were forced to make strategic withdrawals in the face of a rapid Japanese advance. Classic examples include *Bataan* (1943) and *They Were Expendable* (1945). Why should the same image be found in *Saving Private Ryan*, a film set against the background of triumphant Allied advance into France? The initial forces landed on the beaches at Normandy are shown to take terrible losses, but this is no Dunkirk or Dieppe. The film depicts no real defeat, so why have recourse to mythic events whose value appears to be largely compensatory? *Saving Private Ryan*'s version of the 'last stand'/Alamo is important to the narrative development of the film, yoking the Ryan mission back into the bigger picture of the post D-Day historic events. But why a motif as specific and loaded as this? Maybe because it is the ultimate signifier of wartime heroics: the brave resistance of a small band against a superior force. In reality the Allied advance was not without its setbacks and serious difficulties, the dramatic stuff of more than one epic reconstruction in the cinema. The 'last stand' framework brings to this context an economical and clear-cut means of resolving the tensions among the characters. It also plays on broader aspects of frontier mythology, of course, pitting a resourceful band of individuals against an enemy equipped with tanks and other heavy weapons. The familiar framework, however contrived in this instance, makes an immediate sense in its own mythic/ ideological terms. While Miller appears to be just an ordinary solider, one of many caught up in the conflict, we should note that he is a Texas Ranger, and so ideally qualified to meet a heroic death at the Alamo.

These war films also establish narrative and spectacular dynamics around the opposition between the frontier-like world of 'last stands' and heightened experience and the sphere of the home and domesticity. Full-scale war offers on a much wider canvas the moments of extremity and dazzling spectacle around which the action film is constructed. In *Apocalypse Now* the tension between war and home is one that cannot be resolved. The young men on the boat crew want to find a way home, Willard observes: 'Trouble is, I've been back there and know it doesn't exist any more.' In Willard's case, to take on the role of the frontiersman is to be transformed, to lose all possibility of a comfortable return to, or relationship with, 'ordinary' life. In this respect he seems close to Kurtz, who pens a scrawled letter to his wife saying: 'Sell the house. Sell the car. Sell the kids. Find someone else. Forget it. I'm never coming back.'

This is another issue where *Saving Private Ryan* seems to offer a more positive recon- ciliation. Miller has repressed his domestic past when we join him and the others on their mission. This is emphasized through references to the pot of money that has accumulated into a betting pool to be scooped by the man who can uncover his background. His refusal to allow his men to be side-tracked into rescuing the French child appears to be part of a resolve to maintain a separation between the worlds of family/domesticity and warfare. Cracks in Miller's armour appear when he dies after one encounter with the enemy and in his shaking hand symptom. It is at the moment of maximum fragmentation among his men that Miller lets out the secret of his other self in the ordinary world. A confrontation at gunpoint arises during an argument about the fate of a German prisoner threatened with summary execution. Miller breaks it up by announcing, abruptly, that he is a teacher of English composition in a small town in Pennsylvania. A speech ensues in which he declares that he has been changed by his experience of war: 'Every man I kill, the farther away from home I feel.' The result of this, bringing the context of normal domesticity and home to bear on the situation, is an immediate resolution of the tension between the men. They combine, romantically backlit in silhouette, to bury a dead comrade.

The film foregrounds the hazardous and sometimes absurd heightened domain of warfare. At the same time, the absent domestic scene remains important, as in the action cinema, as an alternative pole, a point of orientation against which can be measured anything that might stray too far from the permissible limits of 'civilized' behaviour. The film presents numerous images of 'savage' killing, at a distance or close quarters. These are not explicitly condemned, but the implication is that they threaten the possibility of a return to the normality figured by domesticity. To suggest that some forms of violent killing between enemies might be more acceptable than others seems to gloss over a contradiction at the heart of any notion of 'civilized warfare'. The location of the domestic hearth at the absent core of a film like *Saving Private Ryan* might also be reassuring to any viewer facing a similar contradiction between the espousal of 'civilized' humanitarian values in everyday life and the enjoyment of spectacles of bloody devastation.

Notes

1 Ron Magid, 'Blood on the Beach', *American Cinematographer*, vol. 79, no. 12, December 1998, 62.
2 Steven Shaviro, *The Cinematic Body*, 32–3.
3 Magid, 'Blood on the Beach', 56.
4 'Blood on the Beach', 66.
5 I am grateful to Richard Franklin and Alan Miller for help in explaining the technical basis of this effect.
6 The association of such camerawork with authenticity has been established in home-video based 'reality' television and is exploited to similar effect in *The Blair Witch Project* (1999).
7 Richard Dyer, *Stars*, 30.
8 For an account of recent demographic trends and their impact on the inter-generation appeal of another kind of Hollywood product, see Robert Allen, 'Home Alone Together: Hollywood and the "family film"', in Melvyn Stokes and Richard Maltby (eds), *Identifying Hollywood's Audiences: Cultural Identity and the Movies*.
9 The degree of freedom granted to filmmakers such as Coppola was limited, in both time and extent. For a fuller discussion of these issues in relation to Coppola's career and the limitations of auteurist approaches to Hollywood, see Jon Lewis, *Whom God Wishes to Destroy: Francis Coppola and the New Hollywood*.
10 Gilbert Adair, *Hollywood's Vietnam*, 118.
11 Frank Tomasulo, 'The Politics of Ambivalence: *Apocalypse Now* as Prowar and Antiwar Film', in Linda Dittmar and Gene Michaud (eds), *From Hanoi to Hollywood: The Vietnam War in American Film*, 156.
12 *Camera Politica: The Politics and Ideology of Contemporary Hollywood Film*, 239.
13 *Camera Politica*, 238.
14 'The Politics of Ambivalence', 153.
15 'The Politics of Ambivalence', 149.
16 'The Politics of Ambivalence', 149.
17 'Antiwar Film as Spectacle: Contradictions of the Combat Sequence', *Genre*, XXI, Winter 1998, 484.

18 'The Politics of Ambivalence', 154.
19 See Eleanor Coppola's memoir, *Notes on the Making of* Apocalypse Now.
20 Richard Slotkin, *The Fatal Environment: The Myth of the Frontier in the Age of Industrialization, 1800–1890*, 501.

The Gulf War Did Not Take Place

24

JEAN BAUDRILLARD

Since this war was won in advance, we will never know what it would have been like had it existed. We will never know what an Iraqi taking part with a chance of fighting would have been like. We will never know what an American taking part with a chance of being beaten would have been like. We have seen what an ultra-modern process of electrocution is like, a process of paralysis or lobotomy of an experimental enemy away from the field of battle with no possibility of reaction. But this is not a war, any more than 10,000 tonnes of bombs per day is sufficient to make it a war. Any more than the direct transmission by CNN of real time information is sufficient to authenticate a war. One is reminded of *Capricorn One* in which the flight of a manned rocket to Mars, which only took place in a desert studio, was relayed live to all the television stations in the world.

It has been called a surgical war, and it is true that there is something in common between this *in vitro* destruction and *in vitro* fertilisation — the latter also produces a living being but it is not sufficient to produce a child. Except in the New Genetic Order, a child issues from sexual copulation. Except in the New World Order, war is born of an antagonistic, destructive but dual relation between two adversaries. This war is an asexual surgical war, a matter of war-processing in which the enemy only appears as a computerised target, just as sexual partners only appear as code-names on the screen of *Minitel Rose*. If we can speak of sex in the latter case then perhaps the Gulf War can pass for a war.

The Iraqis blow up civilian buildings in order to give the impression of a dirty war. The Americans disguise satellite information to give the impression of a clean war. Everything in *trompe l'oeil*! The final Iraqi ploy: to secretly evacuate Kuwait and thereby mock the great offensive. With hindsight, the Presidential Guard itself was perhaps only a mirage; in any case, it was exploited as such until the end. All this is no more than a stratagem and the war ended in general boredom, or worse in the feeling of having been duped. Iraqi boasting, American hypocrisy. It is as though there was a virus infecting this war from the beginning which emptied it of all credibility. It is perhaps because the two adversaries did not even confront each other face to face, the one lost in its virtual war won in advance, the other buried in its traditional war lost in advance. They never saw each other: when the Americans finally appeared behind their curtain of bombs the Iraqis had already disappeared behind their curtain of smoke . . .

The general effect is of a farce which we will not even have had time to applaud. The only escalation will have been in decoys, opening onto the final era of great confrontations which vanish in the mist. The events in Eastern Europe still gave the impression of a divine surprise. No such thing in the Gulf, where it is as though events were devoured in advance by the parasite virus, the retro-virus of history. This is why we could advance the hypothesis that this war would not take place. And now that it is over, we can realise at last that it did not take place.

It was buried for too long, whether in the concrete and sand Iraqi bunkers or in the Americans' electronic sky, or behind that other form of sepulchre, the chattering television screens. Today everything tends to go underground, including information in its informational bunkers. Even war has gone underground in order to survive. In this forum of war which is the Gulf, everything is hidden: the planes are hidden, the tanks are buried, Israel plays dead, the images are censored and all information is blockaded in the desert: only TV functions as a medium without a message, giving at last the image of pure television.

Like an animal, the war goes to ground. It hides in the sand, it hides in the sky. It is like the Iraqi planes: it knows that it has no chance if it surfaces. It awaits its hour . . . which will never come.

The Americans themselves are the vectors of this catalepsy. There is no question that the war came from their plan and its programmed unfolding. No question that, in their war, the Iraqis went to war. No question that the Other came from their computers. All reaction, even on their part (as we saw in the episode of the prisoners, which should have produced a violent reaction), all abreaction against the program, all improvisation is abolished (even the Israelis were muzzled). What is tested here in this foreclosure of the enemy, this experimental reclusion of war, is the future validity for the entire planet of this type of suffocating and machinic performance, virtual and relentless in its unfolding. In this perspective, war could not take place. There is no more room for war than for any form of living impulse.

War stripped of its passions, its phantasms, its finery, its veils, its violence, its images; war stripped bare by its technicians even, and then reclothed by them with all the artifices of electronics, as though with a second skin. But these too are a kind of decoy that technology sets up before itself. Saddam Hussein's decoys still aim to deceive the enemy, whereas the American technological decoy only aims to deceive itself. The first days of the lightning attack, dominated by this technological mystification, will remain one of the finest bluffs, one of the finest collective mirages of contemporary History (along with Timisoara). We are all accomplices in these fantasmagoria, it must be said, as we are in any publicity campaign. In the past, the unemployed constituted the reserve army of Capital; today, in our enslavement to information, we constitute the reserve army of all planetary mystifications.

Saddam constructed his entire war as a decoy (whether deliberately or not), including the decoy of defeat which even more resembles a hysterical syncope of the type: peek-a-boo, I am no longer there! But the Americans also constructed their affair as a decoy, like a parabolic mirror of their own power, taking no account of what was before them, or hallucinating those opposite to be a threat of comparable size to themselves: otherwise they would not even have been able to believe in their own victory. Their victory itself in the form of a triumphal decoy echoes the Iraqi decoy of defeat. Ultimately, both were accomplices as thick as thieves, and we were collectively abused. This is why the war remains indefinable and ungraspable, all strategy having given way to stratagem.

One of the two adversaries is a rug salesman, the other an arms salesman: they have neither the same logic nor the same strategy, even though they are both crooks. There is not enough communication between them to enable them to make war upon each other. Saddam will never fight, while the Americans will fight against a fictive double on screen. They see Saddam as he should be, a modernist hero, worth defeating (the fourth biggest army in the world!). Saddam remains a rug salesman who takes the Americans for rug salesmen like himself, stronger than he but less gifted for the scam. He hears nothing of deterrence. For there to be deterrence, there must be communication. It is a game of rational strategy which presupposes real time communication between the two adversaries; whereas in this war there was never communication at any moment, but always dislocation in time, Saddam evolving in a long time, that of blackmail, of procrastination, false advance, of retreat: the recurrent time of *The Thousand and One Nights* — exactly the inverse of real time. Deterrence in fact presupposes a virtual escalation between the two adversaries. By contrast, Saddam's entire strategy rests upon de-escalation (one sets a maximal price then descends from it in stages). And their respective denouements are not at all the same. The failure of the sales pitch is marked by evasive action: the salesman rolls up his rug and leaves. Thus, Saddam disappears without further ado. The failure of deterrence is marked by force: this is the case with the Americans. Once again, there is no relation between the two, each plays in his own space and misses the other. We cannot even say that the Americans defeated Saddam: he defaulted on them, he de-escalated and they were not able to escalate sufficiently to destroy him.

Finally, who could have rendered more service to everyone, in such a short time at such little cost, than Saddam Hussein? He reinforced the security of Israel (reflux of the Intifada, revival of world opinion for Israel), assured the glory of American arms, gave Gorbachev a political chance, opened the door to Iran and Shiism, relaunched the UN, etc., all for free since he alone paid the price of blood. Can we conceive of so admirable a man? And he did not even fall! He remains a hero for the Arab masses. It is as though he were an agent of the CIA disguised as Saladin.

Resist the probability of any image or information whatever. Be more virtual than events themselves, do not seek to re-establish the truth, we do not have the means, but do not be duped, and to that end re-immerse the war and all information in the virtuality from whence they come. Turn deterrence back against itself. Be meteorologically sensitive to stupidity.

In the case of this war, it is a question of the living illustration of an implacable logic which renders us incapable of envisaging any hypothesis other than that of its real occurrence. The realist logic which lives on the illusion of the final result. The denial of the facts is never one of them. The final resolution of an equation as complex as a war is never immediately apparent in the war. It is a question of seizing the logic of its unfolding, in the absence of any prophetic illusion. To be for or against the war is idiotic if the question of the very probability of this war, its credibility or degree of reality has not been raised even for a moment. All political and ideological speculations fall under mental deterrence (stupidity). By virtue of their immediate consensus on the evidence they feed the unreality of this war, they reinforce its bluff by their unconscious dupery.

The real warmongers are those who live on the ideology of the veracity of this war, while the war itself wreaks its havoc at another level by trickery, hyperreality, simulacra, and by the entire mental strategy of deterrence which is played out in the facts and in the images, in the anticipation of the real by the virtual, of the event by virtual time, and in the inexorable confusion of the two. All those who understand nothing of this involuntarily reinforce this halo of bluff which surrounds us.

It is as though the Iraqis were electrocuted, lobotomised, running towards the television journalists in order to surrender or immobilised beside their tanks, not even demoralised: de-cerebralised, stupefied rather than defeated — can this be called a war? Today we see the shreds of this war rot in the desert just like the shreds of the map in Borges' fable rotting at the four corners of the territory (moreover, strangely, he situates his fable in the same oriental regions of the Empire).

Fake war, deceptive war, not even the illusion but the disillusion of war, linked not only to defensive calculation, which translates into the monstrous prophylaxis of this military machine, but also to the mental disillusion of the combatants themselves, and to the global disillusion of everyone else by means of information. For deterrence is a total machine (it is the true war machine), and it not only operates at the heart of the event — where electronic coverage of the war devoured time and space, where virtuality (the decoy, programming, the anticipation of the end) devoured all the oxygen of war like a fuel-air explosive bomb — it also operates in our heads. Information has a profound function of deception. It matters little what it "informs" us about, its "coverage" of events matters little since it is precisely no more than a cover: its purpose is to produce consensus by flat encephalogram. The complement of the unconditional simulacrum in the field is to train everyone in the unconditional reception of broadcast simulacra. Abolish any intelligence of the event. The result is a suffocating atmosphere of deception and stupidity. And if people are vaguely aware of being caught up in this appeasement and this disillusion by images, they swallow the deception and remain fascinated by the evidence of the montage of this war with which we are inoculated everywhere: through the eyes, the senses and in discourse.

There are ironic balance sheets which help to temper the shock or the bluff of this war. A simple calculation shows that, of the 500,000 American soldiers involved during the seven months of operations in the Gulf, three times as many would have died from road accidents alone had they stayed in civilian life. Should we consider multiplying clean wars in order to reduce the murderous death toll of peacetime?

On this basis, we could develop a philosophy of perverse effects, which we tend to regard as always maleficent whereas in fact maleficent causes (war, illness, viruses) often produce beneficial perverse effects. They are no less perverse as a result, but more interesting than the others, in particular because it has been a matter of principle never to study them. Except for Mandeville, of course, in *The Fable of the Bees*, where he shows that every society prospers on the basis of its vices. But the course of events has drawn us further and further away from an intelligence of this order.

An example: deterrence itself. It only functions well between equal forces. Ideally, each party should possess the same weapons before agreeing to renounce their use. It is therefore the dissemination of (atomic) weapons alone which can ensure effective global deterrence and the indefinite suspension of war. The present politics of non-dissemination plays with fire: there will always be enough madmen to launch an archaic challenge below the level of an atomic riposte — witness Saddam. Things being as they are, we should place our hopes in the spread of weapons rather than in their (never respected) limitation. Here too, the beneficial perverse effect of dissemination should be taken into account. We should escalate in the virtual (of destruction) under penalty of de-escalating in the real. This is the paradox of deterrence. It is like information, culture or other material and spiritual goods: only their profusion renders them indifferent and neutralises their negative perverse effects. Multiply vices in order to ensure the collective good.

That said, the consequences of what did not take place may be as substantial as those of an historical event. The hypothesis would be that, in the case of the Gulf War as in the case of the events in Eastern Europe, we are no longer dealing with "historical events" but with places of collapse. Eastern Europe saw the collapse of communism, the construction of which had indeed been an historic event, borne by a vision of the world and a utopia. By contrast, its collapse is borne by nothing and bears nothing, but only opens onto a confused desert left vacant by the retreat of history and immediately invaded by its refuse.

The Gulf War is also a place of collapse, a virtual and meticulous operation which leaves the same impression of a non-event where the military confrontation fell short and where no political power proved itself. The collapse of Iraq and stupefaction of the Arab world are the consequences of a confrontation which did not take place and which undoubtedly never could take place. But this non-war in the form of a victory also consecrates the Western political collapse throughout the Middle East, incapable even of eliminating Saddam and of imagining or imposing anything apart from this new desert and police order called world order.

As a consequence of this non-event and living proof of Western political weakness, Saddam is indeed still there, once again what he always was, the mercenary of the West, deserving punishment for not remaining in his place, but also worthy of continuing to gas the Kurds and the Shiites since he had the tact not to employ these weapons against those Western dogs, and worthy of keeping his Presidential Guard since he had the heart to not sacrifice them in combat. Miraculously (they were thought to have been destroyed), the Presidential Guard recovers all its valour against the insurgents. Moreover, it is typical of Saddam to prove his combativity and ferocity only against his internal enemies: as with every true dictator, the ultimate end of politics, carefully masked elsewhere by the effects of democracy, is to maintain control of one's own people by any means, including terror. This function embodied by dictatorships — that of being politically revealing and at the same time an alibi for democracies — no doubt explains the inexplicable weakness of the large powers towards them. Saddam liquidates the communists, Moscow flirts even more with him; he gasses the Kurds, it is not held against him: he eliminates the religious cadres, the whole of Islam makes peace with him. Whence this impunity? Why are we content to inflict a perfect semblance of military defeat upon him in exchange for a perfect semblance of victory for the Americans? This ignominious remounting of Saddam, replacing him in the saddle after his clown act at the head of the holy war, clearly shows that on all sides the war is considered not to have taken place. Even the last phase of this armed mystification will have changed nothing, for the 100,000 Iraqi dead will only have been the final decoy that Saddam will have sacrificed, the blood money paid in forfeit according to a calculated equivalence, in order to conserve his power. What is worse is that these dead still serve as an alibi for those who do not want to have been excited for nothing, nor to have been had for nothing: at least the dead would prove that this war was indeed a war and not a shameful and pointless hoax, a programmed and melodramatic version of what was the drama of war (Marx once spoke of this second, melodramatic version of a primary event). But we can rest assured that the next soap opera in this genre will enjoy an even fresher and more joyful credulity.

What a job Saddam has done for the Americans, from his combat with Iran up to this full scale debacle! Nevertheless, everything is ambiguous since this collapse removes any demonstrative value from American power, along with any belief in the Western ideologies of modernity, democracy, or secularity, of which Saddam had been made the incarnation in the Arab world.

We can see that the Western powers dreamt of an Islamic perestroika, on the newly formed model of Eastern Europe: democracy irresistibly establishing itself in those countries conquered by the forces of Good. The Arab countries will be liberated (the peoples cannot but want to be liberated), and the women of Saudi Arabia will have the right to drive. Alas! this is not to be. The conquered have not been convinced and have withdrawn, leaving the victors only the bitter taste of an unreal made-to-order victory. Defeat can also be a rival bid and a new beginning, the chain of implication never stops. The eventual outcome is unpredictable and certainly will not be reckoned in terms of freedom.

No accidents occurred in this war, everything unfolded according to programmatic order, in the absence of passional disorder. Nothing occurred which would have metamorphosed events into a duel.

Even the status of the deaths may be questioned, on both sides. The minimal losses of the coalition pose a serious problem, which never arose in any earlier war. The paltry number of deaths may be cause for self-congratulation, but nothing will prevent this figure being paltry. Strangely, a war without victims does not seem like a real war but rather the prefiguration of an experimental, blank war, or a war even more inhuman because it is without human losses. No heroes on the other side either, where death was most often that of sacrificed extras, left as cover in the trenches of Kuwait, or civilians serving as bait and martyrs for the dirty war. Disappeared, abandoned to their lot, in the thick fog of war, held in utter contempt by their chief, without even the collective glory of a number (we do not know how many they are).

Along with the hostage or the repentant, the figure of the "disappeared" has become emblematic in our political universe. Before, there were the dead and traitors, now there are the disappeared and the repentant: both blanks. Even the dead are blanks: "We have already buried them, they can no longer be counted," *dixit* Schwarzkopf. At Timisoara, there were too many of them, here there are not enough, but the effect is the same. The non-will to know is part of the non-war. Lies and shame appeared throughout this war like a sexually transmitted disease.

Blank out the war. Just as Kuwait and Iraq were rebuilt before they were destroyed, so at every phase of this war things unfolded as though they were virtually completed. It is not for lack of brandishing the threat of a chemical war, a bloody war, a world war — everyone had their say — as though it were necessary to give ourselves a fright, to maintain everyone in a state of erection for fear of seeing the flaccid member of war fall down. This futile masturbation was the delight of all the TVs. Ordinarily we denounce this kind of behaviour as emphatic or as empty and theatrical affectation: why not denounce an entire event when it is affected by the same hysteria?

In many respects, this war was a scandal of the same type as Timisoara. Not so much the war itself but the manipulation of minds and blackmail by the scenario. The worst scandal being the collective demand for intoxication, the complicity of all in the effects of war, the effects of reality and false transparency in this war. We could almost speak of media harassment along the lines of sexual harassment. Alas! the problem always remains the same and it is insoluble: where does real violence begin, where does consenting violence end? Bluff and information serve as aphrodisiacs for war, just as the corpses at Timisoara and their global diffusion served as aphrodisiacs for the Romanian revolution.

But, ultimately, what have you got against aphrodisiacs? Nothing so long as orgasm is attained. The media mix has become the prerequisite to any orgasmic event. We need it precisely because the event escapes us, because conviction escapes us. We have a pressing need of simulation, even that of war, much more than we have of milk, jam or liberty, and we have an immediate intuition of the means necessary to obtain it. This is indeed the fundamental advance of our democracy: the image-function, the blackmail-function, the information-function, the speculation-function. The obscene aphrodisiac function fulfilled by the decoy of the event, by the decoy of war. Drug-function.

We have neither need of nor the taste for real drama or real war. What we require is the aphrodisiac spice of the multiplication of fakes and the hallucination of violence, for we have a hallucinogenic pleasure in all things, which, as in the case of drugs, is also the pleasure in our indifference and our irresponsibility and thus in our true liberty. Here is the supreme form of democracy. Through it our definitive retreat from the world takes shape: the pleasure of mental speculation in images equalling that of capital in a stock market run, or that of the corpses in the charnel house of Timisoara. But, ultimately, what have you got against drugs?

Nothing. Apart from fact that the collective disillusion is terrible once the spell is broken; for example, when the corpses at Timisoara were uncovered, or when awareness of the subterfuge of the war takes hold. The scandal today is no longer in the assault on moral values but in the assault on the reality principle. The profound scandal which hereafter infects the whole sphere of information with a Timisoara-complex lay in the compulsory participation of the corpses, the transformation of the corpses into extras which in the same moment transforms all those who saw and believed in it into compulsory extras, so that they themselves become corpses in the charnel house of news signs. The odium lies in the malversation of the real, the faking of the event and the malversation of the war. The charnel houses of Timisoara are such a parody, so paltry by contrast with the real slaughterhouses of history! This Gulf War is such a sham, so paltry: the point is not to rehabilitate other wars, but rather that the recourse to the same pathos is all the more odious when there is no longer even the alibi of a war.

The presumption of information and the media here doubles the political arrogance of the Western empire. All those journalists who set themselves up as bearers of the universal conscience, all those presenters who set themselves up as strategists, all the while overwhelming us with a flood of useless images. Emotional blackmail by massacre, fraud.

Instead of discussing the threshold of social tolerance for immigration we would do better to discuss the threshold of mental tolerance for information. With regard to the latter, we can say that it was deliberately crossed.

The delirious spectacle of wars which never happened: the transparent glacier of flights which never flew. All these events, from Eastern Europe or from the Gulf, which under the colours of war and liberation led only to political and historical disillusionment (it seems that the famous Chinese Cultural Revolution was the same: a whole strategy of more or less concerted internal destabilisation which short-circuited popular spontaneity), post-synchronisation events where one has the impression of never having seen the original. Bad actors, bad doubles, bad striptease: throughout these seven months, the war has unfolded like a long striptease, following the calculated escalation of undressing and approaching the incandescent point of explosion (like that of erotic effusion) but at the same time with-drawing from it and maintaining a deceptive suspense (teasing), such that when the naked body finally appears, it is no longer naked, desire no longer exists and the orgasm is cut short. In this manner, the escalation was administered to us by drip-feed, removing us further and further from the passage to action and, in any case, from the war. It is like truth according to Nietzsche: we no longer believe that the truth is true when all its veils have been removed. Similarly, we do not believe that war is war when all uncertainty is supposedly removed and it appears as a naked operation. The nudity of war is no less virtual than that of the erotic body in the apparatus of striptease.

On the slopes at Courchevel, the news from the Gulf War is relayed by loudspeakers during the intensive bombardments. Did the others over there, the Iraqis in the sand bunkers receive the snow reports from Courchevel?

February 22 was the day of the Apocalypse: the day of the unleashing of the land offensive behind its curtain of bombs, and in France, by a kind of black humour, the day of the worst traffic jam on the autoroutes to the snow. While the tanks advanced to the assault on Kuwait, the automobile hordes advanced to the assault on the snowfields. Moreover, the tanks went through much more easily than the waves of leisure-seekers. And the dead were more numerous on the snow front than on the war front. Are we so lacking in death, even in time of war, that it must be sought on the playing fields?

Stuck in traffic, one can always amuse oneself by listening to the Gulf radio reports: the time of information never stops, the slower things are on the roads the more things circulate on the wavelengths. Another distraction was that of the young couple who switched between watching the war on TV and their child to be, filmed and recorded in the mother's womb and made available on ultrasound cassette. When the war stops, they watch the kid. At the level of images it is the same combat: war before it has broken out, the child before it has been born. Leisure in the virtual era.

The liquidation of the Shiites and the Kurds by Saddam under the benevolent eye of the American divisions mysteriously stopped in their lightning advance "in order not to humiliate an entire people" offers a bloody analogy with the crushing of the Paris Commune in 1871 under the eye of the Prussian armies. And the good souls who cried out for seven months, for or against the war but always for the good cause, those who denounced the aberrations of the pro-Iraqi policy ten years after the event when it was no longer relevant, and all the repentants of the Rights of Man, once again do nothing. The world accepts this as the wages of defeat, or rather, on the American side, as the wages of victory. The same Americans who, after having dumped hundreds of thousands of tonnes of bombs, today claim to abstain from "intervening in the internal affairs of a State."

It is nevertheless admirable that we call the Arabs and Moslems traditionalists with the same repulsion that we call someone racist, even though we live in a typically traditionalist society although one simultaneously on the way to disintegration. We do not practise hard fundamentalist traditionalism, we practise soft, subtle and shameful democratic tradition-alism by consensus. However, consensual traditionalism (that of the Enlightenment, the Rights of Man, the Left in power, the repentant intellectual and sentimental humanism) is every bit as fierce as that of any tribal religion or primitive society.

It denounces the other as absolute Evil in exactly the same manner (these are the words of François Mitterrand apropos the Salman Rushdie affair: whence does he derive such an archaic form of thought?). The difference between the two traditionalisms (hard and soft) lies in the fact that our own (the soft) holds all the means to destroy the other and does not resile from their use. As though by chance, it is always the Enlightenment fundamen-talist who oppresses and destroys the other, who can only defy it symbolically. In order to justify ourselves, we give substance to the threat by turning the *fatwa* against Salman Rushdie into a sword of Damocles hanging over the Western world, sustaining a dispropor-tionate terror in complete misrecognition of the difference between symbolic challenge and technical aggression. In the long run, the symbolic challenge is more serious than a victorious aggression. If a simple *fatwa*, a simple death sentence can plunge the West into such depression (the vaudeville of terror on the part of writers and intellectuals on this occasion could never be portrayed cruelly enough), if the West prefers to believe in this threat, it is because it is paralysed by its own power, in which it does not believe, pre-cisely because of its enormity (the Islamic "neurosis" would be due to the excessive tension created by the disproportion of ends; the disproportion of means from which we suffer creates by contrast a serious depression, a neurosis of powerlessness). If the West believed in its own power, it would not give a moment's thought to this threat. The most amusing aspect, however, is that the other does not believe in his powerlessness either, and he who does not believe in his powerlessness is stronger than he who does not believe in his power, be this a thousand times greater. The Arab *Book of Ruses* gives a thousand examples of this, but the West has no intelligence of such matters.

This is how we arrive at an unreal war in which the over-dimensioned technical power in turn over-evaluates the real forces of an enemy which it cannot see. And if it is astonished when it so easily triumphs this is because it knows neither how to believe in itself nor how to ruse with itself. By contrast, what it does know obscurely is that in its present form it can be annihilated by the least ruse.

The Americans would do well to be more astonished at their "victory," to be astonished at their force and to find an equivalent for it in the intelligence (of the other), lest their power play tricks with them. Thus, if the cunning but stupid Saddam had conceded one week earlier, he would have inflicted a considerable political defeat on the Americans. But did he want to? In any case, he succeeded in his own reinstatement, whereas they had sworn to destroy him. But did they swear it? Saddam played the Americans' game at every turn, but even defeated he was the better player at ruse and diversion. The *Book of Ruses* still harbours many secrets unknown to the Pentagon.

Brecht: "This beer isn't a beer, but that is compensated for by the fact that this cigar isn't a cigar either. If this beer wasn't a beer and this cigar really was a cigar, then there would be a problem." In the same manner, this war is not a war, but this is compensated for by the fact that information is not information either. Thus everything is in order. If this war had not been a war and the images had been real images, there would have been a problem. For in that case the non-war would have appeared for what it is: a scandal. Similarly, if the war had been a real war and the information had not been information, this non-information would have appeared for what it is: a scandal. In both cases, there would have been a problem.

There is one further problem for those who believe that this war took place: how is it that a real war did not generate real images? Same problem for those who believe in the Americans' "victory": how is it that Saddam is still there as though nothing had happened?

Whereas everything becomes coherent if we suppose that, given this victory was not a victory, the defeat of Saddam was not a defeat either. Everything evens out and everything is in order: the war, the victory and the defeat are all equally unreal, equally non-existent. The same coherence in the irreality of the adversaries: the fact that the Americans *never saw* the Iraqis is compensated for by the fact that the Iraqis never fought them.

Brecht again: "As for the place not desired, there is something there and that's disorder. As for the desired place, there is nothing there and that's order."

The New World Order is made up of all these compensations and the fact that there is nothing rather than something, on the ground, on the screens, in our heads: consensus by deterrence. At the desired place (the Gulf), nothing took place, non-war. At the desired place (TV, information), nothing took place, no images, nothing but filler. Not much took place in all our heads either, and that too is in order. The fact that there was nothing at this or that desired place was harmoniously compensated for by the fact that there was nothing elsewhere either. In this manner, the global order unifies all the partial orders.

In Eastern Europe, global order was re-established in accordance with the same paradoxical dialectic: where there was something (communism, but this was precisely disorder from a global point of view), today there is nothing, but there is order. Things are in democratic order, even if they are in the worst confusion.

The Arabs: there where they should not be (immigrants), there is disorder. There where they should be (in Palestine) but are not, there is order. The fact that in the Arab world nothing is possible, not even war, and that Arabs are deterred, disappointed, powerless and neutralised, that is order. But this is harmoniously compensated for by the fact that at the marked place of power (America), there is no longer anything but a total political powerlessness.

Such is the New World Order.

A variant on Clausewitz: *non-war is the absence of politics pursued by other means* . . . It no longer proceeds from a political will to dominate or from a vital impulsion or an antagonistic violence, but from the will to impose a general consensus by deterrence. This consensual violence can be as deadly as conflictual violence, but its aim is to overcome any hegemonic rivalry, even when cold and balanced by terror, as it has been over the last forty years. It was already at work in all the democracies taken one by one; it operates today on a global level which is conceived as an immense democracy governed by a homogeneous order which has as its emblem the UN and the Rights of Man. The Gulf War is the first consensual war, the first war conducted legally and globally with a view to putting an end to war and liquidating any confrontation likely to threaten the henceforward unified system of control. This was already the aim of dualistic (East and West) deterrence; today we pass to the monopolistic stage under the aegis of American power. Logically, this democratic and consensual form should be able to dispense with war, but it will no doubt continue to have local and episodic need of it. The Gulf War is one of these transitive episodes, hesitating for this reason between hard and soft forms: virtual war or real war? But the balance is in the process of definitively inclining in one direction, and tomorrow there will be nothing but the virtual violence of consensus, the simultaneity in real time of the global consensus: this will happen tomorrow and it will be the beginning of a world with no tomorrow.

Electronic war no longer has any political objective strictly speaking: it functions as a preventative electroshock against any future conflict. Just as in modern communication there is no longer any interlocutor, so in this electronic war there is no longer any enemy, there is only a refractory element which must be neutralised and consensualised. This is what the Americans seek to do, these missionary people bearing electroshocks which will shepherd everybody towards democracy. It is therefore pointless to question the political aims of this war: the only (transpolitical) aim is to align everybody with the global lowest common denominator, the democratic denominator (which, in its extension, approaches ever closer to the degree zero of politics). The lowest common multiplier being information in all its forms, which as it extends towards infinity, also approaches ever closer to the degree zero of its content.

In this sense, consensus as the degree zero of democracy and information as the degree zero of opinion are in total affinity: the New World Order will be both consensual and televisual. That is indeed why the targeted bombings carefully avoided the Iraqi television antennae (which stand out like a sore thumb in the sky over Baghdad). War is no longer what it used to be . . .

The crucial stake, the decisive stake in this whole affair is the consensual reduction of Islam to the global order. Not to destroy but to domesticate it, by whatever means: modernisation, even military, politicisation, nationalism, democracy, the Rights of Man, anything at all to electrocute the resistances and the symbolic challenge that Islam represents for the entire West. There is no miracle, the confrontation will last as long as this process has not reached its term: by contrast, it will stop as though of its own accord the day when this form of radical challenge has been liquidated. This was how it happened in the Vietnam war: the day when China was neutralised, when the "wild" Vietnam with its forces of liberation and revolt was replaced by a truly bureaucratic and military organisation capable of ensuring the continuation of Order, the Vietnam war stopped immediately — but ten years were necessary for this political domestication to take place (whether it took place under communism or democracy is of no importance). Same thing with the Algerian war: its end, which was believed to be impossible, took place of its own accord, not by virtue of De Gaulle's sagacity, but from the moment the maquis with their revolutionary potential were finally liquidated and an Algerian army and a bureaucracy, which had been set up in Tunisia without ever engaging in combat, were in a position to ensure the continuation of power and the exercise of order.

Our wars thus have less to do with the confrontation of warriors than with the domestication of the refractory forces on the planet, those uncontrollable elements as the police would say, to which belong not only Islam in its entirety but wild ethnic groups, minority languages etc. All that is singular and irreducible must be reduced and absorbed. This is the law of democracy and the New World Order. In this sense, the Iran-Iraq war was a successful first phase: Iraq served to liquidate the most radical form of the anti-Western challenge, even though it never defeated it.

The fact that this mercenary prowess should give rise to the present reversal and to the necessity of its own destruction is a cruel irony, but perfectly justified. We will have shamefully merited everything which happens to us. This does not excuse Iraq, which remains the objective accomplice of the West, even in the present confrontation, to the extent that the challenge of Islam, with its irreducible and dangerous alterity and symbolic challenge, has once again been channelled, subtilised and politically, militarily and religiously deflected by Saddam's undertaking. Even in the war against the West he played his role in the domestication of an Islam for which he has no use. His elimination, if it should take place, will only raise a dangerous mortgage. The real stake, the challenge of Islam and behind it that of all the forms of culture refractory to the occidental world, remains intact. Nobody knows who will win. For as Hölderlin said. "where danger threatens, that which saves us from it also grows." As a result, the more the hegemony of the global consensus is reinforced, the greater the risk, or the chances, of its collapse.

In the Combat Zone

25

MARILYN YOUNG

Saving Private Ryan, directed by Steven Spielberg. Dreamworks, 1998.

Pearl Harbor, directed by Jerry Bruckheimer. Buena Vista Home Entertainment, 2001.

Black Hawk Down, directed by Ridley Scott. Columbia Pictures, 2001.

We Were Soldiers, directed by Randall Wallace. Paramount Pictures, 2002.

In the aftermath of the U.S. victory in the Gulf War, the first president George Bush was optimistic that the country had "kicked the Vietnam syndrome." But the syndrome continued to manifest itself in the popular imagination of war. The *Rambo* series had tried to reverse the verdict of defeat, but it left standing the public conviction that Vietnam was not a good war. Despite a victory intended to vanquish the memory of Vietnam, the only notable movies made about Desert Storm—*Courage Under Fire* (dir. Edward Zwick, 1996) and *Three Kings* (dir. David O. Russell, 1999)—were haunted by it. *Courage Under Fire*, in its insistence that post-Vietnam America must have heroes, underlined their absence. *Three Kings* explains why, opening with black-and-white text informing us that the war is over, even as a soldier shouts the question: "Hey! Are we still killing people?" No one seems to know the answer. The soldier peers through the scope on his gun and sees an Iraqi on a distant hilltop, white flag in one hand, weapon in the other. Before either the audience, or the soldier, can tell whether the man intends to shoot or surrender, the American fires and the man falls dead. "Congratulations," his buddy says. "You got yourself a raghead. I didn't think I'd get to see anyone shot in this war."

We next observe one of those interviews with the troops that, like ads for the military, punctuated television coverage of the war. Both the press and the troops who so enthusiastically performed for them are mocked: "They say you exorcised the ghost of Vietnam in [this war with its] clear moral imperative," the reporter informs the soldiers, who readily agree: "We liberated Kuwait." The rest of the movie makes deadly fun of this answer. "I don't know what we did here," George Clooney's Special Forces officer bitterly complains to a friend, "just tell me what we did here." "Do you want to occupy Iraq," the friend answers, "and do Vietnam all over again?" But in effect, the Gulf War, as *Three Kings* presents it, *is*

Vietnam all over again. No clear moral imperative exists; on the contrary, Shiites and Kurds are cynically encouraged to rebel against Saddam Hussein and then abandoned to their fate. Even the bad guys drive the point home: "Do [sic] your army care about the children in Iraq?" one of Saddam's Republic Guard soldiers, pausing in the act of torturing an American captive, asks. "Do your army come back to help the people? . . . My son was killed in his bed. He is one year old. He is sleeping when the bomb come. . . . Can you think how it feels inside your heart if I bomb your daughter?" Individual Americans, like Clooney, through their honesty, virility, and disregard for authority, redeem the country's honor, but only in opposition to, or apart from, the government, never in support of its stated aims. In this, *Three Kings* is a sardonic retelling of what Pat Aufderheide has described as the "noble-grunt" Vietnam War movie. The enemies are not Vietnamese or Iraqi, but rather "the cold abstract forces of bureaucracy and the incompetence of superiors."[1]

For the past few years, the only refuge for the righteous fighting man has been World War II.[2] Unsurprisingly, George W. Bush used it as his first point of reference in the immediate aftermath of September 11 (as had his father, on the eve of Desert Storm): the attack was another Pearl Harbor; the enemy was fascist, totalitarian, a spoke in an axis of evil. Only in World War II, the film historian Thomas Doherty pointed out, can Americans find "the consolation of closure and the serenity of moral certainty. For Hollywood and American culture the Second World War would always be a safe berth."[3] Fought for an unquestionably just cause, ending in total victory, World War II could be reliably invoked to remind Americans of their own best selves. Vincent Canby observed that movies about Vietnam had made war itself seem bestial; *Saving Private Ryan* made war "good again."[4] This was war as men of Steven Spielberg's generation played it on the street when they were boys: storming beaches, house-to-house fighting, sharpshooters in doorways, vulnerable human beings against tanks, always outnumbered.[5]

No one can identify with a B-52 and, as Michael Sherry pointed out long ago, we rarely witness bombing raids from below.[6] Ground combat proves much more satisfying. The camera always faces out against the enemy, or inward at the grievous wounds enemy fire causes. The individual soldier fighting for his life becomes the victim of war; those he kills, since they are so evidently bent on his destruction, the perpetrators of violence. His innocence is ours. Spielberg's achievement went beyond nostalgia. By enabling identification with the individual combat soldier, his World War II epic extended a pardon to soldiers everywhere. On the large and small screens of the country, a handful of heroes fight off the enemy horde (variously composed of Germans, Japanese, Iraqis, Somalis, or Vietnamese), World War II tropes mixing freely with those of old-fashioned Westerns. While Ryan's war has nothing to do with contemporary American high-tech military tactics, *Saving Private Ryan* established a useful paradigm. The tight focus on the situation of the combat solider is inherently dramatic and, by screening out everything save the immediate context in which he fights, recent war movies, wherever they are set, serve as all-purpose propaganda instruments. The Vietnam War movies of the late 1980s similarly kept the focus on the individual fighting man, erasing history and politics in favor of "an emotional drama of embattled individual survival."[7] But the differences prove crucial: in *Platoon* (dir. Oliver Stone, 1986), *84 Charlie Mopic* (dir. Patrick Sheane Duncan, 1989), *Full Metal Jacket* (dir. Stanley Kubrick, 1987), and *Casualties of War* (dir. Brian de Palma, 1989), the mission is explicitly meaningless, the officers useless or worse, the men abandoned by authority, the struggle a civil war. "We didn't fight the enemy," the hero of *Platoon* concludes, "we fought ourselves and the enemy was us." The mission in Saving Private Ryan is assumed to be good, the Germans are the enemies, and who wouldn't want to fight under Tom Hanks?

So attractive, in retrospect, is this old-style ground war that HBO made it into a ten-hour series based on the book credited to Stephen Ambrose, Band of Brothers. I watched only one-third of the episodes; after that the rituals of male bonding become wearying. It is not that one missed the presence of women, since, except for sex, men, who cared for each other as tenderly as any woman could, competently handled the things women usually do. The often gentle universe of Band of Brothers reinforces the manifest content of the series: once upon a time, America was very, very good. Magically, its old goodness constitutes an ongoing one as well, if only Americans can be brought to remember and cherish the good past. Like the cold war movies of the 1950s—and in direct contrast to the late Vietnam War movies—Band of Brothers and Saving Private Ryan revel in a "sentimental militarism" that relies not on ideology, but faith in benevolent male authority.[8]

And something more interesting goes on in Band of Brothers than this filiopious history. At the very end, a defeated German general is allowed to address his massed troops, now, like himself, prisoners of war. He tells them how proud he is of them and how well they have fought, with what courage and bravery. The listening Americans are moved: he has described their war as well as his own. War stories written from inside out vary by geography, but they always tell the same story: death, fear, brotherhood. Bravery, courage, and the capacity to commit atrocities are not determined by the cause in which they are displayed. "It's about the man next to you," one of the characters in Black Hawk Down says, "that's all it is." The flat statement, that one kills and dies for the man next to you, never leads to the obvious question: what are both of you doing there? Some historians, like Gerald Linderman, have written the inside story of war with attention to its contradictions, as tragedy rather than heroic epic.[9] Contemporary war movies, from Saving Private Ryan to We Were Soldiers, follow Ambrose's lead. They abstract war from its context, leaving it standing on its own, self-justifying, impervious to doubt, a fact of nature.

The Pacific theater has been a less popular location in which to revisit World War II; perhaps jungle warfare recalls Vietnam too directly. Terrence Malick's The Thin Red Line (1998) was a resounding box office failure, in part because, as Neil Gabler pointed out, in its sharp caricature of the indifference of military authority to the lives of the troops, it was the "last of the Vietnam-era movies."[10] Jerry Bruckheimer chose a safer subject, the attack on Pearl Harbor. The only way to watch Pearl Harbor is on video, with your finger poised over fast-forward. The product of $127 million worth of special effects, Pearl Harbor seems oddly dated. The computer graphics look as unreal, in their high realism, as the tiny galleons that fought on the Spanish Main in Hollywood's days of yore. The love story is faithful to the genre as it was practiced in the 1940s magazine True Romance. The acting is silent-movie grandiose; the sentiments neo-Hallmark. The only surprise is that the filmmakers, intent on a happy ending to the carnage of Japanese-wrought destruction, offer us only Doolittle's raid on Tokyo rather than Hiroshima.[11]

Hollywood nostalgia for World War II is not only about doing an end run around Vietnam or salvaging war as a fruitful human activity. It is also intended to hold a mirror to our own corrupt times. In the fat, soft days before the recession and September 11, the generation that fought World War II was praised, in antique slang, as "the greatest." Succeeding generations could aspire to being good, maybe great, but by definition they could not be the greatest. "It is as though," Ian Buruma wrote after seeing Pearl Harbor, "we should feel nostalgic for times when dying for the nation was called for. We are supposed to believe that people at war were better human beings, and we should be more like them." The filmmakers, Buruma concluded, were not cynical, but something worse: "I have a feeling |they| are deeply sincere. They believe in their own spectacle. . . . So who needs reality? Just sit back and enjoy the show. Until the next war. And then we die, ingloriously."[12] Though not, Buruma should have added, in the movies.

Having waved the flag for so many years before September 11, Hollywood's first reaction was to put the industry at the government's disposal.[13] Less than a month later, forty Hollywood executives made the pilgrimage to the White House for a two-hour discussion with Chris Henick, deputy assistant to the president, and Adam Goldman, associate director of the Office of Public Liaison. Leslie Moonves, president of CBS, explained their mission: "I think you have a bunch of people here who were just saying, 'Tell us what to do. We don't fly jet planes, but there are skill sets that can be put to use here.'" With its usual relaxed attitude toward historical accuracy, the New York Times stated that while "not new to Hollywood," such patriotic sentiments had been "rarely in evidence since World War II." But in one particular, the reporter, Jim Rutenberg, had it exactly right: World War II was the "era to which executives are now looking for guidance." More specifically, "several people who had attended the meeting referred, as models for cooperation, to the director Frank Capra." Others hoped to produce contemporary versions of movies like Mrs. Miniver (dir. William Wyler, 1942), although comparing September 11 to the blitz seems a dubious comfort. There was a clear need, both "domestically and internationally to tell the story that is our story."[14]

On November 8, a smaller group of Hollywood executives responded to an invitation from Karl Rove, senior White House advisor, for a more focused and "high-powered" discussion of how Hollywood might help the war effort. While denying any interest in making propaganda films, the executives reiterated their desire to add a new chapter to Capra's Why We Fight series.[15] Meanwhile, the Los Angeles Times reported that Sylvester Stallone, who has had extensive experience in recycling World War II themes through new wars, was working on a script that would parachute Rambo into Afghanistan to fight the Taliban. Actually, this would constitute Rambo's second visit to the country; in 1988 he fought with the Afghan Warriors Previously Known As Freedom Fighters.[16]

The meeting with Rove took place in Beverly Hills and included not only high-powered movie executives, but representatives of the networks, labor unions, and Cineplex owners as well. Movie content, all agreed, was not up for discussion. However, Rove did suggest that Hollywood could help clarify certain issues: "That the war is against terrorism, not Islam . . . that this is a global conflict requiring a global response, and that it is a fight against evil rather than a disagreement between nations." In addition, the movies could join in issuing a "'call to service'" to all Americans and "aid in the process of reassuring children and families in these uncertain times." Jack Valenti, president of the Motion Picture Association, was pleased by the "seamless web of unity" created at the meeting: "It was really quite affectionate to behold."[17] The affection was mutual. Hollywood and Washington, Rick Lyman reported, had come "closer together" and "political sniping over issues of violence and vulgarity" had "virtually ended." After all, who, other than Jerry Falwell, would want to join Osama bin Laden in an attack on American pop culture?[18]

Television played a minor role in the Korean War and was blamed for losing the Vietnam War. Things went better in the Gulf. High-tech war, war as a video game, played well. The entire population had the experience of being in the nose cone of a missile as it descended toward its target, and all but those on the ground were spared what happened next. It was difficult to imagine what greater service the news media could offer a warring state. But that was before *Survivor*. According to Felicity Barringer, the Pentagon plans to "promote its war effort through television's genre of the moment, the reality series." Over the protests of its news division, whose reporters, like others covering the Afghan war, have been subject to tight restrictions, the ABC entertainment division will work with Jerry Bruckheimer and Bertram van Munster on a thirteen-part series. "There's a lot of other ways to convey information to the American people than through news organizations," Rear Admiral Craig R. Quigley pointed out. "That's the principal means," the admiral went on, "but if there is an opportunity to tell about the courage and professionalism of our men and women in uniform on prime time television for 13 straight weeks, we're going to do it. That's an opportunity not to be missed."[19]

Meanwhile, films whose themes proved too close for comfort, like *Collateral Damage* (dir. Andrew Davis, 2002), about a terrorist attack, were delayed, while movies about old wars were advanced. The chair of Paramount explained why *Black Hawk Down*, about the intervention in Somalia, would appear on local screens sooner than expected: "It's about the sacrifices that soldiers make so the rest of us can be safe." Mark Bowden, who wrote the book on which the movie is based, pronounced himself well satisfied with the treatment. "Many people read *Black Hawk Down* as an argument not to use military force," Bowden told the *Times* reporter, "which I never intended. . . . This movie says that we have the capability of doing this kind of thing. It's ugly and it's terrible, but we have these very brave young men who do this, and we need to use them now and then."[20]

Black Hawk Down begins with a scrolling text informing the audience of the humanitarian purpose of the U.S. intervention—-famine relief—a purpose that could not be fulfilled so long as the evil warlord Aidid controlled the capital Mogadishu.[21] The film wisely skips the unopposed made-for-TV amphibious landing on the beach at Mogadishu.[22] Instead, it focuses entirely on the effort to rescue the crew of a helicopter shot down in the course of a mission to snatch several of Aidid's key lieutenants from their meeting place in the crowded city. Thousands and thousands of armed and apparently crazed Somalis (called, throughout the movie, "skinnies," a reference to the famine, though in fact, most of the Somalis look more like stereotypical muscled boys in the hood) besiege the small band of American troops. The film makes no reference to the constant and indifferent use of excessive force by the United States that led Alex de Waal to conclude that "literally every inhabitant of large areas of Mogadishu considered the UN and U.S. as enemies, and were ready to take up arms against them" by the time of the rescue mission.[23] But then, as Jerry Bruckheimer explained, "We never set out to tell that story. We wanted to make a film about what these young guys were sent out to do and what they did to survive."[24]

Initially, the makers of *Black Hawk Down* considered drawing an explicit connection between U.S. withdrawal from Somalia and the growth of al-Qaeda, but they dropped the idea because they thought "the connections were apparent."[25] Vice president Cheney, secretary of defense Rumsfeld, deputy secretary of defense Paul Wolfowitz, secretary of the army Thomas E. White, assorted generals, and Oliver North, identified in the ArmyLINK News as a "political analyst," attended a special screening of the movie. Ridley Scott told the audience he had made the movie to "set the record straight." He wanted to disabuse the public of the notion that the military had "messed up on Somalia," when in fact "it was heroic in a very unstable part of the world." White agreed: the movie reflected the "values of valor and self-sacrifice" of the military in its current war against terrorism and indeed throughout its history.[26] Yet with all its patriotic trappings, the implications of *Black Hawk Down* are potentially dangerous to warmakers: what is it about America's good intentions that they go so quickly awry? What, after all, did the deaths of a thousand Somalis and eighteen Americans accomplish? The implication of the film's ending, that the United States should not have withdrawn its troops so precipitously, does not resolve but compounds the confusion. What, other than more dead Somalis and Americans, would continued military action have achieved? Could something have been wrong with American intentions?[27]

For all its heroics, *Black Hawk Down* could not erase Vietnam, another war said to have begun with good intentions that went unaccountably wrong. Nor did *Saving Private Ryan* do the job. Giorgio Mariani may be correct when he writes: "the 'monument' that Spielberg erects to his father's generation ties past and present together in a seamless web, thereby absolving the nation not only from the sin of Vietnam, but also from all the other 'mistakes' of the half century separating us from the end of World War II."[28] But this is only generally true. Absolution, to be effective, must be specific. To erase Vietnam, Hollywood would have to go back to Vietnam, where the unraveling of the war story began. In 1941, in an effort to take the bad taste out of World War I and the powerful antiwar movies that dominated the interwar years, Hollywood released *Sergeant York* (dir. Howard Hawks, 1941), a moving tale of a pacifist turned war hero. "We can sit in the theater and see [York] go fight a better World War I for us," Jeanine Basinger has written. Films like *Sergeant York*, she explained, "wipe out earlier images and replace them with new ones, appropriate for the times."[29] To create a "new mythos" for World War II, Thomas Doherty wrote, "Hollywood had to recast the Great War as a reasonable national enterprise, not as the crazy slaughterhouse depicted in literature and film for the previous twenty years. . . . Outright obliteration was a prerequisite."[30]

To fight this new war, the films, literature, and histories of Vietnam must be obliterated. *We Were Soldiers*, in what may be the first of many returns to Vietnam, is the twenty-first century's *Sergeant York*.[31] Like *Black Hawk Down*, *We Were Soldiers* was released ahead of schedule and the test screening pleased Paramount: "The movie has very, very patriotic American values. The audience embraced those values." Joseph Galloway, who, with Lieutenant Colonel Harold Moore, wrote the book on which the movie is based, expressed delight with the film. As he explained to a reporter, "audiences would be drawn to the story because it is not defeatist about what eventually became the misadventure of Vietnam." The book, like the movie, is relentlessly patriotic. "This," the prologue reads, "is about what we did, what we saw, what we suffered in a thirty-four-day campaign in the Ia Drang Valley of the Central Highlands of South Vietnam in November 1965, when we were young and confident and patriotic." It was a "love story," about men "proud of the opportunity to serve [the] country." It was also a story about the "far more transcendent love" that comes to men "unbidden on the battlefields. . . . We killed for each other, we died for each other, and we wept for each other. And in time, we came to love each other as brothers. In battle our world shrank to the man on our left and the man on our right and the enemy all around."[32] The film version makes it also a story about family values, a manly reporter ready to pick up a gun, and worthy enemies.

As it happens, Moore's unit, the First Battalion, Seventh Cavalry Regiment, First Division, was also Custer's, and in the movie, before leaving for Vietnam, Moore is shown thoughtfully leafing through an illustrated account of the battle of Little Big Horn, along with a French book describing what is called the "massacre" of French troops in a battle along Route 19, near where he will soon find himself fighting for his life. Mel Gibson's brow furrows as he contemplates the fate of the French (a brief scene shows Vietnamese soldiers slaughtering French prisoners) and of Custer's men.[33] The domestication of the Vietnamese enemy, common during the war itself, strikes an odd, discordant note. After all, the Indians, in the last couple of decades of films and novels, have been victims, which would make Moore and his men the executioners, and that can't be right. Still, the scene is crucial, the first of many reversals of the images of the Vietnam War. The victims of massacres in Vietnam, it turns out, were white men. My Lai disappears; instead of burning villages, the film shows well-armed, uniformed Vietnamese regulars; napalm strikes burn Americans and Vietnamese alike (the B-52 sorties crucial to the battle are never shown); the American commander is everywhere in the midst of the battle, barely protected and always in danger; the Vietnamese commander gives his orders from the safety of a clean, well-kept, underground tunnel complex (in fact, the Vietnamese command post was not sheltered).[34] Americans die in great numbers, but they are anyhow victorious over the far more numerous Vietnamese, and a soldier's last words express gratitude that he has sacrificed his life for his country. Gone is the resentment of authority the Vietnam movies of the late 1980s expressed; in this Vietnam, as in *Black Hawk Down*, no one gets left behind.[35]

Vietnam has become a war of which Americans can feel proud.[36] The pride derives from the demonstration of courage and the memory of suffering, irrespective of the cause in which the one is displayed and the other endured. Both are proof that the nation, if it would only embrace its heritage, now explicitly including Vietnam, has not gone soft. Ridley Scott, the director of *Black Hawk Down*, decided not to depict the dragging of a dead American through the streets of Mogadishu. Instead, he showed a helicopter pilot, naked from the waist up, his arms out flung, being lifted out of his craft by the mob, a contemporary deposition scene. After watching the film, George Monbiot wrote that the United States had cast itself "simultaneously as the world's savior and the world's victim, a sacrificial messiah on a mission to deliver the world from evil."[37] Monbiot called it a "new myth of nationhood." I am not sure how new it is, but I agree that it "contains incalculable dangers" and that it will be playing on movie screens everywhere in the months and years to come and, more disastrously, in the "real" world as well.

There is something odd about these recent representations of America's messianic mission. From Private Ryan to the Delta Force officers in Somalia and Hal Moore in Vietnam, these Americans sacrifice their lives only for one another. Private Ryan's war, for example, proves the obverse of movies made during World War II, when the individual had sometimes to be sacrificed for the sake of the mission. Ryan reverses the moral of the story; the lives of a group of men are risked for the sake of a single individual. "In the new metaphor war movies seem to be presenting," Neil Gabler wrote, "Americans are no longer distrustful of authority and no longer doubt the cause. Rather, we trust each other and see the cause as us."[38] And who can doubt that "we" are a worthy cause? The legitimacy of the state, incarnate in the nation-at-war, is vested in the wars the United States has waged and the new ones the Bush administration plans to wage, all of them justified by the way they are fought for the "man on our left and the man on our right and the enemy all around." Hollywood, and the government, would seem to have "kicked the Vietnam syndrome."

Notes

1 Pat Aufderheide, "Good Soldiers," in *Seeing through Movies*, ed. Mark Crispin Miller (New York: Pantheon, 1990), 84.

2 One could argue that this has been the case, with interesting variations, since 1945. See Christian Appy, "'We'll Follow the Old Man': The Strains of Sentimental Militarism in Popular Films of the Fifties," in *Rethinking Cold War Culture*, ed. Peter J. Kuznick and James Gilbert (Washington, DC: Smithsonian Institute, 2001), for a particularly interesting analysis of the way Hollywood translated the "sentimental militarism" of World War II films for cold war use, a translation marked by ambivalence and ambiguity.

3 Thomas Doherty, *Projections of War: Hollywood, American Culture, and World War II* (New York: Columbia University Press, 1993), 271.

4 Vincent Canby, "The Horror and Honor of a Good War," *New York Times*, August 10, 1998.

5 For an especially eloquent evocation of this culture, see Tom Engelhardt, *The End of Victory Culture: Cold War America and the Disillusioning of a Generation* (Amherst: University of Massachusetts Press, 1998).

6 See Michael S. Sherry, *The Rise of American Air Power: The Creation of Armageddon* (New Haven, CT: Yale University Press, 1987).

7 Aufderheide, "Good Soldiers," 86.

8 Appy, "'We'll Follow the Old Man,'" 94.

9 Gerald F. Linderman, *The War Within: America's Combat Experience in World War II* (New York: Free Press, 1997).

10 Neil Gabler, "Seeking Perspective on the Movie Front Lines," *New York Times*, January 27, 2002.

11 There are a few good moments in the movie, lines that seem to have wandered in from some other script. It is as if, below the level of consciousness, even Jerry Bruckheimer and Michael Bay had doubts about the enterprise. Early on, a veteran of World War I remembers fighting in the trenches and fervently hopes no one will ever again have to see what he saw. But the holder of this potentially antiwar sentiment is the brutal father of one of the two boys who grow up to be heroes, and we need not pay it undue attention. Similarly, the Japanese responsible for planning the attack on Pearl Harbor protests when he is praised as a genius. A genius, he says, would have figured out how to avoid war. Obviously he was a man not destined to win a war, since, as the actor impersonating (one cannot call it acting) Jimmy Doolittle tells us: "Victory belongs to those who believe in it the most and believe in it the longest."

12 Ian Buruma, "Oh! What A Lovely War," *Guardian*, May 28, 2001. Buruma compared *Pearl Harbor* to patriotic Japanese war movies, which, unlike their American counterparts, stressed duty, courage, sacrifice, and purity of will rather than the evil of the enemy.

13 Hollywood's response to June 25, 1950, the day war broke out in Korea, was much the same. On June 28, 1950, the Title Registration Bureau of the Motion Picture Association announced it had received five hand-delivered titles from various producers: *Korea, South Korea, Crisis in Korea, Formosa* and, rather ominously, *Indochina*. *Film Daily* boasted of the industry's instant response to the call to battle: "For the third time in a generation, the awesome shadow of Mars shot full across the American industry . . . and . . . the industry fell into line and asked for its marching orders from the government." More formally, Francis S. Harmon, who had chaired the coordinating committee between Hollywood

and various government agencies during World War II, returned to act as liaison for the duration of this one. David Detzer, *Thunder of the Captains: The Short Summer of* 1950 (New York: Crowell, 1977), 153; Doherty, *Projections*, 276.

14 Jim Rutenberg, "Hollywood Seeks Role in the War," *New York Times*, October 20, 2001. The reference to Capra was more precise than the reporter is likely to have realized. Capra, according to Saverio Giovacchini, was chosen by the government because of his "conservative political background. . . . The series makes no effort to understand the causes of the war as anything more than an unexplained assault on the world." See Saverio Giovacchini, *Hollywood Modernism: Film and Politics in the Age of the New Deal* (Philadelphia: Temple University Press, 2001), 150.

15 Rick Lyman, "White House Sets Meeting with Film Executives to Discuss War on Terrorism," *New York Times*, November 8, 2001.

16 John Harlow, "Hollywood Joins the Campaign: Rambo Gets Call-up As Movies Catch War Fever," *Los Angeles Times*, November 11, 2001.

17 Rick Lyman, "Hollywood Discusses Role in War Effort," *New York Times*, November 12, 2001.

18 Rick Lyman, "At Least for the Moment, a Cooling Off in the Culture Wars," *New York Times*, November 13, 2001.

19 Felicity Barringer, "'Reality TV' About GI's on War Duty," *New York Times*, February 21, 2002. To illustrate the complaints of newsmen, Barringer cites the problems of Doug Struck, a *Washington Post* reporter; who had been held at gunpoint when he tried to reach the site of a missile attack on an alleged al-Qaeda target. The military denied the allegation, claiming that Struck had misunderstood. The soldier had not threatened to shoot him at all, but had rather warned him that he should not go any further for his own safety.

20 Kim Masters, "Against the Tide, Two Movies Go to War," *New York Times*, November 4, 2001.

21 In fact, the famine had largely abated before U.S. intervention, and the targeting of Aidid restored his waning power, transforming him into "the aggrieved party in a war with UN colonialists." See Stephen R. Shalom, "Gravy Train: Feeding the Pentagon by Feeding Somalia," *Z Magazine*, November 1993, available at www.zmag.org/ZNET.htm.

22 See Shalom, "Gravy Train." The landing was pure public relations for the Marines. Indeed, the entire operation can be seen as an effort by the Pentagon to demonstrate the need for high defense budgets despite the end of the cold war—use it or lose it. See also Scott Peterson, *Me Against My Brother: At War in Somalia, Sudan, and Rwanda* (New York: Routledge, 2001), 54.

23 Alex de Waal, "U.S. War Crimes in Somalia," *New Left Review* 230 (1998): 131–44.

24 Chelsea J. Carter, "'Black Hawk Down' Movie Turns Grim Somalia Fight into a Dramatic Tale of Heroism," *Valley News* (White River Junction, VT), February 2, 2002.

25 Robert K. Elder, "The War Stories of Black Hawk Down," January 21, 2002, available at www.metromix.com/movies.

26 Joe Burlas, "'Black Hawk Down' Reflects Army Values," *Army LINK News*, January 16, 2002, available at www.dtic.mil/armylink/news/Jan2002/a20020116bhdown.html.

27 In one of the endless migration tales of the American empire, Sinp Sithavaday, an eighteen-year-old whose family had fled Laos in 1979, found himself in Somalia, a member of the Tenth Mountain Division's second battalion, Eighty-Seventh Infantry. Interviewed by his local newspaper, Sithavaday, without directly criticizing the movie,

talked about the "growing hubris" of U.S. troops: "We thought, we have rocket launchers, night goggles, infrared designators, all kinds of technical stuff. We are the meanest." After a few months, he had become dubious about his mission: "There was a lot of anger at the U.S. They saw us flexing our muscles and killing them." Like the soldiers sent to Indochina a decade before his birth, Sithavaday complained: "How can you tell a farmer from a militia member?" Melanie Leslie-Finn, "Lyme Man Looks Back on His Tour of Duty in Somalia," *Valley News*, February 2, 2002.

28   Giorgio Mariani, "'Mission of Mercy/Mission of Murder': Spielberg's *Saving Private Ryan* and the Culture of Baby Boomers," *Acoma* 18 (2000): 4, English version available at www.acoma.it/n18/inglese/mission2a.htm.

29   Jeanine Basinger, *The World War II Combat Film: Anatomy of a Genre* (New York: Columbia University Press, 1986), 100.

30   Doherty, *Projections*, 100.

31   The passage of time has made the displacement easier. For example, *Coming Home*, a 1978 antiwar movie, was summarized in the February 25, 2002 *New York Times* TV late movie listings this way: "Jane Fonda, Jon Voight, Bruce Dern. Strong, stinging triangle of wife and Vietnam vets."

32   Kim Masters, "Against the Tide, Two Movies Go to War," *New York Times*, November 4, 2002; Harold G. Moore and Joseph Galloway, *We Were Soldiers Once . . . and Young: Ia Drang—the Battle that Changed time War in Vietnam* (New York: HarperPerennial, 1993), 3–4.

33   See Charles J. Hanley et al., *The Bridge at No Gun Ri* (New York: Holt, 2001). The history of the Seventh Cavalry includes several massacres going the other way: the Battle of the Washita, in 1868, when the cavalry ordered a large group of Amerindians into a constricted area and then slaughtered them; Wounded Knee, in 1890, when it massacred 370 Sioux, many of them women and children; the massacre of Korean villagers in July 1950.

34   The ABC documentary, *We Were Young and Brave*, produced in 1994, is very clear on this point: air power was the deciding factor in the battle. A Vietnamese colonel describes watching, unprotected, as a "sea of fire" engulfed his troops: "If you saw it you would think we all died."

35   See Aufderheide, "Good Soldiers," especially 94.

36   This is in direct contrast to the documentary, in which some of the survivors of the battle returned to the Ia Drang along with their Vietnamese counterparts. The mood is elegiac, sometimes bitter, and the overall effect is of the terrible waste of lives, however bravely sacrificed. Moore and Galloway both accuse the military of stage-managing the post-battle assessments of Ia Drang. "You can almost date the rot at the heart of the American effort in Vietnam to that week," Galloway insists. By depicting the battle as a victory the ABC narrator explains, the military "pulled an unsuspecting nation further into war." Postbattle newsreels described the Ia Drang as proof that the "best of the enemy's forces could be stopped dead in their own territory." Survivors were expected to join in a ghastly charade—clips of which are included—in which Westmoreland congratulated them on their victory. The men are unsmiling and many of them look away, refusing eye contact with the general. The battle itself is brilliantly depicted, using both North Vietnamese and U.S. Army film footage, and the critical commentary of Moore, Galloway, and other combatants is far more stark than anything in the movie.

37   George Monbiot, "Both Saviour and Victim," *Guardian Weekly*, February 7–13, 2002, 13.

38   Neil Gabler, "Seeking Perspective."

A Cultural History of War Without End

26

MELANI McALISTER

. . . . What most Americans knew about terrorism on September 10, 2001, was shaped by . . . earlier wars, which had been waged on television, made meaningful through culture, and brought home through violence. U.S. involvement with terrorism and anti-terrorism emerging out of the Middle East began in the 1970s as an emotional engagement with Israel's response to Palestinian violence against civilians. These concerns expanded dramatically in 1979, with the taking of American hostages at the U.S. embassy in Iran and the ensuing hostage crisis. In the popular culture of the 1980s—particularly but not only in the emerging genre of action movies there was a sustained fascination with the problem of terrorism and the construction of a U.S. response. As the 1980s progressed, anti-terrorism became the glue of a directly politicized popular culture, which worked to imagine American national power in a global context. By the turn of the twenty-first century, the contests and complexities of three decades of struggle with the problem of terrorism and the role of military power were all but invisible. In their place, especially after September 11, was the promise of clear, effective action against definable, defeatable enemies.[1]

Near the end of *Imagined Communities*, Benedict Anderson describes one aspect of the process of consolidating national identities in times of crisis: "All profound changes in consciousness, by their very nature, bring with them characteristic amnesias. Out of such oblivions, in specific historical circumstances, spring narratives."[2] Such narratives, born of amnesias, promise to stitch together a patchwork past. They are forged not just by policy makers, but at the intersection of news accounts, policy developments, and cultural texts such as films, novels, and even video games. Of course, the "memories" constructed and reconstructed in the public sphere are never distributed evenly or unproblematically. But they *are* powerful.

This essay explores the politics of the diverse representations of terrorism in recent decades. It is not a study of policy making per se or of public opinion, as that is measured in public opinion polls or oral histories. But it does find links between popular culture, news accounts, and public understandings of the meaning and significance of political events, though those links are neither direct nor easily measured empirically. I analyze the politics of representation, on the understanding that culture is a crucial site for the negotiation of political and moral values and for the development of an often uneven and contested public understanding of history and its significance. Cultural texts do not inject ideologies into their audiences, but they do figure in the process of constructing frameworks that help policy make sense in a given moment. Policy makers do not control representations; in fact, any given policy (or policy maker) may be deeply at odds with the views presented in contemporary news accounts or with the apparent ideology of any given cultural text. But as policy makers make difficult choices in often complex situations, they must negotiate the fractured terrain shaped by the intersection of conflicting material interests, government actions, political organizing, and cultural texts.[3] What I examine here is not a conspiracy nor a set of functionalist representations in the service of power, but a process of convergence, as historical events, overlapping representations, and diverse vested interests come together in a powerful, if historically contingent, accord that is productive of a new common sense. Cultural texts enter into that process: they are integral aspects of both history and politics. This essay traces how a history was made meaningful; that is, it explores the public activity of devising a particular narrative of anti-terrorism and U.S. power.

Beginnings: Munich

The issue of Middle East terrorism entered U.S. public life in a profound way in September 1972, when Palestinian guerrillas broke into the Israeli compound at the Olympic Games in Munich. There, they killed two members of the Israeli Olympic team and took nine hostage. Immediately, ABC, the network that televised the games in the United States, began continuous live coverage. There were tense negotiations throughout the day, but in the end the plan to capture the attackers went terribly wrong, and the Palestinians killed all of their hostages.

The massacre had an unprecedented impact in the United States, as people watched events unfold on TV and then mourned the athletes. Other terrorism had been more deadly, but nothing had quite this effect on Americans. Perhaps, as some commentators suggested, it was because the spirit of the Olympics had been destroyed. Or perhaps it was because, unlike earlier terrorist attacks, this one was covered live by U.S. television, which had crews already on the scene reporting events as they happened. But at that moment the intractable politics of the Middle East conflict also resonated unexpectedly with Americans, who in 1972 were facing their own protracted and seemingly indecisive end game in Vietnam. Israel and the Palestinians, too, were fighting a long, unconventional war over control of territory. The outcome in both cases was uncertain.

Looking back thirty years later, what is striking about the U.S. response to the Munich Olympics tragedy is that a shared outrage over brutal attacks on civilians did not lead to a uniform view of how to respond. Instead, the divided reactions to the assassinations at the Munich Olympics mirrored debates emerging out of the Vietnam conflict. Many U.S. commentators suggested that a military response would be both appropriate and effective and expressed sympathy with what they took to be Israel's inevitable counterattack (it immediately bombed villages in Syria and Lebanon that, it said, housed guerrilla bases). As one ABC news reporter explained: "Israel will not stand by while its citizens are victims of terror. . . . Time will ease their grief, but time will not weaken their determination to punish the terrorists and their supporters."[4]

Yet there was also an argument, made strongly by liberals, that in the new, multipolar world that was emerging, the battle against terrorism, like the guerrilla war in Vietnam, could not be won merely by overpowering force. This new world was one in which military victories were elusive and moral categories fuzzy. The solution to escalating violence was to respond to root causes, to negotiate, and, in the words of presidential candidate George McGovern, to "Stop the killing! Stop the killing everywhere around the world!" In this argument, specifically in the context of the mainstreamed opposition to the Vietnam War, the emergence of terrorism as a mode of conflict was one symptom of the need to rethink military power as a means for pursuing U.S. interests. Thus liberals and some moderates pointed to Vietnam (and now Palestinian terrorism) to argue that the United States (and now Israel) relied too heavily on force in situations where political, economic, or diplomatic solutions were more likely to be effective. That argument gained considerable strength with OPEC's (Organization of Petroleum Exporting Countries) display of economic power the following year, with the 1973 oil embargo.[5]

There was also the question of how to evaluate actions such as the one in Munich—how to define what should be called terrorism, as opposed to liberation struggle, guerrilla activity, or simply war. To name something terrorism is a condemnation, distinguishing it immediately from actions against civilians that one might justify in certain contexts. Scholars and journalists have debated what kinds of actions would fall under a fully consistent definition of terrorism: Why a massacre in an airport but not a bombing of a village? When is an action terrorism, and when is it simply terrifying for the civilians under attack? Those debates are important, politically and morally, if one is to take a principled position in a particular conflict. But when we ask how the category of terrorism functioned historically in U.S. public life, we see that the definitions have mattered less than the emotions and values that swirled around the events that became exemplary. In practice, the fear and anger about terrorism in the 1970s developed from a specific set of images and stories, not through a consistent, worked-out categorization of types of violence. When an action evoked fear and horror, it was understood to be terrorism—it was as if the force of the emotion itself generated the working definition.

Entebbe

It was not until four years later, in 1976, that the terms of the debate about terrorism shifted decisively with one of the most famous hijackings in history. In June 1976 hijackers associated with the Popular Front for the Liberation of Palestine took over a flight from Tel Aviv and forced it to fly to Entebbe, Uganda. The hijackers demanded the release of pro-Palestinian prisoners held in jails in Israel and several other countries. Israel at first refused to negotiate for the hostages or to release the prisoners it held. But over the next several days, the guerrillas released 140 of the hostages, keeping only the Israelis (including dual citizens) and the French crew. On July 1, under pressure from the families of the hostages (some of whom broke into the military compound where Prime Minister Yitzhak Rabin lived and angrily demanded to see him), Israel agreed to negotiate. As negotiations opened, however, the Israeli government was also planning its military operation. Israeli commandos secretly flew to Uganda on July 4, 1976. There they attacked the airport, fought off Ugandan soldiers, killed all of the hijackers, and loaded the hostages onto planes to Israel. During the raid, three hostages and one Israeli soldier were killed.[6]

U.S. responses to the Israelis' military operation were remarkable for their level of emotional engagement. Of course, the raid *was* an impressive feat, not only technically and logistically, but also in its audacity. The Israelis not only took the political risk of invading another country to rescue their citizens; they also took the very real risk that many hostages and rescuers would be killed in the process. In the United States admiration mixed with joy, and the raid was celebrated across the political spectrum, with enthusiastic responses in the left-liberal *Nation*, the conservative *National Review*, and the mainstream *Newsweek*, among others. *Newsweek* enthused, "Once again, Israel's lightning-swift sword had cut down an enemy, and its display of military precision, courage, and sheer chutzpa won the applause and admiration of most of the world." The *Nation* declared, "The fact is that Israel was doing the work of the rest of the so-called civilized world when it staged that coup against the hostage-holding hijackers." How-they-did-it stories, complete with detailed maps and illustrations, were produced in virtually every major newspaper and magazine in the country, where they competed with television specials, quickie books, and a spate of movies immediately put into production. The response to terrorism had hardened considerably since Munich. When the eleven athletes were killed, there were calls for Israel and the Palestinians to negotiate. Four years later, when scores of people were taken hostage, but no one killed (until the rescue raid), the enthusiasm for military response had increased considerably. Some of the responses suggested not only enthusiasm, but an appropriation of the Israeli success as a shared victory.[7]

While analogies to Vietnam remained very much a part of the public response to Entebbe, the general tenor of U.S. understandings of Vietnam had shifted. Americans had witnessed the disastrous final pullout from Saigon the year before, and comparisons were everywhere. By 1976, conservative intellectuals were already promoting the concept of the "Vietnam syndrome," which suggested that not only had the United States failed to use adequate force to win the war, but that in the wake of the failure, the nation suffered from a failure of nerve, an unwillingness to act decisively. Israel's decisive action in *its* unconventional war was taken as an example of the successful use of force. It became a commonplace after 1976 that the United States should not only act *with* Israel on foreign policy but *like* Israel in matters of unconventional war. . . .[8]

Yet even with this level of enthusiasm, there remained a genuine debate about whether Israeli tactics could or should be a model for the United States. Two weeks after the Entebbe rescue, the journalist Judith Miller (who fifteen years later wrote a well-publicized exposé of Saddam Hussein) reported in the *New York Times Magazine* that many diplomats were concerned about the uncritical embrace of a get-tough-with-terrorists policy. Faced with the mixed results of such policies in the early part of the 1970s, the Ford administration hired the RAND Corporation (a conservative think tank generally tied to the U.S. Army) to review U.S. policies. Brian Jenkins, a senior RAND analyst, concluded that U.S. policy makers should show flexibility in dealing with terrorism. The United States had a firm policy not to negotiate with terrorists; the assumption was that such refusals would deter other terrorism in the future. Jenkins argued that evidence for that assumption was "'squishy' at best." The wringing of concessions is only part of what terrorists want, he argued, and it may not be the most important thing. Describing well the emerging consensus about the impetus to and meanings of terrorism, he surmised that most hijackers and hostage takers did not want mass murder. Instead, "terrorists want a lot of people watching and a lot of people listening, not a lot of people dead." Their target was not so much the hostages as it was the larger audience. "Terrorism is theater," he said. Some U.S. officials argued that the types of raids or assassinations that Israel could carry out would never be possible, politically, for a superpower. But the appeal of quick, clean military action, particularly in hostage situations, was undeniable. Shortly after President Jimmy Carter took office in 1977, he directed the Pentagon to develop anti-terrorist capabilities similar to those of Israel and West Germany (which had just pulled off a successful rescue at Mogadishu, Somalia). Within a month, the Delta Force was created—the first special forces detachment specifically organized to fight "unconventional warfare" against terrorism.[9]

The United States was not often targeted by Arab guerrillas in the 1970s, but Palestinian terrorism against Israel had a cultural salience far beyond its limited strategic importance. Redeploying Israel's war against terrorism from the context of the Israeli-Palestinian conflict, American observers used it to do the cultural work of reimaging U.S. power after Vietnam. Thus Israeli actions mattered in U.S. public culture largely due to internal considerations—*not* the political influence of American Jews, but the legacy of Vietnam and fears of U.S. weakness.

Iran

The presumption of a single appropriate response to the terrorist violence of September 11 evoked the embrace of Israeli tactics but ignored the layered debates that had linked responses to terrorism to the changing understandings of U.S. global power after the Vietnam War. In addition, Bush's notion of an entirely new kind of war depended on a similar mix of memory and forgetting in the face of the most significant American encounter with terrorism in the late twentieth century, the Iran hostage crisis.

In November 1979 Iranians loyal to the Ayatollah Ruhollah Khomeini overran the U.S. embassy in Tehran and took fifty-two Americans hostage. For 444 days the hostages remained captive, while the Carter administration worked furiously to gain their release. And every night for more than a year, Americans watched as Iranians held demonstrations outside the embassy, chanting their anger at the United States and burning U.S. flags.

Television news coverage of the Iran crisis was remarkable for being at once absolutely ubiquitous and remarkably innocent of any historical sense. The long history of U.S. involvement in Iran—thirty years of military and political support for the ruthless Mohammed Reza Shah Pahlavi, who had just been overthrown by a coalition of Islamic activists and leftist opponents—was subordinated to a story of the Iranians' irrational rage. U.S. soil (the embassy) had been attacked and Americans had been made victims; the fate of the hostages became the single most discussed issue in U.S. public life. Television news highlighted the personal aspects of the crisis, focusing particularly on the family members of the hostages. Gary Sick, an official in the Carter administration, described the coverage as "the longest running human interest drama in the history of television." The hostage families became a collective icon in the U.S. media: They gave interviews, held their own press conferences, and confronted political officials.[10]

The hostages soon became a national symbol, but their public status came about precisely because they were understood first and foremost as private individuals—in part, because they were represented first and foremost by their families. Though all of those held were "official Americans," embassy employees or marine guards, that was not what mattered about them: it was just the opposite. They represented the United States because they were ordinary. Television helped to render them as such, identifying them with a private sphere, allied with family, emotions, and domesticity and thus imagined as outside of politics.

In popular culture anti-Arab stereotypes were recycled to apply to (non-Arab) Iran, from the "rich oil sheik" rhetoric that emerged out of the oil crisis in the mid-1970s to the images of the fanatic Arab terrorist. Americans could buy "Nuke Iran" or "Don't Waste Gas, Waste Khomeini" bumper stickers or dart boards and toilet paper with Khomeini's image. (After September 11, there was a similar but smaller-scale business in items such as Osama bin Laden piñatas and "Osama Yo' Mama" hats.) . . .[11]

On April 24, 1980, about six months after the hostages were taken, President Carter appeared on national television to announce that the Delta Force special operations team had aborted an attempted rescue mission after several of the helicopters that were supposed to evacuate the hostages had malfunctioned. As the rescue team was preparing to withdraw from the desert outside Tehran, a helicopter accidentally collided with a transport plane, and eight military personnel were killed. Those deaths and the failure of the rescue ignited a storm of protest from all over the political spectrum, and media coverage of the events was notable for its overt expressions of outrage. Many policy makers and pundits had strongly supported the idea of a rescue but now angrily discussed the mission's failures of planning and execution. Meanwhile, both television and print media produced detailed accounts of the planned raid, with detailed maps, step-by-step illustrations, and charts and arrows explaining what went wrong, where, and why. A special commission was formed to investigate the failure; after it released its report in August 1980, a new flurry of articles appeared. No one who had seen the gleeful enthusiasm that greeted similar illustrations after Entebbe, three and a half years earlier, could have missed the contrast. With the onset of the Iran crisis, the embrace of Israel's military actions did not disappear, but Israeli success could no longer serve a prosthetic function: now Americans were not vicarious victors, but victims.[12]

The hostages were finally released, after intense, final-hour negotiations with the Carter administration, on January 20, 1981, the day Ronald Reagan was inaugurated president. Reagan used his inaugural address to announce that "terrorism" would replace Carter's focus on "human rights" as the nation's primary foreign policy concern. Over the next decade, that first U.S. "war against terrorism" had many fronts. There was continued instability in the Middle East, and Arab- or Iranian-sponsored attacks on U.S. targets increased noticeably. Hijackings and airline bombings were the most visible: In 1985 a TWA flight carrying mostly American passengers was hijacked from Athens to Beirut and one American was killed, and the cruise ship Achille Lauro was hijacked, also with one passenger killed. In 1988, Pan Am flight 103 was blown up over Lockerbie, Scotland, killing 270 people, mostly Americans.

The campaign against such terrorism was a major component of the theoretical structure that supported the Ronald Reagan–George Bush military buildup in many parts of the world (including Latin America and Europe) and the determined reassertion of U.S. political and military hegemony in the Middle East. That reassertion included, among other things, military intervention in Lebanon (1981–1983)—effectively ended by the bombing of the U.S. Marine barracks in Beirut by Shiite militants, in which 243 marines were killed. Other U.S. involvements centered on political and military interventions in the Iran-Iraq war (1980–1988), including political and logistical support for Iraq (1980–1984) and the sale of arms to Iran (the Iran-Contra deal, 1985–1986). In addition the United States expanded arms sales to Saudi Arabia (1985–1988) and in 1986 bombed Libya in retaliation for what the Reagan administration said was Libya's involvement in the bombing of a disco in Berlin.[13]

Moreover, throughout the 1980s, Middle Eastern terrorism was a major concern of foreign policy makers and pundits, and rescue from terrorists was a primary theme in U.S. popular culture. Yet this concern differed in important ways from the focus on Israel in the 1970s. First, the focus was no longer on Israel, but on the United States, which was now represented as the primary victim and the most important warrior in a worldwide battle against terrorism. Second, professional definitions of terrorism took on a new political and cultural force. By the mid-1980s, a new public figure had emerged, the "terrorism expert," and the production of literature on terrorism had become its own industry. There was, among those professionals, a marked change in the moral geography of the Middle East, one heralded by a reclassification: Islam, rather than Arab nationalism or political radicalism, became highlighted as the dominant producer of terrorism. Of course, Islam had indeed become more important as a political force in the Middle East, as the hopes for secular nationalism failed and religious revivalism became one response to the new pressures of globalization, the reach of superpowers, economic crises, and the displacements of modernization. But there was a tendency, especially among experts promoted by the conservative foundations and think tanks, to reassign political struggles as religious ideology and then to search for the "nature of Islam" as the source of the problem. The task was then to discover How the West Can Win, to quote the subtitle of one of the best-known anti-terrorism studies.[14]

Third, the sheer proliferation of policy studies was replicated in popular culture, from films to television specials to popular books. In the 1970s, terrorism had been quite visible— when there was a crisis, newspapers and television covered it intensively—but the focus was periodic rather than sustained. By the 1980s, terrorism, particularly the rescue of hostages taken by Middle Eastern terrorists, became a near obsession. These stories inevitably took the Iranian hostage crisis as their reference point, either directly or indirectly, but they enacted a crucial transformation: now, the hostages in question were rescued, not negotiated for. In these cultural texts, hostages returned home as symbols of victory; they did not linger as nightly reminders of the impotence of the United States.

Terrorism had certainly been represented in films before the Iran hostage crisis. Terrorist attacks, often from domestic groups, figured centrally in the plots of several well-known films in the 1970s, such as The Taking of Pelham One Two Three (1974), about the takeover of a New York City subway, and Black Sunday (1977), about a terrorist plot to explode the Goodyear blimp over a Super Bowl game. And in 1976, the critically acclaimed Network included a running joke about a terrorist sitcom, in which a radical terrorist group (a parody of the SLA [Symbionese Liberation Army] of Patty Hearst fame) contracts to get a weekly half-hour show to broadcast their attacks on television. After 1980, however, terrorism and the rescue of hostages became a stock trope in a new and popular style of action thriller. The theme of hostages and terrorism structured action films ranging from the B-movie military genre—Missing in Action (1984), Iron Eagle (1986), Navy SEALS (1990), Rambo III (1988)—to big-budget thrillers such as Patriot Games (1992) and the film version of John Le Carré's best-selling novel, The Little Drummer Girl (1984). The Chuck Norris vehicle The Delta Force (1986) opened with a scene of the failed rescue of U.S. hostages in Iran. The film then unfolded a hijacking plot almost identical to that of the 1985 Athens-Beirut TWA hijacking, except that this time, rather than the hostages being freed by negotiation, they were rescued by the Delta Force team in an impressively pyrotechnic operation.[15]

There were, of course, many negative stereotypes of Middle Easterners in those films—they were awash in cartoonish portrayals. But that is not the most interesting or most important aspect of the anti-terrorist action genre. Instead, the cultural work emerges from the fact that, of all the potential "actions" in the action genre, the predominant theme is hostage rescue. In other words, unlike action films in the late 1990s, which might have focused on efforts to prevent a bombing or on vengeance for a previous act of violence, the issue for many of these films was not just terrorists, but hostages—particularly, hostages who were marked by their positions in families. In *The Delta Force*, the hostages aboard the TWA flight are carefully delineated in terms of their personal relationships: the father with a little girl, the happily married older couple, the two nuns and the priest who love each other. In *Die Hard* (1988), the people being held are not a family; they work together in an office building. But the most important hostage is the estranged wife of Bruce Willis's character; he will rescue her, and their marriage will be saved. In these films, the uncertain and messy outcomes of real-life hostage and terrorist situations were reimagined in the simpler language of defined threat and unambiguous victory. The rescue of families from terrorists becomes so common, so banal, that its origins as a response to a specific event are submerged and invisible.[16]

What made the terrorist-rescue films *work* so powerfully in this period was not their policy statements, nor their images of Arabs, nor even the military solutions inevitably posited for the problems they depicted. Instead, it was a deep commitment to this simple proposition: It is time to get our people out of there. The presentation of American identity as essentially private, located in family ties and protected by love, means that even films that seem to have deeply political commitments—whether *Rambo* III or *Navy SEALS*—make their most profound political statements in their *depoliticization* of the activities they depict. In U.S. political culture, emotions are imagined as spontaneous and internal to the self; they are naturalized. Thus the desire, the right, to save loved ones by any means can be presented as if it falls beyond explanation. Loved ones return home, and hostage rescue works in their service. Of course, such rescue requires military and political action, but that action is framed as an essentially personal matter, one located in the family and in affect—both love and anger—and therefore outside history.

What the hostage films imagined, the political world eventually provided. With the 1990–1991 Gulf War against Iraq, the United States was able to put together a large multinational coalition to launch one of the largest military operations of the postwar period against Iraq, which had invaded Kuwait. That war was not a hostage rescue (though there was a brief hostage incident) but it was an answer to the hostage story. The Gulf War was understood by almost everyone, its supporters and its opponents, as proof that U.S. military power was back in force—and that it could, and would, be used to shape the political landscape of the Middle East.

Conclusion

In the immediate aftermath of September 11, many Hollywood executives suggested that there could be no more violent action movies after such a national trauma. The planned releases of several action films were delayed, as producers predicted a return to musicals and family drama. But those predictions soon proved wrong. In December 2001, *Entertainment*

Weekly previewed winter film releases with a simple summary: "Hollywood Goes to War." This return to the action genre would not have been a surprise had Hollywood remembered its own history. It was the national drama of the Iran hostage crisis that had helped fuel development of the new hyperviolent action films, which promised military action without the constraints of public debate.[17]

But the two most prominent action films of early 2002 seemed to offer diametrically opposed visions of the nature of U.S. power, and they received quite divergent public responses. The Arnold Schwarzenegger vehicle *Collateral Damage* had received a great deal of publicity when its planned October 2001 release was postponed due, producers said, to the sensitive nature of several scenes. The plot revolves around a fireman (Schwarzenegger) whose wife and child are killed in a terrorist attack by Colombian drug lords. Realizing that the incompetent and/or unconcerned agencies of the U.S. government will never catch the man who killed his family, Schwarzenegger goes on a one-man revenge mission to Colombia, where, without carrying a gun or speaking Spanish, he manages to find the terrorists, destroy a cocaine plant, and get his revenge. The film makes some perfunctory efforts to show "both sides of the story" by giving the terrorists a chance to make statements criticizing U.S. policy, but political nuance quickly disappears as the bad guys reveal themselves to be fundamentally evil and Schwarzenegger enacts justice with "his bare hands and a handy ax." When the film opened in early February 2002, the box office was middling (the film opened at number one, but the receipts plummeted 40 percent in the second week) and the reviews were worse. Reviewers almost uniformly referred to the resonances to September 11 in negative terms (for example, the fact that the hero is a firefighter, and the film's untimely reference to "the first terrorist attack on our nation's capital"). If the filmmakers could not have known what kind of terrorism would happen in the real world, the painful realities had nonetheless, it seemed, rendered the simplicities of Schwarzenegger's trademark action formula unpalatable. One might have expected the opposite, and some audiences did seem to revel in the sense of moral and satisfying violence. Yet reviewers seemed to be speaking for a rather unimpressed public when they announced that the basic story, of one man seeking revenge for his family, making his justice into a personal affair yanked from the jaws of indifferent police and security agencies, "had been played out even back when everyone thought exploding buildings were cool." As Paul Clinton wrote for CNN.*com*, "Without September 11, *Collateral Damage* would have been just another bad movie. Now it's a bad, embarrassing movie."[18]

While *Collateral Damage* was postponed as potentially too painful for viewers, Ridley Scott's *Black Hawk Down* was moved up several months before its planned March 2002 release, appearing on December 28, 2001, just in time both to qualify it for the Oscars and to cash in on the more militaristic mood of a country that had just routed the Taliban from Afghanistan. The plot was based on the *Philadelphia Inquirer* reporter Mark Bowden's account of the October 1993 raid by the U.S. Army Rangers and Delta Force into Mogadishu. While participating in a United Nations program responding to large-scale famine, they attacked and attempted to capture two deputies of the warlord Mohammed Farah Aidid. What was supposed to be a simple strike turned into a large-scale day-long street battle, in which 18 American soldiers and perhaps 1,000 Somalis were killed.[19]

The film did extremely well at the box office (it was number one for five weeks, far outgrossing *Collateral Damage*), and although reviews were mixed, there was a broad sense that *Black Hawk Down* presented much of the complexity of fighting in a war, particularly the horror and the camaraderie. Many reviewers commented on the arresting spectacle of the battle scenes—beautiful in their staging and use of color as well as nightmarish in their intensity. "*Black Hawk Down* has such distinctive visual aplomb that its jingoism starts to feel like part of its atmosphere," wrote the *New York Times* reviewer Elvis Mitchell, echoing a common sentiment that while the movie showed images of war particularly well, it was so focused on presenting the battle that the political background remained undefined and the characters of the U.S. soldiers were virtually indistinguishable. Scott himself was not unaware of the issue, insisting that his movie was not about the political issues at stake in Somalia or the soldiers' lives back home, but about the valor of those who, in the face of danger, found courage and performed their duty.[20]

Of course, no one missed the wartime political resonance of this "apolitical" approach to the story. The Pentagon fully cooperated with the film, providing helicopters, technical support, and even soldiers to serve as extras. The political valence did not come simply or even primarily from the fact that Somalia had been named by the Bush administration as a potential hiding place for Osama bin Laden and thus as a potential target in the next stage of the U.S. war on terror. Instead, it was the film's view of the moral righteousness of U.S. motives and the inherent honorableness of military virtues that made it so seemingly right for its moment. In fact, the filmmakers themselves had considered adding a postscript to the movie that explicitly linked it to the September 11 attacks, suggesting that the Clinton administration's decision to remove the troops in the wake of the raid and the subsequent "irresolution" in Rwanda, Bosnia, and Kosovo had emboldened U.S. enemies. In the end, they removed the explicit statements, asserting that the connection was clear enough for those who wanted to make it.[21]

Yet others saw a different lesson. Andrew O'Hehir, writing for *Salon.com*, suggested that *Black Hawk Down's* refusal to develop the political background to the action in Somalia had reproduced an American tendency to assume that good motives are enough to justify any action. Early in the movie, one earnest young sergeant speaks in favor of the U.S. presence, saying, "Look, there are two things we can do. We can help these people or we can watch them die on CNN." O'Hehir comments, "There was a third option, as it turned out. Armed with good intentions and expensive weaponry, we could blunder into a situation we only partly understood, causing a lot of death and destruction and making a bad situation even worse."[22] It is notable that it was on the Internet, and not on television or in print media, that this dissenting voice appeared.

Yet, by January 2002, enthusiasm for the war against terrorism was beginning to be mixed with precisely such doubts about its long-term outcome. In the immediate aftermath of the attacks, statements of doubt or dissent were often treated as traitorous, as when Attorney General John Ashcroft remarked that those who criticized U.S. policy were only aiding the terrorists. But in December reports about the number of civilian deaths in Afghanistan led one *Time* columnist to suggest that the danger to American troops arose when locals did not share Americans' views of their own actions, especially given that, in Afghanistan, the "collateral damage" that resulted from U.S. bombings was every bit as horrifying for its victims as the attacks on New York and Washington had been for the Americans who died. The fear of a long Vietnam-style entanglement (a fear shared, in different ways, by liberals and conservatives) began to merge with a conservative political discourse that increasingly warned against peace keeping and nation building, indeed *any* humanitarian involvement by U.S. troops.[23]

This layered discourse of refusal and remembrance suggests that when Bush administration officials insisted that there was no relevant history for the "new war" against terror,
they did not intend that Americans forget entirely the conflicts outlined here. Indeed, they
could operate confidently from the assumption that the sedimented cultural impact of
those earlier encounters would help focus Americans' deep moral outrage and desire for
justice toward support for a specific policy that called for immediate and far-reaching
military action, including a bombing campaign, removal of the Taliban, and, ultimately, military action that would reach well beyond Afghanistan. The narratives that had emerged from
the wars against terrorism of the 1970s and the 1980s were personalized tales, organized
around captivity and rescue, in which the protection of private life, even the promise of
a right to be protected from politics itself, appeared as the preeminent value for the very
public activities of the state and the military. They were, at their heart, displacements: Israeli
rescues appropriated as part of U.S. responses to Vietnam, the claim to private life pushing
aside the political nature of the embassy in Iran, and the promise of valiant rescue displacing
the reality of limited military success.

At the same time, neither the public statements of official policy makers nor most of the
media have engaged just how politically and militarily complex those earlier battles against
terrorism really were. A public acknowledgement that there *had* been a debate, not only
about how to respond to terrorism but about the nature of Middle East politics and the
terms of U.S. world power, might have opened up the possibility for an expanded political
discussion—about the military and diplomatic options available and about the possible
long-term political effects of U.S. actions.

If, after September 11, such a discussion seemed impossible for most people to imagine,
that boundary of thought was forged in part by our narratives of the past. With the memory/
forgetting of captivity and rescue behind us, it became time for Americans to win the thirty
years' war—by pretending it had just begun.

Notes

Melani McAlister is associate professor of American studies at George Washington
University. Readers may contact McAlister at <mmc@gwu.edu>.

1   On the politics of "certainty" as it emerged after September 11, 2001, see Peter Alexander
    Meyers, "Defend Politics against Terrorism," *Social Science Research Council* <http://www.
    ssrc.org/sept11/essays/meyers.htm> (May 15, 2002).
2   Benedict Anderson, *Imagined Communities: Reflections on the Origin and Spread of Nationalism*
    (New York, 1991), 204.
3   In recent years, foreign policy scholars have increasingly analyzed the importance of
    culture to studies of international relations. See, for example, Emily Rosenberg, *Financial
    Missionaries to the World: The Politics and Culture of Dollar Diplomacy, 1900–1930* (Cambridge,
    Mass., 1999); John Dower, *War without Mercy* (New York, 1987); Penny Von Eschen, *Race
    against Empire: Black Americans and Anticolonialism, 1937–1957* (Ithaca, 1997); John Fousek,
    To Lead the Free World: American Nationalism and the Cultural Roots of the Cold War (Chapel Hill,
    2000); and Robert Vitalis, "The Graceful and Generous Liberal Gesture: Making Racism
    Invisible in American International Relations," *Millennium*, 29 (Sept. 2000), 331–56.

4 ABC *Evening News*, Sept. 7, 1972 (videotape), Television News Archive (Vanderbilt University, Nashville, Tenn.).

5 ABC *Evening News*, Sept. 6, 1972 (videotape), Television News Archive; *Atlanta Constitution*, Sept. 7, 1972, p. A20. For others who drew the connection between Munich and Vietnam, see *New York Times*, Sept. 8, 1972, p. A22; *Washington Post*, Sept. 8, 1972, p. B1; and *ibid.*, Sept. 10, 1972, p. B7. For the argument about the reliance on force, see Jerry Wayne Sanders, *Peddlers of Crisis: The Committee on the Present Danger and the Politics of Containment* (Boston, 1983), 191–276.

6 Edgar O'Ballance, *Language of Violence: The Blood Politics of Terrorism* (Novato, 1979). See also *Atlanta Journal-Constitution*, July 4, 1976, p. 1.

7 Milton R. Benjamin, "The Fall Out from Entebbe," *Newsweek*, July 19, 1976, p. 41; "Israel's Skill and Daring," *Nation*, July 17, 1976, p. 37. Newspaper and magazine coverage included James Burnham, "Reflections on Entebbe," *National Review*, Aug. 6, 1976, p. 834; Raymond Carroll, "How the Israelis Pulled It Off," *Newsweek*, July 19, 1976, pp. 42ff; *New York Times*, July 11, 1976, sec. 4, p. 7; and "Rescue at Entebbe: How the Israelis Did It," *Reader's Digest*, 109 (Oct. 1976), pp. 122–28. Books included William Stevenson, *Ninety Minutes at Entebbe* (New York, 1976); and Ira Peck, *Raid on Entebbe* (New York, 1977). The race to make movies about the event is discussed in "Entebbe Derby," *Time*, July 26, 1976, p. 82.

8 For a discussion of the idea of a "Vietnam syndrome," as it developed among conservatives, see Sanders, *Peddlers of Crisis*, 235–311. See Robert Holtz, "Israel Points the Way," *Aviation Week and Space Technology*, July 12, 1976, p. 7; and "When the U.S. Rescue Mission Fizzled," *U.S. News and World Report*, July 19, 1976, p. 32. See also my more detailed analysis of this admiration for Israel in McAlister, *Epic Encounters*, 178–97.

9 Judith Miller, *Saddam Hussein and the Crisis in the Gulf* (New York, 1990); Judith Miller, "Bargain with Terrorists?," *New York Times Magazine*, July 18, 1976, pp. 7ff.; David C. Martin and John Walcott, *Best-Laid Plans: The Inside Story of America's War against Terrorism* (New York, 1989).

10 Gary Sick, *All Fall Down: America's Tragic Encounter with Iran* (New York, 1986), 258.

11 The anti-Khomeini items are mentioned both by Edward Said, *Covering Islam* (New York, 1981), 117; and Hamid Naficy, "Mediating the Other," in *The U.S. Media and the Middle East*, ed. Yahya Kamalipour (Westport, 1995), 81–82. On bin Laden items, see *St. Petersburg Times*, Oct. 28, 2001, p. 1F.

12 *Washington Post*, April 26, 1980, p. A1; "Tragedy in the Desert: Rescue That Failed," *U.S. News and World Report*, May 5, 1980, pp. 6ff.; Alan Mayer et al., "A Mission Comes to Grief in Iran," *Newsweek*, May 5, 1980, pp. 24ff. See also *New York Times*, Aug. 24, 1980, p. 1; and *Washington Post*, Aug. 24, 1980, p. A1.

13 Edward Herman and Gary O'Sullivan, *The Terrorism Industry: The Experts and Institutions That Shape Our View of Terror* (New York, 1989), 44. See also Marc Celmer, *Terrorism, U.S. Strategy, and Reagan Policies* (Westport, 1987).

14 On the development of expert ideologies about terrorism, see McAlister, *Epic Encounters*, chap. 5. A collection developed from an anti-terrorism conference held in Washington, D.C. in 1984 included contributions from Israelis, Europeans, and Americans. Prominent U.S. contributors included George P. Schultz, Daniel Patrick Moynihan, Jeane J. Kirkpatrick, Bernard Lewis, Charles Krauthammer, Daniel Schorr, and Edwin Meese III. See Benjamin Netanyahu, ed., *Terrorism: How the West Can Win* (New York, 1986).

15 *The Taking of Pelham One Two Three*, dir. Joseph Sargent (Palladium Productions, 1974); *Black*

Sunday, dir. John Frankenheimer (Paramount Pictures, 1977); *Network*, dir. Sidney Lumet (MGM/United Artists, 1976); *Missing in Action*, dir. Joseph Zito (Cannon Group, 1984); *Iron Eagle*, dir. Sidney J. Furie (TriStar Pictures, 1986); *Navy SEALS*, dir. Lewis Teague (Orion Pictures Corporation, 1990); *Rambo III*, dir. Peter MacDonald (Carolco Pictures, 1988); *Patriot Games*, dir. Phillip Noyce (Paramount Pictures, 1992); *The Little Drummer Girl*, dir. George Roy Hill (Warner Bros., 1984); *The Delta Force*, dir. Menahem Golan (Golan-Globus, 1986). There were also several docudramas, including at least one made-for-television film, about the Munich massacre (*21 Hours at Munich*, dir. William A. Graham [Filmways Motion Pictures, 1976]), as well as several movies about the Israeli raid on Entebbe.

16 *Delta Force. Die Hard*, dir. John McTiernan (20th Century Fox/Silver Pictures, 1988).

17 *Chicago Tribune*, Sept. 13, 2001, p. 13. Dave Karger, "Calling Out the Troops," *Entertainment Weekly's* EW.com, Dec. 3, 2001 <http://www.ew.com/ew/report/0,6115,186560~1~~,00. html> (June 11, 2002).

18 *Collateral Damage*, dir. Andrew Davis (Warner Bros./Hacienda Productions, 2002). *Seattle Post-Intelligencer*, Feb. 8, 2002 <http://seattlepi.nwsource.com/movies/57462_collateral 08q.shtml> (May 15, 2002); "Box Office Preview: Mommy Dearest," *Entertainment Weekly's* EW.com, Feb. 15, 2002 <http://www.ew.com/ew/report/0.6115,203263~1~0~,00.htm> (June 3, 2002); Dave Karger, "Box Office Report," *Entertainment Weekly's* EW.com, Feb. 18, 2002 <http://www.ew.com/ew/report/0,6115,203642~1~~,00.htm> (June 3, 2002); Mark Caro, "Movie Review: *Collateral Damage*," *Metromix* <http://www.metromix.com/top/1,1419, M-Metromix-Home-X!ArticleDetail-15175,00.html> (May 15, 2002); Paul Clinton, "Review: New Schwarzenegger 'Damaged' Goods," CNN.com, Feb. 7, 2002 <http:// www. cnn.com/2002/SHOWBIZ/Movies/02/07/review.collateral/index.html> (May 15, 2002).

19 *Black Hawk Down*, dir. Ridley Scott (Columbia Pictures/Jerry Bruckheimer Films/ Revolution Studios, 2001); Mark Bowden, *Black Hawk Down: A Story of Modern War* (New York, 1999).

20 Elvis Mitchell, "Film Review: Mission of Mercy Goes Bad in Africa," *New York Times*, Dec. 28, 2001, Sec. E, p. 3, available from the *New York Times* Premium Archive <http://www. nytimes.com/premiumproducts/archive.html> (May 15, 2002). Jamie Malanowski, "Film: War, without Any Answers," *ibid.*, Dec. 16, 2001, sec. 2, p. 3, available from the *New York Times* Premium Archive.

21 Rick Lyman, "An Action Film Hits Close, but How Close? Second Thoughts Prevail against a Political Message," *New York Times*, Dec. 26, 2001, sec. E, p. 1, available from the *New York Times* Premium Archive.

22 Andrew O'Hehir, "Fog of War: *Black Hawk Down's Gripping Images of* U.S. *Military's Missteps in Somalia Grope About in a Context-Free Void*," Salon.com, Dec. 28, 2001 <http://wwwsalon. com/ent/movies/review/ 2001/12/28/black_hawk_down/> (May 15, 2002).

23 "Ashcroft: Critics of New Terror Measures Undermine Effort," CNN.com, Dec. 7, 2001 <http://www.cnn.com/2001/US/12/06/inv.ashcroft.hearing> (May 15, 2002). Tony Karon, "What the Army Can Learn from *Black Hawk Down*: Danger Lurks When the Locals Don't Share the U.S. View of Its Own Actions," TIME.com, Feb. 12, 2002 <http://www.time. com/time/columnist/printout/0,8816,202706.00.htm> (June 3, 2002). On the number of civilian deaths, see Carl Conetta, "Operation Enduring Freedom: Why a Higher Rate of Civilian Bombing Casualties," *Project on Defense Alternatives Briefing Report #11*, Jan. 18, 2002 <http://www.comw.org/pda/0201oef.html> (May 15, 2002).

Bibliography

Adair, Gilbert (1989) *Hollywood's Vietnam: From 'The Green Berets' to 'Full Metal Jacket'* Rev. and expanded ed. London: Heinemann (original edition 1981).

Adler, Renata (1969) *A Year in the Dark* New York: Berkeley.

Agamben, Giorgio (1998) *Homo Sacer: Sovereign Power and Bare Life*, trans. Daniel Heller-Roazen, Stanford: Stanford University Press.

Agee, James ([1944] 2000) "March 11, 1944 [Review in *The Nation*]" in David Denby, intro. *Agee on Film: Criticism and Comment on the Movies* New York: Modern Library.

Allen, Tim (1999) "Perceiving Contemporary Wars" in Tim Allen and Jean Seaton, ed., *The Media of Conflict: War Reporting and Representations of Ethnic Violence* London: Zed.

Anderegg, Michael, ed. (1991) *Inventing Vietnam: The War in Film and Television* Philadelphia: Temple University Press.

Anderson, Benedict (1991) *Imagined Communities: Reflections on the Origin and Spread of Nations and Nationalism* London: Verso.

Ankersmit, Frank R. (1994) "Historiography and Postmodernism" *History and Topology* Berkeley: University of California Press.

Arlen, Michael J. (1982) *The Living-Room War* New York: Penguin (revised 1969).

Auster, Albert and Leonard Quart (1988) *How the War Was Remembered: Hollywood & Vietnam* New York: Praeger.

Baker, M. Joyce (1980) *Images of Women in Film: The War Years, 1941–1945* Ann Arbor, MI: UMI Research Press.

Barthes, Roland (1977) *Image-Music-Text* New York: Hill and Wang.

Basinger, Jeanine (1986) *The World War II Combat Film: Anatomy of a Genre* New York: Columbia University Press.

Barnouw, Erik (1974) *Documentary: A History of the Non-Fiction Film* New York: Oxford University Press.

—— (1998) "Translating War: The Combat Film Genre and *Saving Private Ryan*" *Perspectives* online (October); *http://www.theaha.org/Perspectives/issues/1998/9810/9810FIL.CFM*.

Bates, Milton J. (1996) *The Wars We Took to Vietnam: Cultural Conflict and Storytelling*. Berkeley: University of California Press.

Baudrillard, Jean ([1995] 1991) *The Gulf War Did Not Take Place* trans. and intro. Paul Patton Bloomington: Indiana University Press.

—— (2003) *The Spirit of Terrorism* New ed. Trans. Chris Turner. New York: Verso.

Bazin, Andre (1967) *What is Cinema?* Trans. Hugh Gray. Berkeley: University of California Press.

Beck, Ulrich (2000) "Risk Society Revisited" in Barbara Adam, Ulrich Beck, and Joost van Loon, ed., *Risk Society and Beyond* London: Sage.

Belton, John (|1994| 2005) *American Cinema/American Culture*, 2nd ed. New York: McGraw-Hill.

Berg, Rick (1990) "Losing Vietnam: Covering the War in an Age of Technology" in Linda Dittmar and Gene Michaud, eds. *From Hanoi to Hollywood: The Vietnam War in American Film* New Brunswick, NJ: Rutgers University Press.

Bernstein, Matthew, ed. (1999) *Controlling Hollywood: Censorship and Regulation in the Studio Era* New Brunswick, NJ: Rutgers University Press.

Biskind, Peter (1983) *Seeing is Believing: How Hollywood Taught Us to Stop Worrying and love the Fifties* New York: Pantheon.

Blair, Clay (1987) *The Forgotten War: America in Korea, 1950–1953* New York: Times Books.

Bordwell, David, Janet Staiger, and Kristin Thompson (1986) *The Classical Hollywood Cinema: Film Style and Mode of Production to 1960* New York: Columbia University Press.

Bordwell, David, and Kristin Thompson (1994) *Film History: An Introduction* New York: McGraw-Hill.

Bottomore, Stephen (2002) "Introduction: War and Militarism. Dead White Males" *Film History* 14.3–4.

Bourke, Joanna (1999) *An Intimate History of Killing: Face to Face Killing in Twentieth Century Warfare* New York: Basic Books.

Bowser, Elaine (1990) *The Transformation of Cinema, 1907–1915* New York: Scribner's.

Britton, Andrew (1986) "Blissing Out: The Politics of Reaganite Entertainment" *Movie* 31/32.

Brownlow, Kevin (1978) *The War, the West, and the Wilderness* New York: Knopf.

Burch, Noël (1979) *To the Distant Observer: Form and Meaning in the Japanese Cinema* Berkeley: University of California Press.

Burgoyne, Robert (1997) *Film Nation: Hollywood Looks at U.S. History* Minneapolis: University of Minnesota Press.

Burke, Edward (|1757| 1968) *A Philosophical Enquiry into the Origin of Our Ideas of the Sublime and the Beautiful* South Bend: University of Notre Dame Press.

Butler, Ivan (1974) *The War Film* New York: A.S. Barnes.

Campbell, Craig W. (1985) *Reel America and World War I: A Comprehensive Filmography and History of Motion Pictures in the United States, 1914–1920* Jefferson, N.C.: McFarland.

Carnes, Mark C. (2004) "Shooting (Down) the Past: Historians vs. Hollywood," *Cineaste* XXIX.2.

——, ed. (1985) *Past Imperfect: History According to the Movies* New York: Henry Holt.

Carruthers, Susan L. (2003) "Bringing it All Back Home: Hollywood Returns to War" *Small Wars & Insurgencies* 14.1.

Chadwick, Bruce (2001) *The Reel Civil War: Mythmaking in American Film* New York: Vintage.

Chambers, John Whiteclay, II (1994) "All Quiet on the Western Front (U.S., 1930): The Antiwar Film and the Modern Image of War" in Chambers and Culbert (1996) *ibid.* 13–30.

Chambers, John Whiteclay, II, and David Culbert, eds. (1996) *World War II: Film and History* New York: Oxford University Press.

Clark, Michael (1985) "Vietnam: Representations of Self and War" *Wide Angle* 7.4.

Coker, Christopher (1993) *War in the Twentieth Century: A Study of War and Modern Consciousness* London: Brassey's.

Combs, James (1993) "From the Great War to the Gulf War: Popular Entertainment and the Legitimation of Warfare" in Robert E. Denton, ed., *The Media and the Persian Gulf War* Westport, CT: Praeger.

Connerton, Paul (1989) *How Societies Remember* New York: Cambridge University Press.

Corrigan, Timothy (1991) *Cinema Without Walls: Movies and Culture After Vietnam* New Brunswick, NJ: Rutgers University Press.

Crandall, Jordan (2003) "Unmanned: Embedded Reporters, Predator Drones, and Armed Perception" CTHEORY 4/9/2003; www.ctheory.net/text_file?pick=378.

Cripps, Thomas (1994) "The Absent Presence in American Civil War Films." *Historical Journal of Film, Radio and Television* 14.4: 367–76.

Culbert, David, ed. (1990) *Film and Propaganda in America: A Documentary History*, Vol. III: *World War II, Part 2* Westport, CT: Greenwood Press.

Cullen, Jim (1995) *The Civil War in Popular Culture: A Reusable Past* Washington, D.C.: Smithsonian Institution Press.

Curley, Stephen J. and Frank J. Wetta (1990) "War Film Bibliography" *Journal of Popular Film and Television* 18.2: 12–19.

Dall'Asta, M. (1995) "Exploiting the War: Preparedness Serials and Patriotic Women" unpublished paper.

Daniel, Joseph (1972) *Guerre et Cinéma; Grandes Illusions et Petits Soldats, 1895–1971* Paris: Armand Colin.

De Antonio, Emile "Year of the Pig: Marxist Film" in Jump Cut 19: 37 (undated).

DeBauche, Leslie Midkiff (1997) *Reel Patriotism: The Movies and World War I* Madison: University of Wisconsin Press.

DeBona, Guerric (2003) "Masculinity on the Front: John Huston's *The Red Badge of Courage* (1951) Revisited," *Cinema Journal* 42.2: 57–80.

De Landa, Manuel (1991) *War in the Age of Intelligent Machines* New York: Zone Books.

Deleuze, Gilles ([1983] 1989) *Cinema 2: The Time-Image* trans. Hugh Tomlinson and Robert Galeta, Minneapolis: University of Minnesota Press.

DerDerian, James (1992) *Anti-Diplomacy: Spies, Terror, Speed, and War* Oxford: Blackwell.

—— (2001) *Virtuous War: Mapping the Military-Industrial-Media-Entertainment Network* Boulder, CO: Westview Press.

—— "War as Game" (2003) *Brown Journal of International Affairs* 10.1.

Devine, Jeremy M. (1995) *Vietnam at 24 Frames a Second: A Critical and Thematic Analysis of Over 400 Films About the Vietnam War* Jefferson, NC: McFarland.

Dibbets, Karl, and Bert Hogenkamp, eds. (1995) *Film and the First World War* Amsterdam: Amsterdam University Press.

Dick, Bernard F. ([1985] 1996) *The Star-Spangled Screen: The American World War II Film* Lexington, KY: University Press of Kentucky.

Dittmar, Linda and Gene Michaud, eds. (1990) *From Hanoi to Hollywood: The Vietnam War in American Film* New Brunswick: Rutgers University Press.

Docherty, I. (2002) "The New War Movies as Moral Rearmament: *Black Hawk Down* and *We Were Soldiers*" in *Cineaste* 27.3: 4–8.

Doherty, Thomas (1988–89) "Full Metal Genre: Stanley Kubrick's Vietnam Combat Movie" in *Film Quarterly* 42.2: 25–30.

—— (1993) *Projections of War: Hollywood, American Culture, and World War II* New York: Columbia University Press.

Donald, Ralph R. (1992) "Masculinity and Machismo in Hollywood's War Films" in Steve Craig, ed., *Men, Masculinity, and the Media* Newbury Park, CA: Sage.

Easthope, Anthony (1986) *What A Man's Gotta Do: The Masculine Myth in Popular Culture* London: Paladin.

Eberwein, Robert (2001) "'As a Mother Cuddles a Child': Sexuality and Masculinity in World War II Combat Films" in Peter Lehman, ed., *Masculinity: Bodies, Movies, Culture* New York: Routledge.

Eberwein, Robert, ed. (2004) *The War Film* New Brunswick, NJ: Rutgers University Press.

Edwards, Paul M. (1997) *A Guide to Films on the Korean War* Westport, CT: Greenwood.

Engelhardt, Tom (1995) *The End of Victory Culture: Cold War America and the Disillusioning of a Generation.* Amherst: University of Massachusetts Press. (|1995| 1998)

Erenberg, Lewis A., and Susan E. Hirsch, eds. (1996) *The War in American Culture: Society and Consciousness during World War II* Chicago: University of Chicago Press.

Evans, Gary (1984) *John Grierson and the National Film Board: The Politics of Wartime Propaganda* Toronto: University of Toronto Press.

Fagelson, William Friedman (2001) "Fighting Films: The Everyday Tactics of World War II Soldiers" *Cinema Journal* 40.3.

Feldman, Allen (2004) "Deterritorialized Wars of Public Safety" in Bruce Kapferer, ed., *State, Sovereignty, War* New York: Berghahn Books.

Ferro, Marc (1988) *Cinema and History,* trans. Naomi Greene, Detroit: Wayne State University Press.

"Films in Vietnam" (1969) in *Film Comment* 2 (Spring): 46–88.

Fitzgerald, Frances (1972) *Fire in the Lake: The Vietnamese and the Americans in Vietnam* New York: Vintage.

Franklin, H. Bruce (1994) "From Realism to Virtual Reality: Images of America's Wars," in Susan Jeffords and Lauren Rabinowitz, eds., *Seeing through the Media: The Persian Gulf War* New Brunswick, NJ: Rutgers University Press.

Fuchs, Cynthia J. (1990) "Vietnam and Sexual Violence" in Owen Gillman, Jr. and Lorrie Smith, eds., *America Rediscovered: Critical Essays on Literature and Films of the Vietnam War* Hamden: Garland.

Fujitani, T., Geoffrey M. White, and Lisa Yoneyama White, eds. (2001) *Perilous Memories: The Asia-Pacific War(s)* Durham, NC: Duke University Press.

Fukuyama, Francis (1992) *The End of History and the Last Man* New York: Free Press.

Fussell, Paul (1989) *Wartime: Understanding and Behavior in the Second World War* New York: Oxford University Press.

Fyne, Robert (1994) *The Hollywood Propaganda of World War II* Metuchen, NJ: Scarecrow Press.

Gessner, Peter (1966) "Films from the Vietcong" in *The Nation* 202.4 (January 24): 110–111.

Gilman, Owen W., Jr., and Lorrie Smith, eds. (1990) *America Rediscovered: Critical Essays on Literature and Film of the Vietnam War* New York: Garland.

Gitlin, Todd (1989) *The Whole World is Watching: Mass Media in the Making and Unmaking of the New Left* Berkeley: University of California Press.

Gray, J. Glenn (|1960| 1970) *The Warriors: Reflections on Men in Battle* New York: Harper Colophon.

Haines, H.W. (1990) "'The were called and they went': The Political Rehabilitation of the Vietnam Veteran" in Linda Dittmar and Gene Michaud, eds. *From Hanoi to Hollywood: The Vietnam War in American Film* New Brunswick, NJ: Rutgers University Press, 81–97.

Hammond, Charles Montgomery, J.R. (1981) *The Image Decade: Television Documentary, 1965–75* New York: Hastings House.

Hammond, Michael (2002) "Some Smothering Dreams: The Combat Film in Contemporary Hollywood" in Steve Neale, ed., *Genre and Contemporary Hollywood* London: BFI.

Hardt, Michael, and Antonio Negri (2000) *Empire* Cambridge, MA: Harvard University Press.

Hedges, Chris (2002) *War Is a Force that Gives Us Meaning* New York: Anchor.

Herr, Michael (1978) *Dispatches* New York: Avon.

Hoopes, Roy (1994) *When the Stars Went to War: Hollywood and World War II* New York: Random House.

Hüppauf, Bernd (1993) "Experiences of Modern Warfare and the Crisis of Representation" *New German Critique* 59.

Huyssen, Andreas (1993) "Fortifying the Heart—Totally: Ernst Junger's Armored Texts" *New German Critique* 59.

Ignatieff, Michael (1997) *The Warrior's Honor: Ethnic War and the Modern Conscience* New York: Henry Holt.

Isenberg, Michael T. (1975) "An Ambiguous Pacifism: A Retrospective on World War I films, 1930–1938" *Journal of Popular Film* 4.2: 98–115.

—— (1981) *War on Film: the American Cinema and World War I, 1914–1941* Rutherford, NJ: Fairleigh Dickinson University Press.

Jeffords, Susan (1988) "Masculinity as Excess in Vietnam Film: The Father/Son Dynamic" *Genre* 21.

—— (1989) *The Remasculinization of America: Gender and the Vietnam War* Bloomington: Indiana University Press.

—— (1994) *Hard Bodies: Hollywood Masculinity in the Reagan Era* New Brunswick, NJ: Rutgers University Press.

Jeffords, Susan and Lauren Rabinovitz, eds. (1994) *Seeing through the Media: The Persian Gulf War* New Brunswick, NJ: Rutgers University Press.

Joas, Hans (2002) *War and Modernity: Studies in the History of Violence in the Twentieth Century* trans. Rodney Livingstone, Cambridge: Polity Press.

Jones, Dorothy B. (1945) "The Hollywood War Film: 1942–1944" *Hollywood Quarterly* 1.1.

Jones, P.G. (1976) *War and the Novelist: Appraising the American War Novel* Columbia: University of Missouri Press.

Kaes, Anton (1989) *From Hitler to Heimat: The Return of History as Film* Cambridge, MA: Harvard University Press.

Kagan, Norman (1974) *The War Film* New York: Pyramid.

Kaminsky, Stuart M. (1974) *American Film Genres* New York: Dell.

Kane, Kathryn (1982) *Visions of War: Hollywood Combat Films of World War II* Ann Arbor, MI: UMI Research Press.

—— (1988) "The World War II Combat Film" in Wes D. Gehring, ed., *Handbook of American Film Genres* Westport, CN; Greenwood.

Kapferer, Bruce, ed. (2004) *State, Sovereignty, War* New York: Berghahn Books.

Kaplan, Amy and Donald Pease, eds. (1993) *Cultures of United States Imperialism* Durham: Duke University Press.

Kelly, Andrew, ed. (1997) *Cinema and the Great War* New York: Routledge.

Kelly, Andrew (1997) "The Brutality of Military Incompetence: *Paths of Glory*" in Kelly, ed., *Cinema and the Great War* New York: Routledge.

Kelly, Andrew and Edward Lawrenson (1998) "A–Z of Cinema, W: War" *Sight and Sound* 8.4.

King, Geoff (2005) "'Just Like a Movie'?: 9/11 and Hollywood Spectacle," in King, ed., *The Spectacle of the Real: From Hollywood to Reality TV and Beyond* Portland, OR: Intellect.

Kinnard, Roy (1988) *The Blue and the Gray on the Screen: Eighty Years of Civil War Movies* New York: Birch Lane Press.

Kinney, Katherine (2000) *Friendly Fire: American Images of the Vietnam War* New York: Oxford University Press.

Kittler, Friedrich A. (1986/1999) *Gramophone, Film, Typewriter* trans. and intro. Geoffrey Winthrop-Young and Michael Wutz, Stanford: Stanford University Press.

Klein, Michael (1990) "Historical Memory, Film, and the Vietnam Era" in Linda Dittmar and Gene Michaud, ed., *From Hanoi to Hollywood: The Vietnam War in American Film* New Brunswick, NJ: Rutgers University Press.

Koppes, Clayton R. (1995) "Hollywood and the Politics of Representation: Women, Workers, and African-Americans in World War II Movies," in Kenneth Paul O'Brien and Lynn Hudson Parsons, eds., *The Home-Front War: World War II and American Society* Westport, CT: Greenwood Press.

—— (1997) "Regulating the Screen: The Office of War Information and the Production Code Administration" in Thomas Schatz, ed., *Boom and Bust: American Cinema in the 1940s* Berkeley: University of California Press.

Koppes, Clayton R. and Gregory D. Black (1987) *Hollywood Goes to War: How Politics, Profits, and Propaganda Shaped World War II Movies* New York: The Free Press.

Koszarski, Richard (1990) *An Evening's Entertainment: The Age of the Silent Feature Picture, 1915–1928* New York: Scribner's.

Lacy, Mark (2003) "War, Cinema, and Moral Anxiety" *Alternatives: Global, Local, Political* 28.5; *https://goliath.ecnext.com/free-scripts/document_view_v3.pl?item_id*

Landon, Philip J. (1989) "From Cowboy to Organization Man: The Hollywood War Hero, 1940–1955" *Studies in Popular Culture* 12.1.

Lasswell, Harold (1927) *Propaganda Technique in the World War* New York: Knopf.

Leab, Daniel J. (1995) "Viewing the War with the Brothers Warner" in Karel Dibbets and Bert Hogenkamp, eds., *Film and the First World War* Amsterdam: Amsterdam University Press.

Lentz, Robert J. (2003) *Korean War Filmography: 91 English Language Features through 2000* Jefferson, N.C.: McFarland.

Leutrat, Jean-Louis (1985) *L'Alliance Brisée; Le Western des Années 1920* Lyons: Presses Universitaires de Lyon.

Lewis, Lloyd B. (1985) *The Tainted War: Culture and Identity in Vietnam War Narratives* Westport, CT: Greenwood.

Lockwood, Dean (2005) "Teratology of the Spectacle" in Geoff King, ed., *The Spectacle of the Real: From Hollywood to Reality TV and Beyond* Portland, OR: Intellect.

Loshitzky, Yosefa, ed. (1997) *Spielberg's Holocaust: Critical Perpsectives on 'Schindler's List'* Bloomington: Indiana University Press.

Luckett, Perry D. (1989–1990) "The Black Soldier in Vietnam War Literature and Film" *War, Literature, and the Arts* 1.2.

Lundberg, David (1984) "The American Literature of War: The Civil War, World War I, and World War II" *American Quarterly* 36.3.

Martin, Andrew (1990a) "Vietnam and Melodramatic Representation" *East-West Film Journal* 4.2.

—— (1990b) "Critical Approaches to American Studies: The Vietnam War in History, Literature, and Film" University of Iowa Ph.D. thesis Ann Arbor: UMI.

Matelski, Marilyn J. and Nancy Lynch Street, eds. (2003) *War and Film in America: Historical and Critical Essays* Jefferson, NC: McFarland.

McAdams, Frank (2002) *The American War Film: History and Hollywood* Westport, CT: Praeger.

McArthur, Colin (1982) "War and Anti-War" *The Movie* 45.

McCrisken, Trevor, and Andrew Pepper (2005) *American History and Contemporary Hollywood Film* Edinburgh: Edinburgh University Press.

McMahon, Kathryn (1994) "Casualties of War: History, Realism, and the Limits of Exclusion" *Journal of Popular Film and Television* 22.1.

Modleski, Tania (1988) "A Father is Being Beaten: Male feminism and the War Film" *Discourse* 10.2.

Mosse, George L. (1990) *Fallen Soldiers: Reshaping the Memory of the World Wars* New York: Oxford University Press.

Muse, Eben J. (1994) "Romance, Power, and the Vietnam War: Romantic Triangles in Three Vietnam War Films" *Durham University Journal* 86.2.

Musser, Charles (1990) *The Emergence of Cinema: The American Screen to 1907* Berkeley: University of California Press.

Neale, Steve (1991) "Aspects of Ideology and Narrative Form in the American War Film" *Screen* 32.1.

—— (2000) *Genre and Hollywood* London: Routledge.

Newsinger, John (1993) "'Do You Walk the Walk?': Aspects of Masculinity in Some Vietnam War Films" in Pat Kirkham and Janet Thumim, eds., *You Tarzan; Masculinity, Movies, and Men* New York: St. Martin's.

Nornes, Abe Mark, and Fukushima Yukio, eds. (1994) *The Japan/America Film Wars: WWII Propaganda and Its Cultural Contexts* Langhorne, PA: Harwood.

Norris, Christopher (1992) *Uncritical Theory: Postmodernism, Intellectuals, and the Gulf War* Amherst: University of Massachusetts Press.

Paris, Michael, ed. (2000) *The First World War and Popular Cinema: 1914 to the Present* New Brunswick, NJ: Rutgers University Press.

Polan, Dana (1986) *Power and Paranoia: History, Narrative, and the American Cinema, 1940–1950* New York: Columbia University Press.

Porteous, Katrina (1988) "History Lessons: Platoon" in Jeffrey Walsh and James Aulich, eds. *Vietnam Images: War and Representation* New York: St. Martin's Press, pp. 153–59.

Ray, Robert (1985) "Classic Hollywood's Holding Pattern: The Combat Films of World War II" in *A Certain Tendency of the Hollywood Cinema, 1930–1980* Princeton, N.J.: Princeton University Press.

Renov, Michael (1988) *Hollywood's Wartime Woman: Representation and Ideology* Ann Arbor, MI: UMI Research Press.

Richman, Liliane G. (1991) "Themes and Ideology in the Vietnam Films, 1975–1983" University of Texas Ph.D. dissertation, Ann Arbor: UMI.

Rist, Peter (1988) "Standard Hollywood Fare: the World War II Combat Film Revisited" in *Cineaction* 12: 23–6.

Roeder, George H., Jr. (1993) *The Censored War: American Visual Experience During World War Two* New Haven: Yale University Press.

Rollins, Peter C. (1997) "America, World War II, and the Movies: An Annotated Booklist" *Film & History* 27:1–4.

Rollins, Peter C. and John E. O'Connor, eds. (1997) *Hollywood's World War I: Motion Picture Images* Bowling Green, OH: Bowling Green University Popular Press.

Rosenstone, Robert (1995) *Visions of the Past: The Challenge of Film to Our Idea of History* Cambridge, MA: Harvard University Press.

—— (1996) "The Future of the Past," in Vivian Sobchack, ed., *The Persistence of History: Cinema, Television, and the Modern Event* New York: Routledge.

—— (2004) "Inventing Historical Truth on the Silver Screen" in *Cineaste* XXIX.2.

"Roundtable on Film and History" (1988) *American Historical Review* 93.

Rubin, Steven Jay (1981) *Combat Films: American Realism, 1945–1970* Jefferson, NC: McFarland.

Ryan, Michael A. and Douglas Kellner (1988) *Camera Politica: The Politics and Ideology of Contemporary Hollywood Film* Bloomington: Indiana University Press.

Sarris, Andrew (1998) "The War Film" in *"You ain't heard nothin' yet": The American Talking Film, History & Memory, 1927–1949* New York: Oxford University Press.

Scarrow, Simon (1991) "The Vietnam Combat Film: The Construction of a Sub-Genre" University of East Anglia Ph.D. thesis.

Schatz, Thomas (1997) *Boom and Bust: American Cinema in the 1940s* Berkeley: University of California Press.

—— (2002) "Old War/New War: *Band of Brothers* and the Revival of the WWII War Film" *Film & History* 32.1.

Schneider, Karen (1995) "Re-Shooting World War II: Women, Narrative Authority, and Hollywood Cinema" *Genders* 21.

Selig, Michael (1993) "Genre, Gender, and the Discourse of War: The A/Historical and Vietnam Films" *Screen* 34.1.

Shain, Russell Earl (1976) *An Analysis of Motion Pictures about War Released by the American Film Industry, 1939–1970* New York: Arno.

Sherry, Michael (1995) *In the Shadow of War: The United States since the 1930s* New Haven: Yale University Press.

Shohat, Ella and Robert Stam (1994) *Unthinking Eurocentrism: Multiculturalism and the Media* New York: Routledge.

Shull, Michael S. and David Edward Wilt (1996) *Hollywood War Films, 1937–1945: An Exhaustive Filmography of American Feature-length Motion Pictures Relating to World War II* Jefferson, NC: McFarland & Co.

Singer, Ben (1995) "Modernity, Hyperstimulus, and the Rise of Popular Sensationalism," in Leo Charney and Vanessa Schwartz, eds., *Cinema and the Invention of Modern Life* Berkeley: University of California Press.

Sklar, Robert (1994) *Movie-Made America: A Cultural History of American Movies* rev. and updated ed. New York: Vintage.

Slocum, J. David (2005) "Cinema and the Civilizing Process: Rethinking Violence in the Combat Film" *Cinema Journal* 44.3.

Slotkin, Richard (1992) *Gunfighter Nation: The Myth of the Frontier in Twentieth-Century America* New York: Atheneum.

—— (2001) "Unit Pride: Ethnic Platoons and the Myths of American Nationality" *American Literary History* 13.3.

Smith, Anthony D. (1981) "War and Ethnicity: The Role of Warfare in the Formation, Self-Images, and Cohesion of Ethnic Communities" *Ethnic and Racial Studies* 4.4.

Smith, Julian (1975) *Looking Away: Hollywood and Vietnam* New York: Scribners.

Sobchack, Vivian, ed. (1996) *The Persistence of History: Cinema, Television, and the Modern Event* New York: Routledge.

Solanas, Fernando and Octavio Gettino (1976) "Towards a Third Cinema" in Bill Nicholas, ed. *Movies and Methods* Berkeley: University of California Press.

Sontag, Susan (2003) *Regarding the Pain of Others* New York: Farrar, Straus, Giroux.

Sorlin, Pierre (1994) "War and Cinema: Interpreting the Relationship" *Historical Journal of Film, Radio and Television* 14.4.

Springer, Claudia (1988a) "Antiwar Film as Spectacle: Contradictions of the Combat Sequence" *Genre* 21.4.

—— (1988b) "Rebellious Sons in Vietnam War Combat Films: A Response" *Genre* 21.4.

Studlar, Gaylin and David Dessor (1990) "Never Having to Say You're Sorry: *Rambo's* Rewriting of the Vietnam War" in Dittmar and Michaud (1990) *ibid.* 101–12.

Suid, Lawrence H. ([1978, 1991] 2002) *Guts & Glory: The Making of the American Military Image in Film* Rev. and expanded ed. Lexington: University Press of Kentucky.

—— (1979) "The Pentagon and Hollywood" in John E. O'Connor and Martin A. Jackson, eds., *American History, American Film* New York: Ungar.

Swofford, Anthony (1993) *Jarhead: A Marine's Chronicle of the Gulf War and Other Battles* New York: Scribners.

Tomasulo, Frank P. (1990) "The Politics of Ambivalence: *Apocalypse Now* as Postwar and Antiwar Film" in Dittmar and Michaud (1990) *ibid.* pp. 148–58.

Tomlinson, Hugh and Robert Galeta ([1983] 1989) "Translators' Introduction" *Cinema 2: The Time-Image*, by Gilles Deleuze, Minneapolis: University of Minnesota Press.

Toplin, Robert Brent (1996) *History by Hollywood: The Use and Abuse of the American Past* Urbana and Chicago: University of Illinois Press.

Trachtenberg, Alan (1982) *The Incorporation of America: Culture and Society in the Gilded Age* New York: Hill and Wang.

Traube, Elizabeth G. (1992) *Dreaming Identities: Class, Gender and Generation in 1980s Hollywood Movies* Boulder: Westview Press.

Turgovnick, Marianna (2005) *The War Complex: World War II in Our Time* Chicago: University of Chicago Press.

"Vietnam and the Media" [Special Issue] (1985) *Wide Angle* 7.4.

Virilio, Paul (1989) *War and Cinema: The Logistics of Perception* trans. Patrick Camiller. New York: Verso.

Walker, Mark Edward (1991) "The Representation of the Vietnam Veteran in American Narrative Film" Northwestern University Ph.D. dissertation, Ann Arbor: UMI.

Waller, Gregory A. (1990) "*Rambo*: Getting to Win this Time" in Dittmar and Michaud (1990) *ibid.* 113–28.

Walsh, Jeffrey (1982) *American War Literature: 1914 to Vietnam* Houndmills: Macmillan.

—— (1988) "First Blood to Rambo: A Textual Analysis" in Alf Louvre and Jeffrey Walsh, eds. *Tell Me Lies About Vietnam: Cultural Battles for the Meaning of the War* Milton Keynes: Open University Press, 50–61.

Walsh, Jeffrey and James Aulich, eds. (1988) *Vietnam Images: War and Representation* New York: St. Martin's Press.

Ward, Larry Wayne (1985) *The Motion Picture Goes to War: The U.S. Government Film Effort During World War I* Ann Arbor, MI: UMI Research Press.

Weschler, Lawrence (2005) "Valkyries Over Iraq: The Trouble with War Movies" *Harper's* (November).

Wetta, Frank Joseph and Stephen J. Curley (1992) *Celluloid Wars: A Guide to Film and the American Experience of War* New York: Greenwood Press.

Wetta, Frank Joseph and Martin A. Novelli (2003) "'Now a Major Motion Picture': War Films and Hollywood's New Patriotism" *The Journal of Military History* 67.

Whillock, David E. (1988) "Defining the Fictive American Vietnam War Film: In Search of Genre" *Literature/Film Quarterly* 16.4.

White, Susan (1988) "Male Bonding, Hollywood Orientalism, and the Repression of the Feminine in Kubrick's *Full Metal Jacket*" *Arizona Quarterly* 44.3.

Wiebe, Robert H. (1966) *The Search for Order, 1877–1920* New York: Hill and Wang.

Winkler, Allan M. (1978) *The Politics of Propaganda: The Office of War Information, 1942–1945* New Haven: Yale University Press.

Winter, Jay M. (1989) *The Experience of World War I* New York: Oxford University Press.

Wood, Robin (1986) *Hollywood from Vietnam to Reagan* New York: Columbia University Press.

Yeats, William Butler (1997) *Collected Works of William Butler Yeats*, Vol I. New York: Scribners.

Zizek, Slavoj (2002) *Welcome to the Desert of the Real: Five Essays on September 11 and Related Dates* New York: Verso.

Films index

Names and Subjects index

Related titles from Routledge

Hollywood Comedians, the *Film* Reader
Edited by Frank Krutnik

Despite the cult status enjoyed by star performers such as Charlie Chaplin, Buster
Keaton, the Marx Brothers and Woody Allen, comedians and the contexts within
which they worked have not always received their due in scholarly discussions of
cinema culture.

Hollywood Comedians, the Film Reader seeks to redress the balance, with
sections including:

- Genre, narrative and performance
- Approaches to silent comedy
- Sound comedy, the vaudeville aesthetic and ethnicity
- Comedian comedy and gender
- Post-classical comedian comedy

Contributors include: Steven Cohan, Philip Drake, Tom Gunning, Bambi L.
Haggins, Henry Jenkins III, Peter Krämer, Patricia Mellencamp, Steve Neale,
William Paul, Joanna E. Rapf, Kathleen Rowe, Steve Seidman, Mark Winokur

ISBN13: 978-0-415-23551-8 (hbk)
ISBN13: 978-0-415-23552-5 (pbk)

ISBN10: 0-415-23551-0 (hbk)
ISBN10: 0-415-23552-9 (pbk)

Available at all good bookshops
For ordering and further information please visit:
www.routledge.com

Related titles from Routledge

Hollywood Musicals, the *Film* Reader

Edited by Steven Cohan

Hollywood Musicals, the Film Reader explores one of the most popular genres of film history. The mainstay of film production throughout the studio era, the musical endures today through animated features, teen dance films and features such as *Evita* and *Moulin Rouge*.

Combining classic and recent articles, each section explores a central issue of the musical, including genre and stardom, gender and spectacle, and race and sexuality. Sections include: *Generic forms, *Gendered spectacles, *Camp interventions, *Racial displacements.

Contributors include: Rick Altman, Lucie Arbuthnot, Steven Cohan, Richard Dyer, Jane Feuer, Patricia Mellencamp, Linda Mizejewski, Pamela Robertson, Martin Rubin, Matthew Tinkcom.

ISBN13: 978-0-415-23559-4 (hbk)
ISBN13: 978-0-415-23560-0 (pbk)

ISBN10: 0-415-23559-6 (hbk)
ISBN10: 0-415-23560-X (pbk)

Available at all good bookshops
For ordering and further information please visit:
www.routledge.com